Knowledge Management and Virtual Organizations

Yogesh Malhotra
@Brint.com, L.L.C. and
Florida Atlantic University

IDEA GROUP PUBLISHING
Hershey USA • London UK

Senior Editor:	Mehdi Khosrowpour
Managing Editor:	Jan Travers
Copy Editor:	Maria Boyer
Typesetter:	Tamara Gillis
Cover Design:	Connie Peltz
Printed at:	BookCrafters

Published in the United States of America by
    Idea Group Publishing
    1331 E. Chocolate Avenue
    Hershey PA 17033-1117
    Tel: 717-533-8845
    Fax: 717-533-8661
    E-mail: cust@idea-group.com
    Web site: http://www.idea-group.com

and in the United Kingdom by
    Idea Group Publishing
    3 Henrietta Street
    Covent Garden
    London WC2E 8LU
    Tel: 171-240 0856
    Fax: 171-379 0609
    Web site: http://www.eurospan.co.uk

Library of Congress Cataloging-in-Publication Data

Malhotra, Yogesh, 1964-
    Knowledge management and virtual organizations / [edited by] Yogesh Malhotra.
      p. cm.
    Includes bibliographical references and index.
    ISBN 1-878289-73-X
      1. Knowledge management. 2. Virtual reality in management. I. Title.

HD30.2 .M3337 2000
658.4'038--dc21   00-024902

British Cataloguing in Publication Data
A Cataloguing in Publication record for this book is available from the British Library.

NEW from Idea Group Publishing

Knowledge Management and Virtual Organizations

Table of Contents

PART TWO: SUCCESS FACTORS FOR KNOWLEDGE MANAGEMENT AND VIRTUAL ORGANIZATIONS

Preface

This book was born out of the need for advancing the current state of research and practice on knowledge management as related to effective design of new organization forms. It integrates cutting-edge research and best practices being defined and improvised by leading worldwide experts, researchers and practitioners. The articles in this book represent a small percentage of about 150 articles and proposals that were selected through multiple phases of editorial review, as well as double blind peer-review process. Each of those articles represents original and unpublished work of authors with reputed backgrounds and expertise relevant to their contributions. The process through which this book was born represents an epitome of the theme of the book: more than 100 persons located in various countries across the world collaborated 'virtually' through the Internet and WWW from the beginning to the completion of this knowledge aggregation, validation, sharing, compilation and dissemination process.

This book is unique in being the first work of its kind that synthesizes the latest original thinking in knowledge management and the design of information technology and Internet-enabled new organization forms. The scholarly and practitioner contributions to this work represent the first focused and integrated attempt to answer the issues about applying knowledge management for enabling 'anytime, anywhere, anyhow' organizations. These issues will be of relevance to all researchers, scholars, managers, executives and entrepreneurs interested in understanding how information technologies and knowledge management can enable effective design and emergence of virtual organizations, virtual teams and communities of practice. Within this perspective, the focus is on understanding how knowledge creation, knowledge sharing, knowledge acquisition, knowledge exchange, and knowledge transfer can be better understood and applied for enabling new organization forms including virtual web, virtual corporation, Net broker, and business networks.

The first section of the book covers frameworks, models, analyses, cases studies and research on the integration of knowledge management within virtual organizations, virtual teams and virtual communities of practice. Key themes covered in this section include business model innovation; design of virtual organization forms, including virtual corporations, Net-based models, virtual teams and inter-organizational networks; strategies and technologies for knowledge management; tools, techniques and methodologies for enabling knowledge capture, knowledge sharing and knowledge transfer as well as related collaboration, competition and co-opetition at intra- and inter-organizational levels. The focus of the second section is on key success factors that are important for enabling knowledge management and realizing virtual models of business transformation. Key knowledge management themes addressed in this section relate to organizational transformation; analysis and design of knowledge systems and processes; role of organizational control systems; creating successful communities of practice; role of internal and external employees and customers in creation of organizational knowledge; knowledge acquisition and management; and information quality issues.

The backdrop of this project is the @Brint.com Web portal and virtual community of practice, which started as a 'real world' prototype of the virtual organization with explicit focus on knowledge management. Over the last three to four years, this portal has been extensively reviewed in worldwide media for defining the first online compilations of content on this topic and serving as a haven for what is now the largest global virtual community of practice on these issues. Our face-to-face and virtual interactions on these issues with worldwide scholars, corporations, governments, conference organizers, publishers, and journalists over the last few years defined the need for this seminal work on the theme of knowledge management and virtual organizations. Several members of the global community of @Brint.com are represented among the authors and reviewers who contributed to this project.

Most of the authors of chapters included in this book also served as referees for articles written by other authors. Thanks go to all those who provided constructive and comprehensive reviews. However, some of the reviewers must be mentioned as their reviews set the benchmark. Besides the editor of this project, reviewers who provided the most comprehensive, critical and constructive comments include in no specific order: Ron Rice of Rutgers University School of Communication, Information and Library Studies; Mark Nissen, George Zolla and Kishore Sengupta, all of Naval PostGraduate School at Monterey; Bishwajit Choudhary of Norwegian School of Management; Kristen Bell DeTienne of Brigham Young University Marriott School of Management; Ulrich J. Franke of Cranfield University School of Management; Karin Breu of Cranfield School of Management Information Systems Research Center; Karim Hirji of IBM Canada; Brendan Kitts of Brandeis University and Datasage; Karen Lyons, a senior information technology and knowledge management consultant; and, Christopher McLachlan of University of Trier Marketing

Department.

Deep appreciation and gratitude is due to Mini Malhotra, president of @Brint.com LLC, for ongoing sponsorship in terms of generous allocation of on-line and off-line Internet, WWW, hardware and software resources; technical and personnel communication infrastructure; and other editorial support services for coordination of this one-year-long project of global proportions. Special thanks also go to the publishing team at Idea Group Publishing, in particular to Jan Travers, who continuously prodded via e-mail for keeping the project on schedule, and to Mehdi Khosrowpour, whose enthusiasm motivated me to initially accept his invitation for taking on this project. Support of the department of Information Technology and Operations Management at Florida Atlantic University is acknowledged for article archival server space in the completely virtual on-line review process.

With the mission of contributing to the substantive issues of relevance to practitioners, researchers and scholars of business, management, organizations and information systems, we are facilitating a multi-channel forum for creation and dissemination of knowledge on these issues. Besides this book, there are a number of other scholarly and practitioner publications that are, and have been, in the works, details about which are accessible at www.brint.com. Based on your interest in knowledge management and new organization forms, I welcome you to join the global community of practice of the Knowledge Management Think Tank (at forums.brint.com) and the Knowledge Executives Network, and share your significant on-line initiatives, events, programs and publications with the world through the WWW Virtual Library on Knowledge Management (at km.brint.com).

Yours virtually,

Yogesh Malhotra
Editor, *Knowledge Management and Virtual Organizations*
@Brint.com: The BizTech Network [www.brint.com]
Knowledge Management Think Tank [forums.brint.com]
WWW Virtual Library on Knowledge Management [km.brint.com]
e-mail: yogesh.malhotra@brint.com

Part One:

Knowledge Management, Virtual Organizations and Virtual Teams

Chapter I

Knowledge Management and New Organization Forms: A Framework for Business Model Innovation

Yogesh Malhotra
@Brint.com, L.L.C. and Florida Atlantic University

The concept of knowledge management is not new in information systems practice and research. However, radical changes in the business environment have suggested limitations of the traditional information-processing view of knowledge management. Specifically, it is being realized that the programmed nature of heuristics underlying such systems may be inadequate for coping with the demands imposed by the new business environments. New business environments are characterized not only by rapid pace of change, but also discontinuous nature of such change. The new business environment, characterized by dynamically discontinuous change, requires a re-conceptualization of knowledge management as it has been understood in information systems practice and research. One such conceptualization is proposed in the form of a sense-making model of knowledge management for new business environments. Application of this framework will facilitate business model innovation necessary for sustainable competitive advantage in the new business environment characterized by dynamic, discontinuous and radical pace of change.

"People bring imagination and life to a transforming technology."
— *Business Week*, The Internet Age (Special Report), October 4, 1999, p. 108

The traditional organizational business model, driven by pre-specified plans and goals, aimed to ensure optimization and efficiencies based primarily on building consensus, convergence and compliance. Organizational information systems – as well as related performance and control systems—were modeled on the same paradigm to enable convergence by ensuring adherence to organizational routines built into formal and informal information systems. Such routinization of organizational goals for realizing increased efficiencies was suitable for the era marked by a relatively stable and predictable business environment. However, this model is increasingly inadequate in the e-business era that is often characterized by an increasing pace of radical and unforeseen change in the business environment (Arthur, 1996; Barabba, 1998; Malhotra, 1998b; Kalakota and Robinson, 1999; Nadler et al., 1995).

The new era of dynamic and discontinuous change requires continual reassessment of organizational routines to ensure that organizational decision-making processes, as well as underlying assumptions, keep pace with the dynamically changing business environment. This issue poses increasing challenge as 'best practices' of yesterday—turn into 'worst practices' and core competencies turn into core rigidities. The changing business environment, characterized by dynamically discontinuous change, requires a re-conceptualization of knowledge management systems as they have been understood in information systems practice and research. One such conceptualization is proposed in this article in the form of a framework for developing organizational knowledge management systems for business model innovation. It is anticipated that application of this framework will facilitate development of new business models that are better suited to the new business environment characterized by dynamic, discontinuous and radical pace of change.

The popular technology-centric interpretations of knowledge management prevalent in most of the information technology research and trade press are reviewed in the next section. The problems and caveats inherent in such interpretations are then discussed. The subsequent section discusses the demands imposed by the new business environments that require rethinking such conceptualizations of knowledge management and related information technology-based systems. One conceptualization for overcoming the problems of prevalent interpretations and related assumptions is then discussed along with a framework for developing new organization forms and innovative business models. Subsequent discussion explains how the application of this framework can facilitate development of new business models that are better suited to the dynamic, discontinuous and radical pace of change characterizing the new business environment.

KNOWLEDGE MANAGEMENT: THE INFORMATION PROCESSING PARADIGM

The information-processing view of knowledge management has been prevalent in information systems practice and research over the last few decades. This perspective originated in the era when business environment was less vacillating, the products and services and the corresponding core competencies had a long multi-year shelf life, and the organization and industry boundaries were clearly demarcated over the foreseeable future. The relatively structured and predictable business and competitive environment rewarded firms' focus on economies of scale. Such economies of scale were often based on a high level of efficiencies of scale in absence of impending threat of rapid obsolescence of product and service definitions, as well as demarcations of existing organizational and industry boundaries.

The evolution of the information-processing paradigm over the last four decades to build intelligence and manage change in business functions and processes has generally progressed over three phases:

Figure 1: Information Processing Paradigm: Old World of Business

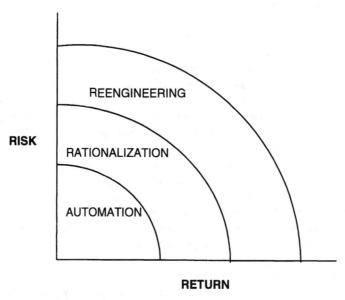

1. *Automation*: increased efficiency of operations;
2. *Rationalization of procedures*: streamlining of procedures and eliminating obvious workflow bottlenecks for enhanced efficiency of operations; and,
3. *Reengineering*: radical redesign of business processes that depends upon information technology intensive radical redesign of workflows and work processes.

The information-processing paradigm has been prevalent over all the three phases that have been characterized by technology-intensive, optimization-driven, efficiency-seeking organizational change (Malhotra 1999c, 1999d, in press). Deployment of information technologies in all the three phases was based on a relatively predictable view of products and services as well as contributory organizational and industrial structures.

Despite increase in risks and corresponding returns relevant to the three kinds of information technology-enabled organizational change, there was little, if any, emphasis on business model innovation – 'rethinking the business' — as illustrated in Figure 1. Based on the consensus and convergence-oriented view of information systems, the information processing view of knowledge management is often characterized by benchmarking and transfer of best practices (cf: Allee, 1997; O'Dell and Grayson, 1998). The key assumptions of the information-processing view are often based on the premise about the generalizability of issues across temporal and contextual frames of diverse organizations.

Such interpretations have often assumed that adaptive functioning of the organization can be based on explicit knowledge archived in corporate databases and technology-based knowledge repositories (cf: Applegate et al., 1988, p. 44; italics added for emphasis):

"Information systems will maintain the corporate history, experience and expertise that long-term employees now hold. The information systems themselves — *not the people* — can become the stable structure of the organization. *People will be free to come and go, but the value of their experience will be incorporated in the systems* that help them and their successors run the business."

The information processing view, evident in scores of definitions of knowledge management in the trade press, has considered organizational memory of the past as a reliable predictor of the dynamically and discontinuously changing business environment. Most such interpretations have also made simplistic assumptions about storing *past* knowledge of individuals in the form of routinized rules-of-thumb and best practices for guiding *future* action. A representative compilation of such interpretations of knowledge management is listed in Table 1.

Based primarily upon a static and 'syntactic' notion of knowledge, such representations have often specified the *minutiae of machinery* while disregarding how people in organizations actually go about acquiring, sharing and creating new knowledge (Davenport 1994). By considering the meaning of knowledge as "unproblematic, predefined, and prepackaged" (Boland 1987), such interpretations of knowledge management have ignored the human dimension of organizational knowledge creation. *Prepackaged* or *taken-for-granted* interpretation of knowledge works against the generation of multiple and contradictory viewpoints that are *necessary* for meeting the challenge posed by *wicked environments* characterized by radical and discontinuous change: this may even hamper the firm's learning and adaptive capabilities (Gill 1995). A key motivation of this article is to address the critical processes of *creation of new knowledge and renewal of existing knowledge* and to suggest a framework that can provide the philosophical and pragmatic bases for better representation and design of organizational knowledge management systems.

Philosophical Bases of the Information-Processing Model

Churchman (1971) had interpreted the viewpoints of philosophers Leibnitz, Locke, Kant, Hagel and Singer in the context of designing information systems. Mason and Mitroff (1973) had made preliminary suggestions for designing information systems based on Churchman's framework. A review of Churchman's inquiring systems, in context of the extant thinking on knowledge management, underscores the limitations of the dominant model of inquiring systems being used by today's organizations. Most technology-based conceptualizations of knowledge management have been primarily based upon heuristics — embedded in procedure manuals, mathematical models or programmed logic — that, arguably, capture the preferred solutions to the *given* repertoire of organization's problems.

Following Churchman, such systems are best suited for:

a) well-structured problem situations for which there exists strong *consensual* position on the nature of the problem situation, and

b) well-structured problems for which there exists an analytic formulation with a solution.

Type (a) systems are classified as Lockean inquiry systems and Type (b) systems are classified as Leibnitzian inquiry systems. Leibnitzian systems are closed systems without access to the external environment; they operate based on *given* axioms and may fall into competency traps based on diminishing returns from the 'tried and tested' heuristics embedded in the inquiry processes. In contrast, the Lockean systems are based on consensual agreement and aim to reduce equivocality embedded in the diverse interpre-

Table 1. Knowledge Management: The Information Processing Paradigm

The process of collecting, organizing, classifying and disseminating information throughout an organization, so as to make it purposeful to those who need it. (*Midrange Systems*: Albert, 1998)
Policies, procedures and technologies employed for operating a continuously updated linked pair of networked databases. (*Computerworld:* Anthes, 1991)
Partly as a reaction to downsizing, some organizations are now trying to use technology to capture the knowledge residing in the minds of their employees so it can be easily shared across the enterprise. Knowledge management aims to capture the knowledge that employees really need in a central repository and filter out the surplus. (*Forbes*: Bair, 1997)
Ensuring a complete development and implementation environment designed for use in a specific function requiring expert systems support. (*International Journal of Bank Marketing*: Chorafas, 1987)
Knowledge management IT concerns organizing and analyzing information in a company's computer databases so this knowledge can be readily shared throughout a company, instead of languishing in the department where it was created, inaccessible to other employees. (*CPA Journal*, 1998)
Identification of categories of knowledge needed to support the overall business strategy, assessment of current state of the firm's knowledge and transformation of the current knowledge base into a new and more powerful knowledge base by filling knowledge gaps. (*Computerworld*: Gopal & Gagnon, 1995)
Combining indexing, searching, and push technology to help companies organize data stored in multiple sources and deliver only relevant information to users. (*Information Week*: Hibbard, 1997)
Knowledge management in general tries to organize and make available important know-how, wherever and whenever it's needed. This includes processes, procedures, patents, reference works, formulas, "best practices," forecasts and fixes. Technologically, intranets, groupware, data warehouses, networks, bulletin boards and videoconferencing are key tools for storing and distributing this intelligence. (*Computerworld*: Maglitta, 1996)
Mapping knowledge and information resources both online and offline; training, guiding and equipping users with knowledge access tools; monitoring outside news and information. (*Computerworld*: Maglitta, 1995)
Knowledge management incorporates intelligent searching, categorization and accessing of data from disparate databases, e- mail and files. (*Computer Reseller News*: Willett & Copeland, 1998)
Understanding the relationships of data; identifying and documenting rules for managing data; and assuring that data are accurate and maintain integrity. (*Software Magazine*: Strapko, 1990)
Facilitation of autonomous coordinability of decentralized subsystems that can state and adapt their own objectives. (*Human Systems Management*, Zeleny, 1987)

tations of the world-view. However, in absence of a consensus, these inquiry systems also tend to fail.

The *convergent* and *consensus building* emphasis of these two kinds of inquiry systems is suited for stable and predictable organizational environments. However, wicked environment imposes the need for variety and complexity of the interpretations that are necessary for deciphering the multiple world-views of the uncertain and unpredictable future.

BEYOND EXISTING MYTHS ABOUT KNOWLEDGE MANAGEMENT

The information-processing view of knowledge management has propagated some dangerous myths about knowledge management. Simplistic representations of knowledge management that often appear in popular press may often result in misdirected investments and system implementations that often do not yield expected returns on investment (Strassmann, 1997; 1999).

Given the impending backlash against such simplistic representations of knowledge management (cf: Garner 1999), it is critical to analyze the myths underlying the 'successful' representations of knowledge management that worked in a bygone era. There are three dominant myths based on the information-processing logic that are characteristic of most popular knowledge management interpretations (Hildebrand, 1999 – interview of the author with *CIO Enterprise* magazine).

Myth 1: *Knowledge management technologies can deliver the 'right information' to the 'right person' at the 'right time.'* This idea applies to an outdated business model. Information systems in the old industrial model mirror the notion that businesses will change incrementally in an inherently stable market, and executives can foresee change by examining the past. The new business model of the Information Age, however, is marked by fundamental, not incremental, change. Businesses can't plan long-term; instead, they must shift to a more flexible "anticipation-of-surprise" model. Thus, it's impossible to build a system that predicts who the *right person* at the *right time* even is, let alone what constitutes the *right information*.

Myth 2: *Knowledge management technologies can store human intelligence and experience.* Technologies such as databases and groupware applications store bits and pixels of data, but they can't store the rich schemas that people possess for making sense of data bits. Moreover, information is context-sensitive. The same assemblage of data can evoke different responses from different people. Even the same assemblage of data when reviewed by the same person at a different time or in a different context could evoke differing response in terms of decision-making and action. Hence, storing a static representation of the explicit representation of a person's knowledge — assuming one has

Figure 2: From Best Practices to Paradigm Shifts

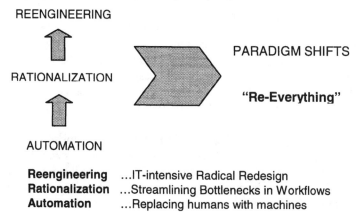

REENGINEERING

PARADIGM SHIFTS

RATIONALIZATION

"Re-Everything"

AUTOMATION

Reengineering ...IT-intensive Radical Redesign
Rationalization ...Streamlining Bottlenecks in Workflows
Automation ...Replacing humans with machines

the willingness and the ability to part with it – is not tantamount to storing human intelligence and experience.

Myth 3: *Knowledge management technologies can distribute human intelligence*. Again, this assertion presupposes that companies can predict the *right information* to distribute and the *right people* to distribute it to. As noted earlier, for most important business decisions, technologies cannot communicate the meaning embedded in complex data as it is constructed by human minds. This does not preclude the use of information technologies for rich exchange between humans to make sense about bits and pixels. However, dialog that surfaces meaning embedded in information is an intrinsic human property, not the property of the technology that may facilitate the process. Often it is assumed that compilation of data in a central repository would somehow ensure that everyone who has access to that repository is *capable* and *willing* to utilize the information stored therein. Past research on this issue has shown that despite availability of comprehensive reports and databases, most executives take decisions based on their interactions with others who they think are knowledgeable about the issues. Furthermore, the assumption of singular meaning of information, though desirable for seeking efficiencies, precludes *creative abrasion* and *creative conflict* that is necessary for business model innovation. In contrast, data archived in technological 'knowledge repositories' does not allow for *renewal of existing knowledge* and *creation of new knowledge*.

The above observations seem consistent with observations by industry experts such as John Seely Brown (1997): "In the last 20 years, U.S. industry has invested more than $1 trillion in technology, but has realized little improvement in the efficiency of its knowledge workers and virtually none in their effectiveness."

Given the dangerous perception about knowledge management as seamlessly entwined with technology, "its true critical success factors will be lost in the pleasing hum of servers, software and pipes" (Hildebrand, 1999). Hence, it is critical to focus attention on the critical success factors that are necessary for business model innovation.

To distinguish from the *information-processing paradigm* of knowledge management discussed earlier, the proposed paradigm will be denoted as the *sense-making paradigm* of knowledge management. This proposed framework is based on Churchman's (1971, p. 10) explicit recognition that "knowledge resides in the user and not in the collection of information…it is how the user reacts to a collection of information that matters."

Churchman's emphasis on the human nature of knowledge creation seems more pertinent today than it seemed 25 years ago given the increasing prevalence of 'wicked' environment characterized by discontinuous change (Nadler & Shaw 1995) and "*wide range of potential surprise*" (Landau & Stout 1979). Such an environment defeats the traditional organizational response of *predicting* and *reacting* based on pre-programmed heuristics. Instead, it demands more *anticipatory* responses from the organization members who need to carry out the mandate of a faster cycle of knowledge-creation and action based on the new knowledge (Nadler & Shaw 1995).

Philosophical Bases of the Proposed Model

Churchman had proposed two alternative kinds of inquiry systems that are particularly suited for multiplicity of world-views needed for radically changing environments: Kantian inquiry systems and Hegelian inquiry systems. Kantian inquiry systems attempt to give multiple *explicit* views of *complementary* nature and are best suited for moderate ill-structured problems. However, given that there is no explicit opposition to the multiple views, these systems may also be afflicted by competency traps characterized by *plurality* of *complementary* solutions. In contrast, Hegelian inquiry systems are based on a synthesis of *multiple completely antithetical* representations that are characterized by intense conflict because of the contrary underlying assumptions. Knowledge management systems based upon the Hegelian inquiry systems would facilitate multiple and contradictory interpretations of the focal information. This process would ensure that the 'best practices' are subject to *continual* re-examination and modification given the dynamically changing business environment.

Given the increasingly wicked nature of business environment, there seems to be an imperative need for consideration of the Kantian and Hegelian inquiring systems that can provide the multiple, diverse, and contradictory interpretations. Such systems, by generating multiple *semantic* views of the future characterized by increasingly rapid pace of discontinuous change, would facilitate *anticipation of surprise* (Kerr, 1995) over prediction. They are most suited for dialectical inquiry based on dialogue: "meaning passing or moving through...a free flow of meaning between people..." (Bohm cited in Senge, 1990). As explained in the following discussion, the *critical role* of the individual and social processes underlying the *creation of meaning* (Strombach, 1986, p. 77) is important without which dialectical inquiry would not be possible. Therein lies the crucial sense-making role of humans in facilitating knowledge creation in inquiring organizations.

Continuously challenging the current 'company way,' such systems provide the basis for 'creative abrasion' (Eisenhardt et al., 1997; Leonard, 1997) that is necessary for promoting radical analysis for business model innovation. In essence, knowledge management systems based on the proposed model prevent the *core capabilities* of yesterday from becoming *core rigidities* of tomorrow (Leonard-Barton, 1995). It is critical to look at knowledge management beyond its representation as "know what you know and profit from it" (Fryer, 1999) to "obsolete what you know before others obsolete it and profit by creating the challenges and opportunities others haven't even thought about" (Malhotra, 1999e). This is the new paradigm of knowledge management for radical innovation needed for sustainable competitive advantage in a business environment characterized by radical and discontinuous change.

KNOWLEDGE MANAGEMENT FOR BUSINESS MODEL INNOVATION: FROM BEST PRACTICES TO PARADIGM SHIFTS

As discussed above, in contrast to the information-processing model based on deterministic assumptions about the future, the sense-making model is more conducive for sustaining competitive advantage in the "world of re-everything" (Arthur, 1996). Without such radical innovation, one wouldn't have observed the paradigm shifts in core value propositions served by new business models.

Such rethinking of the nature of the business and the nature of the organization itself characterizes paradigm shifts that are the hallmark of business model innovation. Such paradigm shifts will be attributable for about 70 percent of the *previously unforeseen* competitive players that many established organizations will encounter in their future (Hamel, 1997).

Examples of such new business models include Amazon.com and e-Toys, relatively new entrants that are threatening traditional business models embodied in organizations such as Barnes and Noble and Toys R Us. Such business model innovations represent 'paradigm shifts' that characterize not transformation at the level of business processes and process workflows, but radical rethinking of the business as well as the dividing lines between organizations and industries.

Such paradigm shifts are critical for overcoming mangers' "blindness to developments occurring *outside* their core [operations and business segments]" and tapping the opportunities in "white spaces" that lie between existing markets and operations (Moore, 1998).

The notions of 'best practices' and 'benchmarking' relate to the model of organizational controls that are "built, *a priori*, on the principal of closure" (Landau & Stout 1979, p. 150, Stout 1980) to seek compliance to, and convergence of, the organizational decision-making processes (Flamholtz et al. 1985). However, the decision rules embedded in 'best practices' assume the character of predictive 'proclamations' which draw their legitimacy from the vested authority, not because they provide adequate solutions (Hamel & Prahalad 1994, p. 145). Challenges to such decision rules tend to be perceived as challenges to the authority embedded in 'best practices' (Landau 1973).

Hence, such 'best practices' that *ensure* conformity by ensuring task definition, measurement and control also *inhibit* creativity and initiative (Bartlett & Ghoshal 1995, Ghoshal & Bartlett 1995). The system that is structured as a 'core capability' suited to a relatively static business environment turns into a 'core rigidity' in a discontinuously changing business environment. Despite the transient efficacy of 'best practices,' the cycle of doing "more of the same" tends to result in locked-in behavior patterns that eventually sacrifice organizational performance at the altar of the organizational "death spiral" (Nadler and Shaw 1995, p. 12-13). In the e-business era, which is increasingly characterized by faster cycle time, greater competition, and lesser stability, certainty and predictability, any kind of consensus cannot keep pace with the dynamically discontinuous changes in the business environment (Bartlett and Ghoshal, 1995; Drucker, 1994; Ghoshal and Bartlett, 1996).

With its key emphasis on the obedience of rules embedded in 'best practices' and 'benchmarks' at the cost of cor-

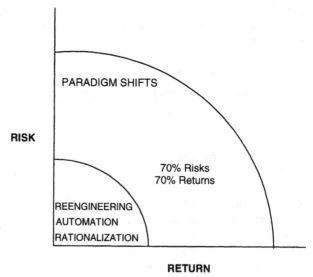

Figure 3: Paradigm Shifts: New World of Business

PARADIGM SHIFTS

RISK

70% Risks
70% Returns

REENGINEERING
AUTOMATION
RATIONALIZATION

RETURN

rection of errors (Landau and Stout, 1979), the information-processing model of knowledge management limits creation of *new* organizational knowledge and impedes renewal of existing organizational knowledge.

Most of the innovative business models such as Cisco and Amazon.com didn't devolve from the best practices or benchmarks of the organizations of yesterday that they displaced, but from radical re-conceptualization of the nature of the business. These paradigm shifts are also increasingly expected to challenge the traditional concepts of organization and industry (Mathur and Kenyon, 1997) with the emergence of *business ecosystems* (Moore, 1998), *virtual communities of practice* (Hagel and Armstrong, 1997) and *infomediaries* (Hagel and Singer, 1999).

HUMAN ASPECTS OF KNOWLEDGE CREATION AND KNOWLEDGE RENEWAL

Knowledge management technologies based upon the information-processing model are limited in the capabilities for creation of new knowledge or renewal of existing knowledge. No doubt, such technologies provide the optimization-driven efficiency-seeking behavior needed for high performance and success in a business environment characterized by a predictable and incremental pace of change. Examples of technologies that are based on a high level of integration such as ERP technologies represent knowledge management technologies based upon the information-processing model. However, given a radical and discontinuously changing business environment, these technologies fall short of sensing changes that they haven't been pre-programmed to sense and accordingly unable to modify the logic underlying their behavior.

Until information systems embedded in technology become capable of *anticipating change* and changing their basic assumptions (heuristics) accordingly, we would need to rely upon humans for performing the increasingly relevant function of self-adaptation and knowledge creation. The vision of information systems that can autonomously revamp their past history based upon their anticipation of future change is yet far from reality (Wolpert, 1996). Given the constraints inherent in the extant mechanistic (programmed) nature of technology, the human element assumes greater relevance for maintaining currency of the programmed heuristics (programmed routines based upon previous assumptions). Therefore, the human function of ensuring the *reality check*—by means of repetitive questioning, interpretation and revision of the assumptions underlying the information system—assumes an increasingly important role in the era marked by discontinuous change.

The human aspects of knowledge creation and knowledge renewal that are difficult —if not impossible—to replace completely with knowledge management technologies are listed below.

- Imagination and creativity latent in human minds
- Untapped tacit dimensions of knowledge creation
- Subjective and meaning-making basis of knowledge
- Constructive aspects of knowledge creation and renewal

The following discussion explains these issues in greater detail and suggests how they can help overcome the limitations of the information-processing model of knowledge management.

Imagination and Creativity Latent in Human Minds: Knowledge management solutions characterized by memorization of 'best practices' may tend to define the assumptions that are embedded not only in information databases, but also in the organization's strategy, reward systems and resource allocation systems. The *hardwiring* of such assumptions in organizational knowledge bases may lead to perceptual insensitivity (Hedberg et al., 1976) of the organization to the changing environment. Institutionalization of 'best practices' by embedding them in information technology might facilitate efficient handling of routine, 'linear,' and predictable situations during stable or incrementally changing environments. However, when such change is discontinuous, there is a persistent need for continuous renewal of the basic premises underlying the 'best practices' stored in organizational knowledge bases. The information-processing model of knowledge management is devoid of such capabilities essential for continuous learning *and* unlearning mandated by radical and discontinuous change. A more proactive involvement of the human imagination and creativity (March, 1971) is needed to facilitate greater internal diversity [of the organization] that can match the variety and complexity of the wicked environment.

Untapped Tacit Dimensions of Knowledge Creation: The information processing model of knowledge management ignores tacit knowledge deeply rooted in action and experience, ideals, values, or emotions (Nonaka & Takeuchi 1995). Although tacit knowledge lies at the very basis of organizational knowledge creation, its nature renders it highly personal and hard to formalize and communicate. Nonaka and Takeuchi (1995) have suggested that knowledge is created through four different modes: (1) *socialization* which involves conversion from tacit knowledge to tacit knowledge, (2) *externalization* which involves conversion from tacit knowledge to explicit knowledge, (3) *combination* which involves conversion from explicit knowledge to explicit knowledge, and (4) *internalization* which involves conversion from explicit knowledge to tacit knowledge. The dominant model of inquiring systems is limited in its ability to foster shared experience necessary for relating to others' thinking processes thus limiting its utility in *socialization*. It may, by virtue of its ability to convert tacit knowledge into explicit forms such as metaphors, analogies and models, have some utility in *externalization*. This utility is however restricted by its ability to support dialogue or collective reflection. The current model of inquiring systems, apparently, may have greater role in *combination* involving combining different bodies of explicit knowledge, and *internalization* which involves knowledge transfer through verbalizing or diagramming into documents, manuals and stories. A more explicit recognition of tacit knowledge and related human aspects, such as ideals, values, or emotions, is necessary for developing a richer conceptualization of knowledge management.

Subjective and Meaning-Making Bases of Knowledge Creation: Wicked environments call for interpretation of new events and ongoing reinterpretation and reanalysis of assumptions underlying extant practices. However, the information processing model of knowledge management largely ignores the important construct of *meaning* (cf: Boland 1987) as well as its transient and ambiguous nature. 'Prepackaged' or 'taken-for-granted' interpretation of knowledge residing in the organizational memories works against generation of multiple and contradictory viewpoints necessary for ill-structured environments. Simplification of contextual information for storage in IT-enabled repositories works against the retention of the complexity of multiple viewpoints. Institutionalization of definitions and interpretations of events and issues works against the exchanging and sharing of diverse perspectives. To some extent the current knowledge management technologies, based on their ability to communicate metaphors, analogies and stories by using multimedia technologies, may offer some representation and communication of meaning. However, a more human-centric view of knowledge creation is necessary to enable the interpretative, subjective and meaning-making nature of knowledge creation. Investing in multiple and diverse interpretations is expected to enable Kantian and Hegelian modes of inquiry and, thus, lessen oversimplification or premature decision closure.

Constructive Aspects of Knowledge Creation and Renewal: The information-processing model of knowledge management ignores the constructive nature of knowledge creation and instead assumes a pre-specified meaning of the memorized 'best practices' devoid of ambiguity or contradiction. It ignores the critical process that translates information into meaning and action that is necessary for knowledge-based performance (Malhotra, 1999a; Malhotra & Kirsch, 1996; Bruner, 1973; Dewey, 1933; Strombach, 1986). The dominant model of inquiring systems downplays the constructive nature of knowledge creation and action. For most ill-structured situations, it is difficult to ensure a unique interpretation of 'best practices' residing in information repositories since knowledge is created *by the individuals* in the process of using that data. Even if pre-specified interpretations could be possible, they would be problematic when future solutions need to be either thought afresh or in discontinuation from past solutions. Interestingly, the constructive aspect of knowledge creation is also expected to enable multiple interpretations that can facilitate the organization's *anticipatory response* to discontinuous change.

CONCLUSIONS AND RECOMMENDATIONS FOR FUTURE RESEARCH

The proposed sense making model of knowledge management enables the organizational knowledge creation process that is "both *participative* and *anticipative*" (Bennis and Nanus, 1985, p. 209). Instead of a formal rule- or procedure-based step-by-step rational guide, this model favors a "set of guiding principles" for helping people understand "not how it should be done" but "how to understand what might fit the situation they are in" (Kanter, 1983, p. 305-306). This model assumes the existence of "only a few rules, some specific information and a lot of freedom" (Margaret Wheatley cited in Stuart, 1995). One model organization that has proven the long-term success of this approach is Nordstrom, the retailer that has a sustained reputation for its high level of customer service. Surprisingly, the excellence of this organization derives from its one-sentence employee policy manual that states (Taylor, 1994): "Use your good judgment in all situations. There will be no additional rules." The primary responsibility of most supervisors is to continuously coach the employees about this philosophy for carrying out the organizational pursuit of "serving the customer better" (Peters, 1989 p. 379).

The proposed model, illustrated in Figure 4, is anticipated to advance the current conception of 'Knowledge-Tone' and related e-business applications (Kalakota and Robinson, 1999) beyond the performance threshold of highly integrated technology-

Figure 4: Knowledge Management for Business Model Innovation

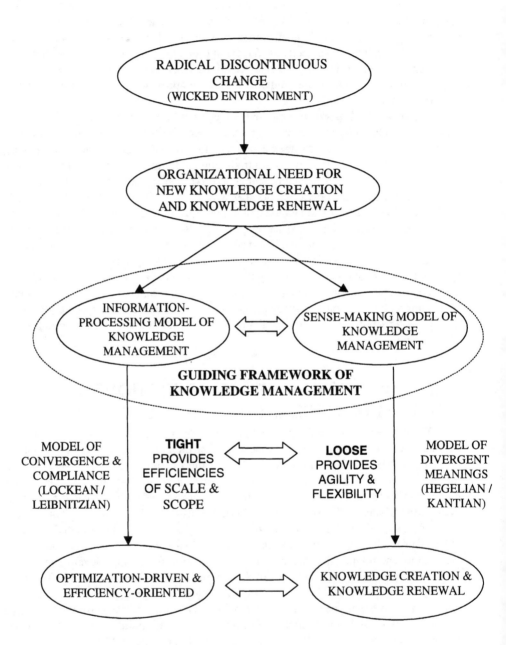

based systems. By drawing upon the strengths of both convergence-driven [Lockean-Leibnitzian] systems and divergence-oriented [Hegelian-Kantian] systems, the proposed model offers both a combination of flexibility and agility while ensuring efficiencies of the current technology architecture. Such systems are *loose* in the sense that they allow for continuous reexamination of the assumptions underlying best practices and reinterpretation of this information. Such systems are *tight* in the sense that they also allow for efficiencies based on propagation and dissemination of the best practices.

The knowledge management systems based on the proposed model do not completely ignore the notion of 'best practices' per se but consider the continuous construction and reconstruction of such practices as a dynamic and ongoing process. Such *loose-tight knowledge management systems* (Malhotra, 1998a) would need to provide not only for identification and dissemination of best practices, but also for continuous reexamination of such practices. Specifically, they would need to also include a simultaneous process that continuously examines the best practices for their currency given the changing assumptions about the business environment. Such systems would need to contain *both* learning and unlearning processes. These simultaneous processes are needed for assuring the efficiency-oriented optimization based on the current best practices while ensuring that such practices are continuously reexamined for their viability.

Some management experts (cf: Manville and Foote, 1996) have discussed selected aspects of the proposed *sense making model of knowledge management* in terms of the shift from the traditional emphasis on transaction processing, integrated logistics, and work flows to systems that support competencies for communication building, people networks, trust-building and on-the-job learning. Many such *critical success factors* for knowledge management require a richer understanding of human behavior in terms of their perceptions about living, learning and working in technology-mediated and cyberspace-based environments.

Some experts (cf: Davenport and Prusak, 1997; Romer in Silverstone, 1999) have emphasized formal incentive systems for motivating loyalty of employees for sustaining firm's intellectual capital and loyalty of customers for sustaining 'stickiness' of portals. However, given recent findings in the realms of performance and motivation of individuals (cf: Malhotra, 1998c; Kohn, 1995) using those systems, these assertions need to be reassessed. The need for better understanding of human factors underpinning performance of knowledge management technologies is also supported by our observation of informal 'knowledge sharing' virtual communities of practice affiliated with various Net-based businesses (cf: Knowledge Management Think Tank at: forums.brint.com) and related innovative business models. In most such cyber-communities, success, performance and 'stickiness' is often driven by *hi-touch* technology environments that effectively address core value proposition of the virtual community. It is suggested that the critical success factors of the proposed model of knowledge management for business innovation are supported by a redefinition of 'control' (Flamholtz et al., 1985; Malhotra and Kirsch, 1996; Manz et al., 1987; Manz and Sims, 1989) as it is relates to the new living, learning and working environments afforded by emerging business models. Hence, business model innovation needs to be informed by the proposed model of knowledge management that is based upon synergy of the information-processing capacity of information technologies and sense-making capabilities of humans.

REFERENCES

Albert, S. (1998). "Knowledge Management: Living Up To The Hype?" *Midrange Systems*, 11(13), 52.

Allee, V. (1997). "Chevron Maps Key Processes and Transfers Best Practices," *Knowledge Inc.*, April.

Anthes, G.H. (1991). "A Step Beyond a Database," *Computerworld*, 25(9), 28.

Applegate, L., Cash, J. & Mills D.Q.(1988). "Information Technology and Tomorrow's Manager," In McGowan, W.G. (Ed.), *Revolution in Real Time: Managing Information Technology in the 1990s*, pp. 33-48, Boston, MA, Harvard Business School Press.

Arthur, W. B. (1996). "Increasing Returns and the New World of Business." *Harvard Business Review*, 74(4), 100-109.

Bair, J. (1997)."Knowledge Management: The Era Of Shared Ideas," *Forbes*, 1(1) (The Future of IT Supplement), 28.

Barabba, V.P. (1998). "Revisiting Plato's Cave: Business Design in an Age of Uncertainty," in D. Tapscott, A. Lowy & D. Ticoll (Eds.), *Blueprint to the Digital Economy: Creating Wealth in the Era of E-Business*, McGraw-Hill.

Bartlett, C.A. & Ghoshal, S. (1995). "Changing the Role of the Top Management: Beyond Systems to People," *Harvard Business Review*, May-June 1995, 132-142.

Bennis, W. & Nanus, B. (1985). *Leaders: The Strategies for Taking Charge*, New York, NY, Harper & Row.

Boland, R.J. (1987). "The In-formation of Information Systems," In R.J. Boland and R. Hirschheim (Eds.), *Critical Issues in Information Systems Research*, pp. 363-379, Wiley, Chichester.

Bruner, J. (1973). *Beyond the Information Given: Studies in Psychology of Knowing*, In J.M. Arglin (Ed.), W.W. Norton & Co., New York.

Business Week (1999). The Internet Age (Special Report), October 4.

Chorafas, D.N. (1987). "Expert Systems at the Banker's Reach," *International Journal of Bank Marketing*, 5(4), 72-81.

Churchman, C.W. (1971). *The Design of Inquiring Systems*, Basic Books, New York, NY.

CPA Journal (1998). "Knowledge Management Consulting Gives CPAs a Competitive Edge," 68(8), 72.

Davenport, T.H. (1994). "Saving IT's Soul: Human-Centered Information Management," *Harvard Business Review*, Mar-Apr, 119-131.

Davenport, T.H. & Prusak, L. (1997). *Working Knowledge: How Organizations Manage What They Know*, Harvard Business School Press, Boston, MA.

Dewey, J. (1933). *How We Think*, D.C. Heath and Company, Boston, MA.

Drucker, P.F. (1994). "The Theory of Business," *Harvard Business Review*, September/October, 95-104.

Eisenhardt, K.M., Kahwajy, J.L. & Bourgeois III, L.J. (1997). "How Management Teams Can Have a Good Fight," *Harvard Business Review*, July-August.

Flamholtz, E.G., Das, T.K. & Tsui, A.S. (1985). "Toward an Integrative Framework of Organizational Control," *Accounting, Organizations and Society*, 10(1), 35-50.

Fryer, B. (1999). "Get Smart," *Inc. Technology*, 3, Sep. 15.

Garner, R. (1999). "Please Don't Call it Knowledge Management," *Computerworld*,

August 9.

Ghoshal, S. & Bartlett, C.A. (1995). "Changing the Role of Top Management: Beyond Structure to Processes," *Harvard Business Review*, January-February 1995, pp. 86-96.

Ghoshal, S. & Bartlett, C.A. (1996). "Rebuilding Behavioral Context: A Blueprint for Corporate Renewal," *Sloan Management Review*, Winter 1996, 23-36.

Gill, T.G. (1995). "High-Tech Hidebound: Case Studies of Information Technologies that Inhibited Organizational Learning," *Accounting, Management and Information Technologies*, 5(1), 41-60.

Gopal, C. & Gagnon, J. (1995). "Knowledge, Information, Learning and the IS Manager," *Computerworld (Leadership Series)*, 1(5), 1-7.

Hagel, J. and Armstrong, A.G. (1997). *Net Gain: Expanding Markets Through Virtual Communities*, Harvard Business School Press, Boston, MA.

Hagel, J. and Singer, M.(1999). *Net Worth*, Harvard Business School Press, Boston, MA, 1999.

Hamel, G. (1997). Keynote address at the *Academy of Management* Meeting, Boston, 1997.

Hamel, G. & Prahalad, C.K. (1994). *Competing for the Future*, Harvard Business School Press, Boston, MA.

Hildebrand, C. (1999). "Does KM=IT?" *CIO Enterprise*, Sep. 15. Online version accessible at: *http://www.cio.com/archive/enterprise/091599_ic.html*.

Hedberg, B., Nystrom, P.C. & Starbuck, W.H. (1976). "Camping on Seesaws: Prescriptions for a Self-Designing Organization," *Administrative Science Quarterly*, 21, 41-65.

Hibbard, J.(1997). "Ernst & Young Deploys App For Knowledge Management," *Information Week*, Jul 28, 28.

Kalakota, R. & Robinson, M. (1999). *e-Business: Roadmap for Success*, Addison Wesley, Reading, MA.

Kanter, R.M. *(1984). The Change Masters: Innovation & Entrepreneurship in the American Corporation*, Simon & Schuster, New York, NY.

Kerr, S.(1995). "Creating the Boundaryless Organization: The Radical Reconstruction of Organization Capabilities," *Planning Review*, Sep-Oct, 41-45.

Kohn, A. (1995). *Punished by Rewards : The Trouble With Gold Stars, Incentive Plans, A's, Praise, and Other Bribes*, Houghton Mifflin Co, Boston, MA, 1995.

Landau, M. (1973). "On the Concept of Self-Correcting Organizations," *Public Administration Review*, November/December 1973, pp. 533-542.

Landau, M. & Stout, Jr., R. (1979). "To Manage is Not to Control: Or the Folly of Type II Errors," *Public Administration Review*, March/April 1979, pp. 148-156.

Leonard-Barton, D. *Wellsprings of Knowledge: Building and Sustaining the Sources of Innovation*, Boston, MA, Harvard Business School Press, 1995.

Leonard, D.(1997). "Putting Your Company's Whole Brain to Work," *Harvard Business Review*, July-August.

Maglitta, J.(1995). "Smarten Up!," *Computerworld*, 29(23), 84-86.

Maglitta, J. (1996). "Know-How, Inc." *Computerworld*, 30(1), 1996.

Malhotra, Y. "From Information Management to Knowledge Management: Beyond the 'Hi-Tech Hidebound' Systems," in K. Srikantaiah and M.E.D. Koenig (Eds.), *Knowledge Management for the Information Professional*, Information Today, Inc., Medford,

NJ, (in press).

Malhotra, Y. (1999a). "Bringing the Adopter Back Into the Adoption Process: A Personal Construction Framework of Information Technology Adoption," *Journal of High Technology Management Research*, 10(1).

Malhotra, Y. & Galletta, D.F. (1999b). "Extending the Technology Acceptance Model to Account for Social Influence: Theoretical Bases and Empirical Validation," in the *Proceedings of the Hawaii International Conference on System Sciences* (HICSS 32) (Adoption and Diffusion of Collaborative Systems and Technology Minitrack), Maui, HI, January 5-8,.

Malhotra, Y. (1999c). "High-Tech Hidebound Cultures Disable Knowledge Management," in *Knowledge Management* (UK), February.

Malhotra, Y. (1999d). "Knowledge Management for Organizational White Waters: An Ecological Framework," in *Knowledge Management* (UK), March.

Malhotra, Y. (1999e). "What is Really Knowledge Management?: Crossing the Chasm of Hype," in @Brint.com Web site, Sep. 15. [Letter to editor in response to *Inc. Technology* #3, Sep. 15, 1999, special issue on Knowledge Management]. Accessible online at: http://*www.brint.com/advisor/a092099.htm*.

Malhotra, Y. (1998a). "Toward a Knowledge Ecology for Organizational White-Waters," Invited Keynote Presentation for the *Knowledge Ecology Fair 98: Beyond Knowledge Management*, Feb. 2 - 27, accessible online at: http://www.brint.com/papers/ecology.htm.

Malhotra, Y. (1998b). "Deciphering the Knowledge Management Hype" *Journal for Quality & Participation*, July/August, 58-60.

Malhotra, Y. *(1998c). Role of Social Influence, Self Determination and Quality of Use in Information Technology Acceptance and Utilization: A Theoretical Framework and Empirical Field Study*, Ph.D. thesis, July, Katz Graduate School of Business, University of Pittsburgh, 225 pages.

Malhotra, Y. & Kirsch, L. (1996). "Personal Construct Analysis of Self-Control in IS Adoption: Empirical Evidence from Comparative Case Studies of IS Users & IS Champions," in the Proceedings of the *First INFORMS Conference on Information Systems and Technology (Organizational Adoption & Learning Track)*, Washington D.C., May 5-8, 1996, pp. 105-114.

Manville, B. & Foote, N. "Harvest your Workers' Knowledge," *Datamation*,42(13), 78-80.

Manz, C.C., Mossholder, K. W. & Luthans, F.(1987). "An Integrated Perspective of Self-Control in Organizations," 19(1), *Administration & Society*, May, 3-24.

57. Manz, C.C. & Sims, H.P. *(1989). SuperLeadership: Leading Others to Lead Themselves*, Prentice-Hall, Berkeley, CA.

March, J.G. (1971)."The Technology of Foolishness" *Civilokonomen*, May, 7-12.

Mason, R.O. & Mitroff, I.I.(1973). "A Program for Research on Management Information Systems," *Management Science*, 19(5), 475-487.

Mathur, S.S. & Kenyon, A. (1997)."Our Strategy is What We Sell," *Long Range Planning*, 30, June.

Moore, J.F. (1998). "The New Corporate Form," In Blueprint to the Digital Economy:

Creating Wealth in the Era of E-Business (Ed. Don Topscott), McGraw Hill, New York, NY, 77-95.

Nadler, D.A. & Shaw, R.B. (1995). "Change Leadership: Core Competency for the Twenty-First Century," In *Discontinuous Change: Leading Organizational Transformation* (D.A. Nadler, R.B. Shaw & A.E. Walton), Jossey-Bass, San Franscisco, CA.

Nadler, D.A., Shaw, R.B. & Walton, A.E. (Eds.) (1995). *Discontinuous Change: Leading Organizational Transformation*, Jossey-Bass, San Francisco, CA.

Nonaka, I. and Takeuchi, H. (1995). *The Knowledge-Creating Company*, Oxford University Press, New York, NY.

O'Dell, C. and Grayson, C.J. (1998). "If Only We Knew What We Know: Identification And Transfer of Internal Best Practices," *California Management Review*, 40(3), Spring 154-174.

Peters, T. (1989). *Thriving on Chaos: Handbook for a Management Revolution*, Pan Books, London, UK.

Silverstone, S. (1999)."Maximize Incentives," *Knowledge Management*, October, 36-37.

Seely-Brown, J. (1997). "The Human Factor", *Information Strategy*, December 1996-January.

Senge, P.M. (1990). *The Fifth Discipline: The Art and Practice of the Learning Organization*, New York, NY, Doubleday.

Stout, R., Jr. (1980). *Management or Control?: The Organizational Challenge*, Indiana University Press, Bloomington, IN.

Strapko, W.(1990). "Knowledge Management," *Software Magazine*, 10(13), 63-66.

Strassmann, P.A. (1997). *The Squandered Computer: Evaluating the Business Alignment of Information Technologies*, Information Economics Press, New Canaan, CT.

Strassmann, P.A.(1999). "The Knowledge Fuss," *Computerworld*, October 4.

Strombach, W. (1986). "Information in Epistemological and Ontological Perspective," in *Philosophy and Technology II: Information Technology and Computers in Theory and Practice*, C. Mitcham and A. Huning (Eds.), D. Reidel Publishing Co., Dordrecht, Holland.

Stuart, A. (1995). "Elusive Assets," *CIO*, November 15, 28-34.

Taylor, W.C. (1994). "Contol in an Age of Chaos," *Harvard Business Review*, November-December 1994,72.

Willett, S. & Copeland, L.(1998). "Knowledge Management Key to IBM's Enterprise Plan," *Computer Reseller News*, Jul 27, 1, 6.

Wolpert, D.H. (19996)."An Incompleteness Theorem for Calculating the Future," Working Paper, The Santa Fe Institute.

Zeleny, M. (1987)."Management Support Systems," *Human Systems Management*," 7(1), 1987, 59-70.

Chapter II

The Knowledge-Based View (KBV) of the Virtual Web, the Virtual Corporation, and the Net-Broker

Ulrich Franke
Cranfield University, UK

This chapter describes virtual organization from an inter-organization perspective. The virtual web is a network of equal and independent companies from which virtual corporations derive. Virtual corporations are temporary partnerships, which are only established in response to market opportunities or customer needs. The net-broker manages and administrates the virtual web and configures virtual corporations. Since knowledge has been identified as a key resource to gain competitive advantage, the knowledge-based perspective of the virtual web / corporation concept is used to argue why virtual corporations have theoretically the potential to build core know-how and therefore to gain competitive advantage. The chapter finalizes with a discussion of whether virtual corporations might be in a better position to achieve competitive advantage than other forms of inter-organizational partnerships.

Today, knowledge is regarded as the key resource to gain competitive advantage. This chapter begins by reviewing the recently emerging new organizational form of virtual organizations. Taking the inter-organizational perspective, the virtual web is a pool of pre-qualified independent companies, which are willing to cooperate. Virtual corporations derive from the virtual web and they are the temporary operating units that create value. The net-broker initiates and maintains the virtual web and formats virtual corporations. Furthermore, this chapter introduces the 'knowledge-based view of the firm', and develops a knowledge-based framework grounded on the existing academic literature. The objective of this chapter is to describe the implications of the knowledge-based view for the virtual web / corporation concept as well as the net-broker. In addition, it analyses and explains why virtual corporations have the potential to build core know-how and are therefore in the position to gain sustainable competitive advantage. In order to support this argument a practical example of the knowledge management of a virtual web/corporation is provided. The chapter concludes with a discussion of why the virtual web/corporation concept is likely to be more efficient in achieving competitive advantages than other forms of cooperations.

THE VIRTUAL ORGANIZATION

Lipman and Stamps (1994) argued that each historical age has its distinct organizational form. Similar to the industrial age and its bureaucracy, the organizational form of the information age will be the 'boundary-spanning networks'. Today's strategic challenge of doing more with less has led firms to look outward as well as inward for solutions to improve their ability to compete without adding internal resources (Kanter, 1989). She proposed three strategic options for firms to cope with increasingly competitive markets. Firms can either pool their resources with others, form alliances to exploit market opportunities, or link their organizational systems in partnerships.

Basically, the 'virtual organization' is a partnership network. The term 'virtual' originates from the Latin word 'virtus' which basically means 'proficiency, manliness' (Scholz, 1994), it defines an attribute of a thing, which is not really existing, but would have the possibility to exist (Scholz, 1996).

Since Mowshowitz (1986) used the term 'virtual organization' for the first time, many other authors have created a variety of different terms and definitions to describe this new form of network organization, such as virtual company (Goldman and Nagel, 1993), virtual enterprise (Hardwick et al., 1996), virtual factory (Upton and McAfee, 1996), and virtual office (Davenport and Pearlson, 1998).

Bultje and Wijk (1998) noted that the different definitions of 'virtual organization' partly depend on the view the authors have of the concept 'virtual' (see Figure 1).

What does the concept of 'Vvirtuality' means for organizations. Venkatraman and Henderson (1996) proposed that: *"Virtualness is the ability of the organization to consistently obtain and coordinate critical competencies through its design of value-adding business processes and governance mechanisms involving external and internal constituencies to deliver differential, superior value in the market place" (p.4).*

Figure 1: The Concept of 'Virtual'

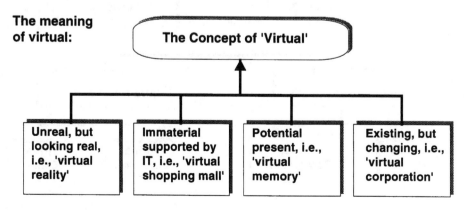

Figure 2 provides an interesting overview of virtual objects. Scholz (1997) distinguished the virtual organization into an intra-organizational and inter-organizational perspective.

The inter-organizational perspective is divided into virtual markets and virtual corporations. Virtual markets means e-commerce: market transactions between actors using sophisticated ICT, i.e., the Internet. In contrast, virtual corporations are basically partnership networks of dispersed organizational units or independent companies.

THE VIRTUAL WEB/CORPORATION CONCEPT

Basically, the virtual web is a pool of independent companies from which operating virtual corporations derive. The major competitive advantage of this concept is that independent companies form partnerships at short notice in response to emerging market opportunities. The virtual web is the organizational framework that deploys a number of organizational mechanisms to facilitate the formation of virtual corporations. The net-broker manages and administrates the pool of independent companies, and performs the role of an architect to establish operative virtual corporations.

The Virtual Corporation

Taking the inter-organizational perspective of virtual organizations we speak about 'virtual corporations' as a concept that organizes collaborative partnerships. Since the idea of 'virtual corporations' is still in its infancy, the description of this organizational concept is very broad. Since so far, there are only a few real virtual webs/corporations existing, i.e., Agile Web, Pennsylvania, USA (Sheridan, 1996), the Virtuelle Fabrik

Figure 2: Virtual Objects, Scholz (1997)

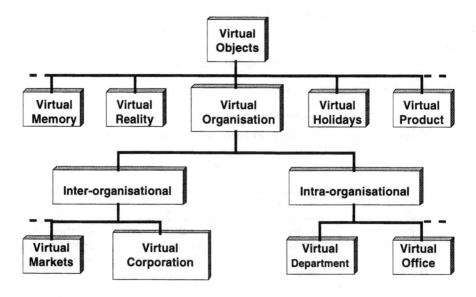

Euregio Bodensee, Switzerland (Schuh et al., 1998), and VIRTEC, Sao Paulo, Brazil (Bremer, 1999), most of the following descriptions are based on the theoretical work of other academics. However, Byrne (1993) has provided the most widely accepted and cited definition of the term 'virtual corporation' within the academic literature.

"A virtual corporation is a temporary network of independent companies— suppliers, customers, and even rivals—linked by information technology to share skills, costs, and access to one another's markets. This corporate model is fluid and flexible—a group of collaborators that quickly unite to exploit a specific opportunity. Once the opportunity is met, the venture will, more often than not, disband. In the concept's purest form, each company that links up with others to create a virtual corporation contributes only what it regards as its core competencies. Technology plays a central role in the development of the virtual corporation. Teams of people in different companies work together, concurrently rather than sequentially, via computer networks in real time" (pp. 36/37).

Following Bryne's (1993) definition the following main characteristics can be identified.

The virtual corporation is a temporary partnership, which is neither set up for an agreed period of time, nor is it an open-ended cooperation, i.e., joint venture. The partnerships last as long as it is beneficial for the cooperation partners. The partnering companies may also be involved in several virtual corporations at any one time (Dess et al., 1995). However, the virtual corporation model provides independent companies with the option to continue their day-to-day business in addition to their involvement in partnerships.

The virtual corporation partners, such as suppliers, customers and even competitors share resources, risks, costs, and access to one another's markets. This relation implies horizontal and vertical value chain integration. Even a partnership with rival companies can be beneficial if, for example, an individual company does not have the necessary resources and know-how on its own that are required to develop, produce and distribute new product developments. The main emphasis of the virtual corporation is to complement and share resources in order to improve competitiveness as a whole.

Another feature of the virtual corporation concept is it enables smaller companies to join forces and to compete, in the form of virtual corporation, with large multinational enterprises on a global scale. Therefore, the virtual corporation model is particularly attractive for small and medium-sized enterprises. It provides them with the opportunity to sustain their independence while at the same time to improve their competitiveness.

The ideal type of the virtual corporation is fluid and flexible, the cooperating partners contributing only their core competencies to the partnership. Once a specific market opportunity is allocated, the partners quickly unite and pool their resources according to customer needs. If the market changes, it might be necessary to change the virtual corporation configuration, if it is to remain competitive. The relationship between the partnering companies has to be flexible and grounded in mutual trust in order to enable rapid market response. A crucial competitive advantage of virtual corporations is that they unite quickly and without the long lasting contract negotiations.

The exchange of information is vital for virtual corporations. A virtual corporation might be feasible without information technology (IT), but recent IT developments in volume, speed and quality have made it possible to synchronize activities which were previously considered hardly possible due to the high costs involved (Mertens & Faisst, 1996). Communication facilitates the coordination of activities between partner companies and generates knowledge, which leads to innovative products and services.

The theoretical concept of virtual corporations includes the global collaboration of distributed cross-functional expert teams. Unlike conventional teams, a virtual team works across space, time, and organizational boundaries enabled by ICT (Lipnack & Stamps, 1997). Virtual teams pursue the aim of concurrent engineering of products, services and business processes. The network form of organizations, supported by ICTs, accelerates and improves the process of R&D, production and distribution.

The virtual corporation is different to other forms of network organizations and cooperative models. To underpin this distinctiveness, Mertens and Faisst (1996) summarized the major differences between the virtual corporation concept and other forms of inter-organizational partnerships (see Figure 3).

The major differences between the virtual corporation approach compared to other forms of inter-organizational co-operations are that the membership is voluntary, partner companies keep their independence and continue their own day-to-day business. Virtual corporations are fluid and flexible, the relationship with other partners is short term, the partnership is temporary and lasts only as long as it is beneficial for the members. The virtual corporation is a co-operation of partners that share costs, risks, and profits. Since the virtual corporation is build on mutual trust, long lasting negotiations between the partners, complicated agreements, and the establishment of new businesses is not necessary. Therefore the virtual corporation is able to react fast to market opportunities or changes, and it pools only the resources it needs to fulfill its destiny.

The Virtual Web

Having described the virtual corporation concept, the subsequent question is about how to find suitable partner companies to form virtual corporations? One way to find possible partner companies is to search in the yellow pages or on the Internet for companies with complementary resources, capabilities, and competencies. The major

Figure 3: Inter-Organizational Partnerships vs. Virtual Corporations. Mertens & Faisst, (1996)

Inter-organizational Partnership	Different Characteristics compared to Virtual Corporations
Strategic Alliance	- a less closed relationship, - hardly any virtual added value processes, - mainly formed by large corporations, - existence beside the core business.
Conglomerate	- dependency agreement
Cartel	- aims to limit competition
Consortium	- existence of formal agreements
Franchise	- long lasting dependency agreement
Joint Venture	- establishment of a new business
Keiretsu	- stable membership of partners

problem involved in this kind of search is that one does not know whether those companies are reliable, even if they have the required complementary resource-base. Companies seeking to form virtual corporations should fit together in terms of mutual trust, organizational culture, business processes and IT/IS systems. To facilitate the partnering process of unfamiliar partner companies, Goldman et al. (1995) introduced the organizational concept of 'virtual webs'. By definition, the virtual web is the home base (hub) of virtual corporations. The web is an open-ended collection of pre-qualified partners that agree to form a pool of potential members of virtual corporations.

Figure 4 illustrates the virtual web and its member companies. Virtual corporations are derived from the pool of member companies. External suppliers and customers are integrated into the value-adding process of the individual virtual corporations.

The main purpose of the virtual web is to facilitate the formation of virtual corporations. The virtual web concept incorporates six key organizational mechanisms, which supports the initiation and operation processes of virtual corporations.

Pre-qualification Criteria. Prior to joining the virtual web each applicant has to match the pre-qualification criteria, which are set by the virtual web members. The pre-qualification criteria aim to select only those companies that are regarded to be fit for future virtual corporations.

Trust and Culture. The virtual web develops its individual dynamic in a stable environment in which a web culture and mutual trust can develop. Successful virtual corporations over a longer period of time accelerate the so-called 'spiral of trust' (Sydow, 1996). Trust mainly depends on experience and reputation, whereby in a stable environment the level of trust develops faster than in an uncertain and dynamic environment. Web members identify themselves with the virtual web organization, which fertilizes the mutual trust process and develops a virtual web culture on its own. Empirical research in Switzerland has shown that personal contact and regular face to face meetings of company representatives are a suitable tool to build a virtual web trust culture (Schuh et al., 1997). Another key factor is the number of web members. Ted Nickel, a net-broker of a virtual web noted that he doesn't see things going much past 25 companies, before, he suggests,

Figure 4: Virtual Web Concept

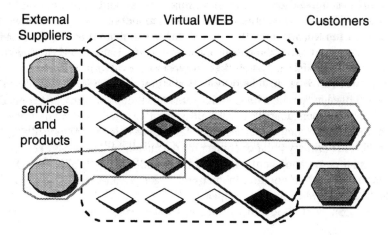

he would start a new web (Sheridan, 1996).

Partner Search. The virtual web can be viewed as a warehouse of distinct resources, capabilities, and competencies kept by its member companies. Web members know each other's strengths and weaknesses, they have the assurance of reliable and trustworthy partners that fit together at short notice.

Quick Formation. Once the suitable partners have been selected for a certain project, the formation process should be not slowed down by long lasting partnership agreement negotiations. Therefore all web members sign a memorandum of understanding, which basically serves as a constitution for the collaboration (Franke, 1998). The memorandum of understanding states the mission and vision of the virtual web, general rules and regulations of the virtual web, but also specific rules as to how risks, costs and profits are distributed between virtual corporation partners.

Fast Operation. One crucial feature of virtual corporations is to reduce the time to market. If the various distributed resources, capabilities, and competencies are 'plug compatible' with one another, that is, if they can perform their respective functions jointly, then the virtual corporation can behave as if it were a single company dedicated to one particular project (Goldman and Nagel, 1993). In order to make newly established virtual corporations operational quickly, the virtual web develops organizational, technical and IT standards as well as reference business processes.

Penalty System. Trust is the key feature of the virtual web concept. If a web member does not behave or perform as expected, it spoils its reputation and damages the trust within the virtual web. The penalty would be that those companies might not be considered for future projects. Exclusion might be very serious for companies, which have been concentrating only on their core competencies, which means that they are not able to create a value chain without cooperation partners. Therefore, such sanctions might endanger the existence of the company. In return, this penalty system motivates all member companies not to disappoint other partners by spoiling the mutual trust in the partnership (Mews, 1997). Web members' commitment to the partnership produces high levels of motivation; it results in high quality products and services.

The Net-Broker

In 1986, Miles and Snow introduced for the first time the concept of dynamic networks. They suggested that a dynamic network needs a coordinator, a net-broker. Since the virtual web/virtual corporation concept belongs to the type of dynamic networks, the net-broker is a fundamental part of it. Reiß (1997) noted that the role of the coordinator of a virtual web is primarily the management of synergy. Hatch (1995) defined the net-broker as a facilitator and catalyst. Brokers help companies to form strategic partnerships, organize network activities and identify new business opportunities. Their task is to spread the network concepts, promote cooperation, organize groups of firms, and connect them to the product designers, marketing specialists, training providers, and industry service programs they need to compete successfully. Karnet and Faisst (1997) added that the net-broker is also the primary point of contact for the customer. The net-broker proposes a suitable virtual corporation configuration and monitors their performance. During the operation of a virtual corporation the net-broker acts as moderator and helps resolve possible conflict between partner companies.

In 1992, Snow et al. identified three net-broker roles: the role as architect, lead operator, and caretaker.

ARCHITECT. In the role of the architect, the net-broker has to perform two primary tasks. The net-broker searches and selects suitable partner companies for the virtual web and also chooses possible web members to form virtual corporations.

LEAD OPERATOR. The net-broker, acting as lead operator, is primarily responsible for the management and maintenance of the virtual web. Furthermore, the net-broker is responsible for the overall project management of virtual corporations. On the other hand, either a partner company of the virtual corporation or the net-broker itself takes over the project management of the virtual corporation on the operational level.

CARETAKER. Partnership networks require continual enhancement if they are to operate smoothly and effectively. The virtual web development process is ongoing; the caretaker monitors the large number of relationships within the virtual web and the virtual corporations. The caretakers' main duty is to support the process of 'learn to cooperate and cooperate to learn' (Prange et al., 1996). Thus, the caretaker is engaged in nurturing and disciplinary behavior. For example, if the net-broker notices that a web member falls behind technologically, or in some other way devalues its usefulness to the web, the net-broker takes appropriate actions to rectify the situation. On the other hand, if the net-broker notes that a web member gains advantages at the expense of other partners, the net-broker's challenge is to point out the dysfunctional effects of such behavior on the overall system and teach the offending web member how to behave more appropriately for the common good (Snow et al., 1992).

Furthermore, the net-broker has to carry out three main management processes.

Initiation of the virtual web. The first task of a net-broker is to search for possible web candidates with a complementary and competitive resource base and the capability to work in partnerships. A clear vision of the future virtual web facilitates the search. In the preparation phase, the net-broker acts as a relationship promoter (Gemünden & Walter, 1995) who contacts people, brings them together, and leads the dialogue and socializing process between them. The main objective is to create a common bond and to promote mutual trust. The final step in the initiation phase is that all participating web members agree on the memorandum of understanding.

Maintenance of the virtual web. Maintenance means that the net-broker manages the relationship between the web members and improves their abilities to collaborate. Therefore, the net-broker together with the web members develops business and technical standards, which aim to facilitate the cooperation between them. The net-broker monitors the web members' performance, and if necessary, the net-broker is involved in nurturing or disciplinary actions. The net-broker also observes the internal and external environment and makes proposals about how to adopt any changes. Since the net-broker is responsible for the competitiveness of the virtual web, the net-broker always searches for new web candidates with missing or complementary resources. Additionally, the internal web-learning process is managed by the net-broker.

Formation and operation of virtual corporations. The formation process starts when an apparent market opportunity is identified. The first step for the net-broker is to create a 'virtual value chain model' (Faisst & Birg, 1997), identifying all the resources needed to match the market opportunity. Since the net-broker keeps track of the web members resource profile, s/he configures the most competitive virtual corporation. Once the virtual corporation is established, the net-broker withdraws from the coordination tasks, unless the net-broker acts as the project manager of the operating unit. When the project has been accomplished the net-broker is also involved in the dissolution process; the net-broker monitors and controls the partners to ensure that they separate in a fair manner.

THE KNOWLEDGE-BASED VIEW OF THE FIRM

In order to identify the implications of the knowledge-based perspective on the virtual web / corporation concept, this section reviews briefly the resource-based theory before it describes the knowledge-based view of the firm in depth.

The idea of looking at firms as a broader set of resources goes back to the seminal work of Penrose (1959). She argued that a firm is more than an administrative unit; it is also a collection of productive resources, the disposal of which between different uses and over time is determined by administrative decisions. The final products being produced by a firm at any given time merely represent one of several ways in which the firm could be using its resources, an incident in the development of its basic potentialities. The essence of the resource-based view of a firm is, not to see the firm as a portfolio of products, i.e. Daimler-Chrysler and its product range of cars, trucks and buses. The resource-based theory identifies the firm as a pool of resources, capabilities and competencies needed to accomplish a task, i.e. physical products or intangible services. The 'resource-based theory' literature is mainly divided into two different streams, one group of researchers are concerned with the internal and external resources of a firm (transaction cost theory), the other group of researchers emphasize how to make the best use of the available resources, i.e. core competence theory (Prahalad and Hamel, 1990).

Drucker (1992) argued that the world is presently in the change towards the knowledge society:

"In this society, knowledge is the primary resource for individuals and for the economy overall. Land, labor, and capital - the economist's traditional factors of production - do not disappear, but they become secondary. They can be obtained, and obtained easily, provided there is a specialized knowledge. At the same time, however, specialized knowledge by itself produces nothing. It can become productive only when it is integrated into a task. And that is why the knowledge society is also a society of organizations: the purpose and function of every organization, business and nonbusiness alike, is the integration of specialized knowledge into common task" (p.95).

Drucker's statement moves knowledge into the center of the resource-based view of the firm. Conner and Prahalad (1996) noted that the central theme emerging in the strategic management resource-based literature is that privately held knowledge is a basic source of advantage in competition. Grant (1997) even claims that the knowledge-based view promises to have one of the most profound changes in management thinking since the scientific management revolution of the early decades of this century. However, it would be wrong to view the firm only as a collection of knowledge; the knowledge-based view of the firm acknowledges the importance of knowledge to seek competitive advantage, but it also recognizes all other resources as supportive elements in creating key competencies or even core competencies. Thus, the knowledge-based view of the firm is not a new theory, it is embedded in the resource-based theory; it responds to the changing view of the world towards the knowledge society. Since the origin of all tangible resources lies outside the firm, it follows that competitive advantage is more likely to arise from the intangible firm-specific knowledge which enables it to add value to the incoming factors of production in a relatively unique manner (Spender, 1996). Therefore, the specific knowledge base, the ability to make use of the available knowledge and to generate new knowledge, determines the competitiveness of the firm in the emerging knowledge society.

Having identified knowledge as the primary resource to gain competitive advantage, Figure 5 combines the traditional resource-based framework and the knowledge-based view of the firm. The resource-based framework uses three levels of abstraction: resources and services, capabilities, and competencies. The knowledge-based view is in the center of the resource-based framework, its implication on the three levels of abstraction follows.

Figure 5: The Knowledge-Based View Framework

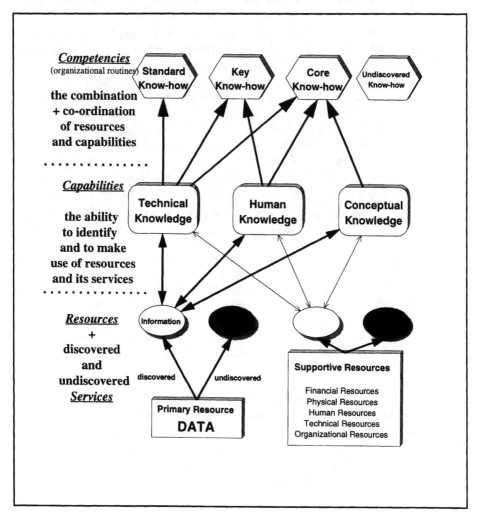

Resources and Services

Richard Hall (1993) distinguished resources and competencies very simply; a resource is something, which one 'has', and a competence is something which one can 'do'. Amit and Schoemaker (1993) defined a firm's resources as stocks of available factors that are owned or controlled by the firm. Resources are converted into final products or services by using a wide range of other firms assets and bonding mechanisms such as technology, management information systems, incentive systems, trust between management and labor, and more. Hofer and Schendel (1978) suggested that all organizations possess five types of resources: (1) financial resources, such as cash flow, debt capacity, and new equity availability; (2) physical resources, such as office buildings, manufacturing plants and equipment, warehouses, inventories, and service and distribution facilities; (3) human resources, such as scientists, engineers, production supervisors, sales personnel, and financial analysts; (4) technological resources, such as high-quality products, low cost plants, and high brand loyalty; and (5) organizational resources, such as quality control systems, short-term management cash systems, and corporate financial models.

However, one important aspect of the concept of resources has been almost neglected in the literature. This is even more surprising since Penrose (1958) stressed the importance of resources delivering services. She wrote:

"Strictly speaking, it is never resources themselves that are the 'inputs' in the production process, but only the service that the resource can render. The services yielded by resources are a function of the way in which they are used — exactly the same resources when used for different purposes or in different ways and in combination with different types or amounts of other resources provides a different service or set of services. The important distinction between resources and services is not their relative durability; rather it lies in the fact that resources consist of a bundle of potential services and can, for the most part, be defined, the very word 'service' implying a function, an activity" (p. 25).

From the knowledge-based perspective 'data' is the primary resource that delivers 'information'. Data on its own is fairly useless; data delivers information that has to be identified in order to make use of it. Therefore, data delivers discovered and undiscovered services, discovered information that has a certain meaning to somebody, and undiscovered information that already exists but has not been discovered as a source to be used for interpretation. The distinction of discovered and undiscovered information has a profound impact on knowledge creation, since each discovery of unknown information adds to the knowledge base of the firm.

Capabilities and Knowledge

Capabilities can be seen as a step between resources and competencies. Amit and Schoemaker (1993) stated that capabilities refer to a firm's capacity to deploy 'resources'. As Penrose (1958) mentioned, a single resource can deliver many different services; some services are very obvious, and some services are hidden and have to be discovered in order to make resources valuable to the firm.

Katz (1974) distinguished between technical, human, and conceptual capabilities.

Technical capabilities imply an understanding of, and proficiency in, a specific kind of activity, particularly on involving methods, processes, procedures, or techniques. It involves specialized knowledge, analytical ability within that specialty, and facility in the use of the tools and techniques of the specific discipline.

Human capabilities or interpersonal capabilities refer to the ability to work effectively as a group member and to build cooperative effort within teams. Human capability is primarily concerned with working with people. This capability is particular important since most of the knowledge is tacit. Tacit knowledge is semiconscious and unconscious knowledge held in peoples' heads (Leonard and Sensiper, 1998). Since tacit knowledge is a subset of information stored in people's minds, human capabilities are needed to make individuals willing to extract their information and to share it with others.

Conceptual capabilities involve the abilities to see the firm as a whole; it includes recognizing how the various function of the organization depend on each other, and how changes in any one part affect all the others; and it extends to visualizing the relationship of the individual firm to the industry, the community, and the political, the social, and economic forces of the nations as a whole.

The knowledge-based perspective identifies capabilities as knowledge. Kogut and Zander (1992) stated that knowledge as information implies knowing **what** something means. Technical, human, and conceptual knowledge is about identifying, understanding, and interpreting information. The second step is to find the appropriate applications for the information and to make use of them in the most beneficial way for the firm.

Competencies and Know-How

In simple terms, competencies are the process of coordinating capabilities and resources in order to fulfill an activity. To build competencies is not simply a matter of pooling resources; competencies involve complex patterns of coordination between people, knowledge and other resources. To understand the anatomy of a firm's competencies, Nelson and Winter's (1982) concept of 'organizational routines' is illuminating. Organizational routines are regular and predictable patterns of activity, which are made up of a sequence of coordinated actions by individuals. A competence is, in essence, a routine, or a number of interacting routines (Grant, 1991). Taking the knowledge-based view, we speak about know-how. Know-how is, as the compound words state, a description of knowing **how** to do something (Kogut and Zamder, 1992). Whereby knowledge is usually thought of the possession of individuals, something people carry around in their heads and pass between each other, know-how embraces the ability to know-what in practice. Thus, know-how is critical in making knowledge actionable and operational (Brown and Duguid, 1998). Similar to competencies, know-how can be distinguished into four different categories, depending on their contribution to customer-perceived value and its defensibility (Deutsch et al., 1997).

Standard know-how is the basis of competency of each organization. It is absolutely necessary to keep a firm operative, but it does not considerably improve the competitiveness of the firm (Deutsch et al., 1997).

Key know-how leads to competitive advantage, but is hardly defensible. For example, the development of an efficient distribution process with a logistics service provider might be a competitive advantage, but on the other hand it might not be difficult for competitors to copy (imitate) this distribution process in a short time.

Undiscovered know-how is what a firm could do, but the firm does not know it. The discovery of new information, or the reconfiguration of information and knowledge generates new know-how, know-how that the firm did not know about, know-how which was unconscious but available within the firm.

Core know-how follows the idea of core competencies (Prahalad and Hamel, 1990). Core competencies are defined as 'an area of specialized expertise that is the result of harmonizing the complex stream of technology and work activity'. Core competencies have special qualities: They exemplify excellence and provide competitive advantage. According to Fischer (1995), coordinating knowledge, human resources, technical resources and physical resources generate core competencies, a combination that is neither easy to imitate nor to substitute, thus it secures a long-term competitive advantage. Core know-how seeks its competitive advantage in very a similar way, except it is about the unique coordination of information and specialized knowledge, which adds superior value to very common input resources in order to be ahead of competitors.

THE KBV OF THE VIRTUAL WEB / CORPORATION CONCEPT

Since the virtual web/corporation approach is a new emerging inter-organizational partnership model, the resource/and knowledge-based view of it differs to that of traditional firms. This section describes the implications that the knowledge-based view has on the virtual web as a pool of knowledge, the virtual corporation as the deriving operational unit which brings the knowledge alive, and the net-broker who acts as knowledge manager. Besides the knowledge management processes, this section identifies mutual trust between partner companies and individuals, as well as a distinct virtual web culture as key facilitator for the exchange of existing knowledge and the generation of new knowledge.

The Virtual Web as a Pool of Knowledge

From a resource-based perspective, the virtual web can be viewed as a warehouse of all sorts of resources kept by its member companies. The basic idea is that virtual web members make their resource base available to their partners. This can range from very basic resources to core competencies. For example, in case one web member reaches the production capacity limits, it would be feasible to partner with other web members and to make use of their production capacity surplus. In such circumstances it would be beneficial for the whole process to also share data and information (i.e., inventory, sales forecast, etc.), to design a smooth supply chain, or even to determine geographical areas to optimize distribution and customer service.

From a knowledge-based perspective the virtual web can be viewed as an inventory of data, information, knowledge and know-how. Again, web members make their knowledge-base available to their partners, they seek cooperation with others to make full use of their knowledge potential, but also to fill their knowledge gap, which might be necessary to accomplish tasks and to compete successfully in existing or future markets.

Grant (1996a) viewed the role of the firm as a knowledge-integrating institution in which specialized knowledge is coordinated. Firms exist as institutions to create conditions under which knowledge transfer and creation is facilitated. Furthermore, he argued that markets are unable to undertake the coordinating role because of their failure in the face of (A) the immobility of tacit knowledge and (B) the risk of expropriation of explicit knowledge by the potential buyer. Liebeskind (1996) even argued that firms, as institutions, play a critical role in creating and sustaining competitive advantage: that of protecting valuable knowledge.

Virtual webs are neither markets nor hierarchies (Thorelli, 1986). The virtual web is an institutionalized partnership network with well-defined organizational boundaries, i.e. pre-qualification criteria. On the other hand the virtual web allows competition between the partner companies to a certain extent and partners also are benchmarked with external suppliers on a regular basis.

The virtual web provides partner companies with a stable trustworthy organizational environment; memorandums of understanding as well as an implemented penalty system protect web members of being expropriated of their specialized knowledge by partner companies. Mutual trust embedded in an idealistic web culture is key for knowledge sharing and transfer between independent web members with opportunistic behaviors outside the partnership network.

This stable virtual web environment also provides a forum for cross-company learning processes, the acquisition and creation of new knowledge. Stuart et al. (1998) provided an empirical example of a cross-company learning network. The mission of this network is that the group of independent companies work together to enable each member to optimize its competitiveness in a win-win environment using shared resources and experiences. If member companies are interested in a certain topic they form a special interest group (SIG). A facilitator helps them to organize meetings, workshops, and hires external consultancy. Special interest group topics included Internet access for group members, access to data for benchmarking performance, the formation of a virtual training center, development of customer service courses, high technology seminar, and many more. Such special interest groups, consisting of individuals from partner companies, overcome the problem of the immobility of tacit knowledge, described by Grant (1996a).

The knowledge-based view of the virtual web provides another interesting feature. Based on empirical research, Mowery et al. (1996) stated that partnership activities could lead to increased specialization. Firms having access to others' capabilities (rather than acquiring them or developing them internally) discovered that the capabilities of partner firms become more divergent in a substantial subset of partnerships. This implies that web members tend to focus on what they do best. By concentrating on their strengths, firms are able to develop key or even core know-how in certain specialized areas. Since firms are involved in a larger resource network, they have the opportunity to drop some of their standard competencies, because those parts of the value chain can be covered by other web partners with better and more sophisticated know-how in such areas. In return, taking over tasks and processes of partners enlarges the scope of business, which enables the firm to acquire even more know-how in its specialized segment. Therefore, the evolution process of the virtual web leads to lean and very specialized firms, firms that pool their specialized know-how to form superior value chains.

The Virtual Corporation Brings the Knowledge Alive

Virtual corporations are the operating units derived from the virtual web. Its a temporary operational partnership that generates value, either physical products or intangible services; by pooling their resources. Per definition, partner companies contribute only their core competencies to the virtual corporation. Since core competencies are very rare and unique, it might be more precise to speak about the strengths web partners pool in virtual corporations. However, virtual corporations are able to create core know-how and core competencies because of the rich resource and knowledge base the virtual web provides to form unique and difficult-to-imitate value chains. An additional aspect is that due to the constant knowledge generation on the virtual web, the virtual corporation enters competition already ahead of its rivals. Joint developments on the virtual web level might open the door to new areas of competition. Furthermore, the virtual corporation is a partnership of specialized companies and individual experts operating in a predetermined trust culture with a predefined set of rules and regulations, (including regulations about knowledge ownership, security and protection), that facilitate the quick formation of the temporary partnerships.

From a knowledge-based perspective the virtual corporation delivers value in a very interesting way to customers. Grant and Baden-Fuller (1995) describe the correlation between the knowledge and product domains of firms. They propose an input-output matrix of knowledge and products, where inputs of specialized knowledge is evaluated to output of products. The knowledge/product matrix provides two perspectives, (A) what knowledge is available within the firm—what products can be produced out of this knowledge base, (B) what are the market needs —what knowledge is necessary to satisfy the market. Traditionally, firms are driven by their resource / knowledge bases. They have looked out on the market and adjusted the resource/knowledge base accordingly. The virtual web / corporation concept follows the second approach. Taking the knowledge-based perspective the following customer needs—knowledge—final product process can be identified (see Figure 6).

The process starts by identifying a market opportunity; the second step is to determine the knowledge requirements; the third step is to allocated the knowledge keepers within the virtual web; the fourth step is to search for additional external knowledge if it is required; the fifth step is to coordinate internal and external knowledge in order to generate key or even core know-how; and the final step is to transferred the new created know-how into operation, the final product.

One of the key subprocesses in the above-described process is the consolidation of existing knowledge and the generation of new knowledge. To operationalize this, virtual corporations form project teams. In order to accelerate the R&D process the virtual corporation assign several expert teams to different tasks which is called modular product design (Sanchez and Mahoney, 1996). This enables concurrent engineering. Since the individual experts of such teams might be geographically dispersed, the virtual corporation would apply the virtual team approach. Unlike conventional teams, Lipnack and Stamps (1997) stated: a virtual team works across space, time, and organizational boundaries with links strengthened by a web of communication technology. Virtual teams are the germ cells of knowledge and know-how creation of virtual corporations. However, Bund (1997) stressed also the importance of regular face to face meetings in order to facilitate the trust building process which is supposed to increase the willingness of virtual team members to share their data and information as well as to articulate their tacit knowledge. Mutual trust among virtual team members lead to high performance. Research has indicated that the teams with the highest levels of trust tended to share three traits

Figure 6: The Virtual Corporation Knowledge Process

The Virtual Corporation Knowledge Process

External Knowledge

② Knowledge Requirements

④

①

③

Market Opportunity

Customer

Virtual Web Knowledge Base

⑤

Virtual Teams

⑥

Final Product

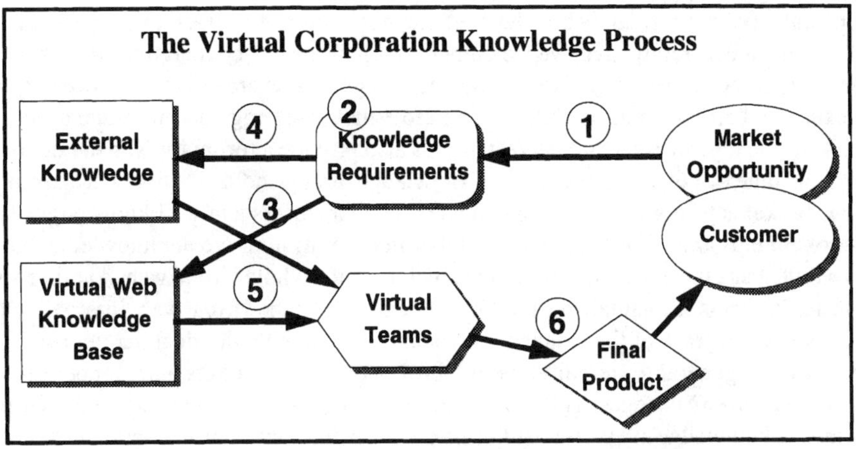

(Coutu, 1998) First, virtual teams began their interactions with a serious of social messages – introducing themselves and providing some personal background – before focusing on the work at hand. This initial period of electronic 'courtship', as the researcher call it, appears to be particularly important in establishing knowledge based trust. Second, they set clear roles for each team member. Assigning members a particular task enabled all of them to identify with one another, forging a foundation for identification-based trust. The third hallmark of the trusting team had to do with attitude: team members consistently displayed eagerness, enthusiasm, and an intense action orientation in all their messages.

The Net-Broker Acts as Knowledge Manager

The main net-broker's task is the management of synergy; synergy which is achieved by the coordination of web members' resource and knowledge bases and the collaboration of partner companies in virtual corporations. From a knowledge-based perspective, the net-broker acts as the knowledge manager of the virtual web. In order to identify the knowledge management activities of the net-broker it is useful to break down the whole net-brokerage process into the three main virtual web management processes: initiation of the virtual web, maintenance of the virtual web, and the formation of virtual corporations.

Knowledge management in the initiation phase. Snow and Thomas (1993) noted that the primary role of the net-broker during the initiation phase is that of an architect. Similar to the design process of a building, the virtual web architect determines the design and resources needed to build a competitive partnership network. The net-broker searches for suitable candidates and selects those with complementary and competitive resource and knowledge bases. Since mutual trust is key for knowledge transfer, sharing, and generation within the virtual web and its deriving virtual corporations, Sydow (1996) stressed the importance to pay attention during the search and selection phase to choose candidates which are somehow similar, but also complementary. Too strong a competition between web members impedes the trust-building process, which would have negative effects on the whole evolution process of the virtual web.

Knowledge management in the maintenance phase. The maintenance of the virtual web is an ongoing process; the net-broker acts mainly as a lead operator and caretaker. The key postulate of the virtual web is that web member companies learn to cooperate with each other and in return that web members learn from the cooperation with others. Therefore, the net-broker organizes special interest groups where web members can learn and exercise their cooperation skills, even before they work together in virtual corporation. Additionally, such special interest groups also provide a forum for web members to learn from others or even to generate new knowledge through collaboration. Furthermore, the net-broker acts as caretaker in case a web member suffers a lack of knowledge. The net-broker helps and advises the web member in order to improve the knowledge base. This would make the nurtured firm again valuable for the whole virtual web. Another task of the net-broker is to maintain the total knowledge base of the virtual web. Internally, the net-broker keeps track of the existing knowledge base of the individual partners and the virtual web in general. Externally, the net-broker observes markets and competitors in order to react to any changes. This could mean that the net-broker realizes that the virtual web misses knowledge in a particular field, i.e. new technology, new markets, etc. In order to fill the knowledge gap the net-broker could either search for new web member companies keeping the required knowledge or the net-broker could organize training or seminars, which would enable existing web members to acquire the missing knowledge.

Knowledge management in the formation and operation phase. The primary role of the net-broker during the formation phase is again that of an architect. Having identified a market opportunity, the net-broker defines a number of tasks, searches for the necessary knowledge within the virtual web and if it is necessary subcontracts external knowledge, and brings all the knowledge elements together in order to form a virtual corporation. In case the net-broker also acts as the project manager, s/he takes over the role of the lead-operator. However, from a knowledge management perspective the integration of the dispersed knowledge is the major challenge. Grant (1996a) pointed out that transferring knowledge is not an efficient approach to integrating knowledge. He identified four mechanisms for integrating specialized knowledge:

Rules and directives. The memorandum of understanding, defined on the virtual web level, determines the rules, regulations, and technical standards for the smooth operation of virtual corporations. The net-broker's duty is to monitor whether partner companies apply to the set of rules and directives and interfere if necessary.

Sequencing. Modular product design and concurrent engineering requires sequencing. The project leader has to determine what and when each expert team has to deliver their results.

Routines, are defined as a complex pattern of behavior (Winter, 1986), the sort of predictable behavior of an actor in organizational settings. Trust, organizational culture and experience lead to routines. Basically, it is about knowing each other, the virtual web provides a forum for individuals to meet and to build social relationships before they work together either in special interest groups of virtual corporations. However, special interest groups are an excellent possibility for training and experiencing routines, which facilitate the later collaboration in virtual corporations.

Group problem solving and decision making. Since the net-broker has a neutral position in the acting virtual corporation, the net-broker acts as moderator between conflicting parties. The net-broker acting as caretaker also supports the decision-making processes if necessary. Even if the net-broker is not involved in the leadership of the virtual corporation, it is the net-brokers' own best interest that the virtual corporation is successful.

The net-broker also acts as caretaker during the dissolution phase of the virtual corporation; s/he is concerned with the storage of acquired and generated knowledge (i.e. database) and property rights of knowledge created.

COMPETITIVE ADVANTAGE THROUGH KNOWLEDGE POOLING

Prahalad and Hamel (1990) argued that:

...in the short run, company's competitiveness derives from the price/performance attributes of current products. In the long run, competitiveness derives from the ability to build, at lower cost and more speedily than competitors, the core competencies that spawn unanticipated products. The real sources of advantage are to be found in management's ability to consolidate corporate-wide technologies and production skills into competencies that empower individual businesses to adapt quickly to changing opportunities (p.81).

Putting it simply, core competencies are the things that some companies know how to do uniquely well and that have the scope to provide them with a better-than-average degree of success over the long term (Gallon et al., 1995). It is very difficult and it might be impossible for the majority of companies to create core know-how on their own. However, the virtual web and its deriving virtual corporations have theoretically the potential to build core know-how by integrating their knowledge bases. If knowledge integration is the basis for competitive advantage of virtual corporations, what are the characteristics of knowledge integration associated with the creation and sustenance of such an advantage? Grant (1996b) identified three characteristics of knowledge integration pertinent to the competitive advantage.

The efficiency of integration. Since the net-broker acts as knowledge-broker, the net-broker keeps track of specialized knowledge available within the virtual web. The net-broker's task is to coordinate specialized knowledge into cooperative teams of experts in which existing knowledge is utilized to generate new knowledge efficiently.

The scope of integration. Since the virtual web comprises the knowledge bases of a number of individual companies, the deriving virtual corporations are configured out of a large pool of specialized knowledge. For each project the net-broker selects only that specialized knowledge from the web members which is needed to accomplish the task. Additional external expert knowledge is acquired if it is needed.

The flexibility of integration. Since virtual corporations are only temporary and very fluid and flexible, the configuration of specialized knowledge is frequently changing. This leads to a dynamic exchange of existing knowledge and a fruitful generation of new ideas, innovations; in short, new knowledge.

Besides knowledge integration as a source of competitive advantage, the knowledge based perspective provides five additional key attributes of the virtual web/corporation concept, which might lead to competitive advantage:

1) Each web member concentrates only on that what it does best; it contributes its specialized knowledge in particular fields to joint projects.

2) The virtual web provides a learning environment, which provides the forum to exchange existing knowledge and to generate new knowledge through multilateral links. This improves the competitiveness of each individual web member company.

3) The virtual corporation pools only that expert knowledge of its members which is needed to complete the task; it insources external knowledge if necessary. Rules, directives, technical standards as well as organizational routines facilitate the formation and operation of virtual corporations.

4) The virtual web and its structure and organizational mechanisms allow the fast and flexible configuration of virtual corporations, partnerships, which are fully functional from the first day on. Core know-how has also a time dimension; to be first on the market can secure the competitive advantage for a longer period of time.

5) Competitive advantage can also be sustained by knowledge protection (Liebeskind, 1996). Compared to adhocracy, the very fluid extreme of virtual corporations, the virtual web provides member companies with a stable environment in which mutual trust, a distinct web culture, and an awareness of knowledge protection against externals can be developed.

From a knowledge-based perspective, one could conclude that the virtual web offers the organizational framework for virtual corporations to build core know-how and to achieve and sustain competitive advantage.

The Bioenergy Cluster

The following case of the Bioenergy Cluster in Austria aims to support the very theoretical concepts discussed earlier in this chapter. This case demonstrates impressively the practical application of the literature-based organizational concepts of the virtual web, the virtual corporation and the net-broker approach. Furthermore, this example provides a practical application of the 'Virtual Corporation Knowledge Process' model (see Figure 6) and its operationalization.

The Bioenergy Cluster was founded in Spring 1999. It is a virtual web with about 45 member companies. All member companies are from the bio-energy industry in Austria and most of them are manufacturers of bio-energy heating systems. The member companies serve different markets, from small firing systems to large district heating systems, from solid fire systems to bio-diesel and biogas systems. This virtual web also unites independent companies that are competitors in certain market segments on the Austrian market. The Bioenergy Cluster was initiated and is today managed by a net-broker organization of six employees. The major aims of the Bioenergy Cluster are to improve the image of bio-energy at the national and international level, to support export of Austrian bio-energy technology and to improve members' competitiveness through cooperation with each other in R&D and production. These three aims are in the interests of each individual member company and bond them together.

Referring to the virtual corporation knowledge process (see Figure 6), the cluster-management (net-broker) spotted a market opportunity. They identified a market for larger turnkey biogas systems. So far, no supplier was able to offer a complete solution to customers. The cluster-management contacted an interested customer and received an inquiry. Based on customers' specification, the cluster-management selected the required knowledge from virtual web member companies and invited external research institutes to participate in the R&D project. In this way, the Bioenergy Cluster created a unique customer solution and developed core know-how that can be used for future business. If the customer accepts the offer, participating member companies are involved in the manufacturing process. This additional business would not have been generated without pooling knowledge with others, and the virtual web provides the organizational framework for fair and trustworthy cooperation.

CONCLUSION

Virtual corporations derived from virtual webs have the potential to build core know-how and to develop core competencies to integrate the total resource potential of partner companies into competitive advantages. Goldman et al. (1995) even compared the virtual corporation with an all-star team. They write: "Imagine the power of an all-star team for every business opportunity, tailored to the challenge of the opportunity and that competitive situation" (p.202). The case of the Bioenergy Cluster provides an excellent example of this notion. Taking the knowledge-based view into consideration, what are the differences between the virtual web/corporation approach and other inter-organizational cooperations? First of all, one can constitute that conglomerates, cartels, consortiums, franchises, and keiretsu are long lasting partnerships based on very tight formal agreements (except cartels), in most cases they are not a partnership of equals and their purpose is neither to share resources nor to generate new knowledge. From a knowledge-based perspective such partnerships are less able to build core know-how and to achieve competitive advantages based on knowledge. Joint ventures have basically the problem that it takes a very long time to establish them. When they are established, joint ventures have a very fixed knowledge base, they depend on their parent companies for additional resources and knowledge, which makes them inflexible. Comparing joint ventures with virtual corporations, joint ventures do not have the potential to build core know-how as fast and as flexible as virtual corporations. There are many different kinds of strategic alliances, but in general, one could say strategic alliances take time to be established, their cooperation is between two or several defined organizational boundaries, and strategic alliances are mainly formed by larger companies. Strategic alliances are opportunistic, companies seeking partnership with others in areas where they have weaknesses, partners do not tend to share their key or core competencies with other. Again, from a knowledge-based perspective, the virtual corporation has a better chance to build core know-how than strategic alliances.

The virtual web/corporation approach has theoretically a better potential to build core know-how and to gain sustainable competitive advantages, but the main inhibitor of such an open cooperation is mutual trust. Only if web members build trustworthy relationships can the joint knowledge base be used to its full potential and gain competitive advantage over traditional firms and other forms of inter-organizational partnerships.

REFERENCES

Amit, R., & Schoemaker, PJH. (1993). Strategic assets and organizational rent. *Strategic Management Journal.* 14(1), 33-46.

Bultje, R., & van Wijk, J. (1998). Taxonomy of Virtual Organizations, based on definitions, characteristics and typology. VoNet: The Netwsletter @ http://www.virtual-organization.net. 2(3), 7-20.

Bund, M. (1997). Forschung und Entwicklung in der virtuellen Unternehmung. *Wirtschaftsmanagement*. 5, 247-253.

Bremer, CF. (1999). Case Study of Virtual Organization in Brazil. VoNet: The Netwsletter @ http://www.virtual-organization.net. 3(1), 35-39.

Brown, JS., & Duguid, P. (1998). Organizing Knowledge. *California Management Review*. 40(3), 90-111.

Byrne, JA. (1993). The virtual corporation. *Business Week*. Feb. 8, 98-102.

Conner, KR., & Prahalad, CK. (1996). A Resource-based Theory of the Firm: Knowledge Versus Opportunism. *Organizational Science*. 7(5), 477-501.

Coutu, DL., (1998). Organization: Trust in Virtual Teams. *Harvard Business Review*. 76(3), 20-21.

Davenport, TH., & Pearlson, K. (1998). Two Cheers for the Virtual Office. *Sloan Management Review*. 39(4), 51-65.

Dess, GG., Rasheed, AMA., McLaughlin, KJ., Priem RL. (1995). The New Corporate Architecture. *The Academy of Management Executive*. 9(3), 7-20.

Deutsch KJ., Diedrichs, EP., Raster, M., Westphal, J. (1997). Gewinnen mit Kernkompetenzen, Die Spielregeln des Marktes neu definieren, Carl Hanser Verlag, München.

Drucker, PF. (1992). The new society of organizations. *Harvard Business Review*. 70(5), 95-104.

Faisst, W., Birg, O. (1997). Die Rolle des Brokers in Virtuellen Unternehmen und seine Unterstützung durch die Informationsverarbeitung. Arbeitspapier der Reihe 'Informations- und Kommunikationssysteme als Gestaltungselement Virtueller Unternehmen. Institut für Wirtschaftsinformatik der Universität Bern / Institut für Wirtschaftsinformatik der Universität Leibzig, Bereich Wirtschafts- informatik I der Universität Erlangen-Nürnberg, 17.

Fischer, K. (1995). Mit Kernkompetenzen im Wettbewerb gewinnen. io management *Zeitschrift*. 64(4), 87-91.

Franke, UJ. (1998). Case study of a virtual corporation of small and medium automobile industry suppliers in Germany as a new way to gain competitive advantage. Conference Paper: 'The 21st century change imperative: evolving organizations & emerging networks'. University of Missouri-Columbia, USA. June 12-14. 12-15.

Gallon, MR., Stillman, HM., Coates, D. (1995). Putting Competency Thinking into Practice. *Research Technology Management*. 38(3), 20-28.

Gemünden, HG., & Walter, A. (1995). Der Beziehungspromotor - Schlüsselperson für inter-organisationale Innovationsprozesse. *Zeitschrift für Betriebswirtschaft*. 65(9), 971-986.

Goldman, SL., & Nagel, RN. (1993). Management, Technology and Agility: The emergence of a new era in manufacturing. *International Journal of Technology Management*. 8(1/2), 18-38.

Goldman, SL., Nagel, RN., Preiss, K. (1995). *Agile Competitors and Virtual Organizations: strategies for enriching the customer*. Van Nostrand Reinhold. New York.

Grant, RM. (1991). The resource-based theory of competitive advantage: Implications for strategy formulation. *California Management Review*. 33(3), 114-135.

Grant, RM. (1996a). Toward a Knowledge-based Theory of the Firm. *Strategic Management Journal*. 17(Winter Special Issue), 109-122.

Grant, RM. (1996b). Prospering in Dynamically-competitive Environments: Organizational Capability as Knowledge Integration. *Organizational Science*. 7(4), 375-387.

Grant, RM. (1997). The Knowledge-based View of the Firm: Implications for Management Practice. *Long Range Planning*. 30(3), 450-454.

Grant, RM. & Baden-Fuller, C. (1995). A Knowledge-based theory of inter-firm collaboration. *Academy of Management Journal. Best Papers Proceedings 1995*, 17-21.

Hall, R. (1993). A framework linking intangible resources and capabilities to sustainable competitive advantage. *Strategic Management Journal*. 14(8), 607-618.

Hardwick, M., Spooner, DL., Rando, T., Morris, KC. (1996). Sharing manufacturing information in virtual enterprises. *Communications of the ACM*. 39(2), 46-54.

Hatch, CR. (1995). *The network brokers handbook*, U.S. Department of Commerce. National Institute of Standards and Technology. Manufacturing Extension Partnership, Gaithersburg, MD 20899, USA.

Hofer, CW., & Schendel, D. (1978). *Strategy Formulation: Analytical Concepts*. West Publishing Company, St. Paul.

Kanet, JJ., Faisst, W. (1997). The role of information technology in supporting the entrepreneur for the virtual enterprise: a life-cycle-oriented description. Internal Working Paper, Clemson University, USA.

Kanter, RM. (1989). Becoming PALs: Pooling, Allying, and Linking across companies. *The Academy of Management Executive*. 3(3), 179-193.

Katz, RL. (1974). Skills of an effective administrator. *Harvard Business Review*. (52)5, 90-102.

Kogut, B., Zander, U. (1992). Knowledge of the Firm, Combinative Capabilities, and the Replication of Technology. *Organizational Science*. 3(3), 383-397.

Leonard, D., Sensiper, S. (1998). The Role of Tacit Knowledge in Group Innovation. *California Management Review*. 40(3), 112-132.

Liebeskind, JP. (1996). Knowledge, Strategy, and the Theory of the Firm. *Strategic Management Journal*. 17(Winter Special Issue), 93-107.

Lipman, J., & Stamps, J. (1994). *The Age of the Network*. Oliver Wight Publication, Inc., Essex Junction.

Lipman, J., & Stamps J. (1997). *Virtual Teams*. John Wiley & Sons, New York.

Mertens, P., Faisst, W. (1996). Virtuelle Unternehmen: eine Organisationsstruktur für die Zukunft?. *Das Wirtschaftsstudium*. 6, 280-285.

Mews, M. (1997). Virtuelle Unternehmen zwischen Anspruch und Wirklichkeit. *IT Management*. 3, 12-17.

Miles, RE., Snow, CC. (1986). Network organizations: new concepts for new forms. *California Management Review*. 28(3), 62-73.

Moshowitz, A. (1986). Social dimensions of office automation. In Myovitz (ed.): *Advances in computers*. 25, 335-404.

Mowery, DC., Oxley, JE., Silverman BS. (1996). Strategic Alliances and Interfirm Knowledge Transfer. *Strategic Management Journal*. 17(Winter Special Issue), 77-91.

Nelson. RR., & Winter, SG. (1982). *An Evolutionary Theory of Economic Change*.

Harvard Business Press, Cambridge.

Penrose, ET. (1959). *The theory of the growth of the firm.* Basil Blackwell, Oxford.

Prahalad, CK., & Hamel, G. (1990). The core competence of the corporation. *Harvard Business Review,* 68(3), 79-91.

Prange, C., Probst, G., Rüling, CC. (1996). Lernen zu kooperieren - Kooperieren, um zu lernen. *Zeitschrift für Organisation.* 65(1), 10-16.

Reiß, M. (1997). Virtuelle Organisation auf dem Prüfstand. *VDI - Zeitschrift.* 139(1), 24-27.

Sanchez, R., & Mahoney, JT., (1996). Modularity, Flexibility, and Knowledge Management in Product and Organization Design. *Strategic Management Journal.* 17(Winter Special Issue), 63-76.

Scholz, C. (1994). Die virtuelle Organisation als Strukturkonzept der Zukunft. Arbeitspapier Nr. 30. Lehrstuhl für Betriebswirtschaft. Universität des Saarlandes, Saarbrücken.

Scholz, C. (1996). Virtuelle Organisationen: Konzeption und Realisation. *Zeitschrift für Organisation.* 4, 204-210.

Scholz, C. (1997). Das virtuelle Unternehmen - Schlagwort oder echte Vision?. *Bilanz Manager.* 1, 12-19.

Schuh, G., Katzy, BR., Eisen, S. (1997). Wie virtuelle Unternehmen funktionieren: Der Praxistest ist bestanden. *Gablers Magazin.* 3, 8-11.

Schuh, G., Millarg, K., Goransson, A. (1998). Virtuelle Fabrik: neue Marktchancen durch dynamische Netzwerke. Carl Hanser Verlag, Munchen, Wien.

Sheridan, JH. (1996). The Agile Web: a model for the future?. *Industry Week.* 245(5), 31-33.

Snow, CC., Miles, RE., Coleman, HJ. (1992). Managing the 21st century network organization. *Organizational Dynamics.* 20(3), 5-16.

Snow, CC., Thomas, JB. (1993). Building Networks; Broker roles and behavior. In: Lorange, P., Chakravarthy, B., Roos, J., Van de Ven, A., (eds). *Implementing Strategic Processes: Change, Learning and Co-operation.* Blackwell Publishers, Oxford.

Spender, JC. (1996). Making Knowledge the Basis of a Dynamic Theory of the Firm. *Strategic Management Journal.* 17(Winter Special Issue), 45-62.

Stuart, I., Deckert, P., McCutcheon, D., Kunst, R. (1998), Case Study: A Leverage Learning Network. *Sloan Management Review.* 39(4), 81-93.

Sydow, J. (1996). Virtuelle Unternehmung - Erfolg als Vertrauensorganisation?. *Office Management.* 44(7/8), 10-13.

Thorelli, H. (1986). Networks: Between Markets and Hierarchies. *Strategic Management Journal.* 7(1), 37-51

Upton, DM., McAfee, A. (1996). The Real Virtual Factory. *Harvard Business Review,* 74(4), 123-133.

Venkatraman, N., Henderson, C. (1996). The architecture of virtual organizing: leveraging three independent vectors. Discussion Paper. Systems Research Center. Boston University, School of Management.

Winter, SG. (1986). The research program of the behavioral theory of the firm: Orthodox critique and evolutionary perspective. In: Gilad, B., & Kaish, S., (eds.). *Handbook of Behavioral Economics.* Vol. A., JAI Press, Greenwich. 151-188.

Chapter III

Implementing Virtual Organizing in Business Networks: A Method of Inter-Business Networking

Roland Klueber, Rainer Alt and Hubert Österle
University of St. Gallen, Switzerland

Virtual organizations and knowledge management have been discussed on a very broad scale in literature. However, a holistic view and methods that support implementation of these concepts are rare. Based on the understanding derived from literature and the experience of many action research-based projects, a method is described that addresses these issues for business networks. This includes the dimensions of strategy, process and IS required for establishing and managing business networks. By providing a systematic and documented procedure model, techniques and results, this method aims to improve the efficiency of setting up business networks, thus improving a company's networkability. In order to illustrate why this method is needed and how it can be applied, a project for implementing a business-networking solution for electronic procurement is described. It shows how a structured approach helps to identify the scenarios, aids implementation and applies previously as well as newly created knowledge. The outlook describes areas for future research and new developments.

INTRODUCTION TO BUSINESS NETWORKING

Essence of Business Networking

Business Networking (BN) has become one of the most powerful strategic business trends. A deconstruction of the economy is taking place, involving a move from vertically integrated hierarchies towards flexible network organizations, and the ability to quickly and efficiently setup, maintain, develop and dissolve partnerships with business partners —a competence we refer to as networkability (Österle et al., 2000) — is a critical success factor. Networkability includes the collaborative advantage termed by Moss-Kanter

(1994) as "the propensity to be a good partner" and aims at pursuing common goals when applied to a specific relationship. Achieving networkability is at the heart of Business Networking, which describes the design and management of relationships between (internal or external) business units.

There are two main driving forces behind the need for Business Networking which are highly interrelated. First, management is being confronted with trends such as globalization, shorter innovation cycles and deregulation leading to increasingly dynamic markets. This requires new strategies, such as core competence focus, outsourcing, and a stronger customer orientation. Business Networking is an inherent element of these strategies. Second, information technology (IT) allows for the efficient exchange of information among organizations and acts as a main enabler for networking among businesses. Wigand et al. describe the consequences as follows: "Classical corporate boundaries are beginning to blur, to change internally as well as externally, and in some cases, even dissolve" (Wigand, Picot, & Reichwald, 1997).

During the last decade companies have integrated their functional information systems (IS) in enterprise resource planning (ERP) systems which provide an integrated database for various functions, such as finance, marketing, and production. These ERP systems have emerged on a large scale and have become the backbone for Business Networking. ERP vendors such as SAP, Baan, Oracle or Peoplesoft are eagerly adding Business Networking functionality for electronic commerce (EC), supply chain management (SCM) and (customer) relationship management (RM). Enhancing and extending existing ERP systems as well as implementing Business Networking strategies is of foremost importance for companies and requires decisions concerning strategy, processes and systems.

Role of Virtual Organizing as a Method in Business Networking

Virtual organizations denote an organizational form which is based on a "temporary network of independent companies – suppliers, customers and rivals – linked by IT to share skills, costs and access to one another's market" (Byrne, 1993; Wang, 1997). This organizational form is largely enabled by IT in order to overcome the limitations of time, space and stable organizational forms (Skyrme, 1998). Following Faucheux (1997), Venkatraman and Henderson (1998) and DeSanctis and Monge (1998), the term virtual organizing is chosen instead of virtual organization in order to emphasize its process-like nature as well as to avoid connotations of a static nature and a limitation to an organizational form. According to Venkatraman and Henderson (1998), virtual organizing is defined as "a strategic approach that is singularly focused on creating, nurturing, and deploying key intellectual and knowledge assets while sourcing tangible, physical assets in a complex network of relationships".

As described by Rockart (1998), virtuality allows for both economies of scale and local innovation as well as a 'single face to the customer'. We see an increasing acceptance of these ideas both in academia and in practice. However, these forms are temporary in nature and require more information and coordination. This can be achieved by a more intensive use of IT, as IT can lead to more coordination-intensive structures due to reduced coordination costs (Malone and Rockart, 1991). This mainly concerns transaction partners and patterns, exchanged products and services as well as the negotiated conditions. Typically, this level is covered by ERP, EC and SCM Systems.

Role of Knowledge Management in Business Networking

Knowledge about setting-up relationships with partners, about their preferences and performance profiles, is not bound to a specific transaction although some knowledge may be derived from individual transactions. This is the domain of knowledge management that aims at making unstructured information, implicit or tacit knowledge available. According to Wiig (1999), "knowledge management is the systematic and explicit management of knowledge-related activities, practices, programs and policies within the enterprise". Multiple phases of the knowledge management process are usually distinguished: goal definition, identification, acquisition, development, distribution, application, maintenance and assessment of knowledge (Probst, Raub, & Romhardt, 1997). In their survey of knowledge management projects , Davenport, De Long and Beers (1998), identified four categories:

- creation of knowledge repositories (e.g. databases with research reports, marketing materials, techniques, competitive intelligence or experiences),
- improvement of knowledge access (e.g. Yellow Pages, competence directories or videoconferencing),
- enhancement of knowledge environment (e.g. guidelines for performing activities) and
- management of knowledge as an asset (e.g. patents database for improved monitoring of licensing revenues).

Knowledge management is a key process for establishing and sustaining networkability. Firstly, knowledge on business partners, their processes and systems is required. Secondly, knowledge of how to set-up and configure these relationships allows rapid identification and qualification of potential partners. Thirdly, it enables an increase in efficiency due to the effects of experience in linking processes and systems. One focus of knowledge management in BN is the identification of relevant cooperative areas and partners, its support with IT and IS tools and the acquisition of knowledge about partners from transaction systems. Therefore, both concepts, knowledge management and virtual

Figure 1: Role of Virtual Organizing and Knowledge Management in Business Networking

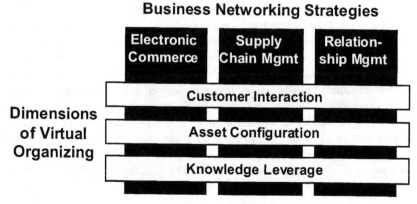

organizing are inherent elements in Business Networking projects. This argument is supported in the model of Venkatraman and Henderson (1998) who distinguish three dimensions of virtual organizing (Figure 1): customer interaction, asset configuration, and knowledge leverage. The advantage of this model is that it already includes knowledge management as an element of all Business Networking strategies.

Business Networking Challenges

Due to the enabling role of IT, Business Networking per se includes the usage of information systems in order to contain increasing coordination costs.[1] This represents a major challenge since Business Networking is not a technological concept and involves decisions concerning strategy and processes as well. As Klein (1996) shows, multiple layers and options have to be included when configuring relationships among businesses. For example, companies can decide to outsource, insource or enter new market segments with Business Networking and they can decide to pursue various networking strategies such as EC, SCM or RM (Alt, Österle, Reichmayr & Zurmuehlen, 1999). More details need to be discussed on the process level when, for instance, an electronic purchasing service or a vendor managed inventory (VMI) process is being implemented. On the systems level, a variety of tools are on the market for performing these activities and choosing the right standards strongly determines networkability.

As outlined above, Business Networking involves a variety of complex issues which have to be tackled. More complexity is added with the different nature of inter-business relationships compared to internal relationships (Alt & Fleisch, 1999). Especially the relative autonomy of business partners permits less direct influence and entails greater potential for conflict. In addition, there is—traditionally—only a lower level of knowledge about the business partner's processes which can be a result of the more frequent change of partners (lower stability) or of less information exchanged between partners.

RESEARCH APPROACH FOR METHOD DEVELOPMENT

In the following we will present four conceptual foundations which are the basis for developing a method for inter-Business Networking. These are action research, business engineering, the business model of the information age and method engineering.

Action Research

In general, a method for Business Networking is only useful when it is applicable in practice. Action research is a research tradition which combines pure (management) action and pure scientific research (Checkland & Holwell, 1998). Action research has two characteristics (Mansell, 1991): "1. The researcher seeks to add to knowledge, but is also concerned to apply knowledge and become involved in the implementation of plans. 2. The problem to be solved is not defined by the researcher but by participants in human activity (e.g. managers in organizations)." Since IT is an applied discipline, action research methods have proven to be appropriate research methodologies in this area (Baskerville & Wood-Harper, 1998). Furthermore, action research provides advantages when studying organizational networks (Chisholm, 1998). Therefore, action research is chosen as the leading research approach.

The setting for the method development project is the Competence Center inter-Business Networking (CC iBN) at the Institute for Information Management of the University of St. Gallen. Eight companies (Bayer AG, Robert Bosch Group, Deutsche Telekom AG, ETA SA, HiServ, Hoffmann-LaRoche, Riverwood International Inc., and SAP AG) are currently collaborating in the field of Business Networking with the researchers from the university. This approach follows the principles of action research as suggested by Probst and Raub (1995): it is problem-driven, action-oriented, and practitioners are actively participating in the projects.

Business Engineering Model

Action research provides the general direction for conducting research, but it does not provide a framework for structuring research in a specific field. An approach which is geared towards the business-oriented conceptualization of information systems is business engineering. The framework of Österle (1995) combines various theoretical disciplines and "structures the organization, data and function dimensions at the business strategy, process and information systems levels". It encompasses business, organizational and information systems aspects in a structured approach that tries to overcome the shortcomings of isolated approaches. Distinguishing these three layers has proved helpful for analyzing and designing ISs. The generic model of business engineering has been enhanced in several aspects. Political and change management have been added (Gouillart and Kelly, 1995) and, as shown in Figure 2, they have been applied to network settings.

Business Model of the Information Age

Closely interrelated with this, the technological and management trends described above are leading towards a business model for Business Networking. This model has

Figure 2: Business Engineering Model Applied to Business Networking

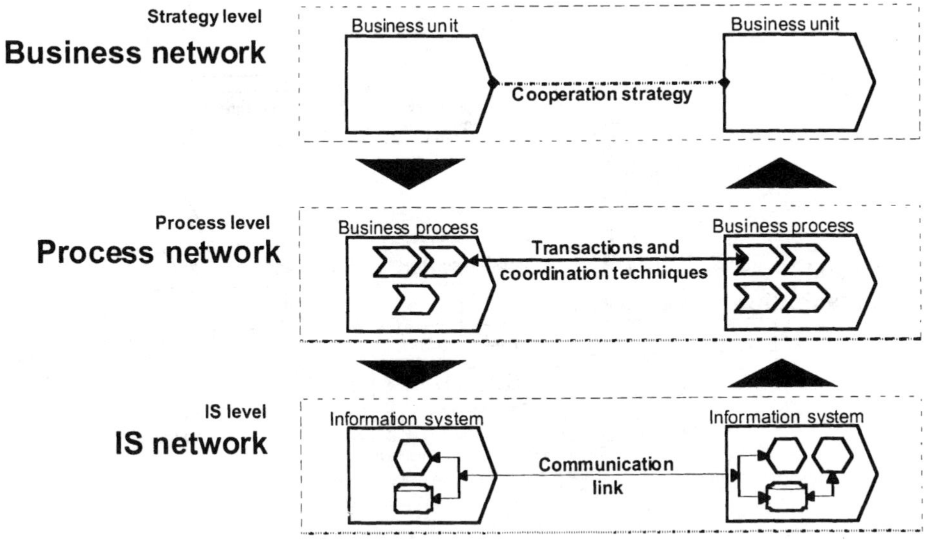

three main characteristics (Österle et al., 2000):

- *Customer processes* determine the design of the value chain. To give an example from the travelling industry, solutions to satisfy a customer's entire demand would include products and services from flight to hotels, cars, theater tickets and the like. Computer reservation systems are models which will become relevant in other industries as well, e.g. the health sector.

- An *aggregator/integrator* which mirrors the customer's processes manages the relationship. This new role forms the basis for new business (Hagel & Singer, 1998). Current examples for such ‚infomediaries‘ are Dell or Amazon.com. Dell also highlights that infomediaries outsource all non-core competencies to suppliers and invest in the management of these supplier relationships.

- A *business bus* supports communication among business partners. The business bus is a concept which is based upon the increasing availability of modular electronic services and standards for processes, data, and interfaces. As shown in Figure 3, the services include not only basic infrastructure services (e.g. messaging) but also directory services (e.g. the database from Dun&Bradstreet), payment and logistics services. Standardization is reflected in the business bus by defining syntactic and semantic standards used by partners. These are implemented by business ports which denote a company's ability to interface with a large number of partners. Examples are standards for catalogs (e.g., RosettaNet, CXML, UN/SPSC) and processes (e.g., SCOR or CPFR).[2] Initial solutions for business ports are already on the market (e.g,. SAP Business Connector) and are expected to develop with the spread of XML-related standards. Electronic services offered via the business bus can be considered as enablers for emerging virtual organizations (Klueber, Alt & Österle, 1999).

Figure 3: Business Model for Business Networking

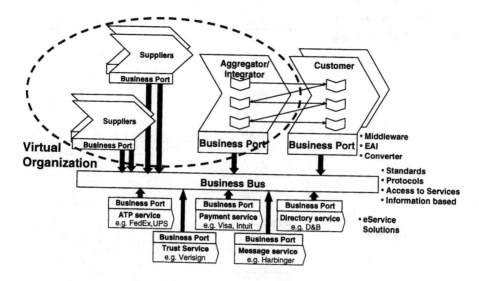

Principles of Method Engineering

In order to structure the method, we rely on the method engineering principles as defined by Gutzwiller (1994), which have been used successfully to define several methods of business engineering (see IMG, 1999). The main objective of a method is to "decompose a project into manageable activities, determine techniques, tools and roles as well as defining results" (Österle, 1995). The procedure model reflects an ideal sequence of top-level activities. Techniques describe how one or more results can be achieved and facilitated with the use of specific tools (e.g., the software selection process). Tools offer conceptual or structural support to produce the result documents with appropriate semantics. For example, the SCOR model facilitates the categorization, modeling and measuring of supply chain processes by providing common semantics for interorganizational supply chain projects. An example for a computer assisted tool is ARIS Easy-SCOR. Finally, roles describe the required know-how and competencies needed to complete the required result documents.

However, the benefits of using a method are not limited to structuring a project. Methods are also used to facilitate training and (self-)learning by example. One major advantage is that they aid coordination and understanding by providing a common language for people with heterogeneous skills, knowledge and backgrounds. Also, a method provides specimen result documents that can be used in similar projects. These benefits should lead to improvements in terms of hard (time, cost, quality) and soft (flexibility and knowledge) factors.

It is a challenge for a method of Business Networking to comply with the principles of action research, to include the analytical layers of business engineering and to take into account the nature of upcoming business models.

TOWARDS A METHOD OF BUSINESS NETWORKING

The motivation to design a method stems from the complexity and novelty of Business Networking projects. Complexity is a function of the number of partners involved, their heterogeneity and the multiple strategies of Business Networking (e.g., EC, SCM, RM). Novelty is based on new approaches towards partnering (i.e., collaborative planning) and processes supported by new software solutions and infrastructures such as the Internet (Rockart, 1998). The method tries to handle these issues and avoids pitfalls and fallacies by offering an ideal but still flexible and customizable path of how to decide and implement one combination of strategies.

Method Overview

It is an assumption of the method that Business Networking projects pursue comparable activities. Figure 4 depicts these activities which can be further detailed in sub-activities. The philosophy of the method is that the first two phases and the last phase are common for all Business Networking projects. Due to their higher degree of process and application-specificity, all other activities are developed in specific procedure models.[3]

Potentials Analysis

Typically, Business Networking projects start with a potentials analysis, which

Figure 4: General Procedure Model

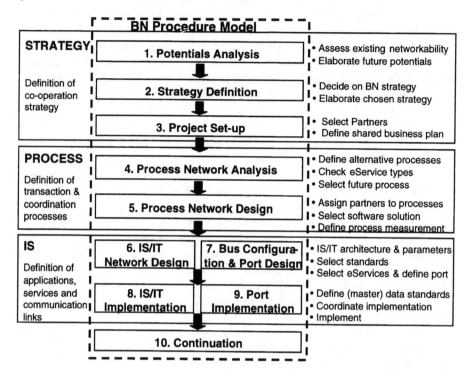

transforms vague ideas on cooperation potentials into specific alternatives. A prerequisite is an initial health check of internal capabilities and processes in order to avoid solutions which address the wrong problems. For example, we have seen that external improvements often require internal excellence. Potentials analysis contains three main sub-activities:

- For the *assessment of networkability, a* clear understanding of corporate resources, customer and market strategies is required. It requires information about cooperation strategies and capabilities as well as future cooperation areas (Stein, 1997; Kuglin, 1998; Hillig, 1997). Networkability includes strategy, cultural, cooperation process, IS connectivity and architectural issues (Rockart, 1998) as well as the human resource and organizational dimension (Hillig, 1997). The degree of networkability can be measured by the time required to establish cooperation, the content of the cooperation and the number of cooperations that can be managed in parallel. It has implications on the strategy level (Doz and Hamel, 1998), the operational processes, and the potentials of innovative information systems. Our findings show that mental models, organizational structures and the information systems and architectures often have to be adapted if a company wishes to reap the benefits and take advantage of the opportunities of virtual organizing. One major result of this sub-activity may be to get a clearer view on the as-is situation as well as to initiate a change of cultural, political and mental frames.

- *Identification of BN areas*. To identify the areas(s) which are attractive for Business Networking, we apply the framework of Venkatraman and Henderson (1998). It can be used to analyze the current state along the dimensions of asset configuration (virtual sourcing), customer interaction (virtual encounter) and knowledge leverage (virtual expertise). The architecture of virtual organizing integrates organizational and exchange considerations with knowledge management. In doing so, it serves as a high-level classification scheme to identify the development potentials.

- The *information intensity analysis* addresses the question of the information-intensity of the product or service group and of its interorganizational coordination mechanism. This is done by adding an aggregated vector to the previous framework (cf. Klueber, 1998) which is determined by the product's/service's information-intensity (X-axis) (Porter and Millar, 1985) and by the information intensity of the interorganizational coordination mechanism (Y-axis) (see Figure 5). Examples of measuring information intensity are: the degree of shared information objects (i.e. shared planning data) (Ludwig, 1997), the degree of mutual adjustment supported via IT (i.e., electronic discussion groups or shared access to knowledge databases), and the support of consumer-producer interdependencies (Malone and Crowston, 1994).

Potentials analysis concerns not only the assessment of the status quo but also helps to define the scenario to-be. This enables an initial assessment of future benefits and completes the understanding of a companies' networkability and the areas with a high potential for Business Networking.

Figure 5: Information Intensity Matrix

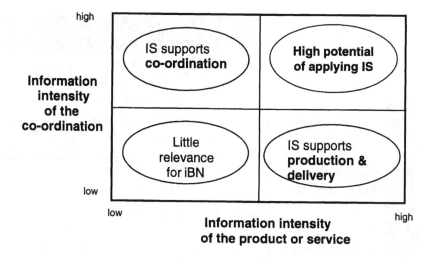

Strategy Definition

Input from potential analysis serves as a starting point to the strategy definition phase which consists of five steps (Figure 6). First, the general strategy (e.g., cost and service leadership) has to be applied to the related organizational areas and the BN goals are identified. The second decision is on the organizational resources that are necessary in order to achieve the goals in the identified area and how they are accessed. The choices are between outsourcing, virtual organization and insourcing (cf. Marakas and Kelly, 1999). Third, a decision about the networking strategy is required to define the category

Figure 6 – Activities in Strategy Definition

of solutions that will be dominantly used to achieve the defined BN goals. The relevant IS-related solution strategies are EC, SCM, and RM. The decision is supported through process categorization and best practices as well as process characteristics that are likely to be achieved with one of the networking strategies.

The result is documented in a matrix which shows the decision on the organizational resource and the networking dimensions for a product group/process/organizational unit combination as alternative future cooperation areas in the portfolio (see Figure 7). If the choice is building a virtual organization, the networking strategies are pursued in collaboration with partners. If it is outsourcing, the cooperation intensity with partners is lower and, if it is insourcing, it is usually higher. The alternatives are assessed and chosen

Figure 7: Major strategy decision

	Organizational Resource Decision		
Networking Decision	**Outsourcing**	**Virtual Organization**	**Insourcing**
Electronic Commerce		eProcurement for C goods	Content Management for Z catalogs
Supply Chain Management		SCM for X parts with Y partners	
Relationship Management			

on the basis of a scoring model which includes multiple dimensions (e.g., cost, time, quality, flexibility, knowledge, strategic fit).

The sequence is ideal but we have assumed that all these interdependent decisions have to be made before a successful BN project can be started. At a minimum it could serve as a checklist if top management decisions are made, the resource questions are solved, the IS potentials are analyzed and the development path is aligned with the overall direction. Furthermore it can be a recursive process, the entry points may vary and results are elaborated in later phases.

Continuation Activity

Finally, continuation activity aims at realizing the whole potential of BN projects identified in the BN project portfolio or at systematically identifying new BN projects. If the strict sequence and starting from the top cannot be applied in a real situation, where a variety of constraints or actual problems have to be taken into account, the clear description of the requirements to start in one activity allows lower starting points, parallel activities and cycles.

Specific Procedure Models

Work with project partners has shown the difficulty of supporting the variety of Business Networking strategies. The challenges vary considerably in the intensity of the cooperation, the quality and quantity of information exchanged and the IS solution categories needed. We decided to introduce specific procedure models as a new element of method engineering, which offers the following advantages:

- Higher problem-specific support and wording,
- Easier comparisons between similar projects,
- Less abstract and more oriented to action, and
- Better basis for capturing and transferring knowledge.

Specific procedure models represent a bottom-up approach compared to the top-down development of the method. They inherit elements of the general procedure model and add specific activities, techniques, result documents, roles and cases (see Figure 8). The underlying common structure and origin from the BN procedure model facilitates the coordination of multiple BN projects.

Link to Virtual Organizing and Knowledge Management

Virtual organizing is the main concept behind the organization strategies in Business Networking. The strategic configurations for internal and external resources are insourcing, virtual organization and outsourcing. A company which plans to introduce a Business Networking strategy would start to analyze its position in the framework of Venkatraman and Henderson (1998). For example, a low level of virtual sourcing implies an improvement potential with EC and/or more intense SCM solutions. The method should help to evaluate *when* virtual organizing is adequate, *what* configuration and combination of EC and SCM solutions are required in specific situations and *how* these could be implemented. The structuring of these new or complementary solutions and guidance towards feasible implementation is at the heart of the method. It adds important elements such as the SCM networking strategy to assess different alternatives and to move further towards an implementation. Thus, virtual organizing is an inherent element in the entire method.

The role of *knowledge management* becomes apparent when use of the method is regarded as a knowledge management tool (Probst et al., 1997). The definition of knowledge goals pursued in BN

Figure 8: Combination of Method and specific procedure models

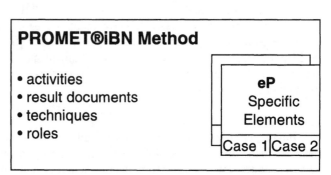

projects is a salient element in the strategy definition phase. The identification of knowledge gaps and sources to fill them is also vital when deciding on BN strategies. Knowledge acquisition is supported by providing a structured approach with context knowledge embedded into the procedure model, techniques and result documents. Furthermore, in using the method, explicit knowledge gets internalized and subsequently supports the knowledge distribution process and its application (cf. Nonaka & Takeuchi, 1995). Also, implicit knowledge that gets codified in cases and best practice examples is made accessible to other individuals. The knowledge application phase is entered when the method is applied to a specific business context. It helps to communicate internalized knowledge by the project members and may aid the externalization and creation of new knowledge for a project. In a second step, knowledge management gains importance after operational processes have been implemented. This is based on better information about business partners that can be used to intensify the relationship in order to develop potentials for further improvements on a win-win basis (Österle et al., 2000).

To summarize, the knowledge management aspect is addressed in two perspectives. First, the method helps to identify process areas where a company has vital knowledge gaps and sustains the processes of knowledge acquisition, development, application, storage and maintenance. Second, the implementation of new BN strategies and processes leads to new operative information systems and provides new information bases that can be used as new areas for knowledge management.

CASE: IMPLEMENTING BUSINESS NETWORKING AT DEUTSCHE TELEKOM AG

Following the principles of action research, case studies undertaken at partner companies (see Chapter 2) are driving ahead the development of the method, especially for specific procedure models. In the following we will present the case of Deutsche Telekom AG which focuses on the procurement of indirect goods via Internet services. We will briefly describe the history and business context of Deutsche Telekom, the procurement process, the project itself, and the procedure map for implementing the Business Networking solution for electronic procurement for indirect goods (eProcurement) which was defined in this project.

Business Context of Deutsche Telekom AG

Deutsche Telekom AG is a formerly state-owned telecommunications company that was converted into a stock corporation on the 1st of January 1995 and went public in November 1996. In 1998, its revenues were DM 69 billion (approx. US$38 billion) with a net income of DM 4.2 billion (approx. US$2.27 billion). The core business is mainly from a national full-service telecommunication business with 179,500 employees (1998). This included 46 million customers in the area of fixed lines and 10.1 million ISDN customers in 1998, which is more ISDN lines than the USA and Japan together. Furthermore, Deutsche Telekom is a major cellular provider with 5.5 million customers, Europe's biggest online and Internet service provider and serves 17.6 million customers with the cable TV infrastructure (Deutsche Telekom, 1999).

The transformation process from a vertically integrated monopolist towards a worldwide active competitive organization involved major changes in all dimensions. This has partly been enforced due to deregulation and liberalization in the European telecommunications market since January 1, 1998. Another major driving force is the convergence of the media, telecommunications and IT industries enabled through digitalization. Two of the challenges Deutsche Telekom faces is to determine (1) what products and services should be provided for which customers and (2) which areas partnerships and alliances are important for competitiveness. As these questions have not been as prevalent in the protected monopolist past, new skills in the management of internal competencies and partnerships have to be acquired in all dimensions of business engineering (cf. Chapter 2). Therefore, a knowledge, skill and IS/IT gap had to be filled in order to sustain success in the global telecommunications marketplace.

One of the first steps in the Deutsche Telekom project concerned the definition of potential areas for Business Networking in terms of knowledge acquisition, internalization and leverage as well as operational improvements and IS/IT innovation. In workshops with Deutsche Telekom, the main strategic options to initiate a networking project were presented as best practice examples. An area which was further examined was the process of procuring indirect goods (eProcurement). The decision to set up the first project to improve the procurement process was based on a high-level scoring model derived from a previous market, resource and strategy analysis.

Procurement Process for Indirect Goods

Indirect goods encompass MRO goods[4], office materials and other C-goods[5]. Figure 10 shows a categorization and some examples of the product range that could be procured electronically via the Internet. We will refer to the electronic procurement process for indirect products as eProcurement. The specifics of the eProcurement process for indirect goods are that demand is not planned, variety of products is large, standardization of products and processes is typically high, value of goods is low, the number of potential users is high and the process involves catalog and authorization processes (Killen and Associates, 1997).

The procurement process for these products consists of a strategic and an operational element (Figure 9). *Strategic procurement* includes customer and supplier management and deals with the selection, contracting and evaluation of the partners. These partners are suppliers of indirect goods as well as content and catalog management service providers.

Figure 9 : Categories of Goods and Services for Electronic Procurement

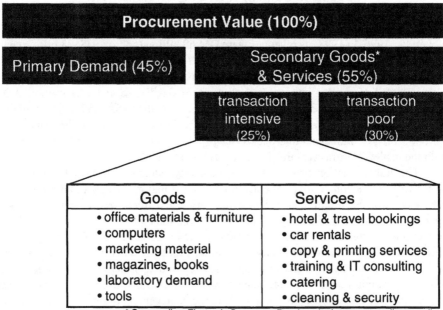

* Compendium Electronic Commerce Benchmarks (www.compendium.   nl)

Although this process has a strong knowledge component, it relies on (operational) transaction data. The goal of knowledge management is to gain information about the performance of partners in order to improve contracts and to establish win-win relationships. The *operational procurement* process consists of five elements (see Figure 10). Desktop purchasing systems (DPS) permit end-users to purchase indirect goods directly via an Internet browser. These systems include conditions which were agreed upon in outline agreements for the goods listed in the catalog. Additionally these systems cover the integration into ERP systems, the authorization workflow as well as the link to procurement departments for exceptional requests. The interorganizational element is the electronic integration and transaction-based monitoring of suppliers, service providers for catalog and content management as well as the integration of payment and logistics services.

Benefits of eProcurement

E-Procurement leads to some major economic benefits. The entire procurement process is IT supported, involves end users and covers products which were not procured electronically before. Three important aspects are:

- *Process improvements.* Systems for indirect procurement such as Ariba's Operations Resource Management System, Commerce One's Market Site and Buy Site or SAP's B2B Procurement allow users to browse and order goods directly which have been pre-configured according to central standards and responsibilities. This not only increases the transparency of the procurement process, thus allowing for the pooling of procurement volume, but also improves the management of suppliers and

Figure 10: Elements of electronic procurement processes

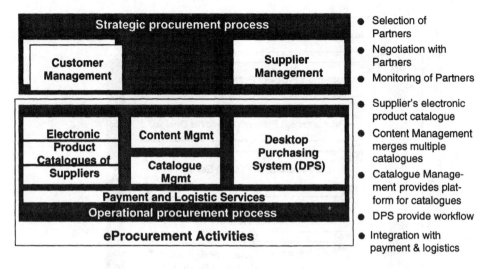

reduces transactions that bypass outline contracts ('maverick buying').

- *Cost savings for buyer.* Findings from software and service providers indicate that systems which support indirect procurement would lead to savings of up to $ 50 per transaction (c.f. Reinhardt, 1998). Other sources report savings of 5-15% of the expenses on indirect goods (Killen & Associates, 1997). Assuming a user population of more than 10.000 and standard installations, savings of several million US$ and a prospective ROI of less than a year were calculated.
- *Opportunities for sellers.* Incentives for suppliers emerge when physical catalogs are replaced and printing and distribution costs are reduced. Suppliers profit from a faster cash-in cycle and suppliers that quickly establish eProcurement capabilities have the opportunity of increasing their turnover with customers (e.g. Deutsche Telekom).

Procedure Model for eProcurement

During the project at Deutsche Telekom, a procedure model was developed for implementing an eProcurement solution. Once the decision was made for the procurement of indirect goods, eight steps were identified (see Figure 11).

In the first activity, *procurement process potentials* were assessed in more detail. After setting-up a joint project team of IT and procurement department, the project portfolio analysis technique showed that similar projects already existed within the Deutsche Telekom group. The generation of alternative scenarios for the procurement process were supported by templates of solutions that have been implemented in the USA (Dolmetsch, 1999). Based on these potentials, scenarios were detailed within the *eProcurement process scenario design* for a catalog and content management service. Since a market survey did not offer any operative solution providers in Germany, the decision was made to enhance internal competencies for establishing an internal service. The strategic procurement technique produced the first feasible scenarios. It helped to identify the potentials and supported the analysis of different scenarios. It includes

Figure 11: Procedure Model for eProcurement

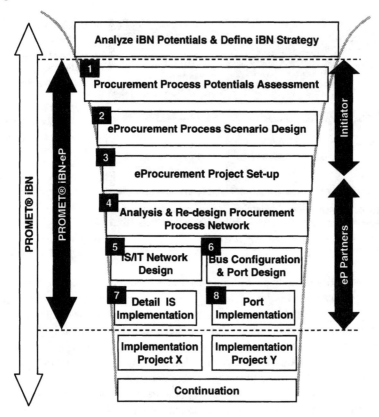

qualitative aspects such as strategic fit, impact on strategic flexibility, knowledge and risk as well as specific categories to assess the more quantifiable benefit and cost implications based on a financial model for eProcurement. The activity led to the evaluation and the decision for one or more feasible scenarios.

The *eProcurement project set-up* converts strategic ideas and scenarios into tangible BN goals and deliverables with the identified partners and settled cooperation contracts. The identification is supported by the partner profiling technique (cf. Alt and Fleisch, 1999) to select appropriate partners. At Deutsche Telekom, early talks with software providers and a reality check with possible suppliers were conducted. Also, a first impact analysis on the IS architecture was performed. The decision on the software solution was not completed, as the value of a customized solution was perceived to be higher than the benefits of implementing existing software processes.

In the more detailed *analysis and redesign procurement process network* activity the to-be processes were defined. The chosen process network was specified in more detail and partner companies or external service providers were assigned. The results were used to detail the software requirements, which were aligned with Deutsche Telekom's strategic IS architecture planning and legacy systems. The idea of the business bus (see Chapter 2) raised the potential not only to create the catalog and content management for internal use but to exploit the buying power, high number of transactions, brand name, critical mass and the IT infrastructure of Deutsche Telekom to establish a dedicated electronic service (eService) for business-to-business eProcurement. Since these requirements increased the complexity the eService was set up as a parallel project. The method supported software requirements analysis and selection, supplier selection and project management by providing best practice examples from the USA and results from desk research. Furthermore the activities and techniques helped to produce result documents to push and document the progress of the project.

The implementation-oriented section of the method envisages four activities. The *IS/ IT network design* activity defines the implementation details such as data, protocol and application standards. It is followed by the *detail IS implementation* activity which provides activities to coordinate the implementation projects. The final implementation may be supported by implementation methods such as PROMET, (IMG, 1999). In parallel, the integration of business bus components, which were identified earlier, is supported by the *bus configuration and port design* activity. Specific eServices are implemented in the *port implementation* activity.

The lessons of Deutsche Telekom reflect the challenges of Business Networking on different levels:

- Early addressing of the IS/IT solution potentials and the integrative process perspective can be considered as a key success factor.
- Knowledge transfer was included by providing successful cases and strategic options for the scenario development to support the decision processes.
- The procedure model and the techniques of the method served as a vehicle to enable this knowledge transfer. They were particularly helpful since the software solutions and the awareness of this area regarding business opportunities was nearly nonexistent in non-English speaking companies in Europe.
- Action research proved beneficial for mutual learning and achieving results and acquiring knowledge that leads to practical solutions.
- Change management and the building of reciprocity and trust as a further enabler for implementation in business networks (Klein, 1996) have also proven to be critical.

CONCLUSIONS AND OUTLOOK

Business Networking is one of the major trends for companies today with virtual organizing and knowledge management as inherent elements. Implementing Business Networking requires multiple decisions on the strategic, process and IS/IT level which have to be taken into account among multiple partners. Therefore, a method which ensures the coherent organization and management of knowledge in virtual organizations has been presented. This method not only helps in identifying and assessing strategic options as some existing organizational approaches do (e.g., the Venkatraman/Henderson model), but also offers a structured route from (strategic) analysis and conceptualization to implementation. It supports solutions for different levels of cooperation intensity by addressing IS solution potentials at an early stage and, therefore, enables organizations to follow a development path towards more virtual and knowledge-based ways of doing business with closer and more intense relationships.

The method has also been described as a knowledge management tool itself since critical configuration and implementation know-how is included—learning from past experiences, lessons learned and best practices. The refinement of the method is performed in close collaboration with the partner companies during the development phase. It is open for further elaboration in specific case studies or company-specific techniques. However, the concept is not limited to the implementation of transactional software solutions. A further implication of the research is that knowledge management in business networks may be addressed after the operative transaction-oriented systems have been improved.

Several foundations were used for method development in order to meet the challenges in establishing a general method for Business Networking which has the flexibility to include all strategic patterns of Business Networking (e.g., EC, SCM, RM). Based on the principles of action research and method engineering, a top-down approach and a bottom-up approach were combined. The former was mainly derived from business and method engineering and the latter from projects pursued with companies. One of the projects, eProcurement at Deutsche Telekom, was presented in this paper. Currently, the project proceeds further towards implementation and the evaluation of extending the eProcurement solution towards an eService offered on the market. This option also includes the definition of a market concept, considerations of critical mass, network externalities and the like. In parallel, other projects are pursued which concentrate on a procedure model for SCM (Klueber et al., 2000).

A future development area might be the application and extension towards learning and more knowledge-oriented cooperations in order to build new competencies or to access specific know-how and other immaterial resources such as patents (Doz & Hamel, 1998). For example, these business relations are common in the pharmaceutical industry where companies work together with many research institutions. In these areas, the organizational form may be closer to the ideal of a virtual organization.

ENDNOTES

[1] Network governance typically involves higher coordination costs than (traditional) hierarchical governance (cf. Wigand, Picot, & Reichwald, 1997)

2 CXML stands for Commerce Extended Markup Language, SCOR for the Supply Chain Operations Reference-model (www.supply-chain.org) and CPFR for Collaboration, Planning, Forecasting and Replenishment.

3 The objective is not to provide a full account of the activities but to focus on the major findings of our research. For more details on the method and its elements see Klueber and Alt (1999) or Klueber et al. (2000).

4 MRO stands for Maintenance, Repair and Operations goods (Dobler & Burt, 1996).

5 C-goods are goods and services with a low procurement value. The C stems from the classification according to a typical ABC-analysis.

REFERENCES

Alt, R., & Fleisch, E. (1999, June 7 - 9). *Key Success Factors in Designing and Implementing Business Networking Systems.* In Proceedings 12th International Electronic Commerce Conference, Bled, Slovenia.

Alt, R., Reichmayr, C., Österle, H., & Zurmühlen, R. (1999). Business Networking in the Swatch Group. *EM-Electronic Markets, 3(9),* .

Baskerville, R., & Wood-Harper, A. T. (1998). Diversity in Information Systems Action Research Methods. *European Journal of Information Systems* (7), 90-107.

Checkland, P., & Holwell, S. (1998). Action Research: Its Nature and Validity. *Systemic Practice and Action Research, 11* (1), 9-21.

Chisholm, R. F. (1998). *Developing Network Organizations: Learning from Practice and Theory.* Reading, Mass.: Addison-Wesley.

Davenport, T. H., De Long, D. W., & Beers, M. C. (1998). Successful Knowledge Management Projects. *Sloan Management Review* (Winter), 43-57.

DeSanctis, G., & Monge, P. (1998). Communication Processes for Virtual Organizations. *Journal of Computer-Mediated Communications, 3* (4).

Dobler, D. and D. Burt (1996). *Purchasing and Supply Management - Text and Cases.* New York, McGraw-Hill.

Dolmetsch, R. (1999). *Desktop Purchasing - IP-Netzwerkapplikationen in der Beschaffung von indirekt/MRO-Produkten.* Ph.D., University of St. Gallen, St. Gallen.

Doz, Y. L., & Hamel, G. (1998). *Alliance Advantage: The Art of Creating Value through Partnering.* Boston, Mass.: Harvard Business School Press.

Deutsche Telekom. (1999). *Company portrait.* Available: http://www.dtag.de/english/company/profile/index.htm [1999, 25.5.1999].

Faucheux, C. (1997). How Virtual Organizing is Transforming Management Science. *Communications of the ACM, 40* (9), 50-55.

Gouillart, F. J., & Kelly, J. N. (1995). *Transforming the Organization.* New York: McGraw-Hill.

Gutzwiller, T. A. (1994). *Das CC RIM-Referenzmodell für den Entwurf von betrieblichen, transaktionsorientierten Informationssystemen.* Heidelberg: Physica-Verlag.

Hagel, J., & Singer, M. (1998). *Net Worth : Shaping Markets When Customers Make the Rules.* Boston: Harvard Business School Press.

Hillig, A. (1997). *Die Kooperation als Lernarena in Prozessen fundamentalen Wandels - Ein Ansatz zum Management von Kooperationskompenz.* Bern: Haupt.

IMG. (1999). *Methods.* Available: http://www.img.com/jscript/E/S_310.htm Mai 25th].

Killen&Associates. (1997). *Operating Resources Management: How Enterprises can Make Money by Reducing ORM Costs* (White Paper). Palo Alto: Killen & Associates.

Klein, S. (1996). The Configuration of Inter-Organizational Relationships. *European Journal of Information Systems.*

Klueber, R. (1998, April 27-28). *A Framework for Virtual Organizing.* Paper presented at the Workshop on Organizational Virtualness, Bern.

Klueber, R., & Alt, R. (1999). *PROMET®iBN Method - Development of a method for inter-Business Networking* (Working Paper 05 (Version 0.5)). St. Gallen: Institute for Information Management, University of St. Gallen.

Klueber, R. et al. (2000). Towards a Method for Business Networking. In Österle et al. (2000) *Business Networking: Shaping Enterprise Relationships on the Internet.* Berlin: Springer, 257-276.

Kuglin, F. (1998). *The Customer-Centered Supply Chain Management - A Link-by-Link Guide.* New York: AMACOM.

Ludwig, H. (1997). *Koordination objektzentrierter Kooperationen - Metamodell und*

Konzept eines Basisdienstes fuer verteilte Arbeitsgruppen. Ph.D., University of Bamberg, Bamberg.

Malone, T. W., & Crowston, K. (1994). The Interdisciplinary Study of Coordination. *ACM Computing Surveys, 26* (1), 87-119.

Malone, T. W., & Rockart, J. F. (1991). Computers, Networks, and the Corporation. *Scientific American, 91* (9), 92-99.

Mansell, G. (1991). Action Research in Information Systems Development. *Journal of Information Systems* (1), 29-40.

Marakas, C., & Kelly, W. (1999). Building the Perfect Corporation: From Vertical Integration to Virtual Integration. *VoNet Newsletter, 3*(1).

Moss-Kanter, R. (1994). Collaborative Advantage: The Art of Alliances. *Harvard Business Review* (July-August), 96-108.

Nonaka, I., & Takeuchi, H. (1995). *The Knowledge Creating Company - How Japanese Companies Foster Creativity and Innovation for Competitive Advantage.* Oxford.

Österle, H. (1995). *Business in the Information Age: Heading for New Processes.* Berlin: Springer.

Österle, H., Fleisch, E., & Alt, R. (2000). *Business Networking: Shaping Enterprise Relationships on the Internet.* Berlin: Springer.

Porter, M. E., & Millar, V. E. (1985). How Information Gives You Competitive Advantage. *Harvard Business Review*(4), 149-160.

Probst, G., & Raub, S. (1995). Action Research - Ein Konzept angewandter Managementforschung. *Die Unternehmung*(1), 3-19.

Probst, G., Raub, S., & Romhardt, K. (1997). *Wissen managen.* Wiesbaden: Gabler.

Reinhardt, A. (1998, June 22). Extranets: Log on, Link up, Save big - Companies Are Using Net Tech to Forge New Partnerships And Pile Up Eye-popping Savings. *Business Week.*

Rockart, J. F. (1998). Towards Survivability of Communication-Intensive New Organizational Forms. *Journal of Management Studies, 35*(4), 417-420.

Skyrme, D. J. (1998, April 27-28). *The Realities of Virtuality.* In. P. Sieber & J. Griese (eds.), Organizational Virtualness (pp. 25-34), Bern: Simowa.

Stein, J. (1997). On Building and Leveraging Competences Across Organizational Borders: A Socio-cognitive Framework. In A. Heene & R. Sanchez (Eds.), *Competence-based Strategic Management* (pp. 267-284). Chichester: John Wiley & Sons.

Venkatraman, N., & Henderson, J. C. (1998). Real Strategies for Virtual Organizing. *Sloan Management Review, Fall,* 33-48.

Wang, H. Q. (1997). A Conceptual Model for Virtual Markets. *Information and Management, 32,* 147-161.

Wigand, R., Picot, A., & Reichwald, R. (1997). *Information, Organization and Management.* Chichester: John Wiley & Sons.

Wiig, K. M. (1999). Introducing Knowledge Management into the Enterprise. In J. Liebowitz (Ed.), *Knowledge Management Handbook* (pp. 1-41). Boca Raton: CRC Press.

Chapter IV

Interorganizational Knowledge Management: Some Perspectives for Knowledge Oriented Strategic Management in Virtual Organizations

Thorsten Blecker and Robert Neumann
University of Klagenfurt, Austria

New organizational approaches like virtual organizations have the potential to provide the flexibility and to reduce the complexity and risk of management necessary to survive in the actual economic environment. A crucial factor for gaining and sustaining competitive advantages in the current economic environment is knowledge. The management of knowledge has been extensively discussed during the past few years. However, there is still a considerable lack of research that addresses innovative ways of managing the transfer of knowledge, best-practices and competence between organizations. In order to partially overcome these conceptual deficiencies we introduce the concept of an interorganizational knowledge management and discuss its implications on knowledge-oriented strategic management in virtual organizations.

INTRODUCTION

Today's management is confronted with ever-increasing dynamics and complexity of the economic field (Ungson and Trudel 1999, pp. 60). This turbulent environment forces enterprises to generate new ideas and to transfer them into processes, structures and products at an increasing pace without having all necessary core competencies. This development leads to a significant rise in business risk. Modern cooperational and organizational forms like virtual organizations enable enterprises to lower complexity and risk as well as to increase flexibility and diversity of available resources simultaneously (Blecker 1999, pp. 1).

Knowledge and its interorganizational management become crucial factors for gaining and sustaining competitive advantages (Preiss, Goldman, & Nagel 1996, pp. 268). Therefore, interactions with other organizations for exchanging and acquiring knowledge become one of the focal points of management. Cooperations are often more powerful and successful, than traditional large enterprises. Empirical evidence to the increased importance of cooperations is provided from the International Motor Vehicle Program (IMVP) of the MIT from the automotive industry (e.g. Womack, Jones, and Roos 1990) as well as certain cases in the electronic field (e.g. De Meyer 1998). However, this discussion lacks a common terminology since different definitions are used to describe the same or similar aspects of modern organizations and cooperations (Blecker 1999, pp. 11; Kaluza/Blecker 1999a, pp. 267). Additionally, there are only gradual differences between these definitions, since almost all of them emphasize the cooperation of economical and/or legally independent companies for commonly achieving competitive advantages by concentrating on core competencies. In this chapter we focus on the concept of the virtual Organizations, which are currently of particular interest to Strategic Management and therefore intensively discussed in literature.

One of the major objectives of this paper consists of providing the theoretical background for explaining the processes taking place within virtual organizations with respect to knowledge. Although this is a rather complex topic, we do not want to reduce our discussion to some pragmatic approaches for the sake of simplicity of manageability. Rather, this chapter tries to thoroughly elaborate the concept of inter-organizational knowledge management by presenting its key contents. In the course of our investigation, we will examine how companies can obtain knowledge-based competitive advantages by participating in virtual organizations. Present research in this field concentrates on a knowledge-oriented management addressing questions regarding elements, characteristics, functions, and possible applications of organizational knowledge.

BACKGROUND

The Concept of Virtual Organizations

The economic literature is characterized by a variety of different meanings of virtual Organizations (Blecker 1999, pp. 23). Most of them follow the common approach of defining the term virtuality analogous to virtual memory management of modern computer systems (Mowshowitz 1997, p. 34). Therefore, virtuality denotes an 'as-if-reality' (Davidow and Malone 1992). This means, that an object has an effect and shows behavior without physically existing in reality (Martin 1996, p. 15).

However, the literature on virtual organization is characterized by heterogeneous definitions and concepts. For instance, Davidow and Malone (1992) define virtuality as the key factor to successful management in the 21st century, but fail to develop a theoretically consistent concept. A concretizing of the construct or even a definition of the virtual organization, which goes beyond general descriptions, is completely missing. Rather, the authors only recite well-known management concepts like just-in-time, lean production, and total quality management as features and/or approaches to the implementation of virtual organizations. Additionally, it is still not obvious whether a virtual organization represents a private firm or a cooperative, enterprise-spreading concept. Byrne, Brandt, & Port (1993, p. 36) define virtual organizations as "a temporary network of companies that come together quickly to exploit fast-changing opportunities. In a virtual corporation, companies can share costs, skills, and access to global markets, with each partner contributing what it is best at." This definition is extended by the authors later to: "a temporary network of independent companies - suppliers, customers, even erstwhile rivals - linked by information technology to share costs, skills, and another's markets." The essence of this definition is that it views virtual organizations as a temporary network of enterprises (e.g. New, Mitropoulos 1995). The companies involved make common use of their resources, share resulting costs, and try to generate common competitive advantages. Based on the large pool of individual core competencies present in a virtual organization it becomes a "best of everything" enterprise.

Despite the large number of publications, neither a common understanding nor consistent concepts of virtual organizations exist. Rather, a literature analysis reveals a substantial uncertainty in dealing with virtual organizations. This is mainly based on the missing of traditional organizational characteristics like exactly defined property rights and organizational boundaries. In order to make the concept of virtual organization more operational Blecker (1999, p. 30) creates a synopsis of the definitions and descriptions being available in the international literature. This synopsis yields a subscription of virtual organizations based on the following characteristics:

- intended temporary cooperation of legally and economically independent companies, which participants concentrate on their core competencies as well as the temporally limited and order-related bundling of these core competencies,
- reciprocal supplement of the actors during the production process,
- mutual agreement on targets,
- high reciprocal trust,
- high value of customer orientation,
- no centralized and/or formalized organizational structure,
- real structures of the virtual organization and its participants are only limited observable by the market partners,
- intensive application of modern information and communication technologies, and
- individualized products.

Additionally, Blecker (1999, pp. 31) emphasizes that virtual organizations cannot be examined in an isolated way but need to be considered as a temporary, project-specific form of a network of enterprises. In virtual organizations the temporary and spatial deployment is achieved by building an enterprise-spreading network based on modern information and communication technologies. Without a network, the search for partners, negotiations regarding the entry of potential partners, the structure of trust as the major instrument of coordination and control in order to create a virtual organization would last too long. Furthermore, the outcome of these processes would be highly uncertain.

However, a virtual organization is only an appropriate organizational concept if it can be created quickly and without complications. Therefore, potential participants need to dispose of a variety of different relationships to other companies prior to joining the virtual organization. These relationships are then bundled. Following the definition of

Figure 1: The Concept of the Enterprise without Boundaries
Source: Blecker (1999, p. 34)

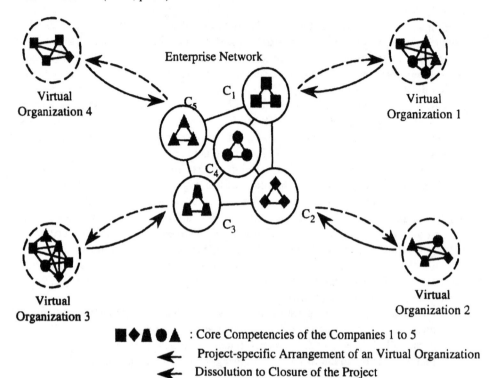

■◆▲●▲ : Core Competencies of the Companies 1 to 5

← Project-specific Arrangement of an Virtual Organization

← Dissolution to Closure of the Project

Sydow (1992, p. 79), Blecker (1999) considers this bundle of complex-reciprocal and rather cooperative than competitive relations as a network of enterprises (Thorelli, 1986; Jarillo, 1988 & 1993; Miwa, 1993). A combination of virtual organizations and network of enterprises leads to a concept we would like to call "enterprise without boundaries". As shown in Figure 1 the enterprise without boundaries is defined as "...a cooperation of legal and economically independent enterprises, which try to achieve competitive advantages together. The cooperative and competitive relations between the enterprises involved form a network, which participants concentrate on their core competencies. On this basis the individual core competencies are temporally linked in market- and project-oriented virtual organizations with the help of modern information and communication technologies" (Blecker, 1999, p. 33).

The Resource-Based View of Strategic Management and the Role of Knowledge

Both the depicted concept of the enterprise without boundaries and our understanding of virtual organizations emphasize the special importance of knowledge and its interorganizational transfer for gaining and sustaining competitive advantages. This importance can be explained by applying the Resource-Based View of Strategic Management (Blecker 1999, pp. 191; Kaluza and Blecker 1999b, pp. 24).

From a resource-based view competitive advantages are based primarily on a different quantity and nature of resources companies are equipped with. Additionally, according to the Resource-Based View companies use their available resources differently from case to case. Due to large deficiencies of factor markets a uniqueness of the enterprises results from this asymmetrical resource allocation. Companies may use their individual resources to generate a variety of different processes and products and, hence, achieve competitive advantages (e.g., Wernerfelt and Montgomery 1998, pp. 246; Montgomery 1992, p. 6, Peteraf 1993, pp. 180, Ring 1996, p. 12, Collis 1996, pp. 154).

We define resources as the companies' specific material and immaterial goods, systems, and processes. These resources are usually divided into the following four categories: physical or tangible resources, intangible resources, financial resources, and organizational resources (e.g., Barney 1991, pp. 101; Nanda 1996, pp. 103). The availability of resources does not necessarily lead to a competitive advantage of the respected company. Therefore, the Resource-Based View examines the basic conditions under which resources generate supranormal rates of return: small or no wearability, transferability of resources needs to be limited, limited imitability, reduced substitution (e.g. Barney 1991, pp. 196, Grant 1991a, pp. 123; Grant 1991b, pp. 111). These four requirements of the Resource-Based View are met by knowledge, since knowledge is weaved in the fabric of the organization. Therefore, knowledge may be regarded as special resource, which enables a company to achieve competitive advantages and supranormal rates of return. This conceptual context is shown by Figure 2.

Recent research in this area focuses on developing sustaining and protecting intangible resources such as knowledge, abilities, and core competencies. Especially Badaracco (1991, pp. 1) considers the potentials for future strategic success in the development, improvement, the protection and the renewal of the companies' specific know-how base. A "knowledge-driven competition" becomes the challenge of the future. This requires strategic management to increasingly focus on factors like personnel and organization, which have been neglected so far.

Following the Resource-Based View, the major function of a company participating in a virtual organization consists of adjusting the current resources configuration with the competitive strategies and of developing these resources according to strategic considerations. Since an individual enterprise has only a limited number of core competencies, it

Figure 2 : A Resource-Based View of Knowledge
Source: Rühli (1994), p. 43; Hillig (1997), p. 94

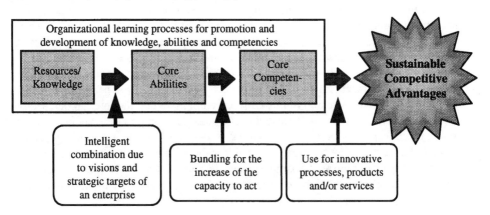

is frequently dependent on the technical, individual and organizational knowledge of its partners.

It is therefore appropriate to temporarily use further knowledge and further core competencies in cooperations like virtual Organizations or even acquire them by means of mutual learning processes (Blecker 1999, pp. 226). Under certain circumstances, the level of process integration among companies involved becomes very strong, leading to a network of processes and/or knowledge. This network executes processes together and/ or generates, gathers and uses knowledge in common. Interorganizational transfer processes and management concepts for explicit and tacit knowledge are necessary and relevant for the success of a virtual organization and its participants.

BASICS OF "KNOWLEDGE-MANAGEMENT"—A NEW PARADIGM OF STRATEGIC MANAGEMENT...?

In economical research and business practice new concepts for competing successfully in today's economic environment have emerged during the past few years. On the one hand, there was a development of heterarchic and adhocratic organizational concepts leading to increased flexibility and a higher degree of intra- and interorganizational decentralization. On the other hand, managerial concepts such as lean management and business process reengineering were introduced, in order to increase organizational efficiency. However, due to the intensive efforts towards downsizing they often lead to a reduction of redundancy and, thus, a loss at Organizational Slack (Cyert/March 1963, pp. 36). Additionally, a large part of company-specific knowledge was uncritically diminished. Thus, not only the waste of resources was reduced, but also the companies' flexibility and efficiency was significantly lowered. Especially, the concept of organizational learning emphasizes the notion that the institutionalizing of learning by means of collective reflection and change processes becomes a critical success factor (e.g. Rheinhardt 1994). For instance, in a virtual organization and also in the Enterprise without Boundaries knowledge can be acquired and used in common which leads to the development of a new Cooperative Slack (Blecker, 1999, pp. 136). In analogy to the Organizational Slack we define Cooperative Slack as all resources within a virtual organization that are at the disposal of every partner but not utilized in the respective period. Based on this new form of slack companies can reduce their Organizational Slack by simultaneously increasing the flexibility. A major obstacle for the realization of this effect is the missing of a theoretically founded and practically usable concept of a "learning enterprise". Thus, the respective reorientation of management did not take place. Current research focuses on two major points of interest: the starting point and the result of learning processes.

In the current discourse regarding the management of knowledge two dichotomic perspectives have emerged: an internal perspective and an external perspective. During the last few years the research in this field has emphasized on the internal perspective. According to this perspective, knowledge is discussed as important strategic resource, core competence or a source for innovations. It views knowledge as a value-generating factor and a starting point for organizational learning processes. In contrast, the external perspective discusses the relationship between the enterprises and the economic environment or the stakeholder, e.g,. knowledge-stakeholder and partners. This analysis concen-

Figure 3: Dichotomy of the Internal and External Perspective of Knowledge
Source: Neumann (1999a p. 34)

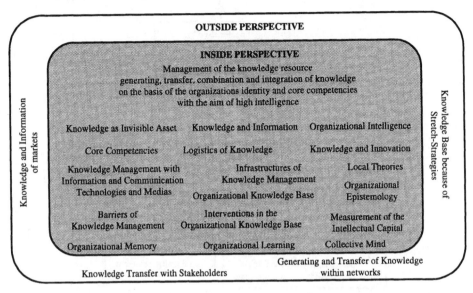

trates on interorganizational knowledge-transfer and knowledge-use processes. Figure 3 shows selected elements of the internal and external perspective.

However, a clear distinction between these two perspectives is still missing in literature. Additionally, based on this different framework a heterogeneous understanding of the term "knowledge" has evolved (Neumann 1999a, p. 53). The resulting uncertainty in using the term knowledge is magnified by the interdisciplinary character of this research field leading to a large variety of attribute-oriented definitions (Neumann 1999a, pp. 62). Therefore, it is appropriate to aggregate the different views of the term knowledge represented in literature. For this purpose three distinct criteria need to be differentiated: the nature of knowledge, the availability of knowledge and the usability of knowledge (Neumann, 1999a, p. 66). Each criteria shows two dichotomic features that need to be distinguished. For instance, knowledge can be of a declarative or procedural nature. In terms of availability, the two possible distinctions are explicit and tacit knowledge. Finally, regarding the usability of knowledge, the two possible perspectives are knowledge as a cognitive item and the conversion of knowledge. Figure 4 shows the resulting typology of knowledge.

In a discussion of knowledge management in virtual organizations or the enterprise without boundaries, all the three dimensions of the typology presented above are addressed. For the discussion of an interorganizational knowledge management, in a first step the tacit or explicit individual and organizational knowledge must be analyzed. In a second step, the required object and process-oriented knowledge needs to be transferred between the enterprises involved. This knowledge-transfer distinguishes intraorganizational knowledge management from interorganizational knowledge management. The major duty of interorganizational knowledge management consists of initiating and managing

Figure 4: The Dimensions of Knowledge
Source: Neumann (1999a), p. 78

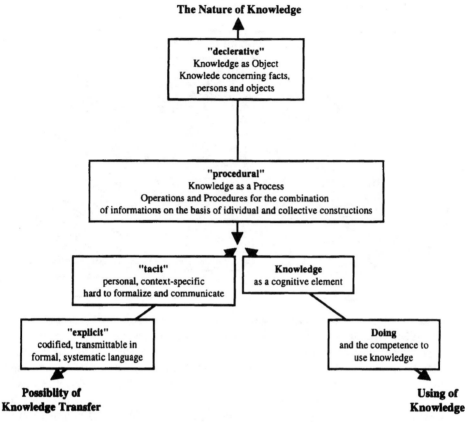

processes of knowledge generation, interorganizational knowledge flow, and a common usage of knowledge. For this purpose, conditions facilitating interorganizational knowledge management need to be created, e.g., procedures for managing conflicts within the cooperation, trust and a common language.

These aspects of interorganizational knowledge management are crucial since cooperative generation and usage of knowledge is very important for the strategic success of a virtual organization. However, only the explicit knowledge can be transferred and used in virtual organizations. Since the exchange of tacit knowledge already encounters substantial barriers within a single organization its interchange within a network is widely considered as being impossible. Additionally, missing common targets, significant differences in corporate culture, competition among partners, missing rules of cooperation, inadequate coordination, and opportunistic behavior render the implementation of virtual organizations more difficult and restrict the interorganizational usage of knowledge.

In the short-term form of virtual organizations, only the outcome of production processes rather than knowledge is shared. However, in the long-term form, a common usage of knowledge is an integral part of a virtual organization. Therefore, the participants need to develop an "Interorganizational Knowledge Management" that addresses the functions discussed. With an Interorganizational Knowledge Management companies can gain and sustain competitive advantages by participating in virtual organizations. Interorganizational knowledge management becomes a new paradigm of strategic management.

INTERORGANIZATIONAL KNOWLEDGE MANAGEMENT

The Concept of Interorganizational Knowledge Management

In practice, there are many examples for different approaches of knowledge management already in place, e.g. 3M, Sony, Skandia ASF, Matsushita, Ford, Arthur Anderson, Mercedes, and BMW. However, these approaches are often only technical solutions for storage and exchange of individual knowledge by means of information and communication technologies (e.g. Wilson snf Snyder, 1999; Hansen, Nohria and Tierney, 1999). Additionally, even in case of integrative approaches, e.g. by the Geneva Knowledge Group (Probst, Buechel and Raub, 1998), significant malfunctions in generating knowledge may occur. These malfunctions mainly derive from counterproductive contextual conditions of the organization like stare department boundaries, unclear competencies, problems of coordination, missing incentives, and a culture of distrust (Figure 5).

Particularly, approaches of knowledge management based on the "ecology of knowledge" (Kirsch 1996, pp. 97), stress the notion of creating conditions that favor the generation of knowledge. Also the model of "organizational knowledge order" (Neumann

Figure 5: Obstacles to Successful Use of Knowledge in Virtual Organizations
Source: Neumann (1999a, p. 28)

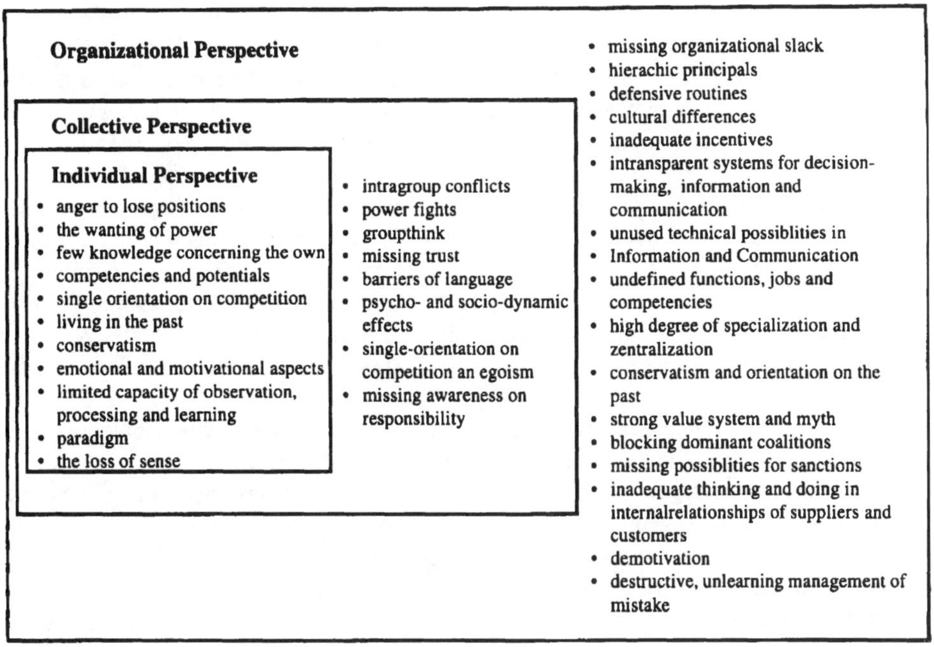

Organizational Perspective

Collective Perspective

Individual Perspective
- anger to lose positions
- the wanting of power
- few knowledge concerning the own
- competencies and potentials
- single orientation on competition
- living in the past
- conservatism
- emotional and motivational aspects
- limited capacity of observation, processing and learning
- paradigm
- the loss of sense

- intragroup conflicts
- power fights
- groupthink
- missing trust
- barriers of language
- psycho- and socio-dynamic effects
- single-orientation on competition an egoism
- missing awareness on responsibility

- missing organizational slack
- hierachic principals
- defensive routines
- cultural differences
- inadequate incentives
- intransparent systems for decision-making, information and communication
- unused technical possiblities in Information and Communication
- undefined functions, jobs and competencies
- high degree of specialization and zentralization
- conservatism and orientation on the past
- strong value system and myth
- blocking dominant coalitions
- missing possiblities for sanctions
- inadequate thinking and doing in internalrelationships of suppliers and customers
- demotivation
- destructive, unlearning management of mistake

1999a, p. 156) emphasize this notion. This model contributes to the development of a knowledge-based organizational theory and describes "knowledge-oriented management" in detail. Based on system-theoretical as well as structuration-theoretical approaches (Giddens 1984) it shows the way of acquiring, generating, integrating and using knowledge in organizations by self-referential and recursive operation and reproduction processes. Simultaneously, these processes are an expression of an "Organizational Epistemology" (Krogh and Roos, 1995; Krogh, Roos and Slocum, 1994). The epistemology describes how organizations gather perceptions and knowledge regarding their identity and their environment. Additionally, existing paradigms, local theories, and established knowledge represent the essential constructive components.

The questions of perception, interpretation and internal processing of knowledge can be primarily attributed to the emergence of differences in the relationship between the system and its environment. For this reason, the theory of self-referential systems provides valuable aspects for the discussion of knowledge in virtual organizations. According to the theory of self-referential systems, organizations are simultaneously open and closed in their relations to the environment. They are open regarding an energetic exchange with the environment and the accommodation of data. However, they are closed regarding the internal allocation and transformation of information into knowledge. Events taking place in the environment may trigger organizational learning processes. However, this mainly depends on self-imposed criteria and rules. Therefore, knowledge derives from the integration of information into a context of relevance. The relevant criteria can be inferred from the experiences that were important for the survival and the reproduction of the organization in the past. An organization's reaction to external knowledge is determined by its institutionalized control system, business processes and standardized procedures, which consist of individual knowledge.

The theory of self-referential systems suffers from a lack of acceptance in the field of economic research. This is mainly due to its biological roots, a high degree of abstraction, and a sociologically dominated language. Nevertheless, this theory supplies valuable epistemological explanations for many economic problems. For instance, questions like how organizations obtain knowledge, what effects it has within the organization, and why a high probability of refusing new knowledge exists are addressed by the theory of self-referential systems.

The phenomenon of self-referential systems can be verified by many real situations of organizations. For instance, enterprises often turn into problems threatening their existence because they fail to notice warning signals from the environment or misinterpret them in a way, so that they fit into the self-interpretation of the organization. Critical signals are frequently displaced consciously or unconsciously, because they do not comply to any patterns of reference of the system. This destructive effect of an operational closeness is also discussed by the crisis research (Hedberg, 1981), the research of organizational pathologies (e.g,. Sorg, 1982), and in the course of phenomenological descriptions of defensive learning routines (Argyris, 1993, pp. 179).

However, the organizational order of knowledge is determined not only by the epistemology of the organization, but also by available resources and structures of an enterprise. These elements are constantly reproduced by a process of interpretation, combination, sense giving and action of the levels of recursion individual, collective and organization. Regarding their actions, all participants of a virtual organization refer to structures in the sense of rules and resources. Additionally, virtual organizations simultaneously reproduce these structures by their behavior. Thus, the duality or recursiveness of structures is emphasized. According to the structuration-theoretical approach of Giddens (1984) structures of knowledge and organizations are both condition and consequence of interactions (Ortmann, Sydow and Windeler 1997, pp. 315). Organizations select, combine, and arrange their available internal knowledge as well as the potential usable external knowledge according to self-imposed criteria. These criteria derive from the specific identity of the organization or the intersubjectively developed paradigm of "dominant coalitions". External knowledge can only be integrated into the system, if it is compatible to existing knowledge and, hence, does not lead to irritations of the members of a virtual organization.

Knowledge produces the definitions of reality and the meaning of reality valid for the system. Therefore, it leads to a preservation and acknowledgment of order. The emergence of knowledge can be viewed as a process of transforming events observed into knowledge within the system (Willke, 1996, p. 265). Thus, knowledge is developed by a context-based linking of information that is considered as relevant by the system. However, what is assessed as relevant or not depends on the identity of the respective system, that is, of experiences, historical lines of development and cognitive structures. In strategic management, a corresponding approach is the path dependency of individual resources in the Resource-Based View. In the understanding of a "resources trajectory" mainly those resources, abilities, and routines are consolidated to core competencies, which are based on the historically grown knowledge of an enterprise. Furthermore, the direction of these processes depends on the historical background and small events in the environment. Thus, the imitation of "organizational capabilities" by competitors or partners becomes extremely difficult within a virtual organization. (Figure 6)

The organizational knowledge order and epistemology of an organization is protected against imitations and, therefore, provides a permanent competitive advantage. This protection is mainly based on a non-imitable identity of the organization as well as individual processes of producing and reproducing knowledge. Knowledge order and epistemology simultaneously represent firm-specific competencies and, hence, belong to the organizational capabilities.

If we apply these principles to long-term oriented relations within a network, the question arises, if a cooperative enterprise-spreading knowledge order can contribute to an increase of the competitiveness of the companies involved. For the materialization of this effect, the companies in a virtual organization require clear, defined arrangements regarding a cooperative generation and usage of knowledge. Additionally, arrangements regarding the integration of the common knowledge into the respective company goals, strategies, and processes need to be made. Therefore, the conscious production of an interorganizational knowledge order is a special management function. Companies involved have to create border-crossing processes for knowledge management and organizational learning.

Thus, knowledge management in virtual Organizations means designing, controlling and developing a purpose-oriented knowledge order together with the partners. According to the systems-oriented management approach (e.g., Gomez and Carpenter, 1992) strategic, normative, operational, and transformative management functions can be distinguished (Bleicher, 1991). Since knowledge management in long-term virtual

Figure 6: Structure of the Knowledge Base of Companies
Source: Neumann (1999a, p. 74)

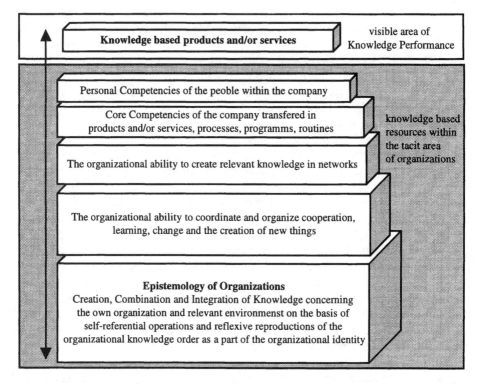

Organizations concerns regular and parallel fulfilled management functions, an iterative process evolves. This process consists of five phases: intention, identification, modification, organization, and internal action. As illustrated in Figure 7, these phases are linked by feedback processes forming a closed loop of an "Interorganizational Knowledge Management".

Phases of an Interorganizational Knowledge Management

Intention

The intention phase consists of determining knowledge targets and measuring criteria. For this purposes in a first step the companies involved need to develop common visions, objectives and strategies of knowledge-oriented management and to communicate them among partners.

For accomplishing this common set of guidelines, two major questions need to be addressed:

- Which importance does knowledge have for the economic success of our company?
- What strategic targets are primarily supported by a more efficient use of knowledge?

In a second step, in addition to already existing targets of the respective company

Figure 7: Process of Interorganizational Knowledge Management in Long-Term Virtual Organizations

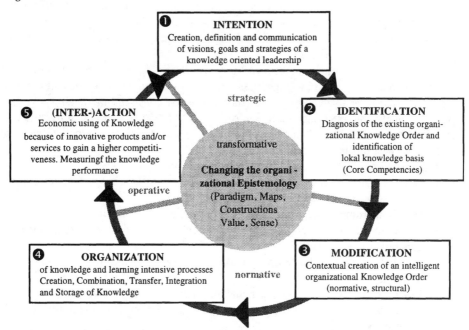

knowledge-oriented objectives have to be established. This notion is also supported by Hamel and Prahalad (1994), who consider a so-called "strategic architecture" as an important prerequisite for the generation of competencies. This architecture determines the way a company will compete successfully on the bases of core competencies in the future. The importance of knowledge and the intention phase is also emphasized by Nonaka & Takeuchi (1995, pp. 156), erecting a "conceptual umbrella" over the whole company. This conceptual umbrella contains common ideas regarding the future of the company, which are expressed as universal metaphors, analogies, symbols, and models. Exact guidelines and procedures as well as concrete measuring criteria are derived from these objectives and strategies. For this purpose methods like the "Balanced Scorecard" (Kaplan and Norton, 1996), the "Intangible Assets Monitor" (Sveiby, 1997) or the "Intellectual Capital Navigator" (Stewart, 1997) can be applied. The respective decisions need to be made on an individual base by each company.

Identification

The phase of identification aims at identifying the existing intraorganizational knowledge order as well as core competencies available in the virtual organization. Furthermore, companies try to assess the core competencies necessary for the future. Thus, this phase focuses on the systematic discussion of the unique elements of knowledge of the own business (North 1998, pp. 28). Divergent knowledge bases often cause differences in performance among the companies involved in a virtual organization. Therefore, it is essential to discover what kind of knowledge a company disposes of.

On the one hand, every company needs to know what kind of knowledge is required regarding its economic environment. On the other hand, also the assessment of the internal knowledge is crucial. This knowledge mainly exists in the form of internal routines, competencies, projects, products, and best practices. It is unveiled by a thorough analysis of all value activities, business process, and interorganizational linkages regarding the associated explicit and tacit knowledge. In this way companies get an overview of their core knowledge, the structure of the knowledge-combining process and the behavior of the knowledge agents involved.

Based on this information, the possibility of forming learning partnerships between companies and external knowledge agents in order to combine internal and external knowledge can be analyzed. Further targets of this phase consist of uncovering cognitive patterns, analyzing inter-subjective representation of reality and the illustration of existing context conditions (Neumann 1999a, pp. 18). In order to achieve these targets, the following questions have to be answered:

- How is knowledge currently managed as a resource?
- What are the most important dimensions of the environment regarding the companies core businesses and future strategic approaches?
- Which instruments are applied in order to monitor these dimensions?
- What are the current organizational conditions and how do they determine the generation of knowledge?
- To what extent does the company make use of formal or informal communication channels?
- What kind of theories influence behavior on different organizational levels?
- What obstacles hinder the perception, accommodation, and integration of new knowledge?
- What mechanisms maintain the existing patterns of knowledge and behavior routines?
- Which factors block the transmission of new knowledge?

Comparing currently existing knowledge resources and competencies necessary for gaining long-term competitive advantages in future companies may identify the major managerial challenges for their functional areas.

Modification
In the course of the third phase an intelligent knowledge order is developed. It contains the creation, organization, and modification of contextual systems. Special emphasis is placed on the knowledge ecology (Kirsch, 1996; Nonaka, Takeuchi and Takeuchi, 1995; North, 1998). This is mainly the duty of the top management. The intra and interorganizational prerequisites consist of a supportive environment. This usually contains:

- the generation and usage of Cooperative Slack (Blecker, 1999, pp. 136; Kaluza and Blecker 1999a, pp. 272);
- flexible process-oriented organizations that aim at modularity, multidimensionality, and multi-functionality (Neumann, 1995, pp. 313);
- the promotion of network-based and cross-functional cooperation in task forces and project teams (Blecker, pp. 314);
- control and sanction mechanisms suitable for networks (Wildemann, 1997);
- the promotion of a high interaction density (Blecker, 1999, p. 151);

- a common languaging (Krogh, Roos and Slocum, 1994, pp. 62);
- institutionalizing of knowledge-links (Badaracco, 1996, pp. 133);
- institutionalizing trust-generating activities (Blecker 1999, pp. 26, pp. 328);
- motivational incentives in order to prevent the "not invented here"-syndrome (Baliga and Sjostrom 1997; Blecker 1999, p. 260, pp. 308);
- establishing feedback systems;
- the active participation in continuing education programs and learning circles of a virtual organization (Blecker, pp. 314);
- the construction of internal and external knowledge cluster (Sydow and van Well 1996, p. 212) and
- institutionalizing of competence centers with comparisons and exchange of best practices.

Modifying an existing interorganizational knowledge order or creating a new one within a virtual organization requires a high level of congruence among assumptions, interpretation patterns, standards, rules, conventions and procedures of a social interaction practice and knowledge-oriented behavior. This contains a conscious re-structuration of the organization, which aims at changing rules and resources as well as established structures of signification and legitimization (Neumann 1999a, pp. 9). Still, changing only structures is not sufficient. Additionally, also interpretation patterns and the corporate culture have to be modified (Neumann 1999a, p. 6).

The paradigms determining organizational behavior are — in the sense of a transformative management — adopted in a way that the companies learn to overcome the contradictions "cooperation versus competition" (North 1998, pp. 75), "order versus modification", and "available versus necessary knowledge". The final objective of every company undergoing this process is the creation of context-sensitive organizational consciousness. Given their individual background regarding identity, companies partici-pating in a virtual organization therefore need to create consciousness and knowledge with respect to those forms of interaction, which aim at existing requirements of the market. Especially in virtual organizations, a lack of consciousness regarding the potential of an existing knowledge order leads to uncertainties and blockades in the exchange of knowledge.

The less a company is conscious about its own knowledge the more a diffuse and irrational fear of imitation or loss of knowledge and competencies takes place. For this reason companies especially need to regenerate those conditions that promote the cooperative thinking and acting of all partners within a virtual organization.

Organization
The fourth phase can be attributed to the normative area of knowledge-oriented management of virtual organizations. In this way, it focuses predominantly on interorganizational knowledge-generating and learning-intensive processes. The de-velopment and creation of knowledge (Nonaka, Takeuchi and Takeuchi 1995) is affected in processes of improvement and renewal learning. The interorganizational implementa-tion and institutionalizing of these processes can be achieved by means of common competence and knowledge clusters (Sydow and van Well 1996, p. 212). They derive from autonomous practices of acting participants and lead to an institutionalized enlargement

and combination of knowledge based on exchange relations.

By collective reflecting on existing experiences (lessons learned) within common projects or by dealing with customer orders, knowledge is accumulated, that has to be documented and distributed. After this process of generating and transferring it is to be integrated into the respective knowledge base of the companies involved, so that it becomes effective (Walsh and Ungson, 1991). Initially, the common interpretation patterns of the communication processes are determined in order to allow the companies involved to become acquainted with external views and experiences and to integrate them into their own interpretation patterns. From a structuration-theoretical viewpoint an integration only takes place, if knowledgeable agents (Ortmann, Sydow and Windeler, 1997, pp. 317) are able to reproduce their behavior modified by the newly acquired knowledge. Additionally, in the course of interaction they need to refer change structures, rules, and resources.

Only if the last prerequisite is fulfilled knowledge becomes relevant for day-to-day behavior as an "accurate or valid awareness" (Giddens 1984, p. 90). Through this behavior, participants in a virtual organization generate new characteristics and features regarding their pool of potential actions. Thus, an imitation and integration of this behavior by other participants is implied. In this way, newly acquired knowledge circulates within the virtual organization as an unintended consequence of behavior and gets ever and ever reproduced. A new knowledge order evolves (Neumann, 1999a, p. 38).

(Inter-)Action

Generation, transfer, and integration of knowledge can only materialize as competitive advantages if knowledge is actively used for innovative products and services. Therefore, the fifth phase aims at a systematic intra and interorganizational utilization of knowledge. In the past, competitive advantages mainly derived from a more efficient combination of traditional factors. In the future, knowledge as a resource will become a major critical success factor. In this way, former highly industrialized economies become knowledge-driven (Drucker, 1994; 1998; Ungson and Trudel, 1999, p. 65).

Conventional market structures change due to significantly shortened half-lives of knowledge, its quantitative and qualitative explosion, as well as the intensification and globalization of competition regarding knowledge resources (Romhardt, 1998). In particular, the innovative development of customer-focused solutions based on the large pool of core competencies at the disposal of a virtual organization represents an attractive opportunity to gain and sustain long-term competitive advantages even in a complex and highly dynamic economic environment (Blecker 1999a; Kaluza, Blecker and Bischof 1998; Kaluza and Blecker 1999a; 1999b).

IMPLICATIONS FOR STRATEGIC MANAGEMENT IN VIRTUAL ORGANIZATIONS

The proverb "who operates alone adds knowledge, who cooperates multiplies knowledge" emphasizes the high importance of a systematic strategic management of the resource knowledge in cooperations. Often this becomes the major principle for the construction of virtual organizations in order to generate and effectively use knowledge within an interorganizational cooperation. Even although the tacit organizational and individual knowledge forms the base for non-imitable and non-transferable core competencies, a successful exchange of knowledge is impossible in short-term virtual organizations. It even implies, that due to the short-termness the necessary basic conditions for knowledge exchange are missing, e.g. common interest and knowledge targets as well as a high interorganizational trust. Therefore, the main function of a knowledge-oriented strategic management is the reduction of institutionalized cooperation conflicts, which appear in the thinking and acting of the respective participants.

In long-term virtual organizations, knowledge represents the decisive basis for the intelligent and competent performance of the partners. Thereby, only a conscious and organized reflection of "lessons learned" from common activities supports a flow back of the acquainted knowledge into the knowledge base of the companies involved. Thus, the functions of a knowledge-oriented strategic management are substantially more extensive than in the short-term form of virtual organizations. First, common knowledge targets and strategies have to be developed and communicated as well as common agreements for a boundary spanning management of knowledge obtained. Simultaneously, the companies have to observe the internal and external available knowledge. Each company and in particular the possible existing focal enterprise must increase and analyze its organizational consciousness in order to become aware of the knowledge that is constitutional for the firm's specific core competencies. Only because of this awareness regarding the own knowledge order and the competencies contained, companies can generate, exchange, and use knowledge interorganizationally in virtual organizations.

In a second step the structures, programs, rules, principles, and processes for an interorganizational order of knowledge have to be compiled and implemented. The respective best practices of the partners are exchanged as explicit knowledge by means of knowledge-links and integrated by communicative interaction-relations. An intelligent form of the strategically aligned and loose "knowledge architecture" is manifested in the organizational structure. Therefore, on a structural level flexible regulation and control systems aiming at learning processes are needed, which support the acquisition, generation, distribution, integration and usage of knowledge in virtual organizations. The help of cross-organizational teams, which take over concrete projects or a common research and development, can achieve this. The knowledge gained in these processes is made available to all companies participating in the virtual organization. However, as these teams mainly consist of specialists, high demands for education and management result. Within the teams a high level of functional trust has to be developed in order to fulfill the expectations efficiently. The ability to permanently manage constantly changing task forces and project teams becomes a central prerequisite to the individual participants in a virtual organization. Additionally, in order to document experiences (lessons learned) during and particularly after working on an interorganizational project regular learning and reflection meetings have to be established. The objective is to share the knowledge contained in the experiences with other project teams. Information and communication technologies like groupware, intranet, knowledge maps, and knowledge databases provide additional support. Consequently, the personnel development has to strengthen the technical and methodical as well as the social and communicative competencies on an individual level. Enterprise-spreading training networks have the function of developing and offering those educational contents, which are needed for an efficient participation in the virtual organization. This common training does not only lead to common knowledge and standards of competence, but also supports cooperative working and the development of a common language. Interorganizational learning is supported also by the exchange of employees (job rotation) on horizontal level between the partners of a virtual organization. Additionally, effective reward and incentive systems for employees can promote competent and knowledge-based acting in an interorganizational network. Finally enterprise-spreading suggestion and improvement processes support the generation of common ideas, which can be transformed into knowledge and transferred into individual competencies.

For the implementation of the outlined approaches to a knowledge-oriented management in virtual Organizations commonly developed and internalized standards and routines are needed. However, each individual company has to create supporting internal conditions in order to realize these standards and routines. For instance, companies may establish new quality and performance standards, e.g. by implementing Total Quality Management concepts (EFQM, Malcolm Baldridge), information and communication systems to support learning processes as well as control principles. Furthermore, companies involved in virtual Organizations can reduce the intraorganizational and interorganizational coordination expenditure by implementing routines and rules, which contain the knowledge from the lessons learned. Thus, the quality of the common performances and knowledge processes is increased.

In summary, a successful participation in a long-term virtual organization requires a common development of an Interorganizational Knowledge Management. In particular top managers are assigned a provocative formative function in this process. Not only must they provide a supporting intraorganizational knowledge order, but also they must represent the respective companies in the emergence of a new interorganizational knowledge order. Knowledge is more and more considered as a critical strategic success factor for long-term virtual Organizations. Thus, effective interorganizational knowledge management becomes crucial for strategic success.

REFERENCES

Argyris, Ch. (1993). Defensive Routinen. In: Fatzer, G. (Ed.): *Organisationsentwicklung für die Zukunft: ein Handbuch* (pp. 179-226), Cologne: Edition Humanist. Psychologie.

Badaracco, J. L. (1991). *The Knowledge Link: How Firms Compete Through Strategic Alliances*, Boston: Harvard Business School Press.

Badaracco, J. L. (1996). Knowledge Links. In: Myers, P.S. (Ed.): *Knowledge Management and Organizational Design* (pp. 133 - 50). Boston: Harvard Business School Press

Baliga, S., Sjostrom, T. (1997). Not Invented Here, Discussion Paper No. 1797, Harvard Institute of Economic Research, Cambridge.

Barney, J. B. (1991). Firm Resources and Sustained Competitive Advantage. Journal of Management, 17(1), pp. 99 - 120.

Blecker, Th. (1999). Unternehmung ohne Grenzen — Konzepte, Strategien und Gestaltungsempfehlungen für das Strategische Management, Wiesbaden: Gabler Verlag.

Bleicher, K. (1991). Das Konzept Integriertes Management, Frankfurt—New York:

Campus Verlag.

Byrne, J. A., Brandt, R., & Port, O. (1993, February 8). The Virtual Corporation. The Company of the Future will be ultimate in Adaptability. *Business Week*, pp. 36 - 40.

Collis, D. J. (1996). Organizational Capability as a Source of Profit. In: Moingeon, B., Edmondson, A. (Eds.): *Organizational Learning and Competitive Advantage* (pp. 139 - 163), London: Sage Publications.

Cyert, R. M., March, J. G. (1963). *A Behavioral Theory of the Firm*, Englewood Cliffs, N.J.: Blackwell Publishers.

Davidow, W. H., Malone, M. S. (1992). *The Virtual Corporation. Structuring and Revitalizing the Corporation for the 21st Century*, New York: Free Press.

De Meyer, A. (1998). Manufacturing Operations in Europe: Where Do We Go Next?, INSEAD Working Paper 98/22/TM, Fontainebleau.

Drucker, P. (1994). *Post Capitalist Society*, New York: Harper Business.

Drucker, P. (1998). Wissen - die Trumpfkarte der entwickelten Länder. Harvard Business manager, (4), pp. 9 - 11.

Giddens, A. (1984). *The Constitution of Society: Outline of a Theory of Structuration*, Cambridge: University of California Press.

Gomez, P., Zimmermann, T. (1992). Unternehmensorganisation. Profile, Dynamik, Methodik, Frankfurt - New York: Campus Verlag.

Grant, R. M. (1991a). The Resource-Based Theory of Competitive Advantage: Implications for Strategy Formulation. California Management Review, 33, pp. 114 - 135.

Grant, R. M. (1991b). *Contemporary Strategy Analysis. Concepts, Techniques, Applications*, Oxford — Cambridge: Blackwell Publishers.

Hamel, G., Prahalad, C.K. (1994). *Competing for the Future*, Boston: Harvard Business School Press.

Hansen, M. T., Nohria, N. & Tierney, T. (1999). What's Your Strategy for Managing Knowledge? In: *Harvard Business Review*, (2), pp. 106 -116.

Hillig, A. (1997). Die Kooperation als Lernarena in Prozessen fundamentalen Wandels. Ein Ansatz zum Management von Kooperationskompetenz, Stuttgart — Wien.

Jarillo, J. C. (1988). On Strategic Networks. *Strategic Management Journal*, 9(1), pp. 31 - 41.

Jarillo, J. C. (1993). *Strategic Networks. Creating the borderless organization*, Oxford: Butterworth-Heinemann.

Kaluza, B., Blecker, Th. (1999a). Dynamische Produktdifferenzierungsstrategie und Produktionsnetzwerke. In: Nagel, K., Erben, R. F., & Piller, F. T. (Ed.): *Produktionswirtschaft 2000 — Perspektiven für die Fabrik der Zukunft* (pp. 261 - 280), Wiesbaden: Gabler Verlag.

Kaluza, B., Blecker, Th. (1999b). Wettbewerbsstrategien — Markt- und ressourcenorientierte Sicht der strategischen Führung. Konzepte — Gestaltungsfelder — Erfolgreiche Umsetzungen, Munich: TCW Transfer-Centrum Verlag.

Kaluza, B., Blecker, Th., & Bischof, Ch. (1999). Implications of Digital Convergence on Strategic Management. In: Dahiya, S. B. (Ed.): *The Current State of Economic Science*, Vol. 4, Rohtak: Spellbound Publications.

Kaplan, R., Norton, D. P. (1996). *The Balanced Scorecard*, Boston: Harvard Business School Press.

Kirsch, W. (1996). Wegweiser zur Konstruktion einer evolutionären Theorie der strategischen Führung. Kapitel eines Theorieprojektes, Munich: Kirsch.

Krogh, G. von, Roos, J. (1995). *Organizational Epistemology*. London: Sage Publications.

Krogh, G. von, Roos, J., & Slocum, K. (1994). An Essay on Corporate Epistemology. *Strategic Management Journal*, 15, pp. 53 - 71.

Martin, J. (1996). *Cybercorp. the new business revolution,* New York et al.: Amacom.

Miwa, Y. (1993). Organizations, Networks, and Network Organizations, Working Paper 93-F-6, University of Tokyo.

Montgomery, C. A. (1992). Resources: The Essence of Corporate Advantage, Harvard Business School Note No. 9-792-064, Boston.

Mowshowitz, A. (1997). Virtual Organization. *Communications of the ACM*, 40(9), pp. 30 - 37.

Nanda, A. (1996). Resources, Capabilities and Competencies. In: Moingeon, B., Edmondson, A. (Eds.): *Organizational Learning and Competitive Advantage* (pp. 93 -120), London: Sage Publications.

Neumann, R. (1995). Risiko Organisation — organisiertes Risiko. Beiträge zur integrativ-systemorientierten Verarbeitung selbsterzeugter Risikopotentiale in und von Organisationen, Frankfurt et al.: Peter Lang Verlag.

Neumann, R. (1999a). Die Organisation als Ordnung des Wissens, Habilitation-Thesis, University of Klagenfurt.

Neumann, R. (1999b). Die Veränderung der organisationalen Wissensordnung. Theoretische Uberlegungen und praktische Erfolgsvoraussetzungen für ein Wissensmanagement und Lernen der Organisation. In: Projektgruppe Wissenschaftliche Beratung (Ed.): Organisationslernen durch Wissensmanagement, Frankfurt: Peter Lang Verlag, pp. 123 - 152.

New, S., Mitropoulos, I. (1995). Strategic networks: morphology, epistemology and praxis. *International Journal of Operations & Production Management*, 15(11), pp. 53 - 61.

Nonaka, I., Takeuchi, H., & Takeuchi, H. (1995). *The Knowledge Creating Company, Oxford,* New York: Oxford University Press.

North, K. (1998). Wissensorientierte Unternehmensführung. Wertschöpfung durch Wissen, Wiesbaden: Gabler Verlag.

Ortmann, G., Sydow, J., & Windeler, A. (1997). Organisation als reflexive Strukturation. In: Ortmann, G., Sydow, J., & Türk, K. (Ed.), *Theorien der Organisation. Die Rückkehr der Gesellschaft* (pp. 315 - 354), Opladen: Westdeutscher Verlag.

Peteraf, M. A. (1993). The Cornerstones of Competitive Advantage: A Resource-Based View. *Strategic Management Journal*, 14, pp. 179 - 191.

Preiss, K., Goldman, S. L., & Nagel, R. N. (1996). *Cooperate to Compete. Building Agile Business Relationships*, New York et al.: Van Nostrand Reinhold.

Probst, G.J.B., Buechel, B., & Raub, S. (1998). Knowledge as a Strategic Resource. In: Krogh, G. von, Roos, J., & Kleine, D. (Ed.): *Knowing in Firms. Understanding, Managing and Measuring Knowledge* (pp. 240 - 252). London: Sage Publications.

Rheinhardt, R. (1993). *Das Modell organisationaler Lernfähigkeit und die Gestaltung lernfähiger Organisationen,* Frankfurt/Main: Verlag Peter Lang.

Ring, P. Smith (1996). Networked Organization. A Resource Based Perspective. Acta Universitatis Upsaliensis, Studia Oeconomiae Negotiorum No. 39, University of Uppsala.

Romhardt, K.(1998). Die Organisation aus der Wissensperspektive — Möglichkeiten und Grenzen der Intervention, Wiesbaden: Gabler Verlag.

Rühli, E. (1994). Der Resource-based View of Strategy. Ein Impuls für einen Wandel im unternehmungspolitischen Denken und Handeln? In: Gomez, P., Hahn, D., Müller-Stewens, G., & Wunderer, R. (Eds.), *Unternehmerischer Wandel. Konzepte zur organisatorischen Erneuerung* (pp. 31 - 57). Wiesbaden: Gabler Verlag.

Stewart, T. (1997). *Intellectual Capital*, London: Sage Publications.

Sorg, S. (1982). Informationspathologien und Erkenntnisfortschritt in Organisationen, Munich: Kirsch.

Sveiby, K. E. (1997). *The new organizational Wealth. Managing and Measuring Knowledge-based Assets*, San Francisco: Berrett-Koehler.

Sydow, J. (1992). *Strategische Netzwerke. Evolution und Organisation*, Wiesbaden: Gabler Verlag.

Sydow, J., van Well, B. (1996). Wissensintensiv durch Netzwerkorganisation — Strukturationstheoretische Analyse eines wissensintensiven Netzwerkes. In: Schreyögg, G., Conrad, P. (Ed.), *Managementforschung 6* (pp. 191- 234). Berlin — New York: Walter de Gruyter.

Thorelli, H. B. (1986). Networks: Between Markets and Hierarchies. *Strategic Management Journal*, 7, pp. 37 - 51.

Ungson, G. R., Trudel, J. D. (1999). The Emerging Knowledge Based Economy. *IEEE Spectrum*, (5), pp. 60 - 65.

Walsh, J. P., Ungson, G. R. (1991). Organizational Memory. *Academy of Management Review*, 16, pp. 57 - 91.

Wernerfelt, B., Montgomery, C. A. (1988). Tobin's q and the Importance of Focus in Firm Performance. *The American Economic Review*, 78(1), pp. 246 - 250.

Wildemann, H. (1997). Koordination von Unternehmensnetzwerken. *Zeitschrift für Betriebswirtschaft*, 67(4), pp. 417 - 439.

Wilson, L. T., Snyder, C. A. (1999). Knowledge Management and IT: How they are Related? *IT Professional*, 1(2), pp. 73 - 75.

Willke, H. (1996). Dimensionen des Wissensmanagement — Zum Zusammenhang von gesellschaftlicher und organisationaler Wissensbasierung. In: Schreyögg, G. & Conrad, P. (Ed.), *Managementforschung 6* (pp. 263 - 304). Berlin—New York: Walter de Gruyter.

Womack, J. P., Jones, D. T., & Roos, D. (1990). *The Machine That Changed The World: Based on the Massachusetts Institute of Technology 5-Million 5-Year Study on the Future of the Automobile*, New York: Rawson Associates.

Chapter V

Computer Mediated Interorganizational Knowledge Sharing: Insights from a Virtual Team Innovating Using a Collaborative Tool[1]

Ronald Rice
Rutgers University, USA

Ann Majchrazak, Nelson King and Sulin Ba
University of Southern California, USA

Arvind Malhotra
University of North Carolina at Chapel Hill, USA

How does a team use a computer-mediated technology to share and reuse knowledge when the team is inter-organizational and virtual, when the team must compete for the attention of team members with collocated teams, and when the task is the creation of a completely new innovation? From a review of the literature on knowledge sharing and reuse using collaborative tools, three propositions are generated about the likely behavior of the team in using the collaborative tool and reusing the knowledge put in the knowledge repository. A multi-method longitudinal research study of this design team was conducted over its ten-month design effort. Both qualitative and quantitative data were obtained. Results indicated that the propositions from the literature were insufficient to explain the behavior of the team. We found that ambiguity of the task does not determine use of a collaborative tool; that tool use does not increase with experience; and that knowledge that is perceived as transient (whether it really is transient or not) is unlikely to be referenced properly for later search and retrieval. Implications for practice and theory are discussed.

How does a team use a computer-mediated technology to share and reuse knowledge when the team is interorganizational and virtual, and when the task is the creation of a completely new innovation?

This is an important set of interrelated questions because of the increasing use of *virtual interorganizational collaboration* and the development and diffusion of *collaborative technologies* (CT) to facilitate the collaboration process (Allen and Jarman 1999; Coleman 1997; Haywood, 1998; Lipnack and Stamps, 1997). Dow, Ford, Chrysler and British Petroleum are well-known examples of companies diffusing CTs to facilitate their work (Ferranti 1997; Hamblen 1998). A Gartner Group (1997) study went as far as to say: "Real-time collaboration use will change from virtually nothing to ubiquity by 1999" (p.26).

The use of CTs is fundamental to making virtual teams work. A CT, also referred to as a virtual workplace, should be able to record, at a minimum, the process of the group, an agenda, libraries of solutions and practices, different forms of interaction, meta-information (such as date, sequence, author of contributions), and provide shared information storage, access and retrieval (Ellis et al., 1991; Field, 1996; Ishii et al., 1994; Kling, 1991; Nunamaker et al., 1993, 1995; Romano et al., 1998; Thornton and Lockard, 1994).

Critical, then, for knowledge-sharing and reuse with CTs is that the CT includes not just a mechanism for exchanging information (such as e-mail), but a mechanism for creating a knowledge repository and a mechanism for accessing the knowledge repository. In this chapter, we report results from a 10-month field study of an interorganizational virtual engineering design team and describe how a CT is used with respect to knowledge-sharing. The two questions we address are: (1) When do members of a virtual, distributed, interorganizational team designing an innovative new product use a CT to collaborate? (2) When and how do team members reuse the knowledge once it is shared in the knowledge repository of the CT?

LITERATURE REVIEW AND RESEARCH PROPOSITIONS

The criticality of CTs to collaborative work has been well-recognized in the literature (see Eveland and Bikson, 1989; Galegher and Kraut, 1990; Hiltz and Turoff, 1993; Johansen, 1988, 1992; Olson and Atkins, 1990; Rice and Shook, 1990; Romano et al., 1998; Schrage, 1990). Among the many factors affecting the use of CTs suggested by these studies, two are of primary concern to us in this study: 1) *experience* with the CT and 2) *task* being accomplished using the CT.

Experience with a CT is a critical factor because, typically, teams use face-to-face media to share crucial knowledge on the extant norms, habits, and political relationships, in addition to content (Ehrlich, 1987; Kraut et al., 1998; Markus, 1992; Perin, 1991; Rice and Gattiker, 1999; Saunders and Jones, 1990). Over time, however, teams have been observed to gradually adjust to conveying richer information through the collaborative tool (Hiltz and Turoff, 1981; Orlikowski et al., 1995; Walther, 1992).

In addition to experience, studies have also found that not all tasks that a team might undertake to accomplish its objective are best suited for use with CTs. Several theories provide foundations for this perspective: "information richness" theory, "social presence" theory (Daft and Lengel, 1986; Rice, 1984, 1987; Short et al.,1976), and the task circumplex model (McGrath and Hollingshead, 1993). These theories argue that organizational information-processing activities are differentially supported by various media; the attributes of certain media match the information processing requirements of some activities better than others. Because of the kind of information they can transmit (nonverbal cues, etc.), some channels (face-to-face, videoconferencing, etc.) are particularly suited for tasks that are unanalyzable, non-routine, equivocal and involve manageable amounts of information. Unanalyzable tasks that teams might perform include strategic direction-setting, brainstorming, and conflict resolution. For such tasks, the theories predict that, given the option, teams will opt to use what can be called "interpersonal" methods of sharing knowledge since such methods provide the most context-rich capability. The most personal of these methods is the face-to-face meeting. For distributed team members, dyadic phone conversations are not nearly as interpersonal, but they provide at least the opportunity to share information in a one-on-one setting with aural cues. In contrast to these interpersonal methods are computer-mediated collaborative tools that share the information with the entire team. Collaborative tools are generally considered less likely to be used for ambiguous tasks because their public text-based, computer-mediated nature makes it more difficult to share the context-rich information needed to understand the task.

Sharing knowledge and putting the shared knowledge into a knowledge repository are an important start in knowledge-sharing and the basis for organizational memory (Davenport et al., 1996; Huber 1991; Walsh and Ungson, 1991). The repository alone is insufficient, however. For shared knowledge to be meaningfully used, the knowledge needs to be coupled with mechanisms for organization, retention, maintenance, search and retrieval of the information (Stein and Zwass, 1995). Such mechanisms are often computer-based, ranging from simple keyword organizing principles to complex intelligent agents and neural networks that grow with the growth of the knowledge repositories (Ellis et al., 1991; Johansen, 1988; Maes, 1994). Common among all these mechanisms is that they are established at the outset of a project (such as keywords) and are not generally modified during use. Thus, the literature indicates that these mechanisms, if established at the outset to promote knowledge reuse, will generally succeed at promoting knowledge reuse.

Although past research has yielded these important suggestions for the use of CTs, the literature on the use of CTs identifies a whole host of individual, technology, organizational, and group process factors that can also affect the use of CTs in sharing and reusing knowledge (DeSanctis and Gallupe, 1987; Furst, Blackburn and Rosen, 1999; Hibbard, 1997; Rice and Gattiker, 1999; Sambamurthy and Chi,n 1994). Because of the many factors that affect the knowledge-sharing and use process, we contend it is difficult to determine which conclusions from the literature apply in all situations. Others (e.g., Kraemer and Pinnsonneault, 1990) have made similar arguments.

One aspect of a situation that has been little studied is the use of CTs among highly creative teams. Most studies of virtual team knowledge-sharing have been conducted on teams working on defined tasks such as software development. We believe that the decision process for creating an entirely innovative design, such as is called for in "discontinuous technology developments" (Iansiti, 1995; Tushman and Anderso,n 1986), is fundamentally different than making decisions about problems for which there is a known solution or process because the brainstorming is neither anonymous nor non-evaluative, the knowledge to be shared is highly contextualized and reliant on informal opportunities of physical proximity, and knowledge-sharing involves not just synthesizing information but dissecting and recreating that knowledge in fundamentally different ways (Allen 1985; Davis 1984; Kraut et al. 1990).

Given these characteristics of knowledge-sharing in creative contexts, conclusions about how CTs are used to share knowledge among team members with more routine tasks may not apply. For example, for creative tasks, the theories noted above all suggest that knowledge-sharing be performed face-to-face. However, for a creative design team, this would mean that most if not all their work be done face-to-face. Such a conclusion seems too extreme and negates the purpose of virtual design teams.

In sum, then, a situation that has particularly been under studied is the use of CTs for knowledge-sharing among: a) distributed team members b) working collaboratively c) across organizations d) via a collaborative tool to e) create a revolutionary new product. As a starting point, we used the suggestions from the literature on using CTs for knowledge-sharing and knowledge reuse as propositions to be examined for this special population of virtual teams.

We examined two propositions for using CTs to share knowledge:

Proposition #1) A distributed virtual team will initially show little use of CT, but its use of CT will increase over time as the members gain more experience with it.

Proposition #2) When a distributed virtual team performs highly ambiguous tasks, the members will use person (face-to-face or phone) more than CT-based media; but when the task is less ambiguous, the members will use the CT more.

We examined one proposition for using CTs to reuse knowledge:

Proposition #3) Establishing technology features and mechanisms for knowledge reuse at the beginning of a project will prompt the virtual team to reuse knowledge during the course of the project.

RESEARCH DESIGN

Site, Sample, and Project

We explored these three propositions through a longitudinal research study of an engineering design team for the 10 months during its conceptual design process. The team involved eight engineers spending a small (<15%) fraction of each of their total work time from three different companies (RocketCo, 6SigmaCo, and StressCo as pseudonyms); the project was referred to by the code name for the product, "Slice". Their goal was to design a new form of a rocket engine thrust chamber. The engineers were organized into a traditional concept development team consisting of a project team leader, conceptual designer, lead design engineer, design engineer, stress analyst, aerothermal analyst, combustion analyst, and a producibility analyst.

The Slice team's design task was a highly innovative one: to design a high-performance rocket injector using combustible fluids that had not been used together previously in RocketCo, at a manufacturing cost that was a significant reduction over what had been previously achieved. The innovation of using a different combination of fluids meant that knowledge of fluid dynamics and combustion behavior acquired from previous designs could not be applied directly to this one. As a result, the design process became more iterative than usual, one in which ideas were generated, analyses performed, guesses made, and ideas thrown out when people didn't seem convinced of the idea's feasibility or analysis results.

In addition to the product innovation, the team was tasked with the explicit objective of innovating in the use of a collaborative tool among geographically dispersed team members; this also represented an innovation for the company. As a result, they saw that part of their effort was not only to design a product (a rocket thrust chamber), but to develop a new process (use of a collaborative tool). Finally, the fact that three companies were involved in this early stage of concept development was new, especially for RocketCo, which considered rocket engine design its core competency. The other companies were included because they had core competencies in producibility engineering and stress analysis, which are crucial components in the initial development of a rocket engine.

Despite all the complexities faced by the team and a poor mid-project review by senior technical managers, by the end of the project, the team was judged by the senior managers in RocketCo as successfully achieving its objectives. The team designed a thrust chamber for a new rocket engine with only 6 parts instead of the traditional hundreds, with a predicted quality rating of 9 sigma (less than 1 failure out of 10 billion) instead of the traditional 2 to 4 sigma, at a first unit cost of $50,000 instead of millions, and at a predicted production cost of $35,000 instead of millions. The team was able to achieve all of this with no member serving more than 15% of his time, within the development budget, with total engineering hours 10 times less than traditional teams, using a new collaborative technology with several partners having no history of working together. Finally, senior management has been sufficiently impressed with the design to approve it for the next step in the development process: a cold flow test assessing the validity of the assumptions of liquid flow through the parts.

Thus, this study provides an excellent opportunity to observe a highly successful virtual team using a CT to accomplish its task.

Description of the Collaborative Technology

Team members had two types of communication channels available to them: interpersonal (which included face-to-face for a few members in RocketCo, three team-wide meetings, and the telephone for all members), and the collaborative tool (e-mail was infrequently used).

The collaborative tool available to them was called The Internet Notebook ("Note-book"). This CT allowed team members access to a project knowledge repository which was housed on a centralized server located at the tool vendor's site. The Notebook was typically launched as a helper application from an HTML browser. Each time a team member would log-on to the central server, he could either just view the notebook without launching the Notebook application, or he could launch the full application. Launching the application provided the engineer with both the knowledge repository as well as such useful capabilities that permitted authoring new documents (called entries), commenting on entries in the Notebook, sorting entries by date, keyword or reference links, navigating to find entries, creating sketches using a whiteboard, "snapshotting" and hot-linking screen displays from other applications, creating a personal profile for email notification of relevant entries, using templates for frequent team activities (such as minutes, agendas), and vaulting documents requiring configuration control.

Team members could use the CT asynchronously or synchronously. Asynchronous use of the Notebook meant that a team member could make an entry into the Notebook with appropriate team members automatically notified of the entry, and then those notified members could comment on the entry and republish it. Team members also used the Notebook for synchronous team meetings which they called "teleconferences". These meetings consisted of the application-sharing Notebook for data only, and audioconferencing on a separate channel, supplemented with the Notebook's full functionalities. This is referred to by the Gartner (1997) group as the "down and dirty" approach to synchronous communication.

Data Collection Methodology

Since virtual teams evolve through different phases depending on the stages of the design project, we used a multi-method longitudinal study design (Menard, 1991):

1. Ethnographic observation (Geertz, 1973; Harvey and Myers, 1995; Hughes et al, 1992; Orlikowski and Robey, 1991) of all 89 one-hour teleconferences and three in-person team meetings (at the kickoff, at mid-project, and at the end).
2. Panel questionnaire surveys of the eight team members at the three stages in the project: inception, for each of the 40 weeks during, and at the project, end to collect data on team members' background, use of communication media, attitudes toward communication media, and satisfaction with team process. Standardized instruments were used and are available upon request.
3. Weekly communication network diaries completed by team members.
4. Interviews with team members after critical events.
5. A "Lessons Learned" group meeting conducted with the team members at the end of the project.
6. Weekly logs of electronic traffic using the Notebook among team members.

FINDINGS FOR PROPOSITIONS FOR USE OF CT IN KNOWLEDGE-SHARING

Findings on Proposition 1: CT Use Will Increase Over Time

Across the entire project, the team members collaborated with others 61% of their time, with the rest of the time spent in activities they could perform themselves (e.g., drawing, analysis, report-writing, etc.). We observed the choices the team members made on whether to use interpersonal media (such as face-to-face or phone) or collaboration tool support when they collaborated with others. Following our initial expectation and that of the literature's, we anticipated that the use of interpersonal media would be high initially and reduce over time while the use of the collaborative tool would be low initially and gradually increase over time.

Figure 1 presents the weekly data over the course of the 10 months of the project. While on the average, across the time-span of the project, the team members used interpersonal methods (face-to-face and phone) 37% and the collaboration tool 63% of the time, there were wide fluctuations in use. Instead of a gradual increase in CT use, we found

Table 1: Modes of Communication

	Primary Method		Secondary Method		Mean %	Mean %
	Personal	Public	Personal	Public	Personal	Public
	FtoF + Phone	TeleConf + Notebook	FtoF + Phone	TeleConf + Notebook	Primary & Secondary	Primary & Secondary
1 ...clarify team members' roles and relationships.	38%	63%	38%	63%	38%	63%
2 ...clarify project objectives and priorities within the team.	13%	88%	50%	50%	31%	69%
3 ...clarify project objectives and priorities with those outside the team.	75%	25%	83%	17%	79%	21%
4 ...change project objectives, priorities, or specification.	13%	88%	50%	50%	31%	69%
5 ...recall technical specifications and constraints.	0%	100%	25%	75%	13%	88%
6 ...sketch out ideas for injector concept.	50%	50%	50%	50%	50%	50%
7 ...transform concept sketch into injector drawing.	50%	50%	67%	33%	58%	42%
8 ...learn about unfamiliar parts of the concept.	25%	75%	38%	63%	31%	69%
9 ...understand the design concerns of other team members.	13%	88%	50%	50%	31%	69%
10 ...get up to speed on current concept.	13%	88%	25%	75%	19%	81%
11 ...share own design expertise with others.	25%	75%	71%	29%	48%	52%
12 ...identify areas requiring more detailed evaluation.	25%	75%	50%	50%	38%	63%
13 ...quickly generate new ideas.	38%	63%	75%	25%	56%	44%
14 ...compare competing concepts.	0%	100%	13%	88%	6%	94%
15 ...focus analysis on important design issues.	13%	88%	38%	63%	25%	75%
16 ...examine design tradeoffs.	0%	100%	25%	75%	13%	88%
17 ...jointly author a document or joint analysis.	25%	75%	63%	38%	44%	56%
18 ...quickly identify disagreements.	13%	88%	88%	13%	50%	50%
19... quickly resolve conflict over design approach.	25%	75%	75%	25%	50%	50%
20... determine next steps in the design process.	38%	63%	50%	50%	44%	56%
21 ..coordinate activities within the team.	0%	100%	88%	13%	44%	56%
22 ...get appropriate team members to participate	75%	25%	63%	38%	69%	31%
23 ..move project forward when stalled.	29%	71%	86%	14%	57%	43%
24 ...resolve design conflicts with others outside the team.	88%	13%	75%	25%	81%	19%
25 ...obtain resources or information outside of team.	88%	13%	100%	0%	94%	6%
26 ...monitor program status and documentation. asking: "To what extent do you believe that ..."	0%	100%	13%	88%	6%	94%

Figure 1: Percent Collaboration Conducted through Computer-mediated Communication by Week (Remaining Percent Conducted through In-person and Telephone)

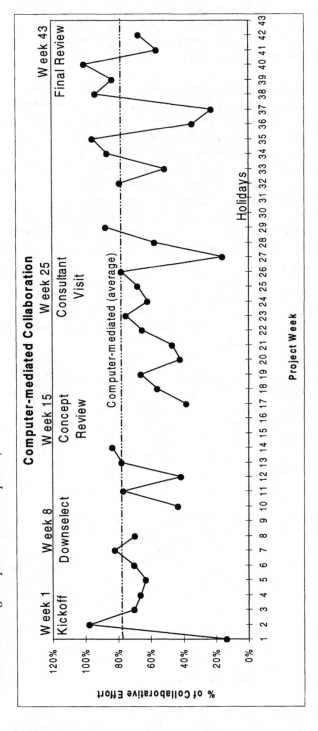

that the members quickly learned the tool and began to use it at a moderate level of use, with enormous peaks and valleys throughout the project, but never showing a consistent trend of increasing. Thus members did not increase their usage over time compared to more interpersonal media of face-to-face and phone.

Findings for Proposition 2: CT Use Will be Less for Ambiguous Tasks

The literature had suggested that face-to-face was more likely to occur with strategic direction-setting, creative brainstorming, and conflict resolution on the design concept. Table 1 shows the results of the questionnaire given to the members at the end of the project asking them to indicate which communication media they actually used primarily and secondarily. Apparent from Table 1 is that, as expected, the team members indicated that they tended to use face-to-face or phone for the more ambiguous tasks of managing external relationships and conflicts (including obtaining resources or information outside of the team, resolve design conflicts with others outside the team, and clarify project objectives and priorities with those outside the team, get appropriate team members to participate), brainstorming (e.g., quickly generate new ideas, transform concept sketch into a thrust chamber drawing), and strategic direction-setting (e.g., move project forward when stalled, clarify project objectives). Also, as expected, they tended to use the synchronous CTs for the more routine tasks of analysis (e.g., comparing competing concepts, examining design tradeoffs, focus analysis on important design issues), and project statusing (monitor program status and documentation, get up to speed on current concept, and recall technical specs and constraints).

In addition, however, the questionnaire data indicated that the CT was used for more ambiguous tasks as well. Such tasks as clarify project objectives, change project objectives, learn about unfamiliar parts of the concept, and understand the design concerns of other team members — clearly non-routine tasks — were performed by the team members, on the average, using the CT 69% of the time (versus face-to-face or phone). This clearly indicates that members were able to adjust to the use of CTs for more ambiguous tasks.

Observations of the team also indicated that the team was able to use CTs for more ambiguous tasks. In particular, the intense, creative "grab-the-pen" variety of brainstorming was initially accomplished only through a face-to-face meeting, but later in the project was accomplished using the CT.

Why was the team able to do brainstorming using the CT at the end of the project while they couldn't at the beginning? We believe it had to do with the artifacts and the shared language that came about from the earlier efforts. At the only face-to-face brainstorm, the team members came up with a first-cut design which, even though was very different from the final design, was instrumental in establishing an artifact around which team members could now work virtually. They used that artifact to explain the underlying physics of combustion and to explain the fundamentals of their disciplines to other team members. In addition, during the earlier meetings, experts spent time explaining the technical reasons for rejecting concepts, which paid off later in the project when other team members detected similar problems encountered earlier. Nonaka and Takeuchi (1995) stress the importance of such shared understanding for enabling knowledge transfer among collaborators.

What created this shared language? Certainly the first two face-to-face meetings provided an important medium. In fact, several members commented that more in-person meetings to resolve conflicts would have been helpful. However, we believe that the ability of the team to create a shared language was also partially attributable to the departure of the initial combustion analyst and conceptual designer — a turnover that eventually led to a more homogeneous team. In a sense, the brainstorming at the beginning was over fundamental differences of opinion, while the brainstorming at the end accepted certain fundamental assumptions. As a result, brainstorming at the end could focus on idea generation and critique, rather than resolution of inherently unresolvable conflicts over assumptions and approaches. Note that in this instance, the richer face-to-face medium can be seen as exacerbating the divergent group norms, while the leaner CT can be seen as facilitating the use of a convergent group norm.

In sum, we learned that sharing knowledge virtually using a CT is not determined solely by the ambiguity of the task but rather by the identification of a common language and artifacts through face-to-face communication. Once the commonality is created, even ambiguous tasks such as creative brainstorming can be performed using CTs. In addition, the use of a CT does not increase as experience with the tool increases, but rather varies with the task at hand, and not necessarily because of task ambiguity.

Findings for Proposition 3: CT Features Will Prompt Knowledge-Reuse

Team members were very interested in encouraging reuse of the knowledge generated by the team. Therefore, at the outset of the project, selected members of the team spent significant time developing a Coordination Protocol that identified ways to use features of the CT that would increase team members' ability to reuse knowledge. This protocol encouraged the use of reference links and keywords when entering knowledge into the CT; using templates for meeting agendas, decisions, action items, and meeting minutes; and being automatically notified when entries relevant to a members' interest were created. The members who created the protocol obtained concurrence from the team to use the protocol and then trained all team members in its use. Thus, we proposed that these features and the protocol would succeed in creating reuse among the team.

Again, the team fooled us. Although in the beginning the members agreed to the standards for keyword use, as the design effort began in earnest, keyword use and reference links quickly fell to the wayside. Only 37% of the entries had two or more keywords and only 27% of the entries had three or more. Members turned off their notification profiles, because, when an entry was republished many times, they would receive too many email notifications (e.g., 621 notifications generated for the keyword "design" in the first 2 weeks of the project). The variety of f templates available were not used as often as expected, with only the "meeting minutes" template still being used midway through the project. Finally, members rarely used the more sophisticated navigation features of the tool (such as the ability to view networks of entries in accordance with the frequency with which they referenced each other); instead most relied on finding entries by reviewing them in their chronological order (looking at those they had arrived since they last looked into the Notebook) with only occasionally even doing a quick top-level keyword search (e.g., search on the keyword "minutes" to find the minutes of a meeting missed).

The questionnaire data from the team members provide additional insight into the use of the CT's features for search and retrieval. Team members were asked the frequency with which they used various features of the CT. Table 2 shows the frequency of use for each. The only feature used relatively frequently (slightly more than 2-3 times a month) was the documentation of work in the public Notebook. In sum, the team made little use of the supposedly powerful organization, search, and retrieval mechanisms provided by the CT.

*Table 2: **Frequency of Notebook Usage during Project***

Feature	Mean	Std Dev
Documentation in public notebook	4.5	1.4
Documentation in personal notebook	2.9	2.0
Navigator	3.3	1.8
Reference Links/Hot Links	3.6	1.2
Templates	2.1	0.9
Snapshot	3.4	1.7
Sketching via Notebook tools	2.4	1.5

Note: Scale consisted of "1" - Never during project, "2" - Less than once a month, "3" - Once a month, "4" 2-3 times a month, "5" - Once a week, "6" - 2-3 times a week, "7" - Daily.

What explains the team's use of the knowledge repository in this way? We found that the design process was so unpredictable that most of the members had no clue as to whether or not the knowledge they were putting into the database would be of value later on and thus those entries did not warrant attempts at categorization and organization. Since designs were changing almost biweekly (with over 20 design concepts generated during the ten months represented in 60 entries), analysis results relevant to a particular design might be obsolete a week later. Since management was seen as changing their directions throughout the project, entries of discussions of strategy and goals were often of limited value a month later. Since drawings were often being redesigned, a drawing might or might not have features and dimensions that would be of use in later designs. We believe that the fact that some knowledge may be perceived to only have what we call "transient utility" has an effect on what gets entered and how it gets entered and recalled.

In other words, because information was changing so rapidly, team members didn't bother to waste their time to attach keywords or reference links. As a result, keyword searches and networks of linked documents quickly became useless. Moreover, because the information was transient, it was hard for them to even see a pattern to the entries in order to suggest new keywords. In fact, at the end of the project, one team member suggested wistfully: "You know, it would have been a good idea if we had created a new keyword for each new concept so that we could search easier"; even this suggestion at structure was critiqued by another member, who pointed out: "How could we? We often didn't even know when we were doing a new concept rather than just a revision to the existing concept".

Was the lack of organization a problem for retrieving needed information? Despite members believing that virtually all entries were transient, in reality, many entries were referenced in conversations later on. By the end of the project, there were almost 1000 entries: 661 generated by the design team, with the remaining for Notebook administration, testing, and pre-kickoff discussions. To look for previous entries, then, took significant amounts of time during a meeting. Moreover, even though reference links were used only 19% of the time, the team members reported, in Table 3, that, when the reference links were created, they were the most useful features for finding information quickly since they helped to trace back to those documents that were the most relevant to their search needs.

Given that the links were considered as having the most potential use for finding information quickly, what barriers need to be removed for engineers to consider using them, especially for what might appear, at first sight, to be "transient knowledge"? To address this question, we asked the team members, at the end of the project, to indicate their agreement with a series of assumptions that tool vendors make about how engineers might use CTs to facilitate their collaboration (Ellis et al., 1991; Grudin, 1988, 1994; Ishii et al., 1994; Johnson-Lenz and Johnson-Lenz, 1982; King and Majchrzak, 1996; Kling, 1991; Malone et al., 1987; Nunamaker et al., 1993). Table 4 shows these results. While team members agreed that a CT and an accessible knowledge repository are valuable assets to their work, such assets will have limited value for

Table 3: Usefulness of Notebook Features in Finding Relevant Information Quickly

Feature	Mean	Std Dev
Authoring Notebook entries	3.6	1.3
Snapshot	3.6	1.3
Sketching	2.8	1.2
Navigator	2.8	0.8
Notify via email of new/changed entries	3.5	1.3
Reference Links	4.6	0.7
Hot Links	4.8	0.4
Template	2.3	1.2
Remote access	3.8	1.3

Note: Scale anchored from "1", definitely useless, to "5", definitely useful.

Table 4: Assumptions About Use of Electronic Notebook

Item	Mean	Std Dev
Engineers need not only a collaborative tool, but also a personal knowledge storage tool.	5.9	0.9
Engineers need to access their own documents while traveling or away from their desk.	5.5	1.7
Engineers want to quickly access old documents.	6.0	1.0
Engineers want to see the connections (links) among old documents.	5.5	1.0
The data structure represented by the links helps engineers understand the content of the document before opening it.	3.3	1.6
When an author publishes a document, he/she will choose the appropriate keywords	3.4	1.5
Set of selected keywords are accurate classifications of the document content.	2.6	1.0
Engineers can easily determine which documents should be linked together.	3.5	1.7
Engineers will make an effort to make (link) the connections among documents.	3.0	1.5
Templates help engineers organize their thoughts.	2.5	1.6
Templates help engineers collect structured data.	3.1	1.8
Engineers want to be automatically informed when documents of interest are published (or changed).	5.8	0.8
When engineers specify their personal profile, they understand the exact meaning of the keywords.	3.3	1.2

Note: 1 to 7 anchored scale from "1" - Not at all to "7" great extent, knowledge reuse unless such knowledge search mechanisms as reference links require less discipline by the team member to maintain, and quickly provide more information to facilitate a search process, and the bulk of knowledge is not of transient utility.

In sum, both the questionnaire and observational data suggest that knowledge reuse by a team using CT is not facilitated with existing mechanisms for search and retrieval when the knowledge informant considers the knowledge to be transient; can not be aided by a set of keywords created in the abstract prior to actual use of the CT; and can not be aided by user-governed reference-linking mechanisms which impose too much burden on the user.

CONCLUSIONS

From our detailed and longitudinal examination of how members of a distributed, virtual, interorganizational creative design team shared and reused their knowledge using a collaborative tool, we found that propositions from the literature were insufficient to inform either theory or practice on the use of collaborative tools.

The information-sharing literature must begin seriously considering the contingent conditions involved in the novel setting of a virtual distributed interorganizational creative team (such as organizational context, team structure, group composition, team norms, building team identity, trust, team cooperation and heterogeneity, process losses, social loafing, groupthink, criteria for group process effectiveness, and material group resources (Furst, Blackburn and Rosen, 1999). However, in spite of the lack of frequent informal or face-to-face interactions, this team was extraordinarily innovative and successful. Very little of the communication here was of the "formal" type (i.e., reports, documents, articles) even if for the simple reason that there were few precedents for the designs, so most of it involved sharing between individuals through attempts at direct solutions. Thus CT designs for such groups should not over-emphasize formal channels, even when technologically possible, and should allow ways to incorporate more "rich" forms of interaction even through the CT itself. Further, it is clear that a fair amount of "mutual expectations" and shared understandings had to be developed before the group could move into a period of focused design process (Krauss and Fussell 1990; Schrage 1990).

In addition to the rejection of commonly accepted propositions in the literature for more routine work environments, our study demonstrated that although most CTs claim to support the exchange of ideas, opinions, and preferences within the group, the document database features that are currently available in most collaborative tools mainly serve as an information repository, not a gateway to the right information, or a process for developing shared cognition. Most navigation tools (search by keywords or links, for example) are not sufficient enough to achieve the purpose. One possible solution to this problem is to create a Knowledge Management role on the team. By organizing the information and collectively monitoring various information sources to ensure information integrity and accuracy, within the rich and transient contexts of the group and the project, the knowledge manager can lower knowledge gathering and monitoring costs of each team member. The fact that early studies of computer conferencing arrived at the same general conclusion — the need for a human process mediator to help support, motivate, and essentially reinforce the group identity and purpose (Kerr, 1986) — reinforces the validity of this suggestion.

ENDNOTE

1 The authors would like to thank the following individuals who generously offered their time and energy throughout this research: Robert Carman, Vern Lott, Hal Buddenbohm, Dave Matthews, Linda Finley, Steve Babcock, Hollis Bostick, Dennis Coston, Bob Corley, Li-Kiang Tseng, Terry Kim, Dave Bremmer. The research was funded by ARPA.

REFERENCES

Allen, G. and Jarman, R.(1999). *Collaborative R&D: Manufacturing's New Tool*. NY: Wiley.

Allen, T. (1985). *Managing the flow of technology, technology transfer and the dissemination of technological information with the R&D organization*. Cambridge, MA: MIT Press.

Coleman, D. (1997). Knowledge management: The next golden egg in groupware. *Computer Reseller News*, March 31.

Daft, R., and Lengel, R. (1986). Organizational information requirements, media richness and structural design. *Management Science, 32*(5), 554-571.

Davenport, T., Jarvenpaa, S.L., and Beers, M.C. (1996). Improving knowledge work process. *Sloan Management Review, 37*(4), 53-65.

Davis, T. (1984). The influence of the physical environment in offices. *Academy of Management Review, 9*(2), 271-283.

DeSanctis, G., and Gallupe, R.B. (1987). A foundation for the study of group decision support systems. *Management Science, 33*(5), 589-609.

Ellis, C.A., Gibbs, S.J., and Rein, G. (1991). Groupware: Some issues and experiences. *Communications of the ACM, 34*(1), 39-58.

Ehrlich, S. (1987). Strategies for encouraging successful adoption of office communication systems. *ACM Transactions on Office Information Systems, 5*(4), 240-357.

Eveland, J.D., and Bikson, T. (1989). Work group structures and computer support: A field experiment. *ACM Transactions on Office Information Systems, 6*(4), 354-379.

Ferranti, M. (1997). Automaker aims for companywide collaborative standards. *Computing*, December 11.

Field, A. (1996). Group think. *Inc., 18*(13), Sept 17.

Furst, S., Blackbrun, R., and Rosen, B. (1999). Virtual teams: A proposed research agenda. Paper presented to Academy of Management, Chicago, August. Chapel Hill, NC: University of North Carolin Kenan-Flagler Business School.

Galegher, J., and Kraut, R.E. (1990). Technology for intellectual teamwork: Perspectives on research and design. In J. Galegher, R.E. Kraut, and C. Egido (eds.) *Intellectual teamwork: The social and technological bases of cooperative work.* (pp. 1-20.) Hillsdale, NJ: Erlbaum.

Gartner Group. (1997). Matter: Summer/Fall 1996 – the future of collaboration. *Gartner Group strategic analysis report*, April.

Geertz, C. (1973). *The interpretation of cultures.* New York: Basic Books.

Gerwin, D., and Moffat, L.K. (1997). Withdrawal of team autonomy during concurrent engineering. *Management Science, 43*(9), 1275-1287.

Grudin, J. (1988). Why CSCW applications fail: Problems in the design and evaluation of organizational interfaces. In *Proceedings of the Second Conference on Computer-Supported Cooperative Work.* (pp. 85-93.) New York: Association for Computing Machinery.

Grudin, J. (1994). Groupware and social dynamics. *Communications of the ACM, 37*(1), 93-105.

Hamblen, M. (1998). Netmeeting cuts Dow travel expenses. *Computerworld*, March 9, 20.

Handy, C. (1995). Trust and virtual organization. *Harvard Business Review, 73*(3), 40-50.

Harvey, L., and Myers, M. D. (1995). Scholarship and practice: The contribution of ethnographic research methods to bridging the gap. *Information Technology and People, 8*(3), 13-27.

Haywood, M. *Managing Virtual Teams*. Boston: Artech, 1998

Hibbard, J. (1997). Knowledge management – knowing what we know. *Information Week*, 653(October 20).

Hiltz, S.R., and Turoff, M. (1993). *The network nation: Human communication via computer, 2nd ed.* Reading, MA: Addison-Wesley.

Huber, G.P. (1991). Organizational learning: The contributing processes and literatures. *Organization Science, 2*(1), 88-115.

Hughes, J. A., Randall, D., and Shapiro, D. (1992). Faltering from ethnography to design. in *CSCW '92: Proceedings of the 1992 ACM Conference on Computer-Supported Cooperative Work: Sharing Perspectives.* (pp. 115-123.) New York: Association for Computing Machinery.

Iansiti, M. (1995). Technology integration - managing technological evolution In a complex environment. *Research Policy, 24*(4), 521-542.

Inkpen, A.C. (1996). Creating knowledge through collaboration. *California Management Review, 39*(1), 123-140.

Ishii, H., Kobayashi, M., and Arita, K. (1994). Iterative design of seamless collaboration media. *Communications of the ACM, 37*(8), 83-97.

Johansen, R. (1988). *Groupware: Computer support for business teams*. New York: Free Press.

Johansen, R. (1992). An introduction to computer-augmented teamwork. In R. Bostrom, R. Watson and S. Kinney (eds.) *Computer-augmented teamwork: A guided tour.* (pp. 5-15.) New York: Van Nostrand Reinhold.

Johnson-Lenz, P., and Johnson-Lenz, T. (1982). Groupware: The process and impacts of design choices. In E. B. Kerr, and S.R. Hiltz (eds.) *Computer-mediated communication systems: Status and evaluation.* (pp. 45-55.) New York: Academic Press.

Kerr, E. (1986). Electronic leadership: A guide to moderating online conferences. *IEEE Transactions on Professional Communications, PC29*(1), 12-18.

King, N.E., and Majchrzak, A. (1996). Concurrent engineering tools: Are the human issues being ignored? *IEEE Transactions on Engineering Management, 43*(2), 189-201.

Kling, R. (1991). Cooperation, coordination, and control in computer-supported work. *Communications of the ACM, 34*(12), 83-88.

Kraemer, K., and Pinnsonneault, A. (1990). Technology and groups: Assessment of the empirical research. In J. Galegher, R.E. Kraut, and C. Egido (eds.) *Intellectual teamwork: The social and technological bases of cooperative work.* (pp. 375-405.) Hillsdale, NJ: Erlbaum.

Krauss, R. and Fussell, S. (1990). Mutual knowledge and communicative effectiveness. In J. Galegher, R.E. Kraut, and C. Egido (eds.) *Intellectual teamwork: The social and technological bases of cooperative work.* (pp. 111-144.) Hillsdale, NJ: Erlbaum.

Kraut, R., Egido, C., and Galegher, J. (1990). Patterns of contact and communication In scientific research collaboration. In J. Galegher, R.E. Kraut, and C. Egido (eds.) *Intellectual teamwork: The social and technological bases of cooperative work.* (pp. 149-171.) Hillsdale, NJ: Erlbaum.

Kraut, R., Rice, R.E., Cool, C. and Fish, R. (1998). Varieties of social influence: The role of utility and norms in the success of a new communication medium. *Organization Science, 9*(4), 437-453.

Lipnack, J. and Stamps, J.(1997). *Virtual Teams.* NY: Wiley.

Maes, P. (1994). Agents that reduce work and information overload. *Communications of the ACM, 35*(11), 30-40.

Malone, T., Grant, K., Turbak, F., Brobst, S., and Cohen, M. (1987). Intelligent information sharing systems. *Communications of the ACM, 30*(5), 390-402.

Markus, M.L. (1992). Asynchronous technologies in small face-to-face groups. *Information Technology and People, 6*(1), 29-48.

McGrath, J.E., and Hollingshead, A.B. (1993). Putting the 'group' back in group support systems: Some theoretical issues about dynamic processes in groups with technological enhancements. In L.M. Jessup and J.S. Valacich (eds.) *Group support systems: New perspectives.* (pp. 78-96). New York: Macmillan.

Menard, S. (1991). *Longitudinal research.* Newbury Park, CA: Sage Publications.

Nonaka, I., and Takeuchi, H. (1995). *The knowledge creating company.* New York: Oxford University Press.

Nunamaker, J., Dennis, A., Valacich, J., Vogel, D., and George, J. (1993). Group support systems research: Experience from the lab and field. In L. Jessup and J. Valacich (eds.) *Group support systems: New perspectives.* (pp. 123-145.) New York: Macmillan Publishing.

Nunamaker, J., Jr., Briggs, R., and Mittleman, D. (1995). Electronic meeting systems: Ten years of lessons learned. In D. Coleman and R. Khanna (eds.) *Groupware: Technology and applications.* (pp. 149-193.) Englewood Cliffs, NJ: Prentice-Hall.

Olson, G. and Atkins, D. (1990). Supporting collaboration with advanced multimedia electronic mail: The NSF EXPRES project. In J. Galegher, R.E. Kraut, and C. Egido (eds.) *Intellectual teamwork: The social and technological bases of cooperative work.* (pp. 429-451.) Hillsdale, NJ: Erlbaum, Hillsdale.

Orlikowski, W. J., and Robey, D. (1991). Information technology and the structuring of organizations. *Information Systems Research, 2*(2), 143-169.

Orlikowski, W., Yates, J., Okamura, K., and Fujimoto, M. (1995). Shaping electronic communication: The metastructuring of technology in the context of use. *Organization Science, 6*(4), 423-443.

Perin, C. (1991). Electronic social fields in bureaucracies. *Communications of the ACM, 34*(12), 75-82.

Rice, R.E. (1984). Mediated group communication. In R.E. Rice and Associates (eds.) *The new media: Communication, research and technology*. (pp. 129-154.) Beverly Hills, CA: Sage.

Rice, R.E. (1987). Computer-mediated communication and organizational innovation. *Journal of Communication, 37*(4), 65-94.

Rice, R.E., and Gattiker, U. (1999). New media and organizational structuring of meanings and relations. In F. Jablin and L. Putnam (eds.) *New handbook of organizational communication*. (in press.) Newbury Park, CA: Sage.

Rice, R.E., and Shook, D. (1990). Communication, collaboration and voice mail. In J. Galegher, R.E. Kraut, and C. Egido (eds.) *Intellectual teamwork: The social and technological bases of cooperative work*. (pp. 327-350.) Hillsdale, NJ: Erlbaum.

Romano, N. Jr,. Nunamaker, J., Briggs, R., and Vogel, D. (1998). Architecture, design, and development of an html/javascript web-based group support system. *Journal of the American Society for Information Science, 49*(7), 649-667.

Sambamurthy, V., and Chin, W. W. (1994). The effects of group attitudes toward alternative gdss designs on the decision-making performance of computer-supported groups (group-decision support systems). *Decision Sciences, 25*(2), 215-241.

Saunders, C., and Jones, J. (1990). Temporal sequences in information acquisition for decision making: A focus on source and medium. *Academy of Management Review, 15*(1), 29-46.

Schrage, M. (1990). *Shared minds: The new technology of collaboration*. New York: Random House.

Short, J., W.E., and Christie, B. (1976). *The social psychology of telecommunications*. New York: Wiley.

Stein, E.W., and Zwass, V. (1995). Actualizing organizational memory with information systems. *Information Systems Research, 6*(2), 85-113.

Thornton, C., and Lockhart, E. (1994). Groupware or electronic brainstorming. *Journal of Systems Management, 45*(10), 10-12.

Tushman, M. L., and Anderson, P. (1986). Technological discontinuities and organizational environments. *Administrative Science Quarterly, 31*(3), 439-465.

Walsh, J. P., and Ungson, G. R. (1991). Organizational memory. *Academy of Management Review, 16*(1), 57-91.

Walther, J. (1992). Interpersonal effects in computer-mediated interaction: A relational perspective. *Communication Research, 19*(1), 52-90.

Chapter VI

The Glue That Binds Creative Virtual Teams

Jill E. Nemiro
Claremont Graduate University, USA

This chapter describes an exploratory, qualitative research project that investigated the work environment necessary for virtual teams to be creative. Nine different virtual teams, with a total of 36 virtual team members (33 of which completed the full study), participated in this study. Three teams were organizational consulting firms, two teams were educational consortiums, three teams were on-line service provider teams, and one team was a product design engineering team. One semi-structured, telephone interview was conducted with each participant. Team members also completed a background survey. Grounded theorizing was used to generate an in-depth understanding of the phenomena under investigation. Connection, defined as the elements that need to be in place for a team to develop and maintain identity and a sense of community, emerged as a key category important to the realization of creativity in virtual teams. Connection was further subdivided into task connection (made up of dedication/commitment, and goal clarity); and interpersonal connection (made up of information sharing, trust, and personal bond). Suggestions for how team designers, team leaders, or managers can establish and develop connection in their own virtual teams are offered.

Creativity is increasingly becoming a critical topic for contemporary organizations. Perhaps one of the most crucial reasons for organizations to promote creativity has been global competition. To meet the demands of fierce global competition, organizational structures are changing, becoming increasingly more flexible. These structures are characterized by such terms as virtual, boundary-less, or networked (Davidow and Malone, 1992; Galbraith, 1995; O'Hara-Devereaux and Johansen, 1994). Advances in information technology have made feasible these types of organizational structures, in which independent firms across the globe join together and function as if they were a single corporation.

Global competition has not only created a dire need for organizational creative efforts; it has forced companies to get products out faster. Teamwork in the virtual corporation is essential to tap into the best talent to create the highest quality and fastest response to customer needs. Virtual teams are groups of geographically dispersed organizational members who communicate and carry out their activities through information technology (Kristof, Brown, Sims, and Smith, 1995; Lipnack and Stamps, 1997; Nemiro, 1998). Alas, the traditional office, conceptualized as a collection of cubicles in a high rise, is shrinking as individuals are finding themselves working in an "anywhere/anytime" mode, connected to coworkers through information technology (O'Hara-Devereaux and Johansen, 1994).

Virtual team structures may lead to higher levels of team creativity as a result of more openness, flexibility, diversity, and added access to information as compared to more traditional group structures. However, it may be extremely difficult to build a sense of personal connection and trust in these types of structures—elements crucial to high levels of creativity (Ekvall, Arvonen, and Waldenstrom-Lindblad, 1983; Geber, 1995; Nemiro, 1998). In designing virtual teams, we cannot ignore the social context of such arrangements. Technology allows for the electronic connection of geographically spread out individuals, but it does not necessarily lead to effective personal connection, communication and creativity. Virtual corporations and teams cannot function without information technology. But technology alone is not the answer to the problems of working across geographical and cultural boundaries. The ultimate answers to these problems lie in the realm of human and organizational relations and creating work environments that bring out the best in people involved in these virtual structures.

What then can team designers, team leaders, and managers do to create a work environment that will help virtual teams realize their creativity? The answer to that question is relatively simple—*create a connection between team members*. Connection involves both task connection (made up of dedication/commitment, and goal clarity) and *interpersonal* connection (made up of information sharing, trust, and personal bond). In this chapter, I will describe a research project that explored the work environment necessary for virtual teams to be creative. The major focus of this chapter will be to illustrate the concept of connection, and the accompanying dimensions, and to offer suggestions on how managers can establish and develop such a connection in their own virtual teams. (The concept of connection was only one of three key categories for a work environment conducive to creativity in virtual teams. For a detailed explanation of the entire model, including the other two major categories—raw materials, and management/team member skills—and their accompanying dimensions, see Nemiro, 1998).

BACKGROUND LITERATURE

The Context for Creativity in Traditional Organizational and Team Structures

As early as 1954, Carl Rogers talked about the social conditions necessary for creativity, which included creating an environment characterized by psychological safety and freedom, high internal motivation, and the absence of external evaluation to allow creativity to flourish (Harrington, Block, and Block, 1987). Since that time, the literature investigating the influence of the social environment on creativity has further demonstrated the importance of creating the appropriate social conditions for enhancing creativity. Experimental research has demonstrated that creativity can be undermined by (a) evaluation (Amabile, 1979; Amabile, Goldfarb and Brackfield, 1990); (b) surveillance (Amabile et al., 1990); (c) reward (Amabile, Hennessey and Grossman, 1986; Kruglanski, Friedman and Zeevi, 1971; McGraw and McCullers 1979); (d) competition (Amabile, 1982); (e) time pressure (Amabile, Dejong and Lepper, 1976); (f) external motivational orientation (Amabile, 1985); and (g) restricted choice (Amabile and Gitomer, 1984; Runco, 1995; Shalley, 1991).

Previous research has also found a strong link between intrinsic motivation and high levels of creativity of individuals (Amabile, 1983; Pelz and Andrews, 1966). Intrinsic motivation has been characterized as an internal locus of control, a sense of being self-driven, an excitement about the work, and a commitment to an idea (Amabile and S. Gryskiewicz, 1987).

An important outgrowth of the examination of social and environmental influences on creativity has been an increasing interest in the ways the work environment might influence the creativity of employees (Amabile, 1989; West and Farr, 1990). From a comprehensive review of the literature, Nemiro and Runco (1996) identified six factors necessary for a work environment that fosters creativity in organizations and work groups. These factors included:

1. *Autonomy and freedom*: Allowing individuals responsibility for initiating new ideas and making decisions, a sense of control over one's work (Amabile and S. Gryskiewicz, 1987; Andrews, 1975; Ekvall et al., 1983; VanGundy, 1987).
2. *Challenge*: Work that is stimulating, engaging, and meaningful, a sense of having to work hard on challenging and important tasks (Amabile and N. Gryskiewicz, 1989; Ekvall et al., 1983).
3. Clear direction: Goals that are clear, negotiated, attainable, shared, and valued facilitate creativity (Amabile, 1988; West, 1990).
4. *Diversity/Flexibility/Tension*: Diversity, both in terms of the work assignments offered and the people one interacts with, and a tolerance of differences (Andrews, 1975; VanGundy, 1987). In order to be tolerant of differences, flexibility is needed (Abbey and Dickson, 1983; VanGundy, 1987). Both diversity and flexibility can lead to a sense of excitement and creative tension (Ekvall et al., 1983; Runco, 1994).
5. *Support for creativity*: An organizational focus on support for or encouragement of creativity (Amabile and N. Gryskiewicz, 1989; Andrews, 1975; Ekvall et al., 1983; VanGundy, 1987).
6. *Trust and participative safety*: Especially crucial for group creativity is trust and participative safety. The emphasis is on encouraging participation in a non-threatening, non-evaluative environment (West, 1990).

Prior research, then, has shown that dimensions of *connection*, both task (clear direction and commitment) and interpersonal (trust and participative safety) are important for enhancing creativity in traditional organizational and team designs. However, these studies did not directly address the specific dimensions that may be necessary when organizations and groups no longer interact in traditional structures.

The Context for Creativity in Virtual Teams

One of the problems with virtual work structures is that electronic interaction eliminates much of the work context, stripping off everything but the message and leaving the rest for inference. A major consideration for virtual teams is how much contextual information do people need to work effectively and creatively, and how much of this information can be communicated across time and distance. O'Hara-Devereaux and Johansen (1994) acknowledged that virtual teams cannot replicate the "water-cooler" information channels that operate for face-to-face teams.

More specifically, one of the contextual factors that is stripped away in virtual interactions is *nonverbal communication*. Although certain etiquettes have been established to communicate some form of nonverbal behavior through text, it can not be ignored that many virtual teams who communicate through media in which the message is shared in text or audio format (faxes, e-mail, phones) lose valuable visual nonverbal cues. Technology such as videoconferencing allows for the transmission of an image of the speaker as well; but, in most cases, the absence of visual nonverbal feedback is a characteristic of virtual interactions (Kiesler, Siegel, and McGuire, 1991). Nonverbal behavior can be used to control, regulate, and modify exchanges. Without such feedback, additional dimensions may be necessary to establish connection, coordination and collaboration for a work environment that will enhance creativity.

Another condition of computer-mediated communication is the level of *dehumanization and social isolation* that may develop in this type of communication. Some research has suggested that communication through electronic means is dehumanizing, creating a sense of social anonymity (Kiesler et al., 1991). As a result, messages in electronic mail tend to be stronger, and more uninhibited and assertive. Additional dimensions, then, may be necessary to establish connection, coordination, collaboration, and unity in the context of possible dehumanization and social isolation.

Finally, another contextual factor that can lead to miscommunication in virtual teams is *cultural differences or diversity*. Virtual teams may be dispersed all over the globe, indicating that these teams may be made up of members from varying cultural backgrounds. For one thing, creativity itself is defined differently in different cultures (Lubart, 1990). Cultural diversity can be a boon for creativity, as individuals from varying backgrounds may offer differing perspectives and insights. However, considering the more or less "context-less" environment of virtual work, dimensions specifically addressing these cultural differences are important to include in a work environment conducive to creativity in virtual teams.

So, what has the research suggested about the dimensions necessary for facilitating creativity in virtual teams? Because the phenomenon of a virtual team is a fairly recent one, no known research (prior to the current study) has directly addressed the social context necessary for fostering creativity in virtual teams. However, some preliminary dimensions may be drawn from existing related research on virtual team effectiveness. This research has suggested that key factors in effective virtual teams have been establishing goal and role clarity, and a sense of trust among virtual team members.

Goal and Role Clarity
Lipnack and Stamps (1997) saw purpose as the essence of a virtual team, "the sine qua non of virtual teams" (p. 41), and the best predictor of virtual team success. Purpose stood for a range of terms, including vision, mission, goals, tasks, and results. Common goals and vision were necessary to build loyalty and trust among geographically dispersed

and culturally diverse virtual team members. Virtual organizations and teams are often made up of competitors, suppliers, and customers all cooperating with one another to accomplish results. This cooperation results from team members who have compatible goals.

George (1996) stressed that specifying the overall direction is crucial for virtual teams. Clear guidelines and expectations up front enable virtual team members to know what and how they need to pursue.

In addition, O'Hara-Devereaux and Johansen (1994) viewed shared goals as important to effective virtual teams. They wrote:

> Distributed team members stay oriented to each other and their tasks through high-level shared vision, goals, and roles rather than through detailed implementation plans. This level of understanding is a critical substitute for the informal, face-to-face meetings that play such an important role in keeping on-site teams in tune with one another. (p. 125)

In addition to having clear, compatible, and shared goals, role clarity appears to be an important factor for successful virtual teams. Lipnack and Stamps (1997) suggested that roles helped geographically dispersed team members to relate. Roles for virtual team members, however, require greater clarification, and expectations need to be more explicit than in co-located teams (Kossler and Prestridge, 1996; Lipnack and Stamps, 1997). George (1996) suggested that one of the best practices for beginning virtual teamwork was to provide a profile of what team members were expected to do, including the roles of both virtual team members and their leaders. While role clarity is important for virtual team members, the roles they play are often multiple, and flexible due to the dynamic nature of virtual teams (Lipnack and Stamps, 1997).

Trust

Trust may be the most crucial dimension necessary for virtual team effectiveness. Davidow and Malone (1992) emphasized trust as a defining feature for virtual corporations:

> The road to world-class supply chain management meanders through a series of cultural changes—to a new plateau of trust. To achieve true partnership, customers and suppliers must share information—on new products, designs, internal business plans, and long-term strategy—that once was closely guarded. (p. 145)

Lipnack and Stamps (1997) stressed that trust is something virtual teams must possess, "In the networks and virtual teams of the Information Age, trust is a 'need to have' quality in productive relationships" (p. 174). Trust is made up of several components: (a) *trusting people*, members need to trust one another's competence and accountability for the work assigned; (b) *trusting purposes*, members generate trust by their commitment to a unifying purpose; and (c) *trusting links*, members need to trust that the information they receive is the best-available information and that the channels through which information is sent will be effective.

Perrolle (1991) emphasized trust to achieve nondistorted communication in electronic interaction. Individuals must trust that other team members are conversing in meaningful and comprehensible ways, and talking about the same thing. In addition, individuals must trust that other team members have the intention of having a rational conversation, and do not intend to mislead or intimidate one another to their advantage. Electronic partners must also trust one another to engage in socially appropriate conversation. In essence, unseen individuals must develop the ability to trust the words they read and the information that is provided.

O'Hara-Devereaux and Johansen (1994) suggested that building trust in the early stages of team development is perhaps the most effective measure in guaranteeing the success of virtual teams. The key rule in building trust is to take the time to build relationships, to create "the human glue of teams" (p. 171). Byrne (1993) also suggested that before companies can routinely engage in virtual work, they must build a high level of trust in each other.

In a case study of one successful virtual team, Kristof et al. (1995) found three elements of trust: (a) trust the company placed in the team members, (b) trust the team members had in the organization, and (c) trust that existed between the members of the team. These three elements of trust combined to create an atmosphere where each team member had both the freedom and responsibility to contribute their best.

Trust may develop more slowly among virtual team members, as compared to face-to-face team members. With less visual contact, it simply may take longer to identify and adjust to the habits, quirks, and skills of team members (Kossler and Prestridge, 1996). George (1996) suggested that lack of trust or mistrust may put a virtual team on a "collision course." And, unfortunately, mistrust is likely, as employees from different locations, cultures and technical backgrounds are apt to question how the information they offer will be used, whether their contribution will be recognized outside the team, and whether other team members will make an equal contribution to the work. Finally, Handy (1995) felt the issue of trust

> does not bode well for the future of virtuality in organizations. If we are to enjoy the efficiencies and other benefits of the virtual organization, we will have to rediscover how to run organizations based more on trust than on control. Virtuality requires trust to make it work. Technology on its own is not enough. (p. 5)

Concluding Remarks

Elements of connection, then, have been shown to be important for enhancing creativity in traditional organizational and group designs, and crucial to the success of virtual teams. However, there is still considerable question about the unique dimensions of connection specific to highly creative virtual teams—those dimensions that will help to create a bond over time and distance, and will allow for a work environment enhancing creativity. The major objective of the current study was to decipher the key dimensions necessary for creating a work environment conducive to creativity in virtual teams. Connection emerged as one of the key categories of the social context for creativity in virtual teams. (The specific dimensions that make up connection will be outlined in the "Findings" section of this chapter.)

METHODS

Data Collection

Nine different virtual teams, with a total of 36 virtual team members, participated in this study. Participation ranged from 100% of the team members in two teams to 25% of the members in one team. For the other six teams, participation ranged between 50-83% of the team members. (*In this chapter, names of the teams, individual team members, and other company specific information have been disguised to ensure the anonymity of the study's participants.*)

One semi-structured interview was conducted with each participant. Interviews were conducted over the telephone and were audio-taped (with the consent of the participant). In the interviews, team members were asked to discuss a variety of topics. Participants were asked to (a) provide background on the organization in which the team resides; (b) discuss their specific role in the team and describe a typical work day; (c) describe the characteristics, behaviors, and norms of their virtual team; (d) describe what they liked and did not like about working in a virtual team; (e) address the strengths and limitations of virtual teams; (f) describe how the creative process evolves in their virtual team; (g) share two stories of projects completed by their team—one story that they felt exemplified high creativity, and one story which exemplified low creativity (Amabile, 1990; Amabile and S. Gryskiewicz, 1987); and (h) comment on how crucial several specific dimensions of the work environment were to the effectiveness of their virtual team (dimensions previously shown as important for the realization of creativity, Amabile, 1990; Amabile and S. Gryskiewicz, 1987; Amabile and N. Gryskiewicz, 1989; Ekvall, 1983; and Ekvall et al., 1983). (Data that emerged from discussion of the last two topics— (g) and (h)—are particularly relevant to this chapter's discussion.)

After the interview, participants were either e-mailed or mailed a background survey. Thirty-three (out of 36) participants returned the background survey. The purpose of the survey was to provide descriptive information on the individual virtual team member, the virtual team, and the organization in which the virtual team resided. The survey was a mixture of both closed-ended and open-ended questions. Section I asked about the individual virtual team member—age, gender, educational level, employment background, and experience and comfort level with information technology. Section II asked for information on the virtual team—size, duration, mission, and specific tasks. It also asked about participants' previous work experience in teams that were not virtual. Section III asked about the frequency with which team members used various methods of communication. It also asked for specific examples of information technology used by the team. Section IV assessed the team's climate for creativity. (This measure was taken from VanGundy, 1984.)

The Sample

Sampling in qualitative research is typically characterized as purposive or theoretical (Miles and Huberman, 1994; Strauss and Corbin, 1990, 1998). Maximum variation sampling is a form of purposive sampling in which the researcher deliberately selects a heterogeneous sample and observes the commonalities in their experiences (Miles and Huberman, 1994). *Maximum variation sampling* was the method that guided sampling in this study. Teams were purposively selected to vary on several key team and individual participant-level characteristics to increase the generalizability of the study's results.

Nature of the work. Teams varied with respect to the nature of their work and the organizations in which they resided. The nine teams fell into four major categories: organizational consulting firms, educational consortiums, on-line service providers, and product design engineers.

Three teams were organizational consulting firms including (a) Alpha Consultants Incorporated (ACI), specializing in assisting clients with organizational change; (b) Vital Training Group (VTG), specializing in personal productivity and time management training, and helping clients streamline their workflow; and (c) Jacobs/Taylor, who assisted clients in technological diffusion.

Two teams were educational consortiums. The Job Search Consortium team was composed of a group of career development professionals from universities with small, but high quality, MBA programs, that had come together to "create the critical mass" to put on an effective, annual recruiting event for their students. The Electronic Learning Consortium (ELC) team was composed of four developers, responsible for developing and maintaining a text-based, educational virtual community for primary, secondary, and university students, dedicated to education, medicine, psychology and disability issues.

Three teams were classified as on-line service providers. Two (of the three) teams resided in the same organization, Worldwide Software Development, a large software development company. The WN-Current Events team was responsible for producing an on-line publication which featured a calendar of events and directory of content of what was happening on the on-line service network. The WN-Religion Forum team managed an on-line chat on religion, sponsored by Worldwide Software Development's on-line service network. The third on-line service provider team resided in OfficeTech, a large, multinational organization that manufacturers business machines and computers. The major work of the OfficeTech team was to develop and sustain a company virtual community to foster knowledge sharing among globally dispersed workers in the corporation.

The final team was made up of product design engineers, all of whom worked full-time for AutoMax, a large auto manufacturing company. The engineers were responsible for designing the electronic side of the car—designing circuit boards for radios, clusters, odometers, anti-lock brakes, and electric windows.

Methods of communication. Teams varied in the methods of communication used, and the degree of face-to-face communication utilized. Results for how frequently each individual team used each of 12 different communication methods are presented in Table 1. The most frequently used communication method for each team is shown in bold. E-mail was the most frequently used method of communication in seven out of the nine teams.

Interview data revealed the degree of face-to-face communication used within the teams varied from none to a few times a week. The AutoMax and WN-Current Events teams had the most frequent face-to-face communication, with members in the same geographic location meeting a few times a week. Jacobs/Taylor was next, with face-to-face communication occurring at least on a monthly basis. Members of ACI, the Job Search Consortium, OfficeTech, and VTG teams met between two to four times a year. There was no face-to-face communication between team members on the ELC and the WN-Religion Forum teams.

Table 1: Mean Frequency of Methods of Communication for Each Team

Method	Org. Cons.			Educ. Cons.		On-line Serv. Prov.			Engineers
	ACI	J/T	VTG	ELC	JSC	OfTch	WN-CE	WN-R	A/Max
Face-to-face	1.2	2.5	1.3	1.0	1.0	1.0	2.3	1.0	3.3
Videoconferencing	1.0	1.0	1.0	1.7	1.0	1.0	1.0	1.0	1.2
Teleconferencing	1.7	1.5	2.3	1.0	1.2	2.7	3.0	1.0	2.5
Telephone	2.9	**4.5**	3.3	1.7	2.3	4.7	3.7	1.5	**3.7**
Voice mail	2.7	4.0	2.3	1.0	1.8	3.3	3.0	1.0	3.0
Remote screen sharing	1.3	1.0	1.0	2.3	1.0	1.3	1.0	1.0	2.5
Computer conferencing	1.0	1.0	1.0	**5.0**	1.0	1.3	1.7	1.5	2.0
Shared database	2.0	2.5	**5.0**	4.3	1.5	3.0	3.3	2.0	2.7
BBS/listserves	1.5	1.5	2.3	4.0	1.0	3.3	2.7	2.0	2.0
E-mail	**3.2**	4.0	**5.0**	4.7	**3.7**	**5.0**	4.7	**5.0**	**3.7**
Fax	2.7	3.0	2.0	1.0	2.0	2.0	1.0	1.0	1.7
Mail (express/regular)	2.2	2.0	1.7	1.0	1.7	1.3	1.0	1.0	1.2

Note. Scale used: 1 = rarely or never; 2 = a few times a month; 3 = a few times a week; 4 = daily; and 5 = several times a day.

Geographic dispersement. Participants were mostly located within the United States, but were widely dispersed across the country. Participants came from Western, Central, and Eastern sections of the United States. California had the most participants, with 10 out of the 36 participants residing there. One participant was from England. Teams also varied in the number of members in each team that were geographically dispersed, ranging from only one member being physically separated from the rest of the group, to all team members residing in different geographic locations.

Work location. While some team members worked out of a company office, others worked out of offices in their homes. Within teams, the combination of home-based and office-based members varied, ranging from teams where all the members worked in an office setting (AutoMax; Jacobs/Taylor), to a team where all the members worked in their homes (WN-Religion Forum).

Team and individual-participant demographics. The size of the teams varied from 3 to 12 individuals. At the time of the interviews, teams ranged in years in existence from as little as six months to as long as 15 years. Team tenure (defined as the time from when the team was initially formed to the time of the interviews) was not easy to determine, as a characteristic of virtual teams is fluid membership (Kristof et al., 1995). Within a team's lifespan, different members join, exit, and sometimes change roles. This was certainly true for several of the teams in this study, especially the more long-lasting teams.

Individual participants varied widely in age, ranging from 23 to 58. The median age for the total sample was 40. Gender was evenly balanced in the overall sample, with 17 females and 19 males. Educational level varied, although all participants had at least some college education. Four participants had some college education, 7 had a bachelor's degree, 11 had some graduate education, 8 had attained master's degrees, and 3 had attained professional or doctorate degrees.

Data Analysis

The overall approach to data analysis followed Glaser and Strauss' (1967; Strauss and Corbin, 1990, 1998) suggestion of using grounded theory techniques to generate an in-depth understanding of the phenomena under investigation. Value was placed on finding what emerged from the data, from what the participants discussed in the interviews, rather than on forcing the data into preconceived, a priori categories. The results of this study, then, are "grounded" in the phenomena at hand, intimately linked to the data being researched. Data analysis involved two major phases—data description and data explanation (Miles and Huberman, 1994).

Data description. The goal of the data description phase was to make "complicated things understandable by reducing them to their component parts" (Bernard, 1988, cited in Miles and Huberman, 1994, p. 90). Specifically, this phase involved coding the interview transcripts. Two levels of coding were involved—first level coding and pattern coding (Miles and Huberman, 1994). In *first-level coding*, descriptive codes were suggested and data were summarized. One of the most useful techniques during this portion of the analysis process was memoing," the theoretical write-up of ideas about codes and their relationships as they strike the analyst while coding" (Glaser and Strauss, 1967, p. 83). Over 100 theoretical memos were constructed on creating and defining new codes, combining codes, and constructing categories. HyperResearch, a computer-assisted data analysis program, was used during the coding process.

After interview transcripts were coded, the process of *pattern coding* began. Codes generated during first-level coding were reviewed for how they could be grouped together or subsumed into categories, thus creating a smaller number of themes or categories. Memoing (Strauss and Corbin, 1990, 1998), visual displays (Miles and Huberman, 1994), and colleague meetings were utilized to view the data from a broader level.

To assess the reliability of coding, two independent raters check-coded (Miles and Huberman, 1994) selected portions of the interview transcripts that were originally coded by the author. Overall, inter-rater reliability was good, with perfect agreement on 69% of the quotes check-coded. Specific areas of disagreement were discussed until either agreement was reached or a code was revised and renamed to resolve the disagreement. [The issue of reliability and validity in qualitative research is recast in the broader construct of trustworthiness (Lincoln and Guba, 1985). A detailed explanation of the procedures used in the current study to establish trustworthiness is included in Appendix A.]

Data explanation. During this phase, the goal was to make "complicated things understandable by showing how their component parts fit together according to some rules—that is, theory" (Bernard, 1988, cited in Miles and Huberman, 1994, p. 90). Writing theoretical memos (Strauss and Corbin, 1990, 1998), and crafting diagrams and visual displays of the data (Miles and Huberman, 1994) were used to examine the relationships between the categories that emerged during the data description phase.

Survey data. Descriptives and frequencies were calculated on the closed-ended survey data questions. Responses to open-ended survey questions were coded and categorized.

Data Presentation

The interview data to be presented in the next section focuses on describing and explaining the environmental features that emerged from what virtual team members shared when asked to discuss high and low creative experiences in their teams. To better describe and explain the answers to these questions, the raw data or the participants' own words are provided. The goal is to provide an absorbing, coherent, and candid account of the virtual teams under investigation. It is also worth noting that in presenting the raw words of the participants, I did minimal editing, favoring authenticity over readability. A few conventions were used to present the words of these virtual team members. Pauses are indicated by three dots (...). Pertinent expressed emotions or nonverbal behavior are included within brackets, for example [laughs]. If irrelevant information was deleted from a quote, it is indicated by four dots (....). On occasion, clarifying information was added to a participant's words, which is enclosed in brackets: [ ]. My own dialog within a quote is indicated by pointed brackets: { }.

FINDINGS

A key category that emerged as important to an environment encouraging the realization of creativity in virtual teams was **connection**, defined as the elements that need to be in place for a team to develop and maintain identity and a sense of community. Connection was further subdivided into *task* and *interpersonal* connection. Environmental features within the overriding category of connection were summarized into five dimensions, each of which ranged from high (facilitates creativity) to low (inhibits creativity), shown in Table 2. Task connection was made up of the dimensions of *dedication/commitment*, and *goal clarity*; and interpersonal connection was made up of the dimensions of *information sharing, trust,* and *personal bond*. Each of these dimensions is described in more detail in the following sections.

Table 2: Dimensions of Establishing Connection for Creativity in Virtual Teams

---

Task Connection:

Dedication/Commitment — a sense of dedication, intense involvement, and commitment to the work; the ability to work hard on difficult tasks and problems, and persevere.

Goal Clarity — clearly defined, developed goals (through constant clarification and feedback) shared by all members.

Interpersonal Connection:

Information Sharing — regular communication; sharing the results of one's efforts; providing needed information; timely updating of information.

Personal Bond — a personal connection among team members; a "family-like" feeling; a sense of connectedness that goes beyond common goals and commitment to the work, to a bond in which team members are also committed to and care for one another.

Trust — a sense of trust that team members will do their designated tasks within the designated time frame; trust in the accurateness of the information provided by other team members; trust that team members will give honest and constructive feedback on ideas, thoughts, and creative efforts shared electronically; trust in one another's expertise and ability to do the work effectively; and trust that team members will hold ideas shared in confidence if requested.

Task Connection

Dedication/commitment. When team members discussed high creativity experiences, they spoke of having a strong sense of dedication, intense involvement, and commitment to the project or task. They worked hard on difficult tasks and problems, and persevered. On the other hand, in low creativity experiences, the degree of commitment to a particular project differed among team members. Differing levels of commitment not only hampered creativity, but caused the mere existence of a project to be in jeopardy. Richard (of OfficeTech) candidly shares how he and his partner differed in terms of their levels of commitment to a project. As a result, a potentially creative outcome was dropped.

Okay, my choice for that [low creativity experience], and I'll be interested if Keith chooses the same thing, was what I would call [the] knowledge sharing model. Keith is the deep thinker and one of his pet areas is simulation. And a particular tool for simulation is something called [name deleted].... Keith was very keen to develop a model of knowledge sharing and learning in a professional services practice, and got the software, did some preliminary work in developing a simulation. He sent me a copy of his model electronically, and I was going to analyze his work and we were going to collaborate on it. I was going to extend the model in ways I felt it needed to be, so on and so forth. The long and the short of it is it didn't work.... The reason for failure is pretty darn simple. And that is, it wasn't as high a priority for me as it was for him.... It's one of those things that I professed to be extremely interested in, but when push comes to shove, other things take precedence. So, I feel a little guilty about it, to be honest with you. And I am genuinely interested in it.... I would like to believe that we will get back to this. But it clearly was an example of low level of creativity and low level of anything.... I really needed to be able to walk away from the office for a week, or more, and say, I'm unreachable, I'm doing something else. And for better or for worse, I didn't choose to do that. (Richard, OfficeTech)

Goal clarity. A team's goals, and the clarity of those goals was a prevalent characteristic of high creativity stories. Interestingly, although goals were crucial for success in creative work, some participants felt it took more effort in a virtual team to make sure those goals were clear. Constant checking, feedback, and asking questions were needed to ensure clarification.

In low creativity stories, participants described situations in which goals were fuzzy or unclear. As a result, misunderstandings and faulty assumptions occurred, and valuable time was wasted. Melissa (of VTG) illustrates how a lack of clarity around the team's goals and roles lead to frustration, misunderstandings, and faulty assumptions.

{Let's turn now to a project that may have been completed by the team in which the creativity was rather low.} It would have to do with a project that we did with a sister company of ours digitally... it was basically a marketing project we did.... It was the least creative project, and it was the least fun. It was the most aggravating, and it was the most... where everybody was just pulling their hair out.... It should have been a very fun project. It was not fun because there were a lot of assumptions made, which I think sometimes a problem with [a] virtual environment is that assumptions are made by one party sitting in their office, closed door, typing away, and they said, oh yes this must be what this meant, so they fire off an e-mail. We interpret it a completely different way. We don't have the luxury of a dialogue back and forth. Instead we have the aggravation of e-mails back and forth, one shot e-mails. So there was a tremendous amount of unclarity, and there was a lot of assumptions made about which party would do what, and who would pay for what, and what the end result would be, and basically what people's roles would be. So potentially it was a good project gone bad. (Melissa, VTG)

Additionally, for some of the teams, creativity suffered due to the indecision that resulted from unclear goals. Consequently, some projects became unwieldy. Cheryl (of ACI) revisits the "Manual from Hell" project to illustrate how lack of goal clarity turned a project into a frustrating, massive undertaking.

{What about an experience then in which you felt the creativity of the group was rather low?} I don't have to think very far for this one. [Laughs] We have had a few little mishaps in my career here. The major one was what was now [we] affectionately refer to as the "Manual from Hell." It was a project where three consultants were writing this manual, and they each had a different section that they were supposed to write. And then I was to edit it and put it together and it was going to go to the client. It was actually pretty simple. But it just turned into this massive undertaking. It was like opening Pandora's box. Once they started writing, it was like, oh, we've got to talk about this and we've got to go out here and then oh well, let's talk about this. So, it just grew and grew and grew and grew. And it got to the point where there was no way that it was going to be finished when it was supposed to be. (Cheryl, ACI)

Finally, even when goals were communicated clearly in initial face-to-face meetings, as team members dispersed, in low creativity experiences goals were sometimes forgotten or dropped.

... we talk about it in January, we plan some things, then we have that May meeting, then we have the agenda, and we're like, oh, yeah, that's great, let's do this, this and this. And then each day that goes by, the more likely people are to forget.... And so I think periodic e-mails or kind of 'to do' lists for the group are really important actually to keep the clarity of the goals 'cause it's real easy to forget about stuff. (Jeff, Job Search Consortium)

Interpersonal Connection

Information sharing. Information is the fuel that feeds the fire of creativity in virtual teams. Information sharing is closely tied to the degree of trust between team members, and both trust and information sharing were perceived by interviewees as crucial for creative work. Highly creative stories described team members who: (a) communicated regularly with one another, (b) shared the results of their efforts, (c) offered open and honest feedback, and (d) updated information regularly.

When people meet in a face-to-face meeting, individuals can be directly asked for information, feedback, or input. In virtual teams, individuals can also be directly asked electronically, but it is easier for individuals to "disappear" or drop out of the discussion.

To avoid this, norms for communicating and exchanging information were created in many of the teams (for example, requiring all team members to return phone calls within 24 hours; or requiring daily updating of project information into shared databases). However, in low creativity experiences, norms for communication were either not established, unclear, or ignored. Communication, and as a result, information exchange, became inconsistent or nonexistent.

Just as too little information can hamper creativity, so too can an *overload of information*. In low creativity stories, team members attempting to deal with the constant flow of information between themselves and their geographically dispersed team members sometimes were overwhelmed with more information than they could effectively comprehend.

Trust. The most frequently-mentioned environmental feature surrounding the high creativity stories was trust. Trust was composed of several elements: (a) a sense of trust that individuals would do what they said within the designated time frame; (b) trust in the accurateness of the information provided by other team members; (c) trust that team members would give honest and constructive feedback on ideas, thoughts, and creative efforts shared electronically; (d) trust in one another's expertise and ability to do the work effectively; and (e) trust that other team members would hold ideas shared in confidence if requested. Participants felt it took a great deal of trust to share ideas and accomplish work electronically: "There's a level of trust with putting everything that you're doing on [the] computer, and knowing everybody's seeing everything you're doing" (Melissa, VTG). In a virtual environment, without the nonverbal indicators available in face-to-face encounters, trust was viewed as essential. Trust was seen as crucial not only for the team to be creative, but for the team to even exist.

Although trust was seen as essential in a virtual environment, it was sometimes difficult to establish, and it developed slowly. Trust developed from a sense of accountability, from seeing that others followed through on what they said they would do. Trust was also based on a belief in the expertise of others, and on positive, ongoing experiences with one another.

In low creativity stories, the level of trust waned, was lost, or did not exist at all. The most frequently mentioned reason for a decline in the level of trust was low accountability, team members not carrying through on their designated work, or not "pulling their weight." For example, in the ACI team, all of the team members interviewed mentioned the same project in their low creativity stories, adoringly named, the Manual from Hell. Lack of accountability was a key factor in why the team members felt the experience was low in creativity.

Personal bond. One of the more intriguing themes that emerged was the ability of virtual teams to establish a personal connection or bond. Team members, even though separated by distance and sometimes time, in many instances suggested they felt like a family. I believe that developing and maintaining this kind of personal connection is critical for creativity to occur in virtual teams. A personal sense of connection can lessen the problematic misunderstandings and faulty assumptions that hamper creativity, and help to develop the trust, respect, understanding, acceptance, and compassion that team members need to feel comfortable sharing ideas and taking risks across distances. This kind of connection goes beyond common goals and commitment to the work. Team members are also committed to and care for one another.

Quite honestly, I was fascinated at the wealth of data that centered around this theme. I had no idea when I began this project that such a strong personal bond could be made between individuals working at distance. And yet these teams proved that it can. A personal connection was established through face-to-face get-togethers; sharing humor and being playful with one another; sharing personal issues and crises with other team members; and, in general, functioning as a support network for one another.

Although one of the teams had never met face-to-face, for the majority of teams *face-to-face contact* was beneficial in beginning to develop a personal bond between team members. Several participants shared how their relationships with team members changed after they had met one another face-to-face. For example,

The fact that we are actually talking to the U.S., and we know names and everything, it really has made a big impact and a big improvement.... Since I went over there [to the United States] last October, and that was the first time anyone had gone over there from our area. I spent 3 weeks with them. When I came back, we've had an excellent relationship since then.... because up until then it was just a name. (Eric, AutoMax)

Sharing humor was another way virtual team members established a personal bond. Even for one of the teams that had never met face-to-face, humor helped to build a sense of community.

We don't feel impersonal, because we translate our humor through the written word.... So we are using little bits of humor, and we're real loose and personal, we're not rigid. And we're very, very comfortable with each other. (Scott, WN-Religion Forum)

Sometimes, playful games were used to develop the team's identity.

We do crazy, silly little game things that build identity, little competitions, or silly things, that we share. And those become the inside jokes that people outside don't know but it forms identity and helps build community. (Chad, Jacobs/Taylor)

In any relationship, taking the time to show *personal interest* in another person helps to create a bond. The same holds true for virtual teams as well. Team members took the time to pass along information they thought other team members might be interested in. At times, taking a personal interest in one another went beyond simply forwarding interesting information or sharing jokes. It involved sharing *personal issues and crises* with one another, and supporting one another through these crises. This kind of sharing was instrumental in creating a "family-like" feeling between team members.

This group of six people is up there close to my family in terms of folks I feel connected with. I mean, and it's not just because we're all in this one life boat called economic survival, but we have been through each other's personal crises. When Pam's husband was sick for so very long, and dying for years, and fighting like heck, and I've been going through some very traumatic times with my older teenage son, and these people are... they're just supportive. I mean, there's just no other way to say it. This is family. (Jason, ACI)

Finally, functioning as a *support network* for one another, both personally and professionally, has solidified the connection between team members.

> The things that I like are the camaraderie. I feel that I have a built-in support system.... I think having people that you know are always going through the same thing that you are, and being able to call and bounce ideas off of each other, that is a very supportive environment, and something that I really enjoy. (Elaine, Job Search Consortium)

So, it is possible to establish a *real* personal connection in a virtual team, even in those teams where no face-to-face contact occurs. Scott, a WN-Religion Forum team member who has never met the other team members, shares:

> {So there's kind of a connectedness between the members?} A very personal one. A very, you know, human one. And I think a lot of people who are not familiar with virtual teams would definitely expect that we're all a bunch of robots, you know what I mean? You just automatically assume that if you're just communicating through a computer, how could there be any connection, how could there [be] anything personal, how could there be anything warm about it, and there is. (Scott, WN-Religion Forum)

LIMITATIONS AND FUTURE DIRECTIONS

It is a humbling experience to consider the limitations of a project that has consumed a major portion of one's time. However, it is crucial to review a study's weaknesses so that future researchers may consider adapting their research designs to avoid these limitations.

A major limitation of the current study concerns the study's methodology. Two methods, semi-structured interviews and a background survey, were used. A good deal of the study's conclusions, however, relied on the interview data. In the interviews, individuals were asked to recall creative experiences in their virtual teams. However, memory biases could have affected the accuracy of reporting, as recollections may have been clouded or incomplete.

This research could be improved by using a case study research design (Yin, 1994). This type of research design is particularly appropriate for pursuing a deep level of understanding of the dynamics within single settings (Eisenhardt, 1989). A key principle of case study research is *triangulation of data*. Triangulation has been defined as the combination of methodologies in the same study. Triangulation rests on the assumption that the weakness in a single method will be compensated by the strengths of another method. Thus, triangulation of data improves the credibility of a study's conclusions (Jick, 1979). In case study research, Yin (1994) outlined six sources of evidence that are typically used—documentation, archival records, interviews, direct observations, participant-observations, and physical artifacts. In the current line of research, data triangulation could be strengthened by incorporating evidence from direct and/or participant observation. Actual observations of the virtual team's creative experiences while they are occurring would add insight beyond the interview data. In addition, as virtual teams now have the ability to document and archive their creative process through electronic mail and shared databases, a review of these documents and electronic communications might be beneficial to future investigations.

A second limitation concerns the assessment of high and low creative experiences. Stories of high and low creativity were shared by the team members themselves. There was, however, no validation of these high and low creativity stories with independent experts or outsiders to the team. External validation of the high and low creativity stories by outsiders to the team would be beneficial in future investigations.

A third suggested improvement would be to utilize *member checks* (Lincoln and Guba, 1985) in the data analysis process. Member checks typically involve verifying the study's data, analytic categories, interpretations, and conclusions with the members from whom the data were originally collected. In particular, it would be important to have virtual team members report on which of the dimensions that emerged in this study they view as most critical to establishing connection while performing creative work.

Fourth, as this was an exploratory study, there were no control or comparison face-to-face teams. However, future researchers may want to explore differences in the impact of the dimensions found in this investigation on virtual and face-to-face teams. The question might be, "Are certain dimensions more crucial for one type of team over the other?" A comparison of traditional team structures with virtual teams from the same organization would assist in deciphering these differences, if any.

A final limitation concerns the study's sample. Background survey data revealed that overall the study's participants felt they had an advanced degree of experience with information technology, and were relatively comfortable with information technology as well. A sample that included individuals who felt they had less experience with information technology, and felt less comfortable with information technology may have yielded different results. In addition, the sample included three organizational consulting teams. Typically, consultants are trained to be analytical and possess excellent communication skills. Future research should include an even more diverse cross section of virtual teams with regards to the nature of their work.

IMPLICATIONS AND CONCLUSIONS

I think because virtual teaming is a comparatively new organizational approach that it definitely adds challenge, and adds stress. I think a lot of companies, mine included, are rushing rather head long into an embrace of the virtual concept. And I must say, even though I am a proponent of an aspect of virtuality, this community business, I do have some reservations about whether people will be able to accommodate the new framework of the virtual workplace as rapidly as management expects it to. (Richard, OfficeTech)

The present research stresses the importance of the human side, and the personal connection in virtual teams. This realization has practical implications for organizations considering moving to a virtual design, and for managers and team leaders of existing virtual teams. As the quote at the top of this section indicates, management in many contemporary companies are "rushing rather head long into an embrace of the virtual concept" (Richard, OfficeTech). However, management cannot assume that they can move workers into their homes and simply leave them there to do work. It is important for managers and team leaders of virtual teams to actively encourage and support a personal bond between virtual team members. This may include providing funds for team members to get together initially to discuss common goals and shared values, and to build trust. Further, once the team is up and running, having periodic face-to-face, social get-togethers or celebrations after completion of particular projects can also help encourage and maintain team identity.

Aside from face-to-face meetings, there are other ways in which organizations, managers, and team leaders can encourage connection, and as a result, creativity in virtual teams. Companies or teams can sponsor team games. Or perhaps one team member may function as a team historian, documenting team stories and sending them out electronically to members. For teams that do not meet face-to-face, even low-tech strategies such as sending all team members pictures of one another can be beneficial (O'Hara-Devereaux and Johansen, 1994). Any number of techniques can be used to help establish a personal connection among team members. The point is it cannot be ignored, but rather must be actively encouraged. The human side of teams does not go away just because members are interacting electronically. As Jason (of ACI) shares:

> I don't think that people should get it in their head that because I'm working at a distance with somebody that the human side and the human issues go away. They don't. All of the personality or what people call personality issues, all of the communication issues, all of the need to respect and be conscious of the other person's feelings and where they're coming from, all of that is still there. Whether you're in the same office building and conference room together, or whether you're on the other end of a telephone or a computer terminal, the person doesn't go away in a virtual team. What we have had to do is to work very hard to keep this a very personal relationship. You have to respect the fact that it's another human being who has feelings and emotions, and ups and downs, and assumptions and lenses. That doesn't go away when you [are] working [at] a distance. And you have to find ways to manage all of that if your team is going to be successful. (Jason, ACI)

To assist in establishing a connection between virtual team members, training is needed prior to moving into a virtual team design. Virtual team members need to be trained in how to use a range of collaborative software and information technology to enhance the team's work. Training, however, needs to go beyond how to use the technology, to incorporate how to communicate effectively through these kinds of technologies. Since many of the traditional nonverbal cues (body language, hand gestures) used in communication are lost in electronic interchanges, virtual team members benefit from training in how to use more linguistic precision in their communications (Townsend, DeMarie, and Hendrickson, 1996). Virtual team members also need training in team management, and interpersonal skills such as maintaining esteem, reaching consensus, and conflict resolution (George, 1996). Lastly, training and educating team members in the different working styles of each of the team members is essential. This type of training, if conducted early on in the team's development, will help eliminate misunderstandings that may be disruptive to the creative process. Team members who understand one another's working styles and trust one another are less likely to attach negative interpretations to incomplete or unclear communications (O'Hara-Devereaux and Johansen, 1994). Training should occur not only at the team's inception, but when new members enter the team as well.

I have emphasized that managers and team leaders need to help create a personal bond between the members of their teams. But managers and team leaders of virtual teams need other skills as well. Team leaders need to take care in the communication of team goals and tasks, making sure their communications are as clear as possible. The development of writing skills for managers has been, and will continue to be, important.

Team leaders must also develop norms for communication within the team. O'Hara-Devereaux and Johansen refer to this as creating "a communications drumbeat" (1994, p. 174). Devising a communication routine, whether daily or weekly, is critical to ensure regular and consistent communication and information sharing. Further, particular attention should be paid to matching the message of the communication with the appropriate method.

Electronic links have increased connectivity so that team members have access to other individuals across the globe. However, as connectivity increases, so does the amount of information provided. Managers must be sensitive to the overwhelming amount of information that can be provided, and develop ways to deal with and eliminate information overload, both for the team members and themselves.

One last, and perhaps most important, future implication of this research was suggested by the participants themselves—the impact working virtually will have on society and its members. This area of proposed research, while perhaps outside of the scope of the current study, will certainly need to be addressed as virtual teams have been predicted to be the wave of the future (Wilson, George, and Wellins, 1994). If this is true, and virtual work will become the standard mode of working in the future, how will this impact society at large? If the trend is toward teams and organizations composed of members that are increasingly working out-of-site of one another, geographically dispersed, and communicating through electronic means, what will happen to the interpersonal skills of those workers? Will they change? Will our society, in general, become too isolated? Some of the participants in this study were not worried about this dilemma.

I think it's [virtual work] a fond hope for the future because I see it as a way of increasing connected[ness] in an otherwise, you know... I think [it] may actually go against the trend of isolation, individual isolation in time. That's sort of a macro social thing, you know what I mean? (Laura, ELC)

For other participants, however, this was a real concern.

But if you look at books about the future, everybody predicted this, that we would get more and more isolated. And it really is happening. We are getting more and more isolated in a physical way. So it's something for people to look out for. (Patricia, WN-Religion Forum)

I personally do not believe that virtual teams will replace conventional teams in performing creative work (or any type of work for that matter). Virtual teams seem to work best when the nature of the work is easily broken down into components or tasks, and those tasks are assigned to individual team members or subgroups, who then work alone on their assigned pieces, and then come together again as an entire team for feedback, revisions, and finalization of the total project (Nemiro, 1998). However, not all creative efforts may be so easily divided into sections. Managers or team leaders will need to consider seriously whether the creative task at hand can be effectively accomplished with a virtual team design, and if so, in what ways they can best establish connection to enhance the creativity of these teams. It will also be the task of future researchers to determine the situations or types of creative tasks in which virtual teams are most appropriate, and when they are not.

APPENDIX A

How Trustworthiness Was Established

For qualitative researchers, issues of reliability and validity are recast into the broader concept of trustworthiness (Lincoln and Guba, 1985). Trustworthiness considers (a) the confidence in the truth of the findings (validity and credibility); (b) the extent to which the findings of a particular inquiry have applicability in other contexts or with other respondents (transferability); (c) the extent to which the findings of an inquiry could be repeated if the inquiry were replicated with the same or similar subjects under the same conditions (reliability); and (d) the degree to which the findings of an inquiry are determined by the subjects and conditions of the inquiry and not the biases of the researcher (neutrality). A variety of techniques were used to enhance this study's trustworthiness.

To establish *internal validity and credibility*, during data analysis I searched for disconfirming evidence and "negative cases," with the intent of constantly revising developing categories (Glaser and Strauss, 1967). To increase *external validity and transferability*, maximum variation sampling was used. Further, emphasis was placed on gathering evidence to produce thick descriptions, in-depth descriptions of the context or setting within which the investigation took place. Thick descriptions are necessary to determine whether the theory that emerged from one context can be transferred to another (Lincoln and Guba, 1985). Information on the experiences of the virtual team members was collected through interviews, background surveys, and in a few cases, company documentation to help create thick descriptions.

Several steps were taken to ensure the *reliability and dependability* of the study. First, both the interview protocol and background survey were piloted and pretested. Second, triangulation, or the use of multiple methods, was incorporated (although on a limited basis) by collecting information through interviews, background surveys, and in a few cases, company documentation. Third, a thorough audit trail was maintained, composed of the following (all recommended by Halpern, 1983):

1. The *raw data*, original tapes of interviews and back-up copies of each; transcribed interviews in both hard copy and on disk; original background surveys and photocopies of each.
2. A *participant recruiting content notebook*, with contact summary sheets which included contact information, logs of each exchange, and all written correspondences (letters and e-mail messages).
3. A *data collection chart*, which tracked the dates of when interviews were scheduled, completed, transcribed, and first-level coded; and also tracked dates of when the background surveys were sent to each participant, when reminders were sent out, when surveys were returned, and when the data was entered into SPSS for Windows.
4. A *methodological journal and memos*: a diary of what was done in the data collection process; memos immediately following each interview to outline reactions and problems; memos written to comment on methodological issues and problems.
5. An *analysis journal and memos*: a diary outlining the data analysis procedure and theoretical development; over 100 memos on codes and their relationships, emerging theory, and on personal biases, feelings and frustrations during the data analysis process.

Colleague reviews and check-coding were also used to establish reliability. Meetings with colleagues were used to discuss the utility of the codes generated, and interpretations created, and to brainstorm possible categories. The reliability of codes within categories was tested with two independent raters coding selected portions of the interview transcripts.

Neutrality was established by reflecting on potential sources of bias and error in method-ological memos, utilizing effective listening skills during the interview process, and being respectful and nonjudgmental of what participants said during their interviews.

REFERENCES

Abbey, A., and Dickson, J. (1983). R&D work climate and innovation in semiconductors, *Academy of Management Journal, 26*, 362-368.

Amabile, T. M. (1979). Effects of external evaluation on artistic creativity. *Journal of Personality and Social Psychology, 37*, 221-233.

Amabile, T. M. (1982). Children's artistic creativity: Detrimental effects of competition in a field setting. *Personality and Social Psychology Bulletin, 8*, 573-578.

Amabile, T. M. (1983). *The social psychology of creativity*. New York, NY: Springer-Verlag.

Amabile, T. M. (1985). Motivation and creativity: Effects of motivational orientation on creative writers. *Journal of Personality and Social Psychology, 48*, 393-399.

Amabile, T. M. (1988). A model of creativity and innovation in organizations. In B. M. Staw and L. L. Cummings (Eds.), *Research in organizational behavior* (Vol. 10, pp. 123-167). Greenwich, CT: JAI Press.

Amabile, T. M. (1989, November). *How work environments affect creativity*. Paper presented at the IEEE International Conference on Systems, Man, and Cybernetics, Cambridge, MA.

Amabile, T. M. (1990). Within you, without you: The social psychology of creativity and beyond. In M. A. Runco and R. S. Albert (Eds.), *Theories of creativity* (pp. 61-91). Newbury Park, CA: Sage Publications.

Amabile, T. M., and Gitomer, J. (1984). Children's artistic creativity: Effects of choice in task materials. *Personality and Social Psychology Bulletin, 10*, 209-215.

Amabile, T. M., and Gryskiewicz, S. S. (1987). *Creativity in the R&D laboratory*. Technical Report #30. Greensboro, NC: Center for Creative Leadership.

Amabile, T. M., and Gryskiewicz, N. D. (1989). The creative environment scales: Work Environment Inventory. *Creativity Research Journal, 2*, 231-253.

Amabile, T. M., Dejong, W., and Lepper, M. R. (1976). Effects of externally imposed deadlines on subsequent intrinsic motivation. *Journal of Personality and Social Psychology, 34*, 92-98.

Amabile, T. M., Goldfarb, P., and Brackfield, S. C. (1990). Social influences on creativity: Evaluation, coaction, and surveillance. *Creativity Research Journal, 3*, 6-21.

Amabile, T. M., Hennessey, B., and Grossman, B. S. (1986). Social influences on creativity: The effects of contracted-for reward. *Journal of Personality and Social Psychology, 50*, 14-23.

Andrews, F. (1975). Social and psychological factors which influence the creative process. In I. Taylor and J. W. Getzels (Eds.), *Perspectives in creativity* (pp. 117-145). Chicago, IL: Aldine Publishing Co.

Bernard, H. R. (1988). *Research methods in cultural anthropology*. Newbury Park, CA: Sage Publications.

Byrne, J. (1993, February 3). The virtual corporation. *Business Week*, 98-103.

Davidow, W., and Malone, M. (1992). *The virtual corporation*. New York, NY: HarperCollins.

Eisenhardt, K. (1989). Building theories from case study research. *Academy of Management Review, 14*, 532-550.

Ekvall, G. (1983). *Climate, structure, and innovativeness of organizations* (Report 1). Stockholm: Swedish Council for Management and Organizational Behavior.

Ekvall, G., Arvonen, J., and Waldenstrom-Lindblad, I. (1983). *Creative organizational climate: Construction and validation of a measuring instrument* (Report 2). Stockholm: Swedish Council for Management and Organizational Behavior.

Galbraith, J. (1995). *Designing organizations.* San Francisco, CA: Jossey-Bass.

Geber, B. (1995). Virtual teams. *Training, 32,* 36-40.

George, J. (1996, November). Virtual best practice: How to successfully introduce virtual team-working. *Teams,* 38-45.

Glaser, B., and Strauss, A. (1967). *The discovery of grounded theory.* Chicago, IL: Aldine Publishing Company.

Halpern, E. S. (1983). *Auditing naturalistic inquiries: The development and application of a model.* Unpublished doctoral dissertation, Indiana University.

Handy, C. (1995, May-June). Trust and the virtual organization. *Harvard Business Review,* 2-8.

Harrington, D., Block, J., and Block, J. (1987). Testing aspects of Carl Rogers' theory of creative environments: Child-rearing antecedents of creative potential in young adolescents. *Journal of Personality and Social Psychology, 52,* 851-856.

Jick, T. (1979). Mixing qualitative and quantitative methods: Triangulation in action. *Administrative Science Quarterly, 24,* 602-611.

Kiesler, S., Siegel, J., and McGuire, T. (1991). Social aspects of computer-mediated communication. In C. Dunlop and R. Kling (Eds.), *Computerization and controversy: Value conflicts and social choices* (pp. 330-349). Boston, MA: Harcourt Brace.

Kossler, M., and Prestridge, S. (1996). Geographically dispersed teams. *Issues and Observations (Center for Creative Leadership), 16,* 9-11.

Kristof, A., Brown, K., Sims, H., and Smith, K. (1995). The virtual team: A case study and inductive model. In M. Beyerlein and D. Johnson (Eds.), *Advances in interdisciplinary studies of work teams: Knowledge teams the creative edge,* (Vol. 2, pp. 229-253). Greenwich, CT: JAI Press.

Kruglanski, A. W., Friedman, I., and Zeevi, G. (1971). The effects of extrinsic incentive on some qualitative aspects of task performance. *Journal of Personality, 39,* 606-617.

Lincoln, Y. S., and Guba, E. G. (1985). *Naturalistic inquiry.* Newbury Park, CA: Sage Publications.

Lipnack, J., and Stamps, J. (1997). *Virtual teams: Reaching across space, time and organizations with technology.* New York, NY: John Wiley and Sons.

Lubart, T. (1990). Creativity and cross-cultural variation. *International Journal of Psychology, 25,* 39-59.

McGraw, K., and McCullers, J. (1979). Evidence of a detrimental effect of extrinsic incentives on breaking a mental set. *Journal of Experimental Social Psychology, 15,* 285-294.

Miles, M. B., and Huberman, A. M. (1994). *Qualitative data analysis* (2nd edition). Thousand Oaks, CA: Sage Publications.

Nemiro, J. (1998). *Creativity in virtual teams.* Unpublished doctoral dissertation. Claremont Graduate University, Claremont, CA.

Nemiro, J., and Runco, M. A. (1996). *Creativity and innovation in small groups.* Unpublished manuscript, The Claremont Graduate School, Claremont, CA.

O'Hara-Devereaux, M., and Johansen, R. (1994). *Global work: Bridging distance, culture, and time.* San Francisco, CA: Jossey-Bass.

Pelz, D. C., and Andrews, F. M. (1966). *Scientists in organizations.* New York, NY: John Wiley and Sons.

Perolle, J. (1991). Conversations and trust in computer interfaces. In C. Dunlop and R. Kling (Eds.), *Computerization and controversy: Value conflicts and social choices* (pp. 356-363). Boston, MA: Harcourt Brace.

Rogers, C. (1954). Towards a theory of creativity. *ETC: A Review of General Semantics, 11,* 249-260.

Runco, M. A. (1994). Creativity and its discontents. In M. P. Shaw and M. A. Runco (Eds.), *Creativity and affect.* Norwood, NJ: Ablex.

Runco, M. A. (1995). The creativity and job satisfaction of artists in organizations. *Empirical Studies of the Arts, 13,* 39-45.

Shalley, C. E. (1991). Effects of productivity goals, creativity goals, and personal discretion on individual creativity. *Journal of Applied Psychology, 76,* 179-185.

Strauss, A., and Corbin, J. (1990). *Basics of qualitative research.* Newbury Park, CA: Sage Publications.

Strauss, A., and Corbin, J. (1998). *Basics of qualitative research.* 2nd edition. Thousand Oaks, CA: Sage Publications.

Townsend, A., DeMarie, S., and Hendrickson, A. (1996, September). Are you ready for virtual teams? *HR Magazine,* 123-126.

VanGundy, A. (1984). *Managing group creativity: A modular approach to problem solving.* New York, NY: American Management Association.

VanGundy, A. (1987). Organizational creativity and innovation. In S. Isaksen (Ed.), *Frontiers of creativity research: Beyond the basics* (pp. 358-379). New York: Bearly Limited.

West, M. A. (1990). The social psychology of innovation in groups. In M. A. West and J. L. Farr (Eds.), *Innovation and creativity at work* (pp. 309-322). New York, NY: John Wiley and Sons.

West, M. A., and Farr, J. L. (1990). Innovation at work. In M. A. West and J. L. Farr (Eds.), *Innovation and creativity at work* (pp. 3-13). New York, NY: John Wiley and Sons.

Wilson, J., George, J., and Wellins, R. (1994). *Leadership trapeze: Strategies for leadership in team-based organizations.* San Francisco, CA: Jossey-Bass.

Yin, R. (1994). *Case study research: Design and methods.* 2nd edition. Thousand Oaks, CA: Sage Publications.

Chapter VII

Using Patterns to Capture Tacit Knowledge and Enhance Knowledge Transfer in Virtual Teams

Karen L. Lyons
Consultant, USA

The virtual team presents a challenging environment in which to share knowledge. These teams can span time zones, geographies, and even cultures. As a result, storytelling sessions and other two-way communications among team members are frequently unachievable. "Maps" to knowledge experts are useless if these experts cannot be reached at the moment when knowledge is needed. In order to transition knowledge from one virtual team member to another, organizations often resort to sharing knowledge in the form of documents or other types of explicit knowledge. However, explicit knowledge typically lacks the context required to be truly useful to the knowledge consumer. A possible solution to this limitation presents itself from another discipline. Patterns and pattern languages, which have their origin in the field of building architecture and urban design, offer a way to enhance explicit knowledge by capturing the context that is typically missing in documented knowledge and by adding a rich, story-like flavor designed to facilitate knowledge transfer.

Documents and other explicit forms of knowledge representation are often a necessary evil when attempting to share knowledge in a dispersed organization or a virtual team environment. Time differences and geographical displacement limit the availability of experts for consultation with knowledge consumers. Moreover, due to the transitory nature of a virtual team, the knowledge created by one team may not always be available to another team. Team members move on and take their knowledge with them unless a determined effort is made to record that knowledge.

There are several advantages to explicitly documented knowledge. This type of knowledge representation can be categorized by subject matter and can easily be distributed to virtual team members. Documents also preserve knowledge for future use if an expert leaves the organization or when virtual communities of practice dissolve. The primary disadvantage of documented knowledge, however, is its lack of contextual richness. The conversion of knowledge into an explicit, documented form typically results in the loss of tacit knowledge. At an APQC conference, Thomas Davenport summarized this reality best when he stated that "... Knowledge dies when it is disembodied" (Stuart, 1995). Any delay in documenting knowledge could impact the capture of tacit knowledge even further. The longer it takes to record knowledge, the more likely it is that key knowledge components will be overlooked. Knowledge consumers can learn from the assumptions made and the alternatives considered during a problem-solving exercise. Unless compelled to consider these key components, knowledge experts may unwittingly omit contextual information that could be useful to the knowledge consumer, information that will help the consumer adapt the expert's knowledge to fit his own situation.

In contrast to documented knowledge, two-way communication and storytelling are often mentioned as the most effective way to transfer knowledge from one person to another. Stories are rich in context and are enhanced with the gestures, expressions, enthusiasm, and other nonverbal techniques of the storyteller. They are enlivened with characters, dramatic conflict, and the setting within which they transpire. In addition, any interaction with a storyteller, such as a question and answer session, allows the people listening to a story to better adapt the message of the story to their own situation.

In order to best share knowledge in a virtual team environment, a happy medium must be found between easily accessible, yet context-poor explicit knowledge and the richness of knowledge that is captured and transferred in the form of stories. An attempt must be made to externalize as much of an expert's tacit knowledge as possible in a form that can be internalized by others and then used to adapt existing knowledge or to generate new knowledge. Patterns and pattern languages may provide the balance between creating a permanent knowledge record and sharing tacit knowledge in a way that enhances learning and new knowledge creation. The goal of this paper is first to review the importance of storytelling as a method for transferring knowledge and then to introduce readers to *patterns*, their story-like nature and teaching components, and the potential they have for facilitating the transfer of knowledge in a dispersed team environment.

BACKGROUND

The Role of Storytelling in Knowledge Transfer

A great deal of research and literature has been dedicated to the role that storytelling plays in effective knowledge transfer. In order to better understand the value of storytelling in the knowledge transfer process, preliminary definitions of "knowledge" and, in particular, *explicit* versus *tacit* knowledge seem appropriate.

Knowledge might be described as "value added" information. It transcends mere information because it is context specific, it contains meaning and purpose, and it is actionable. Knowledge about previous mistakes, as well as the various assumptions and thought processes taken to arrive at a solution, is just as important as knowledge of successful actions. *Explicit knowledge* is knowledge that has in some way been documented or codified. It is easily classified, categorized, combined, and distributed to others. This is the type of knowledge that is typically stored in a knowledge base or document management system.

Tacit knowledge is knowledge held by human beings. It is based upon personal experience that is accumulated over an extended period of time, perhaps even over a lifetime. This type of knowledge is influenced by intangible factors such as personal beliefs, perspectives, and values. An individual's or an organization's tacit knowledge takes the form of rules of thumb, intuition, tips and techniques, internalized skills, best practices, gut instinct, and even knowledge about who to contact for information which is not in one's own area of expertise. Tacit knowledge is extremely difficult to formalize or communicate. "...It reflects the things that people are learning but have been unable (or perhaps just too busy) to articulate and share with others" (Horvath, 1999). Any attempt to communicate tacit knowledge is complicated further by the fact that even those people who hold a great deal of personal knowledge have a hard time expressing exactly how they do what makes them experts in their fields. "To understand tacit experience, try explaining in detail how you swim or ride a bicycle" (Davenport & Prusak, 1998). This type of knowledge typically defies embodiment in an information technology based system.

The primary means of creating new tacit knowledge is through the *socialization process*. Socialization provides the tacit to tacit knowledge transfer described in Nonaka and Takeuchi's (1995) model for knowledge creating organizations, the Spiral of Knowledge Creation. Knowledge is transferred from one person or group to another person or group. Shared mental models and skills are developed as a result of this process. In addition, new knowledge is frequently created when existing knowledge is seen through a new set of eyes and is adapted to new situations. In this socialization process, knowledge transfer occurs through repeated observation and imitation, often without using any formal means of communication (Nonaka & Takeuchi, 1995). Storytelling, informal meetings, brainstorming sessions, on-the-job training, and mentoring/apprenticeship relationships are all examples of socialization.

In recent years, there is increasing recognition that storytelling is one of the most effective methods to transfer tacit knowledge within an organization. "...Knowledge is communicated most effectively through a convincing narrative that is delivered with formal elegance and passion.... [Stories] embody experience and apply it to future expectations..." (Davenport & Prusak, 1998). Several organizations such as 3M, Xerox, IBM, and British Petroleum use stories to share knowledge. 3M Corporation in particular has recognized the fact that "... there's a close, natural relationship among stories, planning, and learning" (Shaw et al., 1999).

Cognitive psychologists have studied the importance of storytelling to human memory and childhood learning. Stories are fundamental to our learning process. Shaw, Brown, and Bromiley's citation of an October 1994 *Scientific American* article describes how a child learns from stories to "'imagine a course of action, imagine its effects on others, and decide whether or not to do it'" (Shaw et al, 1999). Stories help us to adapt to a number of different situations in today's world; they help us survive. "We are basically storytelling creatures. We experience and comprehend life as a series of ongoing narratives, sometimes as conflicts with characters, plots and storylines."

(Shadle, 1998) Stories are part of our heritage as humans. "From the first accidental wiener roast on a prehistoric savanna, we've understood things by telling stories." (Weinberger, 1999)

Language researchers have confirmed that the story-based approach of *Newsweek* and *Time* magazine can enhance learning among high school students. (Shaw et al, 1999) Stories can also facilitate learning in a business environment. An IBM Institute of Knowledge Management (IIKM) research proposal, entitled "Better Knowledge Management through Storytelling", suggests several uses for stories in this environment. These uses include: (IIKM, 1999)

- *Learning what "works" in a certain set of conditions in the business environment. This learning occurs from analyzing both successes and failure.*
- *Just in Time training*
- *Scenario planning*
- *Clarification of organizational roles and responsibilities in an environment where cultural change management is occurring*
- *Improved awareness regarding the needs of both existing customers and potential clients. Better understanding improves foresight regarding future needs of clients.*
- *Familiarization with and adjustment to a new corporate culture or the personality of a new decision-maker in an organization*

Shadle also recommends the use of storytelling as an effective tool for communicating corporate culture. She has found stories to be very effective in teaching new employees and remote workers (telecommuters) about organizational values and acceptable behavior (Shadle, 1998). Other researchers have uncovered even more uses for stories as part of a knowledge sharing strategy. According to Weinberger (1999), "...every meeting with a potential partner, every exciting sales meeting, every important encounter with customers can best be told as a story." Davenport and Prusak (1998) describe how a major securities firm broadcasts daily messages in the form of stories in order to convey information about a certain event, sale, or customer feedback. They also discuss how Verifone distributes stories of "desirable business behavior" to widely dispersed workers.

3M Corporation has recently reinvented its strategic planning process to incorporate storytelling techniques. Prior to this process redesign, 3M's business plans consisted of outlines, lists, and bullet points. "Cognitive psychologists have established that lists, in contrast [to stories], are remarkably hard to remember.... People mainly remember the first and last items on a list but not the rest of it, and – more dangerous yet – ... they remember what they like or find interesting; they do not recall the whole" (Shaw et al, 1999). Because 3M has a corporate culture that values storytelling and because it has used stories extensively in other parts of the organization, key executives recognized the need to enhance the strategic planning process. As described in Shaw, Brown, and Bromiley (1999), the new planning process, called "planning by narrative", incorporates a number of traditional storytelling techniques. First, a strategic planner "sets the stage", then she "introduces the dramatic conflict", and finally a resolution to the conflict is achieved (Shaw et al, 1999). The thought processes and assumptions that influenced the strategic plan are explicitly stated and can therefore be more easily reviewed and discussed. The resulting strategic plan is much "richer" in nature and provides a better transfer of knowledge to those who must execute the plan. It also serves to create a sense of commitment and enthusiasm.

To briefly summarize the role of storytelling with regards to knowledge transfer, stories provide an effective means of capturing tacit knowledge and contextual information. They then present this knowledge in a way that promotes assimilation and adaptation by the knowledge consumer. "A good story has a point that becomes clear through the telling ... [It] defines relationships, a sequence of events, cause and effect, and a priority among items - *and those elements are likely to be remembered as a complex whole*" (Shaw et al., 1999). Stories are based on real events and tell us how something actually "works". They help us solve real problems. As discussed in the next section, a good pattern strives for much of the same.

Patterns 101: The Basics

According to Williams (1997), patterns are "...one of the hottest and most useful concepts to come out of object technology." However, patterns and pattern languages are not new concepts. They have their origin in the work of a practitioner in a totally unexpected field. Patterns were first identified in the work of architect Christopher Alexander and have their roots in urban design and building architecture (Coplien, 1996). Two classic books on patterns, *A Pattern Language* (Alexander et al, 1977) and *The Timeless Way of Building* (Alexander, 1979), were published in the late 1970s by Alexander and his colleagues.

In its most basic form, a pattern is a three-part rule that describes the relationship between a design problem, a general solution for that problem, and a specific problem context (Coplien, 1996). Vlissides (1997) states that at least three additional components are required to make a pattern: "... (1) *Recurrence*, which makes the solution relevant in situations outside the immediate one; (2) *Teaching*, which gives you the understanding to tailor the solution to your variant of the problem...; and (3) A *name* by which to refer to the pattern. The ability of a pattern to be customized to solve a new problem was first noted by Alexander. He stated that "...each pattern describes a problem that occurs over and over again in our environment and then describes the core of the solution to that problem in such a way that you can use this solution a million times over without ever doing it the same way twice" (Alexander et al., 1977).

A pattern is a piece of literature; it tells a story and engages the reader. The primary components of any literary work are embedded into the formal structure of a pattern. According to Coplien (1996), "... if a pattern is literature, it is like a play in that the solution section should provide catharsis. The Context introduces the 'characters' and the 'setting'; the Forces provide a 'plot', and the Solution provides a resolution of the tension built up in the conflict of the 'Forces'." Beck describes a pattern as another type of literature. For him, a pattern is an "essay" in which the context must be described, the problem and constraints are identified, and a solution is suggested (Beck, 1996).

Several forms of patterns and pattern languages have been developed. The most prevalent forms are the Alexandrian form, the Portland form, the Coplien form, and the "Gang of Four" ("GOF") form, which is designed to facilitate object oriented programming. Although a single pattern form is not appropriate for all types of expertise, the basic concept of a pattern as a "vehicle for capturing and conveying expertise" is suitable for a variety of fields (Vlissides, 1997). According to Coplien (1996), the most universal sections of a pattern are:

- Name
- Intent
- Problem
- Context
- Forces
- Solution
- Sketch
- Resulting Context

The Coplien form of a pattern is depicted below in Table 1. The Intent section, which is not actually included in the Coplien form, typically provides a brief description of what the pattern does and the problem it addresses. This section provides enough information to help a knowledge consumer determine which pattern might be most relevant to his own problem. The Intent section might therefore be considered as a pattern "abstract".

As noted earlier, patterns are created in a story-like format with a formalized language. The purpose of this format is to guarantee inclusion of key components for

Table 1: Coplien Pattern Form (Adapted from Coplien, J.O. Software Patterns, *SIGS Management Briefings, 1996, pp. 7, 14. Published by SIGS Publications, New York, New York)*

Pattern Name	A short, well-chosen name which encodes the pattern's meaning. A noun phrase or verb phrase describing the problem or solution may be used.
Problem	A description of the design problem or issue, often stated as a question or design challenge. Alternatively, a scenario may be described that illustrates the problem or issue.
Context	A situation in which a problem might arise and where the solution might be viable. Context should also include anything that might invalidate where a pattern is usable or which would limit potential reusability. Include any pitfalls, hints, techniques that one utilizes when applying the pattern as well as any subtleties associated with reuse in a different environment. A different context may suggest a different solution to the same problem.
Forces	A more detailed description of the problem. Forces identify design trade-offs as well as what pulls the problem in different directions and therefore towards different solutions. Understanding forces helps knowledge asset consumers better understand the problem, the solution, and how to apply a pattern effectively.
Solution	" A good solution has enough detail so the designer knows what to do, but is general enough to address a broad context." A sketch may be included in the solution to communicate "structure".
Rationale	Information about why a pattern "works". The rationale can include a history of the thought processes behind the creation of the pattern. This information is key to providing a "source of learning" to others.
Resulting Context	A "wrap-up" of the knowledge asset. This section describes what forces were resolved, which ones were not resolved, and any solution which might be considered in the future.

knowledge transfer. A distinct teaching component is typically found in the pattern sections that provide a description of the "forces" surrounding a problem, the resolution of these forces, the problem context, and the solution rationale. (Vlissides, 1997) The goal of patterns is to provide enough insight into a problem and its solution in order that future solutions can be tailored to new problems that are similar in nature. A simple, natural language enhances the degree of knowledge transfer possible. Dr. Richard Gabriel notes that "... The use of common sense and everyday language in a pattern language 'puts you in the mood to begin applying it'.... Simple statements have great force because people understand, remember, and act on them" (Petzinger, 1999).

In the architectural community, patterns have been used to describe problems that occur repeatedly in the building of towns, cities, parks, buildings, and both public and private gardens. These architectural structures ".... didn't grow through master plans or lump-sum construction. They acquired their wholeness, their "living" quality, though piecemeal development..." (Petzinger, 1999). Software systems are also "architected" from smaller components such as programs or program modules. The use of patterns in conjunction with object-oriented computing is well documented. Vlissides (1997) has identified four key benefits of patterns in the software development field. These benefits are:

1. Expertise is captured and made widely accessible to others.
2. A common vocabulary is formed from pattern names. This common language facilitates communication between software developers.
3. A software system can be understood more quickly when it is documented with the patterns that are its building blocks.
4. Patterns can facilitate the restructuring of a software system, even if it was not originally designed with patterns.

Patterns have proven useful in a number of other problem-solving domains as well. In fact, Coplien (1996) states that " ... patterns may be useful to any problem-solving domain with a legacy of experience. Narrowly defined domains, such as those whose structure can easily be captured in frameworks, lend themselves well to integrated pattern languages." Patterns have been used in the description of project management skills, business process reengineering (Beedle, 1998) and business organizational structures. Vlissides (1997) tells how a pattern that addressed music composition was submitted to the 1996 PLoP (Pattern Languages of Programming) conference. A pattern has even been created to describe how someone might become a better downhill skier and reduce his or her risk of a fall. This "Hands in View" pattern is documented in Appendix A. This pattern attempts to resolve underlying issues, rather than directly attacking only the symptoms of the problem.

KNOWLEDGE CODIFICATION FOR VIRTUAL ORGANIZATIONS

State of the Practice: Knowledge Sharing Challenges

As alluded to earlier in this chapter, the sharing of experiences and knowledge among members of a virtual organization or distributed team presents a real challenge.

The water cooler conversation and the coffee room tête-à-tête have become denizens of the past. Storytelling opportunities are limited. One of the major problems with the socialization process in general and with storytelling in particular is that physical proximity is typically required in order for knowledge transfer to occur. It is this very proximity, physical and temporal, that is no longer a luxury in today's business environment.

Some distributed teams do attempt to share stories. As mentioned earlier, Verifone and an unnamed securities firm, as well as several other business organizations, have attempted to transmit stories in electronic form. However, unless a story is relevant to the knowledge consumer at the other end of the transmission, internalization of the knowledge embedded in these stories may not actually occur. Davenport and Prusak (1998) "... have seen many examples of these sorts failing because the speaker lacks the insight or imagination to understand where his listeners are coming from, ... the context in which they interpret his words." Clear, concise, jargon-free, *relevant*, and *meaningful* communication is required for a knowledge consumer to take another person's knowledge to heart, internalize it, adapt it, and make it their own.

Another shortcoming of transmitting stories electronically may simply be the media used for transmission. If stories are converted into text form, many of the benefits of live storytelling sessions are lost. The body language, expressions, and vocal intonation of the storyteller are no longer available to enhance the story. Shadle (1998) "... noted that stories are most powerful when they involve all the senses. A face-to-face story lets you see, hear, touch, and perhaps even smell the storyteller so the story really has impact. 'The next best thing to doing it in person is a well-done video'.... that will capture the body languages and the nuances of voice tone." Question and answer sessions are also not feasible when stories are transmitted electronically. As a result, the enhanced knowledge transfer that could result from a lively discussion between knowledge consumer and knowledge expert cannot be realized.

The most common *state of the practice* for knowledge sharing in virtual teams does not even include an attempt to distribute stories. If any managed effort to share knowledge actually exists, this effort usually takes the form of a document management system or a knowledge base of documents, presentations, templates, and other forms of explicit knowledge. Several major consulting firms have frequently used this method to share best practices. There are several benefits to this approach. First, knowledge assets are permanently recorded when added to a knowledge base. If a consultant leaves the firm, his knowledge is not totally lost. Secondly, since explicit knowledge can be easily categorized by subject matter, team members who are looking for a particular type of knowledge can search a knowledge base from a number of perspectives. By providing flexible search mechanisms, the knowledge consumer has an improved chance of success when trying to locate relevant knowledge. Finally, the most significant benefit in a dispersed organization is that team members can share knowledge without consideration to differences in time zones or geography.

On the other hand, knowledge bases typically have several disadvantages. The quality of the contents can vary significantly if there is not a concerted effort by an organization to monitor and control quality, relevance, and timeliness of the knowledge that is stored. Contributors may simply attempt to meet a contribution quota with little regard to actual content. One of the most significant limitations of a knowledge base is the lack of associated context required to interpret and adapt its contents. Think of a time when you tried to make sense of a presentation without actually hearing the speaker or without, at a minimum, having access to the speaker notes associated with the presentation. Presentations typically consist of several screens of bulleted lists, which we already know are not effective ways to transmit knowledge.

Although they probably provide a better way to embed knowledge than disembodied presentations can provide, documents are also lacking in rich contextual information. "Contrast [a business document] with the works of the novelist or essayist... In conveying their message, [they don't] just record a series of observations, the results of an analysis, or the description of a process; what they do is help us *feel what they feel*" (Newman, 1997). Business documents are notoriously poor at capturing context, assumptions, alternatives, and other key components of any decision making process. They tend to focus on facts and figures. "...Today's business documents leave out as much, or more, than they convey. This missing knowledge is the tacit knowledge" (Newman, 1997). Without context and actual relevance to the problems of the knowledge consumer, all of the hard work required to store "knowledge" becomes meaningless as that knowledge is downgraded into mere information. One woman's knowledge may become simply another woman's information if it is not meaningful to her particular situation. Horvath (1999) provides several examples where disparities in intended use and context can depreciate the value of knowledge.

Abstracts are often used to supplement documents and other types of information stored in a document management system or knowledge base. They are used to summarize the contents of a particular document, presentation, template, or other knowledge asset. However, abstracts are typically too brief to provide the contextual information required for a knowledge consumer to decide whether a piece of explicit knowledge is important to him, if he can use the information provided, and how he might adapt it to his own situation. It would be difficult to capture the thought processes or the trials and tribulations that contributed to the creation of a knowledge asset within the typical confines of an abstract. The creator of a particular knowledge asset knows what works for him and why, what does not work and (again) why, and what limitations exist with regards to a particular solution. This is the type of knowledge that must be conveyed for true knowledge transfer and internalization to occur.

As noted repeatedly, "... the primary difficulty encountered in codification work is the question of how to codify knowledge without losing its distinctive properties and turning it into less vibrant information or data.... Some structure for knowledge is necessary, but too much kills it" (Davenport & Prusak, 1998). With the limitations of both explicit knowledge and dispersed organizations in mind, the challenge is to find a way to externalize and distribute as much tacit knowledge as possible in a form that can be preserved and internalized later. We look next at how that challenge might be met.

A "Literary" Approach to Codifying Knowledge

To find innovative solutions to problems, one must often "think outside of the box" and explore new disciplines. In my search for new metaphors that might facilitate the transfer of knowledge, especially where the sharing of tacit knowledge is hindered by geography or by the distribution of team members across various time zones, patterns certainly showed promise. The similarities that exist between stories and patterns imply that patterns have real potential to enhance the knowledge externalization process.

Patterns have repeatedly been linked to stories or other literary forms in the growing volume of knowledge management literature. For example, Davenport and Prusak (1998) state that "... rules of thumb... are shortcuts to solutions to new problems that resemble problems previously solved by experienced workers. Those with knowledge see known patterns in new situations and respond appropriately.... Like play scripts, [... these rules of thumb provide] efficient guides to complex situations. Scripts are patterns of internalized experience." Patterns allow for the same degree of flexibility in interpretation that is provided by stories. They also enable the evaluation and consideration of alternatives. As a result, patterns can save time and trouble that would otherwise be spent analyzing each new situation that is encountered.

The similarity between patterns and effective stories is also apparent when one considers the suggestions made by Bednar regarding ways to improve a story's ability to transfer knowledge. Bednar (1999) recommends that:

- A story should be as descriptive as possible. It should be given a conversational tone, which can be enhanced through the use of questions.
- A story should also be as simple as possible. It can be clarified and explained through the use of charts, graphs, and other visual representations of information.
- The storyteller should state what might be considered obvious conclusions. It is important to explicitly state what is meant and to minimize the possibility of misinterpretation.
- A story should be organized in some logical manner.
- Whenever possible, potential solutions to the problems described in a story should be suggested by the storyteller.

Patterns incorporate these suggestions into their very structure. First of all, questions or design challenges are typically used to describe the problem that will be addressed by a pattern. The structure of a pattern is simple and sketches are often used to illustrate a solution. "Obvious" assumptions and conclusions are documented in the Forces section of a pattern. The formal language of a pattern provides organization and structure. Finally, a solution to the problem is always provided. *Perhaps the structure of a pattern provides the very way to improve stories for the purposes of knowledge transfer.*

It is my belief that patterns, because of their literary nature, tackle the main problem encountered when encoding knowledge to create a permanent knowledge record, the problem where tacit knowledge "dies" or otherwise loses much of its value and meaning. "Once we recognize that narratives are the best way to teach and learn complex 'stuff', ... we can often encode the stories themselves so as to convey meaning without losing much of its leveragable value" (Davenport & Prusak, 1998). Patterns provide a consistent style and structure to the storytelling process. As a result, they force the author of a knowledge asset to include key components that might otherwise be overlooked simply due to ignorance regarding the importance of those components. Patterns compel their "authors" to stop and think about assumptions that were made and conclusions that were reached.

The potential of patterns to facilitate knowledge transfer is also exemplified by the type of questions raised and then answered within a pattern's basic structure. The richness of the comparisons, contrasts, connections, and outcomes recorded within a pattern contributes to its capacity to transfer knowledge. This "richness" helps a pattern transcend from mere documented information into documented knowledge. Davenport and Prusak (1998) have identified four "C" words that actually describe key requirements for the transformation of information into knowledge. These are:

1. *Comparison*: The information about a particular situation or problem is compared and contrasted with other situations that have been previously encountered.
2. *Consequences*: The implications and potential results of certain actionable information are identified. These consequences have a direct bearing on decisions and actions.
3. *Connections*: The interrelationships between distinct pieces of knowledge or information are explored.
4. *Conversation*: Group discussions or other communications are held in order to learn what other people think about new information.

The very structure of a pattern addresses the first three of these four "C" words. In particular, the *Context, Forces, Rationale,* and *Resulting Context* sections of a pattern can be used to compare, connect, and describe the consequences of a particular problem and its solution. The "conversation word" is addressed by pattern discussions. These discussions are typically held between a pattern author and pattern readers in order to debate, refine, and learn from a particular pattern.

Patterns facilitate the two modes of interaction, *externalization* and *internalization*, which are concerned with the conversion of knowledge back and forth between tacit knowledge and explicit knowledge. These two knowledge transformation processes are key components of Nonaka and Takeuchi's (1995) Spiral of Knowledge Creation. *Externalization* is the process whereby tacit knowledge is translated into explicit concepts, often using metaphors, analogies, or models. Patterns provide a new way to model tacit knowledge in explicit form. The *Internalization* process translates explicit knowledge back into an individual's or an organization's personal, tacit knowledge base. This process is facilitated when knowledge that has been captured in explicit form, whether in a document, manual, or written story, can be reexperienced, "appreciated", adapted, and adopted by the knowledge consumer. The teaching components of patterns seek to enhance the ability of the reader to internalize the knowledge of the pattern creator. These components also support the creation of new knowledge. "[This] creation of knowledge occurs with the transfer of what's inside a person's head (his or her tacit knowledge – thoughts, ideas, actions and experiences...) to another individual or group in such a way that the recipient's future actions and decisions are influenced by the transfer" (Bednar, 1999).

Patterns are also applicable to the other two processes, *combination* and *socialization*, described in the Spiral of Knowledge Creation. First, patterns can be *combined* into a pattern language. "Pattern languages go much further [than individual patterns], dealing with rich interactions between patterns to indirectly generate solutions for more fundamental problems, much larger than any one pattern can address by itself" (Appleton, 1997). The interrelationships between patterns are identified in the "teaching" sections of the pattern, such as the Forces or Rationale sections. A pattern language is then developed based on these interrelationships. Through the use of pattern languages, it may therefore be possible to support the *Combination* process where explicit knowledge assets are reconfigured, integrated, and merged (Nonaka & Takeuchi, 1995).

Patterns also provide a focal point for the socialization process. Several "pattern groups" in the object oriented programming (OOP) community meet regularly to "read" and discuss patterns, much as a literary discussion group might meet to discuss the work of a new author. These discussion groups are learning communities. The process of "reading patterns" in a group setting results in the refinement of a pattern. The pattern author can learn more about how his or her pattern will be interpreted by others and can then gain insights into better ways to "write" a pattern. Pattern discussion also increases knowledge for the entire group as group members learn potential solutions to problems that they have either encountered or may soon encounter. This discussion can also lead to the identification of new ways to apply a pattern.

Patterns could become a useful focal point for knowledge sharing discussions in a community of practice. Patterns might even prove to be a way to structure and provide a common language for discussions with business clients during the software application design process. Beck (1996) explores pattern-directed design sessions in his paper. Because it appears that all phases of the knowledge creation spiral can be facilitated through the use of patterns, it may be possible to create a continuous learning loop. A creator of knowledge may actually increase his own knowledge by rethinking the process that he used to create a particular knowledge asset.

How Patterns Facilitate Knowledge Transfer in the Virtual Team

Although patterns and pattern languages can be used to capture and share tacit knowledge in any team environment, the non-virtual organization has the option to sponsor knowledge-sharing events such as storytelling sessions, brainstorming activities, and informal coffee breaks that are designed to facilitate knowledge transfer. In these social settings, tacit knowledge can be transferred without first being stored electronically. The very nature of a virtual organization, however, implies that it is difficult, if not impossible, to share knowledge by means of face-to-face communication. Members of a virtual team may work at home, at customer locations, or at offices located in other parts of the country or even other parts of the globe. They cannot be located in the same room without incurring some travel expense, either in terms of time or dollars. In addition, teams in virtual organizations may be transitory in nature. As teams are disbanded and members are further dispersed, the tacit knowledge that is created and shared by team members may be lost to the organization unless it is codified and preserved in explicit form. Finally, cultural impediments to knowledge transfer are enhanced in a virtual organization that has members located in a wide range of geographic locations. A shared language may not even exist. It is well known, however, that the lack of a common language is a severe impediment to knowledge transfer. Davenport and Prusak (1998) report that "... research shows time and again that a shared language is essential to productive knowledge transfer. Without it, individuals will neither understand nor trust one another. "

Patterns address the three obstacles to knowledge sharing in a virtual organization that were identified above. As described earlier in this chapter, patterns capture and codify tacit knowledge in a literary form that is enhanced with many of the same beneficial aspects found in stories. Patterns also simulate bidirectional communication by asking questions that are then answered in the solution section of the pattern. By effectively representing tacit knowledge in documented form, it can be distributed across the boundaries of a virtual organization in a timely manner to those who might need it. This knowledge can also be recorded for future use in the event that a virtual team is disbanded and dispersed. According to Davenport and Prusak (1998), "knowledge transfer involves two actions: transmission (sending or presenting knowledge to a potential recipient) and absorption by that group or person." Patterns are concerned with both of these actions. The teaching aspect of patterns is especially valuable in virtual organizations where brainstorming sessions, mentoring, storytelling and observation/ imitation cannot readily occur. Finally, patterns provide a common "language" for team members. They offer a familiar literary structure for representing a problem, the context of the problem, and a solution to that problem.

The software engineering community is a superb example of a virtual "community of practice" that has been able to adopt a common language (a "pattern language") in order to share knowledge across community boundaries. Petzinger (1999) states that patterns provide a "...simple, straightforward grammar.... Design principles spread easily through programming groups, giving members a language spanning their special-ties."

A specific example of pattern use within the technology community is provided by the efforts of Dr. Gabriel and Dr. Goldman at Sun Microsystems. These innovative individuals have been using pattern languages to facilitate the development of a new technology (Jini). For this project to succeed, people from several different industries, even previous competitors, need to freely share knowledge. "...Building a richly interconnected Jini world demanded openness and trust across a huge and far-flung community of device makers." (Petzinger, 1999) This community of Jini developers was structured and managed by using a pattern language to describe how different groups should interact in order to ensure the success of the project. For example, a pattern entitled "Coalitions form markets" was built to describe why competitors should collaborate in order to develop a technology such as Jini. (Petzinger, 1999)

If one looks back in time to the 1970s, another example of the exemplary use of patterns in a virtual community can be found. The architectural community was the original "virtual organization" that benefited from the use of patterns. With the aid of a pattern language, Christopher Alexander and his colleagues were able to represent architectural best practices that could be used by anyone to build more functional buildings, create more effective parks, and design better cities and towns. These architectural patterns are useful today across a wide range of cultures for the simple reason that they were developed based on their repeated occurrence in the architecture of several civilizations.

Perhaps the best way to illustrate the power of patterns for a virtual organization is to create a pattern that describes the precise problem that we have been discussing in this paper. This problem occurs repeatedly whenever we try to codify knowledge so that it can be shared across time and space. This new pattern, Patterns Add Context, is illustrated in Table 2. It discusses the "forces" encountered when trying to share knowledge in a dispersed organization.

A Personal Experience with Patterns

As noted earlier in this paper, the software development community, especially the

Table 2: "Patterns Add Context": A New Pattern

Pattern Name	Patterns Add Context
Pattern Intent	This pattern describes how patterns can be used to enhance explicit knowledge to improve knowledge transfer in a dispersed organization or virtual team.
Problem	How can the explicit knowledge shared by distributed teams be augmented to facilitate knowledge transfer and internalization?
Context	Distributed teams typically rely on knowledge bases of explicit knowledge in order to share information and best practices. Explicit knowledge lacks the richness of contextual information required to add meaning and value to the knowledge that these teams are trying to share. This pattern is most applicable in the distributed team environment where people cannot interact directly. However, applying the structure of a pattern to the telling of stories may even enhance knowledge transfer where proximity is not an issue.
Forces	• Two-way communications and storytelling are the most effective ways to transfer tacit knowledge. • Two-way communications are not possible when teams are dispersed across time and geography. • Virtual teams resort to sharing explicit, documented knowledge. • The conversion of knowledge into explicit form results in the loss of context and tacit knowledge.
Solution	When documenting knowledge, utilize patterns and pattern languages to capture assumptions, context and rationalizations.
Rationale	Patterns add the benefits of storytelling to any effort to document knowledge. They explore the "forces" surrounding a problem that is solved with a particular type of knowledge. Insight into these forces helps a knowledge consumer understand the problem and how to apply the knowledge to their own problems. Patterns also document assumptions, risks, and the reasons that alternative solutions were rejected. Patterns add structure to the storytelling process so that key teaching components are not accidentally omitted.
Resulting Context	Forcing the capture of contextual information and a knowledge expert's thought processes helps overcome the limitations of explicit knowledge. As a result, the benefits of storytelling can be realized even in a distributed team environment.

object-oriented programming community, has adopted patterns and pattern languages to "document" software modules. "The leap from building architecture to program architecture is intuitive to many: both concern themselves with structure" (Coplien, 1996). The use of patterns contributes to productivity in the software design world. Patterns eliminate the need for a developer to determine how a program or a software system currently functions when assigned the responsibility for maintenance. Coplien (1996) stated that "... patterns strive to bring ... knowledge into the open" and to relieve the human communication bottleneck in software development. The type of information documented in a pattern appears to be particularly useful for determining the reuse potential of software modules and for documenting and sharing knowledge about them.

Recently, I led a knowledge management initiative within an Information Management organization at a Fortune 100 company. This effort sought to address software reusability issues. Our goal was to preserve and share knowledge about "executable assets" (software modules) as well as the "non-executable assets" associated with an application development project. Non-executable assets include such documents as project charters, work plans, user guides, and other project deliverables. The scope of this knowledge sharing effort was global in nature. Ultimately, it was anticipated that software developers in the United States, Europe, and Latin America would share and reuse software modules. Exemplary project charters would serve as a document template as well as a model for other charters. Comprehensive work plans would be used as a checklist of project tasks that must be included to ensure on-time, on-budget delivery of an application. The ultimate goal was to share the knowledge and experiences of software development teams in order to expedite future software development efforts.

The challenge for this effort was to capture as much tacit knowledge as possible and yet to create a permanent record of the thought processes used during a software development project. Software developers are notoriously transient and might not be employed with the company when the next application development project is initiated. Even if a developer is still with the company and the name of that developer is stored in conjunction with the software module he coded, the realities of a dispersed organization would limit the possibility for two-way discussion with another developer. Our approach was to create a web-enabled knowledge base of "knowledge assets". This technique is similar to the knowledge bases being created by consulting firms that specialize in application development projects for their clients. However, we felt that the "knowledge bases" of some of these consulting firms bordered on mere document management and did not really enable knowledge transfer. They did not adequately tackle the challenge of capturing tacit knowledge. We made the capture of this type of knowledge our special mission. The knowledge management team then explored other disciplines to identify new metaphors that might facilitate the transfer of knowledge from one developer to another.

For the simple reason that we were using object oriented programming for our software development efforts, the concept of patterns was revealed to us in the literature of the object community. The formal language of patterns showed promise as a discipline that could enhance our knowledge sharing efforts. It seemed possible that patterns could be used to augment abstracts or could even be directly incorporated into a documentation style for recording best practices, competitive intelligence, tips and techniques, or other explicit forms of knowledge representation. A decision was made to experiment with patterns in order to tell a "story" about a knowledge asset. For example, we wanted to describe how a particular code module was developed or how project scope was defined. When documenting a software module, we attempted to capture as much knowledge as possible regarding context and forces. From a software reuse perspective, context includes any factor that might invalidate where a module is usable or that could limit potential reusability. Possible factors include the choice of programming language, vendor package, or development platform (i.e. Unix, NT, or Novell). When describing forces, we tried to identify design trade-offs as well as business rules that might impact the way a module is coded.

Developers in our software development team formed a community of practice and met regularly to discuss and brainstorm about software assets under development. As noted earlier, groups of pattern creators in the Object Community have been known to meet regularly to "read", review, discuss, and refine patterns. We considered using patterns as a focal point for our own discussions, but the opportunity did not arise to explore this possibility further.

Considerable progress was made during the duration of this knowledge management effort. Although some developers on the team were initially uncomfortable with "pattern writing", continuous encouragement and coaching reduced their concerns. The ability to write good patterns increased with repetition. Work habits also began to change. One developer commented that she started to think about how to develop code with reuse in mind rather than embedding application specific requirements within the code that could limit potential reuse. Using patterns to document a software module caused this developer to take a step back, to rethink the way in which she developed a module. The actual documentation process caused her to reevaluate the potential applicability of a module as well as design trade-offs and design limitations. This developer learned through the pattern writing process and will probably write better code in the future.

Although this project was in many ways a success, the duration of the project was limited due to redeployment of information technology personnel to address Year 2000 issues. I invite other software development teams to explore the use of patterns to model their knowledge.

State of the Future: Possible Next Steps

A number of research opportunities are suggested by our initial study of patterns and pattern languages. Certainly, as noted above, a more definitive study about the use of patterns in dispersed software development teams is warranted. A new project within my company is charged with creating a community of practice for Web developers. This project would be an ideal opportunity to reevaluate the use of patterns for documenting best practices and other knowledge about the Web development process. It would also be worth researching the applicability of patterns to facilitate knowledge transfer in any number of non-software disciplines. For example, research to determine the capability of patterns to capture the special expertise of sales and marketing teams or the knowledge of research and development work groups could be of interest to several corporations.

Another research opportunity was suggested earlier. Just as literary groups meet to discuss stories, communities of practice might meet to discuss "patterns" related to the knowledge of their community. Members of the object-oriented programming (OOP) community already meet to discuss patterns. These discussion groups are learning communities. Their review, discussion, and refinement of patterns could lead to the development of new knowledge and, perhaps, better software development practices. This suggests that research about the effectiveness of patterns as a tool for structuring discussions might provide valuable information for communities of practice.

Although patterns have been demonstrated to capture isolated pieces of knowledge, little documented research exists with regards to creating pattern languages that can link these morsels of knowledge into a coherent, meaningful whole. Pattern languages have certainly been developed in the fields of architecture and city planning. They have also been used extensively to link software patterns into a pattern language that can describe an entire software system. The combination of patterns to create pattern languages for other disciplines should be explored.

Any research designed to explore the role of stories in the knowledge transfer process may also provide us with some tips on how to enhance patterns. Two large communities of knowledge management practitioners are already involved in research about storytelling. The Knowledge Management Consortium, Inc. (KMCI) provides a link to a storytelling project from its Web site. The IBM Institute of Knowledge Management (IIKM, 1999) is also sponsoring a research project entitled "Better Knowledge Management through Storytelling". The purpose of this study is to help people write better stories, organize them in a meaningful way, and then retrieve them for use in other situations. The study is structured into three phases. The deliverables from the first phase include a repository of stories on knowledge management topics as well as requirements for a tool designed to facilitate the creation, indexing, and retrieval of stories. The key deliverable of the second phase is a prototype of the tool whose requirements are defined in phase I. The last phase of this project acknowledges the significance of human pattern finding capabilities. One anticipated result of this research is a "pattern language" of problem solving heuristics or "rules of thumb."

Another area for research is the use of multimedia to augment patterns. As noted by Davenport and Prusak (1998), "multimedia computing and the hypertext capabilities of intranets have created the possibility of effectively capturing at least some meaningful fraction of an expert's knowledge, making the tacit explicit." Various types of multimedia (graphics, audio clips, or even movie clips) might be added to the "sketch" section of a pattern. Alternatively, an entire pattern might be transmitted using multimedia. It could be stored on a CD or captured on film. In the Internet world, we are not limited to sharing stories in written form. Therefore, why should patterns always be written?

Finally, patterns might provide a way to link individuals into a virtual community of practice. Currently, Internet-based book retailers such as Amazon.com utilize information stored about purchase preferences in order to suggest additional books that might be of interest to a consumer. A similar effort could be made to recommend patterns that might be of interest to a "reader" based on their previous pattern selections. Taking the Amazon.com model one step further would suggest that individuals who read the same patterns have similar interests or problems and should be "introduced" to each other. The result of this introduction might be, at a minimum, the formation of a community of interest.

CONCLUSION

This chapter has explored the considerable potential of patterns to augment knowledge transfer in dispersed organizations. Teams in these organizations cannot effectively engage in face-to-face meetings and storytelling sessions due to the limitations of time, geographic space, and even cultural space. This very type of interactive communication, however, reportedly provides one of the most effective methods for transferring tacit knowledge. Virtual teams must find a way to overcome their impediments to sharing tacit knowledge.

Patterns can help facilitate knowledge transfer in a virtual organization in three key ways. When "virtual" storytelling sessions are possible, via the use of the Internet, CD-ROM, or some other form of multimedia, the formal language of patterns can add structure and consistency to the process. Key components required for knowledge transfer are less likely to be omitted. The second way that patterns can help is to enhance documentation by capturing and codifying tacit knowledge. Most dispersed organizations resort to sharing knowledge in explicit, documented form. However, it is well known that explicit knowledge is not the most effective way to transfer knowledge so that it can be internalized and then used to generate new knowledge. The very structure of a pattern contains teaching components and can enrich standard forms of documentation by adding context and tacit knowledge. This ability of patterns to capture tacit knowledge that can then be internalized by others is especially relevant for virtual organizations with limited opportunities for face-to-face meetings. Finally, patterns and pattern languages provide the common language that is essential to knowledge transfer. A pattern language may provide the shared language that is otherwise lacking in a culturally dispersed organization. It can certainly provide a consistent, familiar way in which to document knowledge.

I hope that this chapter has created a sense of enthusiasm regarding patterns and their role in knowledge management. The few discussions that I have had regarding patterns with others in my organization have sparked considerable interest. Now that the seed of interest has been planted, it will be interesting to see what will grow from that seed. Further opportunities abound for exploring the use of patterns to facilitate the capture and transfer of tacit knowledge.

REFERENCES

Alexander, C. (1979). *The Timeless Way of Building*, New York: Oxford University Press.

Alexander, C., Ishikawa, S. and Silverstein, M. (1977). *A Pattern Language: Towns, Buildings, Construction*, New York: Oxford University Press.

Appleton, B. (August 5, 1997). *On the Nature of The Nature of Order*, Chicago Patterns Group: notes taken on James O. Coplien's presentation on Christopher Alexander's latest work titled: *The Nature of Order*, Chicago, Illinois.

Beck, K. (January 1996). Patterns 101, *Object Magazine*, pp. 25-63.

Bednar, C. "Capturing and Packaging Knowledge", printed in the collection *The Knowledge Management Yearbook: 1999 – 2000*, edited by James W. Cortada and John A. Woods (Boston: Butterworth-Heinemann, 1999), pp. 211-220.

Beedle, M. (1998). *BPR Pattern Language*, Lucent Technologies, Available at Internet location: http://www.bell-labs.com/cgi-user/OrgPatterns?BPRPatternLanguage

Coplien, J.O. (April 1996). *Software Patterns*, SIGS Management Briefings, Published by SIGS Publications, New York, New York.

Davenport, T. and Prusak, L. (1998). *Working Knowledge: How Organizations Manage What They Know*, Boston: Harvard Business School Press.

Horvath, J. A. (April 1999). *Working with Tacit Knowledge*, An IBM Institute for Knowledge Management White Paper.

IBM Institute for Knowledge Management (IIKM). (1999). *Better Knowledge Management through Storytelling*, Research Proposal of the IIKM.

Knowledge Management Consortium, Inc. Web Site. Internet location of home page: http://www.km.org

Lyons, Karen L. (April 1997). *Beyond Theory: Implementing a Knowledge Management Approach for an IM Organization*, Masters Thesis, Stevens Institute of Technology, Hoboken, New Jersey.

Newman, B. (February 27, 1997). *The Siamese Twins – Documents and Knowledge*, Panel Presentation given at Documation '97: Documents and Knowledge Management, reproduced in *Knowledge Praxis*, Internet location: http://www.media-access.com/Siamese_Twins.htm

Nonaka, I. and Takeuchi, H. (1995). *The Knowledge-Creating Company*, New York: Oxford University Press.

Petzinger, T. (Received by NewsEDGE/LAN 5/14/99). *To Get Machines to Talk To Each Other, Two Men Write Human Language*, The Wall Street Journal via Dow Jones and Company, Inc. (1999).

Shadle, C. (April 1998). Tell me a Story, Teach me the Organization, *Telecommuting Review: the Gordon Report 15*(4), Available: Computer Select, record #20 529 103.

Shaw, G., Brown, R. and Brolimey, P. "Strategic Stories: How 3M is Rewriting Business Planning", reprinted in the collection *The Knowledge Management Yearbook: 1999 – 2000*, edited by James W. Cortada and John A. Woods (Boston: Butterworth-Heinemann, 1999), pp. 233-244.

Stuart, A. (November 15, 1995). Meeting in Houston, business leaders address the challenges of managing knowledge, *CIO Archives*, Available Internet location: http://www.cio.com.

Vlissides, J. (March 1997). Patterns: The Top Ten Misconceptions, *Object Magazine*, pp. 31-33.

Weinberger, D. (February 2, 1999). Narrative Knowledge, *KM World*, Available at Internet location: http://www.kmworld.com/feature.articles

Williams, J. (March 1997) Introduction: Patterns, *Object Magazine*, p. 29.

APPENDIX A: SKIING PATTERN

Pattern Name	Hands in View
Pattern Intent	This pattern addresses how to become a better downhill skier and to reduce falls.
Problem	The skier fails to commit to downhill on steeps and bumps, resulting in slides, backward falls, and "yard sales".
Context	In order to explore the entire mountain environment, a skier must be comfortable and adaptable in any terrain and rapid terrain change. To take advantage of this pattern, the skier should be skiing at a level at which parallel turns can be linked consistently.
Forces	• Fear of falling is the most basic of all responses • Reliance on equipment is essential • Continuous movement is essential • Fatigue can be a factor in long descents • Commitment downhill over skis is essential for skis to function as designed
Solution	Concentrate on keeping hands in view. Bring them into sight immediately after each pole plant and turn.
Rationale	As steepness increases, the natural tendency of any sane person is to sit back against the hill and retain the perpendicularity the inner ear prefers. Unfortunately, skis must be weighted to perform as designed, the weight causing flex, which in turn pushes the edges into the snow in an arc, making a turn. Therefore it is essential to "throw" oneself down the mountain over the skis, depending on them to "catch" the fall as they bite into the snow underneath the perpetually falling skier. Intellectually this can be clearly understood but fear prevents execution. Concentrating on something as simple and indirect as "look at your hands" causes the desired behavior without directly confronting the fear. This is directly analogous to what occurs when an individual walks: the weight is thrown forward in a fall, with consequent forward thrust of the leg to catch this fall, repeated for left and right sides in a continuous tension and release of yeilding to gravity in order to defy it.
Resulting Context	Keeping the hands in view changes the alignment of the body from sitting timidly back and allowing the edges to skid out from under the skier. Thus, keeping the hands in view pulls the body forward and thus downhill, bringing the skier's weight over the downhill ski, forcing the edge to bite and turn.

(Adapted from Coplien, J.O. Software Patterns, *SIGS Management Briefings, 1996, p. 33. Published by SIGS Publications, New York, New York)*

Chapter VIII

Managing Knowledge for Strategic Advantage in the Virtual Organisation

Janice M. Burn and Colin Ash
Edith Cowan University, Australia

This chapter looks at the virtual organisation and suggests that the basic concepts of virtual management are so poorly understood that there are likely to be very few such organisations gaining strategic advantage from their virtuality. The authors begin by providing some clear definitions of virtual organisations and different models of virtuality which can exist within the electronic market. Degrees of virtuality can be seriously constrained by the extent to which organisations have preexisting linkages in the marketplace and the extent to which these can be substituted by virtual ones, but also by the intensity of virtual linkages which support the virtual model. Six virtual models are proposed within a dynamic framework of change. In order to realise strategic advantage, virtual organisations must align their virtual culture with the virtual model for structural alignment. This paper further proposes a model for virtual organisational change which identifies the factors internal to the virtual organisation that need to be managed. Critical to this is the role of knowledge management. The authors develop this concept within a framework of virtual organising and relate this to organisations using ERP in an Internet environment. Specific examples will be used relating such developments to organisations employing SAP and illustrating strategic advantage.

Virtual organisations are very much in vogue but there is very little empirical research to show how "virtuality" can provide a strategic advantage to organisations. There is even less guidance provided with respect to the management of change in organisations that embrace some degree of virtuality by leveraging their competencies through effective use of information and communication technologies (ICT). It could be argued that there is a degree of virtuality in all organisations but at what point does this present a conflict between control and adaptability? Is there a continuum along which organisations can position themselves in the electronic marketplace according to their needs for flexibility and fast responsiveness as opposed to stability and sustained momentum? To what extent should the organisation manage knowledge both within and without the organisation to realise a virtual work environment?

While there may be general agreement with regard to the advantages of flexibility, the extent to which virtuality offers flexibility and the advantages which this will bring to a corporation have yet to be measured. There is an assumption that an organisation that invests in as little infrastructure as possible will be more responsive to a changing marketplace and more likely to attain global competitive advantage, but this ignores the very real power which large integrated organisations can bring to the market in terms of sustained innovation over the longer term (Chesbrough and Teece, 1996). Proponents of the virtual organisation also tend to underestimate the force of virtual links. Bonds which bind a virtual organisation together may strongly inhibit flexibility and change rather than nurture the concept of the opportunistic virtual organisation (Goldman, Nagel and Preiss, 1995). Aldridge (1998), suggests that it is no accident that the pioneers of electronic commerce fall into three categories:

- Start-ups, organisations with no existing investment or legacy systems to protect;
- Technology companies with a vested interest in building the channel to market products and services;
- Media companies, attracted by low set-up costs and immediate distribution of news and information.

When is a virtual organisation really virtual? One definition would suggest that organisations are virtual when producing work deliverables across different locations, at differing work cycles, and across cultures (Gray and Igbaria, 1996; Palmer and Speier, 1998). Another suggests that the single common theme is temporality. Virtual organisations centre on continual restructuring to capture the value of a short term market opportunity and are then dissolved to make way for restructuring to a new virtual entity(Byrne, 1993; Katzy, 1998). Yet others suggest that virtual organisations are characterised by the intensity, symmetricality, reciprocity and multiplexity of the linkages in their networks (Powell, 1990; Grabowski and Roberts, 1996). Whatever the definition (and this paper hopes to resolve some of the ambiguities) there is a consensus that different degrees of virtuality exist (Hoffman, Novak, and Chatterjee, 1995; Gray and Igbaria, 1996; Goldman, Nagel and Preiss, 1995) and within this, different organisational structures can be formed (Palmer and Speier, 1998; Davidow and Malone, 1992; Miles and Snow, 1986). Such structures are normally inter-organisational and lie at the heart of any form of electronic commerce yet the organisational and management processes which should be applied to ensure successful implementation have been greatly under researched (Finnegan, Galliers and Powell, 1998; Swatman and Swatman, 1992).

It could be argued that there is a degree of virtuality in all organisations but at what point does this present a conflict between control and adaptability? Is there a continuum along which organisations can position themselves in the electronic marketplace according to their needs for flexibility and fast responsiveness as opposed to stability and sustained momentum? To what extent should the organisation manage knowledge both within and without the organisation to realise a virtual work environment?

A virtual organisation's knowledge base is inevitably distributed more widely than a conventional one, both within the organisation and without – among suppliers, distributors, customers, and even competitors. This wide spread can deliver enormous benefits; a wider range of opportunities and risks can be identified, costs can be cut, products and services can be improved and new markets can be reached by using other people's knowledge rather than recreating it. However, this does make it both more important and more difficult to manage knowledge well. It is harder to share knowledge and hence exploit it in a dispersed organisation and there is an increased risk both of knowledge hoarders and of duplication leading to possible loss of integrity and wasted effort. While competencies and their associated knowledge may be more effectively bought from business partners or outsourced if there are economies of scale, expertise or economic value, care must also be taken to avoid losing the knowledge on which core competencies are based or from which new competencies can be developed quickly.

The ability of the organisation to change or to extend itself as a virtual entity will reflect the extent to which an understanding of these concepts has been embedded into the knowledge management of the virtual organisation as a Virtual Organisational Change Model (VOCM). Managing these change factors is essential to gain and maintain strategic advantage and to derive virtual value.

This chapter addresses these aspects as follows. Firstly, a definition of virtual organisations is developed and related to the concept of virtual culture which is the organisational embodiment of its virtuality. This may take a variety of different virtual models which will reflect the strength and structure of inter-organisational links. The paper identifies six virtual models—the Virtual Alliance Models (VAM)—and suggests that each of these will operate along a continuum and within a framework of dynamic change . In order to maximise the value derived from the VAM the organisation needs to ensure that there is a consistency between the alignment of its Virtual Strategic Positioning and the VAM and the organisation and management of internal and external virtual characteristics. The ability of the organisation to change from one VAM to another or to extend itself as a virtual entity will reflect the extent to which an understanding of these concepts has been embedded into the knowledge management of the virtual organisation as a Virtual Organisational Change Model (VOCM). Managing these change factors is essential to gain and maintain strategic advantage and to derive virtual value (Burn and Barnett, 1999).

The authors expand these concepts by using case examples of organisations using SAP and illustrate the three levels of development mode – virtual work, virtual sourcing and virtual encounters and their relationship to knowledge management, individually, organisationally and community wide through the exploitation of ICT.

VIRTUAL ORGANISATIONS AND VIRTUAL CULTURES

Virtual organisations are electronically networked organisations that transcend conventional organisational boundaries (Barner, 1996; Berger, 1996; Rogers, 1996), with linkages which may exist both within (Davidow and Malone, 1992) and between organisations (Goldman, Nagel and Priess, 1995). In its simplest form, however, virtuality exists where IT is used to enhance organisational activities while reducing the need for physical or formalised structures (Greiner and Mates, 1996). Degrees of virtuality (the extent to which the organisation operates in a virtual rather than physical mode) then exist which will reflect:

- The virtual organisational culture (strategic positioning)
- The virtual network (the intensity of linkages and the nature of the bonds which tie the stakeholders together as internal and external structures)
- The virtual market (IT dependency and resource infrastructure, product, customer)

Culture is the degree to which members of a community have common shared values and beliefs (Schein, 1990). Tushman and O'Reilly (1996) suggest that organisational cultures that are accepting of technology, highly decentralised, and change oriented are more likely to embrace virtuality and proactively seek these opportunities both within and without the organisation. Virtual culture is hence a perception of the entire virtual organisation (including its infrastructure and product) held by its stakeholder community, and operationalised in choices and actions which result in a feeling of *globalness* with respect to value sharing (e.g., each client's expectations are satisfied in the product accessed) and time-space arrangement (e.g., each stakeholder has the feeling of a continuous access to the organisation and its products). The embodiment of this culture comes through the Virtual Strategic Perspective (VSP) which the organisation adopts.

Networks can be groups of organisations but also groups within organisations where the development and maintenance of communicative relationships is paramount to the successful evolution of a virtual entity (Ahuja and Carley, 1998). However, the ability to establish multiple alliances and the need to retain a particular identity creates a constant tension between autonomy and interdependence, competition and cooperation (Nouwens and Bouwman, 1995). These relationships are often described as value-added partnerships based on horizontal, vertical or symbiotic relationships. These in turn relate to competitors, value chain collaborators and complementary providers of goods and services, all of whom combine to achieve competitive advantage over organisations outside these networks. The nature of the alliances which form the virtual organisation, their strength and substitutability define the inherent virtual structure.

Markets differ from networks since markets are traditionally coordinated by pricing mechanisms. In this sense, the electronic market is no different, but further "central to the conceptualisations of the electronic marketplace is the ability of any buyer or seller to interconnect with a network to offer wares or shop for goods and services. Hence, ubiquity is by definition a prerequisite" (Steinfield, Kraut and Plummer, 1995). There are different risks associated with being a market-maker and a market-player and different products will also carry different risks. Criteria for successful electronic market development include products with low asset specificity and ease of description, and a consumer market willing to buy without recourse to visiting retail stores (Wigand and Benjamin, 1995). Necessarily, the most important asset to an electronic market is the availability of pervasive ICT infrastructures providing a critical mass of customers. A virtual organisation is both constrained and supported by the electronic market in which it operates and the stage to which its business environment has developed as an e-business. Figure 1 shows this set of relationships.

Despite the growth of on-line activity, many firms are nervous of the risks involved and fear a general deterioration of profit margins coupled with a relinquishment of market

Figure 1: Virtual Organisations and Virtual Cultures

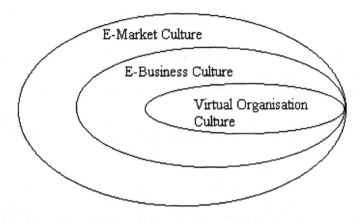

control (Burn and Barnett, 1999). Nevertheless, as existing organisations are challenged by new entrants using direct channels to undercut prices and increase market share, solutions have to be found that enable organisations to successfully migrate into the electronic market. The authors suggest that there are six different models of virtuality which may be appropriate.

MODELS OF VIRTUALITY

This section identifies six different forms of virtual organisations as :
Virtual faces
Co-alliance models
Star-alliance models – core or satellite
Value-alliance models – stars or constellations
Market-alliance models
Virtual brokers

Put simply, virtual faces are the cyberspace incarnations of an existing non-virtual organisation (often described as a "place" as opposed to "space" organisation, Rayport and Sviokola, 1995) and create additional value such as enabling users to carry out the same transactions over the Internet as they could otherwise do by using telephone or fax, e.g., Fleurop selling flowers or air tickets by Travelocity. The services may, however, reach far beyond this enabling the virtual face to mirror the whole activities of the parent organisation and even extend these, e.g., the Web-based versions of television channels and newspapers with constant news updates and archival searches. Al-

Figure 2. The Virtual Face

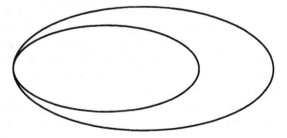

ternatively they may just extend the scope of activities by use of facilities such as electronic procurement, contract tendering or even electronic auctions or extend market scope by participating in an electronic mall with or without added enrichment such as a common payment mechanism. There is obviously an extremely tight link between the virtual face and the parent organisation. This model can be actualised as an e-shop, e-auction or even e-mall.

Figure 3. Co-alliance Model

Co-alliance models are shared partnerships with each partner bringing approximately equal amounts of commitment to the virtual organisation thus forming a consortia. The composition of the consortia may change to reflect market opportunities or to reflect the core competencies of each member (Preiss, Goldman and Nagel, 1996). Focus can be on specific functions such as collaborative design or engineering or in providing virtual support with a virtual team of consultants. Links within the co-alliance are normally contractual for more permanent alliances or by mutual convenience on a project-by-project basis. There is not normally a high degree of substitutability within the life of that virtual creation.

Figure 4. Star -alliance Model

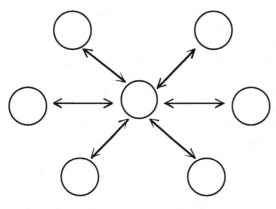

Star-alliance models are co-ordinated networks of interconnected members reflecting a core surrounded by satellite organisations. The core comprises leaders who are the dominant players in the market and supply competency or expertise to members. These alliances are commonly based around similar industries or company types. While this form is a true network, typically the star or leader is identified with the virtual face and so the core organisation is very difficult to replace whereas the satellites may have a far greater level of substitutability.

Value-alliance models bring together a range of products, services and facilities in one package and are based on the value or supply chain model. Participants may come together on a project by project basis but generally coordination is provided by the general contractor. Where longer term relationships have developed the value alliance often adopts the form of value constellations where firms supply each of the companies in the value chain and a complex and continuing set

Figure 5. Value-alliance model

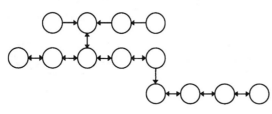

of strategic relationships are embedded into the alliance. Substitutability will relate to the positioning on the value chain and the reciprocity of the relationship.

Figure 6. Market-alliance Model

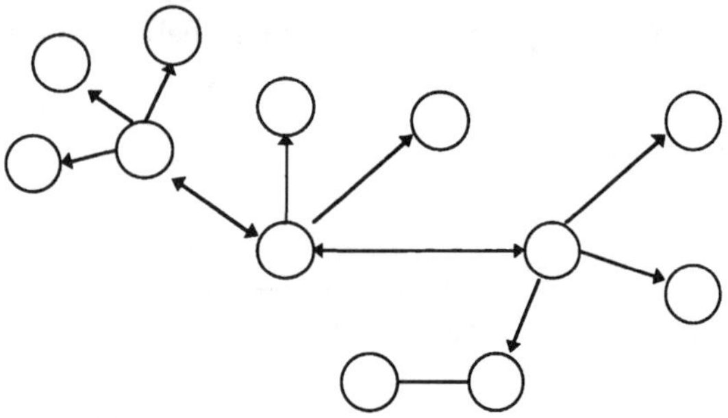

Market-alliances are organisations that exist primarily in cyberspace, depend on their member organisations for the provision of actual products and services and operate in an electronic market. Normally they bring together a range of products, services and facilities in one package, each of which may be offered separately by individual organisations. In some cases the market is open and in others serves as an intermediary. These can also be described as virtual communities but a virtual community can be an add-on such as exists in an e-mall rather than a cyberspace organisation perceived as a virtual organisation. Amazon.com is a prime example of a market-alliance model where substitutability of links is very high.

Virtual Brokers are designers of dynamic networks (Miles and Snow, 1986). These prescribe additional strategic opportunities either as third-party value-added suppliers such as in the case of common Web marketing events (e-Xmas) or as information brokers providing a virtual structure around specific business information services (Timmers, 1998). This has the highest level of flexibility with purpose built virtual organisations created to fill a window of opportunity and dissolved when that window is closed.

As discussed previously each of these alliances carries with it a set of tensions related to autonomy and interdependence. Virtual culture is the strategic hub around which virtual relationships are formed and virtual links implemented. In order to be flexible, links must be substitutable, to allow the creation of new competencies, but links must be established and maintained if the organisation is going to fully leverage community expertise. This presents a dichotomy. The degree to which virtuality can be implemented effectively relates to the strength of existing organisational links (virtual and non virtual) and the relationship which these impose on the virtual structure. However, as essentially net-

Figure 7. Virtual Broker

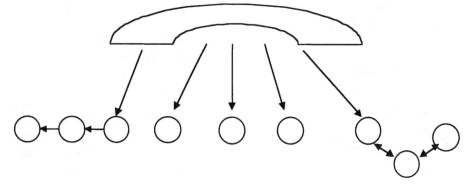

Figure 8. Virtual Alliance Models

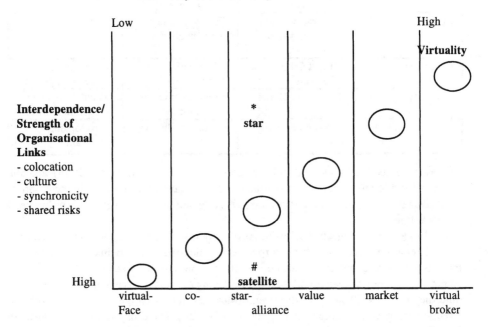

Autonomy/Substitutability of virtual links

worked organisations they will be constrained by the extent to which they are able to redefine or extend their virtual linkages. Where existing linkages are strong e.g. co-located, shared culture, synchronicity of work and shared risk (reciprocity) these will both reduce the need for or perceived benefits from substitutable linkages and inhibit the development of further virtual linkages. Figure 8 provides a diagrammatic representation of these tensions and their interaction with the Virtual Alliance Models (VAM).

These six models are not exclusive but are intended to serve as a way of classifying the diversity of forms which an electronic business model may assume. Some of these are essentially an electronic re-implementation of traditional forms of doing business, others are add-ons for added value possibly through umbrella collaboration and others go far beyond this through value chain integration or cyber communities. What all of these have in common is that they now seek innovative ways to add value through information and change management and a rich functionality. Creating value through virtuality is only feasible if the processes which support such innovations are clearly understood.

VIRTUAL ORGANISATIONAL CHANGE MODEL

These six forms of virtual organisations all operate within a dynamic environment where their ability to change will determine the extent to which they can survive in a competitive market. Organisational theorists suggest that the ability of an organisation to change relates to internal and external factors (Miles and Snow, 1986), including the organisation's technology, structure and strategy, tasks and management processes,

Table 1. E-Market Ecosystem

EcoSystem Stage	Leadership Challenges	Cooperative Challenges	Competitive Challenges
Birth	Maximise customer delivered value	Find & Create new value in an efficient way	Protect your ideas
Expansion	Attract Critical Mass of Buyers	Work with Suppliers and Partners	Ensure market standard approach
Authority	Lead co-evolution	Provide compelling vision for the future	Maintain strong bargaining power
Renewal or Death	Innovate or Perish	Work with Innovators	Develop and Maintain

individual skills and roles, and culture (DeLisi, 1990; Venkatraman, 1994) and the business in which the organisation operates and the degree of uncertainty in the environment (Donaldson, 1995). These factors are also relevant to virtual organisations but need further refinement.

Moore (1997) suggests that businesses are not just members of certain industries but parts of a complex ecosystem that incorporates bundles of different industries. The driving force is not pure competition but co-evolution. The system is seen as "an economic community supported by a foundation of interacting organisations and individuals. Over time they coevolve their capabilities and roles, and tend to align themselves with the direction set by one or more central companies" (p. 26). The ecosystems evolve through four distinct stages:
- Birth
- Expansion
- Authority
- Death

And at each of these stages the system faces different leadership, cooperative and competitive challenges.

This ecosystem can be viewed as the all-embracing electronic market culture within which the e-business maintains an equilibrium. The organisational "virtual culture" is the degree to which the organisation adopts virtual organising and this in turn will affect the individual skills, tasks and roles throughout all levels of the organisation. Venkatraman and Henderson (1998) identify three vectors of virtual organising as:
- Virtual Encounters
- Virtual Sourcing
- Virtual Work

Virtual encounters refers to the extent to which you virtually interact with the market defined at three levels of greater virtual progression:
- Remote product/service experience
- Product/service customisation
- Shaping customer solutions

Virtual Sourcing refers to competency leveraging from:
- Efficient sourcing of standard components
- Efficient asset leverage in the business network
- New competencies through alliances

Virtual Work refers to:
- Maximising individual experience
- Harnessing organisational expertise
- Leveraging of community expertise

Figure 9 is an adaptation of the 'Virtual Organising' model proposed by Venkatraman and Henderson (1998). The component parts of this paper have been embedded into their original diagram. As a holistic model it summarises the way the four dimensions (activities) work together with synergy, to enable an ERP organisation to delivery information-rich products and services—sustainable competitive advantage. Observe the value and complexity increases for each activity as you step up axes away from the origin. The small triangle as it moves away from the origin represents an ERP organisation able to deliver its products and services with increased value.

As organisations step up the ICT axis, there is a cause and effect or pull of 'enabling technologies' on the other axes. This is illustrated in the model by a shift of the small triangle (ERP organisation) away from the origin along this axis. It also means a shift to higher levels in the other three dimensions of competency, management, and market behaviour, thus migrating the organisation towards an *electronic consultative enterprise*. Furthermore, there is the potential to take the organisation beyond an electronic consultative enterprise, where collaboration and competition are in tension with each other at all levels.

To obtain returns on investment, the networked organisation or virtual organisation

Figure 9: Information rich Products and Services by ERP Organisations

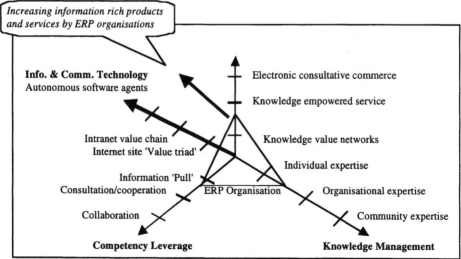

must establish explicit processes to increase collaboration and to facilitate the flow of knowledge throughout the enterprise. In an organisation where an Enterprise Resource Planning (ERP) package is used to align usage of ICT with the virtual alliance model, the stages of development which would be involved in virtual organising are shown in Figure 9 where the third levels all relate to an organisation with an "information rich" product and the highest degree of use of ICT. The component parts of ERP have been embedded into their original diagram. As a holistic model it summarises how the four dimensions (activities) work together with synergy, to enable an ERP organisation to deliver information rich products and services - sustainable competitive advantage. Observe the value and complexity increases for each activity as you step up axes away from the origin.

Where the third levels all relate to an organisation with an "information rich" product and the highest degree of use of ICT. If we view this as the virtual culture of the organisation then this needs to be articulated through the strategic positioning of the organisation and its structural alliances. It also needs to be supported by the knowledge management processes and the ICT. These relationships are depicted in a dynamic virtual organisation change model as shown below.

The degree to which virtuality can be applied in the organisation will relate to the extent to which the VOCM factors are in alignment. When these are not aligned then the organisation will find itself dysfunctional in its exploitation of the virtual marketspace and so be unable to derive the maximum value benefits from its strategic position in the VAM framework.

The organisation needs to examine the VOCM factors in order to evaluate effectiveness and identify variables for change either within that VAM or to move beyond that

Figure 10. Virtual Organisational Change Model (VOCM)

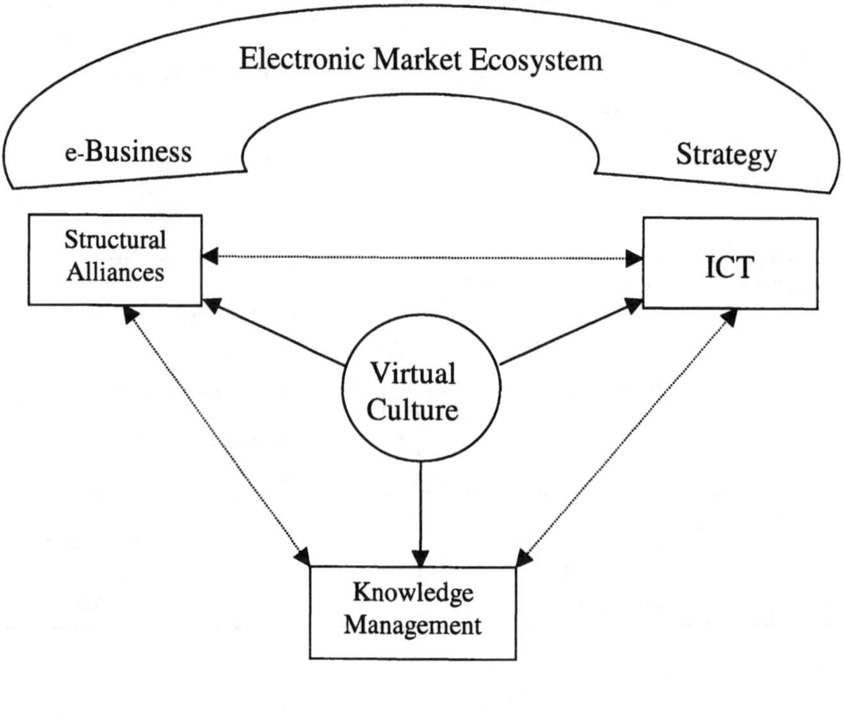

VAM according to the virtual culture. Change directions should be value led but there is as yet very little empirical research to identify how value is derived in a virtual organisation and even less to identify how that knowledge should be built into the management of the virtual organisation.. For virtual organisations performance measurements must cross organisational boundaries and take collaboration into account but it is also necessary to measure value at the individual level since it is feasible that one could be effective without the other (Provan and Milward, 1995).

VIRTUAL KNOWLEDGE MANAGEMENT DEVELOPMENT MODELS

This new world of knowledge based industries is distinguished by its emphasis on precognition and adaptation in contrast to the traditional emphasis on optimisation based on prediction. The environment is characterised by radical and discontinuous change demanding anticipatory responses from organisation members leading to a faster cycle of knowledge creation and action (Denison and Mishra, 1995).

Knowledge management is concerned with recognising and managing all of an organisation's intellectual assets to meet business objectives. It " caters to the critical issues of organisational adaptation, survival and competence in the face of increasingly discontinuous environmental change. Essentially, it embodies organisational processes that seek synergistic combination of data and information processing capacity of information technologies, and the creative and innovative capacity of human beings." (Malhotra, 1997). Knowledge does not come from processes or activities; it comes from people and communities of people. An organisation needs to know what knowledge it has and what knowledge it requires – both tacit and formulated—who knows about what, who needs to know and an indication of the importance of the knowledge to the organisation and the risks attached. The goal of a knowledge management strategy should be to understand the presence of knowledge communities and the various channels of knowledge sharing within and between them, and to apply ICT appropriately. This takes place at the level of the individual networks of knowledge within the organisation and community networks.

EMPOWERING THE INDIVIDUAL

The key characteristic of ICT is it enables a shift in the control of information flow from the information creators to the information users (Telleen, 1996). Individuals using the Web are able to select the information they want, a model of retrieval referred to as information pull. This contrasts with the old 'broadcast' technique of informa-

Figure 11: Deploying Web Technology

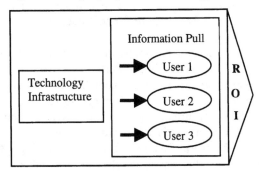

Table 2: A Summary of Traits of Knowledge Workers

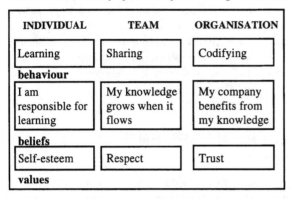

INDIVIDUAL	TEAM	ORGANISATION
Learning **behaviour**	Sharing	Codifying
I am responsible for learning **beliefs**	My knowledge grows when it flows	My company benefits from my knowledge
Self-esteem **values**	Respect	Trust

tion push where the information is sent to them 'just-in-case', normally determined by a prescribed list. Such technology empowers individuals. (Figure 11).

For success in deploying ICT management needs to focus on internal effectiveness. In particular, effective integration of the technology into the enterprise infrastructure and a shift in the control of information flow to the users. To be effective and not just efficient (high ROI), requires not only a new information infrastructure, but also a shift in individual attitudes and organisational culture. This can be summarised as in Table 2.

To supplement the ideas expressed in Figure 11, Gonzalez (1998), gives two key factors for successful intranet development. Firstly, the intranet must fulfill its value proposition. Secondly, employees must want to pull content to themselves. Here the term value proposition is used to expand the requirements for a successful web site:

- satisfy employees' communication and information needs, e.g., helps me do my job better,
- possess outstanding product features, e.g. intuitive navigation and visually pleasing,
- exhibit operating excellence - e.g. convenient, reliable.

These three elements referred to as the Value Triad, work together to create a value proposition. If any one of the three is weak or fails, then the value proposition is reduced.

KNOWLEDGE VALUE NETWORKS

Prior to the development of the Internet manufacturing companies successfully utilised the value chain approach to increase their ability to compete. Faced with increasing cost pressure from global competitors with significantly more favourable labour costs, companies understood that pure price competition was not a viable option. Through the use of the value chain model, companies determined that speed and service would offer the best hope for continued success and growth. But are they able to sustain their success?

The sustainable competitive advantage of the firm derives from the "synergy" of the firm's various capabilities. Porter (1985) has proposed a similar concept in his notion of "complementarities." He argues that the various competitive capabilities of the firm should be "complementary" or "synergistic" so that the synergy resulting from them cannot be easily imitated by current or potential competitors.

Carlson (1995) uses the idea of synergy to develop a 'totally new' model called the Value Network. This model involves creating a shared knowledge infrastructure that enables and "harnesses the flow of knowledge within and between communities". The premise used here is that sustainable competitive advantage can only be attained through a careful integration of activities in a firm's value chain (network), and with knowledge being the basis for this activity integration. Whereas a chain implies sequential flow, a network carries a "connotation of multidimensional interconnectedness". He has developed a model for guiding or managing the change of an old world enterprise through three stages of migration to a knowledge based enterprise that is able to deliver information rich products and services, namely:

- **Knowledge Value Networks**—extend the value chain model for competitive advantage to a highly interconnected internet of knowledge flows;
- **Knowledge Empowered Service**—builds on the value network, enabling customer service representatives to become more effective agents of the organization by giving them better access to the shared knowledge;
- **Electronic Consultative Commerce**—creates competitive advantage by taking e-commerce to the next higher plane, where customers have direct access to the organization's intelligence.

The knowledge value network and knowledge empowered service, are the first steps towards *electronic consultative commerce*. With electronic consultative commerce a customer would engage in a collaborative process, where human and computer software agents both perform tasks, monitor events, as well as initiate communication.

In Figure 12, the diagram illustrates how the various communication links or channels are assisted by software agents and/or human consultants. The various channels for doing business are usually categorised as: consumer-to-business, business-to-business, and Intranet employee-relationships interactions. Together they contribute to an increasing level of knowledge creation.

Many organisations are expanding the role of consultative customer interaction beyond sales to include consultation in every customer contact. For example, SAPNet is SAP's main medium for information and communication between SAP and its customers and partners. SAPNet contains nearly everything you may wish to know about SAP AG; products and processes, partners and solutions, news groups and SIGs. Most of these roles

Figure12: Electronic Consultative Commerce (adapted from Carlson, 1995)

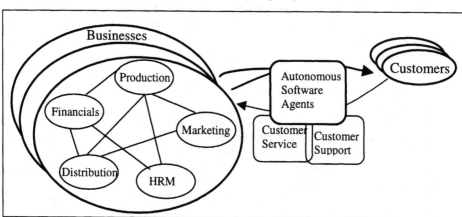

can be supported, at least partially, with a simple Internet site design that includes an underlying information base and a consultative interaction (SAPNet, 1998).

However, more advanced solutions are being developed that employ knowledge-based system technology traditionally found in expert systems. To bring consultative sales directly to the customer is through use of *autonomous agents* (software) that provide assistance to users. 'Instead of user-initiated interaction via commands and/or direct manipulation, the user is engaged in a cooperative process in which human and computer agents both initiate communication, monitor events and perform tasks (Carlson, 1995).

Market niche players like Radnet provide tools and expertise to develop collaborative enterprise applications that fully leverage relational database technology and the entire range of intranet, extranet, and Internet standards. Radnet's InternetShare products and technology help companies realise their competitive advantage by bringing advanced Internet-based collaborative features to their core product offerings (Radnet, 1998).

Autonomous agents can make decisions on a set of options learned from past experiences. So they are fundamentally knowledge-based and belong to the world of artificial intelligence. These agents can be classified in two types: business agents that perform tasks based on business practices, and learning agents that act as electronic teachers. For example, business agents can search product catalogs or 'smart catalogs' while learning agents can assist in configuring products of all combinations, all accessible via an Internet browser (Curran and Keller, 1998).

It's often appropriate, and necessary, for organisations to supplement an electronic commerce strategy with human involvement. A software agent underlying the customer's system interface determines when human assistance is necessary and automatically establishes a telephone connection with a service representative. A more advanced use of learning agents for product configuration can be extended to solve problems associated with R/3 installations. Learning agents have the capacity to search out irrelevant detailed information and deliver the most appropriate information for the user to learn— addressing the problem of information overload. R/3 installation learning agents would greatly reduce the time for business consultants to implement R/3 as well as radically change the way industry-specific applications are deployed. In response to this problem SAP has developed employee self-service intranet application components that deliver preconfigured access to R/3 application servers, making implementation simple and fast (SAP, 1998).

Ultimately the learning agents will enable the non-technical employees to configure new business processes. This assumes IT specialists and employees come together to perform the activities of the value chain so that it becomes possible for users to have a part in the enterprise reengineering. Furthermore, this merging of roles represents a change in ownership of the electronic consultative enterprise's business processes.

There are many claims about enabling technologies which can help to capture and leverage knowledge within the organisation but little about explicit knowledge sharing strategies. Although knowledge is a strategic asset (Eisenhardt and Schoonhoven, 1996; Winter, 1987), embedded or tacit knowledge is difficult to transfer and also vulnerable to loss through misfortune or asset transfers and terminations. Such an important asset should be cultivated and measured but this becomes an impossible task without trust and a close relationship at all levels of the organisation (Scott and Gable, 1997; Badaracco, 1991). This is particularly true of the virtual organisation.

To leverage the benefits of supply chain modeling and management via the Internet, you need to be aware of the influences beyond your company. Success in exposing your business partners to enterprise systems depends as much on people issues–trust, understanding and communication–as it does on technology (Chirgwin, 1998). This implies a shared vision of culture across all levels of the enterprise.

CONCLUSIONS

The virtual organisation is recognised as a dynamic form of interorganisational systems (Burn, Marshall and Wild, 1999) and hence one where traditional hierarchical forms of management and control may not apply. Little, however, has been written about the new forms which management and control might take other than to espouse a "knowledge management" approach. Managing knowledge about what? In an organisation where change is the only constant, there has to be a system which can capture the organisational core competencies and leverage these to provide strategic advantage. This may be a competitive advantage or a strategic advantage in collaboration with the competition. Knowledge has become the major asset of the organisation, and its recording, communication and management deserve attention. Without the ability to identify who has the key information, who the experts are, and who needs to be consulted, management decisions are unlikely to be optimal. Both the importance and the difficulty of the issue are magnified by virtuality in the form of decentralisation and dispersion, empowerment and continual change. In interdependent organisations the synergy of knowledge may be the principal benefit of the interdependence and the issue is again magnified.

In dispersed organisations more conscious efforts and explicit procedures are needed. Skills may not be available where they are wanted, data may not be shared and might be used inefficiently or wrongly. New skills need to be developed quickly and employees will have to take personal responsibility for their own knowledge development. This implies that the virtual organisation will need a number of managers with converging expertise in the areas identified within the VOCM. There may no longer be a separate ICT or knowledge management function. Indeed there may no longer be any management function which does not explicitly demand expertise in these areas. The implications for IS professionals are quite frightening. Whole areas of new skills need to be acquired and these skills are themselves constantly in a process of development, demanding continual updates. We are still struggling with the information age as we are being thrust into the knowledge age but without the intermediation services to support this. Opportunities abound for skilled IS professionals at every level of the organisation but this must be supported by an on-going education programme at the heart of every organisation. The virtual organisation that succeeds will be the learning organisation where people are regarded as their greatest core asset.

REFERENCES

Ahuja, M. K., & Carley, K. M. (1998). Network structure in virtual organizations. *Journal of Computer-Mediated Communication* [On-line], 3 (4). Available: http://www.ascusc.org/jcmc/vol3/issue4/ahuja.html.

Aldridge, D. (1998). Purchasing on the Net – The New Opportunities for Electronic Commerce. *EM – Electronic Markets*, 8(1), 34-37.

Badaracco, J.L. The Knowledge Links, in Myers, P.S. (1996) *Knowledge Management and Organisation Design*, Butterworth-Heinemann, USA, 133.

Barner, R. (1996). The New Millenium Workplace: Seven changes that will challenge managers and workers. *Futurist*, 30(2), 14-18.

Berger, M. (1996). Making the Virtual Office a Reality. Sales and marketing Management, *SMT Supplement*, June, 18-22.

Burn, J. M. and Barnett, M. L., Communicating for Advantage in the Virtual Organisation, *IEEE Transactions on Professional Communication*, 42(4), 1-8.

Burn,J., Marshall, P. & Wild, M., (1999). Managing Change in the Virtual Organisation, *ECIS,* Copenhagen Denmark, Vol. 1, 40-54.

Byrne, J. (1993). The Virtual Corporation. *Business Week*, 36-41.

Carlson, DA (1995). Harnessing the Flow of Knowledge, [http://www.dimensional.com/~dcarlson/papers/KnowFlow.htm]

Chirgwin, R. (1998). The Culture of the Model Enterprise, *Systems,* February, Australia; 14-22.

Chesbrough, H. W. and Teece D. J. (1996). When is Virtual Virtuous? *Harvard Business Review*, Jan-Feb,65-73.

Davidow, W. H. and Malone, M. S. (1992). *The Virtual Corporation*, New York: Harper Business.

DeLisi, P. S. (1990). Lessons from the Steel Axe: Culture, Technology and Organisation Change. *Sloan Management Review*.

Denison, D.R. and Mishra, A.K. (1995) 'Toward a Theory of Organizational Culture and Effectiveness', *Organization Science*, 6(2), March-April, 204-223.

Donaldson, L. (1995). *American Anti-Management theories of Organisation*. Cambridge UK., Cambridge University Press.

Eisenhardt, K M. Schoonhoven, C B (1996). Resource-Based View of Strategic Alliance Formation: Strategic and Social Effects in Entrepreneurial Firms, *Organization Science* (7:2), March-April, 136-150.

Finnegan, P., Galliers, B. and Powell, P. (1998);. Systems Planning in an Electronic Commerce Environment in Europe: Rethinking Current Approaches. *EM – Electronic Markets*, 8(2), 35-38.

Goldman, S. L., Nagel R. N. and Preiss, K. (1995). *Agile Competitors and Virtual Organisations: Strategies for Enriching the Customer*, New York: Van Nostrand Reinhold.

Gonzalez, J.S. (1998) *The 21st-Century INTRANET*, Prentice-Hall, N.J. 189-215, 240.

Grabowski, M. and Roberts, K. H. (1996). Human and Organisational Error in Large Scale Systems. *IEEE Transactions on Systems, Man and Cybernetics*, 26(1), 2-16.

Gray, P. and Igbaria, M. (1996). *The Virtual Society*, ORMS Today, December, 44-48.

Greiner, R. and Metes, G. (1996). *Going Virtual: Moving your Organisation into the 21st Century*. Englewood Cliffs, NJ: Prentice Hall.

Hoffman, D.L., Novak, T.P., & Chatterjee, P. (1995). Commercial scenarios for the Web: Opportunities and challenges. *Journal of Computer-Mediated Communication* [Online], 1 (3). Available: http://www.ascusc.org/jcmc/vol1/issue3/hoffman.html

Katzy, B. R. (1998). Design and Implementation of Virtual Organisations. *HICSS*, Vol, 44-48 .

Malhotra, Y. (1997). *Knowledge Management for the New World of Business*, [http://www.brint.com/km/whatis.htm].

Miles, R. E. and Snow, C. C. (1986). Organisations: new concepts for new forms. *California Management Review* 28(3), 2-73.

Moore, J. F. (1997). *The Death of Competition: Leadership and Strategy in the Age of Business Ecosystems.* New York, Harper Business.

Nouwens, J., & Bouwman, H. (1995). Living apart together in electronic commerce: The use of information and communication technology to create network organizations. *Journal of Computer-Mediated Communication* [On-line], 1 (3).vailable: http://www.ascusc.org/jcmc/vol1/issue3/nouwens.html

Palmer J. W. and Speier, C. (1998). Teams: Virtualness and Media Choice, *Proceedings of HICSS*, Vol IV.

Porter, M.E. (1985) *Competitive Advantage*, Macmillan, N.Y.

Powell, W. W. (1990). Neither Market nor Hierarchy: Network Forms of Organisation. *Research in Organisational Behaviour*, 12, 295-336.

Preiss, K., Goldman, S. L. and Nagel, R. N. (1996). *Cooperate to Compete.* New York: Van Nostrand Reinhold.

Provan, K. and Milward, H. (1995). A Preliminary Theory of Inter-Organisational Network Effectiveness: A Comparative Study of Four Community Mental Health Systems. *Adminstrative Science Quarterly*, 14, 91-114.

Rayport, J. F. and Sviokola, J. (1995). Exploiting the Virtual Value Chain. *Harvard Business Review*, 73 (6), 75-86.

Radnet, (1998) [http://www.radnet.com/]

Rogers, 1D. M. (1996). The Challenge of Fifth generation R and D. *Research Technology Management*, 39(4), 33-41.

SAP, (1998) [http://www.sap.com/internet/]

SAPNet, (1998) [http://www.sap.com/SAPNet/]

Schein, E. (1990). Organisational Culture. *American Psychologist*, 45(2), 109-119.

Scott J.E and Gable, G.(1997) Goal Congruence, Trust, and Organizational Culture: Strengthening Knowledge Links, *ICIS 97 proceedings*, 107-119.

Steinfield, C., Kraut, R., & Plummer, A. (1995). The impact of electronic commerce on buyer-seller relationships. *Journal of Computer-Mediated Communication* [On-line], 1 (3). Available: http://www.ascusc.org/jcmc/vol1/issue3/steinfld.html

Swatman, P. M. C. and Swatman, P. A. (1992). EDI System Integration: A Definition and Literature Survey. *The Information Society* (8), 165-205.

Telleen, S.L. (1996). Intranets and Adaptive Innovation, [http://www.amdahl.com/doc/products/bsg/intra/adapt.html]

Timmers, P. (1998). Business Models for Electronic Markets. *EM – Electronic Markets*, 8(2), 3-8.

Tushman, M. L. and O'Reilly, III, C. A. (1996). Ambidextrous Organisations: Managing Evolutionary and Revolutionary Change. *California Management Review*, 38(4), 8-29.

Venkatraman, N. (1994). IT-Enabled Business Transformation: From Automation to Business Scope Redefinition, *Sloan Management Review*, Winter.

Venkatraman, N. and Henderson, J. C. (1998). Real Strategies for Virtual Organizing, *Sloan Management Review*, Fall, 33-48.

Wigand, R.T., & Benjamin, R.I. (1995). Electronic Commerce: Effects on electronic markets. *Journal of Computer-Mediated Communication* [On-line], 1 (3). Available:

Chapter IX

Virtual Organizations That Cooperate and Compete: Managing the Risks of Knowledge Exchange

Claudia Loebbecke
Copenhagen Business School, Denmark

Paul C. van Fenema
Erasmus University, The Netherlands

'Co-opetition' describes the phenomenon that firms engage in a virtual form of interaction where they cooperate *and* compete with their counterparts. Such hybrid relationships challenge traditional notions of firm boundaries and strategic resource management. There seems a contradiction in the fact that partners are supposed to share knowledge which is at the same time a key determinant of their competitive advantage. This balancing act suggests the need for special competencies that enable companies to reap the benefits of temporary synergy, while avoiding risks associated with making knowledge available to external partners.

This chapter explores the art of controlling knowledge flows in 'coopetitive' relationships. We conceptualize types of knowledge flows and dependencies, resulting in four configurations. For each of these, risks in terms of deviations from the original agreement are examined. We propose control strategies that allow companies engaged in co-opetition to anticipate deviant trajectories and define adequate responses. Directions for future research on this topic are indicated.

THE VIRTUAL ECONOMY

Digital technologies are changing economic relationships for the exchange of products, services, and knowledge. Electronic interaction facilities and information environments complement and substitute traditional business models for customer transactions (Venkatraman & Henderson, 1998). Clients start to experience the Internet as a vast resource of information and a facilitator of their consumption cycles. This ranges from *a priori* obtaining information on products, services and outlets, to purchasing and ex post support (Schwartz, 1999). In turn, companies approach existing and new clientele on the Web with a digital identity and experience environment (Breen, 1999).

Behind the emerging digital façade, organizations are changing their operations. 'Virtuality' impacts companies along two lines. First, companies start to operate in a distributed fashion. Electronic media and infrastructure allow employees to interact remotely on the same project or business process (Evaristo & van Fenema, 1999). Digital communication infrastructures make real time and asynchronous connectivity possible, independent of the location of actors involved (Dertouzos, 1999). New organizational forms emerge that translate the advantages of electronic communications into flexible modes for organizing work (DeSanctis & Fulk, 1999).

Virtuality also has a second connotation that is different but often interacts with the first one. It implies cooperation among multiple companies in such a way that a quasi-organizational entity emerges. Traditional business models assume that each firm is responsible for a well-defined and complete portion of the supply chain. This relative independence is transformed to a tissue of firms that are strongly connected. Market opportunities trigger combinatorial processes that result in ad hoc forms of cooperation (Meyerson, Weick, & Kramer, 1996). Each firm contributes interactively to a coherent, aggregated performance that individual organizations could not achieve (Goldman, Preiss, & Nagel, 1997). The intricate connectivity among contributing firms implies exchange of valuable resources like knowledge and information. In this chapter, we are interested in organizations that form a quasi single entity but have interests that partially diverge (Preiss, Goldman, & Nagel, 1997).

KNOWLEDGE EXCHANGE AND CO-OPETITION

Theorists adopting a resource-based approach to strategic management have emphasized a firm's need for unique, internal resources and competencies (Nelson & Winter, 1982; Wernerfelt, 1984). Further refinements and extensions stress the role of corporate competencies to enable dynamic adaptation and competitive advantage (Barney & Hesterley, 1996). Ever since the contribution from Penrose (1959), this approach has recognized the importance of knowledge as one of the supreme enablers of competitive differentiation. Recently, some papers in *Strategic Management Journal*, in particular the Winter Special Issue 1996, and in *Organization Science* proceeded along this route by investigating synergies of knowledge management and strategic management theory (Grant, 1996a). From multiple perspectives this growing body of literature contributes to our understanding of managing knowledge transfer, integration and creation within corporations (Nonaka & Takeuchi, 1995).

In addition to intra-corporate knowledge sharing, some academics have started to investigate knowledge sharing processes *across* organizational boundaries (Loebbecke & van Fenema, 1998; Wathne, Roos, & von Krogh, 1996). Knowledge sharing has been defined as "the transfer of useful know-how or information across company lines" (Appleyard, 1996: 138). Research on inter-organizational knowledge sharing recognizes the fact that firms are nowadays involved in multiple temporal or more permanent agreements for cooperation (Kodama, 1994). Organizations find temporary modes for leveraging knowledge as one of their primary resources.

However, inter-organizational collaboration may confront companies with a paradox (Hamel, Doz, & Prahalad, 1989). On the one hand, reciprocal knowledge sharing may enhance the summed and individual added value. Partners can translate unique, hardly accessible resources from their counterparts into new business opportunities. However, from a resource-based perspective, inter-firm knowledge sharing may affect the uniqueness and thus competitive contribution of a firm's knowledge repository. Opportunistic behaviors of counterparts may erode anticipated benefits of cooperation and result in unevenly distributed value. In their book *Co-opetition* Brandenburg and Nalebuff (1996) point to the potential tension of relationships where firms cooperate and compete, the latter possibly in other markets or at other points of time. Since companies increasingly open up to engage in these hybrid organization modes, it becomes important to understand and develop the phenomenon (Loebbecke, van Fenema, & Powell 1999).

The purpose of this chapter is to investigate strategies for controlling knowledge as one of the primary resources in 'coopetitive' relationships. We investigate inter-firm collaboration involving knowledge with assumed operational and business value *beyond* the context of the cooperative agreement. We assume that *both* parties can translate the collaborative knowledge into adjacent or overlapping business capabilities and hence exploit *additional opportunities beyond the collaboration*. This suggests partially diverging interests between collaborating partners and motivates the development of a strategic perspective on managing knowledge flows across organizational boundaries.

We discuss background theory on inter-organizational governance and elaborate modes for controlling inter-firm transactions. We interpret the strategic issues and paradoxes of inter-firm knowledge sharing as a problem of coordinating and controlling the behaviors of people *within* the corporation as well as exchanges *across* organizational boundaries. The chapter then develops a concept for distinguishing knowledge flows, and presents four configurations of knowledge exchange in virtual organizations. For each of these we examine potential risks and control strategies.

GOVERNANCE OF INTER-FIRM TRANSACTIONS

Virtual organizations operate in a fluid environment with little enduring connectivity among participating firms. For that reason, transactions among these firms become a pivotal unit of analysis (Williamson, 1994). Transaction Cost Economics (TCE) has structured our understanding of governance transactions by contrasting markets and hierarchical forms of exchange (Williamson & Ouchi, 1981). Determinants of economic governance modes include environmental factors like uncertainty and the number of transactions. In addition, a set of assumptions concerning human behaviors play a role, like bounded rationality and opportunism (Williamson, 1975). Market governance typically applies to situations where reciprocal performances are specified in detail (Williamson, 1994). Contracts thus facilitate the process of ensuring compliance between intended and actual exchange, leaving little room for opportunistic deviations (Ouchi, 1979).[1] An alternative to market governance are internal organizations which are characterized by extensive horizontal and vertical differentiation (Rice & Shook, 1990). The functioning of individuals being part of such a 'bureaucracy' is closely prepared, tracked, and evaluated. Moreover, the availability of collective experience implies refined communication processes that allow actors to economize on problem solving. For that reason, internal governance forms are apt to handle transactions that concern incompletely specified activities (Williamson, 1975).

New Perspectives on Transaction Governance

Scholars have extended the original premises of TCE in several directions. First, the rational perspective on the operation of bureaucracies is complemented with insights from Japanese firms (Ouchi, 1979). Ouchi suggests a clan mode of organizing. The selection and promotion of individuals is not only based on task-related competence, but also relies on their commitment to company goals. In the *Academy of Management Review*, More, Ghoshal and Moran (1996) critique the underlying assumption of TCE that individual behavior is driven by opportunism. They warn that organizations may translate this assumption into coercive control systems that rely on measurable behaviors and work outcomes. As a consequence, firms may recede from work that requires fluid adaptation and instead focus on specifiable work. In turn, companies may fail to leverage one of their original advantages over markets: their capability to accomplish innovative work and achieve dynamic efficiency (Ghoshal & Moran, 1996; Williamson, 1991).

Second, researchers nuance the opportunistic drive of firms operating in markets (Macneil, 1978). Organizations may decide to build sustainable relationships and focus on common interests (Kumar & van Dissel, 1996). Situations where instantaneous exchanges of tightly controlled performances are not feasible may necessitate closer examination of the counterpart's identity to still ensure quality (Ben-Porath, 1980). For example, transactions evolve over time and need reciprocal interactions among firms to identify expectations (Rousseau & McLean Parks, 1993; Thompson, 1967). This occurs in large, complicated projects where parts of the work are outsourced or even subcontracted to different firms (Bryman, Bresnen, Beardsworth, Ford, & Keil, 1987). Similarly, empirical research claims that relational contracts provide the primary means for governing transactions in regional network structures (Powell & Smith-Doerr, 1994), like the Italian industrial districts (Kumar, van Dissel, & Bielli, 1998; Lazerson, 1995).

A third stream of research claims that firms mix elements of 'price' (market governance), 'authority' (hierarchy) and 'trust' (clan modes) to sculpt their internal operations and exchanges with other companies (Bradach & Eccles, 1989). Bradach elaborates examples of these hybrid or plural forms. His research on restaurant chains shows that these organizations combine internal bureaucracy with a franchising network to create large numbers of outlets that have the same outward appearance to customers (Bradach, 1997). In fact, this quasi single entity provides an example of a virtual organization as different governance forms are combined to pursuit (temporarily) shared business objectives.

Finally, researchers have explored the variety of coordination mechanisms employed in inter-firm relationships (Grandori & Soda, 1995). Depending on contingencies like the type of workflow interdependence and structurability, organizations choose modes for interacting and planning exchanges (Grandori, 1997; Kumar & van Dissel, 1996).

CONTROL STRATEGIES

Coordination and control approaches have dominated organization theory, and are still at the core of scholarly thinking on organizational phenomena. Theorizing has long followed two separate lines of inquiry, with one group focussing on intra-corporate linkages (Chandler Jr. & Daems, 1979), and other scholars studying inter-firm strategies for managing transactions (Williamson, 1975). As indicated, the field starts to intermingle both perspectives as more complex, hybrid forms emerge that combine elements of both (Bradach & Eccles, 1989). In the spirit of that emerging tradition, we categorize control strategies along four dimensions. We briefly introduce both intra and inter-firm equivalents, to be used later on when we investigate the control of knowledge exchanges. Intra-organizational coordination and control refers to the mechanisms that structure, execute and evaluate organizational task accomplishment (Ching, Holsapple, & Whinston, 1992). Management of inter-firm tasks includes contractual formalization as well as inter-organizational roles like liaisons or project teams (Grandori, 1997).

Procedural strategies indicate a process of conceiving work beforehand, and documenting that understanding in formal boundary objects like schedules, plans, and generic work instructions (Star & Griesemer, 1989). The same principle returns in case of inter-firm transactions; classical contracts govern exchanges that are "sharp in by clear agreement; sharp out by clear performance" (Macneil, 1974: 738). The fact that work is *a priori* conceived and prescribed implies that control efforts are simplified to monitoring for deviations in the actual execution of work (O'Reilly & Chatman, 1996).

Organizational structures stand for the design of roles that are interconnected and intended to enact the control process (Gupta, Dirsmith, & Fogarty, 1994). Within organizations, vertical control relationships are embedded in a managerial hierarchy, while lateral roles include peer assessment (McCann & Galbraith, 1981). The responsibility for inter-firm transactions are often exclusively delegated to liaisons or formal linking pins (Grandori, 1997).

Social control strategies refer to norms governing interpersonal communications in working relationships (Gabarro, 1990), groups (Barker, 1993) or organizations (Kunda, 1992). Actors shape norms for behaviors and monitor each other to ensure compliance (Schein, 1992). Organizations may also foster relationships across their boundaries as actors on both sides get to know each other (Ben-Porath, 1980), and can identify with their counterparts' preferences and interests (Bryman et al., 1987).

Technology supports the process of work definition, and monitoring actual behaviors and outputs. Traditional forms like mechanization (Edwards, 1981) have been complemented with advanced monitoring devices and integrated business applications like ERP (Orlikowski, 1991). Technology also supports inter-organizational transactions with EDI, supply chain applications, and access to intranet or databases (Kumar & van Dissel, 1996).

KNOWLEDGE-INTENSIVE TRANSACTIONS IN VIRTUAL ORGANIZATIONS

Research on strategic knowledge management has predominantly focused on cognitive processes within a firm's boundaries (Nonaka & Takeuchi, 1995). These processes include creation of knowledge, making tacit knowledge explicit (Nonaka & Takeuchi, 1995), knowledge transfer (Szulanski, 1996) and knowledge integration (Grant, 1996b). The importance of knowledge management for intra-organizational processes equally applies to inter-firm transactions. Companies are engaged in diverse modes of external cooperation (Bradach & Eccles, 1989), and the life cycle of goods and services becomes more knowledge intensive (Grant, 1996b). Our analysis of knowledge exchange in inter-firm relationships proceeds along three lines. First, we expand on the distinction between tacit and explicit knowledge, and provide examples for our argument. Second, the direction of knowledge flows between organizations is elaborated. Finally, we propose a model that combines these dimensions and provides a steppingstone for analyzing risk control strategies.

Tacit and Explicit Knowledge Flows

Literature provides a rich basis for exploring the different types and characteristics of knowledge. Defining the concept itself seems a more feasible challenge for philosophers and social scientists. Hence, as an alternative, we pursue Grant's (1996b) suggestion to focus on *types* of knowledge and their consequences for managerial actions (Machlup, 1980). Knowledge is commonly distinguished in explicit and tacit knowledge, as initially proposed by Polanyi (1967). These two types have influenced subsequent conceptual and empirical research on strategic and organizational knowledge management (Kogut & Zander, 1992; Nonaka & Takeuchi, 1995). *Explicit knowledge* refers to concepts, information and insights that are specifiable, and that can thus be formalized in rules and procedures (Walsh & Dewar, 1987). Access, storage and transfer of this knowledge is achieved by corporate documents and information systems like databases. Examples include detailed engineering specifications for software development or product manufacturing which capture and support inter-human communications (Star & Griesemer, 1989).

On the other hand, implicit or *tacit knowledge* refers to less specifiable insights and skills which are carried in individuals' minds or embedded in an organizational context (Weick & Westley, 1996). Employees develop and refine collectively routines to achieve organizational adaptation and learning (Nelson & Winter, 1982). March and Simon (1958: 142) referred to 'programs' to describe these routines: "Most programs are stored in the minds of the employees who carry them out, or in the minds of superiors, subordinates, or associates." Understanding and transferring this type of knowledge depends on direct participation and inclusion in the context where it resides (Tyre & von Hippel, 1997). Researchers refer to this phenomenon as 'stickiness' (Szulanski, 1996), and pointed to the arduous process of explaining or even integrating tacit knowledge (Grant, 1996a). Exchanging tacit knowledge across organizational boundaries is supposed to exacerbate these issues as professionals lack a set of commonly shared concepts and values provided by an organization's culture (Weick & Westley, 1996).

Direction of Knowledge Sharing

Inter-organizational knowledge sharing is achieved by patterns of transmitting and receiving information. These knowledge-based workflows may take the characteristics of one-way traffic. For example, in an outsourcing agreement, clients share knowledge with their vendors to enable delivery of the product or service (Hamel et al., 1989). This does not necessarily mean that a reverse flows exists, that is, vendors sharing knowledge with their clients. We call this *unidirectional* knowledge sharing. One-way knowledge flows also occur in organizations like marketing research or news agents that even make their business of selling knowledge and expertise.

On the other hand, in many cases the underlying logic of collaboration suggests bidirectional or *reciprocal* knowledge flows. The legacy of such cooperative endeavors relies on integration of complementary knowledge and competencies. Hence, reciprocal sharing of knowledge is a principal determinant for reaping the anticipated benefits of cooperative synergies. These include taking advantage of complementary knowledge and synergistically creating knowledge. An example is collaboration of R&D units where companies share costs by jointly investing in development and manufacturing facilities. Often, like in the semiconductor industry, collaboration is required as investments would exceed an individual firm's resources and require economies of scale.

On an operational level, the different modes of knowledge exchange are associated with different types of workflow interdependencies (Thompson, 1967). Unidirectional, one-way knowledge flows are of a pooled or sequential nature. They comprise subsequent steps of identifying and transferring in a single direction priorly agreed-upon knowledge and information. On the other hand, organizations engaged in reciprocal knowledge sharing face more complicated workflows. Managing these requires inter-firm taskforces of professionals to elaborate and control knowledge exchanges. The work of such a team flows back and forth between both organizations and has been referred to as reciprocal (Thompson, 1967) or team interdependence (Van de Ven, Delbecq, & Koenig Jr., 1976). This intricate mode of cooperation implies that specifying the scope and content of the flows is often not feasible (Kumar & van Dissel, 1996).

Model for Analysis

When the two dimensions are combined, an interesting model emerges as depicted in Table 1. We refer to each type of interaction among the variables as a *configuration*. The use of configurations for investigating organizational phenomena is a common approach in organization science (Meyer, Tsui, & Hinings, 1993). Scholars like Burns and Stalker (1961) and Mintzberg (1979) have built typologies of organizational forms. Choosing relevant variables, they reduce real-life complexity to a limited set of templates. In our case, each configuration epitomizes how virtual organizations can be interconnected. Their distinct properties have different implications for potential risks and control strategies. After the next section, we explore and illustrate each configuration successively.

CO-OPETITION AND THE RISKS OF KNOWLEDGE FLOWS

Virtual organizations involved in cooperative-cum-competitive relationships may experience deviation between intended and actual knowledge flows. Be it deliberately or unconsciously, parties may have different perspectives on the direction and boundaries of

Table 1. A model for inter-firm knowledge flows

	Unidirectional knowledge sharing	Reciprocal knowledge sharing
Explicit, structured knowledge flows	**Configuration 1** Outsourcing strategies: Client-supplier software specifications	**Configuration 2** Exchange of complementary market research information between competitors
Tacit, nonstructured knowledge flows	**Configuration 3** Client-supplier nexus in automotive industry	**Configuration 4** Collaboration of R&D units in semi-conductor industry

the knowledge component in their exchange relationship. Understanding these risks is important to avoid undesirable distribution of valuable knowledge at the end of the cooperative life cycle. We assess here for the dimensions presented in Table 1 potential deviations between originally assumed and actually evolving knowledge interactions.

Explicit Knowledge Flows

Knowledge that is *explicit* can be specified and documented. This enables storage, transfer and sharing by means of corporate documents or information systems. Coordinating these flows requires determining which knowledge companies are willing to share, and reaching agreement on transfer modes. Contracts formalize the contents, the procedures and the deliverables, supplemented by control procedures to verify that actual delivery of knowledge occurs within contractually predefined standards. However, as earlier indicated, our focus is on companies sharing knowledge that both can leverage to adjacent business opportunities beyond their initial agreement. Hence, access to partners' knowledge repository seems a tempting opportunity to absorb knowledge in excess of priorly agreed-upon boundaries as defined in the contract. This may include collecting more knowledge of the same type parties formalized in the contract. Alternatively, a company tries to pull tacit knowledge on top of the explicit knowledge that was specified in the contract. An example of such 'overgrazing' behavior is an outsourcing agreement in which the vendor indicates its need for more detailed specifications and in-depth corporate knowledge that does not bear direct relevance to the execution of the contract (Hamel et al., 1989).

Risks of Tacit Knowledge Flows

Virtual organizations that agree to share *tacit knowledge* expose themselves to the risk of minimally specified interactions. The embedded, intricate nature makes it difficult to confine these knowledge exchanges in advance. Assuming some degree of opportunistic behavior, the receiving firm may employ dynamic tactics to enlarge the flows beyond initial agreements. Similarly, an organization pretending to share tacit knowledge may in practice structure knowledge flows and thus reduce the value of cooperation to its counterpart.

Risks Related to Direction of Knowledge Flows

Unidirectional knowledge flows occur when companies subscribe to a research agency to keep them updated on market trends and developments. At the outset, the agency is supposed to deliver valuable information to its clients, for example by means of a controlled Internet environment. Yet in an attempt to customize its products or resell client-related information, it may track and trace clients' search behaviors. Unilateral provision of knowledge thus transforms into reciprocal exchanges, a possible deviation from the clients' original intentions.

The inverse situation occurs when partners agree upon reciprocal exchanges. Firms formally agree upon collegial collaboration and the necessity of bidirectional information flows. However, if firms pursue a resource-based strategy, they may attempt to restrict mutual sharing to one-way knowledge absorption. Hamel, Doz and Prahalad (1989: 138) quote managers from a Japanese firm employing this strategy: "We don't feel any need to reveal what we know. It is not an issue of pride for us. We're glad to sit and listen. If we're patient we usually learn what we want to know."

Of course, combinations of the risks discussed so far may surface. The next four sections assess for each configuration possible deviation strategies and modes for controlling these.

UNIDIRECTIONAL, STRUCTURED KNOWLEDGE FLOWS (CONFIGURATION 1)

In a strategy aimed at concentrating and nurturing core competencies, increasingly firms outsource peripheral business services like IT projects, marketing, and investment management (McFarlan & Nolan, 1995). To some extent, vendors need corporate knowledge and information to provide their services, and client firms will hence allow vendors to pull from their know-how repository. Our focus here is on the unidirectional transmission of explicit knowledge, like specifications for building and maintaining software. In principle, the outsourced activities do not bear strategic relevance to the client's business, implying a low-risk knowledge flow. Yet both client and vendor may run the risk that exchanges evolve in an undesirable manner.

First, vendors may attempt to absorb more (tacit) knowledge than initially agreed upon, a change to Configuration 3 in Table 1. As they are nestled in a particular industry and serve clients with competitive positions, they may build increasingly sophisticated industry-specific knowledge and use it synergistically in their network. If a client's knowledge is thus leveraged to the vendor's clientele, it becomes a commonly shared good and may lose its uniqueness. In addition, vendors may collect industry-specific know-how to strengthen their competitive position. This enables them to bypass clients and enter their market. Second, clients may change the direction of knowledge flows from unidirectional to reciprocal, encouraging vendors to display their internal competencies (a shift to configuration 4 in Table 1). Incorporation of this know-how decreases the uniqueness of the vendor's performance and hence its competitive position.

Control Strategies

We outline strategies for controlling transitions of exchange relationships using Figure 1. Continuing our example, Company A stands for the client, Company B for the vendor. Knowledge is supposed to flow one-way from A to B. At each organization three teams are involved in the transaction process. Since the transaction concerns the structured transmission of knowledge, it is formalized in detail. The contract specifies which knowledge will be shared, how transmission will be organized, and what procedure will be followed for special requests. The structure of the process substitutes for direct interactions between staff. The articulated character of the knowledge

Figure 1: Controlling the unidirectional flow of structured knowledge

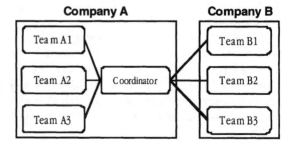

enables transfer modes with low information processing capacity, such as document handovers or controlled access to databases (Daft & Lengel, 1986). Company A reinforces prevention of undesirable knowledge leakage by indirect organizational structures (Perrow, 1999). That is, a centralized coordinator assembles knowledge intended for the external partner prior to the actual exchange process (Allen, 1984). Interaction with Company B is exclusively handled by this gatekeeper, either in person or by controlled access to a digital environment.

Unilateral flows imply that teams at Company B (the vendor) have only direct contact with A's liaison. B can avoid reciprocal interactions between teams at both sides by sticking to that procedure. Enforced by internal guidelines, this approach substitutes for an elaborate safety structure like A has.

RECIPROCAL, STRUCTURED KNOWLEDGE FLOWS (CONFIGURATION 2)

Presence in, and knowledge of local markets often differs between companies having comparable R&D and marketing competencies. In order to enable both companies to leverage their competencies, exchange of complementary local knowledge often seems a viable strategy. This may trigger a process of exchanging for example marketing and sales information, and knowledge of local business opportunities.

From a strategic point of view, such exchange processes make sense. However, when it comes to the actual execution, partners may choose two deviation trajectories. First, each partner can attempt to limit outgoing knowledge flows. As long as only one actor succeeds in pulling knowledge while holding back deliverables, a shift to Configuration 1 occurs. Bilateral attempts to abuse the transactional agreement results in a deadlock situation. Second, one of the firms may try to collect more extensive, tacit knowledge on top of the structured information as agreed upon. In response, the counterpart may choose to pursue the same strategy. Lacking sufficient *a priori* mandate, the cooperation tends to evolve in an intricate exchange relationship (shift to Configuration 4).

Controlling Reciprocal Exchange

The fact that both partners receive and deliver knowledge provides for a complex form of interdependence with recurrent interactions (Thompson, 1967). Still, they can formalize the exchange process as a basic form of transaction governance. The contract stipulates how reciprocal deliveries are intertwined across the life cycle of cooperation. Teams at both sides do not cooperate directly, but funnel their interactions through

Figure 2: Bilateral control strategies

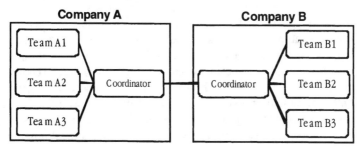

respective coordinators (Figure 2). Internal control procedures stress the exclusive use of coordinating liaisons and technology to submit knowledge for external use (Jaeger & Baliga, 1985).

Exchange between partners is *quid pro quo*: "I will share this with you if you share that with me" (Hamel et al., 1989: 136). Hence, coordinators closely monitor and document knowledge flows to avoid uneven accumulation of know-how. Since the behaviors of partners are complexly interlocked, deviations from the planned exchange process easily occur (Van de Ven et al., 1976). This leads to feedback loops to assess mutual constraints and feasible action patterns. Technology may support the coordinating liaison to plan, monitor and document exchanges. Coordinators have a pivotal role to funnel interactions between teams from both sides. As a substitute for direct interactions between teams, this procedure helps avoid the risk of flow expansion; that is, partners attempting to collect additional, tacit knowledge contrary to initial agreements.

UNIDIRECTIONAL, TACIT KNOWLEDGE FLOWS (CONFIGURATION 3)

The automotive industry has featured many examples of adaptive coordination between a focal organization and its network of suppliers. Pivotal organizations like Toyota tend to intertwine with suppliers to share tacit knowledge in a *keiretsu* network structure (Powell, 1996). In turn, this enables the supplier network to fine-tune their strategic development and business processes (Reve, 1990). In this example, the focus is not on reciprocal knowledge sharing in local industrial networks. Instead, this section analyzes one-way adaptive behavior of a supplier to the client's processes. This induces the client to share knowledge that is intricate, contextual and tacit, enabling adjustment and integration of the supplier's operational processes.

The knowledge we discuss here resides in a tissue of actors used to cooperate on a daily basis (Asch, 1952). The fluid evolution of interaction patterns implies that know-how resides in the minds of participants rather than being sedimented in extensive documentation (Kogut & Zander, 1992). Hence, access to this knowledge tissue can hardly rely on remote electronic communications. People need to explain the context of their know-how, and show artifacts like drawings (van Fenema & Kumar, 1999; von Hippel, 1994). Moreover, unlike the previous configurations, knowledge transfer cannot rely on mediating coordinators because contextual information would get distorted. Besides, clarifying feedback loops would suffer from long turnaround times as coordinators need to screen and pass on reciprocal exchange flows.

Possible Deviation Trajectories

As teams from both sides start to interact directly, a number of risks emerge. First, the supplier in our example may try to pull more information from the client than agreed upon. The supplier's legitimate access to tacit knowledge enables gaining an in-depth understanding of the client's competencies and integrative capabilities (Grant, 1996b). If the supplier maintains connections to firms competing with the client organization, this access becomes rather undesirable. The supplier may share, leverage or even sell its understanding to these competing firms. For the supplier this is a tempting option as tacit knowledge is assumed to provide more intricate and thus valuable information. Alterna-

Figure 3: Controlling one-way tacit knowledge flows

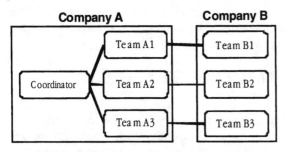

tively, under the guise of a temporary role as a supplier, a firm can copy the client's competencies and subsequently intrude their market (Hamel et al., 1989). The distinction between permissible and excessive knowledge absorption is not easy as partners can only prespecify broad dimensions of interaction flows.

Second, the client may attempt to limit and quasi-structure outgoing knowledge flows, a vertical shift to Configuration 1. For the supplier this implies a dysfunctional restriction that undermines his process of identifying with client's needs and concerns. Third, as teams from both organizations interact directly, the transmitting client organization may attempt to absorb knowledge from the receiving vendor, a shift to Configuration 4. Client teams may abuse requests for clarifications to pull additional information from the supplier context. Reciprocal flows enable the client to decrease the uniqueness of the supplier's competencies and their business.

Tacit Knowledge Control Strategies

The need for direct exchange among teams changes the nature of the contract. As the contractual specifications necessarily remain vague and general, control strategies will focus on progressively managing the dynamics of inter-firm cooperation. The position of the coordinator also changes as team members take over his role of facilitating external connectivity (Ancona, 1992). His role of mediating knowledge flows alters to coaching teams from a background position (Figure 3). That includes promoting a clan-type of environment to make sure that team members remain committed and comply to organizational goals (Ouchi, 1979). As Hamel, Doz and Prahalad (1989: 138) point out: "Limiting unintended transfer ultimately depends on employee loyalty and self-discipline." This suggests people-based strategies that cover selection, socialization and training of people to internalize organizational values and commitment (Pfeffer, 1978). The purpose is to develop and internalize collective routines and commitment that enables staff to define the boundaries of tacit knowledge sharing. Bureaucratic control strategies bear less relevance in this environment since detailed specification and observation of appropriate behaviors is not feasible (Kunda, 1992). Still, the organization's interests and goals are translated into generic rules for external knowledge transfer. This so-called *semi structure* 'exhibits partial order, and lies between the extremes of very rigid and highly chaotic organization' (Brown & Eisenhardt, 1997: 28). The client can impose generic structure to the supplier organization. For example, supplier personnel are only granted access for a limited period of time or to distinct locations.

The supplier organization must avoid that the client limits the type of knowledge shared, or even triggers reverse information flows. As Figure 3 depicts, a more complex interaction environment arises between firms. Hence, the client may attempt to abuse the multiplicity of available channels between teams to press for more information on the supplier's organization. At the same time, outgoing flows may be unduly codified and deliver insufficient resources for the supplier's processes. Similarly to the client organization, supplier teams should relate in a clan type of fashion to avoid these risks. Maintaining lateral contacts, they reinforce and enact external behaviors that are consistent with company goals. At the same time, internal procedures specify escalation processes in case the client organization violates earlier agreements. Managers are alerted when deviations occur to liaise with counterparts from the client.

RECIPROCAL, TACIT KNOWLEDGE FLOWS (CONFIGURATION 4)

In hi-tech industries that thrive on rapid R&D developments, information and knowledge sharing is crucial to remain on the competitive edge. Examples include semiconductor industry in which knowledge transfer has a prominent role (Appleyard, 1996). In conjunction with the pace of technological progress, such industries often require considerable investments in R&D. This motivates external cooperation to mutually benefit from complementary know-how and resources (Powell, 1996). Co-opetition implies here that although partners shape some form of sustainable entity, they may use final results to compete, like the examples of NEC/ Honeywell, GM/ Toyota show (Hamel et al., 1989). A similar business model is becoming common in the airline industry. Partners leverage resources to achieve economies of scale and enhance the quality of their products and services (Jain, 1999).

Often, these virtual organizations start an exploratory process of exchanging resources without having a clear notion of operational consequences and risks. Staff at both sides are expected to team up together and connect. As team members materialize strategic objectives, an intricate form of connectivity unfolds (Van de Ven et al., 1976). Incomplete specification of the scope and content of knowledge transfer necessitates heedful interrelating to adjust and refine progress (Weick & Roberts, 1993). Hence, a quasi single team emerges consisting of staff from both sides. Subsequent phases of socialization and interpersonal contacts promote feelings of collegiality and commitment to the group's functioning (Katzenbach & Smith, 1993). Such a context induces team members to share their know-how as a natural part of the cooperative effort.

Yet the successful formation of inter-organizational teams also increases the risk that partners loose grip on the knowledge exchange process. Co-opetition implies that the cooperation may end at some point of time with each partner counting their take home value. A cohesive team may lose sight of that strategic context and share valuable resources in excess of initial agreements and intentions (Hamel et al., 1989). In addition, their exclusive contacts outside the firm may alienate them from the internal organization,

Figure 4: Organizing two-way tacit knowledge flows

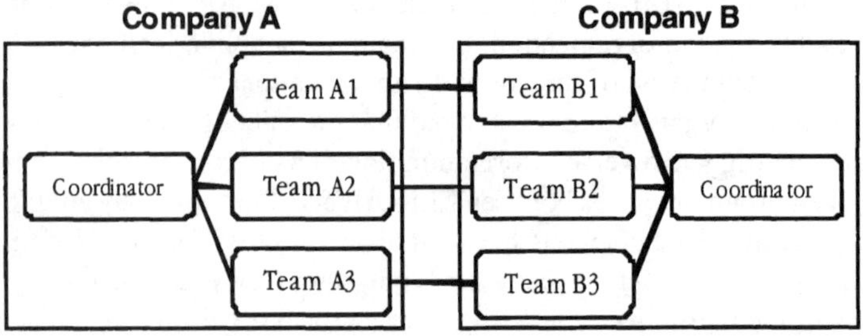

and reduce incorporation of newly acquired knowledge across other business units.

A different type of risk occurs when partners deliberately deviate from the initial agreement. Because organizations can leverage information beyond their cooperative relationship and have partially conflicting interests, they are tempted to free ride on their counterpart's input, for example by providing less or inaccurate information. They may also structure and restrict outgoing knowledge flows contrary to initial agreements. This strategy obviously undermines the partnership as it results in asymmetrical distribution of know-how.

Bilateral Control Strategies

As virtual organizations engage in a fluidly evolving exchange process, they need adjustable and flexible control strategies. A similar control structure will emerge at both sides as knowledge flows back and forth, and each partner runs comparable risks. Prior to starting operational connections, some form of relationship or reciprocal familiarity will probably exist. The intention to cooperate is translated into a relational contract that broadly outlines areas of exchange and codes of conduct (Macneil, 1978). It roughly structures scope, duration and content of exchange to provide a minimal backbone for steering the actual interaction process over time (Brown & Eisenhardt, 1997).

Complementary strategies are required to cater for the remaining open ends and risks. Both companies install a coordinator who regularly meets with team members involved in the exchange process, and mediates between project teams and the stable organization (Figure 4). As the figure depicts, the coordinator is not directly involved in operational exchanges but has an internal role.

The purpose of that role is to enhance and ensure knowledge reception from the partner organization. He also makes sure that novel resources are leveraged to the rest of the organization. In fact, this liaison role may require a small group that interfaces between the company and its teams that interact with the partner firm. Maintaining regular contact with the team, the coordinator keeps them focused on organizational goals. Although his role is on the background, he traces and guards knowledge exchanges to ensure reciprocity and quality of the flows. Team members are put into contact with other staff from their organization to share recently acquired insight (Hamel et al., 1989). To some degree experiences can be summarized and documented. Technologies like intranets or groupware facilitate controlled circulation of relevant information to others in the company. Long-term or remote cooperative endeavors suggest job rotation of team members to foster company-wide learning (Edström & Galbraith, 1977). Novel insights are leveraged and anchored to prepare the organization for subsequent competitive phases. Rotation also maintains the relationship between the organization and employees working on the fringe, and may avoid unwelcome turnover.

Reciprocal, tacit exchange in virtual organizations calls for gradually adapting and elaborating control strategies. Temporary partners juggle to make a hybrid focus work. The complexity they face traces back to their effort to combine temporary collegiality with a 'coopetitive' relationship.

DISCUSSION AND CONCLUSION

The virtual economy changes the mode of organizing transactions between firms. The traditional notion of individual organizations taking care of well-defined portions of supply chains is making place for an open and embedded perspective on their functioning. One implication is that firms seek to cooperate with partners in adjacent business domains, even including competitors. Cooperation means that firms combine specific resources to take advantage of novel opportunities. For virtual organizations that cooperate and compete, this exchange process introduces a complex decision environment. Each organization can use knowledge made available for purposes beyond the definition of their hybrid relationship. As long as both partners comply with the original agreement of cooperation, temporary exchanges evolve without too much risk. Yet at the same time, access to unique knowledge from the counterpart seems a tempting opportunity to enhance benefits derived from the relationship. Mastering this balancing act seems to be one of the novel competencies required in the virtual economy.

This chapter extends earlier literature by focussing specifically on knowledge exchanges. We elaborate a model for knowledge flows and identify four configurations of coopetitive transaction modes. Each configuration features its own risk profile depending on the deviation trajectory counterparts may choose. Control strategies are proposed to anticipate and monitor the actual exchange processes. Uneven distribution of knowledge resources is avoided by a combination of control strategies. These apply to both the internal organization and the external relationship with the partner firm. Four categories of control mechanisms are distinguished: bureaucratic mechanisms like work specification and monitoring; organizational roles like coordinators; social relationships and interpersonal exchanges; and technology employed for organizing transfer of, and access to knowledge.

The analysis extends the field of co-opetition in virtual organizations and has relevance to professionals and academics alike. Professionals may use the analysis to determine feasible configurations and anticipate risk profiles. In addition, they can detect eventual patterns of deviation, and implement remedies to increase the likelihood of a satisfactory coopetitive relationship.

From an academic point of view, the model provides a starting point for conceiving and empirically investigating the complexity of hybrid relationships between firms. Academics may use the proposed line of thought for elaborating connections with other theoretical areas like supply chain management, management of information systems, innovation management, management of joint ventures, and strategic management. In addition, researchers may want to introduce time as a variable to assess the evolution of cross-company interactions over time. Empirical observation may include survey type of research to validate hypotheses derived from the model. Another opportunity is (longitudinal) case study research where exchange processes are documented and analyzed. Finally, grounded research in the spirit of Burgelman (1983) may shed light on intra- and inter-organizational communications that help shape co-opetitive relationships.

ENDNOTE

[1]   As a spin-off from transaction cost economics, *incomplete contracting theory* elaborates on situations where parties cannot specify their transaction in advance. In particular this theory investigates the consequences of contingencies for the distribution of unanticipated value differences among parties (Hart, 1991).

REFERENCES

Allen, T. J. (1984). *Managing the Flow of Technology*. Cambridge, MA: MIT Press.

Ancona, D. G. (1992). Bridging the Boundary: External Activity and Performance in Organizational Teams. *Administrative Science Quarterly, 37*, 634-665.

Appleyard, M. M. (1996). How Does Knowledge Flow? Inter-firm Patterns in the Semiconductor Industry. *Strategic Management Journal, 17*(Winter), 137-154.

Asch, S. E. (1952). *Social Psychology*. Englewood Cliffs, NJ: Prentice-Hall.

Barker, J. R. (1993). Tightening the Iron Cage: Concertive Control in Self-Managing Teams. *Administrative Science Quarterly, 38*(3), 408-437.

Barney, J. B., & Hesterley, W. (1996). Organizational Economics: Understanding the Relationship between Organizations and Economic Analysis. In S. R. Clegg, C. Hardy, & W. R. Nord (Eds.), *Handbook of Organization Studies*. London: Sage.

Ben-Porath, Y. (1980). The F-Connection: Families, Friends, and Firms and the Organization of Exchange. *Population and Development Review, 6*(March), 1-30.

Bradach, J. L. (1997). Using the Plural Form in the Management of Restaurant Chains. *Administrative Science Quarterly, 42*(2), 276-303.

Bradach, J. L., & Eccles, R. G. (1989). Price, Authority, and Trust: From Ideal Types to Plural Forms. *Annual Review of Sociology, 15*, 97-118.

Brandenburger, A. M., & Nalebuff, B. J. (1996). *Co-opetition*. New York: Doubleday.

Brown, S. L., & Eisenhardt, K. M. (1997). The Art of Continuous Change: Linking Complexity Theory and Time-paced Evolution in Relentlessly Shifting Organizations. *Administrative Science Quarterly, 42*(1), 1-34.

Bryman, A., Bresnen, M., Beardsworth, A. D., Ford, J., & Keil, E. T. (1987). The Concept of the Temporary System: The Case of the Construction Project. In S. B. Bacharach & N. Ditomaso (Eds.), *Research in the Sociology of Organizations* (Vol. 5, pp. 73-104). Greenwich, Connecticut: JAI.

Burgelman, R. A. (1983). A Process Model of Internal Corporate Venturing in the Diversified Major Firm. *Administative Science Quarterly, 28*, 223-244.

Burns, T., & Stalker, G. M. (1961). *The Management of Innovation*. London: Tavistock Publications.

Chandler Jr, A. D., & Daems, H. (1979). Administrative Coordination, Allocation and Monitoring: A Comparative Analysis of the Emergence of Accounting and Organization in the U.S.A. and Europe. *Accounting, Organizations and Society, 4*(1/2), 3-20.

Ching, C., Holsapple, C. W., & Whinston, A. B. (1992). Reputation, Learning and Coordination in Distributed Decision-Making Contexts. *Organization Science, 3*(2), 275-297.

Daft, R. L., & Lengel, R. H. (1986). Organizational Information Requirements, Media Richness and Structural Design. *Management Science, 32*(5), 554-571.

DeSanctis, G., & Fulk (Eds), J. (1999). *Shaping Organization Form: Communication, Connection, and Community*. Walnut Creek, CA: AltaMira.

Edström, A., & Galbraith, J. R. (1977). Transfer of Managers as a Coordination and Control Strategy. *Administrative Science Quarterly, 22*(June), 248-263.

Edwards, R. C. (1981). The Social Relations of Production at the Point of Production. In M. Zey-Ferrell & M. Aiken (Eds.), *Complex Organizations: Critical Perspectives*. Glenview, IL: Scott, Foresman.

Evaristo, R., & van Fenema, P. C. (1999). A Typology of Project Management: Emergence and Evolution of New Forms. *International Journal of Project Management, 17*(5), 275-281.

Gabarro, J. J. (1990). The Development of Working Relationships. In J. Galegher, R. E. Kraut, & C. Egido (Eds.), *Intellectual Teamwork: Social and Technological Foundations of Cooperative Work*. Hillsdale, New Jersey: Lawrence Erlbaum Associates.

Ghoshal, S., & Moran, P. (1996). Bad for Practice: A Critique of the Transaction Cost Theory. *Academy of Management Review, 21*(1), 13-47.

Goldman, S. L., Preiss, K., & Nagel, R. N. (1997). *Agile Competitors and Virtual Organizations: Strategies for Enriching the Customer*. New York: John Wiley.

Grandori, A. (1997). An Organizational Assessment of Inter-firm Coordination Modes. *Organization Studies, 18*(6), 897-925.

Grandori, A., & Soda, G. (1995). Inter-firm Networks: Antecedents, Mechanisms and Forms. *Organization Studies, 16*(2), 183-214.

Grant, R. M. (1996a). Prospering in Dynamically-competitive Environments: Organizational Capability as Knowledge Integration. *Organization Science, 7*(4), 375-387.

Grant, R. M. (1996b). Toward a Knowledge-Based Theory of the Firm. *Strategic Management Journal, 17*(Winter), 109-122.

Gupta, P. P., Dirsmith, M. W., & Fogarty, T. J. (1994). Coordination and Control in Government Agency: Contingency and Institutional Theory Perspectives in GAO Audits. *Administrative Science Quarterly, 39*, 264-284.

Hamel, G., Doz, Y., & Prahalad, C. K. (1989). Collaborate With Your Competitors - And Win. *Harvard Business Review* (January-February), 133-139.

Hart, O. D. (1991). Incomplete Contracts and the Theory of the Firm. In O. E. Williamson & S. G. Winter (Eds.), *The Nature of the Firm: Origins, Evolution, and Development*. New York: Oxford University Press.

Jaeger, A. M., & Baliga, B. R. (1985). Control Systems and Strategic Adaption: Lessons from the Japanese Experience. *Strategic Management Journal, 6*, 115-134.

Jain, M. (1999). SOC Success Needs 'Coopetition'. *Electronic Business, 25*(7), 28.

Katzenbach, J. R., & Smith, D. K. (1993). *The Wisdom of Teams: Creating the High-Performance Organization*. Boston, MA: McGraw-Hill, Harvard Business School Press.

Kodama, F. (1994). Technology Fusion and the New R&D. In K. B. Clark & S. C. Wheelwright (Eds.), *The Product Development Challenge: Competing Through Speed, Quality, and Creativity*. Boston: Harvard Business School Press.

Kogut, B., & Zander, U. (1992). Knowledge of the Firm, Combinative Capabilities and the Replication of Technology. *Organization Science, 3*(3), 383-397.

Kumar, K., & van Dissel, H., G. (1996). Sustainable Collaboration: Managing Conflict and Co-operation in Inter-Organizational Systems. *MIS Quarterly, 20*(3).

Kumar, K., van Dissel, H., G, & Bielli, P. (1998). The Merchant of Prato - *Revisited*: Towards a Third Rationality of Information Systems. *MIS Quarterly, 20*(3).

Kunda, G. (1992). *Engineering Culture: Control and Commitment in a High-tech Corporation*. Philadelphia: Temple University Press.

Lazerson, M. (1995). A New Phoenix? Modern Putting-out in the Modena Knitwear Industry. *Administrative Science Quarterly, 40*, 34-59.

Loebbecke, C., & van Fenema, P. C. (1998). *Interorganizational Knowledge Sharing during Co-opetition*. Paper presented at the European Conference on Information Systems (ECIS), Aix-en-Provence, France.

Loebbecke, C., van Fenema, P. C., & Powell, P. (1999). Co-opetition and Knowledge Transfer. *Database, 30*(1).

Machlup, F. (1980). *Knowledge: Its Creation, Distribution, and Economic Significance*.

Princeton, NJ: Princeton University Press.

Macneil, I. R. (1974). The Many Futures of Contracts. *Southern California Law Review, 47*, 691-816.

Macneil, I. R. (1978). Contracts; Adjustment of Long-Term Economic Relations under Classical, Neoclassical, and Relational Contract Law. *Northwestern University Law Review, 72*, 854-906.

March, J. G., & Simon, H. A. (1958). *Organizations.* New York: Wiley.

McCann, J. E., & Galbraith, J. R. (1981). Interdepartmental Relations. In P. C. Nystrom & W. H. Starbuck (Eds.), *Handbook of Organizational Design.* New York: Oxford University Press.

McFarlan, F. W., & Nolan, R. L. (1995). How to Manage an IT Outsourcing Alliance. *Sloan Management Review*(Winter), 9-23.

Meyer, A. D., Tsui, A. S., & Hinings, C. R. (1993). Configurational Approaches to Organizational Analysis. *Academy of Management Journal, 36*(6), 1175-1195.

Mintzberg, H. (1979). *The Structuring of Organizations.* Englewood Cliffs, N.J.: Prentice-Hall.

Nelson, R., & Winter, S. (1982). *An Evolutionary Theory of Economic Change.* Cambridge, MA: Belknap Press.

Nonaka, I., & Takeuchi, H. (1995). *The Knowledge-Creating Company*: Oxford University Press.

O'Reilly, C. A., & Chatman, J. A. (1996). Culture as Social Control: Corporations, Cults, and Commitment. In L. L. Cummings & B. M. Staw (Eds.), *Research in Organizational Behavior* (Vol. 18, pp. 157-200). Greenwich, Connecticut: JAI Press.

Orlikowski, W. J. (1991). Integrated Information Environment or Matrix of Control? The Contradictory Implications of Information Technology. *Accounting, Management & Information Technology, 1*(1), 9-42.

Ouchi, W. G. (1979). A Conceptual Framework for the Design of Organizational Control Mechanisms. *Management Science, 25*(6), 833-848.

Penrose, E. (1959). *The Theory of the Growth of the Firm.* Oxford: Oxford University Press.

Perrow, C. (1999). Organizing to Reduce the Vulnerabilities of Complexity. *Journal of Contingencies and Crisis Management, 7*(3), 150-155.

Pfeffer, J. (1978). *Organizational Design.* Arlington Heights, IL: AHM.

Polanyi, M. (1958). *Personal Knowledge: Towards a Post-Critical Philosophy.* Chicago, IL: University of Chicago Press.

Powell, W. W. (1996). Trust-Based Forms of Governance. In R. M. Kramer & T. R. Tyler (Eds.), *Trust in Organizations: Frontiers of Theory and Research.* Thousand Oaks, CA: Sage.

Powell, W. W., & Smith-Doerr, L. (1994). Networks and Economic Life. In N. J. Smelser & R. Swedberg (Eds.), *The Handbook of Economic Sociology.* Princeton, NJ/New York: Princeton University Press/Russell Sage Foundation.

Preiss, K., Goldman, S. L., & Nagel, R. N. (1997). *Cooperate to Compete: Building Agile Business Relationships.* New York: John Wiley.

Reve, T. (1990). The Firm as a Nexus of Internal and External Contracts. In M. Aoki, M. Gustafsson, & O. E. Williamson (Eds.), *The Firm as a Nexus of Treaties.* London: Sage.

Rice, R. E., & Shook, D. E. (1990). Voice Messaging, Coordination, and Communication. In J. Galegher, R. E. Kraut, & C. Egido (Eds.), *Intellectual Teamwork: Social and Technological Foundations of Cooperative Work.* Hillsdale, New Jersey: Lawrence Erlbaum Associates.

Rousseau, D. M., & McLean Parks, J. (1993). The Contracts of Individuals and Organizations. In L. L. Cummings & B. M. Staw (Eds.), *Research in Organizational Behavior* (Vol. 15, pp. 1-43). Greenwich, Connecticut: JAI Press.

Schein, E. H. (1992). *Organizational Culture and Leadership*. (Vol. 2). San Fransisco: Jossey-Bass Publishers.

Schwartz, E. (1999). *Digital Darwinism: Seven Breakthrough Business Strategies in the Cutthroat Web Economy*. New York: Broadway Books.

Star, S. L., & Griesemer, J. R. (1989). Institutional Ecology, 'Translations' and Boundary Objects: Amateurs and Professionals in Berkeley's Museum of Vertebrate Zoology, 1907-39. *Social Studies of Science, 19*, 387-420.

Szulanski, G. (1996). Exploring Internal Stickiness: Impediments to the Transfer of Best Practice within the Firm. *Strategic Management Journal, 17*(Winter), 77-91.

Thompson, J. D. (1967). *Organizations in Action*: McGraw-Hill.

Tyre, M. J., & von Hippel, E. (1997). The Situated Nature of Adaptive Learning in Organizations. *Organization Science, 8*(1), 71-83.

Van de Ven, A. H., Delbecq, A. L., & Koenig Jr, R. (1976). Determinants of Coordination Modes Within Organizations. *American Sociological Review, 41*(April), 322-338.

van Fenema, P. C., & Kumar, K. (1999). Coupling, Interdependence and Control in Global Projects. In F. Hartman, R. A. Lundin, & C. Midler (Eds.), *Projects and Sensemaking*. Hingham, MA: Kluwer Academic Publishers. (forthcoming)

Venkatraman, N., & Henderson, J. C. (1998). Real Strategies for Virtual Organizing. *Sloan Management Review, 40*(1), 33-48.

von Hippel, E. (1994). "Sticky Information" and the Locus of Problem Solving: Implications for Innovation. *Management Science, 40*(4), 429-439.

Walsh, J. P., & Dewar, R. D. (1987). Formalization and the Organizational Life Cycle. *Journal of Management Studies, 24*(3), 215-231.

Wathne, K., Roos, J., & von Krogh, G. (1996). Towards a Theory of Knowledge Transfer in Cooperative Context. In G. von Krogh & J. Roos (Eds.), *Managing Knowledge: Perspectives on Cooperation and Competition*. London: Sage.

Weick, K. E., & Roberts, K. (1993). Collective Mind in Organizations: Heedful Interelating on Flight Decks. *Administrative Science Quarterly, 38*, 357-381.

Weick, K. E., & Westley, F. (1996). Organizational Learning. In S. R. Clegg, C. Hardy, & W. R. Nord (Eds.), *Handbook of Organization Studies*. London: Sage.

Wernerfelt, B. (1984). A Resource-Based Theory of the Firm. *Strategic Management Journal, 5*(2), 171-180.

Williamson, O. E. (1975). *Markets and Hierarchies: Analysis and Antitrust Implications*. New York: Free Press.

Williamson, O. E. (1985). *The Economic Institutions of Capitalism: Firms, Markets, Relational Contracting*. New York: Free Press.

Williamson, O. E. (1991). Comparative Economic Organization: The Analysis of Discrete Structural Alternatives. *Administrative Science Quarterly, 36*, 269-296.

Williamson, O. E. (1994). Transaction Costs Economics and Organization Theory. In N. J. Smelser & R. Swedberg (Eds.), *The Handbook of Economic Sociology*. Princeton, NJ/New York: Princeton University Press/Russell Sage Foundation.

Williamson, O. E., & Ouchi, W. G. (1981). The Markets and Hierarchies Program of Research: Origins, Implications, Prospects. In A. H. Van de Ven & W. F. Joyce (Eds.), *Perspectives on Organization Design and Behavior*. New York: John Wiley.

Chapter X

Knowledge Management and Organization Design

W. Jansen, G.C.A. Steenbakkers and H.P.M. Jägers
Royal Netherlands Military Academy, The Netherlands

This chapter examines the relation between organization design and knowledge management. Choosing a certain organization form implies a way of dealing with knowledge. The adopted strategies for knowledge management must concur with this form. Knowledge management should always constitute a good 'mix' of strategies applied in the organization form and its information and communication technology (ICT). A model enables organizations to determine their type and implied consequences for their knowledge management. It offers an explanation of why a specific form of knowledge management will or will not work in certain situations, and suggests measures for an appropriate knowledge management.

INTRODUCTION

Practice indicates that many organizations tend to move toward change and seek a multitude of new collaboration forms. When examining external cooperation, we note an increasing tendency among organization networks to develop into virtual organizations. Internally, a change appears toward teams (often self-directed) and organization forms which bear close resemblance to Mintzberg's adhocracy (Mintzberg, 1979). Recent publications, usually under the common denominator of network forms and/or virtual organizations, bestow a great deal of thought upon these developments (Hedberg, Dahlgren, Hansson, Olve, 1997; Ten Have, 1997; Mowshowitz, 1997; Peters, Fisart, 1996; Hale, Whitlam, 1997). In conjunction with this, they pay much attention to the ever-increasing role of knowledge in the functioning of individuals and their affiliated organizations (refer to Davenport, 1998). Experts propose strategies within the fields of Organization Design and Information and Communication Technology (ICT) in order to better utilize the knowledge present in organizations and, in addition, to promote its development. Managers sense that they cannot simply ignore a production expedient of such apparent importance as knowledge. Knowledge must be 'managed' and the organization requires a set up which allows the optimal expression of this knowledge.

In this chapter, we focus on knowledge management as a design issue. Although managers and employees do not always realize it, the choice of an organization form implies a certain manner of dealing with knowledge. The adopted strategies in the area of knowledge management must concur with this form. Knowledge management should always constitute a good 'mix' of strategies applied in the organization form and its information and communication technology (ICT), supplemented by specific HRM aspects (which will not be described in this chapter). The organization-design 'building blocks' proposed in this chapter are not new in themselves. However, the perspective on knowledge management does result in a new line of approach. Viewing the organization as a knowledge-processing system enables us to analyze and explain why the importance of the knowledge management and its structure is dependent on factors in the environment as well as the management model and organization form associated with these factors.

In the second section, we will briefly explain the concept of knowledge and of the creation and processing of knowledge within organizations.

Next, we will present a model which sheds light on the role of knowledge in different types of organizations. The organization types, each dealing in different ways with knowledge, are distinguished on the basis of their degree of complexity and variability.

The elaboration of our model indicates that each of these types requires a different knowledge management structure. Forms such as the virtual organization will play a significant role in knowledge management, specifically in the case of organizations and networks in a highly dynamic environment. The model presented in this chapter is not static; it allows migration between the various quadrants. The dynamics have a strong influence on organization design and knowledge management.

This chapter closes with a number of implications and recommendations.

KNOWLEDGE

There have been many publications on knowledge in recent years. Almost all authors fail to define knowledge in absolutely clear terms, or they suggest that we adhere to the concept as defined in everyday life. By doing this many publications avoid the differentiation between implicit and explicit knowledge (Nonaka, 1995; Choo, 1996; Den Hertog & Huizinga, 1997). We presume the reader is familiar with the substance of this concept.[1]

HAK company is a Dutch market leader in the industry of glass-jar conservation of vegetables and fruit. At first sight this would seem to be a 'low tech' (knowledge utilizing) rather than a 'high tech' (knowledge creating) industry. The quality and food-safety is, however, extremely critical. Until recently, detection devices with which to trace product-contrary elements in a closed jar, such as glass splinters, did not exist. This firm has taken the initiative to construct this device. A search was conducted for technologies which would enable a very precise detection. HAK decided on advanced X-ray technology and image-recognition techniques, originally applied by the U.S. defense industry in the design of cruise missiles. HAK made contacts with suppliers of

technical-inspection installations. An Italian company has created an initial detection-device prototype, based on knowledge from various sectors (knowledge creation). HAK is the first company in the Netherlands to make use of this system (knowledge utilization).
Example borrowed from "The Knowledge Factor", Den Hertog and Huizinga, 1997, pp. 76

Galbraith (1973) usefully viewed organizations as systems that process information. Organizations should be designed to optimally support the decision-making process, by enhancing the information processing capacity or by reducing the need to exchange information. However, we propose that this notion is too limited in the current context in which organizations find themselves. Firstly, knowledge is of a higher level than information, and this level should be the point of departure for the designing of organizations. Secondly, in speaking of information processing within organizations, there is no consideration for the fact that a growing number of organizations find themselves in the process of creating new knowledge (Nonaka, 1995). Information processing does not do justice to the fact that organizations continually gather, convey, utilize and create knowledge, with the aid of information. Only focusing on the processing of information when designing organizations renders this transformation a bad service. In this chapter, we suggest that organizational design should optimally support the creation and/ or processing of knowledge.

A CONTINGENCY MODEL FOR KNOWLEDGE MANAGEMENT

Model Objective

In this section we describe a new contingency model for organization design aimed at creating an insight into the relation between knowledge management, environment and organization form. A contingency model entails taking into consideration the situation (peripheral conditions and environmental characteristics, the contingency factors) during the design process. Many publications about knowledge management propose possible measures for knowledge management in general. We postulate that generalized knowledge management strategies are not effective. More than ever before in the management of knowledge it is the environment in which an organization functions that will have to be taken into consideration. Thus, in highly complex and variable situations the content of knowledge management will necessarily be fundamentally different to those with a low complexity and variability.

This model enables organizations to determine their organization type and the implicit consequences for its knowledge management. Although this model deals with the inherent dynamics, its main focus is on the analysis of a situation. It can explain why a specific form of knowledge management will or will not work in certain situations, and which measures must be taken in order to attain an appropriate knowledge management. This model can be applied to multiple levels in the organization. It may be that an organization has organized its knowledge management by dividing itself up into business units which utilize knowledge of various markets. In their turn, the business units may have, for example, contracted the knowledge creation out to specific knowledge domains outside the organization. Thus, each organization level ('system boundary') within the same organization can be distinguished on that level as a different type of organization form, with attendant different knowledge management choices.

Complexity and Variability

Many organizations cannot limitlessly reduce uncertainty stemming from complexity and

Figure 1. Design Choices; Dealing with knowledge[2]

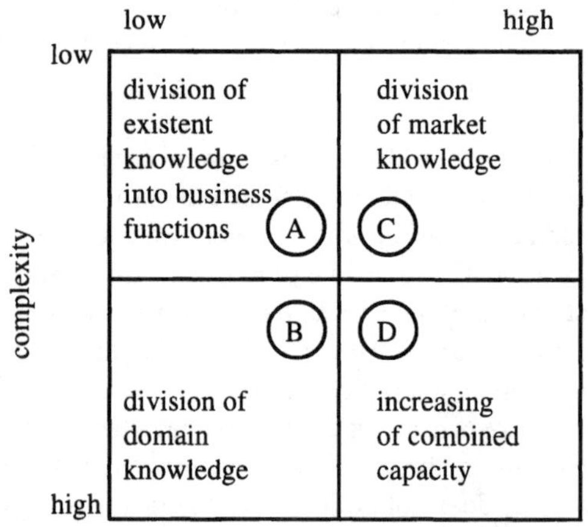

changes in their environment. It may be an effective strategy in the case of a low complexity/low variability situation, where the issue is more one of utilizing existent knowledge, rather than creating new knowledge. It is certainly not an adequate strategy where the organization is facing high complexity and high variability. From the point of view of knowledge management, a beneficial uncertainty conducive to the creation of knowledge is generated by variability and complexity. The aspects of complexity and variability are positioned on the axis in Figure 1.

Complexity concerns the degree to which an organization is confronted with complicated issues and the number of factors which it needs to take into consideration. These can stem from the environment as well as from the work itself. We see variability as the speed and unpredictability of developments in the environment, e.g., the speed of change in market demand. These situational factors determine the design. Organizations which insufficiently adapt to the degree of complexity and variability will, ultimately, not be able to meet the demands of the environment (Mintzberg,1979; Jansen & Jägers, 1991).

It is obvious that an organization (-unit) will never make a perfect 'fit' with one of the model quadrants, and, therefore, the model should not be viewed as a precise tool of measurement. It is a model with which we attempt to determine the relative positions of organizations and to illustrate their transition from one quadrant to the next.

STRATEGIES FOR KNOWLEDGE MANAGEMENT

This section offers a clarification of the four types of organization in Figure 1. We will indicate the most effective knowledge management strategies for each of the types. Right from the start the choice of organization form already implies a (largely unconscious) choice of knowledge management form. As knowledge is crucial to the survival of organizations nowadays, an awareness of this often implicit choice of knowledge management form and the strategies for further development is essential.

A. The Division of Existent Knowledge Into Business Functions

In a situation that is neither complex nor dynamic, an organization will have been designed in such a way as to optimally utilize knowledge. It does not, or barely, create knowledge itself. The knowledge used for the primary process either came from outside or was developed in the initial phase of the organization and subsequently 'frozen' (Hedlund, 1994). The staff organs are highly occupied with the continued refinement of this 'frozen' knowledge in the form of rules and procedures. The knowledge management choice in this type of organization form is to split up the knowledge into business functions such as buying, personnel, and finance and hence, in the organization-design, to relegate this knowledge to departments that become responsible for these business functions.

As a result of this choice, these types of organization often have difficulty in adapting to the environment in case it changes. The implicit strategy of these organizations in their management of increasing complexity and variability often involves ignoring the environment and going on as usual for as long as possible.

> The organization of the Dutch Ministry of Defence is divided into business functions. All affairs concerning personnel are concentrated in the Personnel Directorate, the activities concerning the procurement, maintenance of matériel is the responsibility of the Directorate of Matériel, while the Financial Directorate sees to the financial affairs, etc.. The knowledge is also concentrated by expert fields in these directorates, both in their implicit (minds of the employees in these fields) and explicit forms, like the financial and personnel information systems (in their turn divided into separate information systems for Navy, Air Force and Army personnel). During the relatively long period in which the enemy was clearly defined and the required activities (and knowledge) of the Defence Organization were crystallized in specific doctrines, this functional organization form was extremely efficient and effective. Nowadays, however, an important part of the total activities of the Defence organization concerns its participation in Peacekeeping Operations all over the world. The existing division of knowledge (and its division into information systems) is not conducive to the ability to respond quickly and flexibly to this new situation, which implies the capacity to quickly form a military unit, aptly

Table 1. Organization Design and ICT Measures for Knowledge Management in Quadrant A

The division of existent knowledge into business functions	
Organization Design	Information and Communication Technology
• centralization • staff organs • rules and procedures to utilize knowledge • special department/functionary for knowledge management	• formal, central info-systems focused on knowledge compilation and retrieval • expert systems • electronic 'knowledge maps' • intranet for the optimization of the access to knowledge

trained and adequately equipped.

Strategies for knowledge management. The organizations in this quadrant are targeted toward the efficient utilization and recycling of knowledge. The strategies for knowledge management serve primarily to make the existent knowledge explicit (codification), thus enabling additional parts of the organization and individuals, as well as those outside the involved business functions to make use of it. Together, the organization design parameters and the use of information and communication technology contribute to organization efficiency in its entirety, and to knowledge management efficiency in particular. The following scheme gives an overview of the primary characteristics of this choice.

B. The Division of Knowledge Into Domains or Areas of Expertise

In a situation that is complex but not dynamic, the organization needs to manage this complexity, an important measure being the division of activities into different areas of expertise or professional domains. By hiring professionals who are specialized in a limited area of expertise and who have the pertinent knowledge at their command, it becomes possible to adequately manage the complicated problems that arise in the environment. Examples of this are teachers, medical specialists and lawyers. The increase of knowledge *within* this type, the professional organization, does not, or barely, occur as the professionals within the organization work autonomously and have little shared communication and coordination. The knowledge remains implicit, belonging to the individual organization members. Knowledge increase in the areas of expertise occurs outside the organization in specific institutes or groups, which focus on the development of these areas of expertise, such as training institutes and professional groups. Moreover, the increase of knowledge occurs during the activities of individual professionals within their specific domain of knowledge. Professional groups often share this knowledge, for instance, by way of modern communication technologies such as news groups, bulletin boards or listservers.

An African woman shows up at the neurologist's surgery with fits and paralytic seizures. She appears to have a swelling in her carotid artery. A tumor is suspected, which must be surgically removed. The woman also suffers from anemia and her blood cell count is higher than normal. The doctor enters this information as key words in Medline. Medline is an Internet site which contains a compilation of all medical publications from 1966 onwards. In response to the entry, a reference is made to an article, which describes a similar combination of symptoms in three women. In each of these women's cases, the swelling was due to a blood clot, a very rare condition. Based on this information, the African woman was given medicine and completely cured, without having to undergo an operation. Without Medline, the chance of information being available regarding such rare conditions is almost nil.

Besides Medline, the Internet makes countless other university-supplemented sites available which try to dam the overflow of information and publications by offering summaries of frequently occurring conditions. These sites are generally organized per speciality/expertise.

Table 2. Organization Design and ICT Measures for Knowledge Management in Quadrant B

The division of knowledge into domains or areas of expertise	
Organization Design	Information and Communication Technology
• decentralization • classified into "independent" knowledge domains • individual knowledge level (implicit) or within pro-groups (general) • facilitation shared methods of knowledge application by conference-groups crossing over domains	• decentralized information systems focused on info-exchange bearing on knowledge domains • generally accessible information systems (expert systems) about methods of knowledge application • news-groups, bulletin boards, listservers within the domains

Strategies for knowledge management. As most knowledge remains implicit, it becomes important for organizations in this quadrant to distribute it to employees, without adversely affecting the content of the knowledge management. Here, knowledge management should not be focused on knowledge content (which has to remain the responsibility of the professionals and their domain) but rather on the application methods of this knowledge. Examples are the instruction methods or conduct towards clients. This quadrant also concerns the *utilization* of the organization's knowledge, rather than the creation of new knowledge. This creation takes place outside the organization. ICT solutions should focus on supporting the knowledge sharing within the domains, by creating electronic channels through which the knowledge can be accessed or passed.

C. The Division of Knowledge Into Markets

In situations with a high degree of variability and a low degree of complexity, organizations are structured in such a way that the presence of knowledge is concentrated within a single business unit (Hedlund, 1994). This knowledge is specifically market-focused. By concentrating the increase and compilation of knowledge within one business unit, rather than distributing it to the remaining business units, the organization attains an special maneuverability and flexibility. Due to this decreased complexity the business unit deals more easily with the changes required by the market. Market knowledge is often quite subjective and has a low predictive value. As a result the role of implicit knowledge becomes larger and can be supplemented with general knowledge such as demographic developments and available income, and specific explicit knowledge like, for instance, business-unit sales figures and competition results.

Strategies for knowledge management. The strongest point of the organization form in this quadrant, the focusing of the knowledge on one market segment, simultaneously forms its weakest point. The division of knowledge leads to a lack of innovation within the entire organization. As business units are largely driven in practice by financial results, in most cases there will be little or no thought for innovation within and between the business units. A results-focused policy always leads to short-term efficiency. In this quadrant the knowledge management will be largely decentralized. It will have to focus

Table 3. Organization Design and ICT Measures for Knowledge Management in Quadrant C

The division of knowledge into markets	
Organization Design	Information and Communication Technology
• decentralization • market grouping • market knowledge on individual or team level • distribution of largely implicit knowledge co-ordinated by knowledge managers per unit	• decentralized (per unit) info-systems focused on exploitation of market knowledge • databases with client information

on the exploitation and codification of the knowledge within the units. This process is organized per business unit, when possible by knowledge-managers.

Organizations that pose themselves the question, 'Why is it that 'boundary crossing' knowledge management is so difficult to get off the ground, may draw their conclusions on the basis of this model. If management decides that innovation is to be important, the organization will have to manage its knowledge on an organization-wide scale. However, this requires a new organization form, because the division form (of which we are actually speaking when referring to business units) determines the implicit choice for knowledge management within the business units so strongly, boundary crossing initiatives do not generally deliver good results in practice.

A business-unit manager in the food industry: "In this business, stacks of reports were written in the past regarding the future of the business and the role of technology. That wasn't what was lacking. But regardless of all the knowledge documentation pertaining to our own business, we were apparently not in a state to put things into order. Everyone had a different vision of the future."
Example in "The Knowledge Factor", Den Hertog and Huizinga, 1997, pp. 56

In this case, the organization shifts from that quadrant over to a more knowledge-creating organization in another quadrant.

D. The Creation of Knowledge Through Increasing Combined Capacity of Units

In situations that are highly dynamic and complex, the knowledge of each independent organization participant is no longer sufficient for the management of this knowledge. The organizations are structured in such a way that projects enable the explication of implicit knowledge, as well as the transformation of 'old' knowledge into new knowledge (projects result in learning and new knowledge). This is called the creation or increase of 'combined capacity'. Organizations must take care to build in sufficient mechanisms to anchor this compiled knowledge (knowledge-banks, for example) and to make it transferable and recyclable, for instance via intranet and symposia. Davenport and Prusak (1998) refer to this as 'fusion' and note that fusion does not reduce complexity but,

Table 4. Organization design and ICT-measures for knowledge management in quadrant D

Increase of combined capacity	
Organization Design	Information and Communication Technology

• organizing in projects
• 'slack' in information and organization form
• focus on new knowledge of/for team
• little control/much freedom
• largely implicit knowledge
• virtual organizations
	• knowledge creation by
	  * idea generation support systems
	  * creativity enhancement systems
	• knowledge spreading by
	  * e-mail
	  * Internet/intranet
	  * discussion databases
	• access to knowledge through:
	  * merging of knowledge banks
	  * intelligent agents/search engines

on the contrary, can even generate new complexity. To enable the principle of fusion or combined capacity to work effectively, one must distinguish five knowledge management principles:

1. Create awareness of the importance of the search for knowledge and invest in the process to promote this.
2. Identify important knowledge-workers that could be brought together.
3. Stress the creative factor that is inherent to complexity and to diversity of ideas, in which differences are judged to be positive rather than condemned as potential sources of conflict.
4. Underline the necessity of knowledge creation and focus it on a joint objective.
5. Introduce standards for success which reflect the value of knowledge.

Strategies for knowledge management. Fusion, or the increase of combined capacity, is the only way in which new knowledge can be created out of existent knowledge. This requires the highest possible degree of freedom built into the organization form and a minimization of rules and procedures. The exploration of new forms of work, organizational design and new knowledge domains, are necessary in order to maximize combined capacity. ICT applications should support the collaboration of the groups inside and outside the organization.

KNOWLEDGE MANAGEMENT AND THE VIRTUAL ORGANIZATION

Nowadays we note that many organizations concentrate on the activities in which they excel, on their core competencies. This focus on core competencies will not in itself serve to enlarge the combined capacity of the organization, but rather tend to reduce it. We note the rise of network forms between organizations with differing, complementary core competencies in the form of virtual organizations to realize the necessary knowledge creation. The virtual organization is a network of organizations, functioning like a single organization, which delivers products or services. Collaboration between various organizations leads to an increase of combined capacities. The creation of added value for the client is an increasingly complicated process, in which divergent types of knowledge need to be fused. Independently, organizations do not have the necessary scale for this; hence collaboration becomes a must. Although the virtual organization generally has a dynamic nature, it also contains stable elements. Due to the necessity of trust, the organization-pool from which the temporarily active virtual organization arises is fairly constant. Organizations will often collaborate with the same partners. Virtual organizations can form a bridge between the creation and utilization of knowledge, as the following example illustrates.

Prolion is a Dutch enterprise which specializes in the management of processes in the agricultural food chain. Prolion wants to play a distinctive role in the process and development of biomechanics, robots for living creatures. Its two main products are the milk robot (AMS: Automatic Milking System) and the freSHopper (a fully automatic slicing delicatessen machine). Prolion realizes these products by bringing together various partners who contribute their own specific competencies in a joint project and collectively form a virtual organization. As a small player, its major weapon in this field is its innovative identity. Although the market determines the demand for products and product-related requirements, it is an unreliable indicator in highly innovative areas. Prolion is permanently engaged in forming a profile of potential needs in this sector, which are totally undetectable in the market. First it develops a concept which it presents to the market. It then attempts to determine the level of feasibility and, at the same time, takes up contact with prospective co-producers. Prolion operates in an extensive network of organizations primarily because it does not have the capability to realize products single-handedly. However, it is also keenly aware that a network generates new perspectives. The company is open to new ideas and tries to project this externally. It was through its participation in the milk robot network that Prolion came into contact with another, which developed the freSHopper delicatessen machine. Prolion's role is not the same in every network. For instance, the product in the freSHopper project does not fall directly within Prolion's core competence (mechatronics in combination with living creatures) so they fulfill a supporting role in the network. Management is entrusted to companies which have 'a better understanding of retail

Figure 2. Measure of Knowledge Sharing in Virtual Organizations (virtuality as perceived by the organizations in the research)

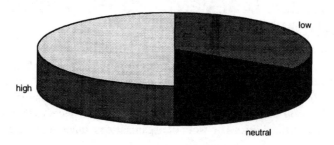

concepts' and Prolion's activities are limited to 'preferred development', steering and the manufacturing of the slicing unit.

In 1999 research among 100 Dutch organizations (profit and nonprofit) was carried out on the relation between virtual organizations and the sharing of knowledge between the participants (Steenbakkers, 1999). The results of this research show a clear link between the organization form (as perceived by the organizations) and knowledge management.

DYNAMICS AND CONSEQUENCES FOR ORGANIZATION DESIGN

The model strategies that are described in the previous section have a dynamic rather than a static nature. The selected strategies 'fit' with a specific environment, but if the environment alters the strategy must alter with it, in order to allow the organization to optimally manage its knowledge. But the dynamics do not originate merely as a passive reaction to a changing situation. Organizations can actively decide to arrange themselves differently, in order, for example, to make the transition from a dynamic market to a more stable environment, or to switch from the production of stable products to more active innovation. This means that, in the long term, knowledge-creating organizations can transform themselves into knowledge-utilizing organizations and vice versa. It is, however, impossible to make such a big step (in the model from upper left to lower right or vice versa) in one go. The three paths of migration are shown in the model. We will describe them consecutively.

Migration path 1

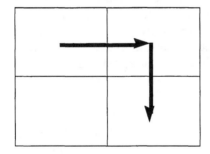

In migration path 1, the organization finds itself in a stable environment, which is, moreover, characterized by low variability. The organization is proficient in the utilization of knowledge. The compilation and distribution of knowledge is anchored in strategies and procedures and the organization is able to use and to recycle this knowledge efficiently. If the variability increases, the organization and its knowledge management will have to alter. The knowledge will then have to be more market focused from the start and, in addition, the compilation process will have to be decentralized. Instead of only utilizing knowledge, the gathering of knowledge and access to this knowledge come to take a more central place.

Migration path 2

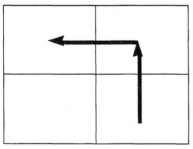

If the complexity increases, it will become more difficult to use measures and procedures for the compilation, distribution or utilization of knowledge. As a result of the high degree of variability, the knowledge has only a temporary life span and, hence, only a temporary usefulness. The knowledge will 'age' in such a way that the organization will have to create knowledge almost perpetually, in order to be or to remain vital.

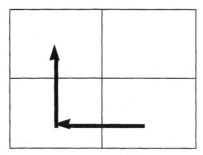

Migration path 3

This situation is completely different in migration path 2. Here we have a knowledge creating organization. Given the complex and dynamic environment, much new knowledge will be created here. After a period of time this knowledge is ready to be utilized. The complexity decreases because the process and knowledge use are familiar. Rules and procedures become necessary to foster more efficiently the knowledge utilization. Standardization constantly increases. If the market also becomes somewhat more stable, giving the product or service its own reasonably stable markets, the knowledge can be fully utilized. The primary business process is thus no longer focused on the creation of new knowledge, but rather, on the efficient utilization of existent knowledge.

Migration path 3 pertains to a knowledge creating organization that is progressing towards a knowledge-utilizing organization. If the variability decreases while complexity remains high, the individual specialists will utilize the knowledge. To an extent, these individuals will also develop knowledge, but this will not be made explicit on the level of the organization. Multiple individuals in different organizations will then utilize the project-group knowledge. The more the complexity decreases, the more individuals in the same organization will be able to utilize the knowledge, with competitive considerations making it advisable to distribute the knowledge while anchoring it centrally.

CONCLUSIONS

Organization forms that have traditionally been chosen by organizations for knowledge utilization lead to the division of knowledge rather than to the fusion of knowledge. In the division of knowledge, those employees and organization-units not directly involved do not have this knowledge at their disposal. This leads to problems when knowledge creation becomes necessary, as combination of knowledge is a prerequisite for the creation of new knowledge. Division also forms a problem for optimal knowledge utilization, as it makes the recycling of knowledge within the organization almost impossible. The solution to the utilization of knowledge is to make the knowledge explicit, making it accessible to a variety of involved parties (through codification, setting up knowledge-banks, and so on). The knowledge utilizing organizations will have to do their utmost to anchor their knowledge at a central level and must develop strategies and procedures that promote the easy accessibility of knowledge, as well as ensure that it is offered in a highly standardized form. This strategy is of importance in stable, uncomplicated organizations.

However, organizations will find themselves increasingly in situations in which the variability as well as the complexity is high. In this case, the organization should focus on creating as much (new) knowledge as possible. It is then of importance to the organization to stimulate the creativity in small, project-oriented groups in which the participants combine their capacities through close collaboration. The creation of virtual organizations is a strategy which has the same result, the sharing and combining of capacities and knowledge across organizational boundaries. Collaboration between various organizations leads to an increase of combined capacities. The creation of added value for the client is an increasingly complicated process, in which divergent types of knowledge need to be fused. On their own, organizations do not have the necessary scale for this; hence collaboration becomes a must.

Knowledge management in the classical sense is not possible in such a case. Knowledge will originate through a process that is spontaneous, uncontrived and unmanageable. In this situation, each form of classic knowledge management will reduce the results of the knowledge creation process.

In this chapter, we postulate that the manner of dealing with knowledge is dependent on the situation in which the organization finds itself. The knowledge management must concur with the organization form, in order to be effective. By using our model, organizations are able to determine whether the desired form of knowledge management and its accompanying strategies will be in harmony with the existent form.

The knowledge management strategies of organizations which function in a stable environment, will work toward the reduction of complexity. In the event of high variability, the reduction of complexity will interfere with the knowledge creation process. Managers should be aware of this fact. Knowledge creation must focus on retaining a vital degree of complexity, something, which as yet, still results in many problems for managers as the goal of management is the reduction of complexity, with an end to reducing uncertainty. This requires a new attitude for the managers of knowledge-creating organizations.

ENDNOTES

1 For definitions and for the distinction between explicit and implicit (tacit) knowledge, we refer the reader to Nonaka (1995), Den Hertog and Huizinga (1997), Jacobs (1996), Choo (1997), Weggeman (1997).
2 In this connection it is worth considering a comparable model in which Blackler describes different types of knowledge encountered in different organization forms. (Blackler, 1995; 1030).

REFERENCES

Blackler, F.(1995). Knowledge Work and Organizations: an overview and interpretation, in: *Organization Studies*, 16(6), 1021-1046.

Choo, C.W.(1996). The Knowing Organization, in: *International Journal of Information Management*, October.

Davenport, T. & Prusak, L.(1998). *Working Knowledge: How Organizations Manage What They Know*, Harvard Business School Press.

Galbraith, J.R.(1973). *Designing Complex Organizations*, Addison-Wesley, Massachusetts.

Hale, R.(1997). Whitlam, P., *Towards the Virtual Organization*, McGraw-Hill Company, London.

Have, S. ten, Lierop, F. van, & Kühne, H.J.(1997). How Virtual Must We Really Be?, in: *Nijenrode Management Review*, Nr. 4. May/June, 85-93

Hedberg, B, Dahlgren, G., Hansson, J.,& Olve, N-G.(1997). *Virtual organizations and beyond; discover imaginary systems*, John Wiley and Sons, Chichester.

Hedlund, G. (1994). Knowledge management and the N-form corporation, in: *Strategic Management Journal*, vol. 15, 73-90.

Hertog, F. den & Huizinga, E.(1997). *The knowledge factor, competing as a knowledge-enterprise*, Kluwer Business Information, Deventer.

Jacobs, D.(1996). *The Knowledge Offensive; competing cleverly in the knowledge economy*, Samson Business Information, Alpen aan den Rijn.

Jansen, W.& Jägers, H.P.M.(1991). *The Design of Effective Organizations*, Stenfert Kroese, Leiden.

Mintzberg, H.(1979). *The Structuring of Organizations*, Prentice Hall Inc., Englewood Cliffs.

Mowshowitz, A., Virtual Organization, in: *Communications of the ACM*, 40 (9), 1997, pp. 30-37

Nonaka, I., Takeuchi, H., *The knowledge creating company*, Oxford University Press, 1995

Peters, S.C.A., Fisart, R., *Network Organizations*, Lansa Publishing, Leiderdorp, 1996

Steenbakkers, G.C.A.(1999). Network Organizations, The relationship between ICT and Organization Design, Ph.D. theses in preparation, Bred.

Weggeman, M.(1997). *Knowledge Management*, Scriptum Management, Schiedam.

Part Two:

Success Factors for Knowledge Management and Virtual Organizations

Chapter XI

Becoming Knowledge-Powered: Planning the Transformation

Dave Pollard
Ernst & Young Canada

In this article, Dave Pollard, Chief Knowledge Officer at Ernst & Young Canada since 1994, relates the award-winning process his firm has used, and which many of the corporations that have visited the Centre for Business Knowledge in Toronto are adapting for their own needs, to transform the company from a knowledge-hoarding to a knowledge-sharing enterprise. The article espouses a five-phase transformation process:

- *Developing the Knowledge Future State Vision, Knowledge Strategy and Value Propositions*
- *Developing the Knowledge Architecture and Determining its Content*
- *Developing the Knowledge Infrastructure, Service Model and Network Support Mechanisms*
- *Developing a Knowledge Culture Transformation Program*
- *Leveraging Knowledge into Innovation*

The author identifies possible strategies, leading practices, and pitfalls to avoid in each phase. He also explores the challenges involved in identifying and measuring intellectual capital, encouraging new knowledge creation, capturing human knowledge in structural form, and enabling virtual workgroup collaboration.

KNOWLEDGE: DEFINITION, TYPES, AND EXAMPLES

Ask most business leaders if knowledge is important to their company's future and they'll say "yes" without hesitation. However most of these leaders can't articulate why it's so important, or how they plan to optimize their organization's knowledge to competitive advantage. The purpose of "Planning the Transformation" is to help business leaders and knowledge officers answer these questions and start to implement the answers.

Our working definition of knowledge is *any intangible resource of a business that helps its people do something better than they could do without it.* Using the models developed by Hubert Saint-Onge[1], Dr. Nonaka[2] and others, we can say that an organization's knowledge (i.e. its intellectual capital) consists of:

1. Tacit Knowledge (Human Capital)—the skills, competencies, know-how, and contextual knowledge in people's heads
2. Explicit Knowledge (Structural Capital)—the knowledge that is captured or codified in the company's knowledge-bases, tools, catalogues, directories, models, processes and systems
3. Customer Knowledge (Customer Capital)—the collective knowledge about, and of, the company's customers, their people, their needs, buying habits etc.
4. Innovated Knowledge (Innovation Capital)—the collective knowledge about as-yet undeveloped or unexploited markets, technologies, products, and operating processes

As Dr. Nonaka[3] has shown, knowledge *creation* is largely a result of the process of converting Tacit Knowledge to Explicit Knowledge (or to Customer Knowledge or Innovated Knowledge), and back again, as shown in Figure 2.

And, as knowledge-focused business games like Celemi's *Tango* and *Apples & Oranges*[4] have shown, the *value* of the organization's knowledge is the incremental discounted cash flow that comes to the organization from applying this knowledge. These games also make it clear that the *amount and balance* of investment of the company in *each type of knowledge* (versus alternative financial and physical investments), and its ability to use (and reuse) this knowledge effectively, will determine its success in leveraging knowledge and creating value for the organization beyond its net tangible book value.

Here are some specific examples of the four types of organizational knowledge, to give you an idea of how difficult it often is for companies to decide which, and how much, knowledge to invest in:

Tacit Knowledge Investments:
- Salaries for new expert hires
- Training programs
- Mentoring and retention programs
- Profit sharing programs

Figure 1: Types of Knowledge

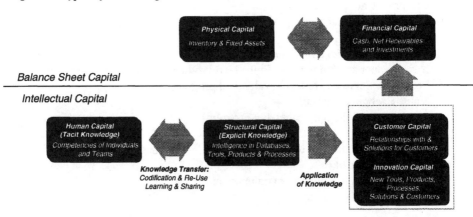

Figure 2: The Cycle of Knowledge Creation

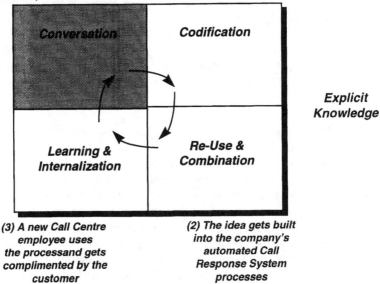

(4) The new employee discusses the process with a colleague over coffee and it provokes a further improvement idea

(1) An employee comes up with & posts an idea to improve response to service calls

Tacit Knowledge

Conversation

Codification

Explicit Knowledge

Learning & Internalization

Re-Use & Combination

(3) A new Call Centre employee uses the process and gets complimented by the customer

(2) The idea gets built into the company's automated Call Response System processes

Explicit (Structural) Knowledge Investments:
- Call centre with customer history database
- E-commerce systems
- Competitive analysis database
- Accelerated solutions centre

Customer Knowledge Investments:
- Customer satisfaction survey with follow-up visit blitz
- Multimedia marketing & branding program
- Customer Care program
- Customer need diagnostic programs

Innovated Knowledge Investments:
- New Product and Knowledge-Embedded Product Incubator
- Product & Service Life-Cycle value-add program
- Value Exchange program
- Pathfinder and thought leadership programs

These investments need to compete for people, time and dollars with physical and financial investments like:
- New distribution centers or extra inventory
- Upgraded staff computers

- Investments in strategic businesses
- Extended credit terms to volume buyers
- Production robotics
- Dividends to shareholders

as well as investments needed to sustain existing capital and legacy programs. It takes a great deal of business acumen, or *knowledge about knowledge* if you like, to be able to objectively and skillfully balance and prioritize the competing demands of these different investments on a company's scarce resources, and forecast and measure the value they produce.

STARTING THE TRANSFORMATION: KNOWLEDGE GOALS, OBJECTIVES AND STRATEGIES

So where does the organization start, to decide what types of intellectual capital investment it should make, and how to improve their existing organizational knowledge?

One of the challenges is that much of the existing legacy knowledge of organizations is widely dispersed, under diverse control. In many cases, even senior management may be unaware of the existence of much of the intellectual capital hidden in the organization. For this reason, many organizations start the transformation to sound knowledge management by cataloguing and assessing current state knowledge, called *knowledge mapping*.

The need and value of such an exercise, however, will vary from company to company, and there is a risk that starting from current state can lead to incremental, rather than innovative, thinking.

Planning the transformation to improved knowledge management usually is best begun by doing these three things, iteratively:

A1. Envision your ideal knowledge Future State ("where are we going")
A2. Ascertain your knowledge Value Propositions ("why")
A3. Determine your Knowledge Strategy ("how will we get there")

The Future State Vision serves several important functions:
- Makes the benefits of knowledge investments more compelling and concrete
- Illustrates the benefits of bringing the company's scattered knowledge resources under a single, virtual organizational umbrella
- Serves as a high-level blueprint for the knowledge improvement plan

It's often useful to lay out the Future State Vision as a "Day in the Life" scenario, showing what knowledge-leveraging activities will be possible in the Future State that are not currently possible. This requires a synthesis of the needs of diverse users in the company, as well as diverse *knowledge behaviours* (ranging from "I do all my own research" to "Do it for me—the only thing I do with my computer is e-mail"), and diverse knowledge sharing distribution channels ("push it out to me" versus "I'll look it up when I need it").

The exercise of canvassing different users in the organization to prepare the Future State Vision is also useful:
- It ensures the CKO or Knowledge Management leaders are aware of the diversity of knowledge needs throughout the organization.

- It helps identify synergy between the knowledge processes and content (both Current and Future State) in various departments of the organization, and identify leading practices that can be deployed company-wide.

Your Future State Vision should, as its name suggests, be far-reaching, ambitious and visionary, rather than focused on quick-wins and short-term projects. The Knowledge Plan will break the improvements suggested by the Vision into manageable (and affordable) chunks, and set priorities for what should be done short-run versus later.

The knowledge Value Proposition(s) will vary from company to company, and even within business units. They specify the reasons, and drivers, behind the knowledge programs and investments of the company. They are the answer to the question that will inevitably and repeatedly be asked at all levels of the company: "Remind me again why we are doing this?"

In line with the quadrants of the Balanced Scorecard[5], knowledge Value Propositions tend to fall into four categories:

- Growth—if the purpose of knowledge investments is to increase company revenues by adding value to the company's products and services, or developing new markets, products and services, or innovations
- Efficiency— if the purpose of knowledge investments is to reduce cost or cycle time through reuse of knowledge objects and process improvements
- Customer—if the purpose of knowledge investments is to strengthen customer relationships or customer satisfaction
- Employee—if the purpose of knowledge investments is to improve employee satisfaction, learning, recruitment or retention

In many cases, it is impossible to demonstrate directly the degree to which knowledge investments contribute to the achievement of the Value Propositions above. If the company achieves its revenue targets, for example, sponsors of company programs other than knowledge management ones will be quick to claim credit for the success.

More direct measures of knowledge creation are: (a) the rate at which tacit knowledge is codified to become explicit (i.e., the rate of new knowledge submissions), and (b) the rate at which explicit knowledge is internalized to become tacit (i.e., the rate of use of codified knowledge). Although these are only surrogate measures of knowledge transfer, they are fairly easy to measure using automated methods, and a strong correlation between the rates of knowledge submission/use, and the achievement of the selected Value Proposition objectives (e.g., increased revenue or employee retention), is fairly compelling evidence that knowledge is being effectively leveraged and knowledge ROI is high.

There are two key tests of the soundness of a company's Knowledge Strategy:

- It must be congruent with and contribute to the company's overall business strategy—a knowledge strategy that takes the company in a different direction from that dictated by the company's other business imperatives is almost certain to fail.
- It must be a true strategy i.e. a selection between alternatives—if the "strategy" claims there is only one way to achieve the company's knowledge objectives and achieve the Value Propositions, it's probably missing something.

KNOWLEDGE ARCHITECTURE AND CONTENT

So now you've decided, at least tentatively, on your Knowledge Vision, Value Propositions, and Strategy. The next two steps in Planning the Transformation are:

B1. Design and Build (or Re-Build) the Knowledge Architecture i.e. how the company's knowledge is organized and stored.

B2. Identify and Acquire the appropriate Knowledge Content, both company-proprietary and externally sourced.

Your Knowledge Architecture includes:

- The way in which your knowledge is indexed and organized (taxonomy).
- The platforms (technical and logical) on which the knowledge content is stored
- The tools by which content is added to, and accessed from, your knowledge repositories.

Taxonomy, at a basic level, specifies the subject matter, date, type, author, and other data for each "knowledge object", so that your catalogues and search tools can find what the user is looking for. Subject matter can further be broken down by the affected business process, business segment, or other indexing and filtering tags relevant to your particular company. While there are many generic subject matter taxonomies, you will need to refine the ways in which you index your organizational knowledge to reflect the most common uses in your company. You must also take care that your taxonomy is not so specialized that new hires and outsiders with whom you want to share your knowledge find your index impenetrable.

At a more robust level, taxonomy should specify *context* about knowledge. Information about a leading industrial practice, for example, can be worthless, or even dangerous, if you don't have information on where, how, how quickly, by whom (so you can get further information if necessary from the source) and at what cost it was developed. Context is what provides the bridge between tacit knowledge (know-how) and explicit, codified knowledge, allowing the user to appreciate the value, risks, and likelihood of successful (re-)deployment of knowledge in another situation.

Your taxonomy must walk a fine line between being too rigid (so that most of your knowledge can't be accurately indexed with the available tags) and too loose (so that the indexing terms are so vague that searches return too many false-positives). Furthermore, the taxonomy must be flexible enough to accommodate changes in your business and in the world at large, but stable enough that you need not constantly re-index everything in your knowledge repositories.

Your knowledge platforms are of two types: technical platforms (the software that "contains" your knowledge objects) and logical platforms (the layout of repositories, and of tools such as your intranet homepage). Again, there is no one right answer for all organizations, and there is a trade-off between power and flexibility. Platforms can vary from massive knowledge warehouses built on established, sophisticated database tools, to individual homepages using common "look and feel" templates that are regularly polled by search tools. Some companies prefer to integrate data and knowledge together, and encourage everyone to submit their knowledge, while others choose filters and submission processes that "promote" only the knowledge deemed by Subject Matter Specialists to be exceptionally valuable and transferable. It is generally wise to try to limit the number of different layouts of knowledge-bases and use standard templates for knowledge-bases. This ensures that users become familiar with their structure and where to find certain types of knowledge, and new knowledge-bases can be launched and populated quickly and easily.

Many IT departments have learned a great deal, very quickly, about how organizational knowledge fits with traditional financial, HR and sales information systems, and the different tools and technologies that enable them to be developed. Nevertheless, close interaction between the organization's knowledge leaders, executive sponsors, and IT management is needed to ensure the architecture design is feasible, affordable, meshes appropriately with legacy IT systems, and is efficiently and effectively built.

Ideally, both the taxonomy and architecture should be all but invisible to end users. Users need to be provided with a suite of knowledge navigation tools that fit their personal knowledge behaviours ("push it out to me" versus "I'll go pull it out when I need it"), and locate and deploy knowledge when and how it is needed.

Knowledge navigation tools Ernst & Young has seen thus far tend to fall into four categories:

- Catalogues and Directories—that allow users to browse sequentially through relevant knowledge (analogous to reading a book's Table of Contents).
- Search Engines—that allow users to find a list of knowledge objects that contain certain keywords or meet other specified search criteria (analogous to reading a book's Index).
- Portals—that point users to a small, organized subset of knowledge from a much larger knowledge warehouse, which can then be browsed.
- Road Maps—that provide users with dynamic step-by-step instructions to learn or find pertinent knowledge about a particular subject.

The tools that users select will depend on the nature of their search situation and on the style of knowledge acquisition they prefer. There are three main styles of knowledge acquisition:

- Browsing—reading through something sequentially until something of value is found (e.g., the way most people read a newspaper).
- Searching—using an index or search term to locate knowledge that meets specific criteria, on a one-time basis.
- Profiling or Subscribing—using a "net" to continuously catch knowledge that meets specific criteria.

The process by which a user navigates through knowledge will often involve both "push" and "pull" mechanisms, one or more of the three styles of acquisition, and the use of one or more of the four knowledge acquisition tool types. Your knowledge architecture must be powerful enough to accommodate these diverse acquisition processes, without being too complex for users to learn easily—this is not an easy design challenge.

Another aspect of knowledge architecture is the development of appropriate vendor management processes (for external-source content) and submission processes (for company-proprietary processes). Negotiation of site licenses with vendors partial to per-head or pay-per-use contracts requires excellent negotiation skills, thorough knowledge of alternative sources of supply, and patience, but can dramatically reduce (or increase) your organization's total knowledge budget depending how well it is done. These contracts also often have complex copyright, redistribution, and indemnification clauses that require competent legal review. The submission process must be simple enough (and ideally transparent) to the end-user to encourage frequent contributions, yet sophisticated enough to capture the taxonomy basics and context needed to enable effective location and reuse of submitted knowledge. The submission process must also be reinforced with measurement, reward and recognition programs that encourage sharing and discourage hoarding of knowledge.

Finally, your knowledge architecture must be *permeable*—it must interface both with existing legacy information systems (FIS, HRIS, SMIS) so that relevant data like personnel and sales information can be shared, and with emerging inter-enterprise systems (Internet, extranets, e-commerce systems) that will use your internal knowledge content and processes as their engine.

Determining the appropriate Knowledge Content for your organization also involves several considerations:

- What types of knowledge to acquire, maintain and deploy.
- What mix of company-proprietary and external-source knowledge to acquire, and how to integrate it.
- What mix of *information* content (e.g. news stories), which is available in huge quantity and relatively inexpensive, versus *knowledge* content (e.g., leading practices), which is scarcer and costlier, to acquire for your organization.
- How long to archive content, and QA processes to ensure accuracy and relevance
- Access security for various types of content and various classes of users.
- How much knowledge to keep in your own domain (secure, proprietary but expensive to maintain) rather than in a vendor's or outsourcer's domain (less secure and proprietary but cheaper).

Categories of business knowledge can include knowledge about:
- Your customers, their needs, businesses and people
- Your industry, markets & competitors
- Your people's competencies & experiences
- Your products & services
- Your processes, practices, policies and procedures
- Your suppliers
- Your tools, models, methods & resources

Within each of these and other categories, there is a continuum of types from raw data (low value, low cost) to sophisticated, synthesized knowledge (high value, high cost).

In addition, as shown in Figure 3, the "raw material" of a knowledge system can contain a mix of user-submitted proprietary and purchased external-source content, which should be integrated in a way that makes them useful, together, for your users.

The process of canvassing your users to ascertain what content is, or would be, valuable to the organization, is not as straightforward as one might expect. If you ask users what they think of current state information and how to improve it, you can get misleading answers:
- Users might not want to admit they don't know what is currently available, or don't know how to access it, or that they delegate knowledge searches to subordinates.

Figure 3: Knowledge Value Chain (© 1999 Ernst & Young)

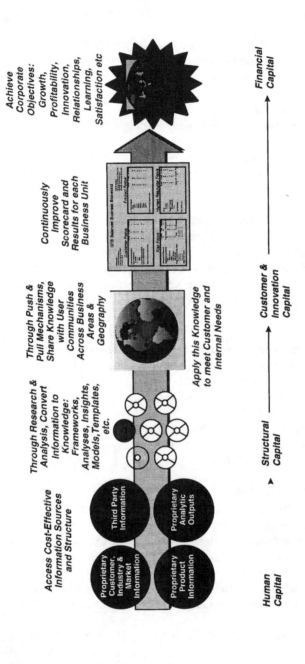

- Users probably don't know what other knowledge could be made available, unless you coach them on the possibilities.
- Users often don't differentiate between knowledge content and the tools and technologies that deliver it, and tend to over-value content when the underlying technology is reliable and powerful, and under-value it when it isn't.
- The "not invented here" and "knowledge is power" syndrome, among other cultural challenges, can make users skeptical of the value of using, or contributing, proprietary knowledge.

The process must be iterative: training users what is currently or could be available, brainstorming with them on what else they might need, and taking them through a Future State "Day in the Life" to make the processes and benefits of knowledge contribution and knowledge use more tangible, will help gradually identify the content, and related processes and cultural obstacles, to be addressed for each user group.

KNOWLEDGE INFRASTRUCTURE AND SERVICES

Once the architecture and content have been put in place, the next three steps in Planning the Transformation are:

C1. Define the roles of knowledge providers, users, and Knowledge Centre support personnel.

C2. Integrate and re-engineer existing library and research functions to reflect the new disintermediated architecture and add more value to knowledge services.

C3. Create, enable, connect and support the company's Communities of Interest.

One of the current tenets of business is "nothing gets done unless it's someone's job" and the new tasks of knowledge management are no exception. Until new knowledge-powered activities and behaviours have been baked into the company's business processes so they become second nature, it is important that all participants in knowledge sharing—providers, users, and support personnel—understand their knowledge roles and how they fit into the company's new knowledge processes. Figure 4 shows a simple example of a Knowledge Centre organization with eight defined roles: knowledge navigation, research, analysis, knowledge-base management, knowledge stewardship, subject matter specialist, network coordination, and user. The user role includes responsibilities to contribute the user's own knowledge as a subject matter specialist, and accommodates both "do it yourself" and "do it for me" knowledge behaviours.

Alternative models of knowledge roles might focus on the customer relationship manager, or on the new product development or production process improvement team, depending on the nature of the business and its knowledge drivers, strategy and value propositions. The important thing is that the new or changed roles be clearly articulated, and performance of those roles appropriately measured and rewarded.

As the new knowledge process allows end-users to access both external-source and company-proprietary knowledge directly (a process Gartner Group calls *disintermediation*)[5] the traditional "rip-and-ship" role of librarians (accessing and forwarding information without any value added) and the unleveraged role of researchers (doing everything from filing to analysis for a small group of users) must give way to new, centrally managed,

Figure Four: Example of Knowledge Roles and Knowledge Centre Organization (©1999 Ernst & Young)

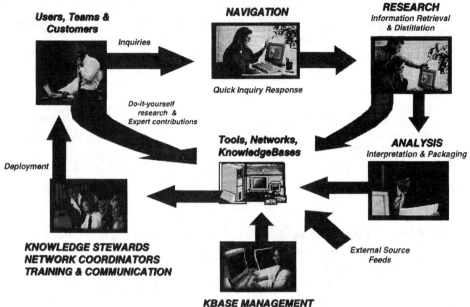

virtually connected, high-value added functions. Researchers previously unconnected and providing similar services with a broad and shallow knowledge (what Gartner calls *T-shape* skills) must now work together, support each other, pool best practices, replace designed-from-scratch deliverables with reusable template deliverables, provide proactive "standing order" services in lieu of just reacting to incoming requests, and sharpen and deepen their knowledge to develop what Gartner calls *I-shape* skills.[6]

Likewise, new knowledge paradigm analysts must work in tandem with researchers, users, other analysts and subject matter specialists to take the researchers' distilled and organized deliverables, add insight and fact-based strategic and implications analysis, and produce much more sophisticated multimedia deliverables ready for presentation to senior management, customers and other key decision makers. New specialty responsibilities in larger knowledge organizations, like content coordination and competitive intelligence, must be developed and deployed.

This is a major reengineering of knowledge functions, but beyond the definition of new knowledge competencies, it is not an especially difficult one, if the people affected are change-resilient and up to the new job. Probably the greatest challenge is getting your knowledge workers' current supervisors to cede authority of those people to the knowledge centre, in return for access to a much larger and more powerful knowledge organization.

It has been noted that, because of internal office politics and jealousies, knowledge often flows more freely between departments, and between organizations, than between people in a single department. Although this is certainly a factor, it is equally true that sometimes the most valuable, objective, and creative knowledge exchanges are extra-organizational, and even within many organizations the most productive and valued "people networks" aren't represented on the organization chart. To encourage this virtual networking activity, enable people with common problems to work together, and allow free cross-pollination of ideas, the knowledge infrastructure needs to be able to create, quickly and on-demand, versatile and powerful "knowledge spaces" where these people can collaborate, share ideas, and capture and post relevant knowledge. Furthermore, the knowledge centre needs to provide network coordinators and/or knowledge stewards that can manage and help populate these virtual spaces for the network team, identify and tie in other possible network members, and otherwise support the effective collaboration of the network team. Some companies with whom the author has worked consider this network support to be potentially the most important function of their knowledge organizations.

CREATING A KNOWLEDGE-SHARING CULTURE

Experts have long warned infrastructure builders to beware of the assumption that "if we build it they will come". This is particularly true in the knowledge arena, where building the appropriate architecture and infrastructure is a necessary precondition to knowledge sharing. But it is not a sufficient condition: once the architecture and infrastructure are in place, the hardest task begins: getting users to willingly contribute their own knowledge, and use others'. The tasks involved in changing this culture are:

D1. Creating a sense of urgency, and obtaining executive leadership and sponsorship
D2. Outreach programs: training, two-way communication, internal marketing
D3. Reinforcement programs: measurement, reward and recognition, early wins
D4. Embedding knowledge activities in your business processes and technologies
D5. Tackling the Collaboration Dilemma

In his book, *Leading Change*[7], John Kotter outlines the steps needed to bring about any kind of change in an organization, and his first two steps are creating a sense of urgency and obtaining executive sponsorship. Creating a sense of urgency is not the same as convincing people that knowledge creation and management are important. At the time of writing most business leaders, judging from the best seller lists of business bookstores, know that knowledge is vitally important to their future, but their spending budgets indicate that Y2K issues, for example, are more urgent. Since it seems to be human nature to look after urgent, unimportant matters before tackling important non-urgent ones[8], it is up to you as a knowledge leader to create the urgency that will bring attention, time and spending priority to knowledge issues.

Compounding the difficulty of making knowledge urgent is the fact that it is intangible, not very sexy (a legacy perhaps of our unfortunate stereotype of librarians), and difficult to tie directly to short-term, bottom-line results. But there are some things that can be done:

- Use a knowledge Future State Vision to make the benefits of knowledge process transformation more concrete; make it daring and enjoyable and suggest the risk to the company if competitors embrace the vision before your company does
- Demonstrate, particularly to key decision makers in your organization, how achievement of your knowledge strategy will go a long way to achieving the company's overall business strategy (and how failure to do so will prevent it)
- Customize your pitch to different audiences: different business leaders have

different knowledge needs and priorities, and different Value Propositions for investments in knowledge that you must appeal to

Once you have top management on-side, give them the material that you used to convince them (in brief, punchy, jargon-free format) to enable them to articulate clearly and push down your message to the rest of the organization. You'll probably find that your new hires won't need much convincing, so as long as your executive sponsors get through to middle management, your selling job is mostly done.

Outreach programs like training, communications, and internal marketing can take, in our experience, as much as 30% of the time of your knowledge transformation team. No matter how simple your knowledge systems may be, it is almost impossible to give people too much training. Some other pointers:

- Combine technology training with knowledge training, using case studies that introduce participants to the most valuable knowledge and learning resources you can offer, and illustrate powerful returns on their learning investment
- Remember that eventually knowledge use must become second nature to your people, so plan to migrate and embed the material from "knowledge training" courses into the mainstream sales, technical, and service training programs of the business
- Consider specialized training sessions or case studies customized to the needs and interests of specific audiences
- Use desktop learning modules instead of or in addition to classroom training if you know your audience can use them and will save time doing so

Communications is of course a two-way street. You should use specialized knowledge communications (ideally in electronic form) to communicate the high-level whats, whys, and hows of knowledge infrastructure. You should plant knowledge-related articles in existing house organs (both general and specialized) as often as possible. You should inform users of any technical or content problems with your knowledge systems before the users stumble on them themselves, and indicate when the problems will be resolved.

You should also spend as much "face-time" as possible with audiences and individuals in your organization, selling them on the value of what you're doing, getting their assessments and ideas for improvement, and reinforcing key training and how-to messages. Regular user surveys should be used to canvass and automate collection of user satisfaction and suggestions. Focus groups of specialized user groups should also be held regularly, so that you can remind them of what you've done for them and brainstorm ideas on what to do next.

As mentioned earlier, surrogate measures of knowledge success (rate of acquisition of new explicit knowledge, rate of use of that explicit knowledge) are not difficult to automate, and can demonstrate progress and quickly pinpoint problem areas (parts of your knowledge system that are not being used, and user groups that are not contributing or using knowledge). At Ernst & Young, we have found the following set of measures, and measurement methods, to be useful, compelling, and inexpensive to collect:

- quantity of new knowledge acquisitions (both bought and submitted), by user group and subject matter area (collected automatically by polling software)
- quantity of accesses of explicit knowledge (number of different users, sessions and

hits), by user group and subject matter area (collected automatically by polling software)

- knowledge success stories (identified and collected by a dedicated member of our communications team from a variety of firm-wide success reports including sales reports, process improvement reports and satisfaction surveys, followed up by "how did knowledge play a role in this success" interviews)
- quality scores from user surveys—surveys of both knowledge repository users and knowledge (research and analysis) service users
- annual penetration surveys and self-assessments by our knowledge management team

To the extent our knowledge success stories reflect "early wins" on new knowledge initiatives they are especially valuable, since they can persuade senior management that not all the returns from knowledge investments are long term. In some cases early wins are vital to move beyond seed funding of controversial or risky knowledge projects.

The reward and recognition processes you use to reinforce the importance of sharing and using knowledge will depend on the nature of your business and how far you have progressed in creating a knowledge culture. We have found that sometimes people are uncomfortable with being overtly rewarded for knowledge contributions, because they feel they are just doing their job. Coercive measures (e.g. minimum knowledge contribution "quotas") can work well in some companies but backfire in others. Companies that use individual Balanced Scorecard-type measures of performance will often welcome new intellectual capital-related measures to add to the Scorecard.

The ultimate goal of most Chief Knowledge Officers is to move knowledge-sharing from "something to do on top of everything else we do" to "the way we do things around here". This means that knowledge activities and behaviours must be embedded in the regular business processes of the organization: sales, new product innovation, production, service, recruiting, performance measurement, training, etc. It has even been suggested[9] that the CKO role may be a temporary one, lasting only until this embedding is complete.

Some of the ways of embedding knowledge in regular business processes include:

- Embedding knowledge training materials into the company's established business training programs
- Embedding knowledge activities into the company's process and procedure manuals
- Ensuring that forms (both paper and online) that must be completed include reference to accessing and contributing applicable knowledge (ideally online forms can include "hot-buttons" that allow you to access and contribute knowledge automatically as you complete the form)
- Programs which, by default, push out or jump to applicable knowledge as part of their routines, and programs which, by default, capture knowledge as it is entered by users, unless overridden by security considerations
- Program changes that simplify work processes (e.g., those that access knowledge-bases and complete fields for you) instead of complicating them

Most of the major corporations that have visited our Centre for Business Knowledge have affirmed that these cultural challenges are more difficult and take longer than building the knowledge architecture and infrastructure, and none is more challenging than creating a culture of collaboration. As most of us who have experienced the frustration and futility of dysfunctional committees and unnecessary meetings can testify, open collaboration, sharing and listening to others' ideas, and objective and egalitarian decision-making between business colleagues is very difficult to achieve, even with an impartial and skilled facilitator. The challenge is even greater when this collaboration is virtual: the body-language is missing, discussion threads can go on tangents, and multiple discussions can go on simultaneously. Until new generations of workgroup tools can be developed, producing a robust, open collaboration environment in (and increasingly between) businesses will remain a huge challenge to the effectiveness of organizational knowledge-sharing.

KNOWLEDGE AND INNOVATION

Earlier in this paper, Innovated Knowledge was identified as one of the four main types of knowledge. Because the link between knowledge-sharing and innovation is not obvious (though it is intuitive), the reader may need to be convinced that almost all innovation is knowledge-powered. Following are five ways of using knowledge to make organizations more innovative:

E1. Employ knowledge to create knowledge-embedded products
E2. Employ knowledge to enhance the New Product Development process
E3. Employ knowledge to innovate business processes and delivery channels
E4. Employ knowledge to tap new markets
E5. Employ knowledge to engineer new business work-tools

What are "knowledge-embedded products"? They are products that contain programmed intelligence that make them more valuable, and (if the programs are upgradable) extend their useful lives[10]. Two examples are the module in some cars that shows current gas mileage, and the software in satellite dish receivers that downloads changes to station and program lineups. The advent of the Internet is allowing many more such products to be developed, such as on-line diagnostic systems. It is codified (structural) knowledge that gives these products their value.

Shared knowledge also allows non-R&D departments to contribute to the new product development process. For example, if in a meeting with a sales representative a customer identifies a need not currently satisfied by existing products, and that knowledge is codified and shared so that the R&D department becomes aware of it, they can work with the sales representative and the client (possibly using a shared extranet) to develop and commercialize the solution.

Knowledge can help businesses innovate processes, not just products. So-called "sales force automation" tools effectively capture and deploy knowledge about customers and products to dramatically streamline and enhance the sales process. The change is sometimes revolutionary, enabling virtual sales-force deployment, allowing effective use of sales call centres, and substantially altering the necessary skill set for an effective salesperson.

Much has been written about how the Internet and e-commerce are allowing local businesses to "go global". Too often the technology is credited with this success, when in fact it is the knowledge shared between the company and its new customers and suppliers (including in some cases knowledge of the very existence of new suppliers) that opens up new markets. On-line surveys and customer knowledge-bases that electronically canvass the product attributes that new customers are prepared to pay for also help identify new niche markets and customer segments.

As illustrated earlier in Figure Two, new knowledge-powered tools like Call Centre software, that captures knowledge about customer needs and buying habits, and matches it to product specifications, can innovate the workplace, using technology to drive process and behaviour change and enhance performance. New data mining tools are also being developed that use knowledge-bases in conjunction with neural network logic to identify and capture sales opportunities, trends and competitive threats.

CONCLUSION

This chapter has attempted to illustrate a five-phase process to plan and navigate the transformation from a knowledge-hoarding organization ("we don't know what we don't know") to a knowledge-sharing organization. As a recap, Figure 5 illustrates these five phases.

The transformation, even in leading-edge organizations, is not yet over. Figure 6 shows a comparison of the changes that have already occurred, and those that are yet to come.

Speaking as someone who has held the Chief Knowledge Officer role at Ernst &

Figure 5: Overview of the Knowledge Transformation Process (©1999 Ernst & Young)

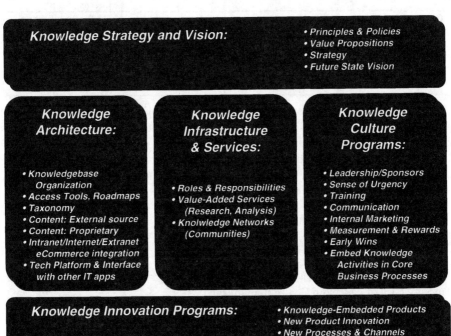

Figure 6: The Evolution of Knowledge Management

	Past	Present	Future
Prevalent Knowledge Sharing Behaviour	Knowledge is power, so don't share anything	Knowledge is valued, so share knowledge content but keep context hidden so users have to come to you	Knowledge sharing is valued, so share everything
Prevalent Knowledge Use Behaviour	Don't use it if it's Not Invented Here	Scavenge knowledge from other sources when there is an obvious re-use saving	Use templated knowledge from others almost always
Prevalent Learning Model	Learn at the foot of the Master	Learn by yourself, from all the sources you can find	Just-in-time collabora- tive team learning
Knowledge Centre Model	People scattered through- out the company with broad, shallow knowledge	Centrally-managed group, collaborating virtually, each with narrow, deep knowledge	Networked, boundary- less, global group using common research and analysis methods & tools
Knowledge Value Model	Knowledge is inherently valuable forever	Knowledge in context is valuable in use, for a limited time	Knowledge in context is valuable in use, for a limited time, and otherwise it's free
Knowledge Access Model	Knowledge is kept within the originating group	Knowledge is kept within the originating company	Knowledge is shared globally, even with "competitors"
Greatest Cultural Obstacle to Knowledge Sharing	"I don't have time" to look at/learn about this	"I don't have time" to look at/learn about this	"We don't collaborate effectively" in using knowledge
Dominant Knowledge Value Proposition	Deploying knowledge reduces cost and cycle time	Deploying knowledge accelerates growth	Deploying knowledge powers innovation

Young for the last five years, and spoken to more than 30 major corporations most of which are just beginning this transformation, I can tell you that there probably isn't a more challenging, important, and ultimately satisfying job to be found in the work world today. I would welcome any questions or continuing dialogue on any facet of knowledge management at Dave.Pollard@ca.eyi.com, and hope to hear from readers visiting the definitive site on knowledge management matters at www.brint.com.

ENDNOTES

1. Tapping into the Tacit Knowledge of the Organization, Hubert Saint-Onge, Toronto, CIBC Leadership Centre (unpublished), 1995
2. The Knowledge-Creating Company, Ikujiro Nonaka & Hirotaka Takeuchi, New York, Oxford University Press, 1995
3. Ba-A Place for Knowledge Creation, Ikujiro Nonaka, in "Perspectives on Business Innovation Vol. 2", Boston, Ernst & Young Center for Business Innovation, 1998 (available through www.businessinnovation.ey.com)

4. These business simulations are more fully described and available through www.celemi.com; much of the work in their development was done by Karl-Erik Sveiby, who is on Celemi's Advisory Board

5. The Balanced Scorecard, Kaplan & Norton, Boston, HBS Press, 1996; the Harvard Business Review has since published several follow-up articles

6. The Knowledge Management Scenario: Trends and Directions for 1998-2003, Gartner Group, Inc., March 18, 1999 (available through their database service)

7. Leading Change, John P. Kotter, Boston, HBS Press, 1996

8. The Urgency Addiction, a chapter in First Things First, Stephen R. Covey, New York, Simon & Schuster, 1994

9. Intellectual Capital: The New Wealth of Organizations, Thomas A. Stewart, New York, Doubleday, 1997

10. As described in Blur-The Speed of Change in the Connected Economy, Stan Davis & Christopher Meyer, Perseus, 1998

Additional Useful Readings:

11. Wellsprings of Knowledge, Dorothy Leonard-Barton, Boston, HBS Press, 1995

12. Perspectives on Business Innovation, Volumes 1-3, Boston, Ernst & Young Center for Business Innovation, 1996-99 (available through www. businessinnovation.ey.com)

13. Jumping the Curve, Nicholas Imparato & Oren Harari, San Francisco, Jossey-Bass, 1997

14. The Knowledge-Enabled Organization, Daniel R. Tobin, New York, AMACOM, 1998

15. California Management Review, Annual Special Editions on Knowledge Management

Chapter XII

Integrated Analysis and Design of Knowledge Systems and Processes

Mark Nissen, Magdi Kamel and Kishore Sengupta
Naval Postgraduate School, USA

Although knowledge management has been investigated in the context of decision support and expert systems for over a decade, interest in and attention to this topic have exploded recently. But integration of knowledge process design with knowledge system design is strangely missing from the knowledge management literature and practice. The research described in this chapter focuses on knowledge management and system design from three integrated perspectives: 1) reengineering process innovation, 2) expert systems knowledge acquisition and representation, and 3) information systems analysis and design. Through careful analysis and discussion, we integrate these three perspectives in a systematic manner, beginning with analysis and design of the enterprise process of interest, progressively moving into knowledge capture and formalization, and then system design and implementation. Thus, we develop an integrated approach that covers the gamut of design considerations from the enterprise process in the large, through alternative classes of knowledge in the middle, and on to specific systems in the detail. We show how this integrated methodology is more complete than existing developmental approaches and illustrate the use and utility of the approach through a specific enterprise example, which addresses many factors widely considered important in the knowledge management environment. Using the integrated methodology that we develop and illustrate in this chapter, the reader can see how to identify, select, compose and integrate the many component applications and technologies required for effective knowledge system and process design.

KNOWLEDGE MANAGEMENT AND SYSTEM DESIGN

The power of knowledge has long been ascribed to successful individuals in the organization, but today it is recognized and pursued at the enterprise level through a practice known as knowledge management (see Davenport and Prusak, 1998). Although knowledge management has been investigated in the context of decision support systems (DSS) and expert systems (ES) for over a decade (e.g., see Shen, 1987), interest in and attention to this topic have exploded recently. For example, knowledge capital is commonly discussed as a factor of no less importance than the traditional economic inputs of labor and finance (Forbes, 1997), and the concept *knowledge equity* is now receiving theoretical treatment through research (e.g., see Glazer, 1998).

Many prominent technology firms now depend upon knowledge-work processes to compete through innovation more than production and service (McCartney, 1998), and Drucker (1995, p. 271) writes, "Knowledge has become the key economic resource and the dominant—and perhaps even the only—source of comparative advantage." This follows his assertion that increasing knowledge-work productivity represents the great management task of this century, on par with the innovation and productivity improvements made through industrialization of manual-work processes (Drucker, 1978). Brown and Duguid (1998, p. 90) add, "Organizational knowledge provides synergistic advantage not replicable in the marketplace." Indeed, some forecasts suggest knowledge work (e.g., performed by professionals and managers) will account for nearly 25% of the workforce soon after the 21st century begins (Labor, 1991). And partly in anticipation, fully 40% of Fortune-1000 companies claim to have established the role of Chief Knowledge Officer (CKO) in their companies (Roberts, 1996). Miles et al. (1998, p. 281) caution, however, "Knowledge, despite its increasing abundance, may elude managerial approaches created in 20th century mindsets and methods."

In fact, knowledge is proving difficult to manage, and knowledge work has been stubbornly resistant to reengineering and process innovation (Davenport, 1995). For one thing, Nonaka (1994) describes knowledge-creation as primarily an individual activity, performed by knowledge workers that are mostly professional, well-educated and relatively autonomous, often with substantial responsibility in the organization. They tend to seek and value their relative autonomy and often resist perceived interference by management in knowledge-work activities (Davenport et al., 1996). Moreover, substantial, important knowledge is tacit, unstructured (Nonaka, 1994) and external to the organization (Frappaolo, 1998). This can greatly impede the identification, acquisition, interpretation and application of such knowledge. Also, corporate knowledge has historically been stored on paper and in the minds of people (O'Leary, 1998). Paper is notoriously difficult to access in quantity and keep current on a distributed basis, and knowledge kept in the minds of workers is vulnerable to loss through employee turnover and attrition. Vulnerability to such loss of knowledge is exacerbated by recent waves of downsizing associated with reengineering (McCartney, 1998) and the constrained labor markets affecting many professions (especially. information technology and software engineering).

Moreover, most information technology (IT) employed to enable knowledge work appears to target data and information, as opposed to knowledge itself (cf. Ruggles, 1997). We feel this contributes to difficulties experienced with knowledge management to date. Knowledge, almost by definition, lies at the center of knowledge work, yet it is noted as being quite distinct from data and information (e.g., see Davenport et al., 1998; Nonaka, 1994; Teece, 1998). Drawing from Arrow (1962) and others, we understand that even information economics has many important differences from standard economic theory (e.g., negligible marginal costs, network externalities, consumption without loss of use), but our understanding of *knowledge economics* is entirely "primitive" (Teece, 1998).

Further, extant IT used to support knowledge management is limited primarily to conventional database management systems (DBMS), data warehouses and mining tools (DW/DM), intranets/extranets and groupware (O'Leary, 1998). Arguably, just looking at the word "data" in the names of many "knowledge management tools" (e.g., DBMS, DW/DM), we are not even working at the level of information, much less knowledge. And (especially Web-based) Internet tools applied within and between organizations provide a common, machine-independent medium for the distribution and linkage of multimedia documents, but extant intranet and extranet applications focus principally on the management and distribution of information, not knowledge per se. Although a great improvement over previous stove-piped systems, islands of automation and other information systems maladies, as Nonaka (1994, p. 15) states, such "information is [just] a flow of messages," not knowledge.

Groupware offers infrastructural support for knowledge work and enhances the environment in which knowledge artifacts are created and managed, but the management of knowledge itself remains indirect. For instance, groupware is widely noted as helpful in the virtual office environment (e.g., when geographically-dispersed knowledge workers must collaborate remotely) and provides networked tools such as shared, indexed and replicated document databases and discussion threads (e.g., Lotus Notes applications), as well as shared "white boards," joint document editing capabilities and full-duplex, multimedia communication features. These tools serve to mitigate collaborative losses that can arise when rich, face-to-face joint work is not practical or feasible, and groupware can facilitate the reuse of knowledge-work artifacts (e.g., successful consultant proposals, presentations and analyses).

However, as we learned through the painful, expensive and failure-prone "first wave" of reengineering (see Cypress, 1994), simply inserting IT into a process in no way guarantees performance improvement. Indeed, many otherwise successful and effective firms experienced process *degradation* as the result of reengineering (e.g., see Caron et al., 1994; Hammer and Champy, 1993). This point is underscored by Hammer (1990), who colorfully refers to such practice as "paving the cowpaths" and "automating the mess" (e.g., making a broken process simply operate broken faster).

Drawing all the way back to Leavitt (1965) and others (e.g., Davenport, 1993; Nissen, 1998), new IT needs to be integrated with the design of the *process* it supports, which includes consideration of the organization, people, procedures, culture and other key factors, in addition to technology. Such integration of knowledge process design with knowledge system design is strangely missing from the knowledge management literature and practice. And what about the information systems (IS) methodologies, techniques and tools used to design and implement knowledge systems? Are they the same, familiar ones employed over the decades for databases, transaction process systems, expert systems, groupware and other applications? Should they be? These are some of the critical knowledge management questions addressed through this chapter.

The research described in this chapter is focused on knowledge management and system design from three integrated perspectives: 1) reengineering and process innovation, 2) expert systems knowledge acquisition and representation, and 3) information systems analysis and design. We integrate these three perspectives in a systematic manner, beginning with analysis and design of the enterprise process of interest, progressively moving into knowledge capture and formalization, and then system design and implementation. Thus, we offer an integrated approach that covers the gamut of design considerations from the enterprise process in the large, through alternative classes of knowledge in the middle, and on to specific systems in the detail.

The central premise of this work is, although knowledge management represents a phenomenon of relatively new widespread interest and attention in research and practice, many of its underlying elements are actually quite familiar and have been effectively addressed for many years (decades in some cases) through work in process redesign (e.g., integration of information technology enablers with organizational design, human resources, information availability, inter-organizational alliance, workflow modification and other process transformations), artificial intelligence (e.g., knowledge capture and formalization, distributed inference, knowledgebase design) and information systems (e.g., structured and object-oriented analysis & design, database development, decision support systems). At this stage of our research, we have developed many compelling examples of well-established methodologies, techniques and tools being composed to support integrated analysis and design of knowledge systems and processes.

In the sections that follow, we outline a three-tier framework for examining alternative methodologies, techniques and tools and employ this framework to provide a high-level overview of well-established approaches from each of the areas above. Drawing from the literature, we examine a number of extant knowledge management systems and practices to classify and analyze current developmental methodologies, techniques and tools. We then outline a contingent feature space of specific elements, levels and stages comprising knowledge management and use this to develop an integrated analysis and design approach tailored to each key aspect of knowledge system and process design. With this, we develop a set of contextual factors (e.g., organizational environment, knowledge characteristics) that draw insight into strengths and limitations of various approaches. This represents a central contribution of the chapter, as it reveals the underlying components of knowledge management and prescribes design guidance specific to each. We then discuss how to employ the design approach developed above through a specific enterprise example, which addresses many factors widely considered important in the knowledge management environment (e.g., cross-functional virtual teams, collaborative work, distributed tacit and explicit knowledge, both routine and non-routine work processes, a dynamic market/organizational environment) and illustrates the use and utility of our integrated approach to analysis and design of knowledge systems and processes. The final section closes with key conclusions and implications for practice, in addition to a focused agenda for future research along these lines.

EXTANT APPROACHES TO SYSTEM AND PROCESS DESIGN

In this section, we outline a three-tier framework for examining alternative methodologies, techniques and tools employed to develop systems and processes, and we present substantive discussion of methods from reengineering, expert systems and information systems domains. This provides background necessary to understand these diverse but overlapping approaches and to appreciate their respective and integrative applicability and potential in the context of knowledge systems and processes.

Analytical Framework

Central to information system and process development are the concepts *methodologies*, *techniques*, and *tools*. These three concepts work together to provide a solid framework for facilitating the development of information systems, expert systems and enterprise processes. Methodologies are comprehensive, step-by-step approaches that guide the development of a system or process. They provide guidance on what should be done, when it should be done, how it should be done and who should do it. Examples of methodologies used in information system development include structured analysis, information engineering, rapid prototyping, object-oriented development and others. Some aspects of these information system methodologies (e.g., prototyping) are also employed for expert systems development, and even reengineering shares some methodological commonality (e.g., through the BPR Life Cycle; see Kettinger et al., 1995). Each methodology generally includes several developmental techniques.

Techniques are specific processes used in conjunction with one or more methodologies that result in well thought-out, complete and comprehensible deliverables. Techniques provide support to a wide range of systems development activities from planning and analysis, through design and implementation, to system maintenance and retirement. Examples of techniques used for information systems development include interviewing, use case modeling, data flow modeling, entity-relationship modeling, structured design, object-oriented programming and others. More so than is the case with methodologies above, several of these information system techniques (e.g., interviewing, use cases) are also employed for expert systems development. But other expert system development techniques (e.g., knowledge acquisition, knowledge representation) focus on knowledge—as opposed to information or data—directly and are unique to the class of knowledge-based systems (e.g., including expert systems, intelligent agents). Likewise, reengineering involves several of the same techniques. But it too has a unique set (e.g., pathology diagnosis, transformation matching) at the techniques level.

Tools are computer programs that facilitate the implementation of techniques within the overall guidelines of a particular development methodology. Examples of information system development tools include program editors, compilers and debuggers, modeling applications (e.g., for data-flow diagrams, entity-relationship diagrams, object models), configuration management modules, test simulators and others. Even more so than above, considerable commonality exists between the sets of tools used for information systems development with those employed for developing expert systems and reengineering engagements.

This relationship between methodologies, techniques and tools employed for the three classes of systems—information systems, expert systems and enterprise processes—is roughly depicted by the Venn Diagrams presented in Figure 1. Notice considerable uniqueness (e.g., very little overlap) at the level of methodologies, increasing commonality through levels of techniques, and substantial overlap at the tools level. The relative sizes of ovals in the figure also depict the relationship from above in terms of numbers; that is, there are relatively few qualitatively different methodologies, but numerous unique techniques and a multitude of diverse tools are employed across the three system classes. From this early examination, we might expect knowledge management methodologies to be quite unique. But they are likely to involve several common techniques and abundant tools used for information systems, expert systems and reengineering. This provides insight into our development of an integrated approach to knowledge system and process development.

Examination of Established Approaches

Here, we focus the discussion on examination of established approaches to analysis and design in the areas of reengineering, expert systems and information systems. The latter two areas serve to represent nearly all IS analysis and design activity—with expert systems approaches oriented directly toward knowledge itself—and incorporation of reengineering discussion serves to integrate both systems and processes into our analysis. This provides the substance for inclusion into our three-tier framework from above.

Reengineering Methodologies. Business process reengineering (BPR) involves radical redesign of enterprise processes (Hammer and Champy, 1993) intended to effect dramatic, order-of-magnitude performance improvement (Davenport, 1993). A number of reengineering methodologies have been developed by BPR experts. They reflect a synthesis of many process redesign endeavors and are generally developed by BPR consultants who are widely acknowledged as the most knowledgeable experts in the field. Admittedly, some of these "methodologies" (e.g., Hammer and Champy, 1993) appear to accomplish little more than motivating the case for BPR (Cole, 1994) and are shown to have substantial room for improved analysis (Hansen 1994); in essence they answer the question of *whether* to reengineer. However, others (e.g., Davenport, 1993) provide a start-to-finish guide to undertaking process improvement, answering questions such as *what* steps need to be taken and in which order. Additionally, a number of academic investigations build upon the kind of knowledge available through expert reengineering methodologies—for example contributing knowledge in terms of frameworks (e.g., Davidson, 1993; Guha et al., 1994) and guidelines (e.g., Henderson and Venkatraman 1993; Klein, 1994) that begin to answer operationalized questions such as *how* to accomplish the redesign steps from above.

Nissen (1998) describes reengineering in terms of process-redesign activities organized as an evolutionary spiral to denote increasing process knowledge and under-standing as the reengin-eering activity progresses. This sequence of activities, delineated in Figure 2, rep-resents a blend of expert reengineering methodolo-gies—particularly those of Andrews and Stalick (1994), Davenport (1993), Hammer and Champy (1993), Harrington (1991) and Johansson et al. (1993)—synthesized together to com-pose an analytical method supporting measurement.

Figure 1: Commonality of Methodologies, Techniques and Tools

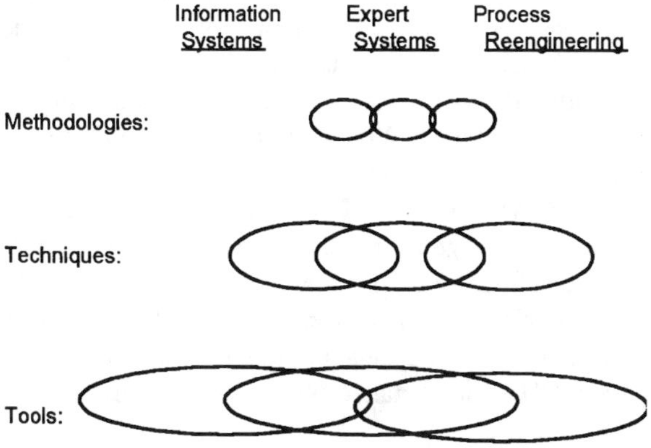

Step one is to identify a target process for redesign. Next, a model is constructed to represent the baseline (i.e., "as is") configuration of this process, and configuration measurements then drive the diagnosis of process pathologies. The diagnostic results are used in turn to match the appropriate redesign transformations available to "treat" pathologies that are detected. This sequence of analytical activities

Figure 2: General Redesign Process

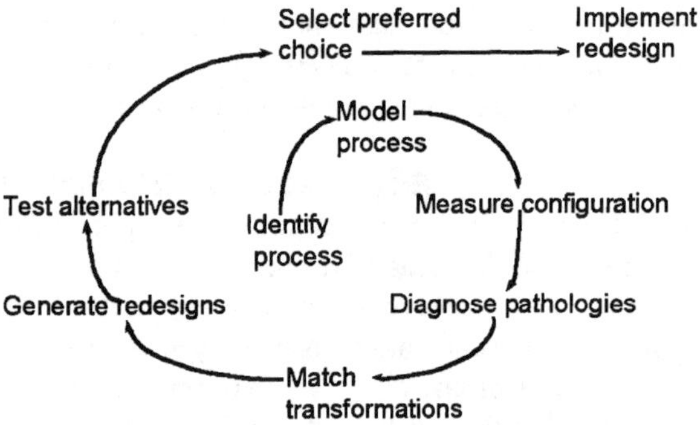

leads systematically to the generation of one or more redesign alternatives, which most experts argue should be tested through some mechanism (especially simulation) prior to selection of a preferred alternative for implementation.

The analysis and design phases of reengineering (generally called "redesign") are followed by implementation and maintenance in what is known as the BPR Life Cycle (Kettinger et al. 1995). And although the life cycle steps are often described as a sequence, their performance is generally very iterative. Generally, process redesign involves analytical activities, whereas implementation and maintenance require making physical and procedural changes in enterprise processes. Redesign requires understanding the objectives and strategies of an enterprise and generally entails process modeling and analysis that results in one or more (re)designs for the process in question. Implementation represents a key stage of activities in the reengineering life cycle and represents a major area of risk in terms of BPR success. Change management is very important for effective implementation, and we now have the benefit of research results such as "preconditions for success" (Bashein et al. 1994), "tactics for managing radical change" (Stoddard and Jarvenpaa 1995), revelations of "reengineering myths" (Davenport and Stoddard 1994) and greater insight into implementation problems (Clemons et al. 1995, Grover et al. 1995).

There is considerable debate regarding how to define "reengineering maintenance." Some experts describe reengineering as an "all or nothing proposition" (Hammer, 1990; p. 105), in which existing enterprise processes are radically transformed through "redesign with a blank sheet of paper" (Hammer and Champy, 1993, p. 131) and "the proverbial clean slate" (Hammer and Stanton, 1995, p. 4). And most researchers agree the radical nature of reengineering makes it an inherently discrete event (e.g., see Cole, 1994, Davenport, 1993 ; Nissen, 1996). But reengineering shares many methodological elements with Total Quality Management (TQM; see Flood, 1993; Harrington, 1991; Hoffherr, 1994), and a number of reengineering methodologies (e.g., see Andrews and Stalick, 1994) include the TQM practice of continuous process improvement (CPI)—an incremental-change approach—as the effective "maintenance" phase of reengineering. Such reengineering maintenance through CPI is justified by Davenport (1993, p. 14): "Lest it slide back down the slippery slope of process degradation, [after process redesign] a firm should then pursue a program of continuous improvement for the post-innovation process." The maintenance phase thus completes the life cycle and often signals the beginning of a new analysis effort (e.g., additional process redesign).

Expert System Development Methodologies. Expert systems are computer programs that emulate the problem solving and experience of experts in specific domains. Expert systems thus provide a way to capture and apply human knowledge, expertise and experience via computer. Because they focus on knowledge directly, expert systems appear to offer particular promise in knowledge management. The process of developing an expert system is called knowledge engineering (Prerau 1990). Similar to the system development life cycle of traditional information systems development, the knowledge engineering process consists of a number of phases, each consisting of several tasks. As with the reengineering life cycle above, although knowledge engineering phases and tasks are usually shown in sequence, in practice they are conducted iteratively. And like the life cycle from above, expert system development can similarly be portrayed in terms of an evolutionary-spiral process. The following is a summary of the essential activities conducted in each of six phases: 1) problem assessment, 2) knowledge acquisition, 3) knowledge representation, 4) system implementation, 5) verification and validation, and 6) maintenance.

Problem assessment pertains to the applicability and feasibility of an expert system solution to a particular problem. A good business case is often required in this first phase. As implied by the name, the knowledge acquisition phase involves acquisition of knowledge from a domain expert and/or other sources of knowledge (Kamel 1999). It also involves interpreting, analyzing and documenting the acquired knowledge. It is well understood that tacit knowledge is more difficult to acquire than its explicit counterpart, and many human experts are truly outstanding at what they do but unable to clearly articulate *how* they accomplish their knowledge work. Knowledge representation involves the selection of a knowledge representational scheme and control strategy. Acquired knowledge is represented using one of several ontologies and representational formalisms (e.g., rules, frames, scripts).

The expert system implementation phase is very much like its reengineering counterpart above and information system counterpart below. This phase involves coding the knowledge acquired as above using appropriate expert system development software (e.g., a development "shell") and one or more of the selected representational formalisms. Verification and validation (V&V) ensures the developed system correctly implements its initial specification and performs at an acceptable level of expertise. This step shares considerable similarity with information systems V&V, except that *knowledge* validation is unique to expert systems development. For example, the Turing Test represents a textbook approach to validating expert knowledge (see Turban and Aronson 1998). Very briefly, if an informed person cannot tell the difference in knowledge-work performance between an expert human and an expert system, such system is deemed validated according to the Turing Test. Finally, maintenance represents an ongoing phase that corrects system errors and deficiencies. It also updates the system knowledge as requirements evolve and completes the development cycle. As with reengineering above, the expert system maintenance phase often signals the beginning of a new analysis effort (e.g., additional knowledge acquisition and representation).

Information System Development Methodologies. A widely used information system development methodology is the system development life cycle (SDLC). The SDLC is a common methodology for system development that consists of phases, subphases and tasks to guide the system analysis and design effort. As above, although the SDLC appears to be a sequential set of phases, its implementation is usually highly iterative. Almost every organization uses a slightly different life cycle model, with a varying number of identifiable phases. Here, we consider a SDLC that consists of six phases: 1) information system planning, 2) project initiation and planning, 3) system analysis, 4) logical and physical design, 5) system implementation, and 6) maintenance.

Information systems planning is usually part of the organization's corporate and systems planning process. It identifies the information needs of the organization as a whole and the potential projects to meet these needs. The project initiation and planning phase defines the scope of the proposed system and specifies the time and resources needed for its implementation. It generally includes an economic feasibility study to ensure the benefits provided by the proposed system outweigh the costs of its development. The main goal of system analysis is to specify complete and detailed requirements of the proposed system. This is accomplished by working closely with current and future system users and by careful study of existing manual or computerized systems (e.g., enterprise processes, legacy information systems). In addition to application requirements, this phase specifies other requirements such as performance, reliability, security, interfaces and more.

The design phase converts the description of system requirements into coherent, well-organized specifications that can be implemented through computer code. The design phase maps the "what" of requirements into the "how" of design specifications, enabling the implementation which follows. Design specifications include all aspects of the system, from databases to software module logic, input and output forms and reports. Design specifications are in turn converted into code, the latter of which is tested and installed in the implementation phase. In addition to coding, testing and installation, this phase includes other activities such as finalizing documentation, user training and system conversion. Finally, maintenance represents an ongoing activity that corrects system problems and adds new functionality as needed. In some sense, maintenance is not a separate phase but a repetition of the other life cycle phases required to analyze, design and implement the needed changes. Thus, as with reengineering and expert system life cycles, maintenance completes the cycle and often signals the beginning of a new analysis effort (e.g., a return to IS planning).

Summary. To summarize this examination of established approaches, reengineering, expert systems and information systems all involve some kind of developmental life cycle. Each respective life cycle begins with some planning and analytical tasks (e.g., reengineering process identification, expert system problem assessment, IS planning). The life cycles proceed through relatively diverse design activities (e.g., reengineering pathology diagnosis and transformation matching, expert system knowledge acquisition and representation, IS logical and physical design). Then each life cycle prescribes some physical and procedural changes through implementation (e.g., change management, V&V, coding) and transitions into a maintenance phase to complete the life cycle.

Despite structural similarities between the three life cycle models, however, the underlying steps and focuses of the corresponding methodologies are quite distinct. For instance, whereas reengineering is oriented toward the enterprise *process*, expert systems methodologies directly address *knowledge*, and IS methodologies focus on systems for *information* processing. Alternatively, one can argue information represents a necessary component of knowledge, which in turn represents a key element of any enterprise process. Thus, the three areas of methodological focus are tightly linked, and a strong argument can be made that all three aspects—process, knowledge and information—should be addressed together when designing knowledge systems and processes. This represents one of the central premises of the chapter.

KNOWLEDGE MANAGEMENT FEATURE SPACE

In this section, we outline a feature space of specific activities and stages comprising knowledge management as a process. We use this to classify and analyze a number of existing systems and practices, drawn principally from the literature, currently employed for knowledge management. The classification elucidates several informative similarities and differences between the diverse sets of systems and practices, and the analysis interrelates the various classes back to the three methodological approaches examined above (i.e., reengineering, expert systems and information systems). This represents a central contribution of the chapter, as it reveals the underlying process elements, levels and phases of knowledge management and links them to methods available for knowledge system and process development. We begin by drawing from the literature to integrate a number of various life cycle models emerging for managing knowledge.

Knowledge Management Life Cycle

Drawing from Nissen (1999), we begin to observe a sense of process flow or a life cycle associated with knowledge management. With some similarity to the developmental life cycles discussed above, although we describe the knowledge management life cycle as a sequence of activities, in practice their performance is generally iterative. Building upon this notion, we outline key elements of several life cycle models drawn from the recent knowledge management literature to develop an amalgamated, general knowledge management process model. We then combine this amalgamated model with other key dimensions and exemplars from the literature to compose a knowledge management feature space for analysis. Results from this analysis are used to make observations pertaining to the current state of the practice in knowledge management and integrate our discussion of extant system development approaches.

Life Cycle Models. In Table 1, we compare the knowledge management life cycles proposed by several researchers (e.g., Nissen, 1999; Despres and Chauvel, 1999; Gartner Group, 1999; Davenport and Prusak, 1998), which all share considerable similarities. For instance, most of the four life cycle models begin with a "create" or "generate" phase; only the Nissen model begins with knowledge capture, an activity appearing in the *third* phase of the Gartner Group model. The second phase pertains to the organization, mapping or bundling of knowledge; Davenport and Prusak omit this organization phase from their model, but it appears very prominently in all the others. Phase three uses different terms across the models, but they all address some mechanism for making knowledge formal or explicit. Likewise, the fourth phase uses different terms but addresses the ability to share or distribute knowledge in the enterprise. Three of the four models include a fifth phase for application or (re)use of knowledge for problem solving or decision making in the organization. Only the Despres and Chauvel model includes a sixth phase for knowledge evolution.

Table 1: Knowledge Management Life Cycle Models

Model	Phase 1	Phase 2	Phase 3	Phase 4	Phase 5	Phase 6
Nissen	Capture	Organize	Formalize	Distribute	Apply	
Despres & Chauvel	Create	Map/bundle	Store	Share/transfer	Reuse	Evolve
Gartner Group	Create	Organize	Capture	Access	Use	
Davenport & Prusak	Generate		Codify	Transfer		
Amalgamated	Create	Organize	Formalize	Distribute	Apply	Evolve

Table 2: Organization Level Systems and Practices

Create	Organize	Formalize	Distribute	Apply	Evolve
Data mining	Knowledge map	Data warehouse	FAQs	BPR	
AI first principles	Semantic network	Reports	Best practices		
R&D	GrapeVines		Lessons learned		
Bench marking			Knowledge brokers		
Business intel			"Yellow Pages"		
			Web publication		
			Document search		

The Amalgamated model integrates the key concepts and terms from the four life cycle models. Comparing the steps above proposed by Nissen (1999) with this Amalgamated model, notice from Table 1 the latter life cycle model makes a distinction between knowledge creation (e.g., as proposed by Despres and Chauvel and Gartner Group) and its capture or formalization (i.e., Phase 3). Whereas knowledge creation involves discovery and the development of new knowledge, knowledge capture requires only that the knowledge be new to a particular individual or organization, and formalization involves the conversion of existing knowledge from tacit to explicit form. The Amalgamated model therefore seems more complete with its beginning at the creation step. Similarly, the Amalgamated model also adopts the evolution step from the Despres and Chauvel model.

These amalgamated life cycle phases are repeated across the tops of Tables 2-5 for reference. The cells of Tables 2-4 contain examples of current knowledge management systems and practices drawn from the literature (e.g., Davenport et al., 1996; Davenport and Prusak, 1998; Gartner Group, 1999; Despres and Chauvel, 1999 and others). We use these exemplars from current practice not only to populate the table cells but to interrelate its underlying dimensions. We have already discussed the life cycle dimension. But higher dimensionality may be required to map the more dynamic knowledge management activities summarized in Table 1. One important dimension along these lines is *knowledge management level*, which draws from Nonaka (1994) and others (e.g., Despres and Chauvel, 1999). The knowledge management level includes both individual and collective entities, the latter of which are further distinguished between groups (e.g., of relatively small collections such as work teams or functional departments) and organizations (e.g., relatively large collections such as enterprises or corporations). This dimension pertains to the scale of knowledge management and extends from a single person, through work groups, to an enterprise as a whole. Combined with the life cycle steps from above, we employ these levels to classify extant knowledge management applications.

Table 2 in particular pertains to organization-level knowledge management, which

Table 3: Group Level Systems and Practices

Create	Organize	Formalize	Distribute	Apply	Evolve
	Engr BoK Knowledge Exchange		Workflow Groupware Community of practice Discussion groups Document sharing Workshops Listservers Tele conference E-mail Meetings	Group DSS	

Table 4: Individual Level Systems and Practices

Create	Organize	Formalize	Distribute	Apply	Evolve
	Keyword extract Online thesaurus KBS	KBS	Information retrieval Document mgmt KBS	Data visualization KBS	

we differentiate from that occurring at the group and individual levels. Tables 3 and 4 are presented to incorporate systems and practices applied at these latter knowledge management levels. In discussing these tables, a number of points merit noting. First, arguably, knowledge creation represents a more difficult and uncertain process than its capture. Indeed, referring to Tables 2-4, few systems exist to support knowledge creation—data mining system conglomerates and artificial intelligence (AI) from first principles represent notable exceptions—but a number of enterprise practices (e.g., corporate research and development (R&D), benchmarking, competitive business intelligence) are widely employed for this purpose.

Second, referring back to Table 1, the Gartner Group collects the organize, formalize and distribute activities under the common heading "knowledge sharing." We use this grouping below to help classify and cluster extant knowledge management technologies and practices. Continuing across the rows of Table 2, examples of systems used for enterprise-wide knowledge organization include knowledge maps and semantic networks. And from Table 3, group-level implementations such as Chrysler's Engineering Book of Knowledge and Anderson Consulting's Knowledge Exchange are also noted in the literature. Table 4 reveals that at the individual level, systems that extract and cluster information by keyword are available, along with the online thesaurus to interrelate key terms and concepts in the enterprise. And as noted above in our discussion of expert systems methodologies, knowledge-based systems (KBS; e.g., expert systems, intelligent agents) address knowledge directly and employ a variety of knowledge representational techniques for its organization. Without going into great detail, notice a number of systems and practices listed under the knowledge formalization and distribution columns. Clearly, this represents the current emphasis of most knowledge management today. Alternatively, the application phase is relatively sparse in terms of supporting systems.

Third, we noted above the Despres and Chauvel life cycle includes a sixth element, called "evolution," to represent the refinement and continued development of existing knowledge. With a little thought, one can see such refinement and continued development is similar in many respects to the "maintenance" phases of the developmental life cycle models above. And as with the former life cycle models—which we note are laid-out sequentially but generally performed in an iterative manner—we can also say that knowledge evolution leads in turn to further knowledge creation, thereby completing the cycle and signaling the beginning of new knowledge capture and sharing (e.g., additional organization, formalization and distribution of knowledge).

Figure 3: Knowledge Management Life Cycle

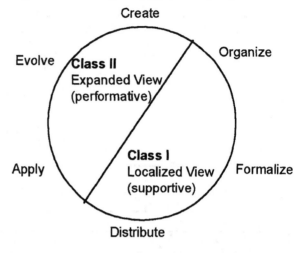

The cyclical nature is more readily discernible when presented as a circle, as opposed to a linear sequence of activities, as depicted in Figure 3. Notice the three "sharing" activities from above—knowledge organization, formalization and distribution—are adjacent on the right-hand side of the cycle. From the tables above, we see these activities correspond with greater support from extant information technologies and hence represent more of a localized view of knowledge management; thus, the grouping under the "Class I" heading in the figure. We note such, localized knowledge management systems are inherently supportive in nature; that is, this class of implementations to organize,

Table 5: Principal Enabling ITs and Transformations

Create	Organize	Formalize	Distribute	Apply	Developmental Approach
Pattern matching					IS, ES
Automatic inference	Automatic inference	Automatic inference	Automatic inference	Automatic inference	ES
Concurrent engr					IS, BPR
Process analysis					BPR
Business research					
	Association lists				IS
	Semantic net				ES
	Database	Database	Database		IS
	Web/Notes	Web/Notes	Web/Notes		IS
	Text search	Text index			IS
			Search engine		IS
			Workflow		IS, BPR
			Groupware		IS
			VTC		IS
			Listserver		IS
			GDSS		IS
			Graphics		IS

formalize and distribute knowledge in the enterprise *support* people in the loop, who in turn apply, evolve and create knowledge in the organization.

Alternatively, the latter three, non-sharing activities are adjacent on the left-hand side of the cycle. But from the tables we see these activities do not correspond well with support from extant information technologies and hence represent an expanded view of knowledge management; thus, the grouping under the "Class II" heading in the figure. We note such, expanded knowledge management systems are inherently performative in nature; that is, this class of implementations to apply, evolve and create knowledge in the enterprise *perform* knowledge-management activities, either in conjunction with or in lieu of people in the organization. Referring back to the tables above, however, we note very few extant knowledge management systems currently capable of performing in this manner. This may highlight a promising area for future knowledge management research and system development.

Table 5 extends the classification of extant knowledge management systems and practices by identifying the principal information technologies (ITs) and redesign transformations used to enable systems and practices from the various classes and life cycle phases. Take the first technology listed under the "create" column, for instance. This entry corresponds with the data mining class of systems identified in Table 2 above. Here, Table 5 indicates most data mining applications are enabled by tools and techniques associated with sophisticated pattern matching. Similarly, AI first-principles reasoning is also listed under the "create" column in Table 2. Here, Table 5 indicates most first-principles applications are enabled through the kind of automated inference performed by KBS. As other instances from Tables 2 and 5, respectively, many corporate R&D processes are transformed through concurrent engineering methods, benchmarking is generally conducted through comparative process analysis, and the collection of most competitive business intelligence is predicated on business research. The other technologies and transformations follow accordingly for Tables 2-4 and should be self-explanatory to the likely reader of this chapter.

Notice, looking across the rows at the rightmost column, we identify one or more of the methodologies from above—reengineering (BPR), expert systems (ES) or information systems (IS)—used to develop each principal IT or redesign transformation. For instance, conventional IS methods are generally employed to develop association lists, and ES approaches are required for implementing most semantic nets. Several important points can be drawn from this table.   First, notice the relative sparsity of applications outside the three "sharing" columns (i.e., beyond knowledge organization, formalization and distribution). At least as described in the literature, the great majority of knowledge management applications pertain to sharing knowledge that already exists in the enterprise. This supports our classification above in terms of a limited view of knowledge management, as it excludes knowledge creation, application and evolution, which are necessary to complete the life cycle. Indeed, we omit the "evolve" column in this table, because a dearth of technologies and practices is presently available for knowledge management at this step of the life cycle.

Second, every principal IT and transformation used to enable knowledge management systems and practices (i.e., listed in the table) is addressed by at least one current methodology. In other words, our current set of BPR, ES and IS methodologies provides the necessary capabilities to design and develop this entire collection of technologies and transformations used to enable extant knowledge management systems and processes. This supports our premise that extant methodologies, techniques and tools can be employed to develop knowledge management systems.

Third, a number of principal ITs and transformations require multiple developmental approaches. For instance, sophisticated pattern-matching tools and techniques employed to develop data mining applications require a synthesis of IS and ES approaches, and transformation of an R&D process to support concurrent engineering involves both information systems and process redesign methodologies and techniques. Indeed, where certain technologies and transformations are developed *together* (e.g., combining concurrent engineering with workflow technology), data from Table 5 indicate all three developmental approaches (i.e., reengineering, expert systems and information systems) are required. The table thus suggests that no single methodology—or pair of methodologies—and related set of techniques and tools is sufficient to develop all knowledge management systems and processes. This supports our premise that an integrated approach to knowledge system and process design is necessary. We address this need in the following section, as we explicitly integrate a number of critical contextual factors into the analysis.

CONTEXTUAL INTEGRATION

The feature space of systems and technologies outlined above defines the broad design space for KM systems. This design space is further defined and constrained by a set of contextual factors that impinge on the implementation of these systems in organizations. We identify and elaborate on two primary factors: 1) the organization, and 2) the nature of knowledge underlying the task.

The Organization

In addressing contextual factors associated with the organization, we divide the discussion into three parts: 1) the role of organizational memory, 2) structure of the organization, and 3) organizational incentives. We discuss each in turn.

The Role of Organizational Memory. Organizations have memory systems that maintain the lessons learned from experience (Levitt and March, 1988). The knowledge resident in an organization's memory constitutes a core mechanism for preserving its history, routines and the lessons learned over time. An organization relies on its memory for maintaining continuity in a changing environment. The elements of an organization's memory are recorded in many ways, formally as well as informally. Formal recording is implemented through artifacts such as memos, reports, files, standard operating procedures and rule books. Informal mechanisms for organizational memory are constituted by individuals and communities of practice (Brown and Duguid, 1991).

The design of knowledge management systems requires an awareness of three aspects of organizational memory. First, not everything that occurs in an organization's life is recorded. Since the amount of experience encountered by an organization is vast, its retention must be necessarily selective. Often, an organization's capacity for sense making and retention imposes a significant constraint toward retaining even knowledge that is vital to its survival and continuity (Weick, 1995). Besides, some of the experiences are ambiguous wherein the link between action and outcome is not clear (Olsen and

March, 1975). In such situations, there is a lack of clarity about the value and content of the lessons learned, raising questions about the necessity of retaining such knowledge. The challenge for designers of knowledge management systems lies in devising ways to augment the existing repositories of organizational memory while at the same time ensuring that the additional knowledge captured is valuable to the organization. Tools such as "yellow pages" and knowledge maps can contribute significantly in this direction.

Second, it needs to be recognized that knowledge captured through informal mechanisms is often richer and more important to the organization than what is stored through formal mechanisms (Weick, 1995). Such knowledge, which is often created outside the realm of institutionally mandated methods and procedures, can dissipate from organizational memory because of factors such as corporate reorganization, turnover in personnel and changes in technology (Brown and Duguid, 1991). The loss of this knowledge can result in organizational de-skilling (e.g., through actions such as corporate downsizing). And such knowledge, once lost, cannot be re-created easily (Hutchins, 1991). The key to building useful knowledge management systems lies in creating solutions that capture the essence of informal knowledge in a way that can be preserved and maintained. Tools such as lessons learned, handbooks of engineering knowledge and knowledge exchanges can perform valuable functions in capturing and distributing informal knowledge.

Finally, the putative effectiveness of knowledge management systems is predicated on the extent to which they are integrated with the nature and content of organizational memory and the underlying work practices. This requirement can be translated into a number of design desiderata. First, in building the conduits for *extracting* knowledge from resident organizational memory or *feeding* into it, designers need to consider whether the knowledge is resident in the formal or informal domains of memory. Often, knowledge management systems are designed to interact only with the formal repositories of organizational memory, in the process neglecting key aspects of knowledge resident in the informal repositories. This can result in a diminution in the actual and perceived relevance and utility of the systems. Second, knowledge management systems need to be integrated within the existing work practices of the organization and its repertoire of tools. Drawing from experiences with groupware (Grudin, 1996), it can be argued that unless knowledge management systems are embedded within the larger context of organizational work practices, they are unlikely to be used. The absence of continued interaction can result in atrophy and obsolescence.

Structure of the Organization. The structure of the organization has important implications for the creation, retention and dissemination of knowledge. As stated earlier, conventional organization structures rely heavily on informal networks and communities of practice for storing and disseminating knowledge. This is particularly the case for tacit and subtle aspects of organizational work practices (Teece 1996). Increasingly, however, organizational activities are being executed in the context of modified organizational forms enabled by information technology, such as virtual and networked organizations (Chesbrough and Teece, 1996; Fulk and DeSanctis, 1995). These organizations, which are typically *ad hoc* in nature, are formed for accomplishing specific objectives by combining multiple functional entities, often from two or more formal (i.e., non-virtual) organizations. Once the objective is accomplished, the virtual organization is disbanded or merged with a more-traditional organization.

The use of virtual organizations can create two specific problems with respect to the creation and retention of knowledge (Sengupta and Ramesh, 1999). The *ad hoc* nature of a virtual organization means that it does not have an established structure or well-developed norms. The members are not familiar with each other, and the task at its initial stages has a high degree of equivocality. Therefore, prior to addressing the task at hand, the organizational participants must first develop a structure as well as routines and channels of communication (Finholt et al., 1990). Second, because of their transient nature, virtual organizations experience difficulties in maintaining continuity; thus, the history of relevant corporate knowledge is not easily available. The problem is perpetuated when the virtual organization is disbanded: the organizational memory is once again lost for future use (Chesbrough and Teece, 1996).

These distinctions in the properties of conventional and virtual organizations can translate to differences in the use and efficacy of knowledge management tools. To illustrate, consider the use of video teleconferencing (VTC). Conventional organizations are usually characterized by clearly established patterns of structure, communication, culture and norms (Carley, 1991). In such organizations, the principal use of VTC lies in facilitating *task-oriented* discussions among individuals who happen to be geographically dispersed. In virtual organizations, on the other hand, these properties of the organization must first be developed. Consequently, the utility of a VTC application in virtual organizations lies not only in aiding task-oriented activities, but also in enabling the more basic activity of *organization-building*.

This distinction-in-use, contingent on organizational structure, can be found in knowledge management technologies across the board. For example, when used in virtual organizations, template-oriented information dissemination tools such as "yellow pages" and knowledge maps serve an additional purpose of providing a scaffold of corporate knowledge around which the new organization can be built (Sengupta and Zhao, 1998). This context-dependent use is often characterized as *bricolage* (Levi-Strauss, 1966; e.g., people make do with what is available and use tools in ways not originally envisaged by the designer). Similarly, drawing from adaptive structuration theory (DeSanctis and Poole, 1994), we argue the use of knowledge management tools can be "faithful" or "ironic", depending on—among other factors—the organizational structure.

Organizational Incentives. In a knowledge management activity, the retention and updating of knowledge is essentially an upstream activity, whereas the benefits from its dissemination and use occur downstream (Davenport and Prusak, 1996; Grudin, 1996). This dichotomy in capture and use can create specific problems. Organizational realities dictate that high proportions of projects or ventures are terminated before they are completed. The decision to continue or terminate is often made on the basis of managerial factors, particularly cost and schedule. Activities such as the capture of knowledge can add to the cost of a project, contribute to its delay and thus increase its prospects for cancellation. Moreover, the benefits of the knowledge accrue only at a later point and typically to a different stakeholder.

The implication for developing tools and processes for knowledge management is that it is insufficient to focus on the technical aspects of application development. Once the technologies are developed, managers may not have adequate incentives to justify devoting resources to the retention and updating of knowledge. Since the utility of knowledge management systems depends on their content, such systems can only succeed if appropriate incentives are provided (e.g., modifying the evaluation procedures for ongoing projects).

The Nature of Knowledge Underlying the Task

Organizations frequently resort to codifying, or making explicit, the processes underlying tasks. The utility of codification is thought to be two-fold (Orr 1990). First, it is a convenient mechanism for the capture and transfer of useful knowledge resident in the organization (Chesbrough and Teece, 1996). Second, it serves as a way of ensuring quality by prescribing uniformity in procedures and practices. Such *canonical* practices are usually contained in devices such as manuals, training programs, organization charts, job descriptions and standard operating procedures.

However, canonical prescriptions are often inadequate for solving complex problems (Bourdieu, 1977). This inadequacy is primarily caused by three factors (Lave, 1988, Lave and Wenger, 1990). First, the amount of effort involved in the acquisition of knowledge required for performing a complex task effectively is non-trivial. Second, knowledge that is acquired and represented in the canonical methods can become obsolete with changes in the underlying technologies (Suchman, 1987). Finally, there often are several different ways in which a task can be performed, and the best way of performing a task is contingent on the context in which it is performed.

Due to inadequacies in canonical descriptions, individuals who perform complex tasks may exercise improvisational skills and resort to *non-canonical* practices in order to bridge the gap between canonical approaches and effective work practices (Zuboff, 1988). As a result, the manner in which complex problems are actually solved often differs from the prescriptive methods, in at least two ways. First, non-canonical practices can serve as extensions of canonical methods (e.g., in compensating for the omissions and inadequacies in prescriptive knowledge). Second, such practices can also modify canonical methods. This can happen if the canonical methods are considered to be obsolete or generally less effective than the corresponding non-canonical methods.

The interplay of prescription and practice results in the creation of a significant body of non-canonical knowledge in organizations. This knowledge is typically embedded in the relevant communities of practice. The knowledge can take various forms, such as vocabularies, knowledge of practical constraints and workarounds relating to specific constraints (Brown and Duguid, 1991). The knowledge resides informally, often in the form of narratives such as "war stories" (Orr, 1990) or simply in the heads of designers, engineers and managers (Lynn, 1992). Such tacit knowledge, which is resistant to efforts at codification (Orr 1990), often forms the core of an organization's distinctive competence (Chesbrough and Teece, 1996) and is preserved and nurtured through communities of practice.

The principal implication of this discussion is, in developing knowledge management systems, a designer is faced with constraints on the types of knowledge that are amenable to capture. While the corpus of explicit knowledge that can be readily codified (and thus captured and distributed through systems) is undoubtedly useful, it is often accompanied by a vast complement of tacit knowledge, which is difficult to capture. This constraint is brought into focus by a recognition that in many instances (as in product design situations), it is the tacit knowledge that constitutes the mother-lode in terms of value.

As a practical matter, the line between explicit and tacit is blurred; often, the distinction is reflected in the way the knowledge is represented (Buckingham Shum, 1994). Formal representations (e.g., in terms of design rules and procedures) lend themselves well to codification, but are difficult to capture. Informal representations (e.g., a videorecording of a design session) do not lend themselves to automated reasoning. However, such representations make the capture of tacit knowledge more feasible. Further, appropriately devised indexing schemes can make context-sensitive retrieval possible.

KNOWLEDGE MANAGEMENT EXAMPLE

To summarize from above, the contextual factors discussed in the preceding section play a critical contingency role in our examination of established approaches; that is, the context of the knowledge management environment and situation has a strong mediating effect on selection of appropriate methodologies, techniques and tools for knowledge system and process development. We illustrate this effect through examination of an example of a knowledge-work process from the literature to articulate, at a high level, our integrated approach to knowledge system and process design. The general example described in this section represents a composite of workflow activities adapted from two extremes of a process family. On the one hand, we have the well-known and relatively well-structured credit financing process described by Hammer and Champy (1993, pp. 36-39). This process is representative of many associated with knowledge and information work and should be familiar to most readers. On the other hand, we also describe its semi-structured counterpart that applies to venture-capital financing of startup technology companies. This latter process depicts the kind of difficulties that often arise with non-routine tasks and helps accentuate both benefits and limitations of our integrated approach to knowledge system and process development. We first outline key aspects of the general process and then discuss it in the context of integrated knowledge system and process development.

General Process

Credit financing represents a key subprocess in support of marketing and sales, as the ability to provide potential customers with in-house financing represents a strong selling point for any company. However, customer feedback suggests the process as practiced in many firms has a number of shortcomings and flaws. For example, it is often associated with long cycle time required to prepare a credit financing package, and many firms lack the ability to report on the status of a particular package while it is being processed. This holds for either routine credit packages (e.g., financing a washing machine) as well as non-routine processes (e.g., syndicating a commercial real estate loan).

Structured Process. Drawing from Hammer and Champy (1993, pp. 36-39), we can characterize the general process through involvement of four value stream participants: 1) field sales groups with representatives that work to secure new customers, 2) the centralized credit financing organization, 3) a third-party delivery company, and 4) the customers themselves. For purpose of this example, say the centralized credit financing unit is organized in terms of four functional departments, each of which is staffed with specialists for the functional areas: 1) credit check, 2) terms development, 3) financial pricing, and 4) quotation packaging.

As a relatively classic, bureaucratic organization, one can understand the process flow is often described as serial, beginning with a meeting between the field sales representative and potential customer. For instance, when customer interest is generated, the process continues with a telephone call from the field sales representative to a contact person in the financing unit, the latter of whom writes down the relevant customer, product and financing information. The paper with this information is then carried to each separate functional department, where a functional manager assigns the job to a specialist from the department. This assignment is accomplished simply by placing the paper in the specialist's in-box. The specialist in each functional department retrieves the paper from his or her in-box and performs the functional tasks required for each potential customer. This functional work is accomplished using specialized, stand-alone computer equipment, but communications are conducted entirely through paper and face-to-face meetings. Once the specialist completes the required functional tasks, he or she writes down the relevant facts and determinations on a separate piece of paper and reviews the results with the department manager.

This kind of functional activity proceeds in series from one department to another until the credit financing package is complete. When complete, the package is reviewed by the unit manager and then carried back to the contact representative, who arranges to have the third party delivery company transport the package to the field sales representative, generally via overnight air service. Once received, the field sales representative schedules an appointment with the potential customer to discuss the financing and other terms of the potential contract. Quality feedback loops at each department indicate packages can be returned for rework at any stage of the process, including return by the salesperson in the field.

Semi-structured Process. The syndicated loan (e.g., for a startup company) proceeds through the same basic steps, but it is far less structured in nature; that is, although the same fundamental tasks need to be completed, the performance of each task may differ depending on the nature of the financing (e.g., amount of loan, type of loan, collateral offered), potential customer (e.g., length of customer relationship, size of customer institution, operating experience) and business proposition (e.g., stability of proposed venture, inherent technological risk, novelty of business model). Where the financing unit has underwritten one or more loans for similar purposes, the process begins with a search for a representative model to use as a starting point for customizing a loan package. This is a manner of case-based reasoning, which generally involves searching through archived documents and asking colleagues about their experiences. Where the requested financing package represents an unprecedented mix of attributes (e.g., financing, customer, proposition), workers from various fields of expertise (e.g., credit determination, contracts, risk assessment, pricing, loan packaging) must meet to determine how to approach the problem. And in the case in which the requested financing is routine, the process essentially collapses into the one described above, through which a package progresses in serial fashion from functional group to group.

Process Analysis

The first stage of knowledge system and process design involves process analysis. Until one understands the process—along with its various redesign opportunities and required knowledge—it makes little sense to begin designing systems. As noted above, many methodologies have been developed for process design. Here, we discuss the measurement-driven redesign method of Nissen (1998), which has been implemented via expert systems technology to automatically diagnose process pathologies and recommend redesign transformations.

Structured Process. The pathologies and corresponding process measurements are shown in Table 6 for the first, structured credit financing process. From measured values presented in the table, one can see the baseline process suffers from a number of serious pathologies. Beginning with the parallelism measurement (1.00), this quantifies the sequential nature of the process and has adverse implications in terms of cycle time. The handoffs fraction measures the relative number of exchanges between workers performing different roles in the process. And the value (1.00) obtained for this process is exceptionally high for a process involving knowledge and information work such as this—on average, a specialist worker (e.g., credit manager, credit analyst, terms manager) performs only a *single* activity before passing work along to the next process step. The associated pathology, process friction, also has adverse implications in term of cycle time, as work sitting in in-boxes and out-boxes, awaiting assignment, pausing for review and approval, undergoing transport and like situations consumes substantial process time. Closely related is the feedback fraction measure, which quantifies the relative number of review and approval steps in a process. The measured value (0.29) is relatively high for a knowledge-work process such as this, as a separate review/approval step is conducted at approximately every third activity. The associated pathology pertains to checking and complexity, which has adverse implications in terms of both cost and cycle time, and reveals relatively little autonomy for the knowledge workers involved in the process.

The three IT fractions are used to measure the relative use of information technology for support, communication and automation, respectively. The relatively low value (0.24) obtained for IT support indicates only one in four process activities is supported by information technology. And notice both the IT communication and automation measurements reflect theoretical minima. The associated pathologies listed in the table (i.e., a manual, paper-based, labor-intensive process) have adverse implications in terms of both cost and cycle time. Moreover, from a knowledge management perspective, knowledge in this baseline process is both

Table 6: Process Measurements and Diagnoses

Configuration Measure	Value	Diagnosis
Parallelism	1.00*	Sequential process flows
Handoffs fraction	1.00	Process friction
Feedback fraction	0.29	Checking & complexity
IT support fraction	0.24	Manual process
IT communication fraction	0.00*	Paper-based process
IT automation fraction	0.00*	Labor-intensive process

* denotes theoretical extremum for a measure

Table 7: Redesign Transformations

Pathology	Transformation
Sequential process flows	De-linearize
Checking & complexity	Asynchronous reviews or empowerment
Process friction	Case manager or case team
Manual process	Integrated databases or workflow
Paper-based process	e-mail or workflow
Labor-intensive process	Expert systems or intelligent agents

tacit and explicit, resides in the minds of specialist workers as well as formal procedures, and where shared at all, it involves paper and face-to-face conversations. This represents a very primitive knowledge management environment.

Semi-structured Process. The semi-structured process involves many of the same activities. And as noted above, it collapses into its structured process counterpart for routine financing requests. Indeed, at the process level, the activities are identical, except for the number of exceptions that affect the semi-structured version and various modes of problem solving used to perform different process activities. For example, the process proceeds along one flow if a prior financing package can be located for use as an exemplar and an entirely different one where such an exemplar cannot be found. Similarly, task performance is quite equivalent to that in the simple process above where specialists can work in relative isolation, but substantial face-to-face interaction is required where collaborative problem solving is required. For ease of discussion and to illustrate our techniques, we focus on the simpler, structured process in the analysis below. But for richness, we weave-in variations and differences to include its more complex, semi-structured counterpart.

Process Redesign. Some representative redesign transformations are summarized for the structured process in Table 7. Beginning with the first pathology listed in the table, redesign transformations involving de-linearization (i.e., performing two or more process activities in parallel) offer good potential to treat this sequential process. Notice these transformations are not mutually exclusive, as de-linearization can also be applied to address the checking and complexity pathology through asynchronous reviews. This is an alternative to empowering analysts in the process to review their own work, fundamentally a TQM idea of building-in quality rather than verifying it through inspection.

The process friction pathology can be addressed through a case manager or case team. In such a transformation, the specialized division of labor and functional organization currently exhibited in the process are dissolved and replaced by a small team—or even a single individual if sufficient knowledge support and expertise can be provided—that performs all the process activities. Manual processes can be addressed by a multitude of information technology transformations. Integrated databases and workflow systems represent good candidates here, and e-mail or workflow can also address the paper-based communications. Regarding the labor-intensive process resulting from negligible automation, expert systems or intelligent agents offer good potential to address these problems, provided the necessary knowledge and expertise can be effectively organized and formalized. Clearly, other redesign transformations also offer potential, and the point is not to exhaustively cover them. Rather, we want to show the importance of addressing the process in conjunction with knowledge and systems.

Additionally, many of these same redesign transformations also apply to the more complex, semi-structured process. The key difference is they apply to different versions or modalities of the latter process. For instance, we noted above the semi-structured process collapses into its structured counterpart for routine credit requests. In such a case, each of the redesign transformations listed in Table 7 also applies here. Alternatively, where more collaboration is required among workers, redesigns such as de-linearization and workflow do not apply as well. However, in this latter case, the group may effectively perform as a case team, essentially transforming itself in this manner as a separate mode of operation. Thus, alternative modalities of execution in the semi-structured process indicate the simultaneous existence of *multiple* redesign alternatives, each of which is instantiated at different times and occasions on the basis of contextual factors (e.g., task familiarity). And to the extent this latter case involves manual, paper-based, labor-intensive process activities—even though collaboratively performed—there exists good opportunity for the kinds of IT-based redesigns noted in Table 7 for the simpler process version above.

Knowledge Analysis

Knowledge analysis is in no way independent of the process analysis above. Rather, the former is fed directly by results of the latter. Looking at the redesign transformations identified in Table 7, for example, nearly all of them address knowledge in some way. For one, to effectively de-linearize process activities, workers such as the field sales agents need to know where work on the various elements of a credit financing packing is in the process. We can express this in terms of our knowledge management feature space above. From the amalgamated knowledge management life cycle model, this involves distributing explicit knowledge at the organization level across the credit unit. As another example, if line workers (i.e., not managers) are empowered to review and approve their own work, they require the kind of knowledge and experience possessed by managers today. From the knowledge management life cycle, this involves formalizing tacit knowledge at the individual level (e.g., the functional managers' expertise) and its subsequent distribution through each functional group.

The case team involves similar knowledge formalization, as generalist workers on a team require access to the detailed knowledge currently possessed by specialists in each functional organization. To work effectively as a team, the group will first need to organize this knowledge, and subsequently it will be distributed across the team members in the group. The case manager (i.e., a single individual) represents the extreme instantiation of a case team and places the most demands in terms of managing knowledge. Say, for instance, this single individual is the field sales agent; that is, instead of relying upon the centralized credit financing organization, field sales agents would become responsible for preparing their own credit packages. Deferring questions of technological feasibility and cognitive limitations for the time being, clearly, the field sales agents would need to be able to apply all the knowledge and reason with all the experience currently employed within the centralized credit organization; otherwise, performance will suffer (e.g., bad loans may increase or promising financing opportunities may be missed by mistake). Referring back to the knowledge management life cycle, no new knowledge needs to be created here, but existing—tacit and explicit—credit financing knowledge needs to be organized for understanding, formalized to be made explicit and distributed for remote application by sales agents in the field. Aside from the creation and evolution steps, this covers the entire knowledge management life cycle and involves knowledge from the level of an individual, through the functional groups, to the entire enterprise.

Contextual Analysis

Here, we draw from the contextual integration section to further refine the analysis of this knowledge management process and associated systems. Considering first the role of organizational memory in the credit financing process, we can identify two principal mechanisms for its recording. Explicit knowledge is well represented through standard operating procedures—though predominately in paper form. And tacit knowledge, which is required to handle novel, complex or unusual financing requests, resides in the minds of each specialist worker and is recorded through communities of practice for each of the four functional specialties (e.g., credit, contracts, pricing, risk).

Drawing from the discussion above, tools such as "yellow pages" and knowledge maps would be appropriate here to formalize and distribute the location and content of knowledge among all the functional workers. Clearly, this would apply more to redesigns such as de-linearization that preserve the functional organization of the process or to virtual coordination of workers who have not previously worked together. But such tools could also be made available to a single case manager, who may need expert assistance with particularly difficult problems. In addition to identifying *who* in the organization possesses various kinds of knowledge (e.g., through the "yellow pages") and *what* kinds of knowledge are possessed (e.g., through knowledge maps), it is also important to begin capturing the corresponding knowledge itself, particularly the tacit knowledge used by specialists to solve difficult problems. "Yellow pages" serve little purpose if the person identified as resident expert is no longer part of the organization (e.g., the de-skilling referred to above). This is an application for which expert systems may be relatively well-suited to make such tacit knowledge explicit and distributable. Other tools, such as lessons learned, handbooks and knowledge exchanges, can also serve a useful purpose by reducing the formalization burden often associated with expert systems.

Recalling the design desiderata from above, we have noted and addressed both tacit and explicit knowledge in the process and the need to develop conduits for feeding and extracting informal as well as formal sources of knowledge in the process. And by redesigning the process before designing knowledge management systems, we address the second design rule arguing such systems must be embedded into the underlying process as well. Here we begin to re-incorporate the methodologies-techniques-tools discussion from above.

Regarding organizational structure, most of the aforementioned redesigns preserve the relatively conventional organizational structure of the baseline credit unit. Although the case manager redesign is radical in terms of shifting responsibility from the organizational level (i.e., the credit unit) to an individual role (i.e., the field sales agent), even this streamlined organization is not particularly virtual in nature. Hence we contrast even the case manager redesign with the kinds of virtual design teams discussed by Sengupta and Ramesh (1999), for instance, and note how the semi-structured credit financing process from above can easily take-on a number of virtual characteristics (e.g., geographically-distributed coworkers, new teams formed for each syndicated loan). When considering VTC, for instance, use of this technology—say by field sales agents needing to interact with functional experts—can focus on task-oriented discussions. Alternatively, where new firms are coming together for the first time to syndicate financing for an Internet startup company, the additional demands and complexities of organization-building would *also* apply in this more complex, virtual case.

This brings us to the issue of incentives. Continuing with the case manager redesign, for instance, the field sales agent clearly represents a consumer of process knowledge and is highly motivated to seek it out. But say that (human) functional specialists are retained in a "help desk" approach to provide such assistance, among other duties. They must be incentivized, not only to provide the requested assistance, but to also be responsive, accurate and thorough in support of field sales agents' questions and problems. This is much more of a human relations issue than the technical questions traditionally addressed by information systems methodologies. But the example should make it clear how important such human relations issues (e.g., compensation, team building) can become in the context of knowledge system and process design. Moreover, say we are interested in capturing such specialist knowledge and experience through expert system technology. Here in particular, specialists require strong incentives to contribute knowledge. For aside from maintaining the resulting expert systems, perhaps, such specialists may effectively be replaced by the knowledge systems they help develop.

The second key contextual factor involves the nature of knowledge underlying each task. Beginning with the kinds of canonical practices from above—which we note are usually contained in devices such as manuals, training programs, organization charts, job descriptions and standard operating procedures—let's presume such practices are formally documented in the structured process. But drawing from the listed pathologies for the process (especially manual, paper-based, labor-intensive), they are unlikely to exist in digital form. Tools to organize, capture and distribute such explicit knowledge include databases, online textual search and retrieval systems, hyperlinked intranet applications and even workflow integration (e.g., through contextualized online help and process information).

However, the non-canonical knowledge is considerably more difficult to manage. Where such tacit knowledge can be identified and articulated, conceivably expert system applications can be employed for its formalization and network technologies used for distribution. The kinds of experience-based knowledge used by managers to review the work of functional subordinates in the structured process, for instance, may fall into this category. Still, as noted above, the knowledge engineering required to develop and maintain such intelligent systems is non-trivial in terms of level and amount. Other kinds of tacit knowledge may be more difficult to identify, and even harder to articulate. Take, for example, problem solving knowledge used by functional specialists—perhaps in a virtual organization—to address novel, complex financing issues. A specialist may not even be aware of the corresponding knowledge until the situation arises, and many experts and professionals are notoriously poor at articulating the manner in which such non-routine problems are solved. For this kind of knowledge, we may have to settle for something of an "80/20" rule. In such a rule, one would strive to capture, formalize and distribute knowledge associated with the 80% of problems that are relatively routine and perfunctory through technology (e.g., expert systems). For the rest, one would instead rely upon the kinds of "yellow pages," knowledge maps, help desks and VTC links required to make such knowledge available among human problem solvers, in either a classical or virtual organization.

To summarize the section thus far, the methodology for designing knowledge systems and processes has progressed through three steps: 1) process analysis and redesign, 2) knowledge analysis, and 3) contextual analysis. Through examination of a general credit financing process, we have identified a number of alternative systems that offer potential to enhance knowledge management in this process context. These include, for instance, "yellow pages," knowledge maps, expert systems, VTC, databases, workflow, textual search and retrieval, intranet and other classes of systems and applications. Returning to one of our original themes in the paper, *individually*, each of these technological artifacts represents a relatively well-known and understood entity, for which extant methodologies, techniques and tools—used for reengineering, expert systems and information systems design—are readily available *at the application level.* In the discussion below, we close the section by briefly illustrating the kinds of methodologies, techniques and tools from above that can be employed to develop some of the knowledge management applications identified through this multi-level (e.g., process, knowledge, contextual) analysis.

Systems Analysis and Integration

At this final stage of analysis, we fix the discussion by focusing on one of the several redesign alternatives from above: case team. As noted above, this redesign is radical in nature—certainly with respect to the baseline, departmentalized organization—and places extreme demands on the designer in terms of knowledge management. The reader may recall the case team also corresponds to one modality associated with the semi-structured credit financing process. Through examination of the corresponding knowledge and contextual factors from above, we can identify several technologies and applications for integration with the case team process.

For instance, case team members need means for formalizing and distributing explicit knowledge (e.g., manuals, procedures, instructions), at the group and individual levels, and applications to help coordinate their respective activities. Drawing from associated group and individual level technologies above (e.g., Tables 3 and 4), knowledge exchange, workflow, groupware, document sharing, e-mail and text-retrieval applications can be implemented across the corresponding phases of the knowledge management life cycle. Individually, each of these applications is common and relatively straightforward to design and implement through conventional IS methodologies, techniques and tools. One could, for instance, iteratively employ the SDLC for this entire set of applications, perhaps using standard IS developmental techniques such as interviews, (e.g., for requirements determination and usage patterns), data-flow modeling (e.g., for mapping process information flows), entity-relationship modeling (e.g., for database design) and structured programming (e.g., for implementation). Associated tools could in turn include structured interview templates, a suite of modeling applications (e.g., as part of a CASE tool), program editors, compilers and debuggers.

Were we to select an alternative process redesign—such as the field sales agent case manager—involving separate knowledge (e.g., tacit managerial and specialist knowledge) and contextual factors (e.g., formal and informal organizational memory requirements, canonical and non-canonical tasks), the systems analysis and integration would necessarily focus on a different set of knowledge management applications (e.g., expert systems, intranets, VTC, others). Nonetheless, methodologies, techniques and tools that are readily available and widely understood can be compared and employed in a straightforward manner. For instance, the applications identified for this latter redesign might integrate expert system development methods with the information system analysis and design techniques and tools from above.

Thus, having reached this level of analysis, one can see traditional, well-understood IS methodologies, techniques and tools can be employed for knowledge management system development. This answers one of the key questions posed in the introductory section. The key to our integrated knowledge management methodology is, such systems are explicitly analyzed, selected and combined to help manage *knowledge* (e.g., explicit work practices), for a particular *process* design (e.g., case team) and set of *contextual factors* (e.g., organizational memory involving canonical knowledge). Most existing methodologies simply begin at this (final) system-development step without consideration of such process, knowledge or contextual factors. Only empirical evidence can confirm that our integrated methodology is in some ways *superior* to extant developmental approaches. But we can certainly argue this integrated knowledge system and process design methodology is more *complete*. This leads us to a number of conclusions and suggestions for future research along these lines.

CONCLUSIONS AND FUTURE RESEARCH

The research described in this chapter has focused on knowledge management and system design from three integrated perspectives: 1) reengineering and process innovation, 2) expert systems knowledge acquisition and representation, and 3) information systems analysis and design. Through careful analysis and discussion, we integrated these three perspectives in a systematic manner, beginning with analysis and design of the enterprise process of interest, progressively moving into knowledge capture and formalization, and then system design and implementation. Thus, we have developed an integrated approach that covers the gamut of design considerations from the enterprise process in the large, through alternative classes of knowledge in the middle, and on to specific systems in the detail.

The central premise of this work is, although knowledge management represents a phenomenon of relatively new widespread interest and attention in research and practice, many of its underlying elements are actually quite familiar and have been effectively addressed for many years through work in information systems, artificial intelligence and process redesign. In the course of our discussion above, we outlined and employed a three-tier framework for examining alternative methodologies, techniques and tools. We then outlined a contingent feature space of specific elements, levels and stages comprising knowledge management, using it to compose an integrated analysis and design approach tailored to each of its key aspects. With this, we developed a set of contextual factors that draw insight into strengths and limitations of various approaches, and we illustrated the use and utility of integrated knowledge system and process design through an example. This represents a central contribution of the chapter, as it reveals the underlying components of knowledge management and prescribes design guidance specific to each.

Through our examination of established approaches, reengineering, expert systems and information systems, all involve some kind of developmental life cycle. Each respective life cycle begins with some planning and analytical tasks, proceeds through relatively diverse design activities, prescribes some physical and procedural changes through implementation, and transitions into a maintenance phase. Despite structural similarities between the three life cycle models, however, the underlying steps and focuses of the corresponding methodologies are quite distinct. Yet, the three areas of methodological focus are tightly linked, and a strong argument can be made that all three aspects—process, knowledge and information—should be addressed together when designing knowledge systems and processes. This represents one of the central premises of the chapter.

A number of other important findings and conclusions emerge from this research. For one, despite the abundance of knowledge management life cycles that now appear in the literature, they all share considerable similarities and can be integrated into an amalgamated model to describe a broad diversity of knowledge management work in the enterprise. As another, if harnessed appropriately, the current repertoire of IT methodologies, technologies and tools has much to offer for the design and development of knowledge management systems. At the same time, as Tables 2-4 show, there are aspects of the knowledge management life cycle where the existing capabilities of IT are inadequate, most notably in the generation and application of knowledge at the organizational and group levels.

Further, contextual factors play a critical role in the design and implementation of knowledge systems and processes. We contend that effective knowledge management is a question of tailoring technical and process solutions to fit the exigencies of the context in which activities are being performed. And we illustrate how our integrated methodology for knowledge system and process design is more complete than existing developmental approaches, the latter of which simply begin at the (final) system development phase and ignore key process, knowledge and contextual factors. Future research along these lines may produce empirical evidence that our integrated method is also superior in some respects to extant approaches.

The research described in this chapter offers several other logical extensions for future research. One important extension would develop IT solutions that address support and performance of knowledge generation and application activities along the life cycle. Recall we found applications for such activities to be largely absent from tables representing the current state of technologies and practices. We may also identify the need for new techniques and tools to support development of the new solutions. Another useful extension would delineate the *contingent* nature of knowledge management. For instance, one could endeavor to specify in greater detail the interaction between information technologies and practices with organizational activities, thereby enabling designers to identify "families" of solutions that are likely to succeed as knowledge system and process implementations. Clearly, this represents only a short, partial list of future research topics. Knowledge management remains a relatively novel focus of research, and much work needs to be accomplished to advance our knowledge and technological level in this area. We hope to have contributed to such knowledge and level by illustrating how current methodologies, techniques and tools can be applied, in an integrated manner, for analysis and design of knowledge systems and processes.

REFERENCES

Anderson and APQC (1996). *The Knowledge Management Assessment Tool: External Benchmarking Version* (Winter).

Anderson, J.R. (1983). *The Architecture of Cognition*. Harvard University Press: Cambridge

Andrews, D.C. and Stalick, S.K. (1994). *Business Reengineering: the Survival Guide* Yourdon Press Computing Series.

Arrow, K. (1962). "Economic Welfare and the Allocation of Resources for Invention," in: R. Nelson (Ed.), *The Rate and Direction of Inventive Activity*. Princeton University Press: Princeton, NJ .

Bashein, B.J., Markus, M.L., and Riley, P. (1994)."Preconditions for BPR success: and how to prevent failures," *Information Systems Management* (Spring), 7-13.

Bourdieu, P. (1977). *Outline of a Theory of Practice* Cambridge University Press.

Brown, J., and Duguid, P. (1991). "Organizational Learning and Communities-of-Practice: Toward a Unified View of Working, Learning, and Innovation," *Organization Science* 2(1), 40-57.

Brown, J.S. and Duguid, P.(1998). "Organizing Knowledge," *California Management Review* 40(3), 90-111.

Buckingham Shum, S. (1996). "Analyzing usability of a Design Rationale Notation,: In T. P. Moran and J. M. Carroll (Eds), *Design Rationale: Concepts, Techniques and Use* Lawrence Erlbaum Associates, Mahwah, NJ.

Carley, K. (1991). "A Theory of Group Stability," *American Sociological Review* 56, 331-354.

Caron, J.R., Jarvenpaa S.L., and Stoddard, D.B.(1994). "Business reengineering at CIGNA corporation: experiences and lessons learned from the first five years," *MIS Quarterly* (September), 233-250.

Chesbrough, H. and Teece, D. (1996). "When is Virtual Virtuous? Organizing for Innovation," *Harvard Business Review* (January-February), 65-73.

Clemons, E.K., Thatcher, M.E. and Row, M.C. (1995). "Identifying Sources of Reengineering Failures: A Study of the Behavioral Factors Contributing to Reengineering Risks," *Journal of Management Information Systems* 12(2), 9-36.

Cole, R.E. (1994). "Reengineering the corporation: a review essay," *Quality Management Journal* 1(4), 77-85.

Cypress, H.L. (1994). "Reengineering - MS/OR imperative: make second generation of business process improvement mode work," *OR/MS Today* (February),18-29.

Davenport, T.H. *Process Innovation: Reengineering Work through Information Technology,* Harvard Press, Boston, MA (1993).

Davenport, T.H. (1995). "Business Process Reengineering: Where It's Been, Where It's Going," in *Business Process Change: Reengineering Concepts, Methods and Technologies,* V. Grover and W. Kettinger (eds.), Idea Publishing, Harrisburg, PA, 1-13.

Davenport, T.H., Jarvenpaa, S.L. and Beers, M.C. (1996). "Improving Knowledge Work Processes," *Sloan Management Review* (Summer).

Davenport, T.H., De Long, D.W. and Beers, M.C.(1998). "Successful Knowledge Management Projects," *Sloan Management Review* (Winter), 43-57.

Davenport, T.H. and Prusak, L.(1998). *Working Knowledge: How Organizations Manage what they Know*. Harvard Business School Press: Boston, MA.

Davenport T.H., and Stoddard, D.B. (1994). "Reengineering: business change of mythic proportions?" *MIS Quarterly* (June), 121-127.

Davidson, W.H. (1993). "Beyond re-engineering: the three phases of business transformation," *IBM Systems Journal* 32(1), 65-79.

DeSanctis, G., and Poole, M.S. (1994). "Capturing the Complexity in Advanced Technology Use: Adaptive Structuration Theory," *Organization Science* 5, 121-147.

Despres, C. and Chauvel, D. (1999). "Mastering Information Management: Part Six – Knowledge Management," *Financial Times* (8 March), 4-6.

Drucker, P.F.(1978). *The Age of Discontinuity*. Harper and Row: New York, NY.

Drucker, P.F.(1995). *Managing in a Time of Great Change*. Truman Talley: New York, NY.

Earl, M.J. and Scott, I.A.(1999). "What is a Chief Knowledge Officer?" *Sloan Management Review* (Winter), 29-38.

Finholt, T., Sproull, L. and Kiesler, S.(1990). "Communication and Performance in Ad Hoc Task Groups," in: J. Galegher, R. Kraut, and C. Egido (eds), *Intellectual Teamwork: Social and Technological Foundations of Cooperative Work* Lawrence Erlbaum Associates, Hillsdale, N.J.

Flood, R.L.(1993). *Beyond TQM* Wiley, New York, NY .

Forbes (1997). Special Focus on Intellectual Capital, *Forbes ASAP* (7 April).

Frappaolo, C. (1998). "Defining Knowledge Management: Four Basic Functions," *Computerworld* 32(8).

Fulk, J. and DeSanctis, G. (1995). "Electronic Communications and Changing Organizational Forms," *Organization Science* 6, 337-349.

Gartner Group (1998). "Knowledge Management Scenario," conference presentation, SYM8KnowMan1098Kharris.

Glazer, R.(1998). "Measuring the Knower: Towards a Theory of Knowledge Equity," *California Management Review* 40(3), 175-194.

Grover, V., Jeong, S.R., Kettinger, W.J. and Teng, J.T.C.(1995). "The Implementation of Business Process Reengineering," *Journal of Management Information Systems* 12(1), 109-144.

Grudin, J. (1996). "Evaluating opportunities for design capture,: in: T. P. Moran and J. M. Carroll (Eds), *Design Rationale: Concepts, Techniques and Use* Lawrence Erlbaum Associates, Mahwah, NJ.

Guha, S., Kettinger, W.J., and Teng, J.T.C.(1994). "Business process reengineering: building a comprehensive methodology," *Information Systems Management* (Spring), 13-22.

Hammer, M. (1990). "Reengineering work: don't automate, obliterate," *Harvard Business Review* (July/August), 104-112.

Hammer, M. and Champy J. *Reengineering the Corporation: A Manifesto for Business Revolution* Harper Business Press, New York, NY (1993).

Hammer, M. and Stanton S.(1995). *The Reengineering Revolution: A Handbook* Harper Business Press, New York, NY.

Hansen, G. (1994). "A complex process: the case for automated assistance in business process Reengineering," *OR/MS Today* (August), 34-41.

Harrington, H.J. (1991). *Business Process Improvement: the Breakthrough Strategy for Total Quality, Productivity, and Competitiveness* McGraw-Hill, New York, NY.

Henderson, J.C., and Venkatraman. N.(1993). "Strategic alignment: leveraging information technology for transforming organizations," *IBM Systems Journal* 32(1), 4-16.

Hoffherr, G.D., Moran, J.D. and Nadler, G.(1994). *Breakthrough Thinking in Total Quality Management* Prentice-Hall, Englewood Cliffs, NJ.

Hutchins, E. (1991). "Organizing Work by Adaptation," *Organization Science* 2(1).

Johansson, H.J., McHugh, P., Pendlebury, A.J. and Wheeler, W.A. III (1993). *Business Process Reengineering: Breakpoint Strategies for Market Dominance* Wiley, Chickster, UK.

Kamel, M.Z. (1999). "Knowledge Acquisition," in: J.G. Webster (Ed.), *Wiley Encyclopedia of Electrical and Electronics Engineering* Vol. 11, New York: Wiley.

Kettinger, W.J., Guha, S. and Teng, J.T.C. (1995). "The Process Reengineering Life Cycle Methodology: A Case Study," in: V. Grover and W. Kettinger (eds.), *Business Process Change: Reengineering Concepts, Methods and Technologies*, Idea Publishing, Harrisburg, PA, 211-244.

Klein, M.M.(1994). "Reengineering methodologies and tools: a prescription for enhancing Success," *Information Systems Management* (Spring), 30-35.

Labor. U.S. Department of Labor Report (1991).

Lave, J. (1988). *Cognition in Practice: Mind, Mathematics, and Culture in Everyday Life* Cambridge University Press.

Lave, J., and Wenger, E. (1990). *Situated Learning: Legitimate Peripheral Participation* Cambridge University Press.

Leavitt, H.J. (1965). "Applying organizational change in industry: structural, technological and humanistic approaches," in: J. March (Ed.), *Handbook of Organizations* Chicago, IL:

Rand McNally.

Levitt, B. and March, J.(1988). "Organizational Learning," *Annual Review of Sociology* 14, 319-340.

Levi-Strauss, C. (1966). *The Savage Mind* University of Chicago Press, Chicago.

Lynn, L.(1992). "Valuing Tradition while Changing: the Japanese Experience," in: Srivastva and Fry (eds.), *Executive and Organizational Continuity* Jossey-Bass, San Francisco.

McCartney, L. (1998)."Getting Smart about Knowledge Management," *Industry Week* (4 May).

Miles, G., Miles, R.E., Perrone, V. and Edvinsson, L.(1998). "Some Conceptual and Research Barriers to the Utilization of Knowledge," *California Management Review* 40(3), 281-288.

Nissen, M.E.(1997). "A Focused Review of the Reengineering Literature: Expert Frequently Asked Questions," *Quality Management Journal,* 3(3), 52-66.

Nissen, M.E.(1998). "Redesigning Reengineering through Measurement-Driven Inference," *MIS Quarterly* 22(4), 509-534.

Nissen, M.E. (1999). "Knowledge-Based Knowledge Management in the Reengineering Domain," *Decision Support Systems* Special Issue on Knowledge Management.

Nonaka, I.(1994). "A Dynamic Theory of Organizational Knowledge Creation," *Organization Science* 5(1), 14-37.

O'Leary, D.E. (1998)."Enterprise Knowledge Management," *Computer* (March).

Olsen, J. and March, J.(1975). "The Uncertainty of the Past: Organizational Learning under Ambiguity," *European Journal of Political Research* 3, 147-171.

Orr, J. *(1990). Talking About Machines: the Ethnography of a Modern Job* doctoral dissertation, Cornell University.

Prerau, D. (1990). *Developing and Managing Expert Systems: Proven Techniques for Business and Industry* New York: Addison-Wesley.

Roberts, B.(1996). "Internet as Knowledge Manager," *Web Week* (9 September), 30.

Ruggles, R. (1997). *Knowledge Management Tools* Butterworth-Heinemann: Boston, MA.

Ruggles, R.(1998). "The State of the Notion: Knowledge Management in Practice," *California Management Review* 40(3).

Sengupta, K., and Ramesh, B. (1999)."Decision Support for Virtual Teams: Issues and Design Principles," *Accounting, Management, and Information Technology.*

Sengupta, K., and Zhao, J. L. (1998). "Improving the Communicational Effectiveness of Virtual Organizations through Workflow Automation", *International Journal of Electronic Commerce* 3, 49-69.

Shen, S.(1987). "Knowledge Management in Decision Support Systems," *Decision Support Systems* 3, 1-11.

Stoddard, D.B. and Jarvenpaa, S.L.(1995). "Business process redesign: Tactics for managing radical change," *Journal of Management Information Systems* 12(1), 81-107.

Suchman, L.(1987). *Plans and Situated Actions: the Problem of Human-Machine Communication* Cambridge University Press.

Teece, D.J.(1996). "Firm Organization, Industrial Structure, and Technological Innovation," *Journal of Economic Behavior and Organization* 31(2), 193-224.

Teece, D.J. (1998). "Research Directions for Knowledge Management, *California Management Review* 40(3), 289-292.

Turban, E. and Aronson, J. (1998). *Decision Support Systems and Intelligent Systems* (Fifth Edition), Prentice-Hall: Upper Saddle River.

Weick, K.(1995). *Sensemaking in Organizations* Sage: Newbury Park, CA.

Zuboff, S.(1988). *In the Age of the Smart Machine* Basic Books.

Chapter XIII

Role of Organizational Controls in Knowledge Management: Is Knowledge Management Really an "Oxymoron"?

Yogesh Malhotra
@Brint.com, L.L.C. and Florida Atlantic University, USA

The mainstream concept of information technology enabled knowledge management suffers from the limitations embedded in the traditional organizational control model. Although importance of organization control is acknowledged by many authors as critical to the success of knowledge management implementations, however the concept of 'control' is often misinterpreted and misapplied. It is the thesis of this chapter that most such assertions are based on incomplete, and often, fallacious understanding of 'control'. Several authors have often suggested that knowledge management is an 'oxymoron,' however such observations are based upon inadequate and incomplete understanding of 'control.' Inadequate and incomplete understanding about organization controls may be often attributed for failure of knowledge management implementations in the new world of business. This chapter sets forth two important goals: first, to develop a richer understanding of organizational controls as they relate to knowledge management; and, second, to propose an organic model of organizational controls that facilitates creation of new knowledge, renewal of existing knowledge and knowledge sharing.

The mainstream concept of information technology enabled knowledge management suffers from the limitations embedded in the traditional organizational control model. Importance of organization control is deemed critical for the success of knowledge management implementations, however the concept of 'control' is often misinterpreted and misapplied. It is the thesis of this chapter that most such assertions are based on incomplete, and often, fallacious understanding of 'control'. Inadequate understanding of 'control' underlies the characterization of knowledge management as an 'oxymoron' by many writers. Inadequate understanding of organization could cause failure of knowledge management implementations in the new world of business. This chapter sets forth two important goals: first, to develop a richer understanding of organizational controls as they relate to knowledge management; and, second, to propose an organic model of organizational controls that facilitates creation of new knowledge, renewal of existing knowledge and knowledge sharing.

The next sections provide a literature review about the concept of 'organizational controls.' Then, the limitations inherent in the mainstream model of knowledge management are discussed. Discussion in this section also expounds how inadequate understanding and application of organizational controls may often lead to failure of knowledge management implementations. The following section proposes and illustrates an organic model of organizational controls that is better suited to creation of new knowledge, renewal of existing knowledge and sharing of knowledge between the organizational members. Based on the preceding discussion, we conclude by underscoring that 'knowledge management' is as much of an oxymoron as any other related notions such as information systems management, human resource management, business management, and so forth.

REVIEW OF LITERATURE ON ORGANIZATIONAL CONTROLS

Based on their review of the concept of organizational controls in diverse areas of management research and practice, Merchant and Simon (1986) had observed absence of any unifying view of control. Flamholtz et al. (1985) define organizational control as the process of influencing the behavior of people as members of a formal organization. Eisenhardt (1989) suggests that control can be accomplished through performance evaluation or by minimizing the divergence of preferences among organizational members. Performance evaluation refers to the cybernetic process of monitoring and rewarding performance and emphasizes the information aspects of control: *"namely to what degree the various aspects of performance can be assessed" or measured.* In contrast, the minimization of divergence (goal congruence) is based on people policies and assumes that members understand and have internalized the organizational goals. The two control strategies are interrelated. An organization can tolerate a work force with highly diverse goals if a precise evaluation system exists. In contrast, a lack of precision in performance evaluation can be tolerated when goal incompatibility is minor, i.e., goal congruence is high (Ouchi, 1979): "people must either be able to trust each other or to closely monitor each other if they are to engage in cooperative enterprise." Within this perspective, the performance evaluation strategy for control can be either behavior based or outcome based. Ouchi (1979) argues that the choice between the two criteria is based upon: (a) knowledge of the transformation process or task programmability (task knowledge), and (b) the ability to measure outcomes. Task programmability implies that behaviors can be explicitly defined and readily measured. If the goals can be clearly stated, then outcomes can be measured and performance evaluations of outcomes can be conducted. If both behaviors and outcomes can be measured, then either can be used (Ouchi, 1979).

Despite lack of a commonly accepted framework or typology of organizational controls (Green and Welsh, 1988, Simons, 1990), invariably, most authors (cf.: Henderson

& Lee, 1992; Kirsch, 1996; Orlikowski, 1991b) have interpreted control in terms of the *influence* exerted on the subordinates to seek their *compliance* with organizational goals. For instance, Lawler (1976, pp. 1248) defined control as a process "to direct, to influence, or to determine the behavior of someone else." Similarly, Tannenbaum (1962, p. 238) defined control as "any process which a person or a group of persons or organization of persons determines, i.e., intentionally affects, what another person or group or organization will do."

Most such interpretations have compared organizational control with the thermostat analogy of the control system (cf.: Anthony, 1988; Grant & Higgins, 1991; Lawler & Rhode, 1976). In most such 'thermostat' models, the performance level of the subordinate is measured and compared with a pre-set standard and the subordinate acts on the feedback received from the superior to decrease the variance between the measured performance and the pre-defined standard. This last element of the process in which the subordinate receives the feedback and tries to modify the measured performance variable is virtually treated like a black box. The alteration of the controllee's behavior (regulation) is assumed to be an intrinsic derivative of the communication (feedback) from the controller. In other words, it has been assumed that the controller seeks compliance by exerting control, say in terms of pre-specified performance criteria, and the desired organizational outcomes are achieved through compliance of the controllee.

Most conceptualizations of control exhibit two common concerns: focus on behavior and actions of organizational actors, and, second, focus on effect of such behaviors and actions on organizational goals or outcomes. In the literature on knowledge management, such behavior and actions of organizational actors is understood in terms of their role in utilization, processing, creation, dissemination and sharing of knowledge. In subsequent discussion, organizational goals and outcomes will be interpreted in terms of not only achievement of such intermediate outcomes, but also in terms of how actors' knowledge behaviors and actions relate to the organizations' competitive advantage.

Existing research has implicitly assumed that the controllee would modify one's behavior to conform to the organizational outcome or performance measures specified by the controller. The implicit assumption in this model is that the controllee's regulation is governed by one's fear of punishment or anticipation of reward and the compliance of the controllee has been considered a *given*.

This framework of management has dominantly interpreted *knowledge management* in terms of *control by compliance* of those entrusted with utilization, processing, creation, dissemination and sharing of knowledge. Examples of operational measures often recommended for facilitating knowledge management, such as bonuses and incentives (cf: Davenport and Prusak, 1997), illustrate such enforcement of knowledge management by fiat.

The dominant model of knowledge management based on *control by compliance* assumes that because compliance is demanded from knowledge workers, it is somehow enforced and achieved. Also, this model has assumed that achievement of compliance of the knowledge workers will lead to positive outcomes for the organization.

More recent awareness about knowledge – in particular tacit knowledge — as being intrinsic to individual knowledge workers (cf: Davenport and Prusak, 1997; *CIO Enterprise,* 1999; Malhotra, 1997; 1999e), has often led writers (cf: *Information Week,* 1999; *Computerworld,* 1998; *Wall Street Journal,* 1998; Sveiby, 1998) to remark that knowledge management is an 'oxymoron.' The reasoning behind this description is often along the following lines: Knowledge is not a "thing" that can be "managed". People responsible for utilization, creation, processing, dissemination and sharing of knowledge cannot be "managed." Our observation about such reasoning is that such reasoning is based on an incomplete, and perhaps inaccurate, definition of management in terms of *control by compliance*.

ORGANIZATIONAL CONTROLS THAT CONSTRAIN KNOWLEDGE MANAGEMENT

The fallacious assumption of the dominant model of knowledge management in terms of *control by compliance* is that compliance is demanded and compliance is achieved. Furthermore, this model has also simplistically assumed that compliance should somehow lead to positive organizational outcomes.

First, the assumption of the passive and compliant knowledge workers is inaccurate given recognition of the *dialectic of control* in which the controllee can "choose to do otherwise" (Giddens 1979, 1984). Second, in the new business environment characterized as the "world of re-everything" (Arthur 1996), passive compliance of existing performance and outcome controls may be detrimental to the health of the organization.

Most conceptualizations of organizational control have assumed alteration of the controllee's behavior (regulation) to be a direct consequence of the communication (feedback) from the controller. Most research on organizational control has not focused on issues such as the knowledge worker's (controllee's) recognition of the feedback sent by the system champion (controller), the interpretation of this feedback, or the impetus of the knowledge worker to act on this feedback *in accordance with the controller's desire*. However, Giddens' (1984) notion of agency, known as the *dialectic of control*, recognizes that: "All forms of dependence offer some resources whereby those who are subordinate can influence the activities of their superiors." In other words, controllees can very well 'game' the process to influence the controller's behaviors and actions. Orlikowski (1991a), too, reaffirmed the validity of the choice of the individual actor in choosing between compliance and non-compliance: "Discussions of organization control often tend to downplay the extent to which individuals retain the potential to act to change a particular situation or form of control" (p. 12). Manz et al. (1987, p. 5) acknowledge controllee's choice between compliance and non-compliance in the observation that: "Persons may exercise self-control even when they choose to acquiesce to external demands, as acquiescence still implies choice." The active role of controllee in choosing between compliance and non-compliance has also received empirical support from the field studies conducted by Malhotra and Kirsch (1996) and Malhotra (1999a; 199b).

Traditionally, organizational controls have been "built, *a priori*, on the principal of closure" (Landau & Stout, 1979, p. 150) to seek compliance to, and convergence of, the organizational decision-making processes (Flamholtz et al., 1985). The fundamental assumption underlying such controls is that the goals have been pre-decided, and the *recipes* for achieving those goals have been pre-decided and translated into procedural guidelines that need to be *followed* by the employees. Such organizational control systems were designed to reinforce stability and maintain the status quo. However, the cycle of doing "more of the same" tends to result in locked-in behavior patterns that eventually sacrifice organizational performance at the altar of the organizational "death spiral" (Nadler & Shaw, 1995, p. 12-13). *The result of this process may not be what is in the best interests of the organization; rather the emphasis of the model is on ensuring that the rules and procedures are meticulously followed.*

The knowledge management system structured as a 'core capability' for a stable business environment may becomes a 'core rigidity' in a discontinuously changing environment. The system that *ensures* conformity by ensuring task definition, measurement and control also *inhibits* creativity and initiative (Bartlett & Ghoshal, 1995). With its key emphasis on the obedience of rules at the cost of correction of errors (Landau & Stout, 1979), the traditional model of organizational control thus constrains creation of *new* knowledge and renewal of existing knowledge.

The problem is compounded by incorrect assumptions about human knowledge underlying the currently popular notion of knowledge management systems that are supposedly expected to "find useful knowledge, bottle it, and pass it around" (Hildebrand 1995; Stewart & Kaufman, 1995). Incorrect representations of knowledge management and related control issues often underlie unrealistic expectations of knowledge management executives. Such representations often assume away the proactive role that knowledge workers need to play in the success of such systems (Newcombe, 1999): "We have 316 years' worth of documents and data and thousands of employees with long years of practical experience. If we can take that knowledge, and place it into the hands of any person who needs it, whenever they need it, I can deliver services more quickly, more accurately and more consistently."

Based on a model of knowledge management that relies upon pre-specification of 'right knowledge' to be provided to the 'right person' at 'right time,' this model is bound for failure (*CIO Enterprise,* 1999). It is not only difficult, but improbable, to predict the validity of knowledge of past in a future that may not be computed based upon the past historical data. The assumption of archival of knowledge is also problematic given that information and bits are archived in data repositories, knowledge is not. Even procedural knowledge, when translated into symbols that are later processed by another human, does not ensure that the outcome of his knowledge will rival that of the original *carrier*. Knowledge needs to be understood as the *potential for action* that doesn't only depend upon the stored information but also on the individual interacting with it.

The dominant conception of technology-based organizational knowledge systems is constrained by the very nature of the knowledge creation processes: it ignores the dynamic and continuously evolving nature of knowledge; it ignores the tacit and explicit dimensions of knowledge creation; it ignores the subjective, interpretative and meaning making bases of knowledge construction; it ignores the constructive nature of knowledge creation; and it ignores the social interactive basis of knowledge creation (Malhotra *in press (b)*).

The model of organizational control embedded in such systems is also overwhelmed by the intense information flows required for (Bartlett & Ghoshal, 1995):

    a) keeping the centralized knowledge base and its custodians (managers) *continuously* current with the *discontinuously changing* external environment,

    b) continually updating the employees on the latest changes in their outputs (goals) and changes in procedures to achieve those outputs.

Business environment characterized by rapid and discontinuous change is not conducive for the viability of the role of managers as custodians of organizational knowledge (Landau & Stout, 1979, p. 148): "...control is a function of knowledge [of managers], and in uncertain environments knowledge [of managers] often does not exist." The knowledge management model of *control by compliance* perfectly suited the bureaucracies or markets within a stable and predictable business environment that allowed knowledge worker performance to be measured with reasonable precision. Being dependent upon explicit monitoring, evaluation, and correction of behavior, this model is also likely to offend the knowledge worker's sense of autonomy and of self-control and, as a result, will probably result in an unenthusiastic, purely compliant response (Ouchi, 1979).

However, the model of *control by compliance* is not suitable for organizations in the new world of business (Malhotra, 1998b; 1998c; 1999c; Ouchi, 1979). Under conditions of ambiguity, of loose coupling, and of uncertainty that characterizes the new business environment, measurement of knowledge worker's performance with reliability and with precision is not possible. A control system based on such measurements is likely to systematically reward a narrow range of maladaptive behavior, leading ultimately to organizational decline.

The new business environments require new models of knowledge management and related organizational controls conducive to sustainable competitive advantage in the face of radical and unpredictable change. The knowledge management model enabled by self-control is discussed in the next section as one such model.

ORGANIZATIONAL CONTROLS FOR SUCCESSFUL KNOWLEDGE MANAGEMENT

Organizations in dynamically changing environments should behave experimentally. Since they will come across few lasting optima, they ought to gear themselves to impermanency and plan as if their decisions were temporary and probably imperfect solutions to changing problems. Knowledge management systems should be set up for experimenting, emphasize evaluations, and be easy to re-arrange and adapt with changing business environment. Decision makers should see themselves as experimenters, and they should keep challenging their findings. In short, organizations in changing environments should have knowledge management processes and systems that are driven by self-evaluation and self-design (Hedberg et al., 1976). Although dynamically changing business environment defies prediction, however, such organizations are more aware of the inadequacy of the forecasts based on historical data and are thus better prepared to adapt accordingly. The knowledge management processes need greater emphasis than specific products that often represent artifacts of partial knowledge management 'solutions'.

Successful implementation of knowledge management systems is driven by the simultaneously processes of ongoing learning and unlearning that I have elsewhere characterized as *loose-tight systems* (Malhotra *in press (a)*). Such systems are *loose* in the sense that they allow for continuous re-examination of the assumptions underlying best practices and reinterpretation of this information. Such systems are *tight* in the sense that they also allow for efficiencies based on propagation and dissemination of the best practices. Such *loose-tight knowledge management systems* (Malhotra, 1998a; 1999d) would need to provide not only for identification and dissemination of best practices, but also for continuous re-examination of such practices. Specifically, they would need to also include a simultaneous process that continuously examines the best practices for their currency given the changing assumptions about the business environment. Such systems would need to contain *both* learning and unlearning processes. These simultaneous processes are needed for assuring the efficiency-oriented optimization based on the current best practices while ensuring that such practices are continuously re-examined for their currency.

All in all, this points toward knowledge management systems design principles that differ considerably from current design ideals, including many system characteristics that were previously considered as 'liabilities.' In addition to striving for order and clarity, consistency and rationality, designers of knowledge management systems for organizations in changing environments should also be concerned with nurturing processes that can counteract and balance these 'old virtues.' The proposed organizational control model "actually exploits benefits hidden within properties that designers have generally regarded as liabilities" (Hedberg & Jonsson 1978, p. 45). This suggestion seems important given that unclear objectives and ambiguous work roles have been suggested by some management scholars (cf: Burns and Stalker, 1961) as *desirable* properties of organismic organizations for thriving in dynamic environments. Design of knowledge management systems thus needs to take into consideration ambiguity, inconsistency, multiple perspectives, and impermanency of existing information. Such systems need to be designed along the principles of *semi-confusing information systems* (Hedberg and Jonsson, 1978) that facilitate exploitation of previous experiences and detected causalities, but ensure that experience of past doesn't hinder ongoing adaptation for the discontinuous future.

The proposed model of organizational control recognizes self-control as the driver of human actors' behavior and actions across all organizational decision and task processes and acknowledges that control over employees is ultimately self-imposed. Instead of emphasizing unquestioning adherence to pre-specified goals or procedures, it encourages the use of intuition through 'playfulness' (Cooper et al., 1981, p. 179). The model of knowledge management through self-control also facilitates error detection and error correction (Stout, 1980, p. 90) instead of compliance with pre-specified rules and procedures. Instead of emphasizing 'best practices,' it encourages development of a large repertoire of responses to suggest not only alternative (complementary and contradictory) solutions, but also different approaches for executing those solutions. In the emerging business world (Wheatley, 1994, p. 151): "solutions...are a temporary event, specific to a context, developed through the relationship of persons and circumstances." The proposed model is based on the premise that (Landau & Stout 1979, p. 152): "solutions to problems cannot be commanded...[they] must be discovered: found on the basis of imagination, analysis, experiment, and criticism." Figure 1 illustrates the comparison between the model of knowledge management by compliance model for industrial organizations with the model of knowledge management by commitment for emergent organizational forms.

Figure 1. Constrasting Knowledge Management for Traditional and Emergent Organizations

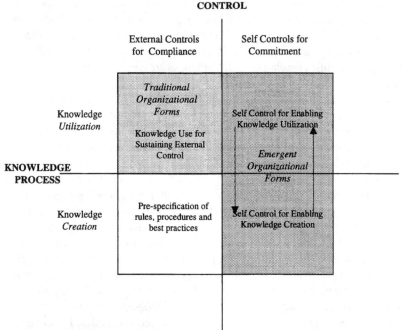

	Traditional Organizations		*Emergent Organizations*
•	Knowledge Utilization as the Antecedent		• Self Control as the Antecedent
•	External Control as the Consequent		• Knowledge Creation as the Consequent
•	Stable Environment		• 'Wicked Environment'
•	Incremental Change		• Increasing Pace of Continual Change
•	Continuous, Predictable Nature of Change		• Discontinuous, Unpredictable Nature of Change
•	Single Loop Learning		• Double Loop Learning with Self Adaptation
•	Static View of Knowledge: Rules, Procedures & Policies		• Dynamic View of Knowledge
•	Knowledge resides with the Management		• More equitable distribution of knowledge
•	Complexity is removed from lower level jobs		• Complexity is handled at grassroots level

IS KNOWLEDGE MANAGEMENT REALLY AN OXYMORON?

As noted earlier, several writers, based upon an inadequate interpretation of management in terms of *control by compliance* have asserted that 'knowledge management' is an oxymoron. They have argued that people responsible for utilization, creation, processing, dissemination and sharing of knowledge cannot be "managed." We contend that those writers are mistaken as they have incorrectly interpreted *control by compliance* as the be all and end all of "management."

Perhaps, they are not alone culpable of such misinterpretations as the dominant paradigm of *control by compliance* has also occupied most management and business texts that were written for the industrial era. Given the same narrow interpretation, management of most organizational activities may qualify as 'oxymoron,' as activities and actors that were previously compliant becomes less compliant. Even when the activities and actors are compliant with pre-specified assumptions and rules, their compliance shows decreasing correlation with organizational performance and competitive advantage. The model of *control by compliance* yields increasingly diminishing returns in an economy driven by increasing returns of intangible assets and intellectual capital.

As the world economies transition from the traditional model of 'workers' to the new model of 'knowledge intrapreneurs' (Malhotra 1998a), we need to re-understand the notion of 'management.' Specifically, we need to understand 'management' in terms of 'self-control.' For effective knowledge performance, we need managers who can nurture the traits of self-leadership and self-regulation. Such managers would need to be adept at influence attempts that are aimed at building satisfaction and commitment of knowledge workers by seeking "proactive self-control" (Manz et al., 1987, p. 5).

The concept of self-control can be contrasted with the concept of external controls such as administrative control and social control (Hopwood 1974). Administrative control refers to the mechanisms designed to regulate the organizational behaviors of individuals toward the attainment of organizational objectives (Flamholtz et al., 1985). When administrative controls are consciously designed to influence individuals' preferences in order to intentionally pass on particular norms or values to them, such forms of administrative control may be called 'social controls' (Hopwood, 1974, pp. 26-27). For social and administrative controls to be effective influences on individuals' organizational behavior, these controls must operate as 'self-controls,' controls people exert over their own behaviors (Hopwood, 1974, p. 31). The norms embodied in the administrative or social controls must be "either directly or indirectly ... internalized by the members of the enterprise and operate as personal controls over attitudes and behavior" (p. 31). Self-control is based on the premise that control can be exercised only through intrinsic individual motivation and the role of external influences is to facilitate the creation of appropriate self-controls (Manz & Sims, 1980, 1987, 1989).

The primary distinction that needs to be drawn here is between the consequence of the control as being *compliance* or *commitment*. Compliance implies the conformity of the knowledge worker who is motivated by a desire of a reward or avoidance of punishment (Kelman, 1961) and generally lasts only until the promise or threat of sanction exists. Control attempts that seek passive acceptance from knowledge workers may be best for achieving compliance. In contrast to *compliance*, *commitment* involves "the internalization of management-derived and sanctioned beliefs, norms and values, in the sense that they become part of the core of the individual's perceptual world" (Johnson & Gill, 1993, p. 36). This is consistent with the view that *control over employees is ultimately self-imposed*, and that external controls are likely to lead only to minimal compliance unless they are designed to seek proactive self-control (Malhotra and Kirsch, 1996; Hopwood, 1974; Manz et al., 1987).

Under conditions of self-control if a certain behavior is motivated intrinsically (Argyris, 1990a, Malhotra, 1998c), the individual will engage in that behavior for intrinsic rewards. Argyris (1990b, p. 120-121) has referred to the transition from traditional external control mechanisms to the paradigm of self-control as "the current revolution in management theory."

CONCLUSION

This chapter was motivated by increasing recognition of critical relevance of 'organizational controls' in successful knowledge management implementation. A review of existing print and online literature on knowledge management suggests that the concept of organizational controls is often misunderstood and misapplied. Specifically, it was observed that the concept of 'management' has been interested in very narrow terms of *control by compliance*. As a consequence of application of this very narrow interpretation of management, some writers have described 'knowledge management' as an oxymoron. This is understandable as control by compliance isn't very effective for facilitating knowledge utilization, new knowledge creation, knowledge dissemination and knowledge sharing by knowledge actors. However, a richer understanding of 'management' in terms of diverse types of control, and 'self-controls' in particular, contributed by this chapter is expected to address this critical void. The framework of knowledge management based on self-controls discussed in this paper advances the managerial thinking from *compliance based knowledge management* to *commitment based knowledge management*. As discussed in the chapter, the model of commitment based knowledge management is more conducive for effective knowledge performance in the new business environments characterized by radical and discontinuous change.

REFERENCES

Anthony, R.N. (1988). *The Management Control Function*, Boston, MA, Harvard Business School Press.

Argyris, C. (1990). *Integrating the Individual and the Organization*,Transaction, New Brunswick, NJ.

Arthur, W. B.(1996). "Increasing Returns and the New World of Business." *Harvard Business Review,* July-August, 74(4), 100-109.

Bartlett, C.A. & Ghoshal, S.(1995). "Changing the Role of the Top Management: Beyond Systems to People," *Harvard Business Review*, May-June, 132-142.

Burns, T. and Stalker, G. M. *(1961).The Management of Innovation*, London, Tavistock.

CIO Enterprise (1999). "Does KM=IT?" written by Carol Hildebrand. Sep. 15. Online version accessible at: http://www.cio.com/archive/enterprise/091599_ic.html.

Computerworld (1998). "Knowledge management: Some 'there' there," written by John Gantz, October 12.

Cooper, D.J., Hayes, D., and Wolf, F. (1981)."Accounting in Organized Anarchies: Understanding and Designing Accounting Systems in Ambiguous Situations," *Accounting, Organizations and Society*, 6(3), 175-191.

Davenport, T.H. & Prusak, L. *(1997). Working Knowledge: How Organizations Manage What They Know*, Harvard Business School Press, Boston, MA.

Eisenhardt, K.M. (1989)."Agency Theory: An Assessment and Review," *Academy of Management Review*, 14(1), 57-74.

Flamholtz, E.G., Das, T.K. & Tsui, A.S. (1985). "Toward an Integrative Framework of Organizational Control," *Accounting, Organizations and Society*, 10(1), 35-50.

Giddens, A.(1984). *The Constitution of Society: Outline of the Theory of Structuration*. Berkeley: University of California Press.

Giddens, A.(1979). *Central Problems in Social Theory: Action, Structure and Contradiction in Social Analysis*, University of California Press, Berkeley, CA.

Grant, R.A. & Higgins, C.A.(1991). "The Impact of Computerized Performance Monitoring on Service Work: Testing a Causal Model," *Information Systems Research*, 2(2), 116-142.

Green, S.G. and Welsh, M.A. (1988). "Cybernetics and Dependence: Reframing the Control Concept," *Academy of Management Review*, 13(2), 287-301.

Hedberg, B.(1981). "How Organizations Learn and Unlearn," In *Handbook of Organizational Design*, P. Nystrom and W. Starbuck (Eds.), Oxford University Press, New York, 1-27.

Hedberg, B. & Jonsson, S. (1978)."Designing Semi-Confusing Information Systems for Organizations in Changing Environments," *Accounting, Organizations and Society*, 3(1), 47-74.

Hedberg, B., Nystrom, P.C. & Starbuck, W.H. "Camping on Seesaws: Prescriptions for a Self-Designing Organization," *Administrative Science Quarterly*, 21, 1976, pp. 41-65.

Henderson, J.C. & Lee, S. (1992), "Managing I/S Design Teams: A Control Theories Perspective," *Management Science*, 38(6), 757-777.

Hildebrand, C. (1995). "Information Mapping: Guiding Principles," *CIO*, 8(18), 60-64.

Hopwood, A.(1974). *Accounting and Human Behavior*, Prentice-Hall, London, UK.

InformationWeek (1999). "Stay In Touch With Information," written by John Eckhouse, April 05.

Johnson, P. & Gill, J.(1993). *Management Control and Organizational Behavior*, Paul Chapman, London, UK.

Kelman, H. (1961). "The Processes of Opinion Change," *Public Opinion*, 25, 57-78.

Kirsch, L.J. (1996). "The Management of Complex Tasks in Organizations: Controlling the Systems Development Process," *Organization Science*, 7(1), 1-21.

Landau, M. & Stout, Jr., R. (1979). "To Manage is Not to Control: Or the Folly of Type II Errors," *Public Administration Review*, March/April, 148-156.

Lawler, E. E.(1976). "Control Systems in Organizations," in M.D. Dunnette (Ed.), *Handbook of Industrial and Organizational Psychology*, Rand-McNally College Publishing, Chicago, IL, 1247-1291.

Lawler, E., E., & Rhode, J.G.(1976). *Information and Controls in Organizations*, Goodyear, Santa Monica, CA.

Malhotra, Y. (2000a)."Knowledge Management & New Organization Forms: A Framework for Business Model Innovation," *Information Resources Management Journal* [Millennium special issue on Knowledge Management], 13(1) .

Malhotra, Y. (in press (b)). "From Information Management to Knowledge Management: Beyond the 'Hi-Tech Hidebound' Systems," in K. Srikantaiah and M.E.D. Koenig (Eds.), *Knowledge Management for the Information Professional*, Information Today, Inc., Medford, NJ.

Malhotra, Y.(1999a). "Bringing the Adopter Back Into the Adoption Process: A Personal Construction Framework of Information Technology Adoption," *Journal of High Technology Management Research*, 10(1), Spring.

Malhotra, Y. (1999b). "Extending the Technology Acceptance Model to Account for Social Influence: Theoretical Bases and Empirical Validation," in the *Proceedings of the Hawaii International Conference on System Sciences* (HICSS 32) (Adoption and Diffusion of Collaborative Systems and Technology Minitrack), Maui, HI, January 5-8.

Malhotra, Y.(1999c). "High-Tech Hidebound Cultures Disable Knowledge Management," in *Knowledge Management* (UK), February.

Malhotra, Y. (1999d)."Knowledge Management for Organizational White Waters: An Ecological Framework," in *Knowledge Management* (UK), March.

Malhotra, Y. (1999e)."What is Really Knowledge Management?: Crossing the Chasm of Hype," in @Brint.com web site, Sep. 15. [Letter to editor in response to Inc. Technology #3, Sep. 15, 1999, special issue on Knowledge Management]. Accessible online at: http://www.brint.com/advisor/a092099.htm

Malhotra, Y.(1998a). "Toward a Knowledge Ecology for Organizational White-Waters," Invited Keynote Presentation for the *Knowledge Ecology Fair 98: Beyond Knowledge Management*, Feb. 2 - 27, accessible online at: http://www.brint.com/papers/ecology.htm.

Malhotra, Y.(1998b). "Deciphering the Knowledge Management Hype" *Journal for Quality & Participation*, July/August, 58-60.

Malhotra, Y.(1998c). Role of Social Influence, Self Determination and Quality of Use in Information Technology Acceptance *and Utilization: A Theoretical Framework and Empirical Field Study*, Ph.D. thesis, July 1998c, Katz Graduate School of Business, University of Pittsburgh, 225 pages.

Malhotra, Y. (1997). "Knowledge Management in Inquiring Organizations," in the Proceedings of 3rd Americas Conference on Information Systems (Philosophy of Information Systems Mini-track), Indianapolis, IN, August 15-17. Accessible online at: http://www.brint.com/km/km.htm .

Malhotra, Y. & Kirsch, L. (1996)."Personal Construct Analysis of Self-Control in IS Adoption: Empirical Evidence from Comparative Case Studies of IS Users & IS Champions," in the Proceedings of the *First INFORMS Conference on Information Systems and Technology (Organizational Adoption & Learning Track)*, Washington D.C., May 5-8, 105-114.

Manz, C.C., Mossholder, K. W. & Luthans, F. "An Integrated Perspective of Self-Control in Organizations," 19(1), *Administration & Society*, May 1987, pp. 3-24.

Manz, C.C. & Sims, H.P.(1989). *SuperLeadership: Leading Others to Lead Themselves*, Prentice-Hall, Berkeley, CA.

Manz, C.C. & Sims, H.P. (1987)."Leading Workers to Lead Themselves: The External Leadership of Self-Managing Work Teams," *Administrative Science Quarterly*, 32, 106-128.

Manz, C.C. & Sims,Jr., H.P.(1980). "Self-Management as a Substitute for Leadership: A Social Learning Theory Perspective," *Academy of Management Review*, 5(3), 361-367.

Merchant, K.A. and Simons, R.(1986). "Research and Control in Complex Organizations: An Overview," *Journal of Accounting Literature*, 5, 183-201.

Nadler, D.A. & Shaw, R.B.(1995). "Change Leadership: Core Competency for the Twenty-First Century," In *Discontinuous Change: Leading Organizational Trans-*

formation (D.A. Nadler, R.B. Shaw & A.E. Walton), Jossey-Bass, San Franscisco, CA.

Newcombe, T. (1999)."Knowledge Management: New Wisdom or Passing Fad?" *Government Technology*. Accessible online at: http://govt-tech.govtech.net:80/gtmag/1999/june/magastory/feature.shtm.

Orlikowski, W.J.(1991a). "Information Technology and Structuring of Organizations," *Information Systems Research*, 2(2), 143-169.

Orlikowski, W. J. (1991b). "Integrated Information Environment or Matrix of Control?: The Contradictory Implications of Information Technology," *Accounting, Management and Information Technology*, 1(1), 9-42.

Ouchi, W.G. (1979). "A Conceptual Framework for the Design of Organizational Control Mechanisms," *Management Science*, 25 (9), p. 833-848.

Simons, R. (1990)."The Role of Management Control Systems in Creating Competitive Advantage: New Perspectives," *Accounting, Organizations and Society*, 15(1,2), 127-148.

Stewart, T.A. & Kaufman, D.C. (1995)."Getting Real About Brainpower," *Fortune*, December 11.

Stout,Jr., R. (1980). *Management or Control?:The Organizational Challenge*, Indiana University Press, Bloomington, IN.

Sveiby, K.E. (1998). "Intellectual Capital and Knowledge Management," Online document at Sveiby Knowledge Management (http://www.sveiby.com.au/).

Tannenbaum, R. (1962). Control in organizations. *Administration Science Quarterly*, 7, 236-257.

Wall Street Journal (1998). "The End of Knowledge Management," in Tom Petzinger's column: 'The Front Lines,' B1, January 9.

Wheatley, M.J.(1994). *Leadership and the New Science*, Berett-Koehler, San Francisco, CA.

Chapter XIV

Beyond Customer Knowledge Management: Customers as Knowledge Co-Creators

Mohanbir Sawhney
Northwestern University, USA

Emanuela Prandelli
Bocconi University, Italy

In the knowledge-based economy, the value of products and services largely depends on the knowledge intangibles they embed (Drucker, 1993). The success of firms is increasingly becoming linked to the intellectual capital they are able to accumulate and re-invest in their markets (Davenport & Prusak, 1998; Nahapiet & Ghoshal, 1998; Sullivan, 1998). In this age of knowledge-based business, it is incumbent upon firms to pay increasing attention to the development of customer knowledge (Balasubramanian et al., 1998; Sawhney & Kotler, 1999).

However, researchers in marketing have generally assumed that knowledge creation happens only within the firm's boundaries or, at the most, within the strategic alliances among firms. We argue that in the knowledge economy we need to move beyond this perspective of the firm as the knowledge creator that learns about customers and creates value for them, to a perspective of the firm as a co-creator of knowledge that learns and creates value with its customers. As already argued only in service marketing literature, customers are a vital source of knowledge and hence competitive advantage. The co-operation with them gives firms the opportunity to renew the source of their competitive advantage constantly. This is significant in a business landscape where unique and lasting competitive advantages are increasingly rare. Through co-operation with their customers, firms can better anticipate market changes (Anderson & Narus, 1991; Nonaka & Takeuchi, 1995), catalyze their innovation processes (von Hippel, 1982, 1986, 1994), and better respond to latent customer needs (Leonard & Rayport, 1997).

Thus, customers can no longer be treated as the "clandestine immigrants' in an ideal economic land with its own pre-defined rules, to which they have to conform passively. On the contrary, they appear like the native citizens of a new borderless country, where production and consumption are deeply inter-linked processes and customers are active participants in defining the firm's offerings. This perspective of customers as knowledge co-creators is consistent with relationship marketing, but goes beyond its traditional conceptualizations. Relationships with customers have traditionally been viewed as one-way: firms import knowledge about customers within their boundaries. In the networked world, firms can establish two-way relationships, defining new mechanisms for direct co-operation in knowledge creation. Entering this new land has deep implications, and requires us to question some of the fundamental assumptions about customer knowledge management. It no longer means only building up rich databases or collecting information through fidelity cards, aimed at understanding customer preferences and buying patterns (Wayland & Cole, 1997; Fournier et al., 1998). In the knowledge-based economy, customers play an active role in the firm's processes of knowledge creation. It is not only important what the firm learns about its customers, but also what customers know.

This way of thinking demands new means to facilitate the participation of customers in the firms' knowledge creation processes. And it demands new competencies on the part of firms. The purpose of this chapter is to explore this emergent phenomenon, and to offer managers a better understanding of the hurdles that arise in customer integration, and how to overcome them. We begin by introducing the traditional concept of knowledge management, and extending it beyond the firm's boundaries. Next, we focus on the pre-conditions that need to be satisfied on the customers' side to allow co-operation in knowledge creation. They include the need for common language, trust and motivation for knowledge sharing. We then turn our attention to the capabilities that firms need after selecting and motivating customers, to integrate customer knowledge, disseminate it within the organization and act on it to translate customer knowledge into new offerings. We introduce and explore the notion of firms' absorptive, sharing and deployment capacities; and argue that if any one of them is missing or if there are disconnects between these steps, the entire mechanism breaks down. We examine the potential process and linkage failures at each stage and we suggest to firms how to overcome them. We conclude the chapter with managerial guidelines, from a technological, organizational, and cultural viewpoint.

BEYOND THE BOUNDARIES OF THE FIRM: NEW PERSPECTIVES ON KNOWLEDGE MANAGEMENT

In a world dominated by information-intensive products, organizations still produce goods, but also individual and social interactions, and several kinds of knowledge (Nonaka, 1991; Vicari, 1991; Nonaka & Takeuchi, 1995; von Krogh & Roos, 1996). The increasing spread of information and of the activities aimed at their production makes strategic knowledge the main source of power and economic revenues. Turbulent environments demand speed and flexibility. Kogut and Zander (1996) argue that *"a firm (can) be understood as a social community specializing in the speed and the efficiency in the creation and transfer of knowledge"*.

The point is that these social communities are becoming increasingly broad: their boundaries are often vague, and the critical sources for their success are often outside the firm's direct control (Prahalad & Hamel, 1990). Hence, the ability to create and manage appropriate inter-organizational relationships has become a key managerial competence: the notion of the intra-firm value chain is being supplanted by the inter-firm "value network" (Hagel, 1996; Moore, 1997; Balasubramanian et al., 1998). Value generation processes are no longer based only on ownership, but more and more often also on partnership (Drucker, 1995). In the post-industrial society, the Learning Organization (Stata, 1989; Huber, 1991; Garvin, 1993; Nayak et al., 1995) is evolving into a Learning Society populated by communities and networks. These communities function bases on distributed processes of knowledge generation.

Several authors have investigated the importance of strategic alliances between the firm and its suppliers and partners[1] in facilitating the process of knowledge spreading (Prahalad & Hamel, 1990; Hamel, 1991; Inkpen, 1998). However, little has been written about the possible contribution of *customers* to such knowledge networks. This is probably because firms either could not directly control such an external source of knowledge, or were not fully aware of its importance to catalyze knowledge creation.

In today's environment, however, three emerging phenomena are driving the need to include customers in social processes of knowledge production (Figure 1). First, there is a growing trend of knowledge socialization[2] as an antidote for overcoming individual cognitive limits and to reduce the uncertainty and the risk of individual knowledge production. On the firms' side, the tendency towards a new division of work, both in its material and cognitive[3] forms, is creating the need to specialize individual competencies and then to socialize them (Sawhney & Prandelli, 1999). On the customers' side, the emergence of communities of consumption in physical as well as virtual spaces, signals the trend towards socialization of individual knowledge.

Second, advances in networking and communications have reduced distances both in time and space, diminishing the barriers to knowledge sharing and transfer (Cairncross, 1997).The virtual organization notion clearly has its roots in these technological means that allow a real globalization of work activities and their re-distribution beyond geographies. This blurring of boundaries makes the distinction between the firm and its customers, suppliers, and competitors less clear. Each of these firm's "interlocutors" represents a holder of specific knowledge, which the firm can capitalize on (Micelli & Prandelli, 2000). From this perspective, creating barriers to "protect a company" from its suppliers and competitors could actually be dangerous, because it could reduce the potential variety of knowledge accessible to the firm, and hence limit its flexibility and innovation potential[4] (Fiocca & Prandelli, 1997).

Finally, increasing information-richness of products enhances the incentives for consumers to connect and communicate with firms. Customers get more timely and reliable information, while firms acquire better knowledge of their needs. For example, outstanding companies like GE Plastics, Intel, Texas Instruments and Cisco offer detailed information to their customers through the Internet. At the same time, they gain important customer feedback on problems with existing products, as well as fresh ideas for new product development. And this is true not only for technology-rich products. Many non-technology-based offerings may also be information-rich, including financial services, healthcare and education (Balasubramanian et al., 1998).

Thus, high environmental uncertainty and the need for knowledge socialization, advances in information technology, and increasing product information-richness all emphasize the inadequacy of a knowledge management approach that is confined within

Figure 1. The New Landscape for Knowledge Co-creation

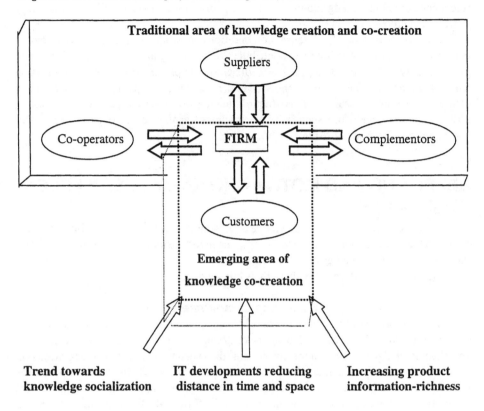

the boundaries of the firm, and excludes customers from knowledge creation activities.

PRE-CONDITIONS FOR CUSTOMER INVOLVEMENT IN KNOWLEDGE CREATION

To assure knowledge co-creation, several pre-conditions have to be satisfied. First, firms and customers have to "speak the same language". In other words, to be able to contribute with their own knowledge, customers first need to "absorb" the firm's specific knowledge and to understand its meaning. This common language should be intended as an *"open semantic system to build up shared meanings"*, beyond mere vocabulary (Di Bernardo & Rullani, 1990). It implies a specific perception of the world. Whether it is absent, co-learning cannot begin.

Second, customers have to deeply trust the firm, being sure that the information they share with it will not be used against their own interests. Such a deterrent could be particularly strong if customers belong to a business-to-business market, where their competitive positioning could be compromised by an opportunistic exploitation of shared information (Anderson & Narus, 1991).

Finally, customers should also have a specific motivation to take part in the firm's knowledge creation process. This motivation can derive either from the awareness of the relevance of their knowledge contribution for the firm's success or – and more frequently —from incentives.

Customers who satisfy all these pre-conditions are what we call "high-involvement customers". They are more likely to contribute to co-learning processes and the improved products they obtain initiate a positive feedback on the pre-existing level of motivation and trust in the firm. The specific knowledge they develop co-operating with a firm can also positively affect usage and satisfaction, leading to increased perceived switching costs. In this way, the firm's specificity of consumer learning can drive customer loyalty and retention (Sawhney & Mittal, 1998).

SELECTING AND MOTIVATING KNOWLEDGEABLE CUSTOMERS

If we accept that customer knowledge is not simply imported by firms, but that it can also feed knowledge co-creation processes, we need to consider how the firm can identify the best customer knowledge assets on the market. We also need to determine how firms can motivate these customers to share their knowledge.

Screening of customers

The first problem firms have to address is the definition of criteria for selecting the best customer knowledge assets. Not all the customers are equally "strategic" because the specific knowledge they hold or the investments they need to support a lasting relationship vary. Nor does every customer want to be involved in the knowledge creation processes enacted by a firm. Thus, the firm needs to be careful in choosing the right set of customers to involve. Initially, a pattern of trial and error can be followed. Over time, the firm should evolve more deliberate criteria to select lead user customers in business-to-business markets and trendsetters in consumer markets. An ideal profile of knowledgeable customers should emerge, together with a selection procedure aimed at creating the optimal conditions for the relationship (Lorenzoni & Baden-Fuller, 1995).

In business markets, lead users are usually firms whose current needs reflect the needs of the segment to which they belong, in the next few months or years. Thus, they derive great benefits from co-operation with the supplier to find customized solutions to their emergent needs (von Hippel, 1986). This is the reason why *"to push out the boundaries of current products concepts, it is necessary to put the most advanced technology into the hands of the world's most sophisticated and demanding users"* (Hamel & Prahalad, 1994: 102). In terms of screening processes, lead users are selected on their capabilities and assets, compatibility of management style, and "cultural fit" with the supplier firm. It is important to note that who most needs a new product – and thus most likely to develop it – is often outside the firm's existing customer base[5].

In consumer markets, trendsetters are customers who occupy a central position within the social network of the community to which they belong (Granovetter, 1985). They generally have superior specific knowledge, and they act as opinion-leaders, influencing the choices of their followers. Because "pre-packed" products do not satisfy their needs, they are often more likely to take part in a process of joint product-definition with a specific firm (Prandelli & Saviolo, 1996). The potential profitability of such a process for the firm is evident: if it is developed with the opinion leaders, the firm can assure itself of a customer-base that is bound to enlarge in time (Itami & Roehl, 1987). As a consequence, firms need to understand the relationships that develop within communities of consumption. Firms should appreciate that, as in a large network composed of many small partners, the center may act as a sort of "evangelist" (Lorenzoni & Baden-Fuller, 1995), influencing the development of the whole community (Sawhney & Prandelli, 1999; Micelli & Prandelli, 2000).

Designing Incentive Mechanisms

The second problem firms face in knowledge co-creation is implementing mechanisms to motivate customers holding the best knowledge assets to take part in this process. Traditionally, literature assumes that the customers who hold the best knowledge assets — i.e., lead users and trendsetters — are also the customers who are the most motivated to co-create new knowledge with the firm (high-involvement customers). This is often the case, but cannot be assumed to be universally true. Clearly, the firm seeks to involve only the best knowledge assets on the market. Otherwise, coordination costs would explode, making the process ineffective. The real problem thus becomes how to motivate such assets to participate in a joint process of knowledge creation.

If the lack of motivation for co-operation arises from a lack of customer absorptive capacity or trust in the firm, one solution is investing in the development of a common language. Firms can take actions to enrich the customers' consumption vocabulary. It can assist customers in encoding, retrieving, and elaborating upon information more easily, thus increasing both the motivation to share knowledge with the firm and the quality of specific customer knowledge (Micelli & Prandelli, 2000). The use of metaphors and analogies can ease the acquisition of new consumption vocabulary. For instance, Microsoft uses "bins" and "folders" to help users to learn the Windows user interface. Ethnographic methods and linguistic-based research techniques can also be useful in developing such vocabularies (Sawhney & Mittal, 1998).

A second approach the firm can take is to increase technological connectivity with its customers. This approach relies on reducing the time and effort that customers have to spend in absorbing the firm's knowledge and sharing their knowledge with it. In fact, to co-operate in knowledge creation, the firm and its customers can also share a virtual space by conducting dialogues online. From this viewpoint, a virtual community of consumption can be an ideal place[6].

A third approach relies on creating trust by investing in the corporate brand and image. The firm's reputation is a key driver of customers' trust in the firm. Thus, by legitimizing itself, a firm can increase customer motivation to share and co-create knowledge.

A final approach to increase customer motivation for knowledge sharing is to clearly identify the payoffs for customers. As the need for knowledge socialization increases, and digitization of information leads to easy copying of ideas, traditional intellectual property law loses much of its relevance (Barlow, 1993). Firms need to recognize new customers' rights to "share payoffs" (Sawhney & Kotler, 1999). Incentives can be economic or non-economic. The former may consist of cash for individuals, research grants to institutions, or discounts on goods that customers help to create (von Hippel, 1982). Incentives can also

Table 1> Approaches to Increase Customers' Absorptive Capacity, Trust and Motivation for Knowledge Co-creation

Problems from the customer point of view	Lack of absorptive capacity	Lack of trust in the firm	Lack of motivation for knowledge co-creation
Possible solutions	Enriching customers' consumption vocabulary, allowing them to better articulate their experiences	Avoiding opportunistic behavior to leverage customer knowledge	Identifying clear incentives, differentiating between business-to-business and consumer markets
	Using metaphors and analogies to improve understanding of new domains	Investing in corporate and brand image	Recognizing customer rights to share payoffs
	Technology investments to improve customer connectivity	Developing a strong reputation and legitimizing the firm	Re-defining intellectual property rights to reward innovation as the output of a joint process

be psychological in nature. In consumer markets, ego-gratification deriving from the identification with a community can be an incentive. In this case, *"the value of participating in a community lies in users' ability to access a broad range of people and resources quickly and easily"* (Armstrong & Hagel, 1996: 138).

We summarize these complementary approaches to increase customers' motivation for knowledge co-creation in Table 1. As it suggests, the common notions of "reciprocity, repute, and altruism" as the pricing mechanisms in the "knowledge market" (Davenport & Prusak, 1998) need to be adapted to the context of customer co-operation in knowledge creation (Table 2).

Reciprocity can be granted through non-monetary mechanisms, like a better customization of goods for lead users (von Hippel, 1994). Customization allows users to reduce their production costs and/or to increase the effectiveness of their production processes. In consumer markets, customization allows trendsetters to introduce new consumption standards, gaining a prestigious position within a specific community. Similarly, reputation for knowledge sharing can help users to improve their positioning in business markets, by gaining an image of innovativeness. In consumer markets, reputation translates into opinion leadership. Finally, altruism in customer knowledge sharing can be associated with the payoff of being recognized as an expert within a specific industry, thereby generating a new potential economic benefit. In consumer markets "authentic" altruism can derive from the simple identification with the community; that is, from pure ego-gratification incentives, beyond a mere economic logic.

UTILIZING CUSTOMER KNOWLEDGE: THE FIRM'S POINT OF VIEW

As a pre-condition for knowledge co-creation, we have argued that customers should be willing to share their knowledge with a firm, developing an absorptive capacity, trust and motivation to take part in such a co-operative process. Then, however, it is up to the

Table 2. Incentives for Knowledge Co-creation in Business-to-Business and Consumer Markets.

Incentive	Business-to-business market (Lead user customers)	Consumer market (Trendsetter customers)
Reciprocity	Better product customization: - Compatibility with internal standards is assured; - Reduced production costs; - Increased effectiveness of production processes	Better product customization: - definition of new lifestyles and consumption standards; - acquisition/enforcement of a prestigious position within the community
Repute	Improved market positioning Improved image as innovative company	Recognition as opinion leader
Altruism	Recognition as an expert Implicit economic benefit	Identification with a community Pure ego-gratification logic

firm to use customer knowledge effectively. Thus, we now need to turn to the firm's viewpoint, suggesting that the firm's ability to utilize customer knowledge is a function of three basic competencies:

- the firm's capacity to absorb customer knowledge (absorptive capacity);
- its capacity to share such knowledge within the organization (organizational sharing capacity);
- its capacity to act on this knowledge and translate it into new offerings (deployment capacity).

Organizational learning theory has analyzed these abilities using more or less similar labels. Here we want to re-consider and re-define such concepts, emphasizing the specific meaning and the managerial implications they assume when they refer to customer knowledge.

Absorptive Capacity

To co-operate with their customers in knowledge creation processes, firms need to develop an absorptive capacity for their customers' knowledge; that is an ability to recognize the value of customer knowledge, sense and incorporate it within their organization. As we said, the first step is a screening process to select the best customer knowledge assets on the market. As the review of literature by Mittal et al. (1997) suggests, from a marketing perspective it implies hearing the voice of the customer, searching and processing market information, and making customer, competitive, or environmental research. Here, however, we suggest going one step further, arguing that the firm's ability to scan should be complemented by a parallel ability to dialogue. The combination of these two abilities constitutes absorptive capacity.

Two factors affect firms' incentives to invest in absorptive capacity (Cohen & Levinthal, 1990). The first is the quantity of knowledge to be assimilated and exploited: the more the knowledge needed, the greater the incentive. The second is the difficulty of learning: the more difficult the learning, the more R&D effort the firm will need to achieve the appropriate level of absorptive capacity. Such a difficulty also depends on the complexity of the network of relationships the firm has enacted. Besides, much of the knowledge the firm has to absorb is tacit, "sticky" (von Hippel, 1994) and thus difficult to communicate. As a consequence, such critical complementary knowledge is acquired only through direct sharing of experiences. For instance, Italian casual-wear company Diesel organizes events to give its customers the opportunity to meet and speak with "Diesel people" directly. They manage a web site to allow customers to interact with the company and among them, socializing their knowledge. No Diesel product is simply "designed at a desk", within R&D labs. Each product is born through a dialogue with trendsetter customers. This ability to "stay on the field", to share customers' experiences is the main strength of Diesel, which has built its competitive advantage on real co-created knowledge.

More generally, absorptive capacity of customer knowledge is essential for any company, because it generates benefits the firm can appropriate. From a marketing viewpoint, this is essential to anticipate complex customer needs. Recognized innovators such as Monsanto, General Electric, and Intel base the success of their new products on this ability to understand latent market needs by developing a deep absorptive capacity (Slater & Narver, 1998).

Organizational Sharing Capacity

Organizational learning processes can benefit from the absorptive capacity for customer knowledge only if the firm is subsequently able to spread this knowledge. In other words, the relationships between the firm and its customers can lead to new knowledge creation only if there are mechanisms for integrating customer and organizational knowledge assets within a unique, idiosyncratic and inimitable network of knowledge. According to the Knowledge-Based View (Wernerfelt, 1984; Vicari, 1991), firms cannot simply import knowledge assets. They have to reproduce them internally, even when customers participate in such a process. Therefore, new knowledge co-creation happens only if firms favor customer knowledge retention, dissemination, re-elaboration and continuous feeding with new, fresh contributions. Multifunctional teams can be particularly useful for this purpose.

In this sense, therefore, by "sharing" we mean *"a process of circulation of knowledge among all and any subject - individual or institutional—that prove to be efficient to this effect and available and/or interested"* (Caraca & Carrhilo, 1996, 772) In particular, as strategy becomes interactive, involving more dialogue and collaboration with customers, there must be greater dispersion of information and decision-making throughout the organization. All business processes need to be strongly focused on customer value, to be more sensitive to the opportunities to create knowledge co-operating with customers (Day, 1998). In fact, most of the success of companies like FedEx, Ritz-Carlton and USAA comes from "enthusiastic customer-oriented organizations", within which customer knowledge is broadly shared among all the functions interested in it (Schultz, 1998). Specific initiatives that can lead to such results include organizing cross-functional meetings that involve senior management, and implementing IT systems that allow for virtual knowledge sharing. For instance, Dell Computer holds regular Customer Advocate Meetings to systematically share what support people have heard from customers with colleagues from product Development, Sales and Marketing (Bohlin & Brenner, 1995). Similarly, Sequent Computer Systems, Inc. focuses most of its knowledge management efforts on supporting its marketing and sales organizations. The company's major vehicle for knowledge management is an electronic library. It is an internal system for capturing, archiving, and providing information to employees, which they can use to increase revenue, reduce cycle time, and put knowledge gleaned from experience to new use. It serves to monitor and measure the flow of knowledge from those who produce it, through those who add value to it, to those who finally consume this knowledge. Prestige motivates people to produce knowledge, and feedback improves its quality (Odem & O'Dell, 1998).

In summary, a firm's customer knowledge sharing capacity refers to the effectiveness of the process and mechanisms by which customer knowledge is transformed into knowledge assets that can be shared within the whole firm, becoming integrated with its existing knowledge base.

Deployment Capacity

If firms really want to improve their new product development processes, they cannot simply absorb and disseminate customer knowledge. They have to develop the ability to act on this knowledge. To transfer customer knowledge into new products, firms need to improve their deployment capacity. They need to overcome the bias "R&D knows best", moving from a passive involvement of customers to an active co-development with customers. The greatest involvement of customers, and thus the greatest likelihood of a product success, is achieved only when firms promote activities of product co-specifications and co-development, including strategic alliances and joint ventures with customers (Wind & Mahajan, 1997).

To explore the firm's deployment capacity of customer knowledge, we need to define how it leverages knowledge assets developed in co-operation with customers. In particular, we need to analyze the processes linking the development of new ideas, the elaboration of prototypes and their fine-tuning in line with customer suggestions. In addition, as we said, we need to consider the implications of co-generated knowledge for intellectual property rights. As incentive for knowledge contributions, firms have to recognize individual inventors participation in the rights to the output created with their knowledge. At the same time, once any piece of knowledge exists, the social incentives are completely reversed. The wider the use and the faster the distribution of that new knowledge, the greater the benefit to the community and, even, to the whole society. Any attempt to manage intellectual property rights should recognize these two inherently conflicting objectives. As monopoly power wanes and social interest encourages the development of new intellectual property, the balance should shift toward favoring the production of new knowledge and be less concerned about the free distribution of existing knowledge (Thurow, 1997). Nevertheless, intellectual property rights management needs to strike the right balance between production and distribution of new ideas.

INTEGRATING CUSTOMER AND FIRM PERSPECTIVES: THE VIRTUOUS CYCLE OF CUSTOMER KNOWLEDGE INTEGRATION

In our analysis of knowledge co-creation with customers, we emphasized the importance of considering the perspective of customers as well as the perspective of the firm. We now propose that these perspectives need to be combined and aligned, to enact a virtuous cycle of co-learning. Customers should be able to absorb a specific firm's knowledge, they should trust it and be motivated to participate in its processes of knowledge creation. If all these pre-conditions are satisfied at the customer end, only then can the capabilities of the firm (absorptive, sharing, and deployment capacities) can be considered. The firm first needs to speak a common language with its customers to be able to absorb their knowledge. It needs to share such knowledge within its organization to facilitate new knowledge generation. Finally, only if the firm's absorptive and sharing capacities are integrated by an effective deployment capacity, the potential for innovation and new product co-development increases. Such co-created products can better satisfy the explicit and implicit needs of the customers who contributed to their definition. This leads to a positive feedback in terms of increased customers' motivation to share their knowledge, making the relationship between such customers and the firm even stronger (see Figure 2, where the different size of cylinders signals different levels of scarcity of the considered assets).

This virtuous cycle of knowledge co-creation processes between a firm and its high-involvement customers increases the uniqueness and the inimitability of the firm's knowledge, thus making it a potentially self-renewing source of entrepreneurial rents (Dierickx & Cool, 1989). A second positive effect of knowledge co-creation processes for suppliers are "short loops" within the mechanisms of learning by errors (Vicari, 1991, 1995). In addition, in consumption contexts where customers have incomplete information and the buying process is complex, co-operation with customers has additional payoffs, reducing evaluation ambiguity. Further, the process of joint definition of product attributes increases customer satisfaction, strengthening customer loyalty to the firm (Siehl & al., 1992). Higher innovation potential, better fine tuning respect of market needs, increased customer satisfaction, major switching costs, shorter loop of learning by errors, and reduced information ambiguity could thus be the most significant output of a knowledge creation process that transcends the firm's boundaries, making organizations

Figure 2. The Virtuous Cycle of Knowledge Co-creation

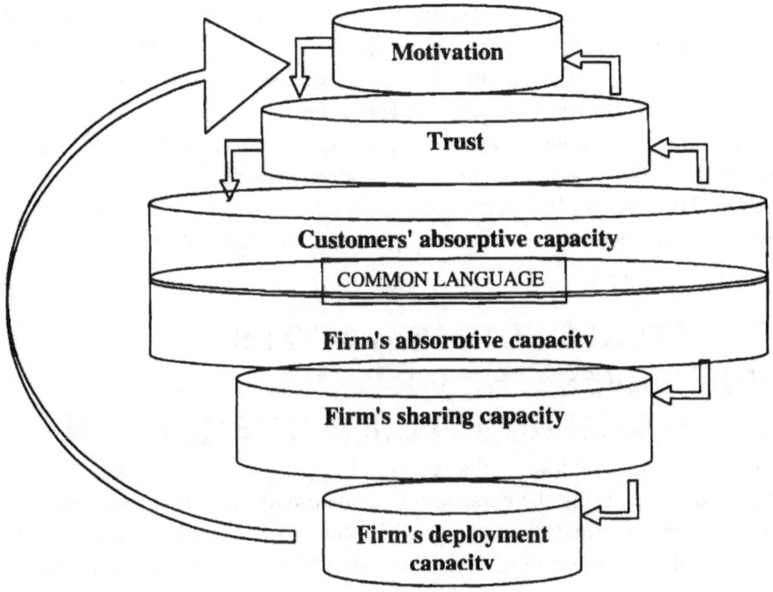

and markets "holonistic systems" of "cooperative, intelligent, autonomous agents" (Miller, 1995).

PROCESS FAILURES AND DISCONNECTS IN THE LEARNING CYCLE

The idealized learning cycle rarely functions as advertised. Modiano et al. (1995) identify a set of "learning disabilities" for each stage of the cycle that transforms knowledge into action. In the first step, they suggest that an "ostrich culture" can prevent many companies from even seeing the problem, inhibiting them from investing in absorptive capacity. That could be because of an exclusive internal focus, limited external contacts, poor information gathering, or a focus on short-term performance that deters people from investigating long-term issues.

Some organizations can "see the problem", but they can not create consensus around it. They suffer from a "donkey syndrome", which manifests itself in an inability to devote sufficient time or effort to customer knowledge sharing. Organizational "chimneys" can inhibit cross-functionally, preventing information from reaching all the people who could use it.

At the third stage, firms may be aware of the relevance of customer knowledge and may create consensus around it, but they may still not be able to act on it. This so-called "snail culture" includes an unwillingness to experiment, inability to take controlled risks and back them if successful, inability to react quickly, and search for stability rather than change.

The point is that it is not enough to overcome just one of these syndromes. The chain is only as strong as its weakest link. To obtain breakthrough performance, firms need to invest in eliminating each of these bottlenecks (Modiano & al., 1995). And if this is true referring to simple learning within a firm, it is much more important considering co-learning processes that extend beyond the firm's boundaries. Coordination mechanisms and alignment efforts are even more relevant here, because the process lacks the control of hierarchical organizations.

Obstacles to effective co-learning can be classified into two categories. First, there

Figure 3. Process and Linkage Failures in the Firm's Customer Involvement Capacity

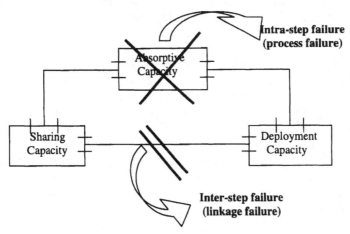

may be an *absence* of one or more capacities. This is an "intra-step failure", a process failure that concerns absorptive, sharing, or deployment capacities. Second, there may be a *disconnect* between stages in the co-learning process. This is an "inter-step failure" or a linkage failure, arising from a lack of alignment between the abilities a firm has developed to interact with its customers (Figure 3).

Process Failures

Absorptive capacity failure: Deficiencies in common language
If an intra-step failure develops within the first step – absorptive capacity – the co-learning process cannot begin. Firms that are not able to develop a common language with their customers cannot build relationships with them. As a consequence, they cannot progress beyond managing spot transactions on the market. This puts firms at a disadvantage at a time when the emphasis in marketing is shifting from customer acquisition to customer retention and from transactional value to lifetime customer value (Valdani, 1995; Sawhney & Kotler, 1999). A process failure at the absorptive capacity stage compromises the first pre-condition for developing co-learning between customers and firms, by inhibiting the dialogue between them.

Sharing capacity failure: Deficiencies in knowledge dissemination
If a firm lacks the capacity to share customer knowledge within its organization, much of the precious knowledge assets developed by cooperating with customers are likely to be dissipated. Managerial slogans such as "Listen to the voice of the customer" are of little use in the absence of concrete tools to encode and disseminate customer knowledge. Customer knowledge tends to be experiential and tacit in nature (Nonaka, 1991). Thus, if firms want to benefit from it, they need to adopt a sort of "expeditionary marketing approach" (Hamel & Prahalad, 1994), involving customers in their knowledge creation process, and helping them to articulate their desires (Leonard & Rayport, 1997). Companies such as Motorola and General Electric maintain strong market positions by utilizing processes of probing and learning" (Lynn et al., 1996).

Thus, a process failure at this step compromises the firm's ability to harness customer knowledge. Further, customers who share knowledge with a firm and then do not find the organization to be responsive will be disappointed, and will perceive their efforts to be a waste of time. In future interactions, they will be likely to stop trusting such a firm, abandoning it and disseminating a negative image of it through word-of-mouth.

Deployment Capacity Failure: Deficiencies in Knowledge Conversion
Finally, if an intra-step failure arises at the deployment capacity stage, the firm cannot convert its learning into profitable innovations. In these firms, customer knowledge has been shared and disseminated within the firm, but the R&D department still functions in a vacuum, believing that it does not need any external contribution. Such a prejudice often comes from a history of market success, which prevents R&D people from "unlearning" the lessons of the past in markets that are changing rapidly (Hamel & Prahalad, 1994). Firms where this is the case still tend to favor early and sharp product definition, and do not adequately emphasize on-going customer feedback. The persistence of a deployment capacity failure prevents the firm from entering into "adaptive co-

development" efforts with its customers. Lack of this capacity is particularly dangerous in markets where competitors have started involving customers throughout the development process. In such markets where speed and flexibility are paramount, this approach is not only undesirable, but also often unfeasible (Balasubramanian et al., 1998).

Linkage Failures

Absorptive-Sharing capacity linkage failure: The "alignment gap"

If the firm has both the capacities to absorb and to share customer knowledge, but a linkage between them is missing, an "alignment gap" would arise (cf. Valdani et al., 1994). This means that the firm is able to dialogue with its customers and to build up strong relationships with them, but the knowledge it absorbs from the market is not the same knowledge shared at the organizational level. In firms that exhibit the alignment gap, customer knowledge gets distorted as it flows from people at the interfaces of the firm to the point at which it needs to be utilized.

It is not always easy to locate the source of distortion of customer knowledge. A deep analysis of the whole process is needed to avoid wastage of energy and frustration among workers who do not perceive improvements in customer satisfaction. If such a disconnect persists, it can lead to a reduced commitment towards customer care.

Sharing-Deployment capacities linkage failure: The "meaning gap"

A different linkage failure develops if the firm is able to share customer knowledge and to act on it, but it finds difficulties in interpreting it. In such a firm, the activities of the whole organization may be inspired by customer knowledge and R&D people are oriented to product co-development, but engineers and designers misinterpret what they learn. For example, customer knowledge could be presented in a format that is not consistent with the terminology or product hierarchies used by the firm's project teams. This is what we call a "meaning gap". It is a cognitive failure that is akin to a "carburation problem": plenty of energy originated by the market feeds the engine of co-development, but people who translate this energy into new offerings do not understand its right nature. The result is an inappropriate use of customer knowledge or, much worse, the "flooding" of the firm's innovation processes; like putting diesel in a car that uses gasoline and then complaining that it does not work. Customers will be disappointed because they do not receive the right output from their knowledge contribution.

Deployment-Absorptive capacities linkage failure: The "capitalization gap"

Finally, a linkage failure can arise when feedback between individual cycles of knowledge co-creation is lacking. If the "energy" from the market flows through the firm's absorptive, sharing and deployment capacities, but then the circuit breaks down, it limits the ability of the firm to "learn about learning". This failure can be termed as a "capitalization gap": the firm is not able to capitalize on accumulated customer knowledge assets, and remains stuck into a short-term approach to knowledge co-creation.

This gap is consistent with what Modiano et al. (1995) define as a "lemming culture", in which there is no effective review of the company's position and recent experiences, so there is no way to re-fuel the learning cycle. Firms that exhibit capitalization gaps tend to continually "reinvent the wheel" in learning, because they are unable

Figure 4. Process and Linkage Failures in Co-learning with Customers

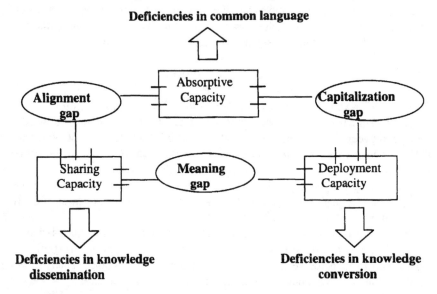

to leverage their learning from high-involvement customers to create improved products for all their customers. Such firms find it difficult to recover the initial costs of knowledge co-creation, and lose the cumulative benefits of learning.

We summarize our discussion of the possible sources of intra-step (process) and inter-steps (linkage) failures in by highlighting the locus of each failure (Figure 4).

APPROACHES TO IMPROVING EFFECTIVENESS OF CO-LEARNING

In the previous section, we identified six sources of failure in knowledge co-creation. We now offer some guidelines to managers for avoiding them. We propose three approaches that couple each process failure with the corresponding linkage failure, as the two are often closely related.

Overcoming Deficiencies in Common Language and Alignment Gaps

The improvement of absorptive capacity and the alignment of the firm's sharing capacity with the absorbed market knowledge require the development of specific marketing competencies.

First, to develop a common language, firms have to develop new approaches to marketing research that emphasize contextual inquiry and role-playing. The premise of the former is very simple: it suggests that observing customers in their native surroundings is much more effective than surveying customers on their consumption behavior, because it provides insights into ongoing experience rather than summary experience. The goal is to make the firm and the customer collaborators understand the latter's deep needs and consumption experience, letting this shape the firm's understanding of customer need (Beyer & Holtzblatt, 1998).

Role-playing is another technique complementary to contextual inquiry. It aims at "entering the minds" of customers through direct interactions with them. For instance, middle management of a Japanese pharmaceutical company periodically spends some time within hospitals, to share the experience of doctors and patients, seeing what it means to live with their problems.

In addition to these techniques, firms should also develop marketing relationships that optimize learning processes. For instance, the National Industrial Bicycle Co. of Japan (NIBC) has transformed its relationships with high involvement customers into strategic learning relationships. NIBC reaps superior returns by employing a system that increases the interaction between its mass production and mass customization factories. *"This gathering and exploitation of information from a segment of 'innovative' users helps the firm to dynamically manage the proliferation of new product designs"* (Kotha, 1996: 446).

Thus, customers' attitudes to cooperate with the firm to create knowledge could represent a new criterion for segmenting the market. Firms could invest in relationships with specific customers, to leverage their individual knowledge contributions better. As a consequence, managers should start thinking in terms of "reverse marketing", that is "reverse segmentation and product design", allowing clients to self-select and co-customize offers with marketers (Sawhney & Kotler, 1999).

Finally, as we said, firms need to design explicit and implicit incentives for customers who share knowledge. These incentives can range from reduced prices (in business markets), to ego-gratification mechanisms and programs to create communities of "special" customers that co-operate with the firm (in consumer markets). These community efforts stimulate collaborative creation of knowledge *among* customers. By organizing customer communities, firms can enter a new social dimension of customer knowledge. This concept is well understood by firms like Harley Davidson and Lego, which every year organize many events to allow their customers to meet and define together their "shared world". The appropriate management of virtual communities of consumption can clearly catalyze such an effect. For example, for some years the kids-wear company Oilily., headquartered in Holland, has created a "fan club" online open to children all over the world, who can write to the company's designers their own suggestions. Generalizing such an approach, the lesson for managers is that marketing people should act like gardeners, who patiently "cultivate" their relationships with the market, rather than hunters, who worry about building the right mousetraps to capture their prey (Sawhney & Kotler, 1999).

Overcoming Deficiencies in Knowledge Sharing and Meaning Gaps

Recent developments in groupware tools like Lotus Notes, as well the increasing diffusion of intranets, favor improved internal sharing of the knowledge grasped at the firm-customer interface. Firms can develop "knowledge catalogs" that can be accessed throughout the firm. For instance, Lucent Technologies has developed a sophisticated system of knowledge mapping. It has created a system for customer relationship management that offers all the information about customers in real-time and in a user-friendly manner. Similarly, USAA has initiated a program to transform its Intranet into a "Knowledge Management and Performance Support". The purpose is overcoming organizational barriers to knowledge sharing. All employees will be able to use it, independent of geography or hierarchy. The key idea is to transform knowledge from a "site" to an "object", building up a library of "data about data", creating tools focused on a community level, and reducing task duplication. Towards this end, USAA is implementing a new "Knowledge Management Intranet", aimed at taking greater advantage from the existing communities of practice, and recognizing individual information needs. Information stewards have assumed a coordination role and customized home pages have been introduced, allowing employees to re-aggregate distributed knowledge stored in a repository of collective memory.

However, these approaches to knowledge management are not enough to ensure knowledge co-creation with customers. Managers need also to foster a customer knowledge-oriented culture. In particular, they should carefully coordinate the process of knowledge transfer from customers to avoid meaning gaps, i.e. misleading interpretation of customer knowledge by engineers and designers. As Beyer and Holtzblatt (1998: 30) argue, *"in fact, understanding a market is fundamentally different from understanding what to design into a system, and the data traditionally collected for marketing has limited usefulness for product design."*

Thus, to avoid a failure at this stage, a new language and a new dialogue are needed not only to improve relationships emerging between customers and the marketing organization, but also to favor better co-operation between marketing, design and R&D. This is not a marketing task; it is a management task. Top managers are the only ones who can provide the resources, facilities, information and tools to create a customer knowledge-centered organization (Schultz, 1998).

Overcoming Deficiencies in Knowledge Conversion and Capitalization Gaps

The first approach to overcoming deficiencies in knowledge conversion and capitalization is to leverage knowledge created from specific customers by making it available outside the relationships that generated it. For instance, Sequent Computer Systems, Inc. makes extensive use of the company's collective skills, knowledge, and experience so that each of its customers benefit from the experience of previous customers (Odem & O'Dell, 1998). Similarly, after working closely with Intel and developing specific packaging design solutions for various chips, Shinko, a Japanese semiconductor packaging manufacturer, was able to re-invest such knowledge on its broader market. In particular, when customers such as IBM adopted a similar technology, Shinko was able to provide them with leading-edge materials and capabilities. As a result, the company increased sales from $68 million in 1980 to $726 million in 1994, recovering the costs initially paid to support the relationship with Intel (Davis & Ueyama, 1996).

Firms can also gain leverage from their customer knowledge assets thinking in terms of "customer platforms", identifying a customer segment that has the most compelling needs for the firm's offering and can serve as a base for further expansion into related segments and application markets. For instance, the success of Sun workstations, Apple Macintosh, the 3Com Palm Pilot organizer, and Lotus Notes was largely attributable to a good choice of customers platforms. The initial customer segments became loyal advocates for the firm and were influential in spreading the word to related segments (Sawhney, 1998).

Finally, firms should capitalize on the knowledge assets accumulated from cooperation with their high-involvement customers, and "re-invest" this learning in the mass market of "knowledge free riders", who benefit from the output of a knowledge-creation process in which they did not participate. As a consequence, firms should charge these "low-involvement" customers a higher price, thus finding a new economic balance between the costs and the revenues deriving from their innovation activities (von Krogh & Prandelli, 1999).

IMPLICATIONS FOR ORGANIZATIONAL DESIGN, INFORMATION TECHNOLOGY, AND MARKETING COMMUNICATION

Some managerial implications emerge from our analysis of knowledge co-creation with customers. We organize them in terms of new product development decisions in the domains of organizational design, information technology (IT), and marketing communication (Table 3).

Implications for Organizational Design

To favor the direct involvement of customers in knowledge creation processes, we have argued that firms should select their customers, focusing primarily on lead-users and trendsetters. As a first consequence, each organization needs people who act as "gate keepers" or "boundary spanners" (Tushman, 1977), filtering knowledge acquired from customers. This is a crucial role to avoid information overload, and to focus attention on the knowledge that is really relevant to catalyze innovation. Once selected customer knowledge has entered their organization, firms need also to identify "knowledge co-creation facilitators", i.e., people who create bridges between customers and specific organizational teams who are working on projects that could benefit from joint learning strategies. The facilitator role is particularly important to avoid alignment gaps. It ensures a common understanding of customer knowledge, and makes the relationship between marketing and R&D more efficient and effective. Finally, firms also need "key integrators and distributors", who re-aggregate the knowledge autonomously produced in several parts of the organization, and make it accessible across the organization. This is essential to avoid not only alignment gaps, but also meaning gaps. For instance, British Petroleum uses a five-person unit reporting to the board of directors to derive lessons learned from past major projects. Similarly, Boeing commissioned a group called Project Homework to dissect its past product development processes, leading to the successful development of the Boeing 757 (Bohlin and Brenner, 1995). In summary, to fully implement the logic of knowledge co-creation involving customers, new organizational roles need to be defined, formally and informally within the company (Figure 5).

Implications for Information Technology

Technology is having a profound impact on how people capture knowledge, achieve understanding, and communicate with one another, activities that are fundamental building blocks of organizational learning. However, firms need to move beyond IT tools that allow for a better information circulation and knowledge transfer within the individual organization. Firms need to develop systems to allow a simpler and more effective

Table 3. Summary of solutions to problems in customer knowledge co-creation

Process failure	Absorptive Capacity	Sharing Capacity	Deployment Capacity
Linkage failure	**Absorptive-Sharing Capacities**	**Sharing-Deployment Capacities**	**Deployment-Absorptive Capacities**
Solution approaches	Shifting from traditional marketing research to contextual inquiry and role-playing mechanisms	Development of a customer knowledge oriented culture	Processes aimed at leveraging co-created knowledge
	Transformation of marketing relationships into learning relationships	Customer knowledge-centered reengineering	Development of "customer platform" thinking
	Development of customer care activities, design of explicit and implicit incentives	Integration between organizational and customer knowledge assets	Criteria to measure value generation based on partnership
Implications for organizational design	Introduction of "gate keeper" or "boundary spanner" roles within the organization	Introduction of "knowledge facilitator" role within the organization	Introduction of "key integrator and distributor" role within the organization
Implications for information technology management	- Training/education support systems - Management of virtual communities	- Collaborative work systems - Knowledge mapping	- Expert systems that encode customer knowledge - Advanced co-design support systems
Implications for marketing communications	- Strengthening of brand value through meaning co-creation - Brand as relationship	- Need for "brand platform thinking" - New brand management culture	- Redefinition of brand extension strategies - Separation between intellectual property associated with the brand and the product
Key functional areas	**Marketing**	**Knowledge Management**	**Strategy**

involvement of external resources and, in particular, of customers, in the firm's processes of learning and innovation. Thus, learning organization applications have to be re-thought and transformed into applications that can support co-operative learning on an extensive basis. These applications can be classified into five categories: training and education; collaborative work; knowledge sharing; decision support and visualization; expert systems (Curtice and Lipoff, 1995).

Each of these categories has to include new tools or, at least, has to admit new kinds of implementation of tools designed to work within the individual organization. For example, training and education support systems can be used to facilitate the development of a common language between the firm and its customers. Similarly, groupware applications have to be developed far beyond bulletin boards, as the experiences of Lucent Technologies, USAA, and Sequent Computer Systems suggest. Repositories of collective memory, knowledge catalogs for knowledge retrieval, and new application of intranet and extranet systems can make knowledge mapping and sharing within and across the organization easier. Further, these systems should be opened to external knowledge contributions. A combination of these systems with the use of IT to create and manage virtual communities can catalyze knowledge co-creation.

Simulation tools also offer promise for knowledge sharing. Management flight simulators can enhance learning by allowing managers to encode customer knowledge and learn from simulated deployments by reflecting on the outcomes. Even if such learning falls short of authentic co-development, it is a useful first step in arriving at a common cognitive understanding of customers and the firm's mental models. Expert systems are another IT tool to encode learning from specific knowledge holders and to make it available to non-experts. For instance, General Motors uses a specialized system to support Quality Function Deployment. The engineering and manufacturing organizations use it to reduce the discrepancy between market information and design specifications, thereby reducing alignment and meaning gaps (Curtice & Lipoff, 1995).

In conclusion, IT tools can greatly enhance knowledge co-creation, but traditional applications have to be modified to allow direct customer involvement.

Implications for Marketing Communication

The final set of implications managers need to consider concerns the firm's communication strategy. The development of a common language between the firm and its high-involvement customers, as well as the building of strong cooperative relationships, requires a new approach to communication and image management. From the perspective of knowledge co-creation, brands are the instruments for creating trust between customers and the firm. Enlightened brand management can allow a firm to exploit its image to become closer to its customers, and to involve them in co-operative knowledge creation. In this perspective the brand is at the basis of the relationship and the intellectual property associated with it can be separated from the intellectual property associated with the product. For instance, Red Hat Inc. has created the Red Hat brand to sell a stable version of the Linux operating system. This is developed by a community of developers, and Red Hat does not own any intellectual property rights on it. However, Red Hat adds its brand and relations with developers and customers to acquire legitimacy and the right to coordinate the activities of the Open Source Software movement (Sawhney & Prandelli, 1999).

Thinking of the "brand as the relationship" also has important implications for brand extension decisions. This viewpoint highlights the importance of the relations embodied in the brand as a platform for expansion into related markets for the same customers (Sawhney, 1998). Instead of thinking of brand extensions in terms of product similarity, this view argues for thinking of brand extensions in terms of relationship similarity. The e-commerce firm, Amazon.com, has proved this idea nicely, by leveraging its customer relationships into areas like auctions that seem to be quite dissimilar from the product standpoint, but are logical extensions of their customer relationships. A key driver of the firm's success is therefore its ability to build trust and relationships with high involvement customers, who are motivated to share their knowledge with the firm.

CONCLUSIONS: TOWARDS CUSTOMER INTEGRATION

In the information economy, knowledge is becoming the only source of competitive advantage. However, increasing uncertainty and complexity in the environment requires continuous adaptation and strategic change, obliging firms to renew the basis of their competitive advantage. Consequently, the firm's knowledge base should be continually fed and enriched. The key theme of this chapter is that co-operation with high-involvement customers in knowledge creation can be a key catalyst for maximizing the innovation potential of an organization.

To enact this process of knowledge co-creation, we argued that customers have to develop a common vocabulary with the firm, they should trust it and be motivated to share knowledge. These are the pre-conditions for transforming customers into knowledge co-creators. On their part, firms also have to develop three fundamental capacities: absorbing customer knowledge, sharing it within the organization, and acting on it to convert knowledge into new offerings.

We identified the process and linkage failures that can compromise the virtuous cycle of knowledge co-creation. The former can be due to a lack of absorptive capacity, which leads to deficiencies in common language; a lack of organizational sharing capacity, which results in deficiencies in knowledge sharing; and a lack of deployment capacity, which leads to deficiencies in knowledge conversion into new products. Linkage failures between absorptive and sharing capacities; sharing and deployment capacities; and deployment and absorptive capacities can result in alignment gaps, meaning gaps, and capitalization gaps, respectively. The solutions we proposed to overcome each one of these intra-step and inter-steps failures require the development of new competencies in marketing, knowledge management, and strategy, as well as re-thinking the ways firms approach organizational design, IT, and communication.

These ideas can be fruitfully extended in several directions. Most importantly, they can serve as the starting point for a deeper and more meaningful linkage between the marketing and knowledge management literatures. This will help firms in moving from customer orientation to customer integration, and from customer relationship management to the management of learning partnerships with customers.

ENDNOTES

1 For instance, Sony Corp. has formed various alliances with computer and telecommunications firms that provide it with access to a wealth of new knowledge, such as how to manage product development cycles. The purpose is to incorporate disparate pieces of individual knowledge into a wider organizational knowledge base (Inkpen, 1998).

2 The sociological concept of knowledge - knowledge as a relationship of sharing between the individual and the groups who developed and possess it – owes its origin to several theoretical disciplines. These include the sociology of knowledge (Boisot, 1995), organizational behavior (Nonaka and Takeuchi, 1995), studies of social impact of advanced technologies (Durand, 1993), theories of learning (Stata, 1989; Huber, 1991), and social system theories (Vicari, 1991; von Krogh and Roos, 1996).

3 Whenever we speak about cognitive activities we refer to activities and labor which aim at knowledge production.

4 In particular, customer knowledge can be considered useful to introduce "perturbations" within the organizational equilibrium state (Vicari, 1991, 1998). Such "disturbing elements" allow the development of a "creative chaos" that favor new knowledge creation in a context always changing (Nonaka and Takeuchi, 1995).

5 In particular, von Hippel (1982: 120-121) argues: *"an auto fastener manufacturer might well determine that those users with the greatest need for reliable fasteners are aerospace companies. Further, one can refine the search as a function of particular product attributes. While the auto fastener manufacturer might well look to aerospace*

companies for more reliable mechanisms, it might more usefully explore toy makers who are primarily interested in keeping costs down".

6 By 'virtual community of consumption' we mean each community arising on-line to serve consumer needs for communication, information and entertainment (Armstrong and Hagel, 1996). They generate a rich web of personal relationships among the members themselves.

REFERENCES

Anderson, J.C. and Narus, J.A. (1991) "Partnering as a focused market strategy". *California Management Review*, 33 (spring): 95-113.

Armstrong, A. and Hagel, J. (1996) "The Real Value of Online Communities". *Harvard Business Review,* (May-June): 134-141.

Balasubramanian, S, Krishnan, V.V. and Sawhney, M. (1998) "New Offering Realization in the Networked Digital Environment". Working paper, Northwestern University.

Barlow, J.P. (1993) "The Economy of Ideas". *Wired,* (4).

Beyer, H. and Holtzblatt, K. (1998) *Contextual Design. Defining Customer-Centered Systems*, Morgan Kauffman Publishers, Inc., San Francisco, California.

Bohlin, N.H. and Brenner, P. (1995) "Measuring Learning: Assessing and Valuing Progress". *Prism,* (Third Quarter): 55-67.

Boisot, M. (1995) *Information Space: A framework for analyzing learning in organizations, institutions and cultures,* Routledge, New York.

Cairncross, F. (1997) *The Death of Distance: How the Communication Revolution Will Change Our Lives.* Harvard Business School Press.

Caraca, J and Carrilho, M. (1996) "The role of sharing in circulation of knowledge". *Futures,* 28 (8).

Cohen, W.M. and Levinthal, D.A. (1990) "Absorptive capacity: a new perspective on learning and innovation". *Administrative Science Quarterly*, 35: 128-152.

Curtice, R.M. and Lipoff, S.F. (1995) "Technology Foundations of the Learning Organization". *Prism,* (Third Quarter): 69-81.

Davenport, T.H. and Prusak, L. (1998) *Working Knowledge. How Organizations Manage What They Know,* Harvard Business School Press, Boston.

Davis, R.J. and Ueyama, S. (1996) "Developing customers before products". *The McKinsey Quarterly*, (3): 72-83.

Day, G. (1998) "Organizing for Interactivity". *Journal of Interactive Marketing,* 12 (1): 47-53.

Di Bernardo, B. and Rullani, E. (1990) *Il management e le macchine,* Il Mulino.

Dierickx, I. and Cool, K. (1989) "Asset Stock Accumulation and Sustainability of Competitive Advantage". *Management Science,* 35: 1504-11.

Drucker, P.F. (1993) *Post-Capitalist Society*, Butterworth Heinemann, Oxford.

Drucker, P.F. (1995) "The Network Society", *Wall Street Journal,* March 29: 12.

Durand, T. (1993) "The dynamics of cognitive technological maps". In *Implementing Strategic Processes: Change, Learning, and Co-operation,* eds. Lorange et al., 165-89, Blackwell, Oxford.

Fiocca, R. and Prandelli, E. (1997) "La reingegnerizzazione dei processi di marketing orientatata alla Time-based Competition". In *La reingegnerizzazione dei processi di marketing,* eds. Valdani and Ancarani, Egea, Milano.

Fournier, S.. Dobscha, S. and Mick, D.G., (1998) "Preventing the premature death of relationship marketing". *Harvard Business Review*, 76(1): 42-44.

Garvin, A.D. (1993) "Building a learning organization". *Harvard Business Review*, (July-August): 78-91.

Granovetter, M.S. (1985) "Economic action and social structure: the problem of embeddedness". *American Journal of Sociology*, 91: 481-510.

Hagel, J. (1996) "Spider versus Spider". *McKinsey Quarterly, 1: 4-18.*

Hamel, G. (1991) "Competition for competence and inter-partner learning within international strategic alliances". *Strategic Management Journal*, 12.

Hamel, G and Prahalad, C.K (1994) *Competing for the Future*, Harvard Business School Press, Boston, Massachusetts.

Huber, G. (1991) "Organizational Learning: The Contributing Processes and The Literatures". *Organization Science*, 2 (1): 88-115.

Inkpen, A.C. (1998) "Learning, Knowledge Acquisition, and Strategic Alliances". *European Management Journal*, 16 (2): 223-29.

Itami, H. and Roehl, T.W. (1987), *Mobilizing invisible assets*, Harvard University Press, Cambridge.

Kotha, S. (1996) "From Mass Production to Mass Customization: the case of the National Industrial Bicycle Company of Japan". *European Management Journal*, 14 (5).

Kogut, B. and Zander, U. (1996) "What do firms do? Coordination, identity and learning". *Organization Science*, 7: 502-18.

Leonard, D. and Rayport, J.F. (1997) "Spark innovation through empathic design". *Harvard Business Review* (November-December): 103-13.

Lorenzoni, G. and Baden-Fuller, C. (1995) "Creating a Strategic Center to Manage a Web of Partners", *California Management Review*, 37 (3): 146-163.

Lynn, G., Morone, J. and Paulson, A. (1996) "Marketing and discontinuous innovation: The probe and learn process". *California Management Review*, 38 (3): 8-37.

Micelli, S. and Prandelli, E. (2000) "Net Marketing: l'innovazione in un mondo senza consumatori", *Economia & Management*, forthcoming.

Miller, W.L. (1995) "A Broader Mission for R&D". *Research Technology Management*, (November-December): 24-36.

Mittal, V, Ross, W.T. and Oliva T. (1997), "Organizational information use and marketing: an integrative framework", working paper, University of Pittsburgh.

Modiano, P., Barbera, M. and Bock, F. (1995) "Converting the Cultural Menagerie: Overcoming Organizational Learning Disabilities". *Prism*, (Third Quarter): 45-53.

Moore, J.F. (1997) *The Death of Competition: Leadership and Strategy in the Age of Business Ecosystems*, HarperBusiness.

Nayak, P.R., Garvin, A.D., Maira, A.N. and Bragar, F.L. (1995) "Creating a Learning Organization". *Prism*, (Third Quarter): 45-53.

Nonaka, I. (1991) "The knowledge-creating company". *Harvard Business Review*, (November/ December): 96-104.

Nonaka, I. and Takeuchi, H. (1995) *The Knowledge-Creating Company*, Oxford University Press, New York.

Odem, P. and O Dell, C. (1998) "Invented here: How Sequent Computer publishes knowledge". *Journal of Business Strategy*, 19 (1): 25-28.

Prahalad, C.K. and Hamel, G. (1990) "The Core Competence of the Corporation". *Harvard Business Review* (May-June): 79-91.

Prandelli E. and Saviolo S. (1996) "Verso il prodotto relazionale. Alcune evidenze dal settore dell'abbigliamento giovane". *Economia & Management*, (6): 53-71.

Sawhney, M. (1998) "Leveraged high-variety strategies: From portfolio thinking to platform thinking". *Journal of the Academy of Marketing Science*, 26 (1): 54-61.

Sawhney, M. and Mittal, V. (1998) "Electronic Information Products: A Learning-Based View of Usage, Satisfaction, and Customer Retention", working paper, Northwestern University.

Sawhney, M. and Kotler, P. M. (1999) "Marketing in the Age of Information Democracy", working paper, Northwestern University.

Sawhney, M. and Prandelli, E. (1999) "Communities of Creation: Managing Distributed Innovation in Turbulent Markets", working paper, Northwestern University.

Schultz, D.E. (1998) "It's the employees, stupid!". *Marketing News*, 32 (20): 6.

Siehl, C., Bowen D. and Pearson C.M. (1992) "Service encounters as rites of integration: an information processing model". *Organization Science*, 3 (4): 537-55.

Slater, S.F. and Narver, J.C. (1998) "Customer-Led and Market-Oriented: Let's Not Confuse the Two". *Strategic Management Journal,* 19: 1001-1006.

Stata, R., (1989) "Organizational Learning-The Key to Management Innovation". *Sloan Management Review*, 30 (3).

Thurow, L.C. (1997) "Needed: A new system of intellectual property rights". *Harvard Business Review,* (September-October).

Tushman, M.L. (1977) "Special boundary roles in the innovation process". *Administrative Science Quarterly,* 22: 587-605.

Valdani, E. (1995) *Marketing strategico: gestire il mercato per affermare il vantaggio competitivo*, etaslibri, Milano.

Valdani, E., Busacca B. and Costabile M. (1994) *La soddisfazione del cliente. Un'indagine empirica sulle imprese italiane*, Egea, Milano.

Vicari, S. (1991) *L'impresa vivente*, etaslibri, Milano.

Vicari, S. (1995) "Verso il Resource-Based Management". In *Brand Equity. Il potenziale generativo della fiducia*, ed. Vicari, Egea, Milano.

Vicari, S. (1998) *La creatività d'impresa. Tra caso e necessità*, etaslibri, Milano.

Von Hippel, E. (1982) "Getting new products from customers". *Harvard Business Review,* (March-April): 117-22.

Von Hippel, E. (1986) "Lead users: a source of novel product concepts". *Management Science*, 32 (7).

Von Hippel, E. (1994) "Sticky information and the locus of problem solving: Implications for innovation". *Management Science*, 40 (4): 429-39.

Von Krogh, G. and Roos J. (1996) *Managing Knowledge. Perspectives on cooperation and competition,* Sage Publications, London, Thousand Oaks, New Delhi.

Von Krogh, G., and Prandelli, E. (1999) "The tacit market of tacit knowledge: new perspectives on customers' knowledge contribution", working paper.

Wayland, R.E. and Cole, P.M. (1997) *Customer Connections. New strategies for growth,* Harvard Business School Press, Boston, Massachusetts.

Wernerfelt, B. (1984) "A Resource-Based View of the firm". *Strategic Management Journal*, 5: 171-180.

Wind, J. and Mahajan, V. (1997) "Issues and Opportunities in New Product Development: An Introduction to the Special Issue". *Journal of Marketing Research,* XXXIV, (February): 1-12.

Chapter XV

Knowledge Management— The Second Generation: Creating Competencies Within and Between Work Communities in the Competence Laboratory

Heli Ahonen, Yrjö Engeström and Jaakko Virkkunen
University of Helsinki, Finland

Knowledge management is in transition. The first theories of knowledge management used the knowledge-carrying individual as the unit of analysis and defined knowledge in terms of discrete skills that can be codified and measured. The key idea of the second-generation theories is that knowledge is embedded in and becomes constructed in collective practices. The challenge is to support the generation of new knowledge and competencies. In this chapter, we will develop further the second-generation competence-management ideas by applying cultural historical activity theory. We will present a new method, the Competence Laboratory, and report the results of its pilot use in a telephone company. With this method, a team of technicians managed to create new forms of joint learning and expand its network of cooperation for learning.

INTRODUCTION: KNOWLEDGE MANAGEMENT IN TRANSITION

In the latter half of the 1990s, knowledge management has become arguably the most dynamic issue in literature on management and organizations. The important books by Nonaka and Takeuchi (1995) and Leonard-Barton (1995) were followed by a number of others, including those by Allee (1997), Boisot (1998), Choo (1998), Davenport & Prusak (1998), von Krogh & Roos (1996) von Krogh, Roos & Klein (1998), Myers (1996), Ruggles (1996), and Sanchez & Heene (1997). The key message of these works is that "the only sustainable advantage a firm has comes from what it collectively knows, how efficiently it uses what it knows, and how readily it acquires and uses new knowledge" (Davenport & Prusak, 1998, p. xv).

An important predecessor of the present literature was the analysis of the core competencies of a firm presented by Prahalad and Hamel (1990; Hamel & Prahalad, 1994). Core competencies are well-defined bundles of skills and technologies that enable a company to generate innovative products. Core competencies are often broken into sets of specific component skills. This easily leads to long, static lists of skills. Other standard implementations of knowledge management have been various techniques of knowledge and competence mapping and the creation of large company-wide databases or knowledge repositories. These, too, tend to become schemes of classification and storage, which do not solve "the problem of providing incentives for people to part with treasured proprietary knowledge, such as sales hints and product ideas" (Lillrank, 1998, p. 3). Finally, the first wave of knowledge management includes attempts to codify and measure the overall knowledge assets of a company, to be included in a "balanced scorecard" or other such framework of accounting for the "intellectual capital" of the firm (Edvinsson & Malone, 1997; Stewart, 1997; Sveiby, 1997).

Allee (1997, p. 218) aptly summarizes the current situation in knowledge management:

> "We cannot solve our Knowledge Era questions with design approaches that came out of Information Age thinking. The current state of practice in 'knowledge mapping' is cumbersome at best. In worst case situations, people are spending much time and resources in an exercise in futility. They lose sight of the self-organizing capability of knowledge. When we don't understand knowledge as a system, we often just get in the way."

The above-mentioned attempts and techniques may be categorized as examples of the first generation of knowledge management. The first generation is largely characterized by (a) using the knowledge-carrying individual as the unit for mapping and enhancing knowledge; (b) defining knowledge as discrete skills or assets that exist, or are required, in the company and can be identified, codified and measured; and (c) using an external, outsider's "objective" point of view in analyzing knowledge and competence. The limits of this stance are becoming increasingly obvious as the life cycles of products and technology become shorter.

The key idea of the second generation is that knowledge is embedded and constructed in collective practices. As Brown and Duguid (1998, p. 2) put it, this leads us "to attend less to the things people apparently know, the information they possess, than to what they actually do—to their work practices." These practices include communication where knowledge is articulated, represented and transferred by means of talk, text, etc. Accordingly, a number of management theorists involved in the construction of the second-generation knowledge management have taken up Lave's and Wenger's (1991) idea of using communities of practice as the prime unit for analyzing knowledge and learning (Allee, 1997, p. 218-219; Choo, 1998, p. 118; Davenport & Prusak, 1998, p. 38-39).

Communities of practice are characterized by mutual engagement, joint enterprise, and shared repertoire (Wenger, 1998, p. 73). Boland and Tenkasi (1995) have proposed a more open concept of communities of knowing, which they relate to Hesse's (1974) idea of a knowledge net. According to them, "it is through the dynamic interactions between such communities that new configurations of the knowledge net emerge by creating new meanings, new linguistic routines, and new knowledge. ... The creation of new knowledge in an organization ... is often the result of an open system transformation of that organization's communities of knowing as they question and revise routines and create new processes and relationships among themselves" (op.cit. p. 352). This idea fits with the finding that informal networks of experts and key users are often decisive for the emergence and successful development of innovations (von Hippel, 1988). The concept of "ba" recently introduced by Nonaka and Konno (1998) is also closely related to the notions of knowledge net and community of knowing. These practice-based ideas are all connected to an emphasis on cycles of knowledge creation (Nonaka & Takeuchi, 1995). Indeed, the central challenge of the second-generation knowledge management is to understand the expansive development of activities and the creation of new knowledge and competencies.

Figure 1 summarizes the two generations of knowledge management. Obviously, a transition to the second generation does not imply abandoning the tools developed in the first generation— it is a stepwise shift in emphasis and interest rather than an abrupt break.

Figure 1: Two Generations of Knowledge Management

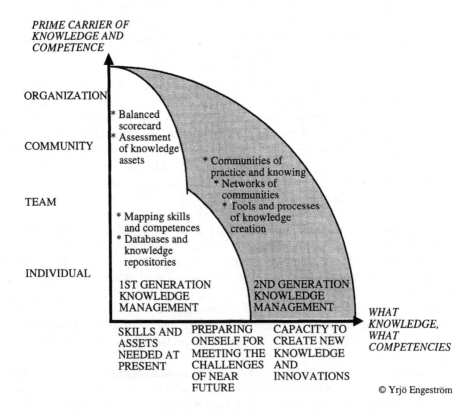

© Yrjö Engeström

COMPETENCE AS A HISTORICALLY CHANGING PHENOMENON

It is a paradox that in the midst of the knowledge management hype and the discussion on the knowledge society, we have few analyses of the historical changes of the quality and form of competencies and work-related knowledge. The task of managing knowledge and competencies is different in different historical forms of work, and the challenge of managing knowledge within one historical type of activity differs from the challenge of navigating the transformation of an activity from one historical form to another. As a tentative basis for historically oriented analysis of competencies, we suggest a general chart of the field of transformation in the organization of work (Figure 2). The chart depicts a succession of historical forms of work from craft production to mass production, to process enhancement/lean production, to mass customization, and to innovation driven co-configuration. Each of these ideal-typical modes is driven by its own central object and motive: from tradition and novelty to commodity, to quality, to precision, to customer intelligent products and services (see Victor & Boynton, 1998).

The chart indicates also two dimensions that are crucial in the strategic decisions faced within each of the ideal-typical modes of production and that also shape the community structure related to the form of the work. The vertical axis in Figure 2

Figure 2. Historical Ideal Types of Production (Engeström, 1999, p. 106)

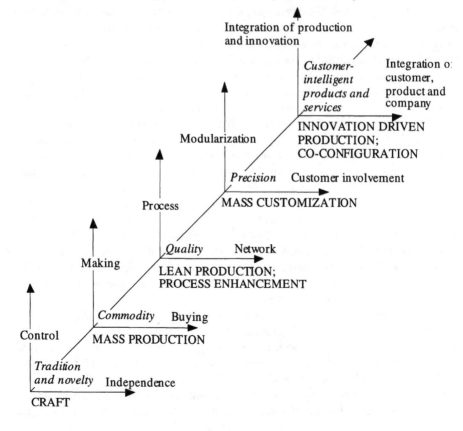

represents internal orientation, the horizontal axis external. In craft production, these two dimensions are condensed in the tension between control and independence. In mass production, the tension builds between making and buying. In lean production, the dimensions are process development and network development. In mass customization, they are modularization and customer involvement. Finally, in co-configuration the internal orientation means the integration of production and innovation inside the company, while the external orientation means the integration of the customer, product, suppliers, and company. While both the dimensions are necessary and mutually dependent in each mode, there is an inherent tension between the two dimensions of each pair.

The transition from one form of work to another is triggered by a contradiction between the needs and possibilities for creating use values for customers and the limitations of the existing form of work. In each transformation, the historically accumulated knowledge of the previous phase is used in a new way to build a qualitatively new type of activity by developing new tools. The transition from craft work to mass production is based on the articulation of the craft worker's knowledge into technical standards, work standards and production process models. These "secondary tools" are used to rationalize and manage the sequentially organized production process. The transition from mass production to process enhancement work is triggered by the need and possibility for low production costs, high quality and greater flexibility, all at the same time. The recourses for this transition are based on the work standards and the production process models created for mass production. The work is so reorganized that the workers use these secondary tools for developing the work-form incrementally (Adler & Borys 1996). They shift repeatedly from the productive work to "secondary work:" a joint analysis of production problems and then experimenting with new arrangements and solutions to eliminate disturbances, waste and quality problems (Hirshhorn, 1986, p. 100). In process enhancement, the functions and processes of the organization become linked to form a well-coordinated whole. In order to accomplish this the actors representing the different processes need a common vision of the future of their activity.

The third transition from process enhancement to mass customization work is triggered by the contradiction between the diversity of customer needs and the rigid product structure. The architectural knowledge of the connections and interdependencies of the different processes, won in the process enhancement, are used to create a qualitatively new form of the activity. The product and the production process are divided into combinable modules in order to make it possible to produce a variety of individualized products without losing the economies of scale of mass production (Pine, 1993). A connecting hub for configuring the relations of the modules is created, and the production is organized into a flexible network of processes. This flexible form of activity would not be possible without the tools and competencies created in process enhancement and the broadening of the workers' horizon from their respective functional tasks to a joint responsibility of serving the customer.

A new form of work based on mass customization is emerging in the medical and software industries. Victor and Boynton call this co-configuration work. The need for this type of work arises from the contradiction between the rapid technological development and the fixed form of the products. Instead of delivering a product, the qualities of which are fully determined by the present-day technology and understanding, the producer and the user engage in a sustaining co-operative learning process. The central medium of the joint learning is the reconfiguration and refinement of the product. An important element in the co-configuration work is the customer intelligence, cumulative real time information about the use and functioning of the product.

Not only are the competencies qualitatively different in different forms of work, but they are also produced in different ways. The ideal-typical form of learning craft work is the apprenticeship system, learning the work by participating in it. The ideal-typical way of learning mass-production work is job training. The competencies in the process enhancement work are created, to a great extent, by the constant co-operative analysis of the problems in the production process as well as developing and experimenting with new solutions in the quality circles.

The theory of the historical development of forms of work gives us an interesting perspective also to the present discussion on competence management. Many of the first generation competence-management methods are developed for the mass-production type of work. The new ideas of the communities of practice and situated learning presented by Lave and Wenger (1991) clearly contain elements that are compatible with the new type of learning and competence development needed in the process-enhancement and mass-customization work. However, more than that, they contain critique of the forms of competence management typical to mass production from the point of view of craft work. The apprenticeship and learning by participating in the work community's activity fairly well depict the way craft work is learned, but do not open perspectives for managing knowledge and competencies in the conditions of rapid technological change. The concept of a community of practice is a step forward from the atomistic, mechanistic and individualistic way of understanding competence, in the regard that it focuses attention to the systemic, situational and interrelated nature of competencies. It is, however, too static to provide us with tools to understand change and transformation of work and competencies. The concept of activity developed in the cultural historical activity theory initiated by L. Vygotsky (1978) and A. N. Leont'ev (1978; 1981; see also Engeström 1987; Engeström et al., 1999) comprises the important insights brought into the discussion with the concept of community of practice, yet giving us better understanding of the change and development of work practices.

A NETWORK OF ACTIVITY SYSTEMS AS UNIT OF ANALYSIS IN KNOWLEDGE AND COMPETENCE DEVELOPMENT

The concept of activity is based on a systemic understanding of life processes. According to A. N. Leont'ev (1978), the fundamental unit of life process is the organism's active interaction with its environment. Activity is not "what an organism does"; rather the organism consists in its activity. Activity is the mode of existence by which the organisms establish themselves as subjects of their life processes. The subject and the object of activity only come into being in the life process as two, interrelated, complementary perspectives on a developing system of subject-activity-object (Fichtner, 1998). The use and systematic manufacture of tools has created a fundamental qualitative change in the form of life activity and its development. The phylogenetically given form of the subject-activity-object interaction has been replaced by the culturally mediated activity systems of a human society. The accumulating information that renders the expedient functioning and reproduction of the system possible is embodied, not in genes, but in cultural artifacts like tools, social institutions and language and is transmitted to new individuals in a process of socialization and education[1].

An activity system comprises the individual practitioner, the colleagues and coworkers of the workplace community, the conceptual and practical tools, and the shared objects of activity as a unified, dynamic whole (Figure 3). The "wholeness" of the system means that its elements are not mechanically assembled together but develop and coevolve complementarily in their mutual relations[2].

Figure 3. The General Model of an Activity System (Engeström, 1987, p. 78)

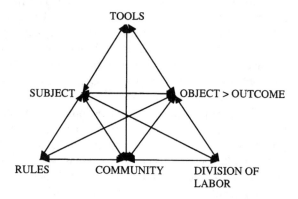

The model in Figure 3 reveals, as the decisive feature, the multiple mediations in an activity. Interaction between the subject and the object is mediated by instruments including symbols and representations of various kinds as well as the less visible social mediators of the activity—rules, community and division of labor. The activity system is much more robust and competent than any of its individual members. The cultural mediators of the activity stabilize the system. On the other hand, the different elements are in constant interaction in the process of activity and keep changing and transforming each other. The activity system incessantly reconstructs itself (Engeström, 1991, 12).

The historically evolved activity system and the material and immaterial artifacts used in the joint activity bear the accumulated knowledge of generations of humans involved in that activity. In the historical development of the activity, an increasing number of the operations needed to produce the outcome have been delegated to the artifacts and tools used in the activity (Latour, 1994). This delegation of operations to artifacts functions in the same way as the automation of human operations during extended practice: the execution and control of operations become automatic and the capacity for conscious attention is freed to other things. Delegation of operations to tools frees the practitioners' capacity to the mastering of large objects of activity and to the development of the activity system. The actor only becomes conscious of the delegated operations and the knowledge inherent in the mediating artifacts when there is a disturbance in the process.

Individuals who join in the activity have to internalize the use and meaning of the tools and the forms of social interaction of the activity. The learning of the newcomer is, however, not confined to the internalization of the existing knowledge and skills. The culturally inherited tools and ideas are always, in some respects, insufficient and incomplete. The object of the activity and the conditions of performing it also change, so that new ways of using the tools and new solutions are needed. A tool always implies more versatile possible uses than the original function for which it was designed and bears possibilities that exceed the needs of the task at hand. The practitioners experiment with new uses of the tools and develop them to meet new requirements. The evolving inner contradictions of the activity system create a motive and set an agenda for this development.

The concept of an activity system seems, at first sight, to be just another way of describing the communities of practice. There is, however, an important theoretical difference between the concepts. The defining characteristic of an activity is not the community, but the object of the activity, which is the societal motive of the activity and connects it to other activities. The analysis of the internal complementary relationships of the elements of the activity system and the internal contradictions within it helps us understand the change and development of an activity system and the formation of new communities of practice.

An activity system is always a node in a network of activities. The basic network of different types of activities around any activity system consists of the object or client activity, tool producing activity, subject-producing activity, such as training, and rule producing activity, such as management or financing. Generally, there are always present culturally more advanced forms of the same activity.

According to Wartofsky (1979), primary artifacts are those directly used in production; secondary artifacts are those used in the preservation and transmission of the acquired skills or models of action or praxis by which this production is carried out. The secondary artifacts are, therefore, representations of such modes of action. They are often also tools used in the tool-, subject- and rule-producing activities which mediate the relationships between the activity systems.

The degree of communication between actors within an activity system and between actors in the network of activities varies. In the routinely coordinated activity of business-as-usual, each actor can focus on the objects of his actions only. In a disturbance situation,

Figure 4. The Basic Network of Human Activity Systems (Engeström, 1987, p. 89).

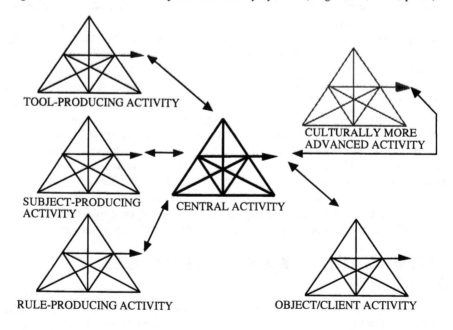

the solving of the problem can become a common concern and a temporary common object for the actors' actions. The common problem solving can, however, lead the actors to see the interrelatedness of their activities and to form an expanded object of their joint activity. When this happens, and the actors begin to develop the form of their mutual exchange and cooperation correspondingly, we can say that the actors in the activity or the network have become a self-conscious, competence developing community.

CHANGING EMBEDDED COMPETENCE: EXPANSIVE LEARNING

Thus far the main focus in the discussion of the embedded and socially constructed nature of competence has been in explaining how an individual learns and masters his or her work and becomes a member of the community. Less has been said of how the work communities and their work practices develop and how new practices are being created. According to the cultural historical activity theory, the development of an activity system is set into motion by inner contradictions within the system, that make it impossible for the subject to continue the historically evolved form of subject-activity-object interaction. The *primary contradiction* within the activity system, which leads to constant changes in it, is created by the double role of its elements as parts of a specific activity system, in which they have a use value, while being also, at the same time, elements in the system of market exchange, where they have a certain exchange value as commodities (Engeström, 1987, 82-92).

In its development, an activity system moves from "business-as-usual" to an unarticulated "need state" and then to a stage of increasingly acute inner tensions. The historical changes of the elements of the activity system can lead to *secondary contradictions* between the elements of the system. These contradictions cause failures, conflicts and tensions in the daily activity, but also prompt individual innovative attempts for overcoming the limitations of the present organization of the activity. At some point, the increasing amount of problems leads to conscious efforts to analyze the causes of the problems and to find a new structure for the activity. In the midst of regressive and evasive attempts to solve the problems, there emerges a novel "germ cell" idea of a new form of the activity that promises to solve the aggravated inner contradictions of the present system. The idea, or prototypic new solution, gains momentum and is turned into a model. The model is enriched by designing corresponding tools and patterns of interaction. The new model is then implemented in practice producing new conflicts between the designed new ways and customary old ways of working. By working through these *tertiary* conflicts, the designed or given new model is replaced by the created new model, firmly grounded in practice (Engeström, 1992, 17-18). The change of the activity, however, leads to *quaternary conflicts* between the central activity and the neighboring activities.

The idealized and simplified phases of a developmental cycle are depicted in Figure 5. The two-headed arrows signify the iterative, nonlinear character of the process.

LEARNING ACTIVITY AND THE CHANGE LABORATORY

The forms of learning and creating competence have changed and developed along the historical development of the forms of work. Joint *learning activity* is a new, emerging

Figure 5. Phases of a Cycle of Expansive Learning (Engeström, 1987, p.189)

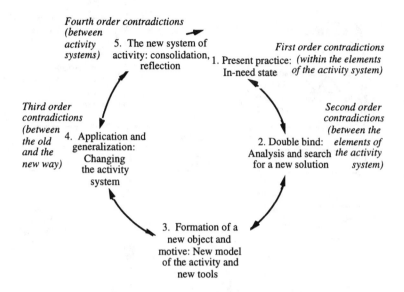

form of learning and competence development (Engeström 1987, p., 131-137). Those involved in an joint activity take, temporarily, distance from their daily work and engage in a related, but separate activity, the object of which is to identify the developmental contradictions in their present system of work activity and to develop co-operatively a new form of that activity, in which the contradictions of the present form have been overcome.

As any activity, learning activity proceeds only through individuals' coordinated actions. The specific learning actions that are needed comprise the questioning of the present practices, analyzing the historical causes and present day manifestations of the problems, generating a new model for the activity, analyzing that proposed new model, concretizing the model and planning concrete implements and solutions for its realization, implementing the new form experimentally, analyzing the results, as well as consolidating and spreading the new form of activity. The outcome of the learning activity is not just new knowledge or understanding, but a new form of the practical activity, new collective competence.

To realize the different learning actions, the practitioners need special tools. The Change Laboratory, which is an activity-theory-based intervention method for collective learning and developing work practices, is designed for providing such tools. The laboratory is a room or space in the vicinity of the daily work, in which there is a wide variety of instruments for analyzing disturbances and bottlenecks in the prevailing work practices and for constructing new models and tools for the work activity (Engeström & al., 1996). The important tools are a 3x3 set of wallboards for representing the work activity, and video equipment. Additional tools include a reference library, databases and statistical data about the operation and performance (Figure 6).

The vertical dimension on the wallboard represents the historical change of the

Figure 6. Prototypical Layout of the Change Laboratory Room (Engeström & al., 1996, p.11)

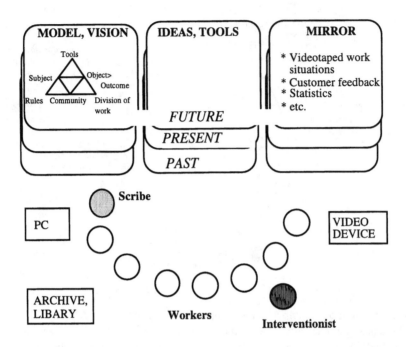

activity from its past form through the present form to its future. The horizontal dimension of the wallboards represents different levels of abstraction and theoretical generalization of visualizations of the activity. At one end, the mirror surface is used to represent and examine the daily work, particularly problem situations and disturbances but also novel, innovative solutions. Videotaped work episodes as well as case histories, interviews, customers' comments and performance indicators, among others, are used in the mirror to help workers observe and analyze their work routines.

At the other end, the Model/Vision surface is used for modeling the activity. The triangular model of the activity system (Figure 3) is used to analyze the interconnectedness of the different components of the activity system. The roots of recurrent disturbances and problems occurring in daily work are traced and conceptualized as inner contradictions of the activity system. The model is also used to analyze the potential for change and to construct a visionary model for the form of the activity in the future. The model of the network of activities (Figure 4) is used to analyze the relationships between the central activity and other activities. The model of the cycle of expansive development of an activity (Figure 5) is used to conceptualize the ongoing historical change in the activity and the nature of the current phase of development.

The third surface in the middle is reserved for ideas and tools. Intermediate tools such as schedules, flowcharts, conceptual distinctions, layout diagrams, organizational diagrams, formulas for calculating costs, and the like, are used for analyzing specific aspects of the activity. The boards are also used for designing new tools and forms of interaction for the activity. As the participants move between the experiential mirror and the theoretical model, they also produce partial solutions and ideas to be experimented with, tested and used as components in the construction of a new model of the activity. These ideas are represented on the "Ideas, Tools" surface.

A natural work unit, or team, uses the laboratory, initially, with the help of an interventionist. The work in the Change Laboratory typically starts from the mirror of the present problems. It then moves to trace the roots of current problems by mirroring changes and experiences from the past and by modeling the past activity system. The work then proceeds to modeling the phase of development of the activity using the model of the development cycle and the current practice and its inner contradictions with the help of the triangular model of activity system. These models enable the participants to focus their efforts on the essential source of trouble, depicted as an inner contradiction in the system. The next step is the envisioning of the future model of the activity and concretizing it by designing new tools and partial solutions. Subsequently, the stepwise implementation of the new vision is planned and monitored in the Change Laboratory. The process typically consists of five to ten two-hour meetings once a week; of one four-week period of experimentation with the new tools and forms of interaction created in the laboratory; and of a follow up meeting. Later on, the laboratory is used, albeit less intensively, for the constant improvement of work practices and, occasionally, again for planning a major change.

The Competence Laboratory is a modification of the Change Laboratory especially planned for developing a work team's or unit's way of learning as well as sustaining and developing its collective competence. A work team or unit reveals in the laboratory the typical ruptures and disturbances in the activity that tell about the deficiencies in its joint mastery and learning. The members of the team analyzed the causes of these deficiencies as contradictions within their own activity system and in its relations to the related activities, and begin to develop a new form for their activity and new ways of joint learning in the network of activities. In this process the practitioners learn to understand the interrelations between the activities, and to identify specific needs for further learning: and build a network of interrelated actors into a community consciously developing its knowledge and competence.

THE COMPETENCE LABORATORY OF THE PC TEAM IN THE TELEPHONE CORPORATION

Telephone Corporation (TC) is a large provider of telecommunications services in Finland. It provides local, long distance, international and GSM mobile calls, data transmission and the planning and implementation of tailored business telecommunications solutions.

In order to meet the increasing competition, the TC had started in 1998 a competence project. As part of this project, the company decided to use, tentatively, the Competence Laboratory Method to establish a second-generation knowledge management tool for increasing at the grassroots-level working communities, the capacity to produce innovations and new knowledge.

The PC Team

The Telephone Corporation began to offer new digital network connections for PCs for private households in the early 1990s primarily to facilitate the use of the Internet. The new network technology increases remarkably the capacity of telephone lines to transmit data. To render this new service, the technicians installing the PC connections have to master both the installation of traditional telephone connections, the new digital network technology and PCs. After the first installations, the TC invited technicians, who were willing to study these technologies and to participate in the development of the new service, to form a new PC Team. The demand for new digital network connections for PCs increased rapidly in the middle of the 1990s. TC trained more technicians and established regional PC installation teams. Some members of the PC Team were transferred to these regional teams to work with the newly hired technicians and to train them. The kernel of the original team was responsible for installing the particularly demanding digital network connections for PCs, maintaining the digital network connections for PCs, and learning the new technologies of the area.

At the time of the Competence Laboratory project, in spring 1999, the PC Team consisted of 15 PC technicians, three dispatchers to allocate jobs ordered by customers to the technicians, and a team leader. The Competence Laboratory process in the PC Team comprised five consecutive weekly meetings of two hours in February to March 1999. A follow up and evaluation meeting was held about two months later. In this process, the team evaluated its present activity system and process of work, created new solutions and a vision of the proximal development for the team's activity and a number of new ways of enhancing the team's learning. The team also made a concrete plan with a time schedule to carry out the intended changes in its activity.

The first author of this chapter led the Competence Laboratory process. She videotaped all the meetings and collected all the documents and materials used or produced during the process. In the following paragraphs, we shall describe concisely the six meetings of the Competence Laboratory on the basis of this material. In selecting the material we have applied the following criteria. First, we are reporting the parts of the discussions that questioned the present practices, involved identification of contradictions in the group's activity and dealt with alternatives to overcome the contradictions. Second, we are reporting those created solutions that effect changes in the group's way of maintaining and developing its competence, and how the group produced these solutions. Third, we have selected the material for the reader to see, how the three different representational tools of the laboratory: the models-, the mirror- and the ideas/tools-surfaces were used. The following description is best understood as a first analysis of the process of a small social experiment that is intended more for testing and developing further the theoretical ideas and the intervention method than for proving a point.

The First Competence Laboratory Meeting:
Questioning the Present Practice

Before the first meeting, the researcher shadowed with a video camera one of the technicians, while he was installing a digital network connection for PCs, and interviewed him during that day. She also interviewed the customer. In the first Competence Laboratory meeting, this authentic installing case was used as a mirror of the present installation practice. It focused the discussion right away on the functioning capacity of the whole network, instead of the skills of an individual technician. The PC technician, whose work the case concerned, told the team openly and realistically about how he had proceeded and what he had intended and thought at each phase of the work. His anticipations, the preparations he had made, the surprises and problems he had met as well as his solutions to overcome them – for instance contacting colleagues by mobile phone – were written down on the Ideas/Tools-board by the scribe of the meeting. It became obvious, that part of the team's competence was its ability to overcome the unexpected problems met in the field by instantly accessing each other's knowledge and tools through informal communication. Various problems in cooperation and process logistics, as well as new ideas to solve them, were brought up and written down on the boards during the lively discussion generated by the case.

The point of view was then transferred to the customer's experience of the service: the team listened to a customer interview conducted by researchers a few days after the installation job. The customer's remarks about the inconsistent information she had received from the person who sold the product and the person who arranged the installation, the lags in the delivery and the need for further guidance in using the new PC, made the team reflect on the division of work and ruptures in coordination of actions within the service network. The members of the team asked, for instance, to whom in the service network the economically unfeasible task of guiding the customer in PC matters should belong. This question brought up, for the first time in the team discussion, the vagueness of the team's task.

More ideas to develop the process and cooperation were presented and written down. The team leader could start to implement some of the proposed changes immediately after the meeting. For the next meeting, the team members agreed to prepare cases dealing with maintenance work.

The Second Competence Laboratory Meeting: Analyzing the Causes of the Problems

The purpose of the second meeting was to examine why problems like the ones identified in the installation case occur in the technicians' work. The researcher introduced the general model of work activity (see Figure 3) as an intellectual tool for analyzing the systemic causes of the problems of the daily work. The models of the activity systems of the technician and the dispatcher who had worked in the installation case were drafted on the board. In the discussion, the team noted that both the technician and the dispatcher had difficulties in mastering their respective tasks owing to mainly two reasons: First, the tools and methods for managing knowledge and for communicating, as well as cooperation within the network of related activities, were insufficient in view of the complicated task. Second, the rules intended to direct the team members' work were too vague.

To further analyze the causes of the problems and to introduce the time perspective, the researcher initiated a discussion of what the installation work used to be like, when the PC service was first started, and how the activity had changed since then. One technician told a case story from that time to inspire the recalling process. The models of the activity system, earlier drafted on the board, were complemented with remarks about those important changes in the history of the installation activity that the team now had discovered. In the beginning, although the job had been just to connect the PC to the telephone network, the technicians had had to orient themselves also to the computers.

This expansion of the technicians' competence was possible only because the formerly separate telephone installing, maintenance and network-linkage functions had been merged organizationally, a few years earlier. The competence of these multi-skilled technicians could then be expanded further with the PC and digital network connection technology know-how.

The analysis of the present work practice was then continued by a detailed case history of the team's maintenance work: fixing an installation error made by a technician of a regional team. A map of the process was drafted on the Mirror-board, and the problems of the process and new ideas were discussed and written down. The team criticized the way the PC installation work had been transferred to the regional teams ("biting off more than they could chew") without making sure that there was enough competent staff in the regional teams. The lack of competence in the regional teams had created extra maintenance work for the team. They had also had to open an informal "help desk" for the regional colleagues, which, in turn, had diminished the time available for them to study the coming next generation technology.

The Third Competence Laboratory Meeting: Defining Tasks to Develop the Team's Service Concept and Work Practices

In the first two laboratory meetings, it had become clear that the PC Team had four separate objects of work: 1) participating in the expanding PC business by installing PC products; 2) PC-connections quality maintenance by repairing complicated faults; 3) distributing competence by training, making instructions and offering "help desk" to the regional technicians; and 4) seizing on new network connection technologies for PCs and new products for the other technicians.

The researcher pointed out that these objects of activity seemed to be in conflict with each other and to compete for the team's limited resources. The team agreed and debated whether the amount of work related to the various objects would, in the future, be likely to increase or decrease. The arguments for both estimates were written down on the board "Ideas, Tools." The general conclusion was that participation in the installation business ("the basic activity") should gradually diminish, thus freeing the team's time for developing its new competence as well as for transferring it further to the regional teams. That would make the demanding maintenance work more efficient and reduce the number of recurring faults. This general scenario contradicted, however, the goals set for the team, because it would reduce the profit created by the team: "Who would allow us to work at a loss?"

The maintenance-work case had revealed shortages in the competence of the service network, especially in the regional teams, and in the notification from the customers with their digital network connection for PC out of order. In the discussion, the team focused especially on the problems of cooperation with the Switching Operator Team and with the management. The Switching Operator Team is an important specialist partner for the team, but cooperation with it was found to be insufficient: "The meetings with the Switching Operator Team are too infrequent, new problems are already at hand before the old ones become solved and the team gets informed about the solutions". From the management, the team expected rules that would clarify its task and objectives. If the team used less time on a single customer, more customers could be served, but the customer-satisfaction rates would definitely drop. On the other hand, "a difficult case is always an opportunity to learn, one wouldn't like to let it go unfinished, even if it took hours".

The team concluded that in order to improve the quality and profitability of service, the customer should get his problem taken care of by one house call. One reason why the technicians spent much time at a customer's was the lack of standardization of the computer cards for the digital network connection. Some of the cards were difficult to fit in the PCs, and the team members questioned how much time a technician should use in trying to do it. The second conclusion was that the dispatchers had to acquire better understanding of the technicians' and the partners' work, in order to better allocate the job assignments to the right persons.

At the end of the third meeting, the researcher asked the team to collect observations about the changes that had occurred in the various elements of the activity system (see Figure 3) of the PC installation in the 1990s, in order to find out whether they could learn from their experiences something of value in meeting the present challenges. One of the team members noted that the team should have started training for the next generation technology earlier "so that we'd not ended up practicing at the customer's." Another team member added: "We should purchase the measuring instruments needed for the installations of the next-generation technology after getting next-generation technology maintenance jobs." One of the members of the team made a more general remark that, at the beginning of the digital installation work, it was possible for the team to spend time for learning because there was not yet much maintenance or help-desk work. "We used to go through experiences immediately in the team. Now everyone is busy and working more on his own." A technician summed up the team's main concerns about learning: "If we have no time to learn the new things, we—and the TC—are stuck on the present level of competence, and cannot support the learning of the other teams, later on."

The researcher asked the team members to organize assignment groups for preparing solutions to the four development issues that were written down during the discussions in this meeting: 1) How could the customer get the digital network connection and PC problems solved during one technician's house call, and what are the limits to spending the technician's work time at one customer's? 2) What training do the dispatchers need, and how should it be arranged? 3) What could be done to enhance the cooperation for learning with the Switching Operator Team? 4) How should the team seize on the next-generation network technology installation and maintenance competence?

The Fourth Competence Laboratory Meeting:
Searching for the New Solutions to the Work Practice

The researcher presented a model of the developmental cycle of the PC Team's work practice in the 1990s, which she had prepared on the basis of the discussion on the changes in the team's work. The object of the team's work had expanded remarkably in four years' time. It included now the whole process from installing to maintenance and from studying new technology to transferring the knowledge to others. Because of the many new tasks and increased workload, the team had lost the way of collective learning it had had in the beginning of its work. Now, under the pressures of daily work, each member of the team took responsibility only for his own learning. The expansion of the object of the team's work had also changed the team's mission to the extent that it needed re-clarification. The team felt that they should put more emphasis on the new competence in TC and less on the short-term business goals.

Much of the meeting was spent to create and refine solutions to the identified development problems. An assignment group presented a detailed proposal of how to limit the technician's responsibility and work in case the customer had a PC computer card which was difficult to install. The team decided also to discuss with the management the rules of using PC cards of different prices.

The second development issue was the dispatchers' need for training. The team stated right away that traditional courses could not provide a solution. The dispatcher's essential competence was based on understanding the work of the other actors in the service network and the information given them in professional terms. The team recognized that the dispatchers gather understanding on the technicians' work by following up their jobs during the day. It was decided that the dispatchers make excursions to the neighboring units in the organization, and to the parallel teams delivering PC service to business customers, and bring the acquired knowledge to the team. The PC Team proposed that a process-development group be put together with the representatives of the sales and marketing function as well as the switching operators.

The Fifth Competence Laboratory Meeting: Searching for the New Solutions to the Work Practice and Creating a Vision for the Team's Future Activity

The team leader had talked with a colleague in the Switching Operators' Team and learned that they would be willing to cooperate for enhancing mutual learning on the basis of the PC Teams initiative (the third development issue).

The proposal of the assignment group of how the next-generation technology and work should be acquired by the team (the fourth development issue) generated a lively debate. The general conclusion was that there would be, in fact, few new things the team had to learn to be able to do the next-generation technology installations. The essential learning challenge seemed to be the use of the new measuring instruments needed in these installations. The team members responsible for learning first the next generation technology installation were asked to collect information about alternative measuring instruments and to evaluate the training possibilities. The team concluded that it is not useful to train the whole team before the demand of the next-generation technology products really starts growing. One of the team members proposed that each technician join one of the team's three experts in their performing next generation technology installing jobs.

The researcher drew a summary of the team's decisions. After that, she drafted a vision of the team's future work practice by placing all the designed new solutions in the model of the team's activity on the Model/Future-board. The most important outcome of the team's work would be the efficient creation and transfer of new competencies within the network of the teams doing the installation and maintenance of the digital network connections for PCs and the next generation technology connections. The economic goal would, then, be the long-term profitability of this activity for the TC. The team suggested that, in addition to those learning tools developed earlier in the Competence Laboratory, they still needed more tools for efficient mastering of the required learning. The team discussed also the rules of learning. They found that the rules applied to customer service were also the most important ones from the perspective of learning. These rules determine how much time the team members can spend on different tasks, and they also standardize the quality of service. The team's vision of its future activity system is presented in Figure 7.

Figure 7. The PC Team's Vision of the Future Form of its Activity

TOOLS
1) weekly team meetings
2) team meetings in the Competence Laboratory two-three times a
   year for improving work practices
3) methods of learning from others: excursions, process groups
   examining actual service cases together, mutual sharing of
   information
4) keeping eyes and ears open
5) the models for seizing on new issues: new technology inquires
   group & training the rest of the team
6) courses
7) the team's developmental projects: assignment group for PC-cards
   and learning cooperation with the switching operators

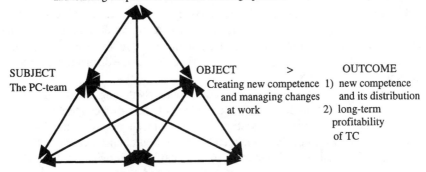

SUBJECT
The PC-team

OBJECT   >   OUTCOME
Creating new competence 1) new competence
and managing changes   and its distribution
at work   2) long-term
                            profitability
                            of TC

RULES
* open information
* criteria for
  assessing
  efficiency of
  team's
  learning
* rules of customer
  service deemed as
  the most important

COMMUNITY
* switching operators
* product development unit
* sales and marketing
* Multimedia Center
* Business Customer
  Services
* management, supervisors

DIVISION OF LABOR
* each team member has a
  special responsibility for
  coordinating and developing
  one aspect of the team's work
* the team sets ad hoc persons/
  groups to make inquiries of
  various things for the team
* each team member is
  responsible for reflecting his/
  her personal development;
  the team leader purchases the
  training

The Follow-up Meeting: Evaluating Changes in the Work Practice

In the follow-up meeting, the team member who had been responsible for implementing each change gave a short report about what had been done and achieved. The team commented on the positive and negative aspects of the change. After this, the team discussed the next steps and prepared a plan for future action.

The team members who were responsible for finding solutions to the problem of the lack of standardization of the digital network connections had defined team rules for using the various digital network connection cards and produced a form for a systematic follow-up of the problems met in the practice. The group had discussed with the salespersons and had realized that many of the problems were caused by the lack of feedback between the sales department and the team. They agreed with the sales unit to intensify their mutual cooperation. The group had also contacted the key supplier of the cards about the problems. The supplier had offered to instruct and train the team. In the near future, the team would hold a meeting in order to generate ideas for a "guidebook" or a checklist for cards installation.

One of the three dispatchers had carried out the study plan that had been prepared for the dispatchers in the fourth meeting. He reported about the valuable tutoring he had received from one of the team's technicians that updated his knowledge about the digital network connection for PC technology. He also told about his visits to colleagues in the digital network connection for PC service for business customers. The dispatcher explained how the Business Customers Team had organized the fault notification service. The colleagues' solution was obviously superior to the one the PC Team had, and this generated discussion about the possibilities of implementing those ideas in the team's work practice. The dispatcher had also recognized a well-functioning system for the follow up and analysis of repaired faults in the other team, which made the team question their own unsystematic practice. The first experiences from the dispatchers' study plan were positive. However, the team found it difficult to free the dispatcher from his regular duties for a day for study.

The first meetings with the representatives of the Switching Operator Team had been promising, since both parties had found the idea of increased cooperation for learning useful. However, it turned out that it is difficult to change the established form of cooperation. There are only few top specialists in the Switching Operator Team and, in the limited time frame, they preferred to support the staff of their own unit. The PC Team did not find out a way to change this situation, but decided to continue the discussion about possibilities to intensify the cooperation with the Switching Operator Team.

The next-generation technology inquiries group had gathered information about alternative measuring instruments and made a purchase proposal. They had also trained themselves in broad band technology and prepared rules for the next-generation technology installation practice. The first next-generation technology jobs were expected to come around in a few weeks, but, the team decided to stay with the original plan of not training the whole team for the time being, but only three months later when every technician would have had the opportunity of familiarizing themselves with the new instrument and there would be next-generation technology jobs available for several technicians.

COMPETENCE AS THE ABILITY TO MANAGE DEVELOPMENTAL CONTRADICTIONS OF THE ACTIVITY

Competence development is commonly viewed as an additive process: the need for new competencies is inferred from the discrepancy between the competencies needed in a task and the competencies already at an individual's disposal. This discrepancy is eliminated by adding to the individual's competencies by training. This view corresponds the task of securing individuals' competence at the present form of the activity. The Competence Laboratory experiment in the Telephone Company focused on preparing the knowledge and competencies that would be needed by the PC team and the network of actors in the near future. This perspective exposed a novel, more contradictory and dynamic view of competence.

In the Competence Laboratory meetings, the team members reflected repeatedly on the tensions between their different tasks and goals: business and service vs. learning; short-term results vs. long-term profitability and customer satisfaction. The PC Team's need and motive for developing its competence, the way of doing it, as well as the form of the created new competence, were shaped by these contradictions. When the team started its work, the contradiction between service and learning was not too prominent. The technicians could learn the installation work through trial and error in the first installing and maintenance jobs by sharing the problems and developing solutions together in frequent team discussions, and by monitoring developments in the field. The contradiction, however, became aggravated as the amount of installation work increased and necessitated the technicians to spend most of their time at the customer's. No longer did they have time for joint learning, as earlier. Each technician had to learn solutions by himself and had only occasionally an opportunity to carry face-to-face discussions about his problems and their possible solutions with his colleagues. For this reason, there was great pressure, in the weekly team meetings, to share all the experiences and to find solutions together.

The increasing workload had slowed down the team's learning. The PC Team, however, still saw as its most important task the creation and distribution of the knowledge and competence about the new network connection technologies for PCs in the TC. Shortly before the Competence Laboratory, the team leader had divided the team into groups of three. Each group was given the responsibility for developing one aspect of the team's work, for informing the team about any new developments in the area, and for collecting the area related ideas and feedback from the other team members. This constituted the first effort to develop the team's way of learning.

In the Competence Laboratory the team took two further steps. First, they began to rationalize their service work to free time for learning. For instance, they agreed upon new rules that reduced the time spent by the technicians at the customer's. This change, obviously, diminished the possibility for individual trial and error learning. Second, the team invented various ways of making learning more effective, for instance, by new forms of sharing and distributing knowledge between its members and cooperation partners. The study program for the dispatchers was one of these, the plan about the way of seizing on the next-generation technology and the search for new forms of cooperation with the switching operators were some of the others. These new forms of learning were based on the distributed responsibility for inquiring, and an effective mutual communication between the team members and the team and its cooperation partners.

The follow-up meeting revealed that the team had been developing further its ideas about the ways of learning. Resorting to a form for the follow up of the digital network connection cards for PCs, the team shifted its learning from individual, solitary problem solving at the customer's to a systematic joint analysis of the gathered data and to a systematic use of the acquired knowledge in the development of its work practices. This innovation clearly moved the team into the direction of a systematic, tool-mediated cooperative mode of learning (Virkkunen & Kuutti, in press). The aggravated contradiction between service work and learning was overcome by this retooling of the learning process.

The contradiction between service work and learning was also in part aggravated because of the openness of the situation: the team did not know when and how rapidly the next generation technology installation work load would increase. A central element in the attempts to solve the contradiction between service work and learning was the timing of the actions. The team had to match together the anticipated future development, the construction of the new activity system and the development of new competencies, and also master the complicated relations between these, in many respects uncertain, elements of the development of its activity.

Although the team was able to find new tools for mastering the contradiction between service work and learning, it failed to improve cooperation with the members of the Switching Operators Team, who were not ready and able to involve themselves in the process of creating competence cooperatively in the network of activities.

One prerequisite for overcoming the acute contradiction between installation service work and learning was that the developed new tools and practices were not merely tools for learning, but also contributed to the management of the service activity. The task of resolving the problems of the present practices, developing the form of the activity and creating new competence were intimately intermingled in the Competence Laboratory process. The process also clearly showed that the work tasks and the competence do not exist as separate entities.

Another aspect of the reframing and remediation that took place in the Competence Laboratory is the team members' new perspective and attitude to their work. In the beginning of the Competence Laboratory, the team took many problematic aspects of its work and the cooperation structures as given. At the end of the Competence Laboratory, these same aspects, for instance the variety of computer cards defined by the product development unit, were questioned more readily and seen as challenges to develop cooperation and to change the situation.

Many of the solutions the team produced in the Competence Laboratory were, in fact, new ways of securing the necessary information and learning. These solutions represent the second-order competence of maintaining and developing work competence. This second-order competence was associated with the expansion of the social contacts and cooperation relationships. The ideas of learning to learn and learning cooperation are frequently expressed in the competence maps typical of the first-generation knowledge management, but these important issues are projected to the individual level as social skills or learning skills. In the Competence Laboratory, the team solved concrete problems of learning and cooperation by creating new tools and new forms of cooperation. The process in which the team developed the new forms of learning was, to a great extent, also a process of building and expanding their work community. It seems that instead of just trying to identify communities of practice, or communities of knowing, we should focus more on analyzing the process in which a number of individual actors become a community, and analyze their different degrees of cooperation, as a community. The creation of common tools for joint learning clearly represents a high degree of being a community, which is only possible when the actors have a common object of activity.

An important question is, what made the above described remediation of the learning actions of the team possible. The integration of the development of the activity system, the new competencies and ways of learning would not have been possible had the team not seen its work in the time perspective, as historically changing, and had it not been able to analyze the historical change of its activity in concrete terms. This was made possible by employing the model of the development cycle of the activity and the triangular model of the activity system which was used to identify the central developmental contradictions. These models would not, however, have become intellectual tools for the team had they not had the concrete installation case-histories as mirrors that made it possible for them to look and analyze their daily work from an outsider's point of view.

ENDNOTES

1. Recently, several authors have tried to surpass the mechanistic view of organization and knowledge by applying Maturana's and Varela's biological theory of autopoetic systems (von Krogh & Roos, 1996). While developing a more systemic approach, these writers seem not to recognize the special, artifact mediated cultural form of human systems that are based on the use and systematic development of tools.
2. The concept of the object of the activity is pivotal in this theory. In management literature, it is customary to speak about objectives rather than objects of activity. The word "object" means "anything that is visible and tangible and relatively stabile in form; a thing, person, or matter to which thought or action is directed; the end toward which effort or action is directed; anything that may be apprehended intellectually" (Random House Compact Unabridged Dictionary, 1996, p 1335). The object of activity comprises all these meanings. "Object" rather than "objective" is used in activity theory to emphasize the opposition and interaction between subject and object—the object is, at the same time, both something psychologically and socially constructed, as an objective, and something existing independently of the actors' thoughts and intentions, as an object.

REFERENCES

Adler, P. S. & Borys, B. (1996). Two Types of Bureaucracy: Enabling and Coercive. *Administrative Science Quarterly*. vol 41. March 1996. Pp. 61-89.

Allee, V. (1997). *The knowledge evolution: Expanding organizational intelligence.* Boston: Butterworth-Heinemann.

Bateson, G., Jackson, D., Haley, J. & Weakland, J.H. (1972). Toward a theory of schitsofrenia. In G. Bateson, *Steps to an ecology of mind.* New York: Balantine Books.

Boisot, M. H. (1998). *Knowledge assets: Securing competitive advantage in the information economy.* Oxford: Oxford University Press.

Boland, R. J. & Tenkasi, R. V. (1995). Perspective Making and Perspective Taking in Communities of Knowing. *Organization Science. 4* (6), 350-372.

Brown, J. S. & Duguid, P. (1998). Invention, innovation, and organization. Manuscript submitted to Organization Science.

Choo, C. W. (1998). *The knowing organization: How organizations use information to construct meaning, create knowledge, and make decisions.* New York: Oxford University Press.

Davenport, T. H. & Prusak, L. (1998). *Working knowledge: How organizations manage what they know.* Boston: Harvard Business School Press.

Edvinsson, L. & Malone, M. S. (1997). *Intellectual capital: Realizing your company's true value by finding its hidden brainpower.* New York: Harper-Collins.

Engeström, Y. (1987). *Learning by expanding*. Helsinki: Orienta-konsultit.

Engeström, Y. (1991). Interactive Expertise. Studies in Distributed Working Intelligence. Helsinki: University of Helsinki. Department of Education. *Research Bulletin 83*.

Engeström, Y. (1999). From iron cages to webs on wind: Three theses on teams and learning at work. *Lifelong Learning in Europe*, 2(4), 101-110.

Engeström, Y., Miettinen, R. & Punamäki, R.-L. (1999). *Perspectives on Activity Theory*. Cambridge: Cambridge University Press.

Engeström,Y., Virkkunen, J., Helle, M., Pihlaja, J. & Poikela, R. (1996). Change Laboratory as a tool for transforming work. *Lifelong Learning in Europe, 1* (2), 10-17.

Fichtner. B. (1999). Activity revisited as an explanatory principle and as an object of study - Old limits and new perspectives. In Chaikling, S., Hedegard, M. & Jensen, U.J. (Eds.), *Activity Theory and Social Practice* (pp.51-65). Aarhus: Aarhus University Press.

Fruin, W. M. (1997). *Knowledge works: Managing intellectual capital at Toshiba*. New York: Oxford University Press.

Hamel, G. & Prahalad, C. K. (1994). *Competing for the future*. Boston: Harvard Business School Press.

Hesse, M. (1974). *The Structure of Scientific Inference*. Berkeley, CA: University of California Press.

von Hippel, E. (1988). *The sources of innovation*. New York: Oxford University Press.

Hirschhorn, L. (1986). *Beyond Mechanization*. Cambridge: The MIT Press.

von Krogh, G. & Roos, J. (Eds.) (1996). *Managing knowledge: Perspectives on cooperation and competition*. London: Sage.

von Krogh, G., Roos, J. & Kleine, D. (Eds.) (1998). *Knowing in Firms. Understanding, Managing and Measuring Knowledge*. London: Sage.

Lave, J. & Wenger, E. (1991). *Situated learning: Legitimate peripheral participation*. Cambridge: Cambridge University Press.

Leonard-Barton, D. (1995). *Wellsprings of knowledge: Building and sustaining the sources of innovation*. Boston: Harvard Business School Press.

Leont'ev, A. N. (1978). *Activity, consciousness, and personality*. Englewood Cliffs: Prentice-Hall.

Leont'ev, A. N. (1981). *Problems of the development of the mind*. Moscow: Progress.

Lillrank, P. (1998). Introduction to knowledge management. In P. Lillrank & M. Forssen (Eds.), *Managing for knowledge: Perspectives and prospects*. Helsinki: Helsinki University of Technology, Industrial Management and Work and Organizational Psychology. Working Paper No. 17.

Latour, B. (1994) On Technical Mediation – Philosophy, Sociology and Genealogy. *Common Knowledge*. 2 (3), 29-64.

Myers, P. (Ed.) (1996). *Knowledge management and organizational design*. Boston: Butterworth-Heinemann.

Nonaka, I. & Konno, N. (1998). The concept of 'ba': Building a foundation for knowledge creation. *California Management Review*, 40, 40-54.

Nonaka, I. & Takeuchi, H. (1995). *The knowledge-creating company: How Japanese companies create the dynamics of innovation*. Oxford: Oxford University Press.

Pine II, B. J. (1993). *Mass Customization. The New Frontier in Business Competition*. Boston. Mass. Harvard Business School Press.

Prahalad, C. K. & Hamel, G. (1990). The Core Competence of the Corporation. *Harvard*

Business Review. May-June, 79-91.

Ruggles, R. L. (1997). *Knowledge management tools*. Boston: Butterworth-Heinemann. Random House Compact Unabridged Dictionary, 1996. New York: Random House.

Sanchez, R. & Heene, A. (Eds.) (1997). *Strategic learning and knowledge management*. Chichester: Wiley.

Stewart, T. A. (1997). *Intellectual capital: The new wealth of organizations*. New York: Doubleday.

Sveiby, K. E. (1997). *The new organizational wealth: Managing and measuring knowledge-based assets*. San Francisco: Berrett-Koehler.

Wartofsky, M. (1979). *Models, representation and the scientific understanding*. Boston: D. Reidel Publishing Company.

Victor, B. & Boynton, A., C.(1998). *Invented Here, Maximizing Your Organization's Internal Growth and Profitability. A Practical Guide to Transforming Work*. Boston. Mass.: Harvard Business School Press.

Virkkunen, J. & Kuutti, K. (in press). Understanding organizational learning by focusing on 'activity systems'. Submitted to *Accounting, Management and Information Technologies*.

Wenger, E. (1998). *Communities of practice: Learning, meaning, and identity*. Cambridge: Cambridge University Press.

Vygotsky, L. S. (1978). *Mind in society*. Cambridge: Harvard University Press.

Chapter XVI

Success Factors in Leveraging the Corporate Information and Knowledge Resource Through Intranets

Karin Breu, John Ward and Peter Murray
Cranfield School of Management, UK

The chapter presents the empirical findings of two large organizations' attempts at competitively leveraging the knowledge and information sharing capabilities of intranets. The work sought to identify the organization and management requirements that are critical to the realization of business benefits of intranet investments. The qualitative analysis suggests that intranets do provide a communications infrastructure that enables communities to exploit their information and knowledge resources for improved business performance provided a number of enabling changes is implemented. Next to the provision of continual user training, the user community must compile the business case, appoint the content manager, and negotiate guidelines for use. Unless these organizational and management changes constitute an integral part of the implementation strategy, the intranet will fail to deliver its investment objectives.

One of the most visible information systems (IS) and information technology (IT) trends of the nineties has been the rapid proliferation of intranet applications in organizations both in the public and private sector. After the downsizing experience of the recent decade, organizations are advised to recognize the growing significance of global information and knowledge sharing to achieving more with fewer resources (Taylor, 1997). In the emerging global economy, organizations need to exploit their information and knowledge resources in supporting individuals and teams to work together effectively across spatial and geographic boundaries. Effective communications, however, bear importantly on a community's capability to share knowledge, ideas and experiences (Bohlin, Shand & Whitehead, 1997). Information and knowledge sharing is a complex process that poses significant challenges to the design of the communications infrastructure and process, especially across spatial boundaries. Among the existing communications technologies, intranets are seen to provide a technological platform capable of providing a solution to this challenge (Wachter & Gupta, 1997).

Because of the crucial role of communications in information and knowledge sharing, the study of the capabilities of intranets in supporting these processes has to build on a conceptual framework that accommodates theories of communications, technologies, and information and knowledge sharing. We consulted the relevant IT-enabled communications, the knowledge sharing, and the business benefits literature of IS/IT investments to frame an analysis of the organization and management conditions that need to be implemented in order to leverage intranet-based knowledge sharing. In the following section, we present a synthesis of that body of knowledge and introduce the research framework we constructed to guide our research.

INTRANET-BASED INFORMATION AND KNOWLEDGE RESOURCE SHARING: A LITERATURE REVIEW

By convention, we start the presentation of the theoretical framework by briefly defining the core concepts employed in this research. The term 'intranet' is used to describe a private computer network that extends Internet standards and protocols to the organization to enable its members to communicate and collaborate independently of spatial and temporal boundaries (Greer, 1998). Compared with internets and extranets, the intranet provides a closed communications infrastructure, access to which is exclusive to the members of the organization. Knowledge management and knowledge sharing are distinct because they relate both empirically and conceptually to different aspects of the knowledge resource. We draw on existing definitions of knowledge management in relating it to "the process of identifying, capturing, and leveraging knowledge to help the company compete" (O'Dell & Grayson, 1998). Knowledge sharing, in contrast, is defined in this paper as the transfer and active exchange of knowledge amongst an organizational community (Nonaka, 1991).

Technologies for Knowledge-Sharing

Reviewing the intranet literature we found the majority of the work is written for technical designers and network managers (cf. Greenberg & Lakeland, 1998; for a World Wide Web-published reference resource cf. Kotlas, 1998). Expert reports that argue the revolutionizing effects of the intranet technology lack any theoretical and empirical foundations (Scott, 1998). In light of the scarcity of inquiries into the effectiveness gains of intranet applications in organizations, we approached the general communications technology literature with the aim of building our study upon theories of effectiveness developed there. The body of literature on communication technologies is voluminous. Our account of that literature is therefore highly selective, but two aspects appeared particularly relevant: views of effectiveness in traditional and in IT-enabled communications environments in organizations.

Communications theory that views communication as a social process focuses on the user of the technology and the social context of use (cf. Fulk, Schmitz & Ryu, 1995; Poole

& DeSanctis, 1990). The social-actor perspective of communications seeks to identify a correlation between peoples' practices of media choice and operational effectiveness. The argument is that effectiveness is the result of the choice that users make from a set of alternative communications channels. Comparative analyses of users' choice behavior discovered a striking disparity in the factors that inform choice in traditional as opposed to IT-enabled communications environments, which have significant implications for communications effectiveness (Webster & Trevino, 1995; Bozeman, 1993; Sitkin, Sutcliffe & Barrios-Choplin, 1992; Fulk & Boyd, 1991).

In conventional communications environments, individuals' choice behavior was found to be largely underpinned by so-called rational determinants. Conventional media such as the telephone, facsimile, and printed documentation have been in use for extensive periods during which views of what are effective, and thus rational decisions of choice, have grown over time, have been validated by experience and are implicitly shared by the user community. Organizational members widely agree on a medium's purpose and use so that their choices from alternative communications channels are predominantly based on rational considerations.

In newly implemented IT-enabled communications environments, however, individual media choice was found to be overwhelmingly informed by so-called sociocultural determinants of how these technologies might most adequately and effectively be used (Webster & Trevino, 1995; Fulk & Boyd, 1991). Because of their novelty they attract a diversity of interpretations of their purpose and use by the user community. Sociocultural choice is oriented by peer practices and individual views of message-medium match. If choice in IT-enabled communications environments is a sociocultural phenomenon, effectiveness can be assumed to hinge on whether users make appropriate choices or not. Low effectiveness in IT-enabled communications environments is seen as the result of inadequate and divergent practices of media use amongst a user community.

Knowledge Sharing as a Social Process

Starting from the premise that people possess a natural proclivity for learning and communicating what they know, one stream of the knowledge-sharing literature seeks to identify the barriers to knowledge-sharing in organizations. Organizational structures that promote silo behavior and enforce boundaries between functions and departments, organizational cultures that value individual contribution over communal success, reward systems that disfavor cooperation and sharing (O'Dell & Grayson, 1998), and the negligence of capturing and transferring of what Polanyi (1966) termed 'tacit knowledge' have been seen as fundamental challenges to the creation of knowledge-sharing communities (Nonaka, 1991). Knowledge sharing is a people-to-people process, a cultural process, and an organizational process (Senge, 1990). To truly leverage the organizational knowledge resource, there is the need to encourage people to share what they know through adequate reward structures, to develop cultures that anchor the sharing of knowledge and ideas as an organizational value, and to design organization structures that enable effective interactions between people (Davenport & Prusak, 1997).

IS/IT-Enabled Business Benefits

Since empirical research has not as yet explored how organizations identify and realize a business contribution from intranet investments, we approached the business benefits research into IS/IT investments to build upon the understanding developed there.

Organizations' failure to realize a business contribution from IS/IT investments has been extensively documented in the practitioner and academic literature and continues to be relevant in practice (cf. Morris, 1996; Willcocks, 1994). IS failures are frequently attributable to a investment decision focus that is restricted to the development and implementation of the technology applications. Organizations rush into the adoption of information and communication technology without building a full business case and without evaluating the project and stakeholder implications (Farbey, Land & Targett, 1993).

Benefits management, as developed by Ward, Taylor and Bond (1996; Ward & Griffiths, 1996), in contrast, takes a processual, evolutionary approach to IS investments that spans the entire project lifecycle from the pre-investment appraisal through to the post-investment evaluation. Benefits management is defined as the process of organizing and managing for the purposive realization of organizational benefits of IS/IT investments (Ward, Taylor & Bond, 1996). Drawing on the view that technology alone cannot deliver organizational benefits because their realization is associated with business changes (Earl, 1992), a fundamental thesis in benefits management thinking is that we realize business benefits of IS/IT investments only when people change their ways of working as a result of the implementation of the technology (Ward, Taylor & Bond, 1996). Under the business benefits approach, the investment objectives are aligned with the drivers of the organization. Next, the set of business benefits is identified that will result from the achievement of the specified investment objectives. The key stakeholders are engaged throughout the process in negotiating and mapping out a network of business benefits that includes the specification of the required changes in working practices and defines the indicators and measures to evaluate their achievement. The benefits dependency network then identifies and locates the IS/IT functionality, which is needed to enable the change. The process also defines roles and responsibilities to ensure the determination of ownership and stakeholder commitment to the business benefits realization plan.

Scholars have been pointing out the difficulties of anticipating the impact of novel technologies. They argue that in the instance of the adoption of new technologies, organizations lack ways of recognizing what its effects and opportunities are for doing things differently and for doing things that were not possible or feasible with the old technology (Bell, 1973; Zuboff, 1988; Orlikowski & Hofman, 1997). Taking the view that the outcomes of the application of novel technology are, in general, uncertain, it can be assumed that the business benefits delivery process is little understood in the context of intranet-based knowledge management.

A Research Perspective on Intranet-Based Knowledge Management

The analysis of the existing literature has shown that, although there are organizations that begin to creatively and successfully use technology to support knowledge management (cf. Hansen, Nohira & Tierney, 1999), few of these claims have actually been substantiated through empirical research. Furthermore, nowhere could we identify research that provided practical advice on how to actually design and implement intranet environments to successfully support the creation of knowledge-sharing communities. We thus designed a research project to study the managerial and organizational aspects that enable the effective adoption and exploitation of intranet infrastructures for information and knowledge sharing in organizational communities. In summary, the review of the relevant literature had established the following core insights:

- While there is an emerging awareness in some of the literature of the crucial importance of building a business case for the adoption of the intranet technology (cf. Greer, 1998), the relevant changes that managers need to implement in order to realize business benefits from the investment have not been identified.
- Few of the claims and propositions suggested in the literature are substantiated by empirical research. There is a clear need for exploring how organizations, in practice, manage their intranets and what results they achieve.
- By implication, the literature relates the effective use of communication technologies to the shift from sociocultural to rational determinants of choice. It fails, however, to spell out the details of managing the transition to perform the effective shift from traditional to IT-enabled communications infrastructures.

The key objective we determined for our study was to seek to identify how to realize business benefits from the knowledge-sharing opportunities that intranets appear to provide. The set of research questions devised to guide our research included:

- Are intranet technologies capable of providing a communications infrastructure for information and knowledge sharing?
- What are the business contributions that intranet technologies can make in this context?
- What changes need to be implemented in order to realize those contributions?

Based on the investigation, we sought to both explore the empirical relevance of the theoretical perspective we developed for researching intranet-supported information and knowledge sharing in organizations and to provide practitioners with useful recommendations on how to manage intranet applications for business benefits.

RESEARCH DESIGN AND METHOD

In the absence of detailed studies of the managerial and organizational aspects of managing the effectiveness of intranets for information and knowledge sharing, we decided to adopt a qualitative approach to the research. From the variety of qualitative designs available in the social sciences, we selected the case study method because it provides the opportunity to both extract in-depth data and study the impact of the context in which these data are grounded (Yin, 1993). Based on existing work into the management of business benefits of IS/IT investments and theories of effectiveness in organizational communications, we developed a semi-structured interview schedule that explored, through the perceptions of the relevant stakeholders, the following areas: the interviewee's role and responsibility within the organization; the business purpose of the intranet application; the patterns and rationales of use of the intranet; the perceived benefits and disbenefits that resulted from its adoption and use; and the learning that emerged from the experience with the intranet and its information and knowledge sharing capabilities. Data was collected in personal interviews with the relevant stakeholders. All of the interviews were tape-recorded and subsequently transcribed for data analysis.

The method of data analysis was selected with a view to the nature of the data and the research objectives. Content analysis was felt to provide a firm method for analyzing the interview transcripts purposively (Weber, 1990). The theoretical framework and the research questions that had been developed from the literature review guided the data analysis aiming to identify the managerial requirements and organizational changes that enable the effective utilization of intranet investments for information and knowledge sharing.

STUDYING INTRANET-BASED KNOWLEDGE SHARING IN ORGANIZATIONS

For the study of intranet-based information and knowledge sharing, we selected two large-sized organizations in different business sectors: the petrochemicals and computer services industries. Both organizations had implemented intranets for sharing their information and knowledge resources across the geographically dispersed organizational communities. The companies are truly multinational organizations so that they provided cases for studying information and knowledge sharing on a global scale. In total, we interviewed 38 individuals: communities of expertise such as the geographically dispersed consultancy, sales and tendering teams, intranet users in a diversity of roles such as communications and call center managers, and, furthermore, content providers, technology managers, knowledge managers, and Chief Knowledge Officers.

FINDINGS

The companies studied had adopted the intranet technology with the objective of increasing competitiveness in the marketplace through supporting a range of business processes with shared information and knowledge resources. We studied the application of the intranet to the business consulting and sales processes intending to improve performance and competitiveness. Although the communications infrastructure in those organizations included conventional and IT-enabled communications such as electronic mail, voice mail and desktop videoconferencing, we focused the analysis on the role of the intranet in information and knowledge sharing. In Table 1 we summarize the cases and projects studied. The column headed 'business imperative' depicts the business process

Table 1: Descriptive Account of Cases and Projects Studied

Company	Business Imperative	Project Purpose
1: Petrochemicals	• Realizing strategic decision of expanding internal consultancy services to external marketplace for revenue increase • Acquisition of core competence of information and knowledge networking in consultancy industry	• Developing capability of global, flexible and responsive project resourcing • Increasing efficiency and productivity in expert resource usage
2: Computer services	• Emulating strategic competence of competitors • Knowledge re-use and sharing in bidding and selling process	• Strategic exploitation of existing information and knowledge resources to increase market share

the intranet technology was designed to support. Under the heading of 'project purpose' we summarize the business objective pursued by the intranet application.

In the following section we will discuss the cases as summarized in Table 1 and present the findings of the within-case and cross-case analyses in detail.

Case One

At the petrochemicals company, the intranet services were introduced to support the international operations of the group's internal consultancy practice. The project was driven by the company's recent decision to enter market competition with external providers of business consultancy services. In order to become truly competitive, the company needed to increase the exploitation of the consultants' expertise and to facilitate the resourcing of consultancy projects, part of which was to overcome the impact of the team's fragmentation across geographic boundaries. In business consulting, information and knowledge resources are stored in historical and contemporary case studies, consultancy project documentation, and project progress reports. Globally connecting and effectively sharing this resource had been identified as a core competence in the industry so that the acquisition of this capability was seen as an absolute necessity for gaining an edge in the marketplace. The envisaged business benefits of achieving a higher utilization of the consultancy resource and of being able to compose project teams faster to win more business were intended to be realized in a number of ways. The global networking of the information resource would increase the consultants' responsiveness to customer de-mands. The intranet-based sharing of problem solving methodologies would increase the efficiency and consistency of the consultancy service provision. The shared learning from successful as well as unsuccessful projects through the publication of best practice on the intranet would result in the community-wide multiplication of knowledge. After a period of 18 months into the intranet implementation, the objective of creating a global information and knowledge resource network that would enable the consultants to 'do a better job' and thus increase performance at individual and group level had not been achieved. The intranet application was agreed to have made no discernible contribution in enabling the consultancy practice to compete effectively.

Reviewing the history of the intranet application provided the company with a valuable learning experience that enabled the identification of a number of factors that are critical to realizing the objectives envisaged with the intranet investment. With hindsight it became clear that the creation of the knowledge sharing community required more than the making available of data and information on the intranet. Prior to the publication of content, there was the necessity of globally connecting and integrating the different ways of working, the different approaches, the different skills in different areas which were fragmenting the coherence and the consistency of the consulting process. Yet to bring these information and knowledge resources meaningfully together, it was realized that the consultancy practice first had to identify its core competencies in terms of the subjects about which it had knowledge and in which it wanted to be expert at. Only after the identification of the information, knowledge and skill resource, the core competencies and the target market, could the intranet infrastructure be usefully designed.

There was the poor structuring, classifying, indexing, retrieving and updating of the published content that had caused the consultants, after an initial period of experimenta-tion with the new form of information and knowledge provision, to revert to the traditional ways of information management and use. It was further recognized that the successful assimilation of the intranet application into the daily working practices was largely a matter of understanding and changing human behavior rather than of merely implementing technology. Inducing behavioral change was seen to include both encouraging people to invest time into the sharing of experience and formally designating the responsibility for contributing through publication to the knowledge base of the team. Capturing knowledge through the consultants reviewing completed projects and publishing it in a form that was useful for others was found central to creating and sustaining the information and knowledge resource network.

The behavioral changes also included cognitive changes. The governing cognitive structure that was traditionally locally focused had to be developed to thinking globally. When the consultants needed information, they would network with peers in the local offices. To truly exploit the global knowledge resource, however, the consultants needed to expand their perspective and start searching for information globally through the intranet. Overcoming individual resistance to knowledge sharing, epitomized in the belief that knowledge is power, was recognized as a further key imperative to realizing the envisaged objectives. This created the awareness that new methods of reward and recognition for knowledge sharing had to be created in order to encourage the behavioral and cognitive changes to occur. Achievements supported by the provision of information and knowledge needed to be reflected back to the contributing individual. The organizational value system had to be developed such that individuals sharing their knowledge were seen to contribute more than others who retained their knowledge.

The learning also included the realization that the current practice of providing user training voluntarily was ineffective because it allowed people not to attend. In order for the intranet application to become a natural way of working, its use needs to be promoted in obligatory training initiatives that ensure a critical mass to build up and to adopt the technology so that its use would eventually become a routinised, self-sustaining process. In the absence of training, users were found to get locked into the limited forms of utilization they knew instead of tapping into the full potential of the application. In order for users to raise their levels of knowledge and systems utilization, their exposure to training had to be continual and also to be, in the future, an integral part to the induction procedure of new members of staff.

The learning further concerned the recognition of the necessity of establishing the new application as a formal channel for communications, of agreeing the types of information and knowledge resources to be provided there, and of implementing a formal process for approving the quality of the published content. Subject matter experts were seen as crucial for ensuring both the quality of the published content and the practical relevance of the classification structure. The meaningful structuring of published content was felt an important design requirement not only for making the resource accessible but also for resolving the current problem of information overload. Only when the changes at the organizational, behavioral and cognitive level are accomplished, will the consultants be able to start to change their ways of working based on a shared understanding of the core business and processes of the consultancy practice. The achievement of these changes will determine whether the investment objectives of increasing the performance and developing external competitiveness of the consultancy practice through the creation of an information and knowledge sharing network will be realized in the future.

Case Two

The adoption of the intranet technology in the computer services company was driven by the imperative of acquiring the strategic competence of information and knowledge reuse, which the firm's competitors had recently built up successfully for winning business. The bidding process is a core knowledge production system for companies competing on the basis of tenders. In the process of compiling a bid, a valuable knowledge resource is created through locating and retrieving relevant sales information, through customer, supplier and bidding team interactions. The location and identification of information and knowledge resources was a time-consuming process with the sales consultants traditionally relying on personal contacts and individual creativity in searching, retrieving and judging its relevance. Since there was no method for extracting and multiplying the knowledge embedded in bids and contracts and which, if shared, would earn the company an efficiency increase and strengthen its competitiveness, the company decided to implement an intranet-based information and knowledge resource network. The organization's customer and supplier information and the historical knowledge accumulated in sales projects are key resources in the bidding and sales process, which if networked effectively would enable project and sales representatives to respond to customer demands flexibly and competitively.

Under the direction of the Chief Knowledge Officer, technicians designed and implemented the intranet infrastructure and continuously expanded the published information and knowledge base. By the time the company's customer, supplier, product and services information was available on the intranet, the sales and bidding consultants were required to exclusively use this resource for compiling bids and drawing up sales contracts. However, the sales teams experienced serious problems in utilizing the intranet-published information resource for processing invitations of tenders. Reviewing the bids, sales managers identified instances where consultants had drawn up offers that included products and services that the company no longer supplied. In other cases, the company's accounting department had realized that cost estimates had been built on incorrect data so that the realization of these bids would have incurred significant loss. As a result, the company was forced to withdraw these offers and suffered a loss of reputation as a professional multinational player in the industry.

Only through exposure to these serious problems did the organization discover the fundamental organizational and managerial conditions that have to be implemented for the intranet infrastructure to provide reliable information resources. They realized the importance of continually managing the currency and relevance of the content published on the intranet along with defining the roles and responsibilities in the content management process. The analysis further revealed that since users had not been trained in the use of the new technology, they lacked knowledge of how to identify and locate relevant information on the net, which ultimately discouraged the use of the technology. In the absence of training, the use of the intranet environment was developed by experimentation, personal views and the emulation of peer practices. Furthermore, inconsistent publication practices across locations, the difficulty in identifying latest updates of Web sites, and the insufficient and incoherent structure of the published content were found confusing. These shortcomings resulted in user distrust of the reliability of the published information resource and their resistance to adopt the intranet and assimilate its information and knowledge resource into their working practices.

Accumulated Learning Through Cross-Case Analysis

The comparative analysis of the levels of investment objective achievement across the two cases revealed that the business benefits envisaged with the intranet implementation had been insufficiently realized. Eliciting the underlying reasons we found similar levels of consistency across the organizations studied. In both companies, the initial phase of the application was one of experimentation in which the potential and the opportunities of the intranet for increasing efficiency and productivity in business operations were explored. In the course of the publication of growing volumes of information on the intranet, the application was increasingly pushed to business-critical processes. Notably, it was the type of information resources published that drove the evolution of its application.

DISCUSSION

Although the companies studied had invested in the intranet with the aim of increasing organizational competitiveness, neither succeeded in strategically exploiting what had started as a high potential application. A useful approach for explaining the observed drift of the intranet application is offered by the IS applications portfolio (Ward & Griffiths, 1996). The IS application portfolio, as represented in Figure 1, categorizes IS projects by their business contribution. By this approach, an organization can differentiate the business value accruing across its range of IS/IT investments. Support applications (e.g. personnel administration or word processing systems) are valuable to the business in delivering efficiency improvements but are not critical contributors to organizational competitiveness. Key operational applications (e.g., production planning and billing systems) are those on which the organization depends to perform its core operations and that are essential to avoid competitive disadvantage. Strategic applications (e.g., enterprise systems) are critical to achieving the future business strategy by changing the conduct of business, enabled by the capabilities of technology. High potential applications (e.g., knowledge management systems) are IS that may become important in sustaining future competitive advantage and success but are, as yet, unproven. The applications portfolio's value is in assessing and articulating the nature of current and future IS investments in terms of the capacity of each to deliver business performance improvements. Naturally, as the systems mature and, depending on the actual business context and industry, their business-criticality and thus significance to the business will change.

Depending on the level of their business contribution and impact, IS applications require diverse levels of resource allocation and management strategies. For high potential applications, as their importance to future success is yet unclear, a limited amount of resources should be deployed until their potential is assessed. The same applies to support applications, as they are only valuable to the business, e.g. through reducing costs, but not critical to sustained organizational competitiveness. Key operational applications, on which the organization currently depends to avoid competitive disadvantage, and strategic applications, as they are critical to achieving the future business strategy, require significant resources and senior management attention.

Typically, novel IS enter the organization as high potential applications. If their high potential business contribution is established through piloting and experimentation, they will migrate to become strategic if advantage can be obtained, then key operational as they become 'business as usual' and, eventually, over time, may become support applications. This migration process is represented by the dotted cycle in Figure 1. Mapping the intranet application pattern identified from our research (as represented by solid lines in Figure 1) against the ideal-typical applications cycle (as represented by dotted lines in Figure 1) graphically highlights the low-level exploitation of this innovative technology in the case companies.

As the analysis has shown, the intranet adoption started off in both case companies as high potential. Through the lack of adequate resourcing and management processes both intranet applications evolved to become only support systems rather than deliver, through enabling effective knowledge sharing, the intended strategic advantages. Eventually and dangerously both then drifted into key operational use even though the application quality and controls were inadequate. The counter-ideal migration path explains why the full business potential of the intranet investment had not yet been realized in the case organizations.

The accumulated evidence across the cases enables the compilation of a set of organizational and managerial conditions whose implementation is critical to avoiding the drift of the application that led to the failure to realize their strategic potential. The success-critical factors identified in the empirical analysis can be clustered into three categories:

1. The *sociocultural factors* such as user training, the negotiation of guidelines for use, and the anchoring of knowledge sharing in the organizational value system.
2. The *organizational and management factors* such as the adequate structuring, archiving and continuous updating of the published information and knowledge resources; the determination of ownership; the specification of roles and responsibilities; and the adaptation of traditional reward systems to encourage knowledge sharing.
3. The *technological factors* such as the provision of appropriate design, bandwidth and platform specifications; user-friendly information access tools; and continual technical support of the user community.

Figure 1: The Intranet Applications Cycle
Source: Based on Ward & Griffiths, 1996: 32.

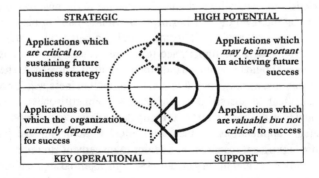

STRATEGIC	HIGH POTENTIAL
Applications which *are critical to* sustaining future business strategy	Applications which *may be important* in achieving future success
Applications on which the organization *currently depends* for success	Applications which are *valuable but not critical* to success
KEY OPERATIONAL	SUPPORT

If these sociocultural, organizational, management, and technological factors were addressed in a detailed business case prior to the adoption, organizations could significantly reduce the risk of benefits realization failure that largely results from technology-driven investment decisions. The finding of the neglect of business scrutiny in justifying and planning intranet adoptions resonates a concern that is well documented in the wider IS/IT literature (Telleen, 1996; Ward & Griffiths, 1996; Ward, Taylor & Bond, 1996). Without the prior demonstration of the technology's contribution to the business and the determination of the stakeholder roles and responsibilities in realizing the investment objectives there is a high risk of failure in achieving business benefits as a result of the implementation of the technology.

IMPLICATIONS

The companies studied accumulated useful insight in their attempts at creating information and knowledge networks through intranet applications. The evidence from these cases provides practical guidance in anticipating the success-critical design, organization, management, and change issues that organizations should address in order to realize business benefits from intranet investments.

The determination of ownership, user community, and new roles and responsibilities needs to constitute an integral part of the intranet implementation strategy. Content managers' and web masters' technical expertise is indispensable but has to be supported by business competence. The IT function should focus its responsibility on the design, implementation, operability, and platform management, as well as the provision of technical support and assistance in user training. Managers with in-depth contextual understanding of the business processes the published information and knowledge resource is supposed to support, are invaluable in contributing from their professional judgment to the determination of what constitutes relevance, criticality and currency and to ensure continual content management. Obsolete and irrelevant information instigates distrust and resistance to assimilate the intranet application into the working practices.

We used the IS applications portfolio to stress the significance of adopting diverse management strategies to different types of applications. Especially when the information and knowledge resource is used in key operational and strategic applications, business managers must assume the responsibility for determining the knowledge management strategy and monitoring content management, in contrast to less business-critical applications such as support functions where this responsibility can be delegated to lower-level management or staff.

Next to the specification of ownership, user community, roles and responsibilities, and the provision of content management, a number of enabling changes at the user level need to be implemented to ensure the realization of the business potential of the intranet application. Especially when intranets are applied to networking the organization's information and knowledge resource for knowledge sharing, this very activity should be anchored in the organizational value system and credibly communicated through the design of reward systems that acknowledge knowledge sharing. Users also need to be exposed to continual training in the use of the intranet application and they should negotiate guidelines for use to ensure consistency and effectiveness in working practices. Of particular value is the definition of a taxonomy of information and knowledge resources for which the organizational members assume a 'pull' or 'push' responsibility.

The findings from our research also suggest a number of theoretical implications. They confirm the claim of media choice theory that users of novel, IT-enabled communications environments base choice largely on sociocultural determinants (cf. Webster & Trevino, 1995). We found that when the intranet technology was adopted, patterns of use evolved in self-directed learning processes and in orientation of use by the social environment. Technology use on this basis is, as our study has shown, not conducive to the purposive realization of business benefits. The findings thus confirm the claim that the successful adoption of novel, IT-enabled communications environments requires the purposive change of organizational and individual practices, shifting the emphasis from sociocultural to rational determinants of technology use (Webster & Trevino, 1995). While there will never be a purely objective, rational use of technology by people, we still need to limit the influence of sociocultural drivers such that the potential of a genuine business contribution of the technology is not eroded. Our findings also expand current understanding of this change process in suggesting the development of rational technology use through the implementation of the organizational, cultural, and user-level changes identified above.

The significance of devising knowledge management strategies that are appropriate to the business process they support has also been confirmed by our findings. Organizations need to take decisions based upon the competitive strategy as to whether they opt for the codification or the personalization strategy for knowledge management (Hansen, Nohira & Tierney, 1999). The choice of strategy has important implications for the role that technology can assume in supporting the knowledge management process. Technology is particularly suitable for the knowledge codification approach, while it is far less effective in supporting the personalization model (Hansen, Nohira & Tierney, 1999).

Finally, the business benefits management thesis, which claims that a business contribution is achieved only when people change their ways of working based on the new technology, was validated in the context of this research. Prior to investments into intranet technologies, organizations need to draw up a business case that demonstrates the contribution the technology will make to the business, how that contribution will be realized and what designates the measures for evaluating the level of achievement.

While the study, based on two in-depth analyses, identified some of the organizational and managerial requirements whose implementation is paramount to the exploitation of the intranet application, we are now in the process of undertaking further case-based research in different organizations to determine the more general validity and applicability of the findings.

REFERENCES

Bell, D. (1973). *The coming of post-industrial society*. New York: Basic Books.

Bernard, R. (1998). *The corporate intranet: create and manage an internal web for your organization*. New York: John Wiley.

Bohlin, R., Shand, D., & Whitehead, R. (1997). *Adding value through intranet applications: a framework for creating and sharing corporate knowledge through the intranet*. London: Business Intelligence.

Bozeman, D. P. (1993). Toward a limited rationality perspective of managerial media selection in organizations. *Academy of Management Best Paper Proceedings*, 278-282.

Davenport, T. H. & Prusak, L. (1997). *Information ecology: mastering the information and knowledge environment.* New York: Oxford University Press.

Earl, M. J. (1992). Putting IT in its place: a polemic for the nineties. *Journal of Information Technology*, 7, 100-108.

Farbey, B., Land, F., & Targett, D. (1993). *IT investment: a study of methods and practice.* Oxford: Butterworth-Heinemann.

Fulk, J., Schmitz, J., & Ryu, D. (1995). Cognitive elements in the social construction of communication technology. *Management Communication Quarterly*, 8(3), 259-288.

Fulk, J., & Boyd, B. (1991). Emerging theories of communication in organizations. *Journal of Management*, 17(2), 407-446.

Gonzalez, J. S. (1997). *The 21st century intranet.* Rhinebeck, NY: Prentice Hall.

Greenberg, J. R., & Lakeland, J. R. (1998). *A methodology for developing and deploying internet and intranet solutions.* Upper Saddle River, N.J.: Prentice Hall PTR.

Greer, T. (1998). *Understanding intranets.* Redmond, WA: Microsoft Press.

Hansen, M. T., Nohira, N., & Tierney, T. (1999) What's your strategy for managing knowledge?. *Harvard Business Review*, 77(2), 106-116.

Kotlas, C. (1998). Intranets: reading and resources, Center for Instructional Technology, March 5, http://www.unc.edu/cit/guides/irg-34.html.

Morris, W. G. (1996). Project management: lessons from IT and non-IT projects. In M. J. Earl (Ed.) *Information management: the organizational dimension.* New York: Oxford University Press, 321-336.

Nonaka, I. (1991). The knowledge-creating company. *Harvard Business Review*, 69(6), 96-104.

O'Dell, C. & Grayson, C. J. (1998). If only we knew what we know: identification and transfer of internal best practices. *California Management Review*, 40(3), 154-174.

Orlikowski, W. J. & Hofman, J. D. (1997). An improvisational model for change management: the case of groupware technologies. *Sloan Management Review*, 38(2), 11-21.

Polanyi, M. (1966). *The tacit dimension.* Garden City, N. Y.: Doubleday.

Poole, M. S., & DeSanctis, G. (1990). Understanding the use of group decision support systems: the theory of adaptive structuration. In Fulk, J. & Steinfield, C. (Eds.) *Organizations and Communication Technology.* Newbury Park: Sage Publications, 173-193.

Scott, J. E. (1998). Organizational knowledge and the intranet. *Decision Support Systems*, 23(1), 3-17.

Senge, P. M. (1990) *The fifth discipline: the age and practice of the learning organization.* London: Century Business.

Sitkin, S. B., Sutcliffe, K. M., & Barrios-Choplin, J. R. (1992). A dual-capacity model of communication media choice in organizations. *Human Communication Research*, 18(4), 563-598.

Taylor, M. (1997). Intranets – a new technology changes all the rules. *Telecommunications*, 31(1), 39-40.

Telleen, S. L. (1996). Intranet organization: strategies for managing change. http://www.iorg.com/intranetorg/.

Wachter, R. M., & Gupta, J. N. D. (1997). The establishment and management of corporate intranets. *International Journal of Information Management*, 17(6), 393-404.

Ward, J. & Griffiths, P. (1996). *Strategic planning for information systems* (2nd ed.). Chichester: John Wiley.

Ward J., Taylor, P. & Bond, P. (1996). Evaluation and realisation of IS/IT benefits: an empirical study of current practice. *European Journal of Information Systems*, 4(4), 214-225.

Weber, R. P. (1990) *Basic content analysis*. Newbury Park, CA: Sage.

Webster, J. & Trevino, L. K. (1995). Rational and social theories as complementary explanations of communication media choices: two policy-capturing studies. *Academy of Management Journal*, 38(6), 1544-1572.

Willcocks, L. (1994). *Information management: the evaluation of information systems investments*. London: Chapman & Hall.

Yin, R. K. (1993). *Applications of case study research*. Newbury Park, CA: Sage.

Zuboff, S. (1988). In the age of the smart machine: the future of work and powers. New York: Basis Books.

Chapter XVII

Creating Knowledge-Based Communities of Practice: Lessons Learned from AMS's Knowledge Management Initiatives

Susan Hanley and Christine Dawson
American Management Systems, Inc., USA

This chapter is a case study of how American Management Systems (AMS) established its current knowledge management program, and the lessons learned during the process. The chapter gives a background on the need for knowledge management at AMS, discusses the challenges of implementation and the AMS Knowledge Management framework, describes the AMS Knowledge Centers (communities of practice), and explains five key lessons learned. Finally, it outlines the results of the knowledge management program for AMS from both internal and external perspectives.

American Management Systems (AMS) today has a successful and widely recognized knowledge management program, but it did not happen overnight. Our journey to become an effective knowledge-leveraging organization has been an evolution, with many challenges along the way. This chapter presents a case study of how AMS established its current knowledge management program and the lessons learned during the process. We provide a brief background on the drivers that alerted us to our need for improving the way we leverage knowledge across the enterprise and discuss the challenges of implementing the knowledge management program we have in place today. The chapter continues with a discussion of the AMS Knowledge Management framework, which outlines how we have integrated people, process and technology to deliver value to our client engagement teams. The chapter emphasizes the "people component" of the framework, the AMS Knowledge Centers®, which are the virtual communities of practice in AMS's eight core business disciplines. Finally, we share the key lessons we have learned from implementing our knowledge management framework, as well as what the results of the knowledge management initiatives have been for the primary stakeholders in the process.

BACKGROUND ON THE NEED FOR KNOWLEDGE MANAGEMENT AT AMS

In the early years of AMS's history, knowledge was shared in the coffee rooms and in the hallways. The company, which was started by a small group of U.S. Department of Defense "whiz kids" in 1970, leveraged its relatively small size for flexibility and efficiency. As AMS grew, however, it began to experience some of the pain associated with the way it was growing—rapidly and across many locations (often thousands of miles apart), with a mix of cultures and personalities that previously did not exist.

In an effort to become a billion-dollar organization, AMS needed to manage its growth and ensure that it would continue to win work by maintaining a competitive advantage and fostering strong relationships with existing clients. In 1992, as part of the management strategy process, senior executives closely examined the way AMS was leveraging its people and their collective knowledge. The company, with thousands of people in offices around the world, was relying on a knowledge-sharing model 20 years old. This "water cooler" model was sufficient when AMS had 500 employees on only 50 engagements, but not with thousands of employees on 500 engagements around the world. Clearly, changes had to be made. Strategies for pursuing engagements were not easily shared; project teams across the company were individually solving similar technical problems; and there was no way of knowing what knowledge resided where within the company.

As a result of the strategy process in the early 1990s, AMS began the implementation of a series of knowledge management initiatives. In their book *Working Knowledge: How Organizations Manage What They Know*, Tom Davenport and Larry Prusak suggest that firms should try to use existing management approaches and initiatives to "jump-start" knowledge management programs (Davenport & Prusak, 1997).[1] This is the approach that AMS used. Values and competencies formed the foundation of AMS's strategy, and our strong company-wide culture of teamwork and knowledge sharing shaped all of our activities. Still, AMS faced a number of challenges during the process of building the knowledge management program it has in place today. First, AMS had to *find* the knowledge that everyone knew already existed both within and outside the company. Next, it had to *capture and organize* this knowledge, and finally, it had to *share* the knowledge globally.

CHALLENGES OF IMPLEMENTATION

Finding the Knowledge

Meeting the challenge of finding AMS's knowledge started with the creation of two formal business groups: the AMS Center for Advanced Technologies ® (AMSCAT®), whose charter includes identifying and researching innovative technologies that deliver practical business value for AMS clients, and the AMS Best Practices Program, a formal effort to discover, disseminate and apply the best methodology and management practices from both inside and outside our organization. In addition to a full-time research staff, AMSCAT also includes advanced technology Associates from across the company, practitioners who each commit to advancing the research agenda of the Center while at the same time sharing their experiences and insights with other members of the community and the company at large. The original group of Associates was identified by AMS business unit managers. Today, Associates "nominate" themselves for membership by describing the contribution they will make. In 1996, AMS established additional communities of Associates, each representing an AMS core competency. These Associates, like AMSCAT Associates, make a formal commitment to contribute to the process of "finding" knowledge within the firm. The communities of Associates together form what is now known as the AMS Knowledge Centers.

Capturing and Organizing the Knowledge

Although knowledge management is not about simply deploying the latest technology, AMS recognized that technology would be the *enabler* to allow us to capture, store and organize the knowledge we were beginning to collect. We embraced several enabling technologies that are still integral to making knowledge management work at AMS today: voice mail, e-mail, video teleconferencing and the most crucial, Lotus Notes. Our Lotus Notes databases are expansive corporate-wide knowledge repositories, organized as the AMS corporate intranet under the umbrella term, the AMS Knowledge Express®.

The Knowledge Express databases include more than ten gigabytes of data, with more than three gigabytes of data accessed every day by AMS staff around the world. These databases are accessible by client teams on site, who can maintain local copies of the databases they need and view others when necessary using our internal network or the Internet. The range of information that is captured by the Knowledge Express is vast—best practices, examples of the best of our work products with key insights and lessons learned in their creation, and continual research into new technologies and techniques. Nearly all of our intellectual capital is stored in the Knowledge Express and a core team, which includes professional librarians, monitors the growing content of key databases to ensure it is accurate, current and useful.

Sharing the Knowledge

Once we found a way to collect and organize corporate knowledge, the third challenge was to ensure that the knowledge could be shared across the company. Today, every AMS employee has access to the AMS Knowledge Express at their desktop. The Knowledge Express includes a growing number of portal interfaces to the content to help ensure that knowledge can be shared effectively. Even with a robust technological infrastructure, however, it soon became clear that there would be times when AMS staff would be unable to get content electronically—and so we developed a people infrastructure as well, AMS Know. AMS Know is a highly efficient information service staffed by professional reference librarians who find vital information for our project teams more quickly and efficiently than they ever could by themselves. As on-line resources have grown both inside and outside AMS, the need for serious research help became imperative. AMS Know staff handle information requests via phone and e-mail for consultants across the company, ranging from questions such as "Who at AMS knows about C++?" to "What are the call-pattern trends in the U.S. telecommunications market?" If the staff is unable to answer a consultant's question directly, then they connect that consultant with another AMS employee who can. AMS Know is an increasingly valuable vehicle for sharing AMS's knowledge.

THE AMS KNOWLEDGE MANAGEMENT FRAMEWORK

The three challenges of building a successful knowledge management program led to the framework AMS eventually embraced: a mixture of people, process and technology. AMSCAT and the Best Practices Program form the process component of the framework—the focus within these programs is on research, discovery, dissemination and practice. The Knowledge Express is the technology component. The heart of AMS's knowledge management initiative, however, is the people component of the framework: the formal communities of practice, the AMS Knowledge Centers.

Even before AMS began undertaking a formal knowledge management initiative, we had a model that worked: networks of people who formed informal communities united by common interest or experience. These groups flourished on their own when the company was smaller; yet, as the company continued to expand at a rapid rate (with many new, experienced people being hired who had lots of information to share), a formal model needed to be developed to ensure that the "heart" of our knowledge sharing culture continued to beat—and that we would still be able to deliver successes for our clients. There are two types of formal "people networks" currently established at AMS: communities of interest and communities of practice.

Communities of Interest: Special Interest Groups (SIGs)

AMS's communities of interest are known as Special Interest Groups (SIGs). Membership in a SIG is open to any person with an interest in learning or sharing more about a business or technology topic. SIGs flourish based on need and tend to be wrapped around either a particular technology (such as object-oriented programming), a concept (such as leadership) or a problem (such as Y2K).

SIGs are not formally funded. The momentum behind them usually comes from an energetic leader and a core group of people with a passion about the topic. Anyone can be a member of any SIG, and of as many SIGs as he or she chooses. There is no expected deliverable from members—the primary goal is to provide a forum for members to share and learn and to apply that knowledge on their engagements. Because there is no commitment, a person can choose to go to meetings or skip them; to participate actively in discussions or "lurk" in the background; or to read group e-mails, yet not respond. These Special Interest Groups are not accountable for tangible blocks of reusable knowledge for AMS's collective knowledge base; however, they do bring together people with knowledge to share and help the company identify who *may* be most interested or experienced in a topic, as a useful starting point when looking for information on that topic.

Communities of Practice: The AMS Knowledge Centers

AMS has always had a culture where people are rewarded for leveraging their knowledge. The company embraces the concept of "one firm," with all employees and clients benefiting from the full range of AMS's experiences and expertise; in fact, it has made that idea part of the corporate business strategy. This knowledge-sharing culture helps define AMS—it has been recognized and praised by people both inside and outside of the company. AMS facilitates knowledge leverage by connecting people through the AMS Knowledge Centers.

Unlike the SIGs, where anyone can join and take a very "low-key" role, participating in the Knowledge Centers communities requires active involvement. The Knowledge Centers are virtual communities of practice in AMS's core disciplines. These disciplines include:

- Business Process Renewal
- System Development and Information Technology Management
- Organization Development and Change Management
- Advanced Technologies
- Engagement and Project Management
- Customer Value Management
- Knowledge Management
- eCommerce

Taken together, the skills and experience developed within the framework of the Knowledge Centers represent the practical way AMS leverages the collective knowledge of all of its employees to bring the best of that collective knowledge and experience to every client engagement.

Because the Knowledge Centers are virtual communities, they traditionally have been supported by only a very small number of full-time staff. Each Knowledge Center community is led by a team of coordinators recognized as leaders in their respective disciplines. Coordinators are full-time practitioners of that competency. Their leadership role in the Knowledge Centers requires a commitment of about 3-4 weeks each year.

Knowledge Centers Associates

Members of the Knowledge Centers, called Associates, are all experienced practitioners in their discipline. They agree to make an explicit contribution to AMS's intellectual capital each year. This contribution, the Associates Project, helps AMS continually grow the knowledge base, with contributions that reflect the direction and strategy of the firm. Associates include not just the company's leading practitioners, but its emerging leaders as well. The most important criterion for membership in a Knowledge Center is the willingness and ability of the member to make a contribution and the value of that contribution to AMS.

What sets members of the Knowledge Centers apart from other employees in the company is that while everyone at AMS is *expected* to contribute and share knowledge, Knowledge Centers Associates are *required* to do so if they wish to remain part of the community. These are communities of experienced practitioners and so Associates' contributions are ones that we want to share across the company.

Reusable Knowledge

Although a commitment to making a knowledge contribution is required, AMS does not simply harvest what its employees know through the Knowledge Centers. The company does not want disconnected bits of information; it does not want content without the context experience provides. The Knowledge Centers program emphasizes that its

Associates must contribute *reusable* knowledge (practical rather than theoretical). The result is that Associates projects have a clear and direct link to practical applications on AMS projects. In the spirit of providing content with context, Associates also agree to be willing to solve problems "in the moment," by responding to e-mails directed to their community as appropriate and by being an acknowledged source of information in their area of expertise.

KEY LESSONS LEARNED

AMS's knowledge management initiatives have become imperative as the company continues to grow. So far, these initiatives have been successful, but their success has not come without challenges. Looking to the future of knowledge management at AMS, we have crystallized five lessons learned from the process of developing AMS's knowledge management program. They are:

1) recognize individual achievement
2) build group identity
3) motivate and reward
4) celebrate successes
5) deliver value

These lessons have provided guidance for developing many facets of the program that still exist, as well as a framework for new enhancements that AMS has just begun to implement.

Recognizing Individual Achievement

Before becoming a Knowledge Centers Associate, a prospective member must first be nominated. For several years, the Associates Program had been structured so that business unit managers nominated only those people who exhibited a superior knowledge of a specific discipline. This model led to the development of small groups of highly skilled practitioners who generally had to gain several years of experience before consideration for inclusion. To be selected was in itself a recognition of the skill that person had attained.

Today, the nomination process has expanded to include not just our current experts, but also those emerging or "next generation" experts whom we want to develop to be our future experts. To help identify these emerging experts, we instituted a self-nomination process so that any person with a sincere interest in a discipline and a meaningful contribution to make could be considered for inclusion. Opening the nomination process stemmed concerns that the program was elitist; yet, the selection process remains rigorous. Knowledge Center Coordinators review all proposed projects to make sure that the proposal has value to AMS and that the nominee meets the basic qualification criteria for each Knowledge Center. Business unit managers must still provide approval and funding for all Associate projects. They also have the opportunity to nominate other candidates for the Program whom they feel would make an excellent contribution (but may require an extra incentive—formal recognition of their ability to make a contribution—to encourage their participation). To be an Associate is still a recognition that an employee has worthwhile knowledge to contribute to the company as a whole. Being recognized for membership in a Knowledge Center comes not just at a corporate level, but at the level in the organization where there is a person who has direct responsibility for performance evaluations and promotion.

AMS recognizes individual contributions in many other ways as well. Aside from special awards for outstanding contributions by individual Associates, we have implemented "Knowledge in Action" awards as a method of recognizing individuals who have successfully leveraged the AMS knowledge base. The winners of the Knowledge in Action award embody the essence of AMS's knowledge-sharing culture. These financial-equivalent awards are distributed at the annual Associates conference.

Building Group Identity

As AMS has tried to replicate the success of the "coffee room" environment on a global scale, the value of building a group identity has become apparent. Building group identity within the Knowledge Centers starts with providing all Associates with immediately identifiable business cards and continues with an infrastructure we've developed that includes e-mail and voice mail distribution lists and collaborative databases to facilitate communications among the members of each Knowledge Center community.

Every AMS employee has access to the repository of knowledge available on the Knowledge Express, but we have also set the Knowledge Centers apart by developing a "home page" database for each community, dedicated to the interests of that community. These databases provide a place where people can request help, post lessons-learned and useful information and engage in discipline-specific discussions. All employees have "read" access to these databases; only Associates have "write" access.

Until recently, it was largely the responsibility of each Knowledge Center to build its own community using the "home page" databases and the energy of the community Coordinators. Inevitably, some communities were more engaged than others; some were more active. We realized that to truly leverage the many Associate "volunteers," we would have to reach out to them, proactively. From the beginning, frequent communications (through e-mail, newsletters, etc.) have played a key role. Recently, AMS also began to address this challenge by developing a role of Knowledge Manager for most of our Knowledge Centers.

The primary mission of the Knowledge Manager is to increase the value delivered by the Knowledge Centers by increasing awareness and use of the assets in each discipline and by building and leveraging AMS intellectual capital. The Knowledge Manager is a subject matter expert in each discipline who proactively contributes content as well as synthesizes knowledge from other sources. The Knowledge Manager will be a key factor in building a group identity because he or she will plan events, work closely with the Knowledge Center Coordinators to encourage active Associate participation and continuously monitor the "home page" database, looking for ways to stimulate discussion in the database and advertise content. Our success with the Knowledge Manager role has been promising so far, and our vision is to have one full-time Knowledge Manager dedicated to each of AMS's core disciplines.

Motivating and Rewarding Participation

Many organizations have found that when undertaking any knowledge management initiative, motivation and reward are among the two biggest issues related to success.

These factors are especially important when the knowledge to be shared is being leveraged through technology, which today requires intellectual capital in written form. After all, the people who are expected to contribute content already have full-time jobs. How do you get people who are already working 10-12 hour days to spend "just a little more time" to write something down so that it may help someone else (someone else whom they may not know and may not even thank them)? Even the most altruistic of people will be forced to prioritize tasks and may not carry through on a good intention. Undoubtedly, motivation is a big challenge.

At AMS, it has helped that our culture historically has tied success (promotions) to how well an individual leverages knowledge. We have also formally motivated people by making the Associates Program (and a tangible Associates project) a requirement for inclusion in a Knowledge Centers community. We learned the value of this requirement through experience. In the first year of the program, when we did not require a contribution for membership, approximately one-half of the 1,100 Associates committed to completing an Associates project. Of those who made a commitment, only 70 percent (or, approximately 400 people) actually completed their proposed project. In contrast, the following year we required that 100 percent of Associates make a commitment. As a result, the pool of Associates became much smaller—only 800 people were willing to become involved and make the commitment. Again, we saw a completion rate of approximately 70 percent. However, that 70 percent amounted to approximately 560 completed projects in the second year. So, although the community was nearly 30 percent smaller, the actual contribution was more than 40 percent larger than in the first year. Since that time, we have continued to make the formal commitment to complete an Associates project a prerequisite to membership in a Knowledge Center. Many employees have the completion of an Associates project written into their formal performance objectives for the year, and thus, have tied their participation to financial incentives external to the program.

Beyond the formal commitment, we have developed a number of other highly successful techniques for motivating and rewarding knowledge-sharing commitments. Every member of a Knowledge Centers community is listed on the "board of Associates" in our headquarters. Every client who visits our facilities stops at the board; most spend time looking for the names of key people on their project. AMS employees realize that inclusion on the board sends a powerful message to clients, and most people don't want to be "left out." We also publicize the most highly leveraged Associate contributions to our on-line collection. Providing visibility is an excellent motivator for participation.

Aside from recognizing Associates by name, we also reward participation in more tangible ways. Last year, we implemented a cash award to the AMS employee whose submission to our "Examples Library" was reused the most times. We also gave shirts, embroidered with the Knowledge Centers name, to every Associate who completed a project. These relatively inexpensive gestures are greatly valued by the Associates who receive them.

Finally, our annual Associates conference has come to be one of the most powerful motivation and reward mechanisms of the entire AMS knowledge management initiative. The conference is an invitation-only, face-to-face event featuring a wide variety of workshops for networking and learning that are planned and organized by Associates across all eight of AMS's disciplines. The conference always features a keynote address by a well-known thought leader; for example, past keynotes have included Tom Davenport, Tom Stewart, John Kao and Marc Andressen. Each year, the conference generates more excitement and enthusiasm among the Associates communities.

Celebrating Successes

Our annual conference has also become a vehicle for celebrating the successes of our Associates, with a number of Associates awards being distributed at the event. At another AMS conference, for senior AMS staff, awards are given for both the creation and reuse of knowledge assets. On a more day-to-day basis, we continuously publish on-line links to Associate papers and publish stories about individuals or project teams who have reused knowledge successfully in both our Associates newsletter and other corporate-wide publications.

Celebrating the successes of individuals has translated into recognition for the program as a whole. AMS has received numerous awards for its knowledge-sharing culture[2] and proudly publicizes these awards to the AMS community. Associates feel pride in these external recognitions of a program that they have worked so hard to nurture. We help to create our own self-fulfilling prophecy that renews itself continually: we show our Associates that we are doing things right and that we have been recognized externally for our successes, they take that knowledge to heart and extend an extraordinary effort to make the program a success, external organizations applaud our success, and so on. Unabashedly celebrating the things we do right goes a long way toward ensuring that they will continue to go right in the future.

Delivering Value

AMS's commitment to both sharing and advancing knowledge as a company enables us to deliver superior value and to increase our effectiveness in serving three primary stakeholders: the clients, the employees and the company. Ultimately, the benefit to these stakeholders is the driver behind every new plan we implement.

All AMS employees, not just Associates, benefit from the lessons and insights that are shared by Associates through the completion of Associates Projects. AMS as a whole benefits from the infrastructure that enables each employee to leverage the entire explicit intellectual capital of the organization. In addition, the company is able to leverage the tacit knowledge of the employees through the directed e-mail messages that are sent not to all employees, but to the specific community of experts who are most likely to be able to provide solutions. The typical "solution time" for an e-mail question sent to a Knowledge Center community is 12 to 24 hours. In 1999, the Knowledge Centers' resources enabled AMS to save close to $5 million in the ability to provide rapid solutions to critical problems and contributed to more than $13 million in revenue. This efficiency allows AMS to deliver rapid, high quality solutions to the most challenging problems on client engagements. Our clients, in turn, can leverage the entire knowledge and expertise of AMS on each and every engagement.

RESULTS OF THE KNOWLEDGE MANAGEMENT PROGRAM FOR AMS

Measuring the value of knowledge management initiatives is almost as challenging as implementing them. We continually work to improve the way we measure this value. Our measurement approach includes tracking key metrics as well as collecting "serious anecdotes" from clients and employees documenting the value of the initiatives.

Clearly, AMS's knowledge management initiatives have had a positive effect on the overall working atmosphere at the company, but the success of the overall program truly can't be measured without looking at what the results of the program have been from a number of different perspectives: the financial, customer, internal business, and innovation and learning perspectives.

Financial Perspective

From the financial perspective, AMS has saved significant labor costs in terms of how we have helped our consultants avoid "spinning their wheels" by providing easy-to-use, fast and effective mechanisms for getting at the knowledge that exists within the company. For example, AMS Know, which was described earlier in the chapter, resolved more than 8,000 knowledge requests in 1998. Funding a team of four highly skilled reference librarians who know where and how to search for information has saved significant labor dollars. The librarian staff's speed and efficiency at performing research resulted in an estimated $500,000 saved in 1998 alone. This financial figure does not take into account the quality of the information they were able to deliver to project teams, which is of inestimable value.

AMS has profited from other components of its knowledge management program as well. A recent survey of users of AMS's corporate intranet indicated that the time saved by AMS consultants through the use of the Knowledge Express databases amounted to a dollar savings of more than $5 million a year.

Customer Perspective

From the customer perspective, AMS has gained positive results from the knowledge management initiatives as well. AMS is focused on delivering business benefits to our clients. As we have grown our expertise in our core disciplines, we have also refined our way of working—organizing our collective knowledge, developing effective delivery channels to share and apply this knowledge, and informing and training consultants in its use. As a result, AMS employees in all of our industry practices know where to find and how to use the rich repository of practical skills and experience that spans the company—across industries, across borders, across time zones and across specialized competencies.

These knowledge management initiatives are more than a way for clients to receive increased information, however. Through our knowledge management initiatives, we are able to make our best practices available to every client engagement. Our clients benefit because they receive *leveraged* knowledge—information of high value to them, based on the best of our global experience, delivered by a team that can apply it.

AMS clients are able to see tangible evidence of our commitment to knowledge management, which is a critical way to provide assurance that AMS pays more than "lip service" to the idea of leveraging knowledge across the company. More than 300 clients visited the AMS Center for Advanced Technologies and AMS Knowledge Centers facility in 1998. Visits such as these allow clients to see how we make it work, and most clients form a very favorable impression:

"Because the challenges we faced impacted many parts of our operation, AMS's multi-disciplinary approach and the resources of their Knowledge Centers helped us achieve the integrated solutions we were seeking."
—*Karla Pierce, Director of Transition for the Kansas Department of Revenue*

We capture feedback from our clients and share it with people across the company, as a reinforcement of the importance of AMS's knowledge management program to AMS's bottom line.

Internal Business Perspective

AMS's groupware infrastructure enables us to respond rapidly to the needs of our clients and the needs of our employees, both for their client work and for business development. Employees electronically shared more than 8,000 deliverable examples in 1998, and exchanged more than 70,000 e-mail messages every day.

How do these statistics translate into true internal business value? Again, testimonials make the picture clear. One AMS employee, a newly hired consultant, wrote about his experience when he sent out a directed e-mail to one of the Knowledge Centers communities, looking for help preparing a requirements traceability matrix for one of his clients:

"I was able to look at the way other projects have done it and, in fact, am currently working to implement an approach that I hadn't originally considered. In the end, I not only received different ideas and considerations, but after deciding what my best approach was, I had a finished, documented product to work with. This saved a week of work—but it isn't a minimal product—it's professionally developed and ready for 100 percent reuse.
— *AMS employee*

AMS's emphasis on reusing knowledge saves project teams significant time and allows all employees to "bring the rest of AMS in their briefcase for every client engagement."

Innovation and Learning Perspective

Through its knowledge management program, AMS offers a number of learning opportunities to the company as a whole. These learning tools include our SIGs, our databases, AMS Know and our knowledge management and technical seminars. One of the most valuable learning components, however, are the conferences and other events that bring together the core group of knowledge-sharing champions—the Associates—to network and share ideas. In the words of one Associate:

"The opportunity to interact with people across AMS who have similar interests as mine, struggling with (or having solved!) the same issues, is absolutely invaluable to me. I also like the feeling of belonging to something that is broader than just my business unit and contributing in a way that helps others at AMS. I really get a better feel for what the whole of AMS is, not just my slice."
—*AMS employee*

Our knowledge management initiatives have nurtured the corporate culture within AMS that values the sharing of knowledge and experience. Similarly, AMS values staff training that goes beyond simple training courses. In 1998, nearly every one of 800 Associates participated in at least one workshop or conference. Sharing information creates a sense of belonging and camaraderie and reduces apathy, ultimately contributing to retention of employees.

Combining our knowledge and expertise with a way of working that provides every AMS consultant and engagement team with access to company-wide resources enables AMS to deliver solutions built through experience. It is how we deliver value to our stakeholders: to the individual, to the company, to the clients. The results of AMS's knowledge management initiatives are highly leveraged engagement teams with AMS's collective knowledge at their fingertips. This *is* knowledge management: people, processes and technology working together to deliver value.

ENDNOTES

1 Davenport, T. & Prusak, L. (1997). *Working knowledge: How organizations manage what they know*. Cambridge, MA: Harvard Business School Press.
2 Moore, A. (1999, February 1). An environment for innovation: American Management Systems. *KMWorld* [On-line]. Available: http://www.kmworld.com/magazine/article.cfm?ArticleID=325

Chapter XVIII

Knowledge Acquisition and Management: Perspectives, Strategic Implications, and Extensions to the Virtual Setting

Jean L. Johnson
Washington State University, USA

This chapter provides an integrative review and synthesis of the knowledge acquisition and management literature. As a starting point, the role of the individual in organizational learning processes is discussed and reconciled. This issue is extended and discussed for the virtual setting. In following sections, the author derives three major theoretical principles from the literature synthesis. These include the knowledge types, knowledge acquisition processes, and organizational memory. Again, each of these principles are extended to the virtual setting. Based on the integration of these principles, a number of conceptual refinements are offered and important strategic implications elaborated. Subsequently, the strategic implications are contrasted and developed for the virtual setting. Communication constraints inherent to the virtual organization bring a unique and likely problematic set of issues with regard to the development and management of organizational knowledge.

The topics of knowledge acquisition and management have assumed a position of importance in both research and theory, as well as in contemporary management practice. This is true to the extent that some firms have now explicitly recognized the role of knowledge acquisition and management by including "knowledge managers" in their organizational charts. Likewise, in the business academy, knowledge acquisition and management have been the topics of numerous articles and several special issues of leading journals in business disciplines.

Some theorists go so far as to suggest that knowledge acquisition and processing are the "raison d'etre" for the firm (Weick & Westley, 1996). Others have worked toward a knowledge-based theory of the firm, advocating knowledge creation and management as the only durable means to competitive advantage (Grant, 1996; Spender, 1996). Many would contend that, at the very least, knowledge acquisition is a strategic imperative for the contemporary firm.

Assuming that such claims have some validity, exploring the implications of knowledge acquisition for the business disciplines and practitioners is a worthwhile endeavor. Osborn & Hagedoorn (1997) strongly urge that we need to "unpack the issue of organizational learning to explicitly deal with what is being learned, the setting in which it occurs, and the types of changes needed..." (p. 271). As such, this chapter aims to provide an overview of knowledge acquisition/organizational learning literature, synthesize it, and derive some unifying observations and fundaments. Based on the theoretical fundaments derived from the literature, the paper offers conceptual refinements and a number of important strategic implications. Importantly, throughout, the paper extends current knowledge acquisition and management theory to a unique, pervasive, and increasingly important managerial setting, i.e., the virtual team or organization. In addition, the chapter offers and extends strategic implications for virtual organizations.

The literature relevant to knowledge acquisition is quite vast. However, in reading the learning literature, several theoretical principles or dimensions emerge as key. These include: knowledge types, knowledge acquisition processes (or learning processes), and organizational memory. Before this chapter commences with the review and synthesis of these three fundamental issues and their extensions to the virtual setting, the beginning section explicates the role of the individual in firm knowledge acquisition. In the remaining sections of the chapter, conceptual refinements and strategic implications involving knowledge conversion, knowledge acquisition as episodic or continuous, knowledge deployment, potential contingent and complementary effects of knowledge bases, deliberateness of knowledge acquisition, and knowledge acquisition speed are developed and discussed. Each of these refinements and strategic implications are extended to the virtual setting. The chapter concludes with a discussion of further research implications.

THE ROLE OF THE INDIVIDUAL IN FIRM LEVEL KNOWLEDGE ACQUISITION

The literature reveals some significant disparities on the role of the individual in firm level processes. Nelson & Winter (1982) imply that the firm is a learning entity unto itself. In their view, the firm is some extra-rational or hyper-rational cognizing entity apart from the individuals who comprise it. Conversely, Dodgeson (1993) suggests that organizations do not learn, only individuals can learn. Basically, Dodgeson contends that the use of the individual analogy has led us astray in believing organizations can learn.

Some consensus seems to be emerging in the middle ground between these two opposing views. Most agree that individuals in the firm play an integral role in organizational knowledge acquisition. Yet, fundamentally, learning at the individual level is a social process, an activity that cannot occur without group interaction in some form. Individuals learn from the collective, while at the same time the collective learns from individuals. Thus, organizational learning involves a complex interplay between the individual and the firm (Cohen, 1991; Grant, 1996; Nonaka & Takeuchi, 1995; Spender, 1996).

Within the firm, individual participants share perceptions and jointly interpret information, events, and experiences (Cohen & Levinthal, 1990). At some point, knowledge acquisition transcends the individual participants and assumes meaning for the collective, i.e. for the firm (Spender, 1996). Without this process, individual knowledge cannot be exploited by the firm. Organizational learning or knowledge acquisition is the amplification and articulation of individual knowledge at the firm level so that it is internalized into the firm's knowledge base (Inkpen, 1995; Nonaka & Takeuchi, 1995).

The interplay between individual level knowledge bases and firm level knowledge bases has important and unique implications in the virtual setting. By definition, interpersonal contact between members in virtual teams or organizations is much less than in traditional settings. The greatly reduced interpersonal contact between managers in virtual situations can greatly inhibit the shared sensemaking, shared experiences and interpretation crucial in amplifying knowledge, thus significantly inhibiting organizational learning in some forms. Some shared sensemaking no doubt will take place in the virtual world; however, interaction between managers exclusively in cyberspace will greatly limit it, perhaps slowing it down or changing its form as well.

The lack of personal contact in virtual settings may result in knowledge stalling at the individual level. Knowledge that should be amplified to the firm level may remain at the individual level. This generates risk for the firm from two perspectives. The first and obvious risk is that when individuals leave the firm, valuable knowledge bases go with them. The firm's losses could be substantial. The second risk is more subtle. As noted, while organizations gain knowledge bases from individuals through the amplification processes, individuals also gain knowledge from the others participating in the shared experience and interpretation, and from the organization itself. This interplay suggests that without the interpersonal contact in the traditional organizational setting, individual knowledge acquisition can be greatly inhibited. The risk is that when individuals do not build and increase knowledge bases, then the firm most certainly cannot.

THE KNOWLEDGE TYPES

Obviously, learning involves the creation or acquisition of knowledge (Argyris & Schon, 1978; Spender, 1996). In addition to Nonaka and Takeuchi's definition of organizational learning as the articulation and amplification of individual knowledge, other popular definitions illustrate this. For example, learning has been defined as concerning the development of insights, knowledge, and associations between past actions, the effectiveness of those actions and future actions (Fiol & Lyles, 1985). According to Huber (1991), an organization has learned if it acquires knowledge that is potentially useful. Thus, however we define it, organizational learning involves some understanding of knowledge and its properties. With Polanyi's (1967) classification of knowledge into explicit and tacit as a foundation, scholars have developed a rich accounting of knowledge with respect to its properties (Grant, 1996; Inkpen, 1995; Nonaka & Takeuchi, 1995; Spender, 1996).

Explicit knowledge is factual and objective. It has been described as discrete or "digital" (Grant, 1996; Spender, 1996). Explicit knowledge is easily articulated and transmitted in a systematic fashion with minimal loss. Explicit knowledge has also been termed articulated knowledge or declarative (Hedlund, 1994; Winter, 1987). We find explicit knowledge in databanks, manuals, and written procedures (for example Grant, 1996; Nonaka and Takeuchi, 1995; Spender, 1996).

Tacit knowledge is knowledge that is difficult to formalize and communicate. It has been characterized as being unarticulated, subjective, and context specific. Spender (1996) suggests that tacit knowledge is knowledge that has not yet been abstracted from practice. Tacit knowledge can be thought of as embedded in the organization, sometimes deeply. As compared to explicit knowledge, tacit knowledge is difficult to codify. Efforts to codifiy it often involve significant knowledge loss (Winter, 1987). This suggests that tacit knowledge is not easily transferred between firms or among functional areas (Spender, 1996).

Nonaka & Takeuchi (1995) further divide tacit knowledge into philosophical, cognitive, and technical knowledge. Philosophical knowledge involves ideals and values that the firm embraces. Cognitive is that form of tacit knowledge that involves mental models, perspectives, paradigms, and beliefs in the firm. Technical knowledge is the tacit knowledge form that comprises skills or craftsmanship, for example of artisans. Hedlund (1994) further divides tacit knowledge into cognitive, skills, and embodied. Cognitive and skills are similar to Nonaka and Takeuchi's cognitive and technical tacit knowledge forms, while embodied knowledge is that which develops through the flow of products (Hedlund, 1994).

In understanding the nature and characteristics of knowledge, we caution that tacitness and explicitness is often not an either/or issue. Rather, tacitness and explicitness are parallel descriptors of knowledge which range in their degree (Winter, 1987). For example, in cases where knowledge is dominated by explicitness, there also exist elements of tacitness. The same can be said for knowledge largely characterized by tacitness; it is often comprised of some component of explicitness. Some knowledge bases, for example those involving technological processes, can stand alone without being embedded in any specific system (organization). However, these cases are more rare. Likewise, the occurrence of knowledge that is totally inarticulate, non-codifiable, and embedded in the firm is infrequent (Winter, 1987).

Because of the means by which tasks are performed and communication takes place in the virtual setting, knowledge bases in virtual firms will more likely be explicit. The ability to codify knowledge is a fundamental necessity in the absence of interpersonal interaction as with virtual settings. Several of the subtypes of tacit knowledge introduced by Nonaka and Takeuchi (1995) especially point to the difficulties of tacit knowledge bases in virtual situations. The development of ideals and values, nebulous concepts in and of themselves, makes philosophical knowledge bases a difficult proposition, likewise with the development of artisan level skill or craftsmanship. The most viable form of tacit knowledge in virtual organizations is the technical knowledge base. Through extremely frequent contact in cyberspace, members in virtual firms or teams may develop embedded, jointly shared mental models and paradigms.

KNOWLEDGE ACQUISITION PROCESSES

A set of issues fundamental in knowledge base development involves the processes by which it is acquired. Unfortunately, a comprehensive discussion of the various means by which the firm acquires or develops its knowledge bases has not been forthcoming. It is intuitively appealing that explicit and tacit knowledge acquisition processes differ. Though Miner & Mezias (1996) discuss several learning processes, they do not focus on differences by knowledge type. They imply that learning processes vary according to

Figure 1: Firm Level Knowledge Acquisition Processes

	Knowledge Acquired/generated WITHIN the firm	Knowledge Acquired FROM Another firm
Predominantly explicit knowledge acquired	**Experiential Processes** Analogous to: Adaptive learning Single-loop learning Low level learning Exploitation	**Grafting Processes**
Predominantly tacit knowledge acquired	**Inferential Processes** Analogous to: Generative learning Double-loop learning Deutero learning High level learning Exploration	**Vicarious Processes**

who is doing the learning, the individual, the group, the organization, or the population. The position here is that whether it is an individual, the firm, or some other subgroup involved, tacit knowledge is obtained in a different manner than explicit knowledge. From the firm perspective, learning can occur through grafting, vicarious, experiential, and inferential processes (Figure 1).

Grafting involves the migration of knowledge between firms. It is a learning process whereby the firm gains access to task or process-specific knowledge not previously available within the firm. The firm gains access by linking with other firms through alliances, mergers, or acquisitions (Huber, 1991). In grafting, the firm learns *from* its partner in a direct passing of knowledge between the firms. A common example of grafting involves technology transfer between partners in a strategic alliance form (Bradaracco, 1991). Implicit in knowledge acquisition through grafting processes is that the knowledge involved is predominantly explicit.

When a firm joins with another firm to observe and participate in the other firm's demonstration of management techniques, or operating procedures and techniques, *vicarious learning processes* are at issue (Huber, 1991; Miner & Mezias, 1996). As with grafting, the process involves the sharing of knowledge between firms, that is, learning *from* another firm. However, the knowledge acquired in vicarious processes by one firm is embedded in the other firm's practices and operation, difficult to codify, and somewhat difficult to transfer without loss (Inkpen & Beamish 1997). It involves learning how to do something, i.e., it is predominantly tacit in nature. An example of this would be when a U.S. firm forms an alliance with a Japanese firm to learn Japanese management techniques.

Experiential knowledge acquisition does not involve the acquisition of knowledge from another firm. Rather, it involves knowledge acquisition by building it *within* the firm. In experiential learning processes, knowledge derives from doing and practicing. Repetition-based experience is a key fundament in experiential learning. As such, it relies to a significant extent on ideas such as the learning curve to establish routines and procedures (Edmondson & Moingeon, 1996; Levinthal, 1991; Levinthal & March, 1993). The firm looks to itself and what it has done in practice and experience for pertinent knowledge (Levinthal & March, 1993; Pennings, Barkema, & Douma, 1994; Starbuck, 1992). The knowledge acquired in experiential learning processes is easily codified and transferred; it is predominantly tacit.

In a complementary view of experiential learning, several theorists have suggested that knowledge acquisition can take place at low or high levels of organizational cognition (Fiol & Lyles, 1985). Low level organizational learning involves changing actions and routine processes. It consists of the development of successful operating procedures and scripts for handling routine situations. It also involves management systems to handle information for unchanging situations and repetition. Low level learning compares to what some theorists have referred to as single-loop learning (Argyris & Schon, 1978; Miner & Mezias, 1996). March (1991) refers to low level learning in terms of exploiting for efficiency based considerations. Slater & Narver (1995) refer to it as adaptive learning.

These descriptions consistently allude to learning as comprised of refinement and improvements in existing procedures and technologies as opposed to developing new ones. In addition, these concepts involve learning that can be considered as deterministic in the sense that existing assumptions, resources, and political strictures within the firm bound it (Miller, 1996). Some authors have suggested that low-level learning likely happens in organizations characterized by rigid and bureaucratized hierarchies (March, 1991; Weick & Westley, 1996).

Inferential knowledge acquisition processes are often alluded to in the literature (Day, 1994; Mintzberg, 1990), but rarely explicated. Like experiential learning, with inferential learning, the knowledge base is built *within* the firm rather than having another firm playing a part in knowledge acquisition. And like experiential knowledge acquisition, inferential processes involve learning by doing. However, it relates only very remotely to the repetition-based experience on which experiential processes are based. In inferential learning processes, firms acquire knowledge by interpreting events, states, changes, and outcomes relative to their own activities and decisions. Knowledge builds through the firm's examination of its activities and decisions, and its own understanding of how those activities and decisions lead to successes or failures. Inferential learning involves a strong deductive and experimental component coupled with the sense making and interpretation of causal linkages between actions and particular outcomes (Huber, 1991; March, 1991; Miner & Mezias, 1996).

As with experiential knowledge acquisition, inferential processes have been viewed by some scholars in terms of the level of organizational cognition where it occurs (Fiol & Lyles, 1985). Inferential knowledge acquisition is consistent with what has been termed as high-level learning in that it involves changing associations and frameworks, and assessments of the in-depth functioning of the organization. It involves the introduction of new and/or different assumptions. In addition to being consistent with inferential learning processes, high-level learning parallels Slater & Narver's (1995) generative type of learning, where the firm questions long-held assumptions and develops new views that are "frame-breaking." In such cases, there is a large latitude for choice and autonomy; learning is essentially free and unbounded by extant cognitive or resource strictures (Miller, 1996). High level learning captures the essence of double-loop or deutero-learning (Argyris & Schon, 1978; Miner & Mezias, 1996). In another view, March (1991) discusses these concepts (high level learning, generative learning, double-loop or deutro-learning) as exploration where new knowledge and new alternatives result rather than refinement of existing competencies and procedures.

It is important to note that we do not intend to associate low versus high-level learning in any way with the level of managerial hierarchy in the firm. Miller (1996) develops a complex typology of learning and suggests that certain types of learning are confined to high-level management while others occur at midlevel or lower level management. Generally, the view here is that experiential (low-level) learning and inferential (high-level) learning can and does occur at multiple levels in the firm's managerial hierarchy and operation. Experiential versus inferential learning can be seen as a trade-off between exploitation of known alternatives for the exploration of unknown alternatives. However, as March (1991) advocates and as was suggested earlier, both exploration and exploitation have a place in the firm.

Knowledge Acquisition Processes in Virtual Settings

Given the premise that the lack of interpersonal interaction in virtual settings makes codification necessary, knowledge acquisition likely involves grafting in alliances involving virtual firms. Vicarious learning requires intensive interpersonal contact to observe and transfer embedded knowledge. Likewise, in the virtual firm, the likely acquisition process for knowledge is experiential. Knowledge gained from repetition and establishment of routines and procedures is likely to be key. In general, virtual settings may be prone to learning where the focus is on incremental adaptation in task performance and procedures. That is not to say that in virtual situations, the tasks are routine, only that the procedures and routines for task performance, once established, are likely to be adapted incrementally.

It is difficult to envision a firm that would never engage in high-level learning, never face the need to break from existing frames of reference and develop new ones. On the other hand, however, it is difficult to picture frame-breaking learning without fairly intensive interpersonal interaction between firm managers. As virtual organizations grow and mature, no doubt they will face situations of "frame-breaking" regeneration and major adaptation. How they accomplish this remains to be seen. This may be an intriguing question with regard to virtual organizations.

ORGANIZATIONAL MEMORY

Though questioned by some (Dodgson, 1993), most theorists agree that firms have knowledge storage capacities (Day, 1994; Hedberg, 1981; Moorman & Miner, 1997; Nelson & Winter, 1982; Walsh & Ungson, 1991). The firm's knowledge storage capacity, i.e., its organizational memory, is the repository for the knowledge developed jointly by multiple individual firm members in the amplification of individual learning to firm level learning. Using human memory as an analog, Walsh & Ungson (1991) propose that organizational memory involves the use of five storage bins: individual firm members, organizational culture, transformation, structure, and ecology.

Each of these bins in the firm's memory have varying implications for the knowledge types and acquisition processes. The storage of explicit knowledge, routine codified material, is likely straightforward. For example, the firm's transformations provide the storage bin where technology-based knowledge or management based standard operating procedural knowledge accumulates (Cohen & Bacdayen, 1994; Walsh & Ungson, 1991). This is where databases would be found and where operating manuals and procedures are documented. Another viable and effective repository for tacit knowledge is the firm's workplace ecology which consists of the physical place in which the organization operates (Walsh & Ungson, 1991).

In contrast to explicit knowledge bases, storage of the non-routine material comprising tacit knowledge is more complex. However, because of the strategic implications involved, it is also more compelling. The three remaining storage bins proposed by Walsh & Ungson (1991)—organizational structure, organizational culture, and individual organizational members—serve as repositories for tacit knowledge bases. Given the pivotal role of individual firm members in firm level learning of all forms, these individuals likely serve as repositories for both tacit and explicit knowledge. The other two remaining bins, organizational structure and organizational culture, play a pivotal role in tacit knowledge base retention.

Organizational structure defines roles and task allocation. It includes the differentiation of production, marketing, boundary spanning, and other operational tasks. Through both formal and informal job descriptions, it defines roles and positions. Thus, the firm's organizational structure serves as an effective storage reservoir for tacit knowledge. Likewise, organizational culture provides a crucial repository for tacit knowledge. Organizational culture is learned and transmitted through language, stories, and shared frameworks. These provide especially appropriate storage bins for knowledge that is non-routine, difficult to codify, subjective, and context specific.

In addition to the various storage bins, Moorman & Miner (1997) suggest that organizational memory has four other dimensions: level, dispersion, accessibility, and content. Level in organizational memory refers simply to the amount of knowledge an organization has accumulated. According to Moorman and Miner, dispersion is the extent to which memory is shared and spread across the organization by the organizational members. Accessibility refers to the extent to which memory can be retrieved for use. Content concerns the meaning of memory in terms of whether it is procedural (involving skills or competencies) or declarative (involving facts or events). As Moorman & Miner (1997) conceptualize it, procedural firm memory content would consist of tacit knowledge bases, while declarative memory content would focus on explicit knowledge bases.

Dispersion of the knowledge stores and access to them are more of a problem with tacit knowledge than with explicit knowledge. Because of its nature, appropriability and transferability are difficult with tacit knowledge. Likewise, tacit knowledge will be generally difficult to pass around in the firm. The properties of tacitness become a disadvantage internally when the firm endeavors to disperse it. Further, some aspects or components of tacit knowledge will be more deeply embedded in the organization structure and culture reservoirs than others. This means that in certain cases, its dispersion and accessibility will be more difficult and inhibited than normal even for tacit knowledge. How much of a problem this is for the firm and how it will be managed varies from case to case.

Organizational Memory in the Virtual Setting

Relative to traditional settings, virtual organizations likely rely on a more limited set of reservoirs for storage and retention of knowledge bases. This pivots to some extent on the types of knowledge in question, i.e., the proness for explicit knowledge bases. In virtual situations, transformations and structure provide the more viable storage bins. The firm's transformations, its routines for task performance, are where the virtual organization accumulates knowledge of procedures, standards, and manuals, etc. With minimal interpersonal contact increasing the need for codification, these bins become the natural reservoirs. The same logic applies to organizational structure for the virtual organization. Role and task allocation, job and operational descriptions can be formalized and codified in the virtual organization. This emphasis on formalization and codification of structure is likely to be greater relative to traditional settings where there is often a strong informal element.

The development of culture in general will be an interesting issue in the virtual organization. Organizational culture pivots on interaction of organizational members. When that interaction is not personal, to a significant extent organizational culture development may be inhibited. Perhaps it will be slowed down and may take different forms. Thus, the role of culture in the virtual firm, at this point is mostly unknown. As a storage bin for firm knowledge stores, it is a less viable candidate.

Having acquired and stored knowledge in the virtual firm, access to and dispersion of memory is perhaps more problematic than in traditional settings. Again, as with knowledge amplification, because of the form communication takes and the limits in interpersonal contact in the virtual setting, organization members will not be able to access firm memory as readily as in traditional settings. In addition, accessibility limits are due partially to there being fewer storage bins and those there having more limited availability.

STRATEGIC ISSUES IN KNOWLEDGE BASE MANAGEMENT

There are a number of important implications surrounding knowledge acquisition processes and management. Here we address the following: conversion between the two predominant forms of knowledge, the extent to which knowledge base acquisition is episodic or continuous, deployment of knowledge bases, complementary and contingent effects of knowledge bases and types, the extent of deliberateness in knowledge acquisition, and speed of the various knowledge acquisition processes.

Conversion Between Tacit and Explicit Knowledge Bases

Recently in the literature there has been some attention given to the idea that conversion between the two major knowledge types can occur. Tacit knowledge can be converted to explicit knowledge and explicit knowledge can be converted to tacit (Nonaka & Takeuchi, 1995; Spender, 1996). The issue of knowledge conversion involves an assumption of some significance—that conversion is desirable. This is questionable especially with regard to the tacit-to-explicit conversion.

The logic for converting from tacit to explicit is fairly intuitive. The conversion into explicit knowledge means that what was difficult to communicate is made easy to communicate. Thus, the conversion to explicit greatly facilitates transference and sharing, and perhaps even the potential use of the formerly tacit knowledge within and between firms. Its accessibility and dispersion is no longer a problem.

However, with regard to the desirability of the tacit-to-explicit conversion several concerns must be questioned thoroughly. First, the tacit-to-explicit conversion cannot be accomplished without considerable knowledge loss (Spender, 1996; Grant, 1996). Thus, in gaining the advantage of easy communication, the value of the knowledge is significantly degraded. A substantial share of the tacit knowledge leaks away as it is converted to explicit. In converting tacit knowledge to explicit, there is some possibility that the advantages of communicability would not outweigh the loss or degradation of the knowledge.

A second and perhaps more important reason to question the desirability of the tacit-to-explicit conversion is strategic. All knowledge is a potential source of competitive advantage. However, relative to explicit, tacit knowledge is the more compelling source. Resource-based theory of the firm suggests that to provide sustainable competitive advantage, a resource should not be easily imitated or acquired by other firms so that its advantage can be competed away (Peteraf, 1993; Reed & DeFillipi, 1990). Thus, the causal ambiguity shrouding a resource such as tacit knowledge serves as a protection. Its value as a source of competitive advantage remains intact and the advantage sustainable by the virtue of its tacitness. Conversely, if knowledge is explicit, it can be transferred or easily passed and acquired by others. Competitors can get it relatively easily. Like any resource that can be easily obtained or imitated, its advantage will be short lived and competed away.

This suggests that greater and more sustainable strategic advantage can be gained by eschewing the conversion of tacit knowledge to explicit. Further, this provides a compelling reason for the reverse, less intuitive conversion, from explicit knowledge to tacit. Because its transfer or imitation is inhibited, converting explicit knowledge to tacit preserves and extends the strategic value of the knowledge. Embedding it as deeply as possible in the organization and shrouding it in causal ambiguity to the greatest extent possible results in a longer strategic life of the firm's knowledge bases in general.

Knowledge Acquisition as Continuous Versus Episodic

The notion of whether knowledge acquisition is continuous or episodic has not been addressed in the literature. However, a review of the examples and case studies on which a vast share of the learning literature is based suggests that such a delineation is warranted and useful conceptually. More important, a continuous versus episodic distinction in knowledge base acquisition has widespread strategic implications.

In a preponderance of the knowledge acquisition examples in the literature, some end or completion is somehow implied. Though not explicitly stated as such, knowledge acquisition is often positioned as task oriented. Theorists have considered learning as a problem solving process or as focused on a specific task (Pisano, 1994). What happens when the problem has been solved or the task completed? For example, in a strategic alliance involving technology transfer, once the technology is transferred, by implication, knowledge acquisition is complete. This builds instability into the alliance from the onset (Inkpen & Beamish, 1997). Also, by implication, when the technology for a new product has been developed and the product launched (Nonaka & Takeuchi, 1995), the learning episode is complete.

These knowledge acquisition episodes imply a static view of knowledge development. Once the process or task is complete, the knowledge base is in place. Having been acquired, the knowledge base is considered a fixed resource to be exploited. Given its static nature, the appropriability of the knowledge base becomes an issue. Again, the strategic value of such a knowledge base would be short lived if it could be acquired by others and/or competed away.

In other learning situations, knowledge acquisition is continuous and more dynamic. These often involve the development of strategic capabilities, or the firm's "skilling" of itself in certain domains such as new product development, distribution, or interfirm networking (Day, 1994). When knowledge acquisition processes are ongoing and involve continual modifications and refinements, even if the modifications and refinements are not radical (Weick & Westley, 1996), causal ambiguity and barriers to imitability are maintained (Reed & DeFilippi, 1990). These knowledge bases are less easily acquired by other firms, less easily emulated and the advantage derived from them less easily competed away. Thus, knowledge bases acquired in the development of strategic capabilities may provide a more viable and enduring source of competitive advantage.

Deployment of Knowledge Bases

As with other resources, knowledge bases must be deployed effectively if the firm is to enjoy enhanced outcomes. Resource-based theory suggests that effective deployment of the knowledge base means maximization of the quasi-rents extracted from the knowledge (Barney, 1991; Peteraf, 1993; Rumelt, 1984). Knowledge acquired and deployed increases the range of behavior for the firm (Huber, 1991). This increased range of behavior is key to the strategic value of knowledge bases to the firm. Essentially, knowledge is a crucial resource because it provides options to the firm. Options arise because the knowledge bases allow preferential access to future opportunities, i.e., choices and activities from which competitive advantage derives (Bowman & Hurry, 1993). However, just because knowledge bases confer strategic options, exercising them effectively or at all may not necessarily follow. Deriving competitive advantage from knowledge bases is not a foregone conclusion of knowledge acquisition. Thus, knowledge deployment becomes a crucial concern.

With regard to tacit knowledge, effective deployment is the conversion of the knowledge into a capability or capabilities salient in the firm's ability to compete. The firm's knowledge base provides the options for future choices (Bowman & Hurry, 1993). However, it must be coupled with the appropriate diagnostics, i.e., managerial sense making and perceptual acuity in recognizing opportunities, identifying the possible courses of action, and matching sets of capabilities and other organizational resources (Bowman & Hurry, 1993; Edmondson & Moingeon, 1996). Through this coupling with managerial diagnostics, the knowledge base not only expands options, but it allows for identification of emerging or previously hidden options (i.e., shadow options and opportunity arrival) and it actually reduces the uncertainty attached to the options. Thus, effective knowledge deployment, its conversion into capabilities and translation into competitive advantage, involves the identification and recognition of the initiating options set and the options chain that results (Bowman & Hurry, 1993). Hofer & Schendel (1978) suggest that resource deployment in and of itself is a unique competence that varies from firm to firm. Viewing knowledge deployment in terms of options theory is consistent with resource deployment as a competence.

Strategic implications for the deployment of explicit knowledge bases differ considerably from those for tacit knowledge stores. Choices and options in applying the knowledge are more apparent and links to deployment outcomes are more identifiable. Effective deployment might result in efficiency gains or in cost decreases. While these can be crucial strategic outcomes, again the concern for appropriability arises. If other firms can appropriate the explicit knowledge base, which is often the case, the advantages soon will be competed away. Explicit knowledge must be rapidly deployed, and it must be rapidly renewed, or recreated, if the competitive advantage is to be retained.

Contingent and Complementary Effects of Knowledge Deployment

Various authors have provided examples of knowledge acquisition that occur in various contexts (Bradaracco, 1991; Inkpen, 1995; Nonaka & Takeuchi, 1995). Likewise, we fully acknowledge that firms can develop multiple capabilities (Day, 1994). The idea of the firm acquiring knowledge in an array of domains seems intuitively appealing. It follows then, that to realize full competitive advantage of capabilities and knowledge resources, firms should deploy them in tandem. As noted above, options theory also implies that optimal strategic gain results from the coupling of various resource bases (Bowman & Hurry, 1993). Resource based views of the firm suggest that when the firm joins an appropriate set of capabilities in pursuit of competitive advantage, the effects would be nonadditive (Peteraf, 1993). Outcome enhancements exceed the sum of the individual capabilities' outcomes. This research, along with options theory applications, opens up an array of strategic implications in terms of coupling capabilities to yield the greatest benefits.

In addition to the potential gains from the complementarity of capabilities, however, explicit knowledge bases can be coupled with capabilities to enhance and extend gains in competitive advantage. Given the potential lack of durability in the competitive advantage gains derived from explicit knowledge, if explicit knowledge such as a technology is coupled appropriately with the right capability or set of capabilities, its life as a source of competitive advantage may be extended. Essentially, deploying explicit knowledge bases in combination with tacit knowledge adds a layer of complexity so that rivals may not appropriate the knowledge as easily, if at all (Peteraf, 1993; Reed & DeFillipi, 1990).

Knowledge Acquisition and Methodological Versus Emergent

Naturally in the course of survival, all firms adapt and adjust (Dodgson, 1993). Thus, in some form, all firms learn whether or not learning is their explicit intent (Fiol & Lyles, 1985). However, the extent or absence of deliberateness in the learning process is an issue of some strategic consequence. Miller (1996) addresses this in terms of method versus emergence. Learning processes in firms, regardless of which type, range on a continuum with methodical at one extreme and emergent at the other. At the emergent end of the spectrum, knowledge acquisition is spontaneous and unplanned. Some knowledge is acquired and some knowledge bases develop. However, acquisition is likely haphazard and the bases may be under utilized because the firm has little or no intent with regard to learning. In general, knowledge bases are less substantial than they could be and less competitive advantage is realized from them than could be. At the other extreme, knowledge acquisition is methical. This means it is intentional, deliberate, and system-atic (Hamel, 1991). The firm motivated in knowledge acquisition likely develops more substantial knowledge stores. When this is accompanied by equal doses of motivation in deployment, optimization of knowledge also likely results.

The Rate of Knowledge Acquisition

The rate of knowledge acquisition by the firm has been cited as important strategically. Hamel (1991) suggested that competitive advantage comes down to the race to learn. The firm that learns faster and more is the firm that will succeed in the market. Because of the characteristics of transferability and appropriability, tacit knowledge acquisition occurs faster. However, as noted previously, the strategic advantage of such knowledge bases is likely less enduring. The implication is that the firm should be reconciled to the possibility that strategic gains from explicit knowledge may be relatively short-term and plan accordingly. The firm's reconciliation involves immediate regeneration and renewal of the knowledge base (Reed & DeFillipe, 1990) or immediate and rapid exploitation for the short-term competitive advantage. In some cases the firm may be able to protect the explicit knowledge base by converting it to tacit or by using legal means such as patents (Liebeskind, 1996).

When rapid knowledge acquisition is imperative, obtaining it from other firms can provide the needed speed advantage. Because the knowledge previously exists, acquiring knowledge from other firms is likely faster than when knowledge acquisition in fact entails knowledge creation within the firm, as with experiential or inferential processes. Thus, grafting and vicarious learning processes may be desirable alternatives when learning speed plays a role in gaining competitive advantage.

Strategic Issues of Knowledge Base Management in the Virtual Organization

In virtual organizations, the major direction of knowledge conversion is from tacit to explicit. The virtual environment hinges on communication that is predominantly not interpersonal and task performance is, for the most part, accomplished without personal contact between organizational participants. This requires that to retain them and to access them, organizational knowledge bases need to be codifiable and codified. Thus, the virtual organization benefits greatly when tacit knowledge is converted to explicit. The difficulties of developing tacit knowledge bases in the virtual setting were previously noted. However, should they be developed, conversion to explicit likely follows quite closely. This leaves the virtual firm more vulnerable to the inevitable knowledge loss and leakage in the conversion process. In addition, it also leaves the virtual organization more vulnerable to the risks of appropriation. The embeddedness and ambiguity that protects tacit knowledge from being easily appropriated by others is gone. The advantages can be competed away more readily.

The vulnerabilities and risks created by 1) the predominantly explicit nature of knowledge bases in the virtual setting and 2) the conversion of the limited potential tacit knowledge bases to explicit, result in even more increased pressures on the knowledge development and management in the virtual firm. In general to be competitive, virtual firms may need to be much more aggressive in knowledge acquisition and management in general. For example, speed and deliberateness of knowledge acquisition and development may be pressured. To gain competitive advantage, virtual firms may need to accelerate knowledge acquisition and development in order to keep ahead of the advantages being competed away. Likewise, pressure will be to acquire knowledge in a continuous and deliberate fashion rather than episodic and emergent. Some pressure may be diminished when the competition is with other virtual firms given that these firms face the same constraints. However, relative to the traditional firm, the virtual firm aggressiveness of knowledge acquisition and management will often remain an issue.

Given the potential limits in the strategic life of knowledge in the virtual setting, acquiring and retaining strong knowledge bases even in a fairly aggressive and continuous fashion does not necessarily lead to a sustainable competitive advantage. Deployment of knowledge bases and effective coupling of complementary knowledge domains completes the picture. Again, both of these are more problematic in the virtual organization. Because of the lack of personal contact, accessing knowledge stores in the virtual organization is more difficult relative to traditional settings, suggesting deployment also may be more difficult. In addition, the lack of interpersonal contact could lead to the atomization of various functional areas in the virtual organization, decreasing the likelihood of joint deployment of various knowledge bases.

The advantages of virtual settings, such as efficiency and cost, may be great. However, these advantages do not come without tradeoffs. The most significant tradeoff may come in terms of the strategically crucial arena of knowledge acquisition and management. At this point in time, for the most part, communication in virtual organizations is limited to some written form. The constraint in communication forms limits the depth and richness of exchanges. Without nonverbal, spontaneous feedback and response in interpersonal interaction, knowledge acquisition, retention, deployment, and the strategic optimization of knowledge bases may prove to be difficult propositions in the virtual environment. Beyond this, acquisition and retention of knowledge will likely focus on the less durable explicit forms. This gives rise to the question of whether or not virtual organizations can develop strategic capabilities.

An issue with regard to knowledge acquisition and management in the virtual organization is the changes that technology will bring. Advances in communication technology will drive the evolution of the virtual firm and likely communication constraints will be temporary. Technological advances will eventually allow for audio and visual interaction in real time, which will facilitate more spontaneous, richer and deeper communication. When communication technologies allow for these types of interactions, knowledge acquisition management in virtual settings may come to parallel that of traditional organizational settings. Cultures can develop, tacit knowledge and all the accompanying issues will become more viable. Meanwhile, as temporary communications deficiencies exist in the virtual setting, they bring fairly widespread implications in important strategic arenas such as learning.

DISCUSSION AND CONCLUSION

Despite widespread belief in the concepts of knowledge acquisition and management by firms, we still know very little about how knowledge is acquired and how the acquisition processes vary in specific contexts important to the firm's well being. Consistent with other scholars (e.g., Slater & Narver, 1995), a central premise of this paper is that consideration of knowledge acquisition processes as varying in different contexts is the key to solidifying and extending our understanding of learning by firms. A critical and little understood context is the virtual organization. This organizational form is becoming increasingly important in the contemporary business environment. However, it brings with it a set of issues and questions even more complex with regard to organizational learning. As such, this chapter synthesizes and integrates a vast and diverse literature in an attempt to delineate important theoretical fundaments. In addition, we offer conceptual refinements and strategic implications. We explore extensions of the theory and implications for virtual settings.

The theoretical fundaments and conceptual refinements presented in this paper suggest an array of directions for investigation. One compelling issue is outcomes. Our ability to help managers in knowledge acquisition and management would be enhanced if we understood learning outcomes. Argyris and Schon (1978) indicate that the outcome of learning is some change in behavior, which is clearly true at an abstract level. Yet, the changes in behavior should link with enhanced performance outcomes for the firm. Like the domains of learning, the domains of outcomes vary. For example, they may involve efficiency or strategic gains.

A related issue concerns the immediacy of the effects of learning. Some scholars have suggested that the benefits of learning may be delayed or masked (Van de Ven & Polley, 1992). Options theory also suggests this could be the case (Bowman & Hurry, 1993). The firm does not realize the enhanced performance outcomes generated by learning until later time periods, or cannot identify emerging options and opportunities. Outcome lags need to be understood so that managers persist in learning efforts and continue allocating resources to knowledge acquisition though benefits are not immediately apparent.

An issue crucial to knowledge acquisition, especially for the virtual organization, involves how the processes are set in motion. Though all firms engage in learning in some form simply in the course of survival, important questions involve moving the firm from the haphazard and unplanned emergent approach to learning toward more intentional, focused, and methodological learning (Miller, 1996). The appropriate management of knowledge acquisition plays a vital role in the process (Van de Ven & Polley, 1992). In some cases, managers must overcome organizational defenses and resistance to learning. Specifically, in virtual firms, managers must overcome the natural barriers to learning that are inherent and introduced by the organization form itself. Considerations in facilitating knowledge acquisition might include the development of firm structures that encourage and evoke knowledge acquisition, setting and understanding knowledge acquisition goals and objectives, allocation of human and financial resources to learning efforts, and evaluation of progress in developing knowledge bases.

Some researchers (Fiol & Lyles, 1985) contend that unlearning may be just as important as learning. Unlearning involves jettisoning old frameworks and breaking away from fixedness. Perhaps as important, unlearning can involve response to mistakes (Van de Ven & Polley, 1992). This suggests that failure can play an important role in knowledge acquisition and deployment if it is viewed as a learning opportunity.

In conclusion, while extremely rich in conceptual treatments and theory, the knowledge acquisition literature has not addressed organizational learning in the important but extremely unique context of the virtual organization. If we continue to unpack the broad topic of organizational learning as some researchers have already begun, we can develop researchable questions that apply to the virtual firm. A tradition of empirical research could then augment the strong theoretical development and the resulting gains would be substantial for both researchers and managers. Intriguing and valuable contrasts between knowledge acquisition and management in traditional and virtual organizational settings will emerge.

REFERENCES

Argyris, C., & Schon, D.A. (1978). *Organizational learning: A theory of action perspective*. Reading, MA: Addison Wesley.

Bradaracco, J.L. (1991). *The knowledge link*. Boston: Harvard Business School Press.

Barney, J. (1991). Firm resources and sustained competitive advantage. *Journal of Management*, 17, 99-120

Bowman, E.H., & Hurry, D. (1993). Strategy through the option lens: An integrated view of resource investments and the incremental-choice process. *Academy of Management Review*, 18, 760-82.

Cohen, M.D. (1991). Individual learning and organizational routine: Emerging connections. *Organization Science*, 2 135-39.

_____, & Bacdayen, P. (1994). Organizational routines are stored as procedural memory: Evidence from a laboratory study. *Organization Science*, 4, 554-68.

Cohen, W.M., & Levinthal, D.A. (1990). Absorptive capacity: A new perspective on learning and innovation. *Administrative Science Quarterly*, 35, 128-52.

Day, G.S. (1994). The capabilities of market-driven organizations. *Journal of Marketing*, 58, 37-52.

Dodgson, M. (1993). Organizational learning: A review of some literatures. *Organization Studies*, 14, 375-94.

Edmondson, A., & Moingeon, B. (1996). When to learn how and when to learn why: Appropriate organizational learning processes as a source of competitive advantage. In B. Moingeon & A. Edmondson (Eds.), *Organizational learning and competitive advantage* (pp. 17-37). London: Sage.

Fiol, C.M., & Lyles, M.A.(1985). Organizational learning. *Academy of Management Review*, 10, 803-13.

Grant, R.M. (1996). Toward a knowledge-based theory of the firm. *Strategic Management Journal*, 17, 109-22.

Hamel, G. (1991). Competition for competence and inter-partner learning within international strategic alliances. *Strategic Management Journal*, 12, 83-104.

Hedberg, B. (1981). How organizations learn and unlearn. In Nystrom, P., & Starbuck, W. (Eds.), *The handbook of organizational design* (pp. 3-27). London: Oxford University Press.

Hedlund, G. (1994), A model of knowledge management and the N-form corporation. *Strategic Management Journal*, 15, 73-90.

Hofer, C.W., & Schendel, D. (1978). *Strategy formulation: Analytical concepts*. St. Paul: West Publishing.

Huber, G.P. (1991). Organizational learning: The contributing processes and a review of the literatures. *Organizational Science*, 2, 88-117.

Inkpen, A. (1995). *The management of international joint ventures*. New York: Rutledge.

Inkpen, A. & Beamish, P.W. (1997). Knowledge, bargaining power, and the instability of international joint ventures. *Academy of Management Review*, 22, 177-202.

Leibeskind, J.P. (1996). Knowledge, strategy, and theory of the firm. *Strategic Management Journal*, 17, 93-107.

Levinthal, D.A. (1991). Organizational adaptation and environmental selection — Interrelated processes of change. *Organizational Science*, 2, 140-45.

Levinthal, D.A. & March, J.G. (1993). The myopia of learning. *Strategic Management Journal*, 14, 95-112.

March, J.G. (1991). Exploration and exploitation in organizational learning. *Organizational Science*, 2, 71-87.

Miller, D. (1996). A preliminary typology of organizational learning: Synthesizing the literature. *Journal of Management*, 22, 485-505.

Miner, A.S., & Mezias, S.J. (1996). Ugly duckling no more: Pasts and futures of organizational learning research. *Organization Science*, 7, 88-99.

Mintzberg, H. (1990). Strategy formation: Schools of thought. In J. Frederickson (Ed.), *Perspectives of strategic management*. New York: Harper Business.

Moorman, C., & Miner, A.S. (1997). The impact of organizational memory on new product performance and creativity. *Journal of Marketing Research*, 34, 91-106.

Nelson, R.R., & Winter, S.G. (1982). *An evolutionary theory of economic change*. Cambridge, MA: Harvard University Press.

Nonaka, I., & Takeuchi, H. (1995). *The knowledge creating company*. New York: Oxford University Press.

Osborn, R.N., & Hagedoorn, J. (1997). The institutionalization and evolutionary dynamics of interorganizational alliances and networks. *Academy of Management Journal*, 40, 261-78.

Peteraf, M.A. (1993). The cornerstones of competitive advantage: A resource based view. *Strategic Management Journal*, 14, 179-91.

Pennings, J.M., Barkema, H.M., & Douma, S. (1994). Organizational learning and diversification. *Academy of Management Journal*, 37, 608-40.

Pisano, G.P. (1994). Knowledge, integration, and the locus of learning: An empirical analysis of process development. *Strategic Management Journal*, 15, 85-100.

Polanyi, M. (1967). *The tact dimension*. Garden City, NY: Anchor.

Reed, R., & Defillippi, R.J. (1990). Causal ambiguity, barriers to imitation, and sustainable competitive advantage. *Academy of Management Review*, 15, 88-102.

Rumelt, R. P. (1984). Towards a strategic theory of the firm. In R.B. Lamb (Ed.), *Competitive strategic management*. Englewood Cliffs, NJ: Prentice Hall.

Slater, S.F., & Narver, J.C. (1995). Market orientation and the learning organization. *Journal of Marketing*, 59, 63-74.

Spender, J.-C. (1996). Making knowledge the basis of a dynamic theory of the firm. *Strategic Management Journal*, 17, 45-62.

Starbuck, W.H. (1992). Learning by knowledge intensive firms. *Journal of Management Studies*, 29, 713-40.

Van de Ven, A.H., & Polley, D. (1992). Learning while innovating. *Organization Science*, 3, 92-116.

Walsh, J.P., & Ungson, G.R. (1991). Organizational memory. *Academy of Management Review*, 16, 57-91.

Weick, K.E., & Westley, F. (1996). Organizational learning: Affirming an oxymoron. In S.R. Clegg, C. Hardy, and W.R. Nord (Eds.), *Handbook of organization studies*, (pp. 440-58). London: Sage.

Winter, S.G. (1987). Knowledge and competence as strategic assets. In D.J. Teese (Ed.), *The Competitive challenge: Strategies for industrial innovation and renewal* (pp.159-84). New York: Harper and Row.

Chapter XIX

Knowledge Needs
of Self-Organized Systems

João Álvaro Carvalho
University of Minho, Portugal

Self-organized systems are capable of changing their own structure in order to adapt themselves to significant changes in their environment. They are at the top of a hierarchy of systems that arranges systems according to the degree of control they have upon their own actions. Self-directed systems, self-regulated systems and uncontrolled systems are the reminder levels of that hierarchy.

The framework developed in this chapter identifies the necessary components at each level of control. These components include operators, coordinators, regulators, directors, organizers and informers. The framework can be described as a model of the general architecture of self-organized systems. It is used to identify and characterize the knowledge needs of self-organized systems by examining the functionality, characteristics and knowledge needs of each of those components.

The use of the term knowledge in contexts related with organizations is becoming increasingly common. Organizational learning and innovation (i.e., organizational innovation capability) are metaphors intimately related with knowledge that are used to study and intervene in organizations. Perspectives on organizations based on such metaphors (e.g., Argyris, 1993; 1994; Senge, 1992; Senge, Kleiner, Roberts, Ross, & Smith, 1994; Nemeth, 1997), led to knowledge to be considered as a corporate resource that, like other organizational resources, has to be managed (Davenport & Prusak, 1998; Stewart, 1997; Myers, 1996; O'Leary, 1998). As a consequence, knowledge management has been emerging as a new professional activity.

This chapter proposes a framework that describes the use of different types of knowledge in organizations. The framework is mainly composed by a *hierarchy of systems* that classifies systems according to the degree of control they have upon their own actions. The hierarchy starts with *uncontrolled systems* and ends with *self-organized systems* which are described as systems that are capable of defining (or changing) their own structure. The different levels of self-control are explained through the existence of components (subsystems) whose functionality and knowledge needs are presented and discussed. The framework can be described as a model of the general architecture of a self-organized system.

ASSUMPTIONS ABOUT KNOWLEDGE

Organizations are the context where *work* is carried out. By work, it is meant purposeful action, i.e., activities executed with the intention of contributing to some purpose or to achieve some goal. Purposeful action is performed by someone, or something, that will be called an *agent*.

It will be assumed that, in order to be capable of acting, agents need knowledge. The definition of knowledge underlying this position will be broad. Knowledge includes whatever an agent knows that enables her/him/it to carry out the activities she/he/it is supposed to perform. It can be related to knowing how to do something, knowing facts or events, past or future, or knowledge resulting from thinking, e.g., ideas, models, judgments.

The identification and explanation of the knowledge needs of active things - agents - will be done using the concept of *system* and other concepts developed by authors that propose systemic approaches to study the "world".

While talking about the knowledge needs of agents, it might be inferred that the term *agent* is standing for *human agent*. That isn't necessarily true, as it is recognized that there are agents capable of automatically performing operations upon knowledge representations. However, the ambiguity is intentional, as it allows eluding the discussion whether knowledge exists only in the human mind or it can also exist in nonhuman entities. Such discussion is considered to be out of the scope of this chapter.

SYSTEMS

System is a concept that is useful to study active things, especially when they are complex. A system is the result of viewing the active world from a certain point of view. Any thing (and especially an active thing) can be viewed as being a system. A system (in general or in abstract) can be defined as an active, stable and evolutionary thing or object that operates in an environment with some purpose (Le Moigne, 1977).

A system converts some input into an output. What is converted can be either a

Table 1: Conversions that a system can produce and the types of objects that can be altered; the table shows some words normally used to refer to some of the alterations

changed objects		form	space	time
passive things	**matter**	transformation	transportation	storage, stocks
	energy	conversion	transportation	accumulation
	information	processing	transmission	storage, memory
active things	**systems**	the alteration of a system addresses its structure		

passive thing (material, energy or information) or an active thing, in which case what is being converted can also be considered as a system (cf. Table 1).

In the first case (passive things), the conversion can change the thing in its form, in space or in time. In the second case, the alteration modifies the structure of the thing.

System is the nuclear concept of *systems theory* that can be viewed as a meta science as it can be applied in almost all the scientific areas. It should be noted that the adoption of a definition of system less strict than the definition provided above is frequent. To some authors, (e.g., Ackoff, 1971; Laszlo, 1983; Boulding, 1985; van Gigch, 1991; Bunge, 1979; von Bertalanffy, 1975; Jordan, 1968) a system is just something whose components are inter-related. The adoption of Le Moigne's definition in this work is justified by the richness it brings to the systemic study of an object.

Simpler systems are mere active objects with no cognitive capacities. More complex systems are capable of learning and making decisions and they can reach a high level of autonomy, i.e., they have independent existence, they are capable of governing themselves and surviving in a changing (and sometimes hostile) environment. Several authors recognize that systems can be more or less elaborate, and propose classifications of systems according to the level of complexity and characteristics they possess (e.g., Boulding, 1956;1985; Ackoff, 1971; von Bertalanffy, 1975; Jordan, 1968; Checkland, 1981; Bunge, 1979; Le Moigne, 1978; van Gigch, 1974; Laszlo, 1983; Skyttner, 1996).

Systems that are autonomous and viable are particularly interesting. Such systems are capable of existing with a high degree of independence from other systems and they are capable of surviving to hostile changes in their environment by adapting their behavior. Some of these are even capable of trying to improve their performance by changing their own structure (or organization) - the self-organized systems[1]. A structure change may be achieved by means, such as: altering the communication patterns among the existing subsystems; substituting some of their subsystems by others capable of performing more effectively or more efficiently; adding or removing subsystems.

SELF-ORGANIZED SYSTEMS

Self-organized systems are at the top of a hierarchy of systems whose classification criteria is related to the degree of control the system has upon its own actions. In this hierarchy, each level encompasses all the levels below it (see Figure 1).

The classification proposed in this work is inspired in a classification suggested by Le Moigne (1978) and it includes the following levels[2]:

Uncontrolled Active System

An uncontrolled active system executes some processing, i.e., it converts the input into the output without any kind of control upon what is being done. This type of system will be called an *operator*.

Self-Regulated System

A self-regulated system is an active system that shows some regularity in its output in spite of the changes in its environment that affect its inputs. The system can be viewed as pursuing some objective.

To be capable of doing this, the system needs to have regulating mechanisms. Two components (subsystems) can then be considered in the system: the operator and the *regulator*. The operator assures the conversion of inputs into outputs, as described in the previous section (uncontrolled active systems). The regulator performs three functions: (i) measures the output produced by the operator; (ii) compares the value of the output with some reference value (the desired output, the objective); and (iii) acts upon the operator so the operator changes the way it acts in order to achieve the objective. The regulator has some decision capabilities as it is able of "deciding" what command to issue to the operator.

Figure 1: Hierarchy of systems according to the level of self-control; each system of a higher degree of control encompasses the system of lower degree of self-control (recursively)

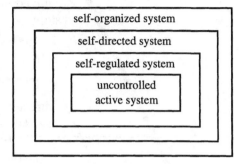

Self-Directed System

While a self-regulated system pursues some objective imposed by an external entity, a self-directed system has the capability of defining its own objective. This is achieved through the action of another subsystem – the *director* – that interacts with the operator and the regulator. The director pays attention to what is happening in the system's environment, what is happening within the system itself, and sets the system's objectives in such a way that its purpose is best accomplished.

Self-Organized System

The self-organized system has the capability of changing its internal structure in order to improve its efficacy and/or efficiency.

Besides the subsystems that incorporate a self-directed system, the self-organized system includes another subsystem— the *organizer*. The organizer introduces changes in the system's structure that aim at the improvement of the system's performance.

Self-control of a system is related to its capability to adapt to changes in its environment. Self-regulated systems have only one adaptation mechanism: changing their behavior so their output remains as constant as possible (through the action of the regulator). Self-directed systems have a second adaptation mechanism: changing their objectives (through the action of the director). Self-organized systems have yet another adaptation mechanism: changing their structure (through the action of the organizer).

Looking inside a self-organized system it's possible to identify the other systems with lower control capabilities and all the subsystems (components) referred to above. Figure 2 attempts to illustrate how these systems (and the different subsystems that compose them) interrelate to each other.

Self-Coordinated System

Sometimes, the accomplishment of the conversions implied by a purpose demands the collaborative action of several operators, either because different skills are necessary or because there are available more that one operator with the same skills. The coordination demanded by such situation might be achieved through the action of another subsystem - the *coordinator*. The coordinator receives work requests from the system

Figure 2: Major relationships between self-organized, self-directed and self-regulated systems: a self-organized system includes a self-directed system, which, in turn, includes a self-regulated system

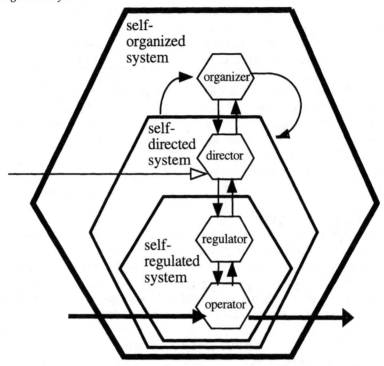

clients, plans the work sequence and distributes the available resources among the operators in such a way that the consumption of resources is minimized and the system performance is maximized. A system with the capability of coordinating the action of several operators will be called a self-coordinated system. A self-coordinated system might be considered to exist within self-regulated systems and, therefore, also within self-directed or self-organized systems.

Components of Self-Organized Systems

The explanation of the behavior of the systems at the different control levels has been done using five *components* or subsystem types: operator, coordinator, regulator, director and organizer. These different subsystems communicate to each other. However, most of the times, the communication among them is asynchronous, i.e., the emission and the reception of a message are not done at the same time. Moreover, a message is often directed to several receivers. These two characteristics of the communication among components lead to the emergence of another subsystem type—the *informer*. Informers perform operations such as: collect messages sent by the emitters (it is useful to consider that informers are also capable of collecting information from direct "observation"); store them in some orderly way (so they can be more easily retrieved when the receivers need them); transmit them to wherever they are required; make them accessible to the receivers;

Table 2 - Systems Components and the Objects They Deal With

Com-ponent	Description	Type of object converted
Operator	Executes the conversion that gives sense to the system's purpose	Passive objects (material, energy, information) and/or active objects
Regulator	Controls the operator in such a way that some objective is sought	Information
Coordinator	Coordinates the action of several operators that have to cooperate in order to fulfill the system's purpose and to achieve the system's objectives	Information
Director	Defines the objectives to be sought by the system in such a way that the system's purpose is fulfilled	Information
Organizer	Introduces changes in the structure of an active object in order to improve its performance	Active objects
Informer	Mediate communication among the other components and collect information	Information

process the content and the format of the messages, so they can better fit the receivers needs, or they can be more easily understood by them.

It is interesting to note that regulators, coordinators, directors and informers are components that deal only with information (cf. Table 1). Operators deal with any kind of object and organizers deal with active objects (which can be viewed as systems).

Table 2 summarizes the role played by each of the six components that have been identified indicating as well the objects they deal with.

Figure 3 attempts to illustrate the relationships among the different components (or subsystems types) identified above. The figure depicts a self-organized system S which converts some input received from its suppliers into some output that is valuable to its clients. This work is carried out by the operators. Three operators are depicted in the figure —O1, O2 and O3. The operators are coordinated by the coordinator C. The coordinator receives work/service requests from the clients through informer I1. Based on the state of the operators - information obtained through the informer I2 (I2 also mediates the communication among operators) - the coordinator allocates workloads and resources to the operators. The results of the decisions made by the coordinator are communicated to the operators through informer I8. The regulator R monitors what is being done by operators (through informers I3 and I2) and sends its commands both to the coordinator and to the operators (through informers I7 and I8, respectively). The director D pays attention to what is happening inside the system (through informers I4, I3 and I2) and in the system's environment (through informer I5) and sends its decisions to the regulator (through informer I6). The organizer ORG intervenes in S' (a subsystem of S) in order to change its structure so it can better respond to changes in its environment. Informer I9 mediates informal communication among any subsystems (an example of such an informer is an e-mail service).

Figure 3 - Relationships Among the Different Components of a Self-Organized System

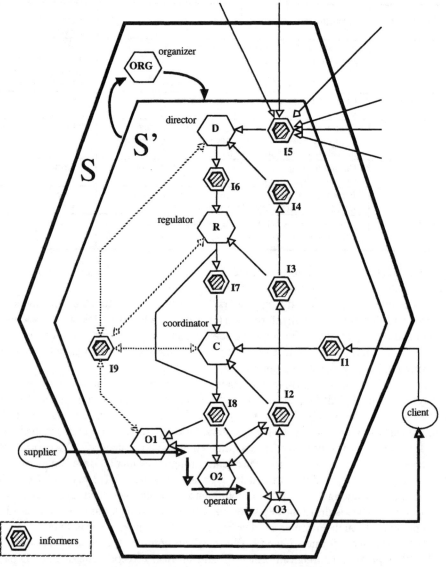

KNOWLEDGE NEEDS OF SELF-ORGANIZED SYSTEMS

The knowledge needs of a self-organized system comprise the knowledge needs of its components. Each of the six components identified in the previous section has its own kind of knowledge needs, depending on its functionality. The identification of their knowledge needs is based on trying to answer the question of *what does each component need to know in order to be capable of doing what it does?*

Three types of knowledge will be considered: behavioral knowledge, factual knowledge and conceptual knowledge (this classification of knowledge is based on a classification of *cognition* proposed by Bunge (1979)):

i) **Behavioral knowledge** is knowledge about how to do something (know how), the knowledge that enables an agent to perform the conversion (i.e., producing the output) it is supposed to (what to do, what actions to undertake). This type of knowledge is therefore necessary to all the subsystems types, although sometimes it is not easy to formalize and communicate. Behavioral knowledge can be presented as ranging from two extreme situations:

Explicitly embedded - the behavioral knowledge is embedded in a system's parts and their interaction; it is not possible to change it without reassembling the system, i.e., changing its parts or the way they interrelate (an example of such situation is a mechanical device).

Tacit - It is not possible to articulate the behavioral knowledge; the agent is capable of acting although it is not capable of describing how she/he does it.

As an intermediate situation, behavioral knowledge can be articulated as a sequence of actions that the agent should carry out systematically and/or a set of rules that the agent should comply to.

ii) **Factual knowledge** is knowledge about facts (events or states), past of future[3]. The values of well established performance measures, are also considered to be factual knowledge.

iii) **Conceptual knowledge** is knowledge that result from thinking (e.g., ideas, models, judgments). It can correspond to classifications, subsumptions or theories that are developed by applying inference mechanisms to factual knowledge.

The knowledge needs of each component are discussed in the following subsections, based on the functionality they provide.

Operator

Operators carry out the conversions that make sense according to the system's purpose. Therefore, all of their characteristics are specific to a particular system and it is not possible to make any kind of generalization (Table 3).

Table 3: It is not possible to generalize the knowledge needs of operators as they depend on the conversion it performs

Operator	
Functionality	Executes the conversion that gives sense to the system's purpose
Objects dealt with	Material, energy and/or information or systems; depend on the system's purpose
Inputs	Depend on the conversion performed by the operator
Outputs	Depend on the conversion performed by the operator
Behavioral knowledge	Depends on the conversion performed by the operator
Factual knowledge	Depends on the conversion performed by the operator
Conceptual knowledge	Depends on the conversion performed by the operator

Table 4 - Knowledge Needs of Regulators

Regulator	
Functionality	Controls the action of operators
Objects dealt with	Information
Inputs	Measure of operators' performance
Outputs	Commands to the operators
Behavioral knowledge	How to compare the "measure of operators' performance" with the "performance reference value" and what rules to follow after that
Factual knowledge	Performance reference value (objective)
Conceptual knowledge	No conceptual knowledge is considered to be needed

Regulator

Regulators attempt to maintain some regularity in the result produced by operators. Regulators implement the action of a basic control loop: they "measure" the operators' performance and compare the obtained measure with some reference value; whenever the operators' performance is different from a reference value, the regulator issues a command to the operators so they change their behavior in order to bring their performance closer to the reference value. Table 4 summarizes the characteristics and knowledge needs of regulators.

Coordinator

Coordinators receive work requests from the system clients, plan the work sequence and distribute the available resources among the operators in such a way that the consumption of resources is minimized and the system performance is maximized. The

Table 5: Knowledge Needs of Coordinators

Coordinator	
Functionality	Coordinates the action of several operators that have to cooperate in order to fulfill the system's purpose and to achieve the system's objectives
Objects dealt with	Information
Inputs	Requests from the system's clients
Outputs	Commands to the operators; these commands are often represented as plans, budgets and other ways of representing resource allocation to operators
Behavioral knowledge	How to combine factual knowledge with the optimization models in order to make the decisions that will lead to the work plans and resource allocation plans
Factual knowledge	Existing operators, their competencies, states, and average performance Available resources (other than the operators) Process models (models of the operations necessary to produce the system's output) Current jobs under operation and their state
Conceptual knowledge	Decision models (optimization models)

coordinators' outputs are commands to the operators. The commands issued by coordinators are different from those issued by regulators. They often have the form of work plans (e.g., operations schedules), budgets or any other way of representing resource allocations.

To make their job, coordinators must combine factual knowledge about the work situation (available resources, work being carried out, work models) with conceptual knowledge that addresses the way work can be optimized. Optimization models such as those developed in areas related to scientific management (e.g., operations research, optimization) are examples of these models.

The behavioral knowledge needed by coordinators corresponds to how to combine factual knowledge with the optimization models in order to make the decisions that will lead to the work plans and resource allocation plans. Table 5 summarizes characteristics and knowledge needs of coordinators.

Director

Directors define the objectives to be sought by the system in such a way that the system's purpose is pursued. The objectives are sent to the regulators that will then use them as their reference value. The inputs of a director (cf. Table 6) can be viewed as information about the outside (system's environment) and the inside (the system). This information is not restricted to recent events and current states because the director also needs to be aware of any kind of change patterns and evolution trends. This implies that the director is capable of remembering past events (both internal and external), and subsuming these events and their occurring sequence to identify change patterns and evolution trends.

To make decisions, directors use conceptual knowledge that corresponds to cause-effect relationships that involve factors both internal and external to the system— decision models. Directors might obtain this knowledge by different ways. They can get it from outside the system, either by hiring people that know it or by acquiring research results. They can also develop this knowledge internally, by engaging in any kind of research

Table 6 - Knowledge needs of directors

Director	
Functionality	Defines the objectives to be sought by the system in such a way that the system's purpose is fulfilled
Objects dealt with	Information
Inputs	Information about the system's environment Information about the system (its state, performance measures) current and past.
Outputs	Objectives to be sought by regulators
Behavioral knowledge	How to subsume information about the system and its environment in order to identify change patterns and evolution trends How to use decision models in order to foresee the actions that best contribute to the accomplishment of the system's purpose
Factual knowledge	The system's purpose
Conceptual knowledge	Decision models - knowledge that enable directors to foresee the likely outcome of the decisions they might make

activity (e.g., marketing research) or by induction, from the system's past experience. To be capable of inducing this knowledge, directors must have advanced reasoning capabilities. They should be capable of remembering past events and states, and the results of decisions made in the past, and also capable of inferring causal relationships based on those facts. Decision models help directors to foresee the likely outcome of their actions, i.e., the decisions they might make.

Decisions are made aiming to contribute to the accomplishment of the system's purpose. So, directors must know the purpose of the systems they direct. The system's purpose is classified as factual knowledge[4].

In what regards behavioral knowledge, the knowledge needs of directors correspond to how to carry out the cognitive operations related to how to subsume information about the system and its environment in order to identify change patterns and evolution trends and how to use decision models in order to foresee the actions that best contribute to the accomplishment of the system's purpose. Table 6 summarizes characteristics and knowledge needs of directors.

Organizer

There is a major difference between organizers and directors, coordinators and regulators. While the latter deal with passive objects, the former deals with active objects. The job of organizers is to change an active object in order to improve its performance. Therefore, the input of the organizer is the active object to be changed and its output is the changed active object.

As an active object can be viewed as a system, most of the times, the organizer creates models (systemic models) of the object it has to change and works upon these models. Initial models correspond to the object "as it is" while later models correspond to the object "as it is sought to be". At some point in time during the change process, there is some work that attempts to make the object being changed to become as described in the "as it is sought to be" models. These models correspond to what has been thought as the most adequate way of organizing the object in order to improve its performance or to solve the problems that led to the organization action. So, during its action, the organizer creates knowledge about the active object being dealt with. Most of this knowledge can be classified as factual (resulting from perceptive activities carried out upon the object, such as models of its structure or its processes) although some conceptual knowledge might also be created. Besides the knowledge created during the change process, organizers also need the following knowledge:

Factual knowledge - what is the system's purpose; system's performance; major problems within the system;

Behavioral knowledge - knowledge corresponding to the change methods the organizer uses to carry out its job; it includes aspects such as how to carry out the change or how to model the object being changed;

Conceptual knowledge - theories about organization and about change processes; this knowledge helps the organizer to foresee the likely outcome of the change decisions it might make.

Table 7 summarizes characteristics and knowledge needs of organizers.

Table 7: Knowledge Needs of Organizers

Organizer	
Functionality	Introduces changes in the structure of an active object in order to improve its performance
Objects dealt with	Active objects
Inputs	The active object to be changed
Outputs	The changed active object
Behavioral knowledge	Change method
Factual knowledge	The system's purpose, performance and major problems Other factual knowledge created during the change process: models of the system's structure and processes
Conceptual knowledge	Theories about organization and change processes

Informer

Informers mediate communication among the other subsystem types and they can also perform perceiving activities, i.e., they carry out operations of information collection through the use of some type of sensor. To carry out those activities they collect, store, retrieve, transmit and deliver information. So, the inputs of an informer are messages or perceptions and their outputs can also be described as messages.

It is reasonable to consider that informers need to know the structure of the information they deal with. Such knowledge can be classified as conceptual knowledge as it results from some kind of reasoning about the structure of the information they deal with. Moreover, informers also need behavioral knowledge corresponding to how to perform the collection, storage, retrieval, transmission and delivery actions. Factual knowledge might be necessary for security reasons. Examples of such knowledge include the emitters from whom the informer should accept messages or the receivers to whom the informer is allowed to send messages. Table 8 summarizes characteristics and knowledge needs of informers.

Table 8: Knowledge Needs of Informers

Informer	
Functionality	Mediate communication among the other sub-systems types and collect information
Objects dealt with	Information
Inputs	Message or perception
Outputs	Message
Behavioral knowledge	How to perform the collection, storage, retrieval, transmission and delivery actions
Factual knowledge	For security reasons: emitters from whom the informer should accept messages or the receivers to whom the informer is allowed to send messages
Conceptual knowledge	Models of messages' structure

Learning Activities Within a Self-Organized System

None of the actions performed by any of the components described in the preceding sections addresses the issue of knowledge acquisition or development. However, it is logic to admit that operators, coordinators, regulators, directors, organizers and informers are capable of improving the way they act by developing the knowledge they use to act, i.e., by learning. So, it is reasonable to consider that, within any of those system components, there are learning activities that are carried out simultaneously with the activities directly related to the role they play. These learning activities can address any of the knowledge types considered: behavioral, factual and conceptual.

Developing behavioral knowledge is often a matter of perfecting the way of doing something resulting from doing it repeatedly. It can also be attained through the adoption of new and better ways of accomplishing one same task (this strategy demands attention to how the task is being performed in other systems and also to technological innovation).

The development of factual knowledge is related to the capacity of remembering a larger amount of facts. This can be succeeded by paying attention to more facts (i.e., by improving perception mechanisms) or by improving or increasing the capability of remembering (i.e., by improving the memorization mechanisms).

Developing conceptual knowledge is perhaps the most interesting situation. It involves the application of inference mechanisms to empirical data in order to improve the existing classifications, subsumptions or theories. The data necessary to perform these reasoning operations is made available by the informers, whose role is to systematically collect and store them.

CONCLUSIONS

The knowledge needs of self-organized systems have been presented as the combination of the knowledge needs of several components whose combined actions confer the system with the capability of adapting to external changes, not only by changing its behavior or its objectives, but also by changing its own structure.

The presentation suggests that the six subsystem types and their knowledge needs are *necessary* and *sufficient* to endow a system with self-organizing capabilities.

It should be noted that the self-organized systems model presented in this work, results from a conceptualization based on a combination of systems theories. Its aim is to provide a framework for understanding complex systems. However, this framework demands experimental validation. Two approaches are being considered to carry out such validation: field studies and simulation using a computational environment based on intelligent agents. The former involves the study of organizations in order to identify the subsystems and their interrelations, and to compare them with the model described in this work. However, difficulties in such a task can be anticipated, namely the complexity arising from the existence of interactions and behavior that result from work dimensions other than those directly related with a pure rational view of work (Santos & Carvalho, 1998). So, the second validation approach turns out to be more promising. Although constituting an artificial setting, it enables the execution of laboratory experiments that are immune to influences from noncontrollable factors related to human behavior.

Other possible research paths address aspects related to extensions and comparisons of the proposed model. The existence of knowledge manipulation activities implies the existence of cognitive capabilities. The identification of the necessary and sufficient cognitive capabilities for each component is a side aspect of the model that can be further explored. On the other hand, it would be interesting to compare the model with other models that also propose architectures for complex systems. Among such models it is worth to refer to Stafford Beer's viable system model (VSM) (Beer, 1984; Espejo & Harnden, 1989).

ENDNOTES

1 This perspective on *self-organized systems* results from trying to explain some pattern of behavior of a system by examining its interior and looking for the components that confer on the system the ability to behave the way it does. The concept of *self-organizing systems* is normally used to refer to some pattern of behavior exhibited by a society of similar systems that results from their spontaneous interaction and not from the action of control mechanisms that compel the system to seek some goal.
2 In Le Moigne's classification, the top level of the hierarchy is filled by systems that are capable of defining their own purpose. It can be considered that such systems pursue *immortality* as they admit to change radically (their purpose) in order to maintain their existence. However, this poses some problems as the change of purpose of a system is perhaps best described as the disappearance of a system and the rise of a new one. As this question is considered out of the scope of this work, such systems won't be considered.
3 Future events or states, either sought or foreseen.
4 Directors must also know facts about the system and its environment. However, such knowledge is described as constituting the input of a director and not as factual knowledge she/he/it must know beforehand.

REFERENCES

Ackoff, R. L. (1971). Towards a Systems of Systems Concepts. *Management Science, 17*(11), 661-671.

Argyris, C. (1993). *Knowledge for Action: A guide to Overcoming Barriers to Organizational Change*: Jossey-Bass Publishers.

Argyris, C. (1994). *On Organizational Learning*. (2ª ed.): Blackwell.

Beer, S. (1984). The Viable System Model: its Provenance, Development, Methodology and Pathology. *Journal of the Operational Research Society, 35*, 7-26.

Boulding, K. E. (1956). General Systems Theory: The Skeleton of Science. *Management Science, 2*(3), 197-208.

Boulding, K. E. (1985). *The World as a Total System*: Sage Publications.

Bunge, M. (1979). *A World of Systems*. (Vol. Treatise on Basic Philosophy, Volume 4, Ontology II:): D. Reidel Publishing Company.

Checkland, P. B. (1981). Systems Thinking, Systems Practice. JACf: John Willey & Sons.

Davenport, T. H., & Prusak, L. (1998). *Working Knowledge: How Organizations Manage What They Know*: Harvard Business School Press.

Espejo, R., & Harnden, R. (Eds.). (1989). *The Viable System Model: Interpretations and Applications of Stafford Beer's VSM*: John Wiley & Sons.

Jordan, N. (1968). *Themes in Speculative Psychology*: Tavistock Publications.

Laszlo, E. (1983). *Systems Science and World Order: Selected Studies*: Pergamon Press.

Le Moigne, J.-L. (1977). *La Théorie du Système Général: Théorie de la Modélisation*: Presses Universitaires de France.

Le Moigne, J. L. (1978, Novembre 1978). La Théorie du Système d' Information Organisationnel. *Informatique et Gestion,* 39-42.

Myers, P. S. (Ed.). (1996). *Knowledge Management and Organizational Design*: Butterworth-Heinemann.

Nemeth, C. J. (1997). Managing Innovation: When Less is More. *California Management Review, 40*(1), 59-74.

O'Leary, D. E. (1998). Enterprise Knowledge Management. *IEEE Computer*(3), 54-61.

Santos, I., & Carvalho, J. A. (1998). Computer-Based Systems that Support the Structural, Social, Political and Symbolic Dimensions of Work. *Requirements Engineering, 3*(2), 138-142.

Senge, P. (1992). *The Fifth Discipline: The Art and Practice of the Learning Organization*: Century Business, London.

Senge, P. M., Kleiner, A., Roberts, C., Ross, R. B., & Smith, B. J. (1994). *The Fifth Discipline Fieldbook: Strategies and Tools for Building a Learning Organization*: Nicholas Brealey Publishing.

Skyttner, L. (1996). *General Systems Theory: An Introduction*: Macmillan Press.

Stewart, T. A. (1997). *Intellectual Capital: The New Wealth of Organizations*: Nicholas Brealey Publishing Limited.

van Gigch, J. P. (1974). *Applied General Systems Theory*: Harper & Row Publishers.

van Gigch, J. P. (1991). *System Design Modeling and Metamodeling*: Plenum Press.

von Bertalanffy, L. (1975). *Perspectives on General Systems Theory: Scientific-Philosophical Studies*: George Braziller, New York.

Chapter XX

Information Quality and Its Interpretative Reconfiguration as a Premise of Knowledge Management in Virtual Organizations

Daniel Diemers
University of St. Gallen, Switzerland

The general objective of this chapter is the attempt to develop solid epistemological foundations for discussions around the subject of knowledge management and virtual organizations. For this purpose the rich and encompassing theoretical complex of the interpretative paradigm in social sciences is adopted and a specific transfer is made from the newer sociology of knowledge, as introduced by Alfred Schutz, Peter L. Berger and Thomas Luckmann. The main thrust of the chapter opens with a discussion of information quality in the context of knowledge management and develops accordingly the concept of common interpretative spaces and a tripartite model of the transformational process, which are both standing at the very heart of any approach to knowledge management in virtual organizations.

Knowledge management deals with basic questions and concepts that have a long epistemological tradition: what exactly is knowledge? Why do we have knowledge? How do we get knowledge? How are we storing, processing and sharing knowledge? If we take a closer look at current literature about knowledge management we observe one common feature that is shared unfortunately by many approaches: a rather weak theoretical foundation of the basic assumptions about knowledge, which are used – and sometimes even in an constituting manner – within the approach.

From my sociological background and a certain affinity to the encompassing thoughts of Alfred Schutz and its scholars Peter L. Berger and Thomas Luckmann came the main thrust to explore an old sociological tradition, namely the study of knowledge, its distribution, its genesis and its function within society, in order to develop theoretical concepts, which can be used within approaches to knowledge management in virtual organizations. The interpretative paradigm, on which the newer sociology of knowledge is based on, has not only methodological relevance for qualitative empirical studies, but it also offers a rich theoretical framework and solid epistemological foundations, which may eventually disclose many fresh, new insights to anyone working within the social discourse around knowledge.[1]

This chapter, thus, deals broadly with interpretative conceptualizations of knowledge management in virtual organizations and tackles specifically the issues of how we are able to apply objective measurements of valuation in the transformational process of organizational knowledge transfer and how we sustain and develop the appropriate common interpretative spaces. In this context the notion of information quality is taken as a point of reference and starting from its interpretative reconfiguration, two concepts of relevance are introduced within this chapter, namely the idea of common interpretative spaces, which constitute the semantic scope of any organizational knowledge flow, and a small model of the transformational process, which turns interpersonally shared information into situated and valued knowledge, a process which lies at the very heart of any knowledge management in virtual organizations.

KNOWLEDGE MANAGEMENT IN VIRTUAL ORGANIZATIONS

The managerial challenge of the coming decades will be influenced significantly by two developments, which can already be identified today: first, management in its original form as an institutionalized mode of managing material resources and long-term employees within regionally segmented markets will increasingly be substituted by more dynamic, knowledge-oriented forms of management. Second, new virtual modes of organizing allow future managers of intellectual assets to operate in new social spaces and allocate appropriate human resources for specific projects instead of life-long employment. This new *modus habituandi* of doing business in the forthcoming decades could be termed accordingly "knowledge management in virtual organizations," a development that is explicitly covered in its different implications and aspects by this book.

Knowledge management, as an independent discipline within business administration, did not attain wide popularity until the 1990s. Although early approaches to the topic have been made before, it is not until this decade that the business world is commonly accepting knowledge management as a main issue of concern. With higher degrees of specialization and division of labor, we are currently living and working in systems and networks, where increased dependency and highly specialized and distributed knowledge prevail. Daniel Bell (1974) coined the term of post-industrial society and described the inherent social changes that led to a shift from the industrial sector to a rapidly growing service sector. Bell spoke in this context of a transformation from the good-producing society to a new information or knowledge-society. Peter Drucker (1993; 1998), who spoke accordingly of a post-capitalist society, coined the term "knowledge worker" and focused his analysis of Western economies on the knowledge dimension.

The second shift has been induced by new technologies and media and comprises new, virtual modes of organizing, which change the way we interact in business contexts and offer new challenges for knowledge management. Within the scope of this chapter the term organization is used as "socially constructed forms of cooperation," which are built actively in order to achieve a specific set of goals. Every organization is built on certain norms and values and has a distinct structure, which coordinates and redirects the activities of organizational members and available resources towards lasting organizational functionality, in the sense that its goals are permanently attained (see March & Simon, 1958; Pugh & Hickson, 1976). To put it more simply, we can say that spontaneous modes of organization evolve, whenever one person alone is not able to solve a specific problem, and that such social forms of cooperation – assuming that they have proven to be adequate problem-solvers – can become institutionalized through repeated social practice. Berger and Luckmann identify the process of increased institutionalization and highly differentiated and specialized organizations as a main feature of modern societies (Berger & Luckmann, 1966). The aspect of both formal and informal dimensions of organizational structures has received increasing popularity in the last decades (Morgan, 1986), and this shift from a functional, instrumental view to the manifold, pluralistic facets of organizations and its culture brought current approaches in closer contact with theories and research on communities and revealed the importance of social interaction and commonly established interpretative spaces for the study and discussion of organizations.

In the last years this development has taken a second, even more dramatic turn: the coming of a new type of organization (Drucker, 1988). New media and communication technologies have led to a significant change of the way we interact and the way we work together, therefore it is essential not to constrain this phenomenon to its technical side, but to consider virtualization as a major social process (Diemers, 1997; 1998). Thus, virtualization has a significant impact on social interaction and relationships within organizational boundaries in a business context and we can increasingly observe the reconceptualization and modification of organizational roles and norms (Cash, 1991). These developments have finally led to new forms of organization, which have been ascribed accordingly to the term of "virtual organizations" (Nohria & Berkley, 1994; Davidow & Malone, 1992). The main feature of these new, virtual modes of organizing is the fact that mediated, virtual forms of communication and interaction play a central role within the organization and substitute direct, face-to-face communication to a large extent, while its structure reflects this constitutive quality of organizational relationships and resembles to a virtual, heterarchical network.

INFORMATION QUALITY AND COMMON INTERPRETATIVE SPACES

One key criterion for knowledge management in virtual organizations is the entire concept of information quality, an expression which links to an established research field on its own that focuses on adequate quality standards to evaluate all sorts of information.[2] While the traditional "fitness for use" (Juran et al., 1974) definition has been enlarged significantly by newer approaches to information quality, they all share the common feature that any attempt to measure an objective quality of information sooner or later has to include concepts about subjective valuation and individual information relevance. Thus, information quality always resides to a significant part within subjective configurations of meaning, which determine the factual value of information in the context of knowledge management in virtual organizations. In order to analyze this subjective dimension of information quality we have first to dwell into the ways and means how intersubjective configurations of meaning are mutually constructed and how common interpretative spaces are accordingly established within organizational boundaries.

For communication we are obviously using alphabets, language, symbols, gestures, words, utterances, intonation and even highly sublime effects ("I felt a certain weakness in his appearance"). These representations, however, are not objective, divine facts, but are interpreted every time by all interacting partners. The criterion for successful interaction is therefore a reciprocal, approximately identical interpretation by all partners of the interactive process. Only then are meanings of representations shared and interaction is feasible in the context of knowledge management in virtual and non-virtual organizations.

In the 1960s Peter L. Berger and Thomas Luckmann (1966) developed, based on Husserl's phenomenology, Weber's conception of an interpretative sociology and Schutz's theory of daily life-world, a comprehensive, influential sociological theory which emphasizes the social construction of what we refer to as our external world. The cornerstone of this theory is the dialectic relationship between the subjective reality of the individual and the objective reality of the society. While language is seen as a self-referential social system of meaning, through which we are able to internalize and externalize socially relevant objectivations, a universe of discourse is constantly constructing, deconstructing and reconstructing the social realms of reality through interaction and conversation. It is important to mention in this context the transcendental nature of language, which is capable of establishing a context beyond the "here and now" of an immediate social situation and thereby construct and make finite provinces of meaning accessible. Given this, we are experiencing our social world as an actual reality, consisting of objectivations created by the processes of internalization and externalization, which are constantly reconciling the individual, subjective reality with the objective, reificated reality. Objectivations, then, are the "bricks of knowledge" out of which our daily life-world is made, and here it is important to notice the social processes of how objectivations are being created and sustained, up to the point where we can speak of an objective social reality.

In social interactions it would be highly inefficient not to establish certain routines, which help us anticipate and structure social situations. Thus, we can observe a process of habitualization as soon as an action is carried out repeatedly. In Schutz's terminology we are sedimenting knowledge of recipes, useful knowledge or even skills of how to do certain things. Once these habitualized actions are reciprocally objectivated by several actors, we can speak of a social institution. Institutions, thus, are something that have their own reality, a reality that is experienced by man as an external, binding fact, and every institution has a corresponding set of knowledge, which constitutes its semantic content. Knowledge, in this sense, is in the center of the fundamental dialectic of society, in that it defines the guidelines through which the process of externalization produces an objective reality. But at the same time, knowledge is constantly being internalized as valid and true objectivations of the realm of reality. Given this conception, it is obvious that our knowledge of these reciprocally institutionalized habitualizations is confined to a temporal and cultural speciality and is especially subject to change. Every knowledge, therefore, has an historic line of institutionalization, which can be traced back accordingly.

This process of internalization of knowledge is called socialization within the terminology of Berger and Luckmann and is basically a twofold process of experiencing the external world as a meaningful and social reality. The primary socialization is responsible for the internalization of typicalities and social objectivations, out of which a specific system of relevancies is constructed, while the secondary socialization is providing role-specific knowledge in an ongoing process, which allows the individual to perform a portfolio of social roles and to live in institutional finite provinces of meaning, *Subsinnwelten* that is, which are fragmenting the daily life-world. Furthermore, in the course of socialization we are internalizing specific legitimations of our institutional knowledge, in the sense that a secondary objectivation of meaning is taking place. This legitimation – which, in the end, is an epistemologically relevant mode of justifying a belief in the truthfulness of my knowledge – can socially be constituted on different levels, depending on the complexity of the underlying theory.

The common interpretative space, then, is a specific set of signs, shared meanings, norms and values of two or more individuals interacting face-to-face, in "co-presence" with each other. It will be created initially based on individual cognitive spaces, but undergoes a transformation during the process of "focused interaction". Assuming that both individuals have a similar cultural background, i.e., their cognitive space has been formed within the same social space of representations, they will use roughly the same code of signs to express themselves or, using Goffman's terminology, to play their roles and establish modes of self-representation. If also their meaning-structures do correspond, i.e., they are both attributing the same meanings to used signs, the interaction will proceed without problems, until a "situational inadequacy" occurs and a role is performed other than expected. At this point there are very probably differences in norms and values relevant to the interactional modality and these differences have to be resolved by modifying the common interpretative space accordingly (Goffman, 1959; 1969). Assuming that a specific interaction is carried out repeatedly, the social situation will turn out to be less and less problematic for two individuals. The process of institutionalization makes interaction easier by improving the shared interpretative space and maybe our two individuals are learning more about each other in the course of time, in that they share knowledge about their system of relevance, their typifications, their values and norms in other areas and former experiences, which are sedimented in their cognitive space. The historical line of their interaction will also become part of the common interpretative space and at a certain point socioemotional contents – emotions, trust, friendship, tradition, bonds, etc. – may become part of the common interpretative space. Within such developed common interpretative spaces, new signs, meaning-structures, values and norms may evolve over time, which are then shared only by the interactional partners and constitute "finite provinces of meaning" (Schutz & Luckmann, 1974; Hall, 1997).

THE TRANSFORMATIONAL PROCESS REVISITED

So far we have identified information quality as a key issue in knowledge management in virtual organizations, in that information's situational value resides in intersubjective configurations of meaning between two or more individuals within organizational boundaries. Common interpretative spaces, thus, constitute semantic or modal-logical spaces, within which the semantic component of information quality is reciprocally determined. But we can go one step further and look at the specific process that transforms quality information into knowledge, a process which stands at the heart of any knowledge management within virtual organizations.

Up to this point we have freely spoken of knowledge without addressing the question of what exactly is meant by knowledge within the scope of this chapter. Obviously many different scientific disciplines are using the term knowledge to their own rights – from cognitive psychology, information sciences, philosophy, to business administration, economics, sociology and even theology, to name just a few – and this led to the current situation, where definitions of knowledge are legion and almost every scientist who has an interest in knowledge management feels an urgent need to deliver and own, new and consolidated definition. Thus any attempt to structure, discuss or simply present all those different approaches to the term "knowledge" would lead inevitably to a chapter – or even a book – of its own. Instead, the three terms data, information and knowledge are outlined briefly, without entering the realm of definitions, and subsequently a focus on subjective knowledge is made according to Schutz's conception, even if the scope of this chapter does not unfortunately allow a thorough analysis.

Let us consider data, derived from the Latin *datum* "that, which is given," as all kinds of sensibly observable phenomenons in our social world, e.g., sounds, letters, figures, pictures, body movements, etc. At a certain point, which we can furthermore differentiate by place and time, data can suddenly become meaningful to an individual. At this stage data becomes information, having the quality to give the information recipient an added value compared to not receiving the information.[3] Given this, Knowledge seems to be a synthesis of perceived information and its cognitive processing, but it remains still vague, what exactly the social dimension of this process is.

Alfred Schutz's grand merit, then, is his effort to carry out a profound scientific inquiry of the daily life-world of man, being the fundamental premise of any knowledge. For any knowledge is always rooted in the believed existence of my daily life-world, being the world of directly experienced, social reality, which thus becomes a paramount reality beyond question. My personal stock of knowledge consists primarily of recipes on how to solve problems in social situations. With my knowledge at hand, I am able to reduce or eliminate the problematic dimension of social situations to an extent that I become part of a social community. Schutz differentiates accordingly skills, useful knowledge and knowledge of recipes, depending on the degree of routinization of the respective type of knowledge.[4] All these are, following Schutz' terminology, constructions of first degree, in the sense that they reflect our natural perception of the daily life-world. Constructions of second degree, then, are all sorts of theoretical knowledge about constructions of first degree, e.g., everyday theories or scientific theories and concepts.

Given this structure, the collective, societal stock of knowledge is composed of all three constructive types of knowledge, while the daily life-world recipes constitute the largest and most important part therein. The same goes for the individual stock of knowledge, which is composed of constructions of first and second degree, and here we have also a dominance of routinized, implicit knowledge, which helps us making our way in our social world. With the abovementioned implicit/explicit dichotomy revisited, it is now evident that all constructions of second degree – in a sense everything we refer to as "scientific" knowledge – are explicit knowledge, while constructions of first degree, i.e. skills, useful knowledge and knowledge of recipes, are to a large extent implicit or *tacit* knowledge. Now that the ontological framework of knowledge is outlined, two questions remain interesting from a knowledge management point of view: how is knowledge socially distributed and how is the transformational process, which lets information become knowledge, embedded in the social dimension.

Tackling the second question first, it is important to notice that my individual knowledge is structured in a system of relevancies and typicalities, based on a subjective configuration of meaning.[5] Schutz made a concise description of how knowledge is permanently valued and revalued according to my projections of acts, with which I am trying to achieve certain goals I have. Thus, plan, act and knowledge go together and this rather pragmatic view on knowledge is central in Schutz' conception of a social epistemology. The transformational process is then the process of acquiring knowledge out of information, which I'm experiencing in my daily life-world. The more I believe that specific information is a valid recipe for a problematic social situation, and the more a successful outcome of this social situation is important for one or several of my projects of acts, the more likely it is that I will incorporate this information in my stock of knowledge and position it prominently within my system of relevancies.[6]

The first question, then, touches a major issue, which has driven the sociology of knowledge ever since: the social distribution and attribution of knowledge. Knowledge in daily life-world is always distributed among people and also my individual, subjective stock of knowledge is to a certain degree shared with other people and part of the social stock of knowledge. My knowledge about sailing, for example, is certainly something, which other people have as well, and if I'm meeting someone with a correspondingly overlapping system of relevancies, we have "something to talk about." Accordingly, the things you learn in school have become highly standardized explicit knowledge, which all persons who attended the same school at the same time should share with each other. On the other hand, I may have ideas or thoughts, which I'm keeping only to myself and which I will never share with anybody.

Essential to any attempt to "manage" knowledge is the fact that a large amount of our stock of knowledge consists of implicit constructions of first degree. A management of explicitly constructed theories, constructions of second degree that is, can only lead to success if we have established an appropriate common interpretative space, which allows us to actually *share* knowledge with others. Assuming that the nature of knowledge resides in social, discursive constructions of what we perceive as reality, the transformational process, which derives knowledge from explicit information,[7] lies at the heart of our analysis of knowledge management in virtual organizations. Thus, we have to ask: What are the respective information quality criteria, which allow information to be successfully internalized by others and become objectivated, social knowledge? As a second step we could then ask, what potentially successful strategies would influence and facilitate this transformational process?

Let me introduce now a small model, which establishes the three major criteria of comprehension, contextualization and valuation for an analysis of the transformational process.

The lowest level is about comprehension and constitutes a common syntactic space as a prerequisite for a successful transformational process. Information is "fit for use" only if it can be cognitively processed with success. If we don't comprehend certain information, because, for example, we are not familiar with the language or the syntax, or information seems devoid any logic or far too complicated to us, the transformational process is already stalled at this lowest level.

The middle level, then, is about the process of internalization and constitutes a

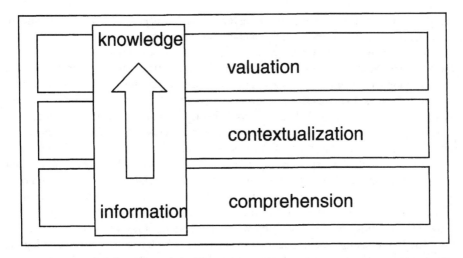

common interpretative space as a major prerequisite for the transformational process. Information is, as a matter of fact, never "stand-alone," but always embedded into a social context and highly personalized. On this level, thus, the transformational process is contextualized, and its success depends heavily on a commonly established interpretative space with a synchronized semantic interpretation and overlapping sets of typifications.

The highest level is about belief and comprises a common space of relevancies, which finally determines our acquisition or non-acquisition of knowledge in the transformational process. As mentioned above, knowledge includes always believing in information to be true or not to be true, and depending on the contextualization we consider persons or labels as "experts" for certain information, in the sense that they have specifically distributed knowledge about the topic in question. Accordingly, information is also valued on its importance and usefulness within my system of relevancies and for my personal plans – here we meet the above stated relation plan-act-knowledge again – and depending on this valuation the transformational process is finally successful or abandoned uncompleted.

With these concepts now sufficiently outlined, it has become obvious on what premises an analysis of knowledge management can alternatively be based. The interpretative paradigm offers a rich and encompassing framework, which draws the focus on subjective components of the knowledge processes in virtual organizations, namely the necessary common interpretative spaces and the transformational process, which can be analyzed with the tripartite approach under consideration.

FUTURE TRENDS

If we consider an increasing importance of methods to manage intangible assets within companies and a predominance of virtual modes of organizing as future and emerging trends, which affect our economies more through their persistency than their ephemeric quality, the two concepts elaborated above will increasingly allow for more sophisticated and appropriate tools. In this context I want to make a strong point on the fact that most attempts to influence the transformational process in contemporary knowledge management are aiming at the lowest level of comprehension, while neglecting or even ignoring the other two levels. Taking into account the theoretical apparatus, which has been presented in this chapter, it becomes strikingly evident that a wider, holistic approach is definitely needed if we want to achieve better results. While strategies aiming at the comprehension level clearly have a supportive, necessary function, they should at least be combined with strategies aiming at higher levels of the transformational process, some of which will be outlined below.

Starting at the level of comprehension, typically useful strategies are a formalization of information; visualization by means of symbols, figures and graphs; the use of analogies and metaphors, which offer alternative, maybe better known schemes of comprehension (Nonaka & Takeuchi, 1995, p. 64); and the thorough explanation or reformulation of information, whenever the recipient has troubles in getting the message.

On the second level strategies have to contextualize information in order to establish a common interpretative space. A good starting point is reciprocal learning about the other's stock of knowledge, its historical line of acquisition and especially its actual self-interpretation by the owner, as past experiences are constantly reinterpreted and modified in order to fit into the currently established system of relevancies. A major strategy on this level, then, is to openly exchange and share our knowledge in the course of the transformational process, and thereby we can achieve a larger overlapping of the respective stocks of knowledge, which in the end leads to an improved common interpretative space.[8] A second approach exploits the dynamics of the process of institutionalization described above. Through constant repetition in a social context we are eventually able to create meaningful rituals, which achieve an internalization through the processes of habitualization and institutionalization. Finally, it is important to notice that an internalization of objectivations is generally more successful if communication takes place in a vis-a-vis situation. Any form of mediated communication is thus inferior to face-to-face communication and in an attempt to synchronize associations and establish a common interpretative space we can make use of the specific dynamics of social interaction in the daily life-world.

The third level of the transformational process is about belief and valuation and surely the most decisive – but of course also most difficult – level for any transformational strategy. As on the second level a good starting point is a reciprocal learning about the other's system of relevancies and especially his projections of plans, his goals and the means with which he thinks he can achieve them. An especially interesting case here are idiosyncrasies, because they reveal a clash of systems of relevancies and allow an analysis of why and how these systems are contradictory and not overlapping in a specific case.[9] Thus, we can include the explication and analysis of idiosyncrasies as a supporting strategy in the course of reciprocal learning. A second, major strategy, then, is to use social discourses that assign the attribute of expert to oneself. In a context of socially distributed knowledge and high degrees of specialization we are increasingly depending on experts, which nevertheless are entirely social constructions. Thus it is important to use such constructions to achieve the status of expert in the respective field and towards the information recipient, which will finally have a very strong impact on the transformational process, because with the help of such a social attribution, we can assign higher levels of importance and truthfulness to our information.

Having outlined now possible strategies on the three levels of the transformational process, one major insight should be that the transformational process is more complex than often described and that the process is highly multidimensional, while the social dimension in its interpretative objectivation of intersubjective configuration of meanings plays a very important role therein. With the same argument we can analyze the ways and means how common interpretative spaces are constructed in the context of virtual organizations, in order to identify opportunities for the management of knowledge.

Newer research of virtual organizations stresses heavily the importance of common interpretative spaces (Davis & Brewer, 1997; Baym, 1995). Handy, for example, identifies trust, a sense of mutuality and reciprocal loyalty as inevitable requirements for virtual organizations. Given the potentially harmful consequences of poorly working common interpretative spaces, he proposes the "concept of community membership," which abandons the traditional notion of organizations as means to an end, where members work in exchange for some sort of payment, and calls for a transformation of organizational structures into communities, where individual efforts and commitment are rewarded with a sense of belonging, mutual trust and identity (Handy, 1995). Given this interesting turn, which is induced by new media and communication technologies, the two concepts of organization and community are no longer opposed to each other and may enter combined discourses. We can thus take a closer look on what actually "community" means and how we can incorporate this social phenomenon into approaches to knowledge management in virtual organizations.

The sociological notion of community usually opens large patterns of diffuse associations, which might include social networks, security, social order, family, neighborhood, clans, emotional bonds, identity and several more. This wide semantic scope combined with a certain historical and normative burden dates back to early sociological uses of the concept of community, for example by Toennies, who opposed the idealistic model of community to a rather pessimistic picture of modern society (Toennies, 1963). With the increasing virtualization of society, however, the term of community has received new popularity, but most authors are not dwelling too much on the different associations and interpretative patterns, which go along with the use of community as an open label for different kinds of social phenomenons. One exception here is Komito, who delivers a distinct analysis of the different facets of communities in the context of virtual modes of social interaction. The basic distinction is made between "proximate communities," where a common interpretative space is constructed on the grounds of physical proximity and involuntary membership, "moral communities," where a shared common interpretative space is based on moral bonds, communal solidarity and a sense of common purpose and commitment, and "normative communities," such as communities of practice or communities of interest, which are not restricted to geographical places and share common values and norms (Komito, 1998). An interesting point is the fact that all three types of community can be found in virtual communities, which sometimes started as normative communities, later developed into moral communities and even social phenomenons of proximate communities appeared. Rheingold uses in this context the expression of "grassroots groupminds" to describe virtual communities, which grew steadily around many virtual fireplaces in the form of Usenet discussion groups or bulletin board systems, where like-minded people came together and evolved into moral communities with high levels of mutual support and solidarity (Rheingold, 1995). Mosco, on the contrary, rates the discourse of caring, virtual communities as a myth, which is used as a legitimizing argument within the current discourse around cyberspace and virtual worlds. With a glance at a long sociological tradition of community research he reminds us that communities are not just about romantic neighborhoods and caring for each other, but also about strong social conventions and processes of exclusion and inclusion, which can eventually lead to social minorities and stigmatization (Mosco, 1998).

The most important point, however, within the scope of this chapter is the fact that virtual networks can be media platforms, where common interpretative spaces of social networks constitute social spaces (Harasim, 1993). A virtual community, thus, establishes a common interpretative space through mediated forms of communication and current research on virtual communities supports the view that these communities show very similar patterns of interaction and share many qualities of non-virtual communities (Turkle, 1994; 1995; 1996). Some virtual communities actually do arrange face-to-face meetings of its members, but there are many other examples of communities where such "real-world grounding" has never taken place. If these ungrounded virtual communities succeed in establishing a common interpretative space of such a quality that typical community functions are satisfactorily performed, this result would be applicable to virtual organizations, which could then be set up within a community-oriented framework.

CONCLUSIONS

This chapter had one main goal in that I wanted to make the theoretical apparatus of the newer sociology of knowledge – as introduced by Alfred Schutz, Peter L. Berger and Thomas Luckmann – accessible for approaches to knowledge management in virtual organizations. Starting from the notion of "information quality" and its relevance for common interpretative spaces and the transformational process, the theoretical apparatus offers a rich and well-founded paradigm, which helps us – regardless of scientific membership and paradigm adherence – building a solid base-theory for practical strategies and concepts in the field of knowledge management in virtual organizations.

Furthermore, our operationalization of the interpretative paradigm delivered the insight that a good deal of traditionally applied strategies to influence transformational processes in knowledge management are mostly not exceeding the lowest of the three criteria, namely the criterion of comprehension. By introducing a tripartite model of the transformational process, the importance and relevance of the upper two levels – which are focusing entirely on the social, interpretative dimension of the process – was made explicit. This approach can furthermore be combined with a conception of common interpretative spaces, which fold up the semantic space for knowledge management in virtual organizations. For a practitioner, thus, these two concepts – combined with the theoretical foundations of the interpretative paradigm – offer a basic, analytical framework and a rich, innovative source for new approaches and new solutions in the field of knowledge management in virtual organizations.

ENDNOTES

1   Classical works involve for example Berger & Luckmann, 1966; Schutz & Luckmann, 1974; 1983; Knorr-Cetina, 1981. For a general, historical overview see Stark (1991), Stehr (1994) and McCarthy (1996) deliver a contemporary, fresh view on the sociology of knowledge, while Kertesz (1993), as an example, demonstrates its relevance in other fields, e.g., in the discourse around artificial intelligence.

2   See for a good introduction and overview Kahn et al. (1997), who start off from classical definitions and Total Quality Management (TQM) literature and introduce a 2x2 information quality product/service model, which maps information quality criteria along the dimensions of specification conformance and meeting/exceeding customer expectations. See also Eppler, 1997; 1995, who tackles the issue of information quality in the context of new media technologies.

3   Or, to be more precise, it changes the condition of the information recipient in a positive *or* negative way. We can say—paraphrasing Bateson—that it achieves differences that make a difference (Bateson, 1979, p. 5). On the same issue see Machlup (1983) for a semantic analysis.

4   Here we have an analogy – or even an identical construct with a different terminology – to Polanyi's vividly cited distinction between *tacit* (or implicit) and explicit knowledge. The higher the pragmatically oriented routinization of knowledge is, the more its use becomes implicit and "hidden", with the result of skills being almost inexpressibly applied ("Sorry, I really can't explain that, I think I'll have to show you"). See on the subject of *tacit* knowledge: Polanyi, 1966; Nonaka & Takeuchi, 1995; Muller, 1997.

5   Schutz attributes the systems of relevance an important role in his epistemological conception. Namely, he differentiates between *thematic*, *interpretational* and *motivational* relevance, which allows —in spite of a postulated interdependence of the three relevance types— a more thorough analysis. See Schutz & Luckmann, 1974, p. 182; Schutz, 1982.

6   Alfred Schutz describes the acquisition of knowledge as the sedimentation of current experiences in meaning-structures, according to relevance and typicality. These in turn have a role in the determination of current situations and the explication of current experiences. (...) This acquisition, as a sedimentation of experiences, results from situations and is biographically articulated (Schutz & Luckmann, 1974, p. 119).

7   Please note that this process is *not* about making implicit knowledge explicit, a process which is also often described as a "transformational process" in knowledge management literature, but the process under consideration here is focusing on *explicit* objectivations, as these are the sole things you can actually "manage" in any form of knowledge management. See accordingly Baecker, 1997, p. 22; Brosziewski, 1999, p. 5.

8   This strategy is supported by newer theories about the nature of knowledge, which abandon the traditional view of organizations as confined containers, where different "pieces" of knowledge are combined and exploited, and see knowledge as residing within heterogeneous networks of social relationships that transcend and bypass conventionally defined organizational boundaries (Araujo, 1998, p. 331). In the same line of fire aims a proposal of Chan Kim and Mauborgne, who advocate a fair process maxime for managing in the knowledge economy (Chan Kim & Mauborgne, 1997).

9   See Knorr-Cetina, 1981, p. 37. Idiosyncrasies - the psychological expression for very strong aversions against something or somebody - are very reliable indicators for situations, where two completely different interpretative schemes or systems of relevance are clashing together and the third transformational level is blocked accordingly. Senge identifies such situations as very harmful in a business context and proposes pro-active surfacing of mental models (Senge, 1990).

REFERENCES

Araujo, L. (1998). Knowing and Learning as Networking. *Management Learning*, 29, 317-336.

Baecker, D. (1997). *Zum Problem des Wissensmanagement in Organisationen*. Discussion paper, Witten/Herdecke: University of Witten/Herdecke.

Bateson, G. (1979). *Mind and Nature. A Necessary Unity*. New York: Bantam.

Baym, N.K. (1995). The Emergence of Community in Computer-Mediated Communication. In S.G. Jones (Ed.), *CyberSociety. Computer-Mediated Communication and Community* (138-163). Thousand Oaks CA: Sage.

Bell, D. (1974). *The coming of postindustrial society. A venture in social forecasting*. Harmondsworth: Penguin.

Berger, P.L., & Luckmann, T. (1966). *The Social Construction of Reality*. New York: Doubleday.

Brosziewski, A. (1999, in print). Wissen über Wissen. Zusammenhänge zwischen Wissensökonomie und Wissenssoziologie. In M. Schwaninger (Ed.), *Intelligente Organisationen*. Berlin: Duncker & Humbolt.

Cash, D.C. (1991). Information Technology and the Redifinition of Organizational Roles. *Research in the Sociology of Organizations*, 9, 21-48.

Chan Kim, W., & Mauborgne, R. (1997). Fair Process. Managing in the Knowledge Economy. *Harvard Business Review*, July-August, 65-75.

Davidow, W.H., & Malone, M. S. (1992). *The Virtual Corporation. Structuring and Revitalizing the Corporation for the 21st Century*. New York: Burlinggame Books.

Davis, B.H., & Brewer, J.P. (1997). *Electronic Discourse. Linguistic individuals in virtual space*. Albany NY: State University Press.

Diemers, D. (1997). *Die Virtuelle Triade. Mensch, Gesellschaft und Virtualität*. Master thesis. St. Gallen: University of St. Gallen.

Diemers, D. (1998). *The Virtual Triad. Society and Man under the Sign of Virtuality*. Essay for the 9th Honeywell Futurist Competition Europe. Munich: Honeywell.

Drucker, P.F. (1993). *Post-Capitalist Society*. Oxford: Heinemann.

Drucker, P.F. (1998). The Coming of a New Organization. In Harvard Business Review (Ed.), *Harvard Business Review on Knowledge Management*. Boston: Harvard Press.

Eppler, M. (1995). *Persönliche Informations-Portfolios. Ein integriertes Konzept für die individuelle Informationsbewirtschaftung*. Master thesis. St. Gallen: University of St. Gallen.

Eppler, M. (1997). Information oder Konfusion. Neue Kriterien für die betriebliche Kommunikation. *IO Management*, 5, 38-41.

Goffman, E. (1959). *The presentation of self in everyday life*. New York: Bantam.

Goffman, E. (1969). *Behavior in Public Places. Notes on the Social Organization of Gatherings*. 4th Ed. New York: Free Press.

Handy, C. (1995). Trust and the Virtual Organization. *Harvard Business Review*, May-June, 40-50.

Hall, S. (1997). The Work of Representation. In S. Hall (Ed.), *Representation. Cultural representations and signifying practices* (13-74). London: Sage.

Harasim, L.M. (1993). Networlds. Networks as social space. In L.M. Harasim (Ed.), *Global Networks. Computers and international Communication* (15-34). Cambridge MA: MIT Press.

Jones, S.G. (1995). Understanding Community in the Information Age. In S.G. Jones (Ed.), *CyberSociety. Computer-Mediated Communication and Community*. Thousand Oaks CA: Sage.

Juran, J.M., Gryna, F.M.J., & Bingham, R.S. (1974). *Quality Control Handbook*. 3rd Ed. New York: McGraw-Hill.

Kahn, B.K., Strong, D.M., & Wang, R.Y. (1997). A Model for Delivering Quality Information as Product and Service. In D.M. Strong, & B.K. Kahn (Eds.). *Proceedings of the 1997 Conference on Information Quality* (80-94). Cambridge MA: MIT Press, p. 80-94, 1997

Kertesz, A. (1993). *Artificial Intelligence and the Sociology of Knowledge. Prolegomena to an Integrated Philosophy of Science*. Frankfurt am Main: Peter Lang.

Knorr-Cetina, K. (1981). *The Manufacture of Knowledge. An Essay on the Constructivist and Contextual Nature of Science*. Oxford: Pergamon Press.

Komito, L. (1998). The Net as a Foraging Society. Flexible Communities. *The Information Society*, 14, 97-106.

McCarthy, E.D. (1996). *Knowledge as Culture. The New Sociology of Knowledge*. London: Routledge.

Machlup, F. (1983). Semantic Quirks in Studies of Information. In F. Machlup, & U. Mansfield (Eds.), *The Study of Information* (641-671). New York: John Wiley & Sons.

March, J.G., & Simon, H.A. (1958). *Organizations*. New York: John Wiley & Sons.

Morgan, G. (1986). *Images of Organization*. Beverly Hills CA: Sage.

Mosco, V. (1998). Myth-ing Links. Power and Community on the Information Highway. *The Information Society*, 14, 57-62.

Muller, K.H. (1997). *Selbstsichten, "implizites Wissen" und Gesellschaftsbilder. Ein kognitionstheoretischer Streifzug durch soziale Wahrnehmungsfelder*. Wien: Institut für Höhere Studien.

Nohria, N., & Berkley, J.D. (1994). The Virtual Organization. Bureaucrazy, Technology, and the Implosion of Control. In C. von Heckscher, & A. Donellon, *The Post-Bureaucratic Organization. New Perspectives on Organizational Change* (108-128). Thousand Oaks: Sage.

Nonaka, I., & Takeuchi, H. (1995). *The Knowledge-Creating Company. How Japanese Companies Create the Dynamics of Innovation*. New York: Oxford.

Polanyi, M. (1966). *The Tacit Dimension*, Garden City NY: Doubleday.

Pugh, D.S., & Hickson, D.J. (Eds.)(1976). *Organizational Structure in its Context. The Aston Programm I*. Farnborough: Saxon House.

Rheingold, H. (1995). *The Virtual Community. Finding Connection in a Computerized World*. London: Minerva.

Schutz, A. (1982). *Das Problem der Relevanz*. Frankfurt am Main: Suhrkamp.

Schutz, A., & Luckmann, T. (1974). *The Structures of the Life-World*. Vol. 1. London: Heinemann.

Schutz, A., & Luckmann, T. (1983). *The Structures of the Life-World*. Vol. 2. London: Heinemann.

Senge, P. (1990). The Leader's New Work. Building Learning Organizations. *Sloan Management Review*, fall, 7-23.

Stark, W. (1991). *The Sociology of Knowledge. Toward a deeper understanding of the history of ideas*. New Brunswick: Transaction Publishers.

Stehr, N. (1994). *Arbeit, Eigentum und Wissen. Zur Theorie von Wissensgesellschaften.* Frankfurt am Main: Suhrkamp.

Toennies, F. (1963). *Community and Society.* New York: Harper and Row.

Turkle, S. (1994). Constructions and Reconstructions of Self in Virtual Reality. Playing in the MUDs. *Mind, Culture and Activity,* 1, Nr. 3, 158-167.

Turkle, S. (1995). *Life on the Screen: Identity in the Age of the Internet.* New York: Simon & Schuster.

Turkle, S. (1996). Virtuality and its discontents. Searching for community in cyberspace. *The American Prospect,* 24, winter, 50-57.

About the Authors

Heli Ahonen is a PhD student in the Centre for Activity Theory and Developmental Work Research at University of Helsinki. She has a long experience as an HRD specialist in a number of public organizations. Her research for the PhD deals with the development of new, second-generation knowledge- and competence-management methods in a large tele company.

Rainer Alt (Dr.), studied business administration (Dipl.-Kfm.) at the University of Erlangen-Nürnberg, Germany. Research Assistant at the Institute for Information Management, University of St. Gallen (Ph.D in 1997). Research Associate at the Department of Computer Science, University of California, Irvine. Senior Consultant with Roland Berger & Partner in Düsseldorf, Germany (1997-1998). Since 1998 he is Project Manager at the Institute for Information Management, University of St.Gallen. His research interests are in Electronic Commerce, Logistics and eServices for business-to-business relationships.

Colin Ash is a lecturer and research associate with the School of Management Information Systems at Edith Cowan University in Perth Western Australia. He has acted as a consultant to numerous organisations in the Asia Pacific region. His current research interest relates to the virtual empowerment that organisations can realise through the effective implementation of Internet based Enterprise Resource Planning systems. Colin consults and publishes in the area of SAP/ERP and e-commerce development and implementation.

Sulin Ba (Master's in Library and Information Sciences, Ph.D. in Management Information Systems, University of Texas at Austin) is assistant professor of information systems at Marshall School of Business at the University of Southern California, Los Angeles, CA 90089 (sulin@sba.usc.edu). Her current research focus is on the design of intermediaries: trusted third parties for facilitating electronic market transactions and knowledge brokers for organizational knowledge acquisition and knowledge sharing. Her research articles have appeared in the *Journal of Decision Support Systems* and *Sun* .

Thorsten Blecker: Dipl.-oec., University of Duisburg, Germany (1994), Majors: Production/Operations Management and Strategic Management; Dr., University of Duisburg, Germany (1998); Current Position: Assistant Professor at the Department of Production/Operations Management, Business Logistics and Environmental Management, College of Business Administration, University of Klagenfurt, Austria, e-mail: blecker@ieee.org. Research Interests: Strategic Management, Production/Operations Management, Modern Information and Communication Technologies, Internet Production, Virtual Organizations.

Karin Breu is Research Fellow in Information Systems at the Cranfield School of Management in the UK. Karin received her Ph.D. in strategic change management at Oxford Brookes University. She earned her Masters Degree (M.A.) with honors in Economic Systems and International Law at the University of Munich, Germany. Prior to joining Cranfield, Karin was a business consultant in a broad range of business development and marketing projects to European Community and US-based industrial organizations. Karin has published in knowledge management, intranet-supported information management and IT-enabled communications based on empirical research in multinational corporations such as BT, Shell International, ICL, Galxo-Welcome, Zeneca and NatWest

Janice Burn is Foundation Professor and Head of School of Management Information Systems at Edith Cowan University in Perth, Western Australia and World President of the Information Resources Management Association (IRMA). She has previously held senior academic posts in Hong Kong and the UK. Her research interests relate to information systems strategy and benefits evaluation in virtual organisations with a particular emphasis on cross cultural challenges in an e-business environment. She is recognised as an international researcher with over 100 publications in Journals and international conferences. She is on the editorial board of five prestigious IS journals and participates in a number of joint research projects with international collaboration and funding.

João Álvaro Carvalho is Associate Professor at Department of Information Systems, School of Engineering, University of Minho, Portugal. He obtained a first degree on Systems and Informatics Engineering at University of Minho (1983) and a PhD on Information Systems at University of Manchester Institute of Science and Technology (UMIST), UK (1991). His current duties include: teaching (undergraduate and postgraduate) courses on fundamentals of information systems and information systems development; project supervision of final (5th) year undergraduate students; dissertation supervision of Master students; and Ph.D. thesis advisor; director of a M.Sc. on Information Systems. His main research interests address the systemic fundamentals of information systems, knowledge management and requirements engineering.

Christine Dawson, an Associate with American Management Systems (AMS), Inc., is a senior writer at the AMS Center for Advanced Technologies (AMSCAT). In this role she leads a number of AMSCAT's knowledge transfer initiatives, including supervising, writing and editing publications and bylines. She is an active member of the AMS Advanced Technologies Knowledge Center, as well as a regular contributor to AMS's corporate newspaper and to the AMSCAT Web site. Her writing has appeared in a number of trade magazines, and in teaching guides and children's books published by Disney Press and Scholastic Books, among others. Ms. Dawson has a BA in English with honors from Cornell University and is currently pursuing her MBA at Johns Hopkins University.

Daniel Diemers studied economics, business adminstration and sociology at the University of St. Gallen, Switzerland and at the Rotterdam School of Management, Netherlands, and holds a lic.oec.HSG and a CEMS master degree. He is currently writing his Ph.D. thesis on knowledge management, virtuality and early warning systems at the chairs of Prof. Dr. Peter Gross and Prof. Dr. Georg von Krogh, University of St. Gallen, Switzerland. Beside his academic activities, Daniel Diemers is working for a well-known German consultancy in the field of strategic management consulting.

Yrjö Engeström is Professor of Communication at University of California, San Diego, and Academy Professor at the Academy of Finland. He is Director of the Center for Activity Theory and Developmental Work Research at University of Helsinki. Engeström applies cultural-historical activity theory in developmental studies of work. His research focuses on transformations in work organizations and formation of collaborative expertise through expansive learning. His recent books include *Cognition and Communication at Work* (1996, edited with D. Middleton) and *Perspectives on Activity Theory* (1999, edited with R. Miettinen and R-L. Punamäki). His current research project deals with the transformation of the multi-organizational field of medical care in the Helsinki area , Finland.

Ulrich J. Franke is a researcher at Cranfield University, England. He has extensive international work experience in the field of logistics management. He has worked for major German blue chip companies with his latest position as the head of logistics of a manufacturing company. He holds German degrees in economics and business information systems. Additionally he received an MBA degree from Oxford Brookes University. Currently, he is conducting comprehensive research in the management of virtual organizations.

Susan Hanley, a Senior Principal with American Management Systems (AMS), Inc, is the Director of Knowledge Management. In this role, she directs the activities of the AMS Knowledge Centers and leads

AMS's Knowledge Management Knowledge Center. Ms. Hanley also provides knowledge management subject matter expertise for AMS's external knowledge management consulting engagements. The AMS Knowledge Centers are virtual communities of AMS's leading practitioners in each of its core disciplines. Ms. Hanley manages the resources, programs, and technology infrastructure of the AMS Knowledge Centers, through which AMS consultants share ideas and know-how quickly and effectively, bringing greater value to AMS clients. Prior to establishing the AMS Knowledge Centers in 1996, Ms. Hanley spent more than 16 years as a project manager and business analyst on a variety of consulting engagements. Ms. Hanley is a frequent writer and speaker on the topic of building communities of practice and measuring the value of knowledge management. Her byline articles have appeared in the July/August 1998 and May/June 1999 issues of *Knowledge Management Review*, the February 1999 issue of *Management Consultant International*, and the April 26, 1999 issue of *Information Week*.

H.P.M. Jägers (Hans), is a Professor in the Faculty of Military Management Sciences at the Royal Netherlands Military Academy. He is also a Professor of Design of Information-Intensive Organizations at the University of Amsterdam. He is a participant in the University of Amsterdam PrimaVera research programme (http://domino.fee.uva.nl/PrimaVera).

W. Jansen (Wendy), is an Associate Professor on Management Information Sciences at the Royal Netherlands Military Academy. Her primary field of study is the relation between organization design and the use of information and communication technology. She is a participant in the University of Amsterdam PrimaVera research programme (http://domino.fee.uva.nl/PrimaVera).

Jean L. Johnson is Associate Professor of Marketing at Washington State University. She received her Ph.D. from the University of Nebraska in 1988 in marketing with emphasis in distribution. Her major research interests focus domestic and across-culture interfirm relationships in marketing. Dr. Johnson studies knowledge acquisition and management in interfirm relationships, the development of strategic partnering capabilities in marketing interfirm relationships, and the strategic role of interfirm partnering for the firm. In the international arena, Dr. Johnson's research focuses on the management of equity and non-equity based strategic alliances between Japanese firms and firms from other cultures, and distribution relationships between Japanese and US firms. Dr. Johnson's research has appeared in the *Journal of Marketing, Journal of International Business Studies, Journal of the Academy of Marketing Science, Journal of Business Research, International Marketing Review, Journal of International Marketing, International Journal of Research in Marketing, Journal of Business-to-Business Marketing*, and *Journal of Marketing Channels*, among others. By invitation, Dr. Johnson co-authored a chapter titled "The Bases and Dynamics of Trust in Cross-Cultural Exchange," which will appear in *The Handbook of Cross-Cultural Management*. She has also presented her work at a variety of domestic and international conferences, and is active in the American Marketing Association and the Academy of Marketing Science. Professor Johnson serves on the Editorial Boards of several leading marketing journals including *Journal of Marketing* and the *Journal of the Academy of Marketing Science*. She is a past Editorial Board member of *The Journal of World Business*. In addition she reviews for other leading journals. Dr. Johnson has been named co-editor of the upcoming *Journal the Academy of Marketing Science* special issue on strategic alliances. Dr. Johnson's consulting activities include projects for the Japanese government, for the State of Washington, and for several private firms in the Pacific Northwest. She has been awarded a number of competitive grants including those from the Institute for the Study of Business Markets and the Direct Marketing Policy Center. Dr. Johnson has been the recipient of several awards within the College of Business and Economics including the most prestigious, College of Business and Economics Outstanding Researcher/Scholar Award. Dr. Johnson teaches strategic marketing at the undergraduate, MBA, and doctoral level. She also teaches special topics seminars on alliancing, distribution channels management, and business-to-business marketing. Before beginning her academic career, Dr. Johnson spent a number of years as a market researcher/ analyst in the advertising industry. She has lived and taught in several different countries (e.g., France and Japan) as well as working on research projects in those countries.

Magdi Kamel is an Associate Professor of Information Systems at the Naval Postgraduate School in Monterey. He received his Ph.D. in Information Systems from the Wharton School, University of

Pennsylvania. His main research interest is in the design and implementation of database and knowledge base systems. Specifically, he is interested in data models and languages; data modeling; knowledge acquisition, representation, and implementation; interoperability and integration issues in heterogeneous database and knowledge base systems; and database and knowledge base connectivity to the Internet. He has consulted in these areas for several organizations and is the author of numerous published research papers on these topics. Dr. Kamel is a member of Association for Computing Machinery and IEEE Computer Society.

Nelson King (B.S. Columbia University School of Engineering, M.S. University of Arizona) is a Ph.D. candidate with the Department of Industrial and Systems Engineering, University of Southern California, Los Angeles, CA 90089 (nelson.e.king@aero.org). He has corporate experience in preliminary design for natural resource, aerospace, and information technology projects. He has published articles in *IEEE Transactions on Engineering Management, Project Management Journal* and numerous conference papers. His current research places conceptual design activities within a social and organizational framework to facilitate the use of collaborative technologies.

Roland Klueber (Dipl. Wirtsch.-Inf.), studied information management at the University of Bamberg (Germany) and business adminstration at the University of Birmingham (UK). In 1997, he joined Coopers & Lybrand as a consultant in Frankfurt, Germany. Since 1998 he is research assistant at the Institute for Information Management, University of St. Gallen. His research interests are in Business Networking, Knowledge Management and eServices.

Claudia Loebbecke holds the KRAK Chair of Electronic Commerce at Copenhagen Business School, Denmark. She received a Masters and a Ph.D. in Business Administration from University of Cologne, Germany, and an MBA from Indiana University, Bloomington, IN, USA, and worked before in France, Hong Kong, Germany, Australia, and The Netherlands. Her research focus is on electronic commerce, knowledge and media management. Claudia Loebbecke has over 100 internationally, peer-reviewed journal articles and conference papers and is associate editor of the Information Systems Journal and on the editorial board of the Journal of Decision Systems, Journal of the AIS, and Computer Personnel. Claudia Loebbecke is a frequent speaker in international academic and practitioner conferences and provided consulting to a dozen of international companies.

Karen L. Lyons has spent more than eighteen years in the information technology field with an emphasis on process improvement and sharing knowledge within virtual teams. Most recently, Ms. Lyons has been responsible for partnering with business units of a pharmaceutical company in order to address organizational change management issues associated with promoting knowledge sharing within these organizations. Prior to her current role, she led a team responsible for developing a knowledge management approach for an IM software development team. Ms. Lyons was previously employed at Chemical Bank NY where she managed a project to evaluate natural language/knowledge-based interfaces to relational databases. Ms. Lyons has a passionate interest in identifying new ways to codify and transfer knowledge. She is also interested in the role of knowledge intermediaries and the challenges associated with management of expertise. Ms. Lyons holds a M.S. in Information Management from Stevens Institute of Technology. Her thesis was focused on *Implementing a Knowledge Management Approach for an IM Organization*. She also holds a M.S. in Computer Science from Stevens Institute of Technology, a Paralegal Certificate in Litigation from UCLA, and a B.A. in Psychology from Florida International University.

Ann Majchrzak (Ph.D. in Social Psychology, UCLA, 1980) is Professor of Information and Operations Management at the Marshall School of Business, University of Southern California , Los Angeles, CA 90089 (p:213-740-4023; majchrza@usc.edu). She conducts research on management of technology with a focus on information systems used for collaboration. One of her recent articles can be found in the *Harvard Business Review* (Sept/Oct 1996).

Arvind Malhotra (B.S. in Electronics and Communication Engineering, M.S. in Industrial Engineering University of Southern California) is a faculty member in the Management area at the Kenan Flagler Business School, University of North Carolina at Chapel Hill. He is completing his Ph.D. in Information

Systems Management at the Marshall School of Business, University of Southern California, Los Angeles, CA 90089 (amalhot@almaak.usc.edu). His current research interests are in the areas of e-commerce business models, value innovation in electronic economy, knowledge management, supply-chain management for e-business, and virtual organizing. He won the SIM International paper award competition in 1997 based on his research on how companies can exploit IT infrastructures to reinvent themselves. His work has been published in *MIS Quarterly*.

Yogesh Malhotra is the founder, chairman and chief knowledge architect of the WWW-based portal and global virtual communities of practice including @Brint.com: *The BizTech Network and Knowledge Management Think Tank*. As a professor of E-Business and Knowledge Management, he has taught at Carnegie Mellon University, University of Pittsburgh and Florida Atlantic University. As a global thought leader on Knowledge Management and E-Business, he has delivered recent invited keynotes to CIOs in Government of Mexico, hi-tech entrepreneurs and professionals network based in Silicon Valley, Baldrige Quality Award winning U.S. corporations, and global corporate executives at most prestigious industry conferences. He is an invited contributing editor and founding member of the GII's Standard for Internet Commerce and has served on Knowledge Management advisory panels for Arthur Andersen managing partners and Government of Netherlands and as council partner of U.S. Federal Government's Inter-Agency Best Practices Council. He is the lead author of two books *Knowledge Management and Virtual Organizations* and *Knowledge Management for Business Model Innovation*, has published in numerous leading scholarly and practitioner journals, and presented at leading world-class conferences. He serves as an editor and reviewer for leading information technology publications, is frequently interviewed by the worldwide business and technology media, and is included in the millennium edition of Marquis *Who's Who in the World*. Over the last 18 years, his worldwide professional experience has primarily focused on design, development and strategy for large-scale information technology and engineering systems with Fortune 100 companies, global multinationals and Internet startups. His credentials include Bachelor of Engineering, magna cum laude; MBA, summa cum laude with Phi Kappa Phi and Beta Gamma Sigma honors and Ph.D. in Business Administration with Beta Gamma Sigma honors from the University of Pittsburgh. He is a Certified Computing Professional of the Institute for Certification of Computing Professionals, a Chartered Engineer and life member of The Institution of Engineers, and award-winning member and doctoral consortium fellow of the Academy of Management. He can be contacted at yogesh.malhotra@brint.com.

Peter Murray has been a Research Fellow in the Information Systems Research Centre at the Cranfield School of Management since 1995. Peter has a B.Sc. in physics and, prior to joining Cranfield, he was with Zeneca Pharmaceuticals in a variety of Information Systems executive roles including world-wide responsibility for Zeneca's R&D systems, having previously held senior management posts in an engineering conglomerate. His current areas of teaching and research are knowledge management, intranet-supported information management, benefits management, and electronic commerce. He is a consultant to a number of global organizations, has published several articles on knowledge management and spoken at many international conferences on the topic.

Jill Nemiro is an Assistant Professor in the Organizational Psychology Program at the California School of Professional Psychology, Los Angeles. She has also served on the faculty at Claremont Graduate University; California State University, Long Beach; California State University, Los Angeles; California State Polytechnic University, Pomona; and Chaffey Community College. Professionally, Dr. Nemiro has worked for twenty years in the entertainment industry, as a film and videotape editor, specializing in management training and corporate videos. She has also published several articles in the field of creativity research. Dr. Nemiro received her Ph.D. in Organizational Psychology from Claremont Graduate University.

Robert Neumann: Mag. rer. soc. oec., Universities of Klagenfurt and Vienna, Austria (1990), Majors: Organizational Development and Strategic Management; Dr., University of Klagenfurt, Austria (1994); Habilitation Thesis to the Topic: "The Organization as an Order of Knowledge" (submitted); Current Position: Assistant Professor at the Department of Organizational Behavior and Management Development, College of Business Administration, University of Klagenfurt, Austria, e-mail: robert.neumann@uni-klu.ac.at. Research Interests: Strategic Management, Learning Organization, Organizational Behavior,

Cognition and Change, Knowledge Management. Professional Background: 1987-1994 Consultant with the Hernstein International Management Institute (Vienna) for Business and Non-Profit-Organizations, Certified Consultant for Competence-Diagnosis and Development and Change Management.

Mark Nissen is Assistant Professor of Information Systems and Acquisition Management at the Naval Postgraduate School. His research focuses on the investigation of knowledge systems for enabling and managing change in areas such as process innovation, electronic commerce and knowledge management. Recently he has been investigating knowledge systems to innovate processes in the acquisition domain and is currently involved with intelligent acquisition agents. Before his information systems doctoral work at the University of Southern California, he acquired over a dozen years of management experience in the aerospace and electronics industry and served as a Supply Officer in the Naval Reserve.

Joe Noone is a currently undertaking a PhD in the Health Informatics Research Group at the Levels Campus of the University of South Australia. His work centres on the effectiveness and suitability of clinical practice guidelines for health practitioners for the care of the chronically ill. He holds an undergraduate degree of a Bachelor of Health Sciences with Honours.

Hubert Österle (Prof. Dr.) studied business economics at the Universities of Innsbruck and Linz, subsequently obtaining his doctorate at the University of Erlangen-Nuernberg in 1973. In 1974, he joined IBM Germany as a systems consultant. From 1975 until 1980, Hubert Österle was an assistant at the University of Dortmund, where he wrote his postdoctoral thesis in the field of Computer Aided Systems Engineering. Since 1980 he has been Professor for Information Management at the University of St. Gallen and, since 1989, managing director of the newly founded Institute for Information Management. Hubert Österle's main topics in publication and research are business engineering, information management, business networking, and knowledge management.

Dave Pollard, B.Sc. (Comp.Sc.), CA, has been the Chief Knowledge Officer for Ernst & Young in Canada since 1994, following twenty years as an Entrepreneurial Services practitioner and partner. Dave has responsibility in Canada for: developing the firmís Knowledge Strategy and Vision, design and deployment of Knowledge Architecture, Tools and Content, management of Research, Analysis, Navigation, and Specialist Network Services, and attainment of a Knowledge-Sharing Culture. He is the new Director for Knowledge Innovation in E&Yís Global CBK (Center for Business Knowledge), a virtual knowledge organization serving E&Y practitioners worldwide and employing over 600 business researchers, analysts, and managers of knowledgebases, networks and the Internet, Intranet, and Extranets. Dave's new role entails: meeting with CBK customers and helping them to anticipate and define their emerging knowledge, learning and new product needs, working with global knowledge thought leaders to identify and deploy leading practices, helping customers reengineer their existing knowledge processes and resources, and design new knowledge tools, to embed knowledge creation and use in E&Y's day-to-day business culture, and hence increase the value of knowledge to the firm, and helping to extend E&Yís world-class "knowledge enterprise" to engage customers, associates and other business partners in the firm in collaborative and innovative activities with each other and with E&Yís people. Dave is also the Global Corporate Finance Knowledge Coordinator, working with the leaders of the firmís Corporate Finance service line to develop knowledge tools, processes and resources to meet the evolving needs of this service line, which provides strategic finance, valuation, litigation support, restructuring and M&A transaction services for clients. Dave has chaired firm committees and focus groups on the Virtual Workplace, Internet/Intranet strategy, and business innovation. He is a subject matter specialist advising clients and client service teams on knowledge management, business innovation and e-commerce. He has written and lectured on a variety of subjects related to knowledge management, innovation and the future of business. Dave lives in the Caledon Hills outside Toronto, and works from anywhere, anytime. An active environmentalist, Daveís hobbies include genealogy, writing short stories and composing music. Ernst & Young is one of Canada's, and the world's, largest integrated professional services firms, and an acknowledged global leader in knowledge management.

Emanuela Prandelli is Professor of Marketing at SDA Bocconi, the Graduate School of Business of Bocconi University, in Milan, Italy. She has just taken her PhD in Business Administration at the same University. She recently has been Visiting Research Scholar at St. Gallen University, Switzerland and at Kellogg Graduate School of Management, Northwestern University, Evanston (Ill., USA).

Ronald E. Rice (B.A. in Literature, Columbia University; M.A., Ph.D. in Communication Research, Stanford University) is Professor at the School of Communication, Information and Library Studies at Rutgers University, 4 Huntington St., New Brunswick, N.J. 08901-1071 (p: 732-932-7381; f: 732-932-6916; e: rrice@scils.rutgers.edu; http://scils.rutgers.edu/~rrice). He has conducted research and published widely in communication science, public communication campaigns, computer-mediated communication systems, methodology, organizational and management theory, information systems, information science and bibliometrics, and social networks. He was associate editor of *Human Communication Research*, and of *MIS Quarterly*, and currently serves as associate editor on *New Media and Society* and *Communication Theory*, and is on the editiorial boards of a half dozen communication, information science, and management journals.

Mohanbir Sawhney is the Tribune Professor of Electronic Commerce and Technology at the Kellogg Graduate School of Management, Northwestern University.

Kishore Sengupta is Associate Professor of Information Systems, Naval Postgraduate School, Monterey, California. In 1996-1997, he was a Visiting Scholar at the Hong Kong University of Science and Technology. Dr. Sengupta received his Ph.D. in Management Information and Decision Systems from Case Western Reserve University, Cleveland, OH. His research interests are in knowledge management for collaborative work, decision support for dynamic tasks, and electronic commerce. Dr. Sengupta has published in leading journals on management and information systems, including *Management Science, MIS Quarterly, IEEE Transactions on Software Engineering, IEEE Transactions on Systems, Man, and Cybernetics, IEEE Transactions on Engineering Management, Accounting, Management and Information Technology, Omega, Decision Support Systems*, and *Concurrent Engineering Research and Applications*.

G.C.A. Steenbakkers (Wilchard), is an Associate Professor on Organization sciences at the Royal Netherlands Military Academy. Virtual and network organizations are the focal point of his current research. He is a participant in the University of Amsterdam PrimaVera research programme (http://domino.fee.uva.nl/PrimaVera).

Paul C. van Fenema is Ph.D. Candidate in Management of Information Systems at the Rotterdam School of Management, Erasmus University in the Netherlands. He holds a MSc degree (cum laude) in Law & Economics from Utrecht University. His current research concerns the management of Global IS Projects from a coordination and control theory perspective. He has published in *ICIS, IFIP 8.2 Proceedings, Database*, and *the International Journal of Project Management*.

Jaakko Virkkunen, PhD, is Docent of Adult Training and Senior Researcher in the Centre for Activity Theory and Developmental Work Research at University of Helsinki. He has a long experience as an HRD specialist and consultant in the Finnish State Administration. His research focuses on intervention methods and tools for joint expansive learning and development of work practices . His recent publications concern organizational learning and a new work development method called Change Laboratory. His current research project deals with the new methods for knowledge and competence management.

John Ward is Professor of Strategic Information Systems and Director of the Information Systems Research Centre at Cranfield University, School of Management. John's main areas of study are the strategic uses of IS/IT, the integration of IS/IT strategies with business strategies, the development of organizational IS capabilities and the management of IS/IT investments. He has published papers on these and related topics in leading journals and is author/co-author of the books, "Strategic Planning for Information Systems", "The Principles of IS Management" and "The Essence of Information Systems". Prior to joining Cranfield in 1984 he worked in industry for 15 years, the last three as Systems Development Manager at Kodak Limited. He acts as a consultant to a number of major international organizations. He has a degree in Natural Sciences from Cambridge, is a Fellow of the Chartered Institute of Management Accountants and is a past President of the UK Academy for Information Systems.

Index